POPULAR MAPS

THE ORDNANCE SURVEY POPULAR EDITION ONE-INCH MAP

of

ENGLAND and WALES

1919-1926

POPULAR MAPS

THE ORDNANCE SURVEY POPULAR EDITION ONE-INCH MAP

OF

ENGLAND AND WALES

1919-1926

Yolande Hodson

With a Foreword by
David Rhind

London
The Charles Close Society
1999

First published December 1999 by The Charles Close Society for the Study of Ordnance Survey Maps c/o The Map Library, British Library, 96 Euston Road, London, NW1 2DB

ISBN 1-870598-15-6

Typeset by the author

Printed and bound by Redwood Books Limited, Kennet Way, Trowbridge, Wiltshire BA14 8RN

Colour printing by Oxford Cartographers, Oasis Park, Eynsham, Oxford OX8 1TP

FOREWORD

About two million Landranger maps are sold every single year by Ordnance Survey. They represent the national mapping agency's flagship product. Landrangers are used for every conceivable (and some inconceivable) purpose(s); they are used for planning of all kinds, for environmental monitoring, for military and state security purposes, for the education of every child in Britain, for walking and other leisure pursuits and for much else.

These maps at 1:50,000 scale replaced the old 'One-Inch' (1:63,360 scale) maps in 1974. Much of the content and some aspects of style derive from that antecedent. It is therefore no exaggeration to say that the present mapping is a lineal descendent of those created from 1801 onwards. In their day, the one-inch maps set worldwide standards for clarity, completeness, accuracy, innovation and breadth of use. And they are exquisite art as well as irreplacable scientific and historical documents.

There is, then, a great story to be told about the creation and evolution of the one-inch map. It is a fascinating one for it involves politics, the effects of changing technology, the changing needs for the maps as society itself changed, and the interplay of powerful and determined personalities - as well as of cartography. Yolande Hodson is the ideal person to write such a story. Dr Christopher Board of the London School of Economics and I saw this clearly when we examined her admirable PhD thesis and urged her to turn it into a more widely accessible book. Readers can move onto the main text confident in the historical accuracy of what she says, relying on her sure judgement and scholarship and revelling in the story she tells.

David Rhind
Director General, Ordnance Survey 1992-8

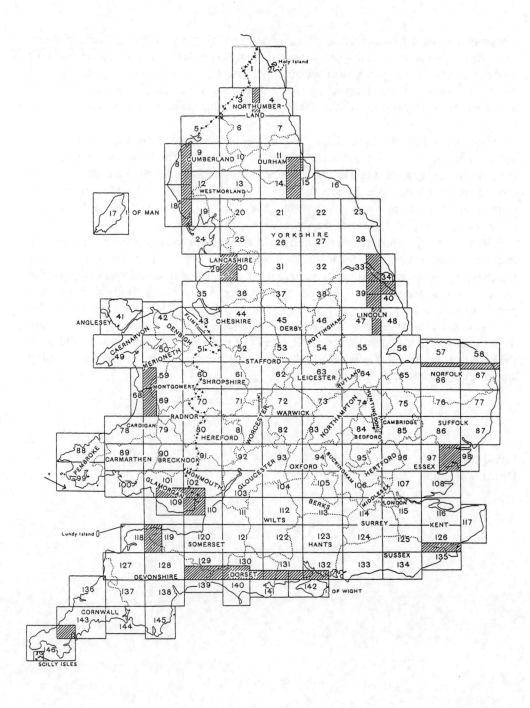

CONTENTS

LIST OF ILLUSTRATIONS

The map extracts have been reproduced to scale unless otherwise stated.

Figures 12, 14 and 38 were drawn by Catherine Lawrence

Colour plates

ABBREVIATIONS and LIBRARY SIGLA

AA	Automobile Association
AOP	Assistant Officer in charge of Printing Department
AR	Ordnance Survey Annual Report
Baker	Printed evidence and reports of the Baker Committee *see* Sources
BL	British Library
BLa	British Library Maps 1175.(149)
BLb	British Library Maps 1175.(258)
BLc	British Library Maps 13.c.24
BLd	British Library Maps 1175.(157)
BLe	British Library Maps 1175.(259)
BLf	British Library Maps 1175.(263)
Bod	Bodleian Library
CB	Companion of the Bath
CC (or C/C)	Chief Clerk's Circulars
CCS	The Charles Close Society for the Study of Ordnance Survey Maps
CEB	Central Electricity Board
Ch	Ordnance Survey Office, Chessington
CMG	Companion, Order of St Michael and St George
Cr	Ordnance Survey Office, Crabwood
CUL	Cambridge University Library
Davidson	Printed evidence and reports of the Davidson Committee *see* Sources
DCL	Doctor of Civil Law
DGOS	Director General of Ordnance Survey
DO	Divisional Officer
Dorington	Printed evidence and reports of the Dorington Committee *see* Sources
DSO	Companion of Distinguished Service Order
EO	Executive Officer
FRS	Fellow of the Royal Society
GPO	General Post Office
GSGS	Geographical Section General Staff
Hayes Fisher	Printed evidence and reports of the Hayes Fisher Committee *see* Sources
HMSO	His/Her Majesty's Stationery Office
HWM	High water mark
IBG	Institute of British Geographers
Ilkeston	Printed evidence and reports of the Ilkeston Committee *see* Sources
IMW	International Map of the World at 1:1,000,000
KBE	Knight Commander of the Order of the British Empire
KCB	Knight Commander of the Order of the Bath
KCMG	Knight Commander of the Order of St Michael and St George
KGM	Guy Messenger map collection, CUL Map Library
LLD	Doctor of Laws
LR	Ordnance Survey Office, London Road, Southampton
LUS	Land Utilisation Survey of Britain
LWM	Low water mark
MCL	Manchester Central Library

MOT	Ministry of Transport
MS	Manuscript
NLS	National Library of Scotland
O/C	Officer in Charge
OE	Officer in charge of the Engraving Department
OID	Officer in charge of the Irish Division
Olivier	Printed evidence and reports of the Olivier Committee *see* Sources
OP	Officer in charge of the Publication Department
OS	Ordnance Survey
OSC	Ordnance Survey Committee
OSCL	Ordnance Survey Cartographic Library
OSG	School of Geography, University of Oxford
OSHS	Ordnance Survey Hill Sketches, Map Library, British Library
OSL	Ordnance Survey Library
OSRML	Ordnance Survey Record Map Library
PC	Private Collection
PEF	Palestine Exploration Fund
PRO	Public Record Office
RAC	Royal Automobile Club
RDC	Rural District Council
RGS	Royal Geographical Society, London. Since 1995: The Royal Geographical Society (with the Institute of British Geographers)
RO	Research Officer, Ordnance Survey
SG	Department of Geography, University of Sheffield
WO	War Office
WP	Waterproof
ZP	Zinc Printing Department

A note on currency

The prices of maps quoted in this book have not been converted to decimal currency. For those unfamiliar with pre-decimal currency there were twelve pennies (12d.) to one shilling and twenty shillings (20s.) to one pound sterling (£1), and thus 240 pennies to a pound. A guinea was one pound one shilling.

Acknowledgements

My professional concern with Ordnance Survey products began in the 1960s when my personal interest in OS maps, acquired during childhood, was fostered during my time at what was then the Survey Production Centre (RE) by Peter Clark and Ian Mumford. They have given me such valuable support over so many years that it is impossible to enumerate here the extent of their largesse with information, maps, and the time given to discuss my ideas with me; I give them my heartfelt thanks.

One of the great pleasures in writing any work is to meet those who are the guardians of the material that is central to the study. The staff of the British Library Map Library have been helpful beyond the call of ordinary service, and I thank them all for their many kindnesses to me. At Cambridge University Library, Roger Fairclough, and then Anne Taylor have gone out of their way to make material available to me, as did Betty Fathers, and then Nick Millea at the Bodleian Library, Oxford. My time in Scotland, researching the Bartholomew Archive, was made especially pleasurable by the friendly efficiency of the staff of the Department of Manuscripts and of Margaret Wilkes, and subsequently Diana Webster and the staff in the Map Library: Bill Todd deserves a special thank you for responding instantly, and patiently, to requests for huge volumes of maps. My friends at Ordnance Survey are, happily, numerous; in particular, Campbell Ballantyne, John Paddy Browne and Pat Poppy, all now retired, Wayne Debeugny and Sheila Caine, have produced gems of information which added sparkle to my many visits there. In the Public Record Office, Geraldine Beech and her staff ensured that the requisite files were always to hand. Francis Herbert, at the Royal Geographical Society (with IBG) has been most generous with his time and in providing material from his research into the firm of Edward Stanford.

When it comes to acknowledging the help which I have received from members of the Charles Close Society, I am tempted to refer the reader to their membership list for so many have given freely of their knowledge. I am particularly grateful to: Peter Chasseaud; Drs Andrew and Karen Cook; John Coombes; John Crutchley; Richard Dean; Brian Dobbie; Peter Ennor; Brian Garvan; Bill Henwood; the late Guy Messenger; Dave Watt; David Webb; Rob Wheeler, and Julian Williams.

I am indebted to those who have given indispensable help: Brian Adams for imparting his profound knowledge of mathematical cartography, and for checking my lists of co-ordinates; Mike Cottrell, for bringing his trained accountant's eye to bear on my financial calculations and on the correct rendering of all the print codes in the catalogue; Cilla Hedderson: the layman who read the entire manuscript without complaint and provided useful corrections; Paul Laming: collector *par excellence*, who ran his meticulous eye over the check-lists. Drs Chris Board, Roger Hellyer, Tim Nicholson and Richard Oliver, as well as lending maps in the customary CCS tradition, also took considerable time to read the manuscript and make many improvements. I have learned much from them.

David Archer has given the author exemplary support for which she is most grateful. It is not possible to overestimate his contribution. His advice, sound judgment, and hours of involvement in this publication have been much appreciated.

Last in this list, but first in my estimation, my dear husband, Donald, and son, Matthew, who had, perforce, to acquire the skills of domestic engineering while I spent months in my study, have provided that quiet environment so necessary to any author's travail. I am deeply grateful to them.

Preface by the Chairman of the Charles Close Society

It is with great pleasure that I commend this study of the Ordnance Survey's Popular Edition One-Inch map to all who are engrossed by maps. Completing a PhD thesis on the Popular Edition in 1995 was already a significant achievement by Yolande Hodson. But no one should underestimate the effort required to turn the thesis into a book which distills all that can be said about a map series for England that was in its day Ordnance Survey's most successful one-inch map. There is no doubt that the Popular Edition, first published eighty years ago, made Britain into the map-minded country it is today. A pictorial cover set the seal on the product through an image of a then typical map user. The pipe-smoking cyclist would no longer be approved of, but in the 1920s he epitomised the newly mobile map owner, the pockets of his Norfolk jacket being almost made for the folded versions. He is as we might wish to remember our grandfathers who escaped from the daily grind and the aftermath of the Great War to enjoy the British countryside and coast armed with this popular new map.

Dr Hodson's book digs deeply into the context of the conception, design and production of a single map series: a set of maps reproduced at a uniform scale and in a common style planned to cover a specified area. That is enough of a tall order when she has to deal with half a century of mapping activity, comprising 146 map sheets in more than 780 distinguishable states personally examined by her. There is no doubt that readers of this book, whether collectors, or travellers, historians, surveyors, geographers or cartographers, will all find here something to enjoy and ponder.

The Charles Close Society exists to exchange information and ideas on Ordnance Survey maps and a key element is the publication of scholarly studies. It is proud to be able to publish this model account of a British map series and believes it will be regarded as a major contribution to the history of cartography in the twentieth century. Long anticipated, Dr Hodson's *chef d'oeuvre* will not disappoint, but only encourage others to follow in her footsteps. I hope we are willing to accept the challenge.

Christopher Board
7 October 1999

INTRODUCTION

> The one-inch should ... be a really complete and authoritative record of the country, and of its administrative organisation at the date of publication ... even if it becomes congested.
> *The British Association for the Advancement of Science* [1935].[1]

This book is the story of a one-inch map series from sheet line construction to shop counter. In the inter-war years, the position of the one-inch map as the most important cartographic interface between Ordnance Survey and its public was always emphasised by the Survey; the map was in 'universal national use', and its bearing on the 'health and holidays of the public' was of the 'greatest significance'.[2] Yet the memorandum from the British Association for the Advancement of Science, quoted above, conveyed a complaint that useful detail was being omitted from the one-inch map, and that a mistaken policy was being followed of seeking clarity of design at the expense of information. In this instance the criticisms that parish boundaries were deleted from the Popular Edition, and that deciduous and non-deciduous woods could no longer be distinguished on its successor, the Fifth Edition, were voiced by many who gave evidence to the Davidson Departmental Committee on the Ordnance Survey in the 1930s. How was it that a national mapping organisation could seem to be out of touch with the needs of its customers, and what were the factors which influenced the production and design of the nation's premier small-scale map?

These were just two among many of the cartographic questions which occurred to me to ask when writing the chapters on the inter-war period of the Ordnance Survey, which were eventually published in 1980 in W.A. Seymour (Ed.) *A history of the Ordnance Survey*. I was struck by how little detail was known then about the cartography of the national survey. Our ignorance as historians did not just apply to that era but, at that time in 1974, to practically the whole spectrum of Ordnance Survey cartography. In that year, a beginning was made with the publication of the late Brian Harley's *Ordnance Survey maps: a descriptive manual*, which summarised the main cartographic points of the major map scales. John Andrews's study of Irish mapping, *A paper landscape: the Ordnance Survey in nineteenth-century Ireland*, was about to be published in 1975, and Brian Harley and I had begun *The Old Series Ordnance Survey maps of England and Wales*,[3] which was, with different authors, to become a massive study of the Ordnance Survey's very first published map series. But in writing what is now known as the 'Seymour history', many of our accounts focused on the organisational aspects of the Survey's work rather than on the particulars of its cartographic products, which were generally accorded only superficial treatment.

---

1   OSL G5186, OSC 134, undated memorandum from the British Association for the Advancement of Science to the Davidson Committee.
2   OSL G5186, Appendix I to OSC 9, 5/12/1934.
3   Margary, (1975-1992).

This is not to say that the maps were totally ignored. For my part, I was more fortunate than most, for I was employed in the British Library's Map Library - the national copyright library - and therefore had ready access to all the maps for the period about which I was writing. However, I soon discovered, to my surprise, that the national repository of Ordnance Survey maps was, in some cases, merely a token collection of what had been published. Far from being complete, as was frequently claimed, it was, in some instances, barely representative. There were two reasons for this. First, copyright deposits were made in paper flat form only; this meant that the rich variety of cover art for the period was not present at all. Secondly, few reprints of sheets were deposited, and therefore the publishing history of the maps could not be reconstructed.

In preparing the text for the Seymour history, time was at a premium, deadlines had to be met. With only four weeks of annual leave, there was little opportunity, in my case, for the detailed cartographic studies which should have preceded any authoritative synthesis such as that envisaged for what was regarded as the 'official' history of the Ordnance Survey. Nevertheless, authors were helped immensely by privileged access to Public Record Office files. Thus the administrative background of the mapping was readily compiled, but not the history of the maps themselves.

Among the wealth of cartographic products of the period about which I was writing, none seemed to me to be more evocative of that time than the Popular Edition one-inch series of England and Wales. Conceived at the end of the Edwardian era, and embodying the cartographic ideals of the Victorian army, it was born into the inter-war period which was one of rapid change, not only in terms of the landscape which it purported to record, but also in terms of printing methods. The Popular Edition of England and Wales lay at the watershed of nineteenth-century map reproduction practice on the one side, and twentieth-century technology on the other. First published between 1919 and 1926, it began as a copperplate derivative and ended as a drawn and photographed map, whereas the Popular Edition map of Scotland was all completely redrawn from start to finish. The specification of the English series was similar to that of the Third Edition, which it superseded, but there were significant differences. The Popular was also the first map series to benefit fully from customer oriented marketing techniques - new covers were designed, promotional literature was devised. Not only that, new tourist and district mapping, based on Popular Edition material, was published - all in the most attractive packaging. But little of this was in the British Library.

Clearly, a thorough study of the maps would have to be undertaken at a later time. In the meantime, the policy was adopted of expanding the Ordnance Survey holdings of the British Library by purchasing folded copies of the states of inter-war small-scale mapping that the national collection lacked. One of the features which most interested me, in making records of these sheets, was the fact that the reprints all carried print codes which gave information on when and how many copies of each sheet were printed. It was immediately apparent that here was not only a useful method of identifying different printing states, but also the raw material for analysing the publication history of the map; from it, perhaps, could be discovered the best-selling sheets, for example.

At the same time, my studies of the methods of production in the eighteenth and early nineteenth centuries of the Old Series one-inch map, and of their conventional signs, which owed much to military cartographic practice, led me to notice some similarities with those of the Popular Edition, and to wonder how it was constructed, and to ask, for example, how it was printed, what were the revision policies in force at the time and, particularly, what influenced its design. In other words, was it possible to reconstruct its specification and explain the reasons for its adoption? There was, for the Popular Edition, no equivalent to the formal documentation for the Seventh Series one-inch map or the present 1:50,000 Landranger series. These documents set out full details of elements such as the series layout, the marginal and border details, magnetic information, conventional signs, and colour of the inks. Many of the files which I had used in writing the chapters for the Seymour history had contained useful technical information on some aspects of all the small-scale maps for the inter-war period, but none had given the specification of the maps; and the significant details of the revision and drawing instructions, which must have governed the content and appearance of the map, were not present either.

The search for supporting documentation therefore began with the departmental instructions. For the most part, these were printed, but unpublished, internal regulations that are seldom found outside the Ordnance Survey. Most of the surviving sets related to scales of 1:10,560 and larger and dated from the 1930s; many could be found in the Ordnance Survey Library. More came to light through enquiries among the staff in different divisions of the Ordnance Survey - the Boundaries Section was particularly rich in historical material. Gradually, the collection increased, but the material for the period before the 1940s was, and still is, rare; the most valuable examples were those which had a succession of dated amendments, usually in manuscript, which chronicled, in effect, the development of the series to which they related. Other instructions were embedded as departmental circulars, either in the large bound volumes, known as the Southampton Circulars, in the Ordnance Survey Library, or within the departmental files in the Public Record Office. One of the aims of the study of the Popular Edition was therefore to bring together all the available evidence on the revision and drawing instructions for the one-inch map from the 1880s to the 1940s.

In reading these instructions for the one-inch map, it became obvious that the study of the Popular Edition would have to take account of the evolution of the one-inch series of England and Wales as a whole, of which it was only a part. In particular, its relationship with its immediate predecessors, the Third Edition and Revised New Series, would have to be established, and this would mean attempting to define a nomenclature for the succession of one-inch maps of England and Wales - a subject fraught with bibliographical pitfalls.

The revision and drawing instructions were therefore primary printed evidence for the depiction of the content of the map. The second fundamental printed source was the evidence and minutes of five departmental committees. Indeed, this study could very well have been entitled 'From Baker to Davidson: the one-inch map 1892-1939', since four of these had a significant impact on the design and marketing of the Popular Edition. The first, held under the Presidency of Lieut.-General Sir T.D. Baker, deliberated in April 1892 and was appointed to inquire into the 'form' of a 'military map of the United Kingdom'; its findings, which were printed later in the year, were to have a direct impact on the specification of the one-inch map in general, and the Popular Edition in particular. The second committee, which sat a month later, and which was therefore influenced, to a certain extent, by the earlier military conclusions, was chaired by Sir John Edward

Dorington. Of its three objectives, the aim which had the most direct effect on the Popular Edition was that of discovering whether the published maps 'satisfy the reasonable requirements of the public in regard to style of execution, form, information conveyed, and price'. Its recommendations were published in 1893.

Two years later yet another committee, chaired by William Hayes Fisher, was summoned, this time to inquire into the methods of selling the Ordnance Survey maps. The evidence of this committee, published in 1896, revealed much about the selling techniques of commercial firms which were to be imitated for the Popular Edition and other small-scale maps in the 1920s. The evidence of the fourth departmental committee (1914), charged with investigating methods of selling the small-scale maps and chaired by Sir Sydney Olivier, was to prove crucial to understanding the genesis of the Popular Edition. While the contents of the preceding three committee reports were well known, those of the Olivier committee had remained unread by historians until they were 'discovered' while I was researching the material for the Seymour history. The reason for the previous neglect of this seminal document was that it had never been published because the information it contained would have revealed too many 'trade secrets'. It was therefore classified as confidential, and only one copy is known. The significance of this report was that it was printed in 1914, just at the time when experimental work on the one-inch map was being carried out; the details of these experiments which it included appeared in no other source.

The value of the final committee, chaired in 1935 by Sir John Davidson and inquiring principally into the state of the large-scale mapping of the country, lay in its retrospective judgements on the merits of the Popular Edition compared with those of its successor, the Fifth Edition. These, together with the then current views of professional map users on the optimum form and content of the one-inch map, were to be found not so much in the published reports as in the files of correspondence and papers which have, as yet, not been systematically studied by other historians, and which remain in the Ordnance Survey Library.

Other primary printed material was to be found in the Parliamentary Papers; the reports of Select Committees on Estimates yielded data on costs of production, for example, while the Hansard chronicles revealed mounting concern at the increased costs to the nation of the Survey, and, in the 1930s, was the vehicle for formal public complaint at the obsolescence of the large-scale plans. The official opinions of those who designed and marketed the Popular Edition could be found in the Public Record Office files and in Ordnance Survey publications, such as the *Professional Papers*. In particular, the *Annual Reports* gave detailed information on all aspects of the Survey's work.

Many of the officers of the Ordnance Survey gave lectures and wrote papers on various aspects of the design of the maps for which they were responsible, and these were published in periodicals such as the *Empire Survey Review*, *The Geographical Journal* and the *Royal Engineers Journal*. In particular, the Royal Geographical Society, of which Colonel Sir Charles Close (Director General, Ordnance Survey 1911-22) was President between 1927 and 1930, was the public platform most used by the Ordnance Survey for announcing and debating the cartographic policy of the national survey. New and experimental maps were often brought to meetings and then deposited in the Society's map collection; this material, together with the correspondence, preserved in the Society's archives, between Survey personnel and Society officers, provided more relaxed personal judgements on the cartographic questions of the day. For more of these private views, I sought out retired officers. Most from this period were no longer alive, but relatives were very helpful. In particular, the late Colonel Richard Arden-Close, son of Sir Charles Close (who was responsible for the design of the Popular Edition), was most generous. I was allowed access to all his father's private papers; these have now been transferred to the Royal Geographical Society and to the Library at the Institution of Royal Engineers at Chatham. I was also given tremendous hospitality by the late Colonel A.B. (Archie) Clough, who was Executive Officer, or Deputy Director General, of the Ordnance Survey in the 1930s. At the age of 91, he would collect me from the railway station, drive me to his home and cook me lunch; I was regaled with good food and entertaining recollections of pre-war days.

These interviews, and the initial collecting of material, were carried out in the late 1970s. But of course, the study of any map requires not only the perusal of documentary sources but also a thorough examination of the map itself. At that time, when I began this study, no detailed cartographic investigation of any one-inch series, or other series for that matter, had been published, apart from the early volumes of the Old Series facsimiles, and the David & Charles reprints of later printings of the Old Series maps. The production of cartobibliographies of Ordnance Survey maps could hardly even be considered to be in its infancy; it was more embryonic, and distinctly unformed. All this was to change within the next decade. By 1979, it was apparent that a series of guides to the Ordnance Survey collections of the British Library would prove invaluable to the readers of the Map Library. While these did not emerge at the time, another plan did crystallize. This resulted from the realisation that some of the readers who consulted the Map Library holdings were avid collectors of Ordnance Survey maps. Perhaps they would have in their own collections copies of states of maps which were missing from the national collection. If so, a knowledge of their holdings would be essential to any serious study of, for example, the small-scale maps. With this in mind, Peter Clark[4] and I suggested the formation of a Society, with the principal object of pooling resources to produce authoritative records of what had been published by the Ordnance Survey.

The Charles Close Society for the Study of Ordnance Survey Maps (CCS) was founded in November 1980. In 1982 a scheme was put forward for providing concise guides to the series of small-scale maps,[5] and since that time, the Society has published a succession of series guides on the one-inch maps which are models of precise recording. These guides are principally the work of Dr Richard Oliver, whose indefatigable enthusiasm for the subject, coupled with comprehensive trawls of Public Record Office files and unremitting scrutiny of the maps themselves, has provided useful summaries and listings of the Fifth Edition, New Popular, Scottish Popular with National Grid, and Seventh Series, all of which have been invaluable in compiling this study of the Popular Edition of England and Wales. Also, the late Guy Messenger provided a

4 Peter Clark, Chief Map Research Officer, Map Research and Library Group, Ministry of Defence, 1964 to 1983; Keeper of the Royal Geographical Society, 1986 to 1992.

5 Charles Close Society Archives, circular letter dated 11/1/1982 from Y. Hodson to Christopher Board, Peter Clark, Brian Garvan, Alan Godfrey, Brian Harley, Guy Messenger, and Richard Oliver.

detailed listing of the Third Edition Large Sheet Series. This used no documentary research, and was based only on the observations of the sheets and their covers; but from this careful record it has been possible to extract much information which otherwise would have taken years to acquire.

From 1981, the Charles Close Society produced, in addition to the series guides, a journal, *Sheetlines*. Its early appearance - small, typed, and entirely homespun - bears no comparison with its present professional format. Successive editors have gradually improved the quality of both content and presentation, and the articles and papers that have been published within its covers, some of which are outstanding contributions to the history of Ordnance Survey cartography, have been another fruitful source of information for this study, which owes an enormous debt to those CCS members who, over the years, have so unselfishly lent me their whole collections of Popular Edition maps so that I could compare different states of sheets side by side. This physical juxtaposition is absolutely essential in any work of this nature, and the opportunities for doing this in public collections are rare.

A map series is a dynamic animal. It is one map, divided into as many sheets as are necessary, depending on the scale, to enable it to be handled easily. Thus the Popular Edition one-inch map of England and Wales which, at the scale of 1:63,360, would produce a map measuring about 33ft x 27ft, is divided into 146 sheets, mostly measuring 18 x 27 inches. These sheets, while together making up the whole, lead independent lives; each can be reprinted at different times and in different numbers. Modifications to the specification are made on some, but not on others; revision is carried out at different times; even the bibliographical information in the margins of the sheets cannot be relied upon to be standardised. There is no point in trying to create order where none exists, but by recording every important feature, both on the map and on the cover, it is possible to analyse the data in order to provide an overall picture of the evolution of the map's design, or, quite simply, to be able to explain an apparent anomaly by saying that a photographer was careless in pinning up the marginal information on such and such a day.

The minutiae of the information thus recorded were transferred to dBase IV. The resulting data analyses have been used to provide, for example, much of the evidence for dating specification changes, or the introduction and use of certain cover styles. But not all aspects of the specification of the Popular Edition have been examined, and this investigation does not claim to be comprehensive in this respect. For example, while lettering is touched on, the subject of place-names has not been covered. This is because so many new settlements with new names sprang up in the inter-war period, that the Popular Edition would provide enough data for yet another book. How many would recognise in 'New Anzac on Sea' the now familiar 'Peacehaven' in Sussex, for example? Both names presumably had First World War connotations, but the former appeared only briefly on the first printing of sheet 134. Many other similar instances await the attention of a student of the development of new settlements in the inter-war period.

Having studied the map as an artefact, the other important and much more difficult question to be answered was, did each sheet really show everything, within the limits of scale, that was on the ground at the time of its publication or reprinting? Was there any evidence that it showed information that was not to be found on the larger scale maps from which it was derived? This would be particularly important in an era when the large-scale plans were becoming progressively out of date with regard to portraying the movement of industry, the spread of urbanisation, and the development of road transport. It was too great a task to compare every state of every one-inch sheet with all the editions of its component six-inch sheets from which it was derived but, by using the survey dates of the large-scale plans, given in Oliver's *Concise guide to Ordnance Survey maps* (1993), it was possible to select areas where it seemed there might be a discrepancy in content between large and small-scale map.

There was also the question of whether or not a study should be made of the derivatives of the Popular Edition. The most important of these, the military edition, or GSGS 3907 as it was known from 1931, was an obvious candidate for inclusion. Indeed, in the original structure of this book it was to have formed a chapter; but, as in so many instances, the more one grew to be acquainted with the subject, the more complex it became. Not only would it be necessary to discuss the background to the cartography and policies of military mapping for this country, but it seemed that the printing plates for the individual sheets sometimes had different printing histories to those of the standard series. In short, the comparative work necessary to achieve reasoned conclusions would have been sufficient to have compiled a book on the military one-inch in its own right. That has therefore been reserved for future toil by others together with the Tourist and District maps, the history of which would occupy a small volume, and other Popular-based maps, such as those of the Land Utilisation Survey of Britain, undertaken by Sir Dudley Stamp in the 1930s.

The purpose of this book is therefore threefold; first, and principally, it is an investigation of the production, specification and publishing history of the standard sheets of the Popular Edition one-inch map of England and Wales. Secondly, it sets out to provide a brief, selective examination of the extent to which the map can be regarded as a useful cartographic tool in the study of the geography of the country between the wars and, in looking at the methods of marketing the map, to attempt to evaluate the commercial performance of the Popular Edition. The third objective is to supply a basis for future geographical and historical studies by providing as comprehensive a catalogue as possible of the states of the individual sheets of the Popular Edition of England and Wales.

This account, then, does not pretend to be complete; it is intended merely as a general introduction to selected technical and social aspects of Ordnance Survey one-inch map production between 1892 and 1939, and, in particular, as a companion to the Popular Edition Ordnance Survey one-inch map of England and Wales.

G R

T H E

Ordnance Survey Maps
of Great Britain

on the scale of

ONE INCH TO ONE MILE

EVER since the foundation of the Ordnance Survey in the 18th Century the One Inch to One Mile has been the standard Small-Scale Map of the country and to-day it is the most complete topographical record in existence. Periodically it has been thoroughly revised and brought up to date and each new edition has been adapted to the needs of the time.

The sheets of the present series (the Popular Edition) are invaluable to Walkers, Cyclists, Motorists and all those who require accurate maps for Scientific or Commercial purposes.

Each normal sheet of the Popular Edition measures 27 x 18 inches and consequently covers an area of 486 square miles.

All roads are shown and are classified by means of distinctive colouring according to the nature of their surface, suitability for fast traffic, etc. Footpaths, towns, villages, railways and stations, rivers, streams, parks, woods, county boundaries, high and low watermark are all accurately delineated. Altitudes above Mean Sea Level are shown along Main Roads and on the summits of high ground, and contours are drawn at 50 feet intervals.

Objects of Antiquarian interest are indicated by Old English or Roman Characters.

ENGLAND AND WALES.—The "One-Inch" Map is available in the following forms :—

(1) 4th (POPULAR) EDITION, Coloured. This Edition is based on the 3rd Revision of the country which took place between 1914 and 1925, but Roads, Railways and minor details are constantly being corrected on the printing plates so that reprints of the map are brought up to date as far as the rapidity of modern development allows. Water is shown in blue, woods green, 1st Class Roads red, 2nd Class Roads (fit for ordinary traffic) brown,

Fig.1 The front of a 1932 Ordnance Survey fold-out leaflet advertising the one-inch maps of Great Britain. *Private collection.*

Chapter I

THE ONE-INCH MAP OF ENGLAND AND WALES 1801-1919

It is possible to make a charming decoration out of the most accurate and efficient of modern maps. The Ordnance Survey printed in five colours is a beautiful thing to look at, and one can imagine a panel, or a whole wall of a study richly and interestingly adorned with a slice of England reduced to the scale of an inch to the mile.
Aldous Huxley, 1925[1]

The one-inch map began, in 1801, as the only cartographic product of the Ordnance Survey; by 1919, it constituted a mere fraction of the output of this 'great map-producing industry'.[2] Yet the one-inch was the most used, and most generally known of Ordnance Survey maps, and served the wide ranging needs of government officials, statisticians, engineers, social legislators, antiquarians - and indeed, as Winterbotham[3] remarked, one could go on for a week - 'finally it ends up with the man in the street'.[4] The one-inch map, as the cartographic flagship of the Ordnance Survey, therefore received attention out of all proportion to its size in relation to the total map production of the Survey. One of the principal reasons for this was that it was the smallest scale at which any useful synthesis of the large scales could be made; it was therefore the smallest scale at which all valuable social and physical data of the nation could be encapsulated in graphic form. Ideally, it should provide, at reasonable intervals, a 'snapshot' of the state of, for example, road and rail communications, urban development, or afforestation. No wonder that Winterbotham concluded that it was 'a scale which we can afford to take very few risks with. It must show everything to everybody.'[5]

The designer's dilemma in creating a map that had to be all things to all men was perhaps best exemplified in the Popular Edition one-inch map of England and Wales (hereafter referred to as the 'Popular Edition' or 'Popular'), for it inherited all the problems associated with devising a new map using existing materials, and eventually led Close to start with a clean slate for the Popular Edition map of Scotland, which was to be entirely redrawn. The production of the England and Wales Popular Edition series was a reaction to growing criticism, voiced earlier in 1890, that the one-inch maps did not meet 'popular requirements'.[6] The Popular was the last one-inch map series of England and Wales to be derived from engraved copperplates, and the first to contain sheets which had been reproduced from original drawings on paper. First on sale to the public in 1919,

---

1   Quoted by Withycombe, (1925), from an unidentified text; Withycombe appears to have assumed that Huxley was referring to the Popular Edition.

2   Ilkeston, (1911a), p.5.

3   Harold St John Lloyd Winterbotham, Director General, Ordnance Survey, 1930-1935.

4   Winterbotham, (1934b), p.104.

5   *Ibid.*

6   Crook, (1890).

it remained as the basic form of the one-inch map of England and Wales for thirty years. Although it was cartographically inferior to its successor, the Fifth Edition, which was introduced in 1931, the latter's incomplete coverage of the country ensured the continuing sales of the Popular Edition throughout the inter-war years. After the war, Popular Edition material, which had been used as the basis for the War Revisions of the one-inch (in areas not covered by the Fifth Edition), was used in the construction of the New Popular (Sixth Edition) for those areas not covered by the Fifth. Therefore much of the Popular survived beyond the introduction of the Seventh Series from 1952 for which it provided the stylistic concept, as revealed in a letter from Cheetham, designer of the Seventh Series, to Close, architect of the Popular Edition:

> I am now starting the design of a new 1" map which will replace the New Popular but be on the same sheet lines. It will not be markedly different from the New Popular, but in some respects is going closer to the design of the original Popular.[7]

The influence of the Popular Edition on the cartography of the one-inch map, and on the First Series of the 1:50,000 map (which was based on Seventh Series material) can therefore be said to have extended from at least 1914, when the first prototypes appeared, to 1974, when the first sheets of the Second Series 1:50,000 map were published. In many ways, the specification of the Popular had evolved from the ideas discussed during the sitting of the two important Baker and Dorington Committees,[8] both held in 1892. Detailed accounts of the specific influence of these committees on the one-inch map are given in the chapters devoted to specification, but we may here note that the major recommendations of both: that the one-inch should be in colour, that extra contours should be inserted, roads be re-classified and publicity for the maps be generated, only came to full fruition with the Popular Edition. A third departmental inquiry, the Olivier Committee,[9] held in 1914 to inquire into the sale of small-scale maps, was to have a lasting effect on the marketing of Ordnance Survey maps and, in particular, was directly responsible for the emergence of the Popular Edition.

The true creator of the Popular Edition was, however, not the joint wisdom of departmental committees, but Colonel Charles Close, who had been appointed Director General in 1911 at the age of 46. In 1893, when both the Dorington and Baker Reports had just been printed, Close, who was then 28, returned from being in charge of the Great Triangulation of India to the School of Military Engineering at Chatham, where he spent the next sixteen months. His primary interest was in surveying, and it is possible that during this time he could have had opportunities to discuss the development of the national mapping with Major-General Sir Charles Wilson (Director General, Ordnance Survey 1886-1894). Close was to spend parts of 1897 and 1899 working at the Ordnance Survey, and had already, by 1898, written the *Text book of military topography*. He spent another brief period with the Ordnance Survey, this time at the division in York, then went on to become Instructor in Surveying at Chatham and, in 1905, he became head of the Topographical (later, Geographical) Section, General Staff. In the meantime, he had

---

7   RGS Archives (Close Correspondence). Maj.-Gen. Geoffrey Cheetham, Director General (1943-1949), to Close 7/5/1948.

8   The fullest account of the Dorington Committee proceedings is in Seymour, (1980), chapter 18.

9   The proceedings are described in Seymour, (1980), pp.225-7.

written more works on geodesy and surveying, and had had considerable experience of surveying abroad.[10] By 1911, therefore, he had a wide knowledge of map production for both civil and military purposes. He believed that the only effective stimulus to the production of topographical surveys was military necessity, and that 'the civil public finds no great need for such surveys'.[11] Even so, he was to provide, in the Popular Edition, a map which was intended to meet military requirements, but which was packaged to appeal to civilian tastes.

However, the now familiar design of the Popular Edition was not Close's preferred cartographic style in 1911, and was certainly not his first choice for the new map of England. Within a few months of his appointment, Close had halted the production of the few dull and unimaginative sheets of the Fourth Edition of the one-inch, which had been initiated by his predecessor Colonel S.C.N. Grant in the traditional mould of the New Series: the one-inch map of the 1870s-1890s. At the same time he stopped work on the Third Revision, which had begun in 1909, and he replaced both with new revision procedures and improved cartographic practices which were designed to revolutionise the appearance of the small-scale maps. Close intended that a new one-inch map should be introduced that should surpass all others at this scale for visual beauty as far as the representation of relief was concerned.

And yet, as O'Brien has said,[12] Close was not a cartographical radical. His views on what constituted the model small-scale topographical map were well formed by 1911, and were set out in a paper entitled 'The ideal topographical map' and delivered to the Royal Geographical Society in 1905.[13] His three-point profile of the qualities possessed by the best topographical maps comprised, first, that all the information should be accurate; second, that as much information should be shown as possible; and third, that the information should be presented as intelligibly as possible. The first element was determined by the field methods used in survey, but the second and third were frequently matters of opinion. For example, Close was convinced that the inclusion of parish boundaries on the one-inch map cluttered the image. His thinking on this (which reflected that of the two 1892 Committees) proved to be misguided, and the consequences of omitting these from the Popular Edition was to become an embarrassment to the Ordnance Survey.[14]

Close's interpretation of map intelligibility, that it 'depends more upon the use of colour than upon anything else'[15], does not sit easily, from a technical point of view, with his strongly-held opinion, to which he remained wedded for many years, that 'for

10 A list of Close's publications is given in Freeman, (1985).

11 RGS Archives (Close Correspondence). Close to Hinks, 20/11/1916.

12 O'Brien, (1992), pp.1-7.

13 Close, (1905).

14 In 1918, Close decreed that only in 'very special cases' would impressions from copper be provided and only then 'if good reason is shown' (OSL G7094, circular dated 1/4/1918); however, hundreds of thousands of Small Sheet Third Edition outline sheets had to be printed in the 1920s and 1930s for the very 'good reason' that they were the only one-inch map to show parish boundaries. Many of these were printed from stone or zinc from about 1936.

15 Close, op.cit., p.635.

Fig.2 Colonel Sir Charles Arden-Close (1865-1952), Director General, Ordnance Survey 1911-1922. Close became Head of the Topographical (from 1907, Geographical) Section, General Staff in 1905. Many of his ideas on small-scale cartography developed from this date. He took the name Arden-Close in 1938 to comply with the terms of a bequest. *Private collection.*

the best work ... paper draughtsmanship is not required, but engraving on copper, which no paper draughtsmanship can touch.'[16] The technical problems associated with producing a coloured map from an engraved base had already been experienced with the Third Edition, yet Close was to continue with engraving for the Popular. Again, this was to have costly repercussions for the Ordnance Survey. One of the reasons for his persistence with engraving may have been his experience on the Survey of India in the 1880s, where he found the style of reproduction was 'weak ... a rather coarse lithography in black which did not compare favourably with European styles of the same date'.[17] Close remained committed, until 1921, to engraving as the only means of producing high quality work. Nevertheless, his introduction of a smaller contour interval and thorough overhaul of the road classification system did transform the one-inch map into a popular product.

He was helped in this by Captain J. Withycombe,[18] the officer in charge of the Maps Branch, whose artistic skills, knowledge of lettering, strong feeling for design and business acumen were 'found useful' in the preliminary trials of the Popular Edition.[19] Close recalled that the Popular Edition had been issued 'under the influence of two ideas': first, the war of 1914-18 had delayed the issue of a new one-inch map, which was to boast an intricate relief system. Instead, a simple, straightforward map, requiring no complex printing plates which took time to prepare, was to be produced in order to minimise the delay of publication; and secondly, the map 'should be as clean and clear as possible, and very easy to read'.[20]

At first sight, the Popular Edition, uncluttered by hachures or shading, certainly did appear to be a clear map. Cartographic clarity is taken for granted today, and is embodied in the specification for the 1:50,000 map; yet eighty years ago the publication of such a map as the standard national map series at the one-inch scale was something of a revolution. In order to understand this, we need to consider what one-inch mapping was available before the First World War. At the beginning of the twentieth century, the Ordnance Survey one-inch map, in published form, was one hundred years old. It had taken seventy years to complete the first edition, which was issued in 110 sheets. Known as the 'Old Series', this first map was derived, in the south, principally from two-inch surveys, but also from six and three-inch surveys which dated back to the eighteenth century. Although this block, south of the Preston-Hull line, underwent revision in the 1820s and 1830s, it was not as rigorously compiled as the northern sheets, which were derived from basic surveys at the scales of six and twenty-five inches to the mile after 1840.[21] By 1873, therefore, when the final sheet of England and Wales was published, much of the map was already out of date.

In 1871, the War Office had complained about the inadequacy of the southern sheets,

16 RGS Archives (Close Correspondence). Close, 'Notes on Draft Evidence on the Education of Geographical Draftsmen', 26/11/1916.
17 Quoted in Freeman, (1985), p.2.
18 John Gidley Withycombe, died 1934. Obituary by Willis, (1935).
19 RGS Archives (Close Correspondence). Close to Jack, 3/2/1934.
20 Close, (1932), p.53.
21 For a comprehensive account of the Old Series see the introductory essays in Margary, (1975-1992).

Fig.3 Officers and principal civilian staff of the Ordnance Survey, taken at some time between March 1926 and March 1929. **Left to right, back row**: Frederick C. Bagley, Chief Clerk and Finance Officer; Capt.? S.F. Turner; Capt. John Gidley Withycombe (not in uniform), in charge of Map Sales and Issues; Capt. H. Bagot. **Second row**: Harold L.P. Jolly, Research Officer; O.G.S. Crawford, Archaeology Officer; Capt. A.W. Heap. **Third Row**: Major? D.R. Martin; Lieut. N.A.M. Swettenham; Capt? H.A. Bazley; unknown; unknown. **Fourth row**, sitting: Major? D.A. Hutchison; Col. G.S.C. Cooke, Executive Officer; Brig. E.M. Jack, Director General; Lt.Col. M.N. MacLeod (Director General, 1935-1943); unknown. *Ordnance Survey*.

and Treasury sanction was obtained to prepare a new one-inch map for the southern block, to be based on the new large-scale surveys as they progressed southwards. The northern sheets, which had already been prepared in this way, were incorporated in the new series without revision, and instead of being numbered from south to north, sheet numbering now began in the north, and the southern sheets which had formerly been of various sizes, now conformed to the dimensions of the northern sheets. The whole was known as the 'New Series', but only the southern sheets (nos 1-90) were 'new', or, it might be more appropriate to say, only the original southern sheets could be termed 'Old Series'. For the north of England, both Old and New Series sheets, with their different numbering systems, were on sale simultaneously, confusing map-seller and customer alike.[22]

With the advent of the New Series began the proliferation of varieties of the standard one-inch map which was to bring further confusion to the map market by 1914. The

22 Hayes Fisher, (1896b), para.403.

facsimile duplication of engraved copperplates had been made possible by the introduction of electrotyping[23] to the map-making process in the 1830s. The new process introduced the ability to separate the component features of the map onto different copperplates, and this facility produced two basic forms of the one-inch map: a contoured outline edition without hachures, and an edition with hachures (sometimes referred to as 'with hills'). It was only a short step to the printing of the hachures in a different colour - brown - and a new sophistication was brought to the appearance of the one-inch map. Experiments in colour-printing had taken place by 1892,[24] and more were made during the First Revision of the New Series,[25] between 1893 and 1898, which produced four versions of the one-inch map: outline; hills in black; hills in brown, and coloured (brown hills, red contours, yellow roads, blue water).

The nomenclature of the one-inch map

This multiplicity of map styles was to generate problems in nomenclature which remain to this day. The Popular Edition was also known as the Fourth Edition - but it was not actually fourth in line from the beginning. A Second Revision had begun in 1901 which was to produce the 'Third Edition' of the one-inch map. This, too, appeared in a variety of guises, and even changed its sheet lines halfway through publication. It was the first one-inch map series of England and Wales to carry a series title - Third Edition - on the sheets other than a sheet name and number and 'Ordnance Survey of England', and was the first to use a numbered edition designation that was to be one of a sequence, with the exception of the Popular Edition, which terminated with the Seventh Series.

This succession was not a straightforward progression from one to seven. There were actually eleven distinct 'editions' of the one-inch between 1801 and 1974, and most of these were published in more than one version. It is inevitable, therefore, that the many inconsistencies in the Ordnance Survey's practice of naming their maps should have generated a persistent confusion of terminology, which has been compounded by the appearance, in a recent history of the Ordnance Survey, of a table which applies the term 'New Series' to all the one-inch maps up to and including the Sixth Edition.[26] In one sense, every new edition was a 'new series', and that, indeed, was how the original New Series came to be named. At the same time, the term 'Old Series' came into being retrospectively. These terms applied only to England and Wales; they were never printed on the map and were first used on the indexes to the one-inch maps of England and Wales which appeared in the Ordnance Survey *Annual Report* for 1873. Such names were the product of a mapping organisation which was pioneering the way in map series production: there was no standard terminology which could be followed, and no thought seems to have been given to the concept of regularly produced, completely revised, editions of the one-inch until the 1890s.

---

23 Electrotyping for engraved map copperplates was first used on the Survey of Ireland between 1837 and 1840. Descriptions of the process are given in *Account of the Methods and Processes ...* (1875), and Sankey, (1995).

24 Dorington, (1893c), paras 2835, 3473, 4266.

25 Hayes Fisher, (1896b), para.1760.

26 Owen and Pilbeam, (1992). The 1995 reprint has amended the tables to conform with the nomenclature used in Hodson, (1995).

Old Series	1805-1874
New Series	1874-1897
Revised New Series (First Revision)	1895-1904
Third Edition (Second Revision)	1903-1913
Fourth Edition (abandoned)	1911-1912
Popular Edition (Third Revision)	1919-1926
Fifth Edition (Fourth Revision)	1931-1939
War Revision 1940	1940-1943
Second War Revision 1940	1940-1944
New Popular (Sixth) Edition	1945-1947
Seventh Series	1952-1961

Fig.4 Table of the one-inch maps of England and Wales. The dates are those of first publication, and do not take account of reprints. Fuller details appear in Appendix 1.

When, therefore, it became the turn of the New Series to undergo revision for the compilation of a new up-to-date one-inch map, it was referred to, loosely, but following a natural sequence, as the 'Revised New Series' or 'New Series, Revised'.[27] Only when this in turn came to be revised does the penny seem to have dropped, and the formal designation of 'editions' was adopted in 1903 with the Third Edition. This very term implies one of two interpretations: first, that the Old Series was being deliberately, and conveniently, ignored. After all, the standards of survey for sheets 1-90 fell far short of their northern counterparts (sheets 91-110), which had been incorporated, lock, stock and barrel, with different sheet numbering, into the New Series. It follows, therefore, that the name 'Third Edition', used in the context of this interpretation, must imply that the New Series was the first edition, and the Revised New Series was the second edition, which, de facto, they undoubtedly were, as long as we, too, ignore the Old Series. The second interpretation is that the Old Series was thought of as the first edition, and both the New Series and Revised New Series were together regarded as the second edition, as suggested by Harley.[28]

An excellent attempt has been made to classify the New Series into first and second editions, treating the Third Edition as a development within the New Series, rather than

---

27 The first official published reference to the 'Revised New Series' appears to have been in *Publications issued from 1-31 March 1895*, when the publication in outline of sheets 274, 306, 315 and 321 was announced.

28 Harley, (1964), p.16, citing Harvey and Thorpe, (1959). Reference is made in Harley to the citing in the Davidson Committee of the Revised New Series as the Third Edition, implying that the Old Series was considered as the First. This simply demonstrates the confusion which arises in applying new terminology retrospectively.

as an evolution of it.[29] There seems to be little doubt that this was the way in which the Ordnance Survey itself considered these maps. As far as the Third Edition is concerned, the title appears only on the map, not on the cover, and, although the publication reports used the edition title,[30] in other descriptions the Third Edition is referred to either as 'the coloured map', or the 'Large Sheet Series' or 'Small Sheet Series'. Even in the official literature of 1917, the identification of the Third Edition, whose description appears under the heading 'New Series', can be inferred only from the physical details given. Oliver has recently extended his classification of the New Series to embrace the Fifth Edition and Seventh Series on the grounds that they were all derived from the larger scales, rather than from a specific survey for the one-inch map.[31] This view appears to take no account of map construction and specification changes, and is not followed here.

In this book, in order to avoid ambiguity and to preserve cartobibliographical accuracy as far as possible, it has been considered preferable not to impose any retrospective classification system on the several series, but to adopt first, titles that appeared on the map itself, and secondly, commonly-used terminology that appeared in official publications. Therefore, this study will refer, for example, to 'New Series' and 'Revised New Series', and 'Third Edition' in order to avoid any implication that the Old Series is being disregarded. None of the one-inch maps can be considered usefully in isolation from its forebears or successors, but there has been, until only recently[32] no full list of the main editions and their variants, nor is there a complete history of this long-lived scale.[33] Since many of these maps are relevant to the Popular Edition, either because it was derived from them, or because it provided material for their compilation, a brief listing of them has been provided in Appendix 1.

A third revision, which began in 1909, produced a named Fourth Edition,[34] which, after the publication of a few sheets, was passed over in favour of the Popular Edition, which was also known as the 'Fourth'. But this designation of Fourth Edition for the Popular, which was used in annual reports and descriptive booklets, was printed on neither map nor cover.[35] Close's proposed new, intricate, relief edition was itself referred to as a new edition of the New Series[36] in 1914, but this term was not used in

---

29 Oliver, (1982b).

30 The first official printed use of the title 'Third Edition' seems to have been in *Publications issued from 1st to 31st July 1903*. The first sheets to be published, in outline, were 1, 2, 4, 5, 317, 331, 332, 333, 344, and 345.

31 Oliver, (1991), [pp.6, 8].

32 Hellyer, (1999).

33 The nearest approach, which is very brief, is Hodson (Ed), (1991b). A Master's thesis, by Roberts (1946), gives a superficial examination of the conventional signs of the one-inch maps up to the Sixth Edition, but uses no original documentary material in the study. In the early 1960s, Major-General A.H. Dowson (Director General 1961-1965) compiled a history of the one-inch map which it was proposed to publish as an Ordnance Survey Professional Paper, but this was not carried through. Other short accounts of the one-inch map appear in Harley, (1964) and Hodgkiss, (1969-70).

34 The publication of this was first announced in *Publications issued 1st to 31st January 1911*. The last sheet was published September 1912.

35 Oliver, (1992b), gives the background to the true Fourth Edition.

36 Olivier, (1914a), para.19.

conjunction with its replacement, the Popular, after about 1918. By then, in spite of its Third Edition small sheet copperplate parentage, its specification was evolving away from the New Series, and relations between the two became distant by the 1930s.

The naming of the Popular Edition, which was sub-titled on the cover 'Contoured Road Map', marked a turning point in Ordnance Survey attitudes towards marketing its maps. The concept of a map which would be popular with the purchasing public, as well as fulfilling military and governmental requirements, grew slowly from the recognition in the 1880s that the contoured outline one-inch map was more popular than the hachured version, and from the suggestions made in 1892 that a coloured one-inch would be a 'pretty, popular map', to the realisation in 1914 that, compared with commercial publications, the Ordnance Survey maps were distinctly unpopular, not only in terms of price, but also in content and presentation. As if to emphasise Close's concern that Ordnance Survey small-scale maps should be more in tune with public requirements, the key word throughout the report of the 1914 Olivier Committee was 'popular'. References were made to 'popular forms of Ordnance Survey maps', and to the fact that the Survey had to compete against the 'popular maps produced by Messrs Bacon, Philip and other enterprising firms of map producers'. In fact, it was wryly observed that the cheaper and poorer the map, the greater seemed to be the sales.[37]

The proposed new road classification was expected to 'increase the popularity' of the Ordnance Survey maps, but some aspects of relief portrayal were 'unsuited to popular use'. Finally, the birth of the Popular Edition Contoured Road Map is anticipated in paragraph 32 of the 1914 Olivier report. The Committee's deliberations had highlighted the need for the Ordnance Survey to produce a competitively priced map. It was not the first time this had been suggested; the concept of the 'cheap' map was mooted at least as early as 1872,[38] and the '6d. map' ethos was frequently debated throughout the 1890s; the nearest it ever came to realisation was with the Popular Edition. Close provided examples of a contemplated 6d. map to show to those giving evidence at the Olivier Committee in 1914. The Committee reported:

> We have had the opportunity of examining a proposed 'Contoured Road Map', a new type of map on the 1-inch scale which ... contains the new system of road classification and shows contours, but is without layers or hill shading ... This map should become a highly popular form of the 1-inch ...'[39]

The Committee did not go so far as to recommend the formal adoption of this map, but in suggesting that it would be 'sold in large numbers', at 6d. a copy, it gave implied authority to the Ordnance Survey to produce a cheap alternative to Close's proposed fully coloured relief series (discussed below). In the event, it was this cheap option which was to become the Popular Edition.[40] The formal designation of the series as 'Popular Edition' was made in the Ordnance Survey catalogue for June 1918. By combining the 'Popular' element with the 'contoured road map' description - a well-used term by

37 Hayes Fisher, (1896b), para.401.
38 Dorington, (1893c), para.225.
39 Olivier, (1914a), para.32.
40 This point was first made in Seymour, (1980), p.231.

commercial map publishers[41] - the Ordnance Survey had hit upon a winning formula, specifically devised to attract Winterbotham's 'man in the street'.

'Novelties in Cartography': the experiments of 1912-16

In 1892 it had been recommended that experiments in the design of the small-scale maps - the trying out of 'novelties in cartography' - should be made with maps of special areas, rather than with a national series.[42] Very little was done to implement this suggestion until Close became Director General, nearly twenty years later. In his first annual report he gives a hint of the break with the past:

> The one-inch map, coloured edition [i.e. the Third Edition Large Sheet Series], is good of its kind, but by no means represents the last word in cartography ... it is certain that improvements can be effected in our standard small-scale maps.[43]

At this time, there were five versions of the one-inch map (Third Edition),[44] based on the Second Revision which was carried on between 1901 and 1912. As well as these, it was still possible to obtain, by special request, and at a cost of ten shillings, copies of the engraved southern Old Series sheets.[45] By April 1912 it had been decided to discontinue the two hachured forms of the black outline Third Edition maps[46] and, within a year, experiments had begun 'to improve the character of the coloured edition of the one-inch map.' Two years later, several sheets of this new one-inch were in an advanced state of preparation, and it was expected that some would be published during the summer. What, then, was the new edition to look like, and what was the background to Close's experiments, and what areas did they cover? In 1911, Close sought to reduce the number of one-inch styles available to the public, and to improve what remained. He regarded the 1897 type of coloured map as occupying 'a high place amongst the maps of the world', but acknowledged that 'owing to recent cartographical progress, its relative position some years ago was higher.'[47] He continued to emphasise his point by commenting that maps had become more complex, 'and our cartographical ideals more exacting', and pointed to the virtual demise of maps printed in black. He cited three apparent defects in the existing one-inch map [i.e. the Third Edition]: first, the road classification did not meet modern standards; second, the hill features fell short of the possibilities of modern cartography, and third, the existence of parish boundaries served only to confuse the detail. In 1912, he therefore initiated a series of experiments with the one-inch map which were designed to improve the representation of hill features, without omitting the hachures. The key to these experiments was the use of colour and in the

41 Gall & Inglis's contoured road books, for example. Bartholomew also produced the 'Contoured Road Map of Scotland' and of England and Wales before 1913; NLS, Bartholomew Printing Archive: Book 52.

42 Dorington, (1893a), recommendation 18, p.xxxviii.

43 *Annual Report*, (1911/12), p.5.

44 Small Sheet Series: outline; hills in black; hills in brown; coloured. Large Sheet Series: fully coloured.

45 *Ordnance Survey maps of the United Kingdom A description of their scales, characteristics &c.*, (1917).

46 The first Ordnance Survey catalogue to record the decision to cease publication was that for 1st April 1912. A printed slip announcing the withdrawal of the two forms is pasted over the original entry on the example in the British Library.

47 *Annual Report*, (1911/12), p.5.

combination of different methods of showing relief. By this time the French had made 'a real study of the Marseilles sheet', an early example of the new 1:50,000 series, and the Ordnance Survey was having 'to look to [its] laurels.'[48] Apart from the representation of relief, there were the roads, whose cartographic depiction was 'one of the greatest defects'[49] and were now seriously out of date. At Close's request,[50] the War Office assembled a committee early in 1912 to decide on a suitable road classification system. Their recommendations (discussed in Chapter VII), slightly modified by Close, were to be adopted for the Popular Edition.

In the thirty years between 1895 and 1925, mapmaking, as Hinks remarked, had been 'profoundly modified by the rapid development of colour lithography'.[51] The 'enormous resulting improvement was conspicuously in the representation of relief', and it was in this sphere that the Ordnance Survey, under Close, was to excel. Close had already worked with Survey of India maps which had employed hill shading techniques, and he was responsible for the enhanced version of the Persia and Afghanistan sheet (GSGS 2149, 1:4,055,040),[52] which added hill shading to the layers, giving a 'far more speaking picture of the country'.[53] Close's experiments with this map had been made in 1907 and 1908;[54] at the same time Walter Coote Hedley, who had reorganised the map printing of the Survey of India and improved its colour printing, had joined the Ordnance Survey where he 'put renewed life and enthusiasm into the printing department'.[55] These two must have exchanged ideas on colour printing, particularly during the experiments with the 1:1,000,000 International Map of the World (IMW; whose central office was at the Ordnance Survey, while much of the cartography was done at the Royal Geographical Society). One of the British contributions to this map was to produce the 'supreme example of skill in layer colour-printing.'[56]

This ultimate model was the 'Gamme', or colour scale, which had been attached to the Report of the Paris Conference on the IMW which had been held in 1913. In referring to it, Hinks added that there were 'infinite possibilities in the combination of layer colouring with contours, hachure, vertical and oblique hill shading'. This particular blend of techniques, now ascribed to Close, was in fact a development by him of an idea by George Philip, who in response to Close's own views on the ideal topographical map said, in 1905, that

48 Winterbotham, (1936b), p.75. A full study of the development of colour printing by the Ordnance Survey in the context of international development in this field is being made by Ian Mumford for a Ph.D. on 'Maps and Lithography'; only passing reference to foreign material is therefore made here.

49 Douglas Freshfield, commenting in the discussion following Close's paper on 'The ideal topographical map' (1905).

50 Olivier, (1914b), p.30.

51 Hinks, (1925). Arthur R. Hinks, Secretary, Royal Geographical Society.

52 RGS Archives (Winterbotham Correspondence). Winterbotham to Hinks, 8/9/1931.

53 Memorandum by Col. Hedley, March 1913. RGS Archives (1/M Map Correspondence).

54 RE Corps Library, 'Outline history of W.O. Map Printing Section. 1897-1930. [signed] J. Crawford, Late Superintendent Map Printing Section. (RE/GSGS/M.I.4). I am indebted to Peter Chasseaud for drawing this file to my attention.

55 Obituary of Sir Walter Coote Hedley, (q.v. in Bibliography) (1938).

56 Hinks, (1925).

if, in addition to the colours advocated by Major Close [i.e. blue for water, etc.], we combine tints, contours, and hachures, we can obtain a still more graphic effect. To my mind a perfect topographical map would be a kind of picture in which the elevations would be shown in detail by hill shading, the relative height by contour-lines ... and the absolute height above sea-level by a system of tinting in 'layers.' I do not think such a combination of flat tints, contour-lines and hill shading has been sufficiently emphasised; it seems to me it would give the most perfect result.[57]

Close expressed a decided interest in 'Mr Philip's suggestion of a combination of shading, tint, and contours', saying that it would be 'a very good thing to try'.[58] Doubtless he had Philip's ideas in mind while experimenting with the Afghanistan map, but it was to be a further eight years before Close was able to apply them to the one-inch map of England and Wales.

In the same year of the Paris Conference, 1913, two maps were published which were quite unlike anything produced previously by the Ordnance Survey. They embodied all of Philip's suggestions and added hachuring; in concept, they were the basis of tourist map production for the next ten years. The first, and best known, was of the Killarney district in Ireland.[59] Now a rare collector's item, this delightful map shows relief by a deft combination of black dotted contours, hachures, layering and a greyish-purple hill shading.[60] The contours were at intervals of 100ft up to 1000ft and thereafter at intervals of 250ft, while the layers ran from pale green through pale browns at bands of 0-300ft, 300-1250ft and 1250ft and over. It was the first colour-printed map to be produced in this country that could be described as a work of art. Thirteen runs through the press were claimed for it,[61] in order to produce the eleven colours that can readily be distinguished.[62] The Killarney sheet was hailed as the most complex system of hill representation yet adopted, and there was 'no hestitation in pronouncing [it] to be a long way the best topographical sheet of gently mountainous country yet published.'[63]

Using a similar specification, but with less subtle colours, a sample covering Keswick and Skiddaw in the Lake District was published in 1913 in the second edition of Close's *Text book of topographical and geographical surveying* (Plate 2). Here the tones are more honey coloured; the contours use the same interval as the Killarney map, but are dotted in brown instead of black, the hachures are a lighter brown, and three layers are used:

---

57 Close, (1905), p.643.

58 *Ibid.*

59 Illustrated in colour in Seymour, (1980), plate 15. The publication of this sheet was first announced in *Publications issued 1st to 30th September 1913*. It sold for 2/- mounted and folded, 1/6 paper folded, 2/- mounted flat, 1/6 paper flat, and 2/6 in folded sections. *Cork*, and *Belfast* (sheets 16, and 17) was also published in this style, but not until 1918.

60 Winterbotham, (1932a), p.21, describes this as 'crayon shading'.

61 Winterbotham, (1936b), p.75.

62 It is not clear how the thirteen printings were made up. The eleven that can be identified are: black, red (roads), orange (roads), solid blue (rivers), ruled blue (lakes), green (woods), brown (hachures), grey/purple (shading), three layers. Even so, it is possible that the two blues were printed from the same plate. It may be that the extra printings, if there were such, may have involved the hill shading and hachuring which is very subtle in its effect.

63 [Hinks], (1913).

a light yellowish green for 0-400ft, a light yellowish brown for land above 400ft, and a very slightly darker colour for ground above 700ft. The change between these last two layers is barely perceptible. The 'sunny side' is lit from the north-west, the shadow is lightly touched in, and the tops are illuminated, giving a cheerful appearance to an often gloomy landscape. Prominence has always been given to the Killarney sheet as the prototype of Close's proposed new one-inch series, but it seems that this example of the Lake District deserves equal, if not primary, status as a model for the new map of England. For while Close referred to the style of the Killarney sheet as 'somewhat similar to that of the new series,'[64] he described the Lake District map as 'an advance specimen' which had been published in 'reasonable anticipation' of the issue of the standard series.[65] This view is further confirmed by the specification given in contemporary instructions for the preparation of the new relief map (Appendix 2) which were printed in March 1913, and which prescribe not only brown contours, but also three 'Ground Tints' in green, light buff, and darker buff. The interval at which these colours were to be used is not stated, but it was intended that 'in sheets of small features' only the first two layers would be used. The Lake District specimen, which was printed in November 1913, conforms most closely to these instructions. For all that, Winterbotham was to claim that the Fifth (Relief) Edition was heir to the Killarney experiment. The true parent, as far as the colouring of the relief was concerned, was the Lake District sample.

We know from Winterbotham that at this time the cartography of foreign mapping was being scrutinised by the Ordnance Survey, and that he himself was 'privileged to talk a good deal to Close about his ideas'.[66] Unfortunately, he did not expand on the content of these ideas; but clues to the thinking behind the development of the future one-inch map, and to the further experiments carried out in 1914, are given in the evidence of the Olivier Committee, which had convened on 9 June 1914. This reinforces the view that the principal object of the experiments was to improve the method of relief representation by using an unprecedented combination of conventions and printing in several colours, epitomised by the Killarney map which was constantly referred to throughout the Committee's Report.

On 7 July 1914, a Mr Southern, giving evidence as the representative of the Federation of Rambling Clubs, was asked if he had seen the new Dorking map,[67] and was shown the Dorking section with Leith Hill. This had contours, layering and hill shading. Close commented that the purpose of the Ordnance Survey with that map had been not to make the colouring 'too heavy, to make it indicative, but not to make it confusing'. The woods were tinted instead of being a heavy green, and Close remarked that it was not 'strictly on the old layer system' which was used as a means of emphasising the altitudes, and the technical term which he used to define the colouring was 'ground tones'.

At least three layers are discernible: 0-300ft light green; 300-600ft pale brown; 600ft and over, slightly darker brown; this was a different interval to that used for the Lake

---

64 *Annual Report*, (1913/14), p.10.
65 Close, 'The new one-inch Ordnance map'. (1931).
66 Winterbotham, (1934b), p.104.
67 Publication first announced in *Publications issued 1st to 30th June 1914*.

District, although the same concept of the three layers prevailed. In what seems to be the earliest version, the colours are muted, and the layers are almost imperceptible, giving a smooth, uninterrupted appearance to the three dimensional aspect of the map, but it did not achieve the delicacy of colouring of the Killarney sheet, and the reason for this was that the contours were printed as solid dark brownish green lines, and this gave the map a very heavy appearance. Apart from the colouring of its layers, roads and water, the Dorking map owed its specification to the Third Edition map. However, it was different enough to impress Mr Southern, who, on enquiring if other sheets were available in this style, was told that there were none.

In fact, the Glasgow sheet had just been published in May,[68] and Ilkley was to follow in July.[69] The Glasgow area (Plate 6) was chosen in response to the criticism that the complex method of showing relief would not work for an urban area because the hachures and shading would obscure the names. But the greatest density in detail for the Glasgow sheet is in the lowland thereby negating, in part, the purpose of the experiment in this area. Like the Dorking map, both Glasgow and Ilkley used the same contour interval of 100ft, the same three layers (both in interval and colouring), and the contours were printed in a dark sage, or brownish green. The water features followed the convention of the Killarney sheet, with rivers in solid blue, uncased, and lakes were shown by horizontal blue lines with blue casing thickened on the north and west sides. This convention was to be introduced to the Popular Edition only after it had been in production for two or three years.

Three more experimental maps were produced in 1914. The third national revision of the Ordnance Survey one-inch map on which the Popular Edition was to be based, began in 1912 with eight sheets in two blocks. One comprised the future Popular Edition sheets 137 (*Dartmoor, Tavistock & Launceston*), 138 (*Dartmoor & Exeter*), 144 (*Plymouth*), and 145 (*Torquay & Dartmouth*) and covered the Dartmoor region. The other, whose sheet lines coincided with sheets 114, 115, 124 and 125 of the Third Edition Large Sheet Series, contained Popular Edition sheets 113 (*Reading & Newbury*), 114 (*Windsor*), 123 (*Winchester*) and 124 (*Guildford & Horsham*), and surrounded the Aldershot area. Both these revision blocks were to produce the material for the experimental work of 1914.

If we look at the evidence of the Olivier Committee, we see that Close flourished an unidentified map in front of Mr Morrison (the Director of the firm of Cornish, of Birmingham) and asked him what he thought of it as a type of district map; it was 'the new type proposed for a cheap district map, with the roads classified in thirteen different forms'. Mr Morrison commented that it was a part of the country with not many first class roads in it; fortunately, he named three settlements: California Cross, Modbury and Kingsbridge, narrowing the search to the Torquay and Dartmouth area. We are also told that the map which Close exhibited showed two road gradients: slopes 1/10 to 1/7 and those steeper than 1/7. No map apparently survives for this area which fits this description exactly - it might have been the first prototype of the Popular Edition - but a unique sheet, based on the Third Revision of 1912-13, printed in 1914 and covering

---

68 *Publications issued 1st to 31st May 1914.*
69 *Publications issued 1st to 31st July 1914.*

Torquay and Dartmouth, is preserved in the Royal Geographical Society[70] (Plate 3). It appears to be the first map to be issued on the sheet lines of the Popular Edition, which had been devised between 1912 and 1914. But this example could hardly have been intended as a cheap road map, for although it carries the superior road classification which differentiated the Popular from the Third Edition, and shows the two slope gradients, the sophistication with which the relief is portrayed could not have been destined for a cheap product.

The black dotted contours, echoing the Killarney convention, are here drawn at 50ft intervals instead of 100ft, foreshadowing the specification for the Popular Edition. But the colouring of the 'ground tints' is a complete departure from the projected three layer convention in green and buff. Here, two layers in grey/buff tones are used for 0-300ft, and 300-900ft, with a very dark greyish buff for the lowest layer, giving an impression of aerial perspective, while two buff tints, increasing in depth with height, show ground from 900 to 1200ft, and over 1200ft; these are combined with faintly printed brown hachures and greyish hill shading, which, together with the use of a light tone to illuminate the 'tops', produced a most unusual effect for that period.[71] The Royal Geographical Society acquired this map from Winterbotham on 17 June 1914, together with some specimens of the International Map of the World. He described the sheet as a copy of 'the new 1" O.S. new style' which was sent 'to add tone to the proceedings'.[72] The letter does not give the background to the map, but Hinks was sufficiently impressed to describe this sheet as 'one of the most interesting and beautiful sheets ever printed by the Ordnance Survey,' and suggested that 'specimens should be secured for collections'.[73] It also demonstrated how much Close's ideas had moved on from the design of the Lake District specimen if the description of the Torquay sheet (assuming that the surviving example is the one referred to) as the 'new style' of one-inch map is accurate. The colouring of the map is indeed subtle, but the substitution of grey tones for green for the lower layers gives an overall subdued effect which might not have worked successfully for lowland Britain, especially in areas of urban development where the dense detail of the black outline plate would have combined to give a heavy appearance.

The other two maps, also based on the Third Revision, to be printed in 1914 were entitled *Aldershot District (North)* (Plate 4) and *Aldershot District (South)*; they were similar in concept to Killarney and Dorking. The importance of Aldershot from a military cartographic point of view is underlined by the constant production of maps of this area for military purposes since the late eighteenth century, and it is possible that the initiative

70 RGS OS Specimen no.49.

71 The effect is very similar to that achieved in a surviving MS hill shading drawing for part of sheet 145. Dated January 1914, and endorsed by J. Henry, it took 5½ days to complete. See Hodson, (1991b), p.22., item III.9b.

72 RGS Archives (1/M Map Correspondence). Winterbotham to Hinks, 17/6/14. The accompanying list of 'sheets forwarded' included 'New Series 1-inch. TORQUAY & DARTMOUTH sheet 145 (Devonshire).' Another map, referred to as a 'half-printed' and 'beautiful and delicately tinted map of the relief of South Devon' is mentioned in Ogilvie, (1915), p.67. It apparently showed relief and outline detail; no example seems to have survived.

73 Hinks, (1923), p.223.

for early revision of the barracks area and surrounding manoeuvre and training grounds came from the War Office. The two sheets were also printed in 1914 with contours only. All these sheets embody the legend and other marginalia of the future Popular Edition, although the alpha-numerical squaring across the face of the sheet, which characterises the later map is absent, as in *Torquay & Dartmouth*. Like this map, the first versions of the two Aldershot sheets show relief by dotted contours at 50ft intervals, but Aldershot and Torquay were treated differently with regard to layering and shading.

The *Aldershot District (South)* sheet has brown hachures printed over three layers; this was combined with a faint grey shading. In some printings the hachures are a dark brown, while in others they appear in a paler, more yellow colour, giving a completely different character to the map. In some versions, the bottom green layer is so faint as to be imperceptible, giving the sheet a subdued appearance. The variations in *Aldershot District (North)* included minor differences, such as more pronounced hill shading. Even in this respect, however, some copies show a marked variation in colouring such as a lighter brown for the hachures, a different green for the woods, a more royal blue for the water. It is therefore possible that other printing modifications, for both sheets, may exist in what could have been a deliberate sequence of colour experiments for which the documentation no longer exists. It is more likely, however, that the marked differences in appearance of these early colour-printed sheets, including Killarney and Dorking, stems more from an inability to control colour printing then as effectively as can be achieved today.

Two examples of the 'North' sheet, both dated 1914, provide particularly noticeable evidence of these colour variations: one includes hill shading which is partially omitted from the other. Like the Torquay map, the fully hill-shaded version of *Aldershot District (North)* shows the gradient of 1/10 to 1/7 in addition to slopes steeper than 1 in 7. On this sheet, as on Killarney, the hill shading is more than a mere boost to the hachuring, for it is present in areas where no hachuring can be discerned. This is particularly evident in the area north-west of Woking; the difference in hill shading between the two examples is pronounced but puzzling, for the partially shaded copy demonstrates a less well-defined shading over much of the map. This would seem to be a straightforward variation in colour control, which can be seen on both states of the hill shaded sheet.[74] The hill shading was presumably derived from the one-inch brushwork studies which had been prepared for the engraved hachured version of the New Series map; if this is so, it provides an interesting study of the extent to which the engraver edited the drawings. There is no doubt that the fully hill-shaded version of the 1914 Aldershot (North) map bears striking testimony to the value of the shading for terrain analysis at this scale, particularly for the lower lying areas below the 100ft contour.

The other versions of *Aldershot District (North)* (Plate 5) and *(South)*, which were printed in 1914, turned out, retrospectively, to be the true precursors of the Popular Edition. Published, as were their companions, 'For Official Use Only', they are characterised by the complete absence of hachures, shading and layering. The relief is shown only by solid line contours, printed in an unusual maroon/brown colour, at 50ft intervals. The water, as in the other Aldershot sheets, is shown in the same style as the

74 Colour photographs of these versions can be found in Hodson, (1995), figs.55a and b.

early Popular Edition sheets (Chapter VI). Apart from the fact that these maps are not on regular sheet lines, and do not, therefore have an index diagram to the adjacent sheets in the bottom margin, the only difference between these sheets and the regular Popular Edition early sheets is the colouring of the contours, the absence of the alpha-numerical squaring across the face of the map and the price note. It is reasonable to conjecture, in view of the area covered, that if a decision was made in 1914 to drop the sophisticated methods of relief portrayal it was because of a military requirement for a clear and uncluttered map. If this were so, it foreshadowed the resolution made in 1936 again, seemingly as a result of military pressure,[75] to abandon the Fifth (Relief) Edition in favour of the contours only version. Apart from a revival in 1932 of a hachured and shaded Aldershot (North) and (South) by Winterbotham, the future military maps of this area used only contours for relief depiction, as in the 1914 Popular prototype.

No other experimental work is recorded for 1914, and only one further trial sheet appears to have been undertaken between 1914 and 1918. Recalling some 'perfectly beautiful experiments of that time in colour printing', Winterbotham remembered one of Somerset 'which would have been of the greatest value to King Alfred in his western battles with the Danes, for the features stand out so that no man can misunderstand'.[76] In another text, Winterbotham recalled Close's experiments

> amongst which the Killarney sheet is the best known. To my mind, however, the most useful thing he produced as an experiment was a map of Somersetshire (Bridgwater) which now hangs in the office of O.Maps. A quite beautiful piece of work.[77]

Until 1991, no example of this Bridgwater sheet was known, but what appears to be at least one version of this experiment has come to light in a private collection.[78] Printed in 1916,[79] and based on the third revision of 1913, it comprises sheet 120 of the Popular Edition, although it is not so titled, but the sheet number, name and title: *Ordnance Survey of England and Wales Bridgwater & Quantock Hills*, are identical with the future published standard Popular Edition sheet.

It is, indeed, a striking map: its principal feature is the single pale buttery yellow colour which covers the land area, and which brings to mind Close's concept of a 'ground tone' which he described to the Olivier Committee. It is also reminiscent of a similar convention used for a few sheets of the half-inch map, which included a darker yellow background tone.[80] This yellow background was not an Ordnance Survey innovation; on the contrary, it seems to have been borrowed from the commercial map

75 Winterbotham, (1934b), p.111.

76 Winterbotham, (1936b), p.75.

77 Winterbotham, (1934b), p.104.

78 A brief description of the map and its discovery appears in Oliver, (1992a).

79 The letters 'C.B.' are lacking from the imprint; the map was therefore possibly printed before the 7th of June, after which the initials 'C.B.' were to be added to Close's name in imprints. Circular, C/C 2726/16.

80 For example, *Ordnance Survey of England New Forest and surrounding country parts of sheets 78, 79, 86, 87, 95, 96*. Scale 1:126,720, (1904).

publishers of the nineteenth century,[81] by whom the convention was in common use. On the Bridgwater sheet, relief is shown by dark brown contours at 50ft intervals and greyish brown hachures. There is no layering, and there appears to be no hill shading. This map is a reasonable example of the superiority of hachures in highlighting the nuances in land levels under 50ft; but it gives no more relief detail than the old Third Edition sheet, and Winterbotham's description that 'the features stand out so that no man can misunderstand' does not ring true if this example of sheet 120 is compared with the shaded and hachured version of *Aldershot District (North)*. It may be that yet another example of the Bridgwater sheet, with shading as well as hachures and layers, remains to be discovered.

Apart from the method of relief portrayal, the other principal difference between this map and the future standard sheet is that the woods are not printed in a solid green, but in a half screen, giving a light, translucent appearance, especially where these are superimposed on upland areas, where grey hachures and brown contours combine to give a predominantly dull appearance, in spite of the underlying yellow. Unlike the later published standard series sheet, this example does not show bathymetric layering, nor are the sand flats coloured, except in the overall blue used for the sea. This is a much greener blue than the more royal blue used for rivers, and this colour convention was to be used in some of the Popular Edition sheets. The price information in the marginalia carries over from the Third Edition, but the legend is, to all intents and purposes, the same as the early Popular Edition, except that it includes a symbol for parish boundaries: these did not appear on the new standard series, nor are they apparent on the face of this map, although the italicised names of parishes, where these do not coincide with village names, remain.

The purpose of the Bridgwater experiment is not recorded and the sheet is something of an anomaly in view of Close's statement that from the moment the War broke out 'the new map was put utterly aside.'[82] The whole idea may well have been Withycombe's brainchild, for he had been born and brought up in Somerset. In 1916 he was serving at the Ordnance Survey, first as the Officer in charge of the War Maps Department which was amalgamated after March 1916 with Map Sales and Issues, and at the same time, he held the position of Officer in charge of the Engraving and Small Scale Division. His finger would therefore have been firmly on the pulse of any planning or experimental work for the new one-inch map.

Several sheets of the new relief map were 'in an advanced state of preparation,' by April 1914.[83] What exactly was meant by this phrase is open to question, but in view of Close's statement in 1931[84] that it was unlikely that any of the plates for these sheets had been preserved, it can be deduced, since we know that the outline plates at least survived, that hachure, layering and hill shading plates had also been completed, and that it was these which had been lost. Nothing in the 1914 Olivier report indicated that any

---

81 For example, W.H. Smith's one-inch map of the Isle of Wight [1887]. Printed by Bartholomew, it closely resembles the Bridgwater sheet, with yellow base, green woods, roads in two colours, and contours. It lacks only the hachures.

82 Close, (1931).

83 *Annual Report*, (1913/14), p.9.

84 Close, *op.cit.*

27

sheets had been printed in their final form by June; however, the evidence given to the Olivier Committee by Lieut.-Col. E. P. Brooker, who was in charge of the Publication Department, gives the fullest contemporary written description of the proposed new style:

> The new 1-inch represents an attempt to combine the advantages of several systems of depicting landforms within the terms of reference that legibility of details and names must not be obscured. The systems to combine are a) contours, representing with scientific accuracy facts portrayed; b) hachures, more or less reliable information as to slopes in detail and under features; c) shading, to assist imagination to model the form, a conventional method broadly true of lighting from some specified direction; d) layers, to give a generalisation of absolute altitude above sea level.[85]

The inclusion of layers was justified on the grounds that they were necessary as an adjunct to the hachures and shading in order to 'confine the latter to their proper work of representing a scale of slope only', otherwise the draughtsmen 'get at sea and show the same slope on higher ground much darker than on low ground, thus departing from a coherent plan.'[86]

The English sheet which came closest to this ideal was the 1914 *Aldershot District (North)*, which combined all four relief methods, and, but for a different contour interval, and a slightly darker green, both for the bottom layer and for the woods, closely resembled the Killarney map. Although the Glasgow and Ilkley maps did use shading, the contours were shown as solid, rather than dotted lines. The instant effect of this was to make the map appear much heavier, so that it lost the 'delicacy', so characteristic of Killarney, the Lake District and Aldershot (North). It was this feature that Hinks referred to when, on reporting the retirement of Sir Charles Close in 1922, he wrote

> the increase in cost of production has forbidden for the time being any further progress with a delicately beautiful one-inch map that has been seen in proof: a triumph of colour printing'.[87]

It would seem, then, that even after the war, Close may have clung, briefly, to the hope that plans for the deluxe relief edition could be revived. Close's personal input to the design of what he was to refer to as his 'lost map',[88] (the Lake District style) was evidently significant, even though we have George Philip to thank for the original idea. The principal objective of the pictorial method was to produce on paper a three dimensional image of the landscape in hues which resembled as closely as possible the natural original. It was a concept which, as far as Ordnance Survey cartography was concerned, was first practised by Robert Dawson at the beginning of the nineteenth century,[89] and was the guiding principle behind the production of the 1959 tourist map of the Lake District.[90] The style was abandoned with great regret by those who had worked to perfect it, and those sheets which were almost complete in 1914, and which,

---

85 Olivier, (1914b), p.32.

86 A description of the planned eleven printings for this map is given in Appendix 2.

87 Hinks, (1922). The proof referred to is not identified, but may have been the Torquay and Dartmouth sheet.

88 Close, (1931).

89 Jones, (1974).

90 Harris, (1959).

according to an index map in the *Annual Report* for that year, embraced the whole of Cornwall, most of Devon and Somerset, all of Monmouthshire and parts of the surrounding counties, were now produced in the style of the popular 'Contoured Road Map', whose publication had been endorsed in 1914.

The Popular Edition, then, was never intended in the first instance to be produced as the principal one-inch map of the country, but was designed as a cheap alternative to a more sophisticated specification which, in the event, never materialised. It was a makeshift map, the product of the financial exigences of the aftermath of the First World War. The force of these cut-backs, and their effect on the Ordnance Survey is summed up in a trenchant retrospective by Close:

> I was directed to reduce the OS budget and I submitted a simple scheme by which we would omit the revision of those counties which had a population of less than 100 to the square mile. This scheme was decisively turned down ... and I was told to submit a much more drastic scheme ... at one time, I thought it possible that the Geddes Committee might recommend the abolition of the OS.[91]

It was into this indigent climate of post-war Britain that the Popular Edition was launched. The decision to name the series 'Popular Edition' was probably not made before 1918; had it been made any earlier, it is possible that the experimental Bridgwater sheet might have carried this name in 1916. However, at that point, it could not have been known that post-war economies would have eliminated the possibility of proceeding with the fuller colour specification.

The outline map

Colour undoubtedly enhanced the legibility of the map message as a whole - the overall distribution of woods, water, roads, settlements and relief could be taken in at a glance. For many, however, a plain black and white base map, on which only the salient features were shown, was essential for superimposing specialist thematic information. The term 'outline' was presumably a throwback to the days of engraving, when engravers with different degrees of skill were allocated discrete areas of work. Thus the writing would be the province of the best letterer, the engraving of the hachures for the hills was the most skilled work, and the outline, that is, the roads, rivers, settlement, and outlines of woods and parks, etc., was undertaken by a third engraver.

The outline one-inch maps first became popular when it was possible to produce the hachures on a separate copperplate, and demand for the unhachured version was always high, principally because the map was less cluttered and therefore more legible. It was also easier to plot different information onto an unhachured map. As colour printing became better established, some features, such as the water, and perhaps the contours, of the originally black and white outline map would be printed in colour; however, the aim was still to avoid the large areas of flat colour, such as layering for relief, and expanses of woodland.

The earliest statement on the form which the outline version of the Popular Edition map was to take appeared in the general instructions for the Third Revision of the one-

---

91 RGS Archives (Close Correspondence). Close to Jack, 18/3/1950.

inch map, which were dated 6 March 1913 (Appendix 2). These described the outline map as being prepared from three printings: outline (now excluding rivers and contours) black; water blue; and contours in red. In 1914, it seems that yet another form of outline

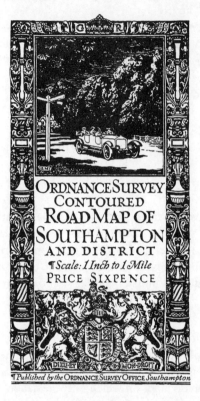

Fig.5 Cover design by Ellis Martin [1918/19] for a 6d. district road map. The formal top and side borders are reminiscent of his 1911 advertisement for Whiteley's. (Browne, 1991, p.62.) The design is printed in black on white, but 'Southampton', the price, and the initial letters O, S, C, R, and M, are printed in red. *Private collection.*

map was being contemplated in which only the roads were to be coloured[92] according to the new classification system (described in Chapter VII). It may have been this map that was originally intended to supply the sixpenny market, and for which Ellis Martin designed a cover (never used for the one-inch map) that emphasised the 'Road Map' element of the title, and which came to be used for the half-inch map (fig.5). This road version of the Popular Edition outline map was never published.[93] In any case, in spite of Close's description, during the proceedings of the Olivier Committee, of this proposed road map as an outline map, it is doubtful whether it is correct to refer to it as such. In the report of the 1914 Committee[94] Close stated that in future the black outline edition, which until June 1914 had been printed from copper in small sheets (12" x 18"), was only to be published, for England and Wales, in large sheets (18" x 27") from zinc or stone, and that it would show parish boundaries.

---

92 Olivier, (1914a), para.772.

93 However, a 'Road Edition' of the Lake District Tourist map, for example, was printed in 1920. Based on Third Edition material, but with Popular Edition-style marginalia, it showed only the roads in three colours and water in blue.

94 Olivier, (1914b), p.30.

Since Close had linked this description to a list of the one-inch maps already available in 1914, it is unclear whether he was referring to outline sheets of the Third Edition Large Sheet Series, or to the forthcoming large sheets of the new (future Popular Edition)

Fig.6 Proof of an Ellis Martin cover design, ca 1918-19, for the outline Popular Edition. The sheet name and price are printed in orange; the other detail is in black on a buff background. While the outline was not, as far as is known, ever sold in folded format in covers (unless, perhaps, made up to special order), this design was modified for the covers of the standard sheets. *Private collection.*

map. Hellyer records that 58 of the Third Edition Large Sheets were printed in Black Outline Edition form from the black and blue plates;[95] since the library accession dates of these sheets are 1918-19, it can be assumed that these were produced in accordance with Close's 1914 decision. At least one sheet of the Popular (sheet 96) was also issued in 1919 in black only format, and showed parish boundaries. It may have been for this format that Ellis Martin designed yet another cover which specified the title 'Popular Outline Edition', the price for which was to have been 7d. (fig.6). This cover seems never to have been used, and it appears that the outline edition of the Popular was usually published in paper flat form; it does not appear to have been advertised in any other way by the Ordnance Survey, although an example in an Ordnance Survey district map cover[96] is known to exist. Any outline sheets found in covers are likely to have been cased to order.

Although one black only outline sheet had been printed in 1919, it seems that this was not regarded as the final design for the map, for in his *Annual Report* to 31 March 1920

95 Hellyer, (1999), p.25.
96 Cover style H8(2) in Browne, (1991).

(p.9), Close announced that the 'exact form which the revised edition of the "*Outline*" *1-inch map* should take' was under discussion with the War Office, Admiralty, the Institution of Civil Engineers, the Surveyors' Institution, and 'other important engineering authorities'. In the following year, he reported that the type of revised outline map had been agreed, and that it was to be printed in black outline with reddish-brown contours - no other colours were to be used.[97] Close had already written to Hinks that the reddish contours had been asked for by the Institution of Civil Engineers 'and others'.[98] In fact, the outline edition of the Popular was produced in eight versions (see p.282), although some of these were distinguished by only minor differences. In 1944, Cheetham ordered an investigation into the reasons which led to the design and variations of the Popular Outline Edition,[99] but if such a study were made, it does not seem to have survived.

Publication of the Popular Edition

Uncertainty has been expressed in the past about the precise date of first publication of the Popular Edition. There are two reasons for this; first, four sheets (119, 120, 128 and 143) carry the initial printing date of 1918,[100] and secondly, chronological lists, compiled in about 1925,[101] have an entry for the Zinc Printing Department which states that the first sheet to be published, on 24 June 1918, was sheet 120 (Bridgwater), while an entry under the Map Department for 1918 reads: '1" England and Wales. Popular Edition. 1 sheet printed, 119 [i.e. sheet 119] published in July.' These departmental records were not carefully compiled, nor were they comprehensive - errors of fact in other entries lead one to be cautious in accepting dates without question. It seems reasonable to assume, however, that four sheets were indeed printed in 1918, but there is no other evidence to confirm that they were actually published, and on sale to the public.[102]

It seems possible that in 1918, the production of two versions of the one-inch map might still have been contemplated. The publication of the 6d. contoured road district map that had been endorsed by the Olivier Committee was evidently seriously considered at this time, otherwise it is difficult to justify the commissioning of the cover design (fig.5) by Ellis Martin (who first produced work for the Ordnance Survey in 1918). This embodies the title and price of the cheap map mentioned in 1914. Within months, this sixpenny map was to become the shilling unmounted Popular Edition sheet. The first formal reference to the official publication of the Popular Edition appeared in the Publication Report for June 1919,[103] where the issue of thirty sheets, including those

97   *Annual Report*, (1920/21), p.6.

98   RGS Archives (Close correspondence). Hinks to Close, 21/3/1921.

99   OSL Director General's Conference, no.3, 13/7/1944.

100 Sheet 118 was first published in June 1919 with a print date of 1919, but on the 1923 and succeeding reprints of the coloured sheet, the date was changed to 1918 (the outline sheet was dated 1924). It is not known if this was an error, or if the sheet really was printed in 1918.

101 PRO OS/18.

102 Seymour, (1980), p.231, quotes the 1918 publication date without question, but this was because there had been no opportunity to study the maps and their related documentation.

103 *Publications issued from 1st to 30th June 1919.*

mentioned above, was announced. Confirmation of 1919 as the date of first publication is found in a letter from Close to Hinks dated 8 January 1919. In reply to a request from Hinks for sight of the new one-inch, Close wrote:

> we will certainly send you specimens of our various new maps and map covers, but I should like to delay sending them until about 1st July. The reason is that they will not be on the market till then.[104]

Thirty-one sheets were published in June 1919 (see Check-list 4, p.377), and a further seven were issued during the remainder of the year. All these early sheets covered areas in the south of England.[105]

Most of the research and development that had gone into the design of the new map between 1911 and 1914 had been focused on the use of colour for relief representation. None of this, with the exception of the work on contours, was to be used for the surrogate series, the Popular Edition. The Popular did, however, inherit the sheet lines, marginalia and conventional signs of the 'lost map'. Close was always to reflect that although the Popular Edition served its purpose, 'it would have been a pleasant thing to have produced the principal national small-scale maps in the style of, say, the Killarney sheet, or of the Torquay and Dartmouth sheet, or others of that general type, as had been intended before the War.'[106] The surviving experimental sheets from this period are ample evidence that Close could have achieved his aim of improving the one-inch map, and it is certainly arguable that the Ordnance Survey has not produced their equal in artistic appearance in the subsequent eighty-five years of the one-inch map in all its forms.

Although it is easy to criticise the decision to use engraving as the base for the new coloured map, one can sympathise with the aesthetic reasons for the choice - it is, for example, difficult to imagine the drawn Popular Edition of Scotland being treated in the Killarney or Lake District style - the linework of that map, as Close maintained, could not be compared for fineness with engraved work, and even the Fifth (Relief) Edition is coarse in comparison with its engraved and coloured ancestors. After the First World War, with the basic form of the cheap alternative waiting in the wings, the Popular Edition, understudy for the Killarney style, made its first public appearance. It was soon to become apparent, once the one-inch map was untrammelled by the apparatus of hachures, layers and shading, that outdated methods of production were to become a liability in producing up-to-date maps.

104 RGS Archives (Close Correspondence).

105 A district map of York, with the heading 'Provisional Popular Edition One-Inch Map' was published in September 1919, but this was based on Third Edition material; it is described in Messenger, (1988), p.237. It was reprinted in 1923 (print code 500/23), and the word 'Provisional' was removed, but no change appears to have been made to the map itself.

106 Close, (1934), p.65.

Fig.7 Bramah's Hydraulic Press, patented in 1795. Copperplate-printed maps were placed between glazed boards and placed in the press to flatten and give shine to the finished impression. Photographed ca 1914. *Ordnance Survey.*

Chapter II

PRODUCTION METHODS

'Although it had a long respite, the copper plate as a means of map production was doomed when lithography was discovered.'   *Capt. J.G. Withycombe* (1929)[1]

First used in 1799 for engraving the one-inch sheets, the copperplate was last employed in the compilation of this series in the 1940s, when the plates which had been made up for the Popular Edition were photographed to provide a basis for the northern sheets of the New Popular (Sixth) Edition.[2] Its 'respite' was perhaps fifty years longer than it might have been, and the apparent error of judgement made in the decision to perpetuate the use of copper engraving for the production of the Popular Edition was to lead to major problems of maintenance in the inter-war period. The Popular Edition spanned forty years of advances in printing technology, but was able to take only limited advantage of new photographic methods because the thinking behind its production was so firmly rooted in the copperplate era. Its component copperplates, which were taken from the Third Edition Small Sheet Series, had their origins in, and the same sheet lines as, the New Series, publication of which began in 1874, and although the map images they produced underwent substantial changes, these plates were a basic element, even if at several removes, of at least part of the one-inch map of England and Wales until the appearance of the Seventh Series. In order to understand the changing face of the Popular Edition, it is therefore necessary to have some grasp of the technical processes by which it was made, and a knowledge of the instructions that framed the revision and drawing procedures which produced the compilation material for the engraver.

The Popular Edition was a compromise between the processes of engraving and lithography, and a parting, albeit prolonged, of the ways between old and new traditions of map reproduction. Three of its sheets (1, 3 and 5) were based, not on copperplates, but on new drawings,[3] and were the first standard series one-inch Ordnance Survey maps of England and Wales to be produced in this way. Like the coloured Third Edition before it, and the earlier coloured sheets of the Revised New Series, the Popular Edition, although based on the engraved copperplate, was lithographically printed. Engraving was to be formally abolished in 1924,[4] but to begin with, the principal problem in the construction of the Popular, given that it was to be based on copperplates, was to find the best method of producing large sheet lines from a small copper original. The Third

---

1   Withycombe, (1929a), p.160.

2   This was for the provisional edition of the Sixth Edition: Cheetham, (1945).

3   This was because they included parts of Scotland, which was a drawn, rather than engraved map.

4   A comprehensive account of the abolition of engraving on Ordnance Survey is given in Seymour, (1980), p.242 *et seq.* The final demise of the engravers' class was signalled in Circular, C.C.819. 5/5/1923; one engraver was retained into the 1930s, see Circular C.C.1065.

Edition Large Sheet Series (see Appendix 1) had been made by taking transfers from the Third Edition Small Sheet Series copperplates, and joining up these transfers on the lithographic stone in order to achieve a bigger sheet size. For the Popular Edition, it was decided to increase the size of the copperplate to avoid the difficulties that had been experienced in matching the transfer sections on the stone, which had, in turn, led to inaccuracies on the map. This was done by cutting up the small sheet matrix (see footnote 32, p.43) plates and rivetting them together: a technique which may have been regarded as satisfactory at the time, but, over thirty years later, standards of map compilation had become more rigorous, and this operation was then described as having been 'performed by mechanics rather than surveyors, and quite apart from any necessary exaggeration of detail, the sheets have no pretensions to precise accuracy.'[5] However, there is evidence to indicate that in 1912 this process of cutting and joining the plates was regarded as a skilled job, which had no counterpart in commercial trade, and the four assistants who carried it out were allowed the privilege of contributing to a pension.[6]

In 1932 it had been admitted that the cutting and joining of unequally worn copperplates had further damaged the detail plate, and had led, here and there 'to singularly unfortunate results'.[7] In addition, subsequent revisions were made upon them, and developments in cartographic ideas had resulted in further alterations to the plates, so that it was inevitable that drawing afresh, rather than engraving, should have become the medium of the Popular Edition for Scotland. The decision to draw, rather than to engrave, the new Scottish map was announced in the *Annual Report* for 1921/2. This followed from the recommendations made by a committee appointed by Close in 1921, and chaired by Lieut.-Col. W.J. Johnston, the officer in charge of the Publication Department.[8] The report of this committee was not, according to Jack,[9] 'so full as it might have been, considering the importance of the subject', and it was never published. This was a mere seven years after the first sheets of the Popular Edition of England and Wales had been put in hand, in 1914. Little new one-inch printing was carried on during the four war years, and so we must conclude that it was the unsatisfactory results obtained from printing the Popular Edition in the first two years following the war, and which are amply demonstrated by the numerous specification changes to the series in its first eighteen months, which led to Close's fundamental change of policy in departing, at last, from engraving as the basis of the one-inch map. But why had it taken so long to arrive at this decision?

The experience of colour-printing on the Ordnance Survey in the 1890s had led to the statement that heliozincography was 'very useful in the production of maps for printing in colour.'[10] But in 1900 it seems that colour-printing on zinc was virtually unknown

---

5 PRO OS 1/111. f.43A. CR9221. MacLeod to Hinks, 6/11/41. The technique of cutting and joining plates had been practised since at least the 1850s.

6 Ilkeston, (1912), p.5.

7 Winterbotham, (1932a), p.18.

8 PRO OS 1/9/5. The report of this committee does not appear to have survived, but it is referred to in 'Report on engraving as a basis for small scale Ordnance Survey maps', (22/3/1923).

9 Colonel, later Brigadier, E.M. Jack, Director General, Ordnance Survey, (1922-1930).

10 *Account of the methods and processes ...*, (1902), p.180.

in the Ordnance Survey,[11] and there seems to be no indication that this method was considered for the production of the coloured Third Edition. Yet, as Jack noted, where no engraved map already existed, as in the case of the half-inch series of England and Wales, that map was successfully produced in 1903 by drawing and heliozincography; but it was still to be some time before it was even suggested that the outline of the one-inch map could be drawn instead of engraved.[12] As far as colour-printing was concerned, in the crucial years of the design of the Popular Edition, 1912-14, the Ordnance Survey was still entrenched in the traditional copperplate mentality of the previous hundred years. This was admitted by Jack, who said that until this time the engraved plate remained almost unquestioned as the basis of the coloured one-inch map.[13] The natural process was to transfer the outline from the copper to the zinc plate, and then to make colour plates to conform. Even the sophisticated experiments with Killarney, Torquay and Aldershot had been firmly based on the engraved image. The criticisms of the poor quality of the coloured Irish one-inch sheets at the turn of the century[14] might have been expected to have prompted some serious investigation into an alternative method of production for the English maps, but this was to be a missed opportunity to take advantage of new techniques.

The Survey's failure to embrace new methods and to invest more heavily, not just financially, but intellectually, in new processes, was to make the maintenance of the one-inch map over the next forty years a financial millstone, which in turn was a brake on the quality (with a brief interval in the unfinished Fifth Edition) of map production at this scale for England and Wales. The price of preserving the copperplate as the basis of map production was cartographic inferiority which, ironically in the economy-conscious inter-war period, was more expensive in upkeep than a redrawn map would have been. Could all this have been foreseen in 1912? It could be argued that it should have been anticipated ten years earlier, in 1902.

In his wide-ranging review of the use of colour-printing by the Ordnance Survey in the nineteenth century,[15] Mumford makes the salient point that even earlier, in 1882, the number of foreign countries publishing coloured maps was extensive, and quotes the following telling passage from the *Notes on the Government surveys of the principal countries*, published by HMSO in 1882:

> The advantages of colours in reading maps is recognised by all ... but the technical difficulties in the process of printing colours are too great for general purposes ... in some foreign countries the tendency is apparent in cartography to adopt chromo-lithographed maps with contours, in the place of maps in black outline with features represented by hachures.

As Mumford remarks, 'these statements appear overly defensive coming from a country which had for long claimed to be the cartographic envy of the civilised world.' Indeed, they seem, more than a century later, hardly defensible at all; but the key to the

11 Farquharson, (1900).

12 PRO OS 1/9/5. Report on engraving as a basis for small scale Ordnance Survey maps, (22/3/1923).

13 *Ibid.*

14 Andrews, (1975), pp.292-3.

15 Mumford, (1991).

Ordnance Survey's backward looking attitude lies in the second part of the above quote: its preoccupation with providing a hachured map of Great Britain which, 'regarded either as a work of art, or as a pictorial representation of ground, is inferior to none of its class in Europe.'[16]

However, achieving first-class work in hill engraving was a slow process. In 1887, the increasing delay in the publication of hill-engraved one-inch sheets, coming, as it did, on top of an already prolonged hold-up in the production of the outline map, was a matter for serious concern. Steps were taken to expedite the progress of the preliminary stages of hill sketching, but little could be done about the length of time taken for work in the office: four to six months to prepare a drawing for the engraver, and a further one to two years to engrave the plate itself. Eventually completed in 1902, the engraved one-inch map with hills was abandoned only ten years later, in 1912; the reason for its demise was its lack of popularity. But, by not buying the hachured map in quantity in the first place, the public had signalled its lack of interest in this version as much as twenty years earlier. Indeed, in 1892, the very year that the Director General, Sir Charles Wilson, had declared to the Dorington Committee that, in spite of the experiments which had shown that the hills could be printed in a cheaper, coloured form, 'it would be a very great misfortune' to abandon the engraved hachures, his *Annual Report* pronounced that public demand for this very map was poor.

This point was brought out when Wilson was questioned in the committee by Lieut.-General Cooke, who had noticed that it was 'a curious thing that, when 1-inch sheets are published with and without hill features, the public buy more without than with.' In Scotland the sale of the outline sheets had been seventeen times greater than for the same sheets with hills.[17] Both soldier and civilian found map reading in the densely hachured areas of upland Britain impossible. For the engraver, correcting the detail on the engraved plate for intermediate revisions meant that hachures were damaged and had to be repaired: the time taken on these sheets lengthened. By 1890, it had become essential to have separate plates for the hachures alone, and from now on, the hill plates led an independent life to the revised detail sheets. But why had this procedure not been in place at the outset of the production of the New Series, in 1872? It can hardly be argued that the need for revision of the plates was in its infancy - the constant changes noted in the states of the Old Series sheets show that periodic revisions to the copperplates were being made long before the first national revision was authorised in 1893.[18] The problems of revising the detail on hachured plates must therefore have been all too apparent even from very early days, and by not considering the technical implications of the need for revision on a plate which combined detail and hills, Sir Henry James, who was Director from 1854 to 1875, and his successors Cameron, Cooke and Stotherd, contributed materially to the inadequacies of the one-inch map in the 1890s.

It seems, in retrospect, that the only justification for retaining the hachures was on artistic grounds; it was a view that was to be perpetuated by Close and Winterbotham,

---

16 Dorington, (1893c), written memorandum by Wilson, p.225.

17 Dorington, (1893c), para.83.

18 See the cartobibliographies in Margary, (1975-1992), Vols I-VIII. The *Annual Report* for 1893 states (p.9) that the revision of the one-inch was 'commenced last year'. The *Report* was written in 1894.

Fig.8 Maj.-General Sir Charles William Wilson, KCB, KCMG, FRS, DCL, LLD. (1836-1905). His tenure as Director General of the Ordnance Survey, from 1886 to 1894 was the last in a succession of distinguished posts, which included Director of the Topographical Department of the War Office (1870-1876). Commissioned into the Royal Engineers in 1855, Wilson's earliest posting was as Secretary to the North American Boundary Commission, where he gained invaluable survey expertise. He undertook the Survey of Jerusalem in 1864-5, the resulting plans of which (known as the Ordnance Survey of Jerusalem) have been the basis for all subsequent topographical studies of that city. After completing the Survey of Sinai in 1869, he devised the surveying instructions for the one-inch survey of Western Palestine in 1870. His views on the content and form of topographical maps, which had shaped the deliberations of the two 1892 committees, clearly also influenced Close who, like him, was to become FRS and Chairman of the Palestine Exploration Fund. *Palestine Exploration Fund.*

who, while acknowledging the unpopularity of the old hachured maps, ignored past experience and produced, in Winterbotham's case, a national hachured one-inch series which sold badly for the same reasons that had obtained forty years earlier. Even the Killarney map, so extolled by its producers, was a flop in the local market-place,[19] and may be reasonable to suggest that the same fate might have befallen Close's projected new one-inch relief map of England and Wales, for which the Killarney map was a model. It is noticeable, too, that the early hachured tourist maps of the 1920s were soon replaced by a simpler, layered alternative.

When the first national revision of the one-inch was begun, in 1893, the specification of the resulting map, the Revised New Series, particularly with regard to roads, was also revised. But the opportunity for a radical re-think of production methods was not taken in spite of the evidence given to the Dorington Committee, and submitted by Wilson himself, that engraving was a dying art and engravers themselves difficult to come by, and by others that there had been a general 'falling off' in all engraved work during the last forty years, and that engraving cost about three times more than lithography. Wilson had said, on the one hand, that in his opinion the abandonment of line engraving would be a very grave mistake, while on the other, he conceded that if a new map of Great Britain were contemplated, considerations of cost and time would doubtless lead to the adoption of other processes.

Wilson's strongly-held opinion, which was to influence his successors into the first two decades of the twentieth century, was that

> In engraving, the lines have a firmness and sharpness which cannot be produced on paper with a pen, and therefore no map produced by heliogravure, photo-etching, or photo-zincography can be so perfect as engraving. Whilst preserving truthfulness in detail, engraving admits of high artistic treatment in the delineation of ground ... it is, however, slow and costly, and this has led to the adoption of cheaper and more rapid though inferior processes on the Continent...[20]

In his defence of what was, in effect, a luxury product, Wilson was not entirely on sound ground in criticizing continental cartography. In 1867, Lieut. J. Waterhouse, Assistant Surveyor General in charge of the photozincographic branch of the Surveyor General's Office in the Survey of India, went through a two-month induction course in photozincography as practised by the Ordnance Survey in Southampton. He followed this by a visit to the Paris Exhibition later that year where he saw specimens of French, Belgian and German cartography which were 'superior to anything I had hitherto seen in England.'[21] In 1868 he visited the official and commercial map publishing organisations on the continent. Here, there was no question but that lithographed maps at the scale of 1:40,000 (Belgium) or 1:50,000 (Holland) were 'scarcely distinguishable from copper-plate engraving' which had virtually been abandoned in favour of lithography and photographic processes in Holland, about fifty years before engraving was abandoned by the Ordnance Survey in 1924.

The real obstacle to technological progress was not so much the cost of

---

19 Olivier, (1914a), para.40. However, this judgement was based on a short sales period of a few months.

20 Dorington, (1893c), 'Memorandum on the 1-inch map', p.226.

21 Waterhouse, (1870), p.x.

superannuating trained engravers - they could, in any case have been retrained for different skills - but the seemingly obstinate adherence to hachuring which was becoming an increasingly outmoded method of hill depiction (the Belgian map, for example, used contours at 5 metre intervals). In this, the Ordnance Survey had been aided and abetted by the Baker Committee (1892), which, in spite of the preference for contours which was stated by some of the officers, recommended that this 'artistic work' (the hachured map) and 'beautiful map should be completed in the most finished style'. It comes as no surprise to discover that one of the members of this military committee was none other than Col. Sir Charles Wilson.

By insisting on the retention of hachuring (and by 1910 it was noted that hill engraving was a speciality almost entirely confined to the Ordnance Survey, and that the highest earners among the civil assistants were the hill engravers, an elite workforce whose maximum pay of £5.2s.0d. per week was £2 more than any comparable commercial pay[22]), the military committee was flying in the face of the decision, taken by another army committee[23] twelve years earlier, to recommend that the principal method of showing relief for military purposes should be by contours. It was never disputed that the same degree of finish of the engraved hachure could be achieved by a drawn and lithographed substitute - the photozincographed editions had nicely demonstrated that point - but the need for finely-engraved hachures had never been proved on economic grounds, and the practical reasons for keeping the hachures, that is, as an aid to reading the lie of the land, were valid only so long as the standard contour interval remained as large as 100 feet. Even though it would have been cheaper to interpolate contours intermediate to the surveyed lines, than to have continued to engrave hachures, no attempt to decrease the interval was made until 1912, with the Popular Edition.

Armed in 1894 with the knowledge that the black and white map was already becoming a thing of the past, and with a brief to produce a coloured one-inch map for the army, the Ordnance Survey could have investigated new methods of producing a coloured one-inch map, especially as it was already apparent that as soon as the engraved image was reproduced by lithography the firmness and sharpness of line was immediately lost. And yet lithography was essential to multi-colour reproduction - this was surely a quandary which merited extensive critical technical exploration. The trials involving the use of colour plates made up from the copper, and described as a 'productive period of cartographic experiment and development',[24] were more a system of 'make do and mend' than a design for a long-term practical solution to coloured map-production. Even Farquharson, Wilson's successor in 1894 as Director-General, had to admit that colour-printing at the Ordnance Survey did not yet approach the best standard of that achieved by the trade.[25]

---

22 Ilkeston, (1911a), p.7.

23 War Office (1880). Discussed in Jones, (1974).

24 Seymour, (1980), p.201.

25 Farquharson, (1900). Farquharson had evidently authorised trials of colour printing by Bartholomew, who printed what appears to be a specimen of Revised New Series sheet 315 (Southampton) with blue water, blue water lining off the coast, red contours, brown hachures and ochre roads. The quality of this printing

By the time that Col. D.A. Johnston replaced Farquharson in 1899, it was even more clear that engraving was unsuitable for producing a coloured map. For although the copperplate was a stable medium, it was almost impossible to obtain a perfect fit, or register, of the various transfers which were needed for the different colours, on the zinc plates. It was, in fact, one of the most serious defects of producing a coloured map from a copperplate, for in order to take a transfer from the copper for laying down onto zinc, the copper had to be heated and the transfer paper damped. The transfer was then put down onto cold zinc. As Jack was to say, not only might the copper be incorrect in its dimensions (a fault apparently not unknown in copperplates), but the heating and damping altered these dimensions. This meant that the outline, when transferred to zinc was not true to scale, and errors were often significant. While this might not be important in a single map, the discrepancies which appeared when joining parts of sheets together to make a special map were often large and produced an 'infinity of trouble'.[26] The appropriate process for colour work - heliozincography - had been introduced in 1893,[27] and was operating in a custom-made printing building by 1903, the year after the second national revision of the one-inch map began. It would have been the ideal moment to seize the initiative, and begin the new century with a new approach. The technology was in place, but, again, there is no evidence to suggest that Johnston even considered a drawn map for the one-inch. Apart from the preoccupation with hachuring, there may be three reasons for this apparent lack of foresight.

First, as we have seen, the practice of engraving the small scales had an unbroken century of tradition behind it in the Ordnance Survey, which, in the beginning, was perpetuating a still older tradition of map engraving going back to the sixteenth century. Although lithographic printing for maps was used from 1808,[28] and had been used for the Ordnance Survey large scales since the 1850s, it was still received opinion, at the beginning of the twentieth century, that none of the foreign lithographed maps equalled the engraved map for crispness of line and clarity of detail. Even in 1928, MacLeod[29] commented that

> The fact of the matter is that Ordnance Survey maps ... were designed for cutting on copper, and our ideas are built up on this foundation. We have got accustomed to symbols, styles and lettering invented by engravers, and we are shocked by departures from the traditions so formed.[30]

Secondly, the principal reason given for retaining the copperplate as the basis for the one-inch map at the turn of the century was that the plate constituted a non-distorting, practically indestructible record, on which changes could be made relatively easily. Yet this opinion turned a blind eye not only to the fact that most of the corrections were made on the transferred image on the stone, but also to the crucial advantage of

---

is first class. Forty copies each were printed on linen-backed paper and thin paper on 18/5/1897. NLS Bartholomew Printing Archive, vol.26.

26 PRO OS 1/9/5. Report on engraving as a basis for small-scale maps, (22/3/1923).

27 Seymour, (1980), p.200.

28 Clark and Jones, (1974).

29 M.N. MacLeod, Director General, (1935-1943).

30 MacLeod, (1929), p.130.

heliozincography over the standard procedure for producing the Popular Edition. This was that corrections could be made to a negative, which in turn was taken by photographing a drawing. The surface of the negative did not deteriorate under constant reworking in the same way as the face of a stone, and a new, distortion-free negative was easy, quick and relatively cheap to make, should the original be destroyed. By contrast, the replacement of a stone involved printing from the copperplate, transferring (with all the inherent distortions of this process) to stone and updating by litho draftsmen - a much more laborious process at that time.

A third, and perhaps less convincing reason was not so much the state of the art of heliozincography itself in 1902 - it was, at that time, being used successfully to produce the six-inch maps - but the hidden costs of preparing work for the process. In 1925, it was suggested that while heliozincography was 'very admirable, and indeed one must use it nowadays'[31] the cost of drawing for the process, which had to be done at twice the scale of the finished map to eliminate coarsening of the final image, was twice as expensive as drawing to scale, because it took a draftsman almost twice as long to draw a square mile at the two-inch scale as it did on the one-inch scale. This argument was something of a red herring for it took no account of the relative ease, and therefore cheapness, with which the master document (the negative) could be corrected compared with making alterations on stone, copper or zinc.

Of course, in 1903, the post-war expansion of road construction and urbanisation, and the consequent increase of revision data could hardly have been envisaged; otherwise a different choice might have been made. In the meantime, the methods used to prepare a map in colour from a monochrome design on copper became ever more complex in the years leading up to the beginning of the Popular format in 1912. Many of the steps in the ladder of one-inch map production were by now directly related to the need for revision. Coupled with a new road classification and extra contours, the compilation work for the Popular Edition in 1919, leaving aside the greater number of procedures that would have been involved for the relief version, had become laborious, for changes were no longer made just to a single copperplate, but to an array of lithographic stones which had, by now, become the master documents for map production.

The Popular Edition, then, inherited a legacy of copperplate engraving which was of gigantic proportions, because every time a plate was brought up to date, a matrix[32] would be taken, on which deletions were made, and a duplicate made of the matrix on which corrections and additions were engraved. Even if each of the 346 sheets of the Third Edition Small Sheet Series had been printed only once, the total number of

---

31 Craster, (1925), comment by Winterbotham, p. 309.

32 A matrix was a non-printing copy in relief of the original copperplate, made by the process of electrotyping. First used by the Ordnance Survey in the 1830s, electrotyping involved the deposit of a layer of new copper over the incised surface of the copperplate. When the two were separated, the old detail stood out in relief on the matrix, and information could easily be deleted before more copper was deposited to make a duplicate intaglio plate on which new detail and corrections could be engraved. For a long time it was difficult to obtain an even deposit unless expensive battery current was used; this problem was resolved when dynamo current was used from about 1885: MacLeod, (1939), p.186.

copperplates accumulated for the series could have numbered about 2076.[33] Doubtless, a comprehensive listing of all the states of the New Series, Revised New Series and Third Edition would reveal a colossal figure for worked copperplates, which, in turn, was an awesome investment in terms of raw materials and manpower. It is no wonder it could not lightly be given up.

It is, of course, a matter of small moment to refer to 'matrices' and 'duplicates', but this was by no means a straightforward process. Intensely laborious, the making of each plate took about eight days of continuous work. This compared with about half an hour for making a glass negative for heliozincography.[34] A heavy workload for one year in the electrotyping department was assessed at about 228 matrices and 270 duplicates,[35] and vagaries in the supply of electric current, such as those experienced in 1903, could lead to poor quality plates. The reason given for not using photography for the preparation of the one-inch map in the 1870s was that all the detail of the six-inch, reduced to a smaller scale, would cause too much confusion for the one-inch draftsman.[36] But by 1884, modern technology prevailed, and the reduction of the six-inch map to the one-inch scale for the engraver, using the pantograph, had been superseded by photography.

Two-colour printing was a straightforward process by 1892, by which time experiments had already been made with printing contours in red and water in blue.[37] In 1913, a brief investigation was made into a three-colour printing process[38] which had been used before 1910 by the Board of Agriculture and Fisheries,[39] but this had been found impracticable for cartography since it used relief plates which would have needed a letterpress machine for printing. By the beginning of the twentieth century the separation of detail onto a number of printing plates, in order to produce four colours and a black outline, required the careful preparation of additional materials which added to the overall production time of the map. So extensive was this extra work that it was used as a justification by the litho-draftsmen for a claim for increased pay. For example, it was

---

33 The sequence would have been: Revised New Series, outline with contours plate (**1**) of which a matrix (**2**) was made; deletions were made on the matrix and a duplicate (**3**) was made; additions would be engraved on the duplicate which then became the new original for the first printing of the Third Edition sheet; however, because (**3**) was regarded as the master plate, and was not usually printed from, another electrotype (involving another matrix (**4**) and duplicate (**5**)) was made to provide a printing plate (**5**) that was a substitute for the original (**3**), which was preserved in order to supply an unworn plate from which further printing plates could be made if needed. Theoretically, future revisions were made to (**3**). Finally, a hill plate (**6**) would be engraved with the hachures. Even were no substitute plate made, each printed sheet would have been produced from four pieces of copper: a minimum total of 1380 copperplates for the first printing of the Third Edition Small Sheet Series with hills. *Account of the methods and processes* ..., (1875, 1902). *Annual Report*, (1902/3), p.26.

34 Workflow diagrams for these procedures are given in Hodson, (1995), Appendix 3.

35 *Annual Report*, (1900/01), p.22.

36 *Account of the methods and processes* ..., (1875).

37 RGS Ordnance Survey Specimens. 'Specimens of Ordnance Survey Maps obtained for the Exhibition in the R.G.S. Map Room 1890'. This list includes New Series sheet 255 (Beaconsfield) with contours in red and water in blue.

38 PRO OS 1/4/3. 'Notes on 3 colour process work as applied to O.S. maps', 25/4/1913.

39 Ilkeston, (1911b), para.2767.

Fig.9 Electroplate shop 1914, OS London Road, Southampton, showing two electrotyping troughs. *Ordnance Survey*.

maintained that the work of the litho draftsmen was exactly similar to copperplate engraving, which was the 'highest classed' production, and that the transferring work for printing the small scales in colour required that the litho draftsman had to be able to assimilate all engraved work - the hills, writing, outline and ornament. This was because in the process of transferring and scraping, the fine hair lines of the lettering were damaged, and whole areas of hachuring would have to be made good.

There was, therefore, just as much work on the stones as there was on the copper-plates; the same situation was true of the Zinc Department, where additional skill was needed to print in colour maps which were originally designed for black and white.[40] Those involved in the production of the small scales claimed that the work was very complicated and trying and demanded special skills, and that the One-Inch Drawing and Revising Department performed some of the most intricate duties on the Ordnance Survey, for which men were specially selected from other departments.[41] All this was recognised before Close became Director General, and the burden of evidence against the use of copper as the basis for a coloured map was well established. If redrawing was not an option for the Popular Edition, it was a logical step, taken by early 1912,[42] to increase the size of the sheets to match that of the Large Sheets of the Third Edition.

The earliest instructions relating to this process are given in a three-page document entitled 'England & Wales, 3rd Revision 1-Inch Maps. General Instructions for guidance of Departments'. Dated 6 March 1913, it gives an outline of the procedures in making up the new one-inch map;[43] these were further described a few months after the first Popular Edition sheets had been published, by Col. W.J. Johnston, who was the officer in charge of the Publication Department. In order to avoid unsightly joins, detail on both sides of the matrix edges was scraped clear and then the contours and water features were removed.[44] The detail along the edges of the former plates was then re-engraved on an electrotyped duplicate plate, and the contours and water features were re-engraved on separate copperplates. The corners of the component six-inch sheets were also scored on the copperplates.[45] On an impression from the black detail plate (water and contours erased) for the Cambridge sheet can be seen the blank crossing lines marking the coincidence of the four Small Sheet Series plates, parts of which went to make up Popular sheet 85 (fig.10).

40 Ilkeston, (1911b), paras 1756, 1818.

41 Ilkeston, (1911b), paras 2813, 2635.

42 Ilkeston, (1912), p.5, para.23; four assistants were employed in joining the copperplates to make the new one-inch sheets.

43 PRO OS 1/4/3. Only one copy of this document is known; it is transcribed at Appendix 2.

44 Johnston, (1920), pp.192-201. RGS OS Specimen no.44 is a pull from the copperplate of Third Edition sheet 266 (1914) showing, in three different areas, the removal of contours and water, leaving the detail; the removal of detail and water, leaving the contours; and the removal of detail and contours, leaving the water.

45 Winterbotham, (1936a), p.322. The function of the intersection marks which can be seen on RGS OS Specimen no. 57 is not clear. This map is a proof from Popular Edition sheet 85, Cambridge, showing detail in black, water in blue, and contours in red; parish boundaries are shown, and squaring is not drawn across the face of the map. The spacing of the intersections would seem to fit a six-inch pattern, but they do not exactly coincide with the position of the actual component six-inch maps.

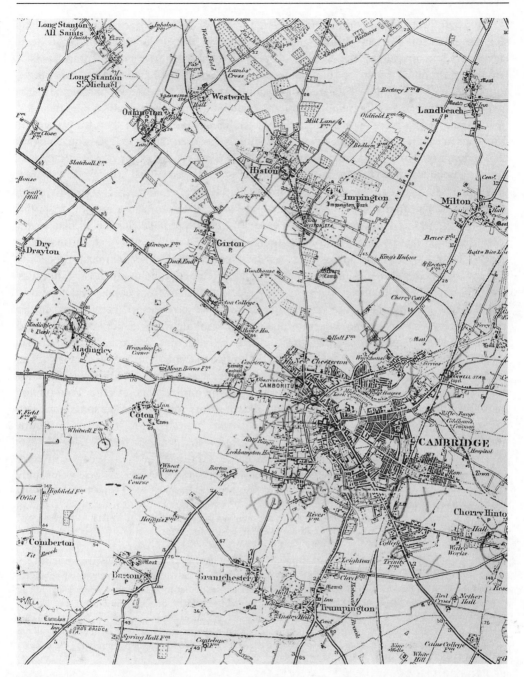

Fig.10 Part of the erasure sheet for Popular Edition sheet 85 (Cambridge). Water and contours have been erased from the joined up matrices of Third Edition Small Sheets 187, 188, 204 and 205. Parish boundaries remain for the moment. The blank lines, marking the joined and scraped clean edges of the component copperplates, can be seen clearly; this is the only erasure sheet known to exist. It is annotated in the bottom margin, in red ink: 'The remarks for erasures are made in the margins of this sheet 22.1.19' and in black ink: 'Attended to on matrix H. Eastman 27.1.19.' *Royal Geographical Society (with IBG) OS Specimen no. 58.*

By 1920, it had been found necessary 'for technical reasons of lithography'[46] to abandon this separation of outline and water. It seems that major difficulties had been encountered in producing a perfect register[47] between the three major components,[48] but by this time, most of the southern sheets had been made up from three copperplates,[49] and many of the remaining northern sheets were now constructed from two engraved plates: outline and water, and contours. This was not all: a singular lack of forethought and planning had led to the plates being joined before they were revised. This caused duplication of work on the overlapping sheets so that over 2000 square miles of overlapping work was drawn, engraved and revised twice before it was decided to revise the plates before they were joined.[50]

In practical terms the originals for the Popular Edition came to be on stones rather than copper. The first stage in the production of a sheet was to take a transfer from the copperplate and lay it down on stone. However, the engraved plate showed all detail, and therefore much that was not wanted was transferred to the outline plate and subsequently had to be removed - a tedious and, as Jack commented, uneconomical process.[51] Offsets[52] were therefore taken from the stone to produce the colour plates. This was one of the major disadvantages of producing a coloured map from copper; another was that if a new outline plate were required - as was to be the case for many sheets in the 1920s and 1930s - it was necessary to make all the colour plates again simply because no two transfers from a copperplate were ever exactly alike. According to Jack, who considered the production of the Popular Edition to be not 'wholly satisfactory',[53] (a model of understatement), there were two methods of achieving colour plates from an engraved base. The first was to make offsets from the outline plate to other zinc plates, on which the detail for the colours was drawn. This was a cumbersome process,

---

46 Johnston, (1920), p.194.

47 Until about 1972, corner registration marks, visible on the Popular Edition sheets, were the principal means of obtaining registration between the different components of a colour set. Without mechanical aids, the accuracy of registration depended on the operators. When visually transferring corner marks from one piece of material to another, errors of positioning could occur, either through parallax or carelessness; when this was combined with inaccurate base material, positioning errors could be further compounded. Bramhall, (1972).

48 It is possible to find examples of misregistration on many sheets; particularly bad instances can be seen on sheet 50 (*Bala*, 1921 printing) where the lakes and tarns frequently transgress the enclosing contours, and the head of Bala lake spills over the road; another tell-tale point to watch for is where gaps, left in the water plate to accommodate names or bridges, do not match the detail of the black plate. Not all instances of misregister could be blamed on printing methods; for example, on sheet 77 (Lowestoft), the 1921 printing shows a pronounced mismatch of contour and water in squares J2/3 (SW of Southolt) where the stream runs across the contour. This has been corrected on the 1937 reprint by redrawing the contour to accommodate the water.

49 PRO OS 1/52. f.1A.

50 PRO OS 1/9/5. '1" revision of Great Britain'. Submission by the Engraving Department to the Director General, (ca Dec. 1922).

51 PRO OS 1/9/5. Report on engraving as a basis for small scale Ordnance Survey maps, (22/3/1923).

52 Offsets were non-printing paper duplicates of the detail which had been transferred to stone from the copperplate. On these offsets, the litho draftsmen inked in any detail required for the colour plate. Ordnance Survey *Methods and processes ...*, (1928).

53 PRO OS 1/9/5. Report on engraving as a basis for small scale Ordnance Survey maps, (22/3/1923).

involving heavy lithographic stones, and the quality of work produced was not always very fine, and accounts for the coarse appearance of some of the sheets of the Popular Edition. The second, and much improved method, which was used for the production of the Popular from about 1922, entailed making drawings for the colour plates and then making zinc plates either by the helio or Vandyke process.

An impression of a Popular Edition sheet was made up from about seven printings (compared with the eleven which had been envisaged for the intricate relief version), as shown in fig.11. These were demonstrated in a colour sequence which was produced in 1920 as a special supplement to the *Caxton Magazine* and the *Modern Lithographer*.[54] This sample, which covers a small part of the east Kent coast from Dover north to Deal, and about five miles inland, was cunningly chosen so that virtually the only inland water visible fell below the 50ft contour, thus avoiding any possibility of a mismatch between outline, contours and water.

The actual number of printings varied throughout the life of the series, as changes were made to the specification. For example, the replacement in 1920 of solid blue for inland water by ruled lines in the same blue as the rivers meant that all inland water could be combined in one printing, but extra plates would still be needed for coastal areas where sea and sand infill were shown. Again, the maps themselves will reveal evidence of different combinations of plates, where printing trials seem to have been introduced for some, but by no means all, sheets. Examples of this are the early combination of first class, and sometimes second class, roads with the contour plate.

In 1924, when the drawing for the last Popular sheets of England and Wales was under way, the process of heliozincography was introduced for the first time in the production of the one-inch map of England and Wales.[55] This method was used when a map was reproduced at a different scale from that to which it was drawn - in this case, the sheets were drawn at the scale of two inches to one mile - and a photographic reduction was made onto a glass negative, which was then printed onto a sensitised zinc plate. The full technical details of precisely how this was done is given in a small pamphlet produced in 1928.[56]

By 1932, the physical condition of the stones of the engraved sheets had deteriorated seriously. All corrections, since the inception of the series, had been made on the stones by scraping off the unwanted detail, so that the original smooth surface was pitted with minute depressions which destroyed any perfect contact when making duplicate plates. The duplicates suffered in clarity as a consequence. This was compounded by the deterioration of the detail itself, which had been subject, in many cases, to frequent alteration. The original clarity of some of the stones was now largely lost, and was in any case so poor that further duplication was out of the question.[57] As a result, new stones

---

54 RGS OS Specimen no. 64, receipt stamp dated 4/4/1921. The order of printing the seven plates for this supplement was: 1, outline: black; 2, roads: red; 3, roads: yellow; 4, woods and parks: green; 5, rivers and inland water and bathymetric contours: blue; 6, sea: a different blue; 7, contours: brown.

55 Ordnance Survey *Instructions to field revisers and draftsmen ...*, (1924).

56 Ordnance Survey *Methods and processes ...* (1928). A synopsis of the main stages of the work appears in Hodson, (1995), Appendix 3e, f.

57 PRO OS 1/52. In fact all the reproduction material for the small scales was in poor condition. Even the

Popular Edition sheet lines traced on matrices of 3rd Edition
Small Sheet copperplates

1st MATRIX
(small sheet matrices cut and joined by rivetting)

detail scraped out on both sides of joins; contours and water scraped out; crowded detail in woods
cleared; badly engraved or placed names deleted; further deletions made according to field documents

1st ELECTROTYPE
impression taken to provide
Erasure Sheet (Fig.10)

further erasures made to 1st Matrix

2nd ELECTROTYPE

engrave: corrections; additions; sheet lines; lat./long.; alpha-numerical references; sheet name;
sheet number; continuous line for railways; adjoining sheet diagram

2nd MATRIX

DUPLICATE (3rd) ELECTROTYPE
(printing plate; sub for original)

[CONTOUR and WATER plates]
Separate copperplates for contour and water were made from drawings prepared from
the Third Edition Small Sheet plates

transfer outline image from 3rd electrotype, or duplicate, to **STONE (A)**
DUPLICATE REVERSE PLATE (ZINC) [BLACK]

offset **roads (primary)** to **STONE (B)**
(scrape out all other detail on STONE B)
DUPLICATE REVERSE PLATE (ZINC) [RED]

offset **roads (secondary)** from STONE A to **STONE (C)**
(scrape out all other detail from STONE C)
DUPLICATE REVERSE PLATE (ZINC) [YELLOW]

transfer **water (lakes, ponds)** from COPPER to **STONE (D)**
(scrape out rivers and streams on transfer or stone)
DUPLICATE REVERSE PLATE (ZINC) [BLUE TINT]

offset **woods** from STONE A to **STONE (E)**
(scrape out all detail except for wood outlines from STONE E)
DUPLICATE REVERSE PLATE (ZINC) [GREEN]

transfer **contours** from copper to **STONE (F)**
DUPLICATE REVERSE PLATE (ZINC) [ORANGE]

transfer **water** (rivers and streams) from COPPER to **STONE (G)**
(scrape out ponds and lakes)
DUPLICATE REVERSE PLATE (ZINC) [BLUE]

ROTARY OFFSET PRINTING: 7 PASSES THROUGH THE PRESS

POPULAR EDITION SHEET

Fig.11 Reconstruction of the general sequence of actions necessary to print a Popular Edition sheet at
the beginning of 1919, before the decision to erase parish boundaries was made, or to combine water
and outline. In the absence of job sheets, this diagram does not claim to be accurate; it is merely
indicative of the procedures involved in the printing process. For example, a third duplicate electrotype
may not have been made, but it was usual not to print from the 'original' copperplate, in order to
preserve the image. Sources: OS *Instructions* (1914); Johnston (1920); Fig.10; *Annual Reports*.

were made up for some sheets from new transfers from the old copperplates. This was a costly and tedious exercise, sometimes involving the separation of outline and water again, and, of course, the incorporation of every item of revision for that sheet since the Popular had begun.

The complex nature of the production of the Popular Edition was underlined when in 1932 the Ordnance Survey conducted an internal enquiry into the financial pros and cons of continuing to produce the next series, the Fifth (Relief) Edition, by redrawing, as against revising the Popular Edition, and preparing negatives (pulls from the existing stones would not be sufficiently sharp to photograph successfully) from new stones, going right back to the original Third Edition copperplate.[58] This procedure would have saved about £250 per sheet; even so, the overall cost of revising the Popular was still more than half the cost of redrawing a Fifth Edition sheet, and it was argued that a Fifth Edition sheet, produced from the Popular Edition in this way, while being faster, so that more sheets per year would be produced, would not even begin to approach the technical superiority that could be achieved with a redrawn map.

Another point in favour of continuing with the redrawing was the impossibility of eradicating on the Popular the large number of displacements which had occurred between the outline, water and contours. Finally, the form of the original: stone for the Popular, and negatives for the Fifth, clinched the argument in favour of redrawing, for in comparison with the stones, the glass negatives, although fraught with their own maintenance difficulties, were still more easily updated and corrected without their condition deteriorating. It might be thought that the need for such an enquiry was superfluous after it had been acknowledged that drawing had been accepted as the only reasonable basis for a coloured map. What, then, prompted the investigation in the first place? The root cause lay not so much in the delay of output of the drawn sheets of the Fifth Edition, as in the policy decision, taken at the outset when the Ordnance Survey introduced heliozincography in 1924 as its normal method of map production, to make corrections to the negative only, and not to the original drawing.[59]

This policy was adopted for three main reasons. First, it was thought that a negative could be corrected easily for an indefinite period, and would not be damaged in the process; secondly, it kept its shape, whereas paper, while easier to correct, was liable to distortion; then the preparation of a printing plate from a negative was fast and cheap, while making a new negative from an original drawing which had been done in several pieces[60] was more intricate and could take about a month to complete. It could take several hours, for example, to pin all the component drawings onto the board, and then the negatives would have to be touched up to eliminate the joins and pins, and any lines

drawings for the half-inch and quarter-inch series were in such a bad state and so out of date, that to revise them and pin them up again would have taken as long as redrawing: PRO OS 1/351, minute dated 11/5/1935. Film negatives were not immune to this kind of degradation for the quality of the fine lines on the Seventh Series was found to have deteriorated after twenty years of repeated photographic and photomechanical processes: Price, (1975), p.22.

58 PRO OS 1/52.

59 The method of correction is described by Craster, (1925), pp.301-14.

60 The Fifth Edition sheets were drawn in sections, Ordnance Survey *Instructions for the revision and and drawing of the one-inch (Fifth Edition) map*, (1936).

that had been erased because they had crossed deleted detail would have to be redone.[61] However, by the time that the Fifth Edition was underway, some disadvantages of the system of correcting on the negatives had become apparent. The initial cost of the negative had proved to be very high; and in spite of a comment made in 1925 that 'the glass is pretty thick; it takes a good deal to break it'[62] only three years later, this very thickness led to their being described as 'heavy, brittle and difficult to handle'.[63] Then again, the cost of correcting it had exceeded early estimates, and even touching up a fresh negative for the new Fifth Edition took a month of skilled work before the map was fit to print.

By the mid 1930s, it was realised that the Fifth Edition, at its current rate of progress, would not be completed until 1965. The immediate implication of this was that the life of the Popular Edition would inevitably be extended for those areas not covered by the publication of the Fifth Edition sheets (this included most of Kent, all of England north of Buckingham, and all of Wales except for part of Glamorgan). But the litho stones which constituted the originals of the Popular were now so worn out that it had become impossible to correct them any further. The solution to these problems, and to those raised by the 1932 inquiry, was to be the production of a stable drawing material which in turn was to enable the maintenance of the Popular Edition to be continued. Fortunately, the experiments aimed at producing this stable drawing support had been successful in 1936, and the result was a metal plate, coated with white enamel, which could be used for manuscript drawings.

Apart from its distortion-free qualities, and the ability of rulings and stipples to be transferred onto it, the enamel plate could be used for duplicating work from old stones from which a reasonable print could still be made. The plate was then touched up, and revisions were put in by hand. The new image was then photographed for the production of a new sheet. Afterwards, further corrections could be carried out either on the enamel, or on the negative, without causing more deterioration of the image. The water and contour plates were prepared by pulling paper impressions from the stones and pasting these down in succession on top of a blue print on glass which had been made from the outline negative. A precise fit between the outline, water and contours was achieved by fitting the paper pulls to the outline before being pasted down and photographed. This formed the basis of the method used for some reprints of the Popular Edition after this date, and by 1939 forty-five sheets had been converted from stones to negatives in this way, and a further seven were scheduled to complete the programme.[64]

Some attempts had been made to photograph the image on the stones which were too worn to print from, in order to try to produce a negative which could then be corrected by hand. These experiments were unsuccessful, and it had then become necessary to go back to pulling transfers from the original copperplates, laying these down onto the

61 Ordnance Survey *Notes on map reproduction*, (1927), p.4.

62 Craster, (1925), p.314. The polished glass plates used in the camera were quarter of an inch thick and measured 45 x 30 inches, Ordnance Survey *Methods and Processes ...*, (1928).

63 MacLeod, (1929), p.129.

64 *Annual Report*, (1938/9), p.36. These figures do not quite tie up with an index on PRO OS 1/219, which indicates that by 1940, sheets 1-42 of the Popular Edition were on negatives.

enamelled plates, and then bringing them up to date by hand. This would have been an extraordinarily labour-intensive process because of the vast amount of revision information which would need to have been incorporated since the copperplates were first produced at least twenty years earlier.[65] The sheets themselves show many traces of the vicissitudes of their production methods and these are discussed in further detail in the chapters on specification.

The new road classification of the Popular Edition, and the introduction of interpolated 50ft contours, together with a different method of showing water in the coloured map, must all have resulted in an increased workload for the one-inch draftsmen and the litho-draftsmen, and an indication of the complexity of one-inch compilation in 1914 is given in the work-flow diagram at Appendix 3. The volume of drawing work required to produce the copperplate from which the Popular Edition was made had grown substantially since the Small Sheet copperplates were first created in the 1870s, and must have made a significant contribution to increased costs. Between 1914 and 1919, the evidence of the impracticality of producing a coloured map from copper at last weighed heavily enough in favour of a redrawn map for production by heliozincography, but this decision was too late for the Popular Edition. The whole position was succinctly summed up by Jack in 1923, when he said that

> It was when the Popular Edition of the one-inch was started (a map in which it was intended to take full advantage of the power given by colour) that it was realised that this was the parting of the ways, and that the engraved map was not suited to form the basis of such a map … it seems clear now, in the light of greater knowledge, that the policy was entirely wrong and that the engraved map ought to have been abandoned at the outset.[66]

Neither Jack nor Close could have foreseen that the copperplates would have remained the basis for the one-inch map of most of England and Wales for so long, nor, in 1912, in spite of late Victorian building speculation and Edwardian urban expansion, could the escalation in the advancement of road transport and housing have been predicted. Otherwise, the scale of revision consequent on such developments could have been anticipated and might have precipitated an early change in one-inch design. Those in favour of the superiority of engraving over drawing were to lose ground rapidly in the 1920s, so that even Jack was able to say in 1923 that there was now 'no need to fear comparison between the drawn map and that produced by transfer from the copperplate; the difference is one of style, not of quality.'[67] The style of the Popular Edition was to be a compromise between the two.

So, in about a quarter of a century the printing methods of the Popular Edition had come almost full circle with the reversion to the original copperplates. Apart from the point that copper was unsuited to colour work, the factor that rendered it even more inappropriate to twentieth century map production was the amount of revision which was needed to keep the sheets up to date. The sheet lines of the copperplates which made up

---

65 *Annual Reports* for 1936/7 and 1937/8.
66 PRO OS 1/9/5. Report on engraving as a basis for small scale Ordnance Survey maps, (22/3/23).
67 *Ibid.*

the Popular Edition had not changed since the inception of the New Series in 1872, and because an old state had always formed the basis for a corrected issue, they had, by 1914, inherited the changes of two national revisions and many intermediate amendments.

Chapter III

REVISION

Ad hoc revision to individual sheets of the one-inch had been carried out from the very beginning, but on a piecemeal basis that seemed initially to lack any coherent policy.[1] Only with the Dorington recommendation, that the map of England and Wales should be revised independently of the survey and revision of the large scales, did it become necessary to set out a formal procedure for the systematic revision of the whole one-inch map. To begin with, in 1893, this was a very simple approach, but by the time the third national revision began in 1912, it had developed into a formidable catalogue of actions necessary to produce the Popular Edition. These steps were, for the most part, detailed in circulars, and in revision and drawing instructions. They are invaluable documents for they reveal many of the *raisons d'être* and dating of the conventional signs used on the maps. A certain degree of caution is needed in their interpretation, however, for while it can be taken that they reflect the status quo at the date of their issue, it is equally true to say that they are invariably an amalgam of past practice and new procedures.

Also, the custom of updating the rules, by the convention of manuscript amendments to the printed regulations, means that it cannot be assumed that a set of printed instructions remained unchanged between one edition and the next. It follows that the most valuable instructions for the purpose of monitoring changes in, say, specification, are those which have been updated by the draftsman or reviser. Many of the instructions and procedures which governed the production of the Popular Edition had been framed by at least 1896, and in order to understand their full context, and to be able to trace the continuity of their implementation and development, it is necessary to examine the revision and drawing policies for the one-inch map from the 1890s to the 1930s. As so few examples of these documents have survived (and where they have, they are not always readily accessible), it has been judged necessary to quote from them, sometimes at length, where appropriate, in this and the succeeding chapters on specification.

The earliest systematic record-keeping relating to the up-dating of the copperplates has so far been traced to the Southampton Circulars,[2] and is dated 1894. Entitled *Instructions for keeping the history sheet of English 1" revision plates*, it lists sixteen stages in the correction of an original plate, and most probably was devised for the new one-inch map, that is, the Revised New Series, which was to result from the first national revision.[3] The instructions referred to three compilation documents which were to feature

---

1   The cartobibliographies in Margary (1975-1992) indicate how widespread this practice was. Margary 6:xiii gives a possible rationale to the methods of revision of the later Old Series sheets.

2   OSL G3693.

3   A history sheet for each map of Close's proposed relief version of the Popular Edition was mentioned in the 1913 *General Instructions* for the third revision of the one-inch map (para.16ii.; see Appendix 2), and

in the reproduction materials for the Popular Edition. These were, first, the manuscript drawing, which, extrapolating from later instructions, was an impression of the copperplate printed in blue on which additions and corrections were drawn; secondly, an erasure sheet, which was a pull from the copperplate on which deletions to be made to the matrix were marked; and thirdly, the road map. The erasure sheet and drawing may well have been a long-standing feature in the history of the one-inch map: they would have been logical adjuncts to any map correction process. The earliest use of the road map is not known; it was certainly in use between 1884 and 1885, when it took the form of a one-inch impression on which were recorded certain roads for large-scale purposes.[4] It was retained in the 1890s, probably as a consequence of the new road classification for the Revised New Series. It became one of the basic revision documents from 1893 onwards, especially for the Popular Edition, for which roads were the most constantly revised features.

For many years it had been the practice to issue instructions on particular aspects of map production in the form of circulars, and while it is certainly possible that many of these were written for the first national revision (1893-9), only a few have survived. Two years after its commencement a comprehensive set of directives was issued. Entitled *Instructions for the revision of the one-inch map in the field*, and dated 16 March 1896, it constitutes the first surviving formal prescription for the one-inch map. These revision regulations which, although printed, were not published, provide a fundamental source on the development of the one-inch.

The lack of a common standard at the beginning of the first revision must have resulted in work of very varied quality, to the extent that it had become necessary to direct that 'no time should be wasted in inserting or correcting detail that, from its minuteness, cannot be reproduced on the one-inch scale.'[5] In 1896, the following objectives were set:

> ...to supply detail that has come into existence since the sheets of the map were published; to remove obsolete or unnecessary detail; to correct errors; to supply details of military importance; to secure uniformity by a systematic classification of the roads, &c.

In order to achieve this, revisers had to 'make themselves thoroughly acquainted with the class of detail shown on the one-inch map'. From now on, formal instructions were the principal guide for one-inch detail, and became part of an increasingly structured routine. New editions of instructions were usually issued with each national revision, but they

    it is reasonable to assume that one was kept, not only for the sheets of the Popular Edition, but also for the Third Edition, but none has been found. In 1937, MacLeod introduced 'job sheets' (a file for each sheet on which all details of the reproduction of that sheet were recorded) as a matter of policy (PRO OS 1/39. 28/1/1937). This was almost at the end of the Popular's life. While no job files for any specific Popular Edition sheet appear to have survived, a few completed 'Revision and specials job sheet' proformas have been preserved for some of the district sheets (e.g. Manchester) from 1939. These are kept in the Charles Close Society Archive of Ordnance Survey Material, at Cambridge University Library.

4   OSL G3962. Circular entitled 'Roads, Carriage Drives, &c', (28/4/1884).

5   Ordnance Survey *Instructions for the revision of the one-inch map in the field*, (16/3/1896). This instruction was almost identical with Major-General William Mudge's (Director, Trigonometrical Survey, 1798-1820) direction before 1820 that 'such things as could not be shown on the 1 inch scale' should be omitted from the field sheets. (PRO OS 3/260 f.237, 2/3/1821. Quoted in Hodson, (1989), p.31.).

were supplemented by office notices and circulars which illustrate how points of detail in a specification could be changed or introduced at any stage during the life of a map series. A copy of the printed 1909 instructions, for example, contains manuscript amendments up to 1913, the year before a new 'edition' was written.[6]

The formal revision policy for the one-inch map, as laid down in 1893, specified a fifteen-year revision cycle.[7] This policy was further amplified in the *Annual Report* for 1893 which stated that

> When the map has once been brought up to date it is intended that no sheet should afterwards represent a survey, or revision, more than 15 years old, and that all sheets should be annually brought up to date as regards railways, canals and important public works.

In other words, every sheet was to undergo a major overhaul at least once every fifteen years. Perhaps the most ambitious aspect of this policy statement was the intended scheme for annual minor revision. The implication of this statement is that sheets would be reprinted every year where sufficient change had taken place - a precursor of the continuous revision procedures envisaged by Davidson for the large scales in the 1930s. Only a detailed cartobibliographical study of the Revised New Series would reveal the extent to which this policy was put into practice, but preliminary studies show that many reprinted sheets had been up dated.[8] However, the Board of Agriculture, in adopting the recommendations of the Dorington Committee, accepted Wilson's views[9] and were careful not to tie the Ordnance Survey to an absolutely fixed fifteen year interval for all sheets of the one-inch map, because, as they acknowledged, while such a space was undoubtedly more than adequate for the sparsley populated portions of England and Wales, 'it was quite possible that revision ought not to be postponed so long' for the manufacturing districts and the south and south-east of England.[10]

In fact, the first national revision took about five years, and was completed in 1899; the second was begun in 1901. To accompany it, a set of *Instructions for the 2nd revision of the 1-inch map in the field* was issued in 1901.[11] These were hardly more detailed than their 1896 predecessors, but gave clearer directions on the documents to be completed. By now it would seem that the six-inch impressions, on which the revision was made, had been cut up and made into cards (the size of these was unspecified, but since there could be sixteen six-inch sheets to a small-sheet one-inch map, the cards must have been much easier to handle). On these cards, everything which was considered to be sufficiently important to include on the one-inch was to be circled or underlined in blue, to which was added the note 'insert on 1-inch'. The one-inch impression on which all alterations to names were shown was now called the 'Reviser's Fair Sheet'. Amendments to road classification were also to be coloured up on this sheet so that the

---

6   Ordnance Survey *Instructions for the revision of the 1-inch map*, (1909). Annotated copy in OSL.

7   Dorington, (1894), p.4.

8   Private communication from R. Oliver, who has made an extensive, but, as yet, unpublished, study of this series.

9   His comments on the recommendations of the committee are given in PRO OS 1/2/5.

10 Dorington, (1894). This view anticipated the variable revision cycles of 7, 15 and 25 years which were adopted for the sheets of the Seventh Series, according to their location. Griffith, (1965).

11 Ordnance Survey *Instructions to one-inch field revisers*, (1901).

extent of the changes could be seen at a glance.

With the exception of a block of sheets in Lancashire,[12] the Second Revision, which gave rise to the Third Edition Large Sheet Series, was completed by 1909. The Ordnance Survey had thus taken full advantage of the opportunity, first offered in 1893, to reduce the theoretical fifteen year cycle substantially: two national revisions had been completed in just twenty years. In 1909 a much more detailed set of revision instructions was produced which contained the only printed announcement of a new policy statement to the effect that it had been 'approved that [the] fifteen year cycle be extended to twenty years'. The revision of the one-inch map was now to be tied to that of the large scales, in just the same way that the New Series had had to wait for the large-scale plans to be completed before it was compiled. It must, to many, have seemed a retrograde step to have taken in face of the compelling reasons given by the Dorington Committee, only sixteen years before, for separating the large and small-scale production. It has been suggested[13] that the architect of the new policy was Grant,[14] who had succeeded Hellard[15] as Director General in 1908. There is probably little doubt that this was so. Grant had been promoted straight from the position of officer in charge of the Reproduction Branch (photography, zinc printing, colouring, letterpress printing and bookbinding). But his relevant experience had been as the officer responsible, from 1893 to 1897, for the First Revision of the one-inch map. He may even, in this capacity, have been the author of the first set of revision instructions of 1896, whose emphasis on unnecessary 'minuteness' is strongly echoed in 1909.

The catalyst for the change from fifteen to twenty years was financial cost. 'Owing to the liberal scale of allowances given', wrote Grant on 8 April 1909,[16] 'the work of the one-inch revisers is now very expensive'. He complained of low productivity because of too great an attention to detail. His ideas on what merited attention in one-inch revision were to set the standard for future revisions, but would appear to be expressed only in this circular:

> For the purpose of the one-inch a cottage more or less in the interior or on the outskirts of a village, the exact number of buildings at a farm, are not material provided the village or farm is indicated in the right place and approximately of the right size and shape. Nor are slight changes in the line of the sea coast, small pieces of rough heather and waste land, or other such minor detail really important. The insertion of new roads or means of communication, the noting of disused or closed roads, the classification of roads, the erection or destruction of buildings, &c, which form or have formed conspicuous features in the country or enable the user of the map to locate his position, are important.

These precepts harked back to the ideas on generalisation of detail at the beginning of the nineteenth century,[17] and in order to cut expenditure even further, Grant then

---

12 Sheets 24, 25, 29, 30, 31, 34-6. Except for sheet 29 (revised between 1911 and 1912), the revision of the other sheets was commenced between 1903 and 1908, but not finished until 1910-12. Messenger, (1988).
13 *Ibid.*
14 Colonel S.C.N. Grant, Director General, (1908-1911).
15 Colonel R.C. Hellard, Director General, (1905-1908).
16 OSL G3964. C.C. 324. 8/4/1909.
17 Hodson, (1989).

proceeded to impose a productivity deal of the kind the future Whitley Council would strongly have disputed. In return for not reducing the reviser's allowances, he expected a higher rate of progress; those who fell behind would be financially penalised, and Sunday allowances were no longer valid.

The object of the new policy was to reduce the time spent in the field by the revisers, and to transfer most of the work of revision to the drawing office.[18] The immediate effect of this would have been a role reversal for the draftsman, who was now responsible, instead of the field reviser, for making the initial selection of one-inch detail from the six-inch sheets. The whole of this work was done in the engraving department. The selection of detail was drawn onto the erasure sheet and the drawing sheet which, from now on, together with the one-inch field sheet (the equivalent of the 1901 'reviser's fair sheet'), were to be the principal field documents of the reviser so that 'practically all the old tedious reference to the 6-inch plots will be done away with.' The financial stakes were potentially high. Most of the English sheets were classed as 'medium' or 'open' work, for which the pay was 2s.8d. and 1s.4d. per square mile respectively.[19] But if the work was drawn up in the office from the six-inch first, then the unit cost per reviser per square mile was reduced to 1s.8d. and 10d. On a total area of about 60,000 square miles for England and Wales, this represented possible savings approaching £5,000, or just over 2%, out of an overall expenditure, in 1910, of over £225,000.[20] However, no estimates appear to have survived for the inevitable increase in costs of the draftsmen's work, which would undoubtedly have cancelled a significant proportion of the economies made on the revisers.

This theoretically streamlined scheme, which included detailed provision for cost returns and the compilation of progress diagrams at the scale of 27 miles to the inch, was not to survive for long; but in the meantime it was noted in the instructions that 'a transition period must necessarily occur between the old and new system', and revisers and draftsmen were cautioned that, while the two methods co-existed, 'the principle remains the same and field revisers must realise that the old order of minute assimilation between the two scales is to give place to a degree of assimilation *sufficiently* close for 1-inch purposes.' Although the 1909 instructions do not in their title associate themselves with a third national revision, the first confirmation that this was officially the case is given in the *Annual Report* for 1909/10,[21] which states, under the heading '1-inch scale, 3rd Revision', that 872 square miles were revised in the nine months following the 31 March 1909.

In fact, as the *Annual Reports* for 1909-11 show, the second and third revisions were carried on side by side: the second in Lancashire, and the third in south-east England. Both areas coincided with the first blocks of the second revision of the large scales,

---

18 As a measure of Grant's cut-backs, the two pages of revision instructions which appeared in the 1908 Ordnance Survey *Administrative regulations and instructions* were reduced, in the 1910 edition, to one short paragraph.

19 In 1908, the minimum rate of progress for revision of 'open work' was 200 square miles a month, or 80 square miles for 'medium work'. No minimum rate was set for urban areas. *Ibid.*, (1908), p.85.

20 *Annual Report*, (1909/10), p.12.

21 At p.7, Tabular statement of Progress to March, 1910.

which had begun in 1907, and it was the first opportunity for Grant to put his new proposals into action. In the case of south-east England, the product of the Third Revision was a group of Fourth Edition small engraved sheets (details are given in Appendix 1). For Lancashire the Second Revision, which may have been carried on according to the 1909 instructions, rather than those issued in 1901,[22] resulted in the final sheets of the Third Edition Large Sheet Series. Thus the official trend towards greater generalisation, first apparent in the 1890s, became, for the first time, much more specific. Whereas, in 1901, for example, no new 'garden character' was to be added, by 1909 it was ordered that 'the garden character formerly applicable to Market Gardens, Allotments, &c., will be discontinued and cancelled where already existing.' This dilution of detail was to become more apparent for the Popular Edition.

Grant's Third Revision, and with it, the twenty-year cycle, came to an abrupt halt in 1911, when Close became Director General. It was as if the first Third Revision had never existed; the final Lancashire sheets of the Second Revision were completed in 1912, and in that year Close began, what was, in effect, a new Third Revision which was to produce the Popular Edition. These sheets were to carry, in their early printings, a reference to the Third Revision, together with dates; none of these dates refers to the work of 1909-11 for the areas of Kent and Sussex which were covered by the earlier revision.[23] It would seem that Close put an immediate stop to a system which would, inevitably, have led to long delays in the production of the one-inch map - a return to the unsatisfactory state of slow publication which was the cause of so much military and public complaint in the nineteenth century.

Close has been credited with initiating a coherent revision policy for the one-inch map,[24] whereby the fifteen-year cycle was restored, together with an orderly geographical pattern of progress from south to north, instead of the piecemeal development which had formerly characterised it. This south to north pattern echoed eighteenth-century practice which in turn was determined by military necessity - the south of England would always be an immediate operational zone in the face of aggression from Europe. In 1912, however, quite apart from the military aspect which was ever present, there was a further, commercial, factor. Bartholomew had begun publishing his series of English half-inch maps in 1895 with sheets covering south Devon, Surrey and Kent.[25] This was virtually complete by the time the Ordnance Survey's unsuccessful competitor at this scale was launched in 1903. By 1912, the Bartholomew series had been through several reprints, and the best-selling sheets (judging by print runs) were in the south of England. If the Ordnance Survey could not compete at the half-inch scale, it must have been hoped that the projected new relief version of the one-inch would take a large slice of the market share in small-scale maps, and it would be an obvious priority to begin, not

---

22 Manuscript additions, dated to 1913, to the 1909 instructions show that they were in use for the Lancashire revision period.

23 Although sheet 135 carries a revision date of 1903-10 under the Second Revision dates.

24 Oliver, (1992b).

25 Among the first counties to be printed were: South Devon: 1523 copies printed on 20/5/1895; Surrey: 1463 copies printed on 14/6/1895; Kent: 930 copies printed on 19/5/1896; Sussex: 2080 copies printed on 7/10/1896; Cornwall: 1537 copies printed on 18/1/1897. NLS, Bartholomew Printing Archive.

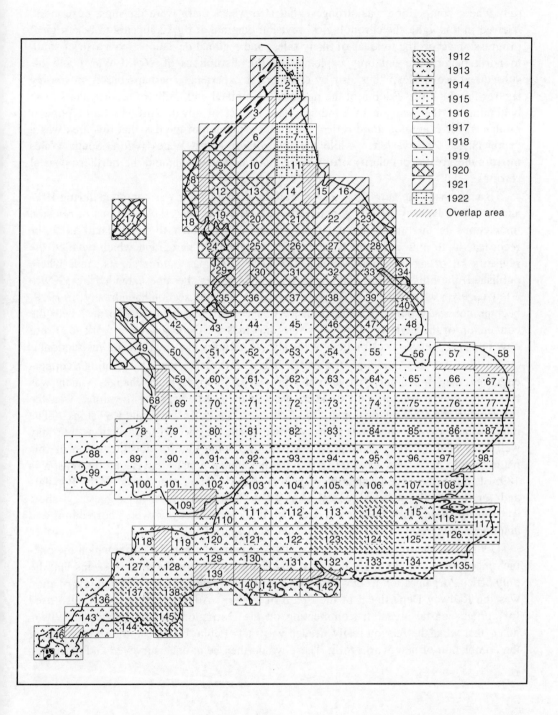

Fig.12 Diagram showing the progress of the Third Revision of England and Wales 1912-1922. The year in which revision was first taken up for each sheet of the Popular Edition is shown. Dates are taken from the maps.

only where competition was strongest, but also where there were the most customers. Viewed in this light, the chronological revision diagram at fig.12 appears to be a logical progression according to areas of likely sales, and regional deviations from a strict south to north pattern are not only explained by the disruptions of World War I and the subsequent economies,[26] but also by commercial experience, perhaps based on trading figures for the Third Edition of the one-inch, combined with military requirements. The beginning of the revision of southern East Anglia in advance of the more popular midlands, for example, could reflect the military opinion of the day that this area was a prime target for invasion,[27] while the revision of North Wales before South Wales mirrors the greater popularity of the tourist area of Snowdonia and the northern coastal resorts.

To accompany the new Third Revision, a set of instructions was compiled during 1913 and issued in January 1914.[28] A noticeable feature of the successive editions of revision instructions is the increasing attention given, not so much to what detail is to be recorded, as to how it should be done. The simple 1896 paragraph which detailed the reviser's kit of six-inch impressions, New Series one-inch outline sheets, and (where published) the hills version, and copies of the Old Series, became extended by 1909 to a few pages in what was now a 22-page manual. A separate section had already, in 1909, become necessary purely for the guidance of the draftsmen who were to deal with the conversion of the revisers' documents into drawings for the engraver to work to. From now onwards, revision instructions were always accompanied by drawing instructions.

This trend reflected not only the greater technical demands made by printing a copper-engraved map in colour, but also the growth of topographical change, which was becoming ever more difficult to keep pace with. A true sign of the times was the inclusion in the 1909 instructions of the first reference to 'Intermediate Revisions'. The intermediate revision sheet was first identified as such in the 1914 instructions, but may well have been of long standing in practice, and some kind of documentation of this nature would have been essential to provide the annual updates envisaged by Wilson in 1893. It was to become a standard component of the revision documents for the Popular, and for the small scales in general after 1914. It was, as its name suggests, a sheet (presumably a one-inch impression, although this is not stated) on which corrections and amendments were noted for inclusion at the next reprint.

Until 1914, the source documents, apart from reviser's material, from which the one-inch maps were compiled, are largely a matter for conjecture. In 1892, it seems that the only official organisation from whom the Ordnance Survey regularly received information was the Railway Department of the Board of Trade;[29] Admiralty charts were also used for certain coastal areas. In commenting on the Dorington recommendations, Wilson noted that what the Survey really needed was that 'Public bodies should send notice of the completion of new works to it. These would then be at once surveyed and placed on

---

26 Oliver, (1992b), p.45.

27 Hodson, (1994).

28 Ordnance Survey *Instructions for the revision of the small scale maps* ..., (Jan. 1914).

29 Dorington, (1893c), para.257.

the one-inch map.'[30] His intention was that such revision should appear immediately on the one-inch, and only subsequently on the large scales as they came up for revision. If this policy were carried out - and clearly this view was behind the decision, referred to earlier, to update the map annually - it has significant implications for the value of the one-inch map as a historical document for the 1890s. The principle certainly appears to have been put partly into action for, in 1893, a more positive approach to regularising data collection was taken when it was announced that the 'Board of Trade and the various Sanitary Authorities have been requested to send early notice of new works and improvements to the Department.'[31]

Of course, the absence from official records of any mention of extra-departmental source materials does not necessarily imply that they were not used, but they are first mentioned in print in Close's 1914 instructions for the third revision. Here we find that, in compiling the Popular Edition sheets, local guide books were to be consulted for information on antiquities; Bradshaw's Guide was to be used for data on railway stations; the Postal Guide was the main source for post and telegraph offices; lighthouses and lightships were compiled from the Admiralty List of Lights; and the Wreck Chart from the *Life Boat Journal* provided information on lifeboat stations. The list was extended in the 1930s to include railway company maps, the *Radio Telegraph* list of stations, the *List of Aerodromes* and the *Air Pilot*, the *National Trust Annual Report*, and the *Youth Hostel Handbook*. These additions were contained in the *Instructions for the revision and drawing of the one-inch (Fifth Edition) map*, which were published in 1936. These were the last set of instructions to be relevant to the compilation of the Popular Edition, because although they were intended for its successor, many of the new features were incorporated in the old map on successive reprints during the 1930s when it was current alongside the Fifth Edition.

These successive editions of instructions provided the framework for furnishing the map with up-to-date detail, but they were intended, primarily, for the complete revision in the field which theoretically occurred once every fifteen years. In this sense, the revision of the small scales was indeed independent of that of the large scales. The policy for the intermediate revisions is less easy to tie down but it would seem, as far as the Popular Edition was concerned, that these did depend on the revision of the large scales and, in particular, the six-inch map. In the *Annual Report* for 1934/5, the intermediate revision is described as one which was carried out in the office and incorporated 'only such additions as are available from the revised large-scale sheets which have been published since the current edition was printed.'[32] However, because the revision of the large scales was in such arrears in the 1930s it meant, as one officer commented, that 'at best our one-inch sheets are patchy, being up to date in parts and possibly 20 years behind the times in others', a compromise which might be satisfactory in theory, but 'lamentable in

30 PRO OS 1/2/5. Memorandum dated 3/3/1893.

31 *Annual Report*, (1893), p.9.

32 Page 15.

practice'.[33]

In the main, where sample comparisons between one-inch and six-inch have been made, this statement is borne out, although there are important exceptions, such as the special road revision, and examples where detail has been published at the one-inch scale in advance of the larger scale. These, together with considerations of specific revision cases, are described in the later chapters, but from a general point of view, it can be said that some confusion seems to have reigned among the Officers in charge of the relevant departments in the Ordnance Survey about what was, or was not, to be included on reprints of the Popular Edition. For example, at one point it was claimed that the Survey did not incorporate 'anything like the amount of information available in the office', and that changes were confined to 'adding new main roads, altering road classification and attending to minor matters such as changing symbols to show whether stations are open to the public or not.'[34] On the other hand, in 1934 it was said that 'we incorporate on the old sheets [i.e. the increasingly obsolete Popular sheets] on intermediate revision a great deal of detail which is of little value to the public'.[35] These conflicting remarks may have been based simply on those sheets which were undergoing revision at the time; if so, they reflect, at the least, an inconsistent policy. It was suggested that the only items to be included on reprints should be new communications information (roads and railways), all housing estates involving the provision of new roads, all woods covering 10 acres or more and important new works such as reservoirs.[36] The evidence of the Popular Edition sheets which were reprinted after 1935 indicate that these proposals were followed.

Revision and methods of map production were, as we have seen, closely tied together. Once the details of the physical and human landscapes had been captured in linear and angular measurements, their presentation in graphic form depended on the judicious selection of projection, sheet lines, symbols, and the design of the marginal information of each sheet. In many of these respects, the Popular Edition leant heavily on the past - the layout of its sheet lines, for example, was circumscribed by the inflexibility of the copperplates on which the series was based. However, at 146 sheets, it was the smallest one-inch series, in terms of numbers of sheets, so far produced of England and Wales.

---

33 PRO OS 1/54. Minute 68.

34 PRO OS 1/312. Memorandum dated 29/10/1934.

35 PRO OS 1/54. Minute 68, [1936].

36 *Ibid.*

Chapter IV

SHEET LINES AND MARGINALIA

Finality in sheet lines is never reached. Even with that clear and excellent Popular Edition as it now exists we have found it necessary to provide numerous tourist or special sheets for the convenience of this or that locality which has fallen awkwardly upon the normal series. *Winterbotham, 1932.*[1]

Until the adoption of the Transverse Mercator (meridional orthomorphic) projection for the Fifth Edition of the one-inch map in 1928, all maps and plans of the Ordnance Survey of England and Wales had been drawn on Cassini's (transverse cylindrical) projection.[2] The reasons for the selection of this projection lie in the Survey's eighteenth-century origins, and perhaps in its professional connections with the French Cassini family of astronomers after whom the projection is named. On this projection, the scale is true only along the central meridian and along great circles perpendicular to that projection, so that scale north and south is exaggerated on all other meridians, and increases away from the central meridian. This distortion, which was considered to be quite unacceptable on the large-scale plans of the national grid era (it was claimed that the distortion of an angle in a triangle of five-mile sides on the Cassini projection might amount to three or four minutes[3]) was not significant at the one-inch scale, amounting, at the greatest distance from the central meridian, to five feet in one mile.[4] The geographical co-ordinate values given in Appendix 7 nicely demonstrate the extent to which projectional distortion affects the position of the sheet corners.

Much depended on the selection of the central meridian. The meridian on which the construction of the Popular Edition sheet lines was based was Delamere - but what was the principle governing its selection? In order to answer what might appear to be a simple question, it becomes necessary to look at the way in which the Popular's antecedents were made. It is a singular omission in the published history of Ordnance Survey mapping that, until recently, the physical construction of the sheet lines of any map series has hardly been touched on[5] except for brief descriptions, some of which are misleading. For example, in order to avoid gross angular errors, the large-scale county plans were

---

1 Winterbotham, (1932b), p.20.
2 A brief description of Cassini's projection together with tables for its construction is given in *Account of the methods and processes ...* , (1902). A further account of the projection and its use by the Ordnance Survey is given in Steers, (1962), pp.134-5, 208-15.
3 PRO OS 1/111. MacLeod to Boulnois, 27/6/1938. A discussion of the angular distortion produced by this projection in the large-scale plans is given in Hotine, (1938), pp.132-3.
4 Winterbotham, (1936b), p.46.
5 An exception to this is an essay by Adams in Hellyer, (1992b), pp.176-84, and in Hellyer, (1999).

based on many local meridians,[6] but a similar multiplicity of origins has been claimed for the construction of sheets 1-90 of the Old Series one-inch map.[7] This, however, would seem to be an invention by Winterbotham, who also mentioned, but did not name, meridians for Kent, Sussex, Essex and Surrey.[8]

Winterbotham appears to have confused the meridians that were observed for the calculation of the triangulation, of which there were ten,[9] with those that were used for the construction of the southern sheets of the Old Series one-inch map, of which there were two: Greenwich and, it was formerly believed, Butterton Hill. An intimation of the unknown second meridian is given by Harley and O'Donoghue,[10] who cite the only known contemporary document on the policy behind the selection of meridians for the construction of the one-inch map at this time in the early nineteenth century.[11] From this it emerges that, apart from Greenwich, another meridian was selected 'at the centre of the Kingdom'. This was not identified by name, but recent work by Adams[12] not only suggests, convincingly, that it was probably 3°W, but also gives a most original account of the construction of the Old Series sheets, whose irregularity of size, shape and layout - which was consequent on the use of more than one meridian - is illustrated by the index at fig.13.

Adams has shown[13] that Mudge's apparent intention in introducing several meridians was to limit the longitude extent of their use in calculating the triangulation. Delamere was, in fact, used as the origin for a great tract of Britain in the north-south direction, extending from Gloucester to Fife. This made, as Adams states, the inevitability of its selection as the origin for the New Series projection all the more certain. Thereafter, from about 1842 until the 1930s, the projection of the one-inch, and smaller scale maps of England and Wales, was constructed on the meridian of Delamere,[14] the geographical co-ordinates of which are 53°13'17"274 N, 2°41'03"562 W.[15] The divergence of the one-inch sheet lines from those of the six-inch, which were constructed on local meridians, is well illustrated by the diagrams of constituent six-inch sheets which appeared in the margins of the Revised New Series.

In 1873, when the Old Series one-inch map of England and Wales was virtually complete, Capt. H.S. Palmer remarked that

---

6 A brief description of the plethora of meridians is given in Winterbotham, (1938).

7 Winterbotham, (1938); Dunnose, Delamere, Clifton Beacon, Burleigh Moor, Moel Rhyddlan, Greenwich.

8 *Ibid.*, p.322.

9 Beachy Head, Black Down, Burleigh Moor, Butterton Hill, Clifton Beacon, Delamere, Dunnose, Greenwich, Moel Rhyddlan, St. Agnes Beacon.

10 Harley and O'Donoghue in Margary, (1975:1992), III: xxx-xxxi.

11 PRO OS3/260. ff.339-40.

12 Adams, (1994a).

13 *Ibid.*

14 The original 1805 station was named 'Delamere Forest'; an attempt to restore the station in 1842 showed it to be 3.7 feet adrift. In Clarke, (1858), it is referred to once as 'Delamere, New', but thereafter, was known simply as 'Delamere'.

15 When the one-inch was derived from the larger scales, which were drawn on different meridians, it would have been a simple job of calculation to transfer the data from one meridian to another. The mathematical basis of the one-inch maps is given in Wolff, (1919).

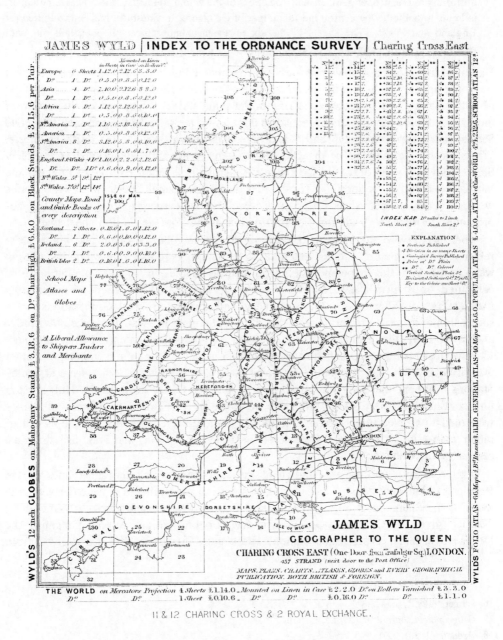

Fig.13 Index to the Old Series one-inch map of England and Wales, issued by James Wyld about 1864. Reduced; scale of original 50 miles to one inch. The use of several meridians in the construction of the Old Series is reflected in the marked discontinuity of adjacent blocks of sheets. Note also the irregular shape and size of many of the sheets. *Private collection.*

it is to be regretted that the early one-inch sheets of England and Wales were not constructed uniformly to one proper geometrical projection for the whole country ... the mistake, however, is being remedied. One central meridian, that of Delamere, in Cheshire, has been adopted for England and Wales. The sheets of the six northern counties have all been laid out with reference to it, on a similar projection to those of Ireland.[16]

Half a century later, a reviewer of the Scottish Popular Edition map was to comment that 'it would appear likely that the Delamere meridian was originally chosen so as to allow of both England and Scotland appearing in the same series.'[17] The earliest indication of the intended use of the Delamere meridian appears on an index to the one-inch map (Old Series) dated approximately 1839,[18] and here it is drawn only for the northern sheets. When the southern sheets of the Old Series were recast and re-engraved as the New Series, they too, were drawn on the Delamere meridian, so that the whole of England and Wales appeared on one meridian for the first time. These small sheets of the New Series were, in terms of their sheet lines which were calculated according to Cassini feet co-ordinates, to form the basis for the construction of the Popular Edition sheet lines.

The maps were therefore laid down using rectangular co-ordinates which were referred to triangulation stations, and it has to be remembered that at this time insufficient was known about the shape and size of the earth to enable a national triangulation to be computed on a firm basis. It was because of this that the concept of calculating rectangular co-ordinates for the secondary and tertiary triangulation stations on a succession of origins, or meridians, at about 60 mile intervals, was introduced by Mudge at the end of the eighteenth century.[19] It is Adams's contention that although astronomical results were not introduced into the adjustment of the triangulation, other than at Greenwich, it is probably significant that six of the ten meridians were at Sector Stations.[20] When, therefore, the production of the Old Series north of the Hull-Preston line continued in the 1840s,[21] after the adoption by the Ordnance Survey of Airy's spheroid, it was clearly preferable that the sheets should be constructed on one meridian, rather than two, as formerly. Delamere was a Sector Station, and was also the most central to Great Britain.

Until recently, nothing was known of the data from which the sheet lines of the Popular Edition were constructed, except, in a general sense, that they were derived from those of the Small Sheet Series of the Third Edition. But a useful series of articles by Adams[22] gives the Cassini co-ordinates in feet for the two-inch square containing the Delamere primary triangulation station. His sources for these data are derived from

16 Palmer, (1873), p.14.
17 *Geographical Journal*, (1925) LXV, 2:161.
18 Hodson, (1989), p.91.
19 Adams, (1989a,b), in Hellyer, (1992b).
20 These were places where astronomical observations of celestial bodies in a zenith position (vertically above the observer) were made. By observing the same stars from places some distance apart, the difference in latitude could be calculated. In the early nineteenth century these measurements were made using Ramsden's zenith sector, hence, 'Sector Station'. Owen and Pilbeam, (1992), p.23.
21 Margary, (1975-1992), VIII:vii-viii
22 Adams, (1989a, b, and 1990).

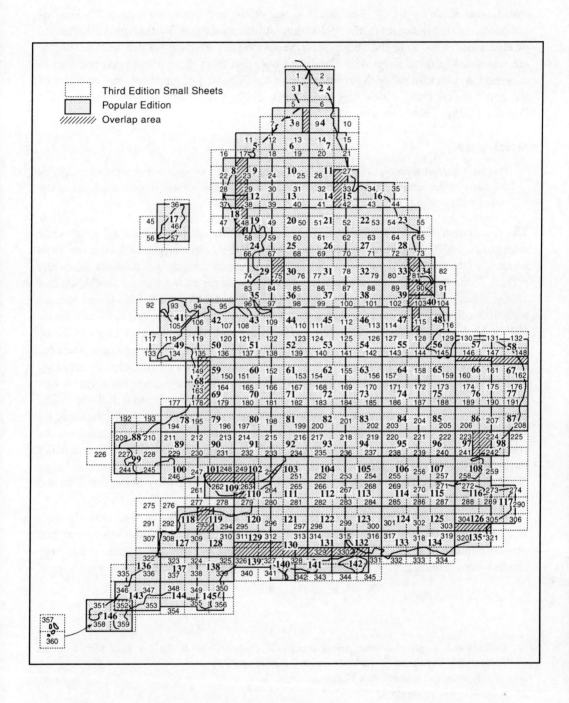

Fig.14 Index showing the relationship between the sheet lines of the Third Edition Small Sheets and the Popular Edition.

calculations made by J.C.B. Redfearn[23] in the 1930s, and from a volume of Cassini co-ordinates, probably begun in the 1930s, and still remaining at Southampton.[24] Separate printed indexes for both the Small Sheet Series and the Popular Edition in this volume are annotated in manuscript with Cassini values, and from these it has been possible to construct an index showing the relationship of the Popular Edition sheet lines to those of the small sheets from which they were derived (fig.14). Each standard sheet of the Popular Edition covers an area of 486 square miles.

Series layout

> The most perfect solution of this sheet line question which I personally can think of is to issue the maps of the country in two editions which cut each other's sheet lines through the centre and at right angles.[25]

The difficulties of using several meridians for the construction of a national small-scale map series had been solved by the substitution of the single origin of Delamere from about the late 1840s, but the other problems inherent in designing a national sheet line system,[26] convenient for the majority of users, only came to the fore in the 1880s and 1890s, when cycling became a mass popular recreation and the cyclist soon found himself travelling off the small one-inch sheets. Until this time, the sheet lines of the small sheets (12″ x 18″) of the New Series, which had been devised for the north of England in the 1840s, were well suited to pedestrians and passengers of horse-drawn vehicles. The total lack of overlaps was tailored to the rigid production methods of copperplate printing. This inflexibility was to mean that the ability to select a sheet layout so that major towns were contained on the least number of sheets was denied to the Popular Edition.[27] The inconvenience of the mid-nineteenth-century scheme was manifested in the demand, by 1892, for maps of special areas of tourist interest, none of which fell happily on the standard sheet lines. The larger maps needed to fulfill this requirement eventually influenced the size of the regular sheets, for even before the advent in 1906 of the Large Sheet Series of the Third Edition, many sheets of the Revised New Series were issued in a combined format.

The larger sheets of the Third Edition (18″ x 27″) had been designed to 'kill off' their smaller siblings;[28] they had been produced at the request of the War Office, and had proved popular with an ever more mobile public. Therefore the dimensions of the large sheets were retained for the Popular Edition, but the sheet lines themselves were altered

23 Redfearn was a gifted amateur mathematician and Deputy Chief of the Far East Section in the Hydrographic Department in the 1940s. Adams, (1994b), p.9.

24 OSL Departmental Records, Box TL23.

25 Winterbotham, (1934b), p.99.

26 Board, (1993), p.120, summarises sheet line design for the one-inch map.

27 Even where modern production methods allow flexibility of choice, it is still difficult to select the best sheet lines. For example, eight trial layouts were made for the 1:50,000 series. Price, (1975).

28 Olivier, (1914a), paras. 307, 308. The creation of these larger sheets was the only contribution to cartography noted by Close, (1929), of Hellard's Director Generalship in his obituary of Hellard.

slightly in order to bring them into line with those of the half-inch series,[29] so that, for inland areas, four Popular Edition sheets would be covered by one half-inch map. Similarly, the sheet lines of the engraved half-inch map had been constructed so that each sheet would cover nine of the small one-inch maps. The relationship of the Popular Edition to its constituent copperplates, and to the derived small scale map, was therefore entirely logical. Another feature of the design of the Popular layout was the provision, made in the 1914 instructions, for extrusions. This stated that 'Where towns are cut through by sheet lines, and there is room to complete them in the margin, they should be so completed, and the marginal lines left broken'.[30] No fewer than forty-six sheets showed settlement or road detail continued into the margin. An added bonus in the change of layout was the reduction in overlaps, which, while being a useful way of dealing with unsympathetic sheet lines, unfortunately entailed complicated revision procedures, especially if adjacent sheets were not brought up to date simultaneously. Even so, it had been necessary to produce forty-seven district and tourist sheets for England and Wales, virtually a third of the total of series sheets, in order to compensate for awkward standard sheet lines. This in itself was an expensive outlay with doubtful commercial returns, which was to lead to a programme of rationalisation in the 1930s.

Of the approximately 340 copperplates which made up the Popular Edition, 118 remained uncut, a further 118 were cut into exact halves, either horizontally or vertically, thirty-four were cut into quarters, and the remainder were unequally divided to provide the non-standard sheets. The first layout of the Popular Edition was devised before March 1913,[31] and the earliest map known to have been printed with the new sheet numbering was the Torquay experimental sheet (sheet 145) in 1914, which covered an area formerly included in sheets 149 and 150 of the Third Edition Large Sheet Series. Also, an undated index showing the relationship of small sheets to the large sheets of the Third Edition[32] carries the manuscript annotation 'see Index ½" map Diagram A Circular 30.9.12 for new numbers of sheets'. The 'new' sheet numbers may have referred to those of the future Popular Edition, and this date can therefore be regarded as a *terminus ante quem*. None of the usual graphic documentation associated with the compilation of new sheet lines appears to have been kept, but the evidence of the maps themselves, and of the printed graphic indexes (Appendix 4), is considerable.

The only contemporary published statement[33] about the design of the sheet lines is in a lecture to the Royal Geographical Society,[34] by Johnston, the officer in charge of the printing department of the Ordnance Survey, who described how the Popular Edition sheet lines were constructed by tracing the cutting lines 'of the 1-inch Large Sheet Series [i.e. the Popular Edition]' onto 'the engraved Small Sheet matrix plates'. The Third Edition Large Sheet layout had been arranged in four staggered blocks, from north to

29 *Annual Report*, (1912/13).
30 Ordnance Survey *Instructions for the revision of the small scale maps ...*, (Jan.1914), p.13, para.72. Extrusions are also discussed in Board, (1993).
31 The announcement of the new sheet lines was made in the *Annual Report*, (1912/13).
32 Kept in the Ordnance Survey Cartographic Library.
33 The sheet lines of the Popular Edition are not discussed in detail in, for example, Winterbotham, (1932b).
34 Johnston, (1920).

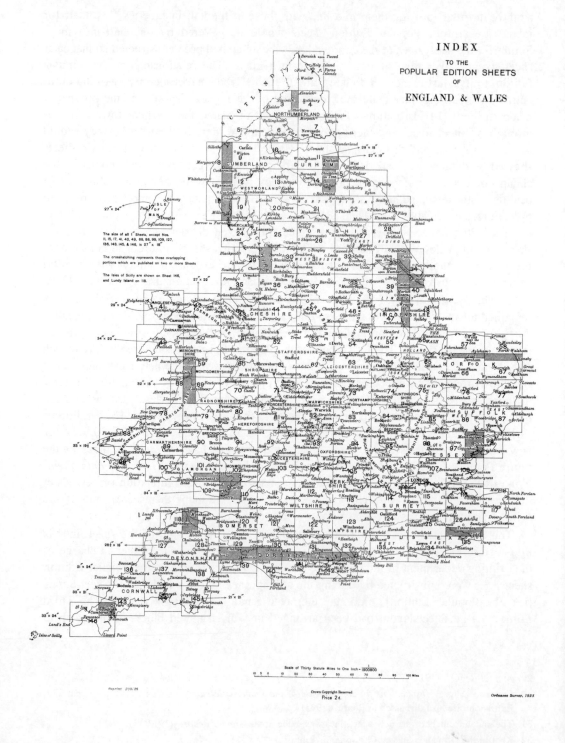

Fig.15 Index to the Popular Edition. Reduced; scale of original 1:1,900,800. *Private collection.*

south. A greater degree of uniformity was achieved for the Popular Edition resulting in a reduction of the number of sheets from 152 to 146 (fig.15; see plate 7 for the relationship between the sheet lines of the two series), but the number of non-standard size sheets was increased from ten[35] to thirteen in the first instance, and then to fifteen.[36] The policy behind this was that, while the inland sheets were to be co-terminous with those of the half-inch map, those on the coastline were to be arranged so as 'to give the best map to the public'.[37] In this way, the rigidity of the Small Sheets, which had produced so many coastal maps with only small areas of land, was avoided. Two changes to the projected sheet lines occurred, probably after 1919, and this was to the layout of sheets 34 *The Mouth of the Humber* and 42 *Llandudno and Denbigh* (fig.16).

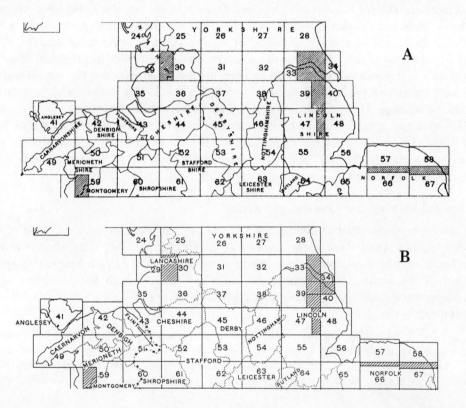

Fig.16 Index **A** from *Catalogue of maps and other publications of the Ordnance Survey* (1924), showing the wrong sheet lines for maps 34 and 42; Index **B**, from *Specimens and Indexes of the Ordnance Survey small-scale maps of Great Britain* (1935), showing the correct layout of sheets 34 and 42. *Private collection.*

35 The non-standard sheets of the Third Edition were: 17, 34, 48, 49, 100, 118, 128, 136, 150 and 151.

36 Sheets 15 and 42 were added to the list of non-standard sized sheets which appeared on the graphic indexes from about 1925. The fifteen were: 11, 15, 17, 41, 42, 49, 68, 88, 99, 109, 127, 136, 143, 145, 146.

37 Olivier, (1914a), para.716.

On some early indexes, sheet 34 was shown as a landscape-shaped sheet, with about a 60% overlap with sheet 33 to the west. It was, however, first published in 1924, in portrait shape. The amount of overlap was not reduced, but was now shared with sheets 39 and 40, as well as 33. The suggestions given by Oliver[38] for this change - that Grimsby and its neighbourhood were no longer spread over three sheets, and that the military installations along the coast could now be shown on one sheet instead of two - are logical. However, the index was not corrected for the Ordnance Survey's annual reports until the year 1929/30, four years after the final sheet in the series had been published.

Sheet 42, first published in 1922, was a non-standard size of 22" x 27". In this case, it would seem that the original standard-sized layout, shown on the early indexes, gave ample clearance for the inclusion of Great Orme's Head, but would not have embraced the off-shore mud banks of West Hoyle Spit. This was the western continuation of West Hoyle Bank, one of a series of banks which stretched across the mouths of the Rivers Dee and Mersey, and which constituted major physical features in Liverpool Bay. The anomaly which existed for sheet 34 between the published map and the way in which it was portrayed on the indexes was repeated for sheet 42. This demonstrates a persistent lack of attention to detail on the smaller scale indexes to the extent that even the early indexes which appeared on the back cover of the map itself, showed the sheet lines in the wrong position. The error was compounded in the annual reports which showed the sheet at the standard size until indexes to the Popular Edition were discontinued in this publication in 1932/3.

The two-inch square referencing system

Each sheet of the Popular Edition was covered with an alpha-numerical system of two-inch squares which were drawn parallel to the sheet lines. This is an ancient form of referencing which had been used as early as the third century in Chinese cartography.[39] One of the earliest English maps to use a two-mile (though not two-inch) square referencing system was Norden's map of Hertfordshire (1598), on which the following explanation was given:

> The figures and letters which followe the names of the places in the alphabeticall tables, are a ready meane whereby to find, any place desired in the Mapp, by referring them to meet, in the squares, very familiarly: without which helpe a place vnkown would be long to find in the Mappe. Betweene the lines is 2. miles, by which a distance may bee found without compasses.[40]

Later, Joel Gascoyne's map of Cornwall, published in 1699 at almost the one-inch scale, carried two-inch squares which were identified by upper and lower case letters.[41] Unlike these early systems, the squaring on the Popular Edition can be regarded as the crude forerunners of our modern national grid because they can be identified with the Cassini

38 Oliver, (1982b), [p.8].
39 Wallis and Robinson, (1987), p.195, and Heawood, (1932).
40 Quoted in Hodson, (1974), p.15.
41 Ravenhill, (1991). The map is illustrated in figs 1.4 and 1.5.

co-ordinates from which the map was constructed. These squares were apparently put on the map for military needs and were not designed, initially, to fulfill any civil purpose.[42] By the 1920s, however, the need for a gazetteer (perhaps prompted by Bartholomew's gazetteer to his half-inch maps) was recognised, and it was planned that one should be compiled which would relate to the squares on the Popular Edition. The project was dropped because it was thought that the referencing 'would be too heavy a task to undertake'.[43] The Popular Edition was used by the English Place-Name Society for referencing, although this must have been slightly unsatisfactory because the squares were specific only to individual sheets, and thus the full reference for any place in England would comprise sheet number followed by the alpha-numeric designation.

It is a curious anomaly, however, that a sheet, two sides of which are measured in an odd number of inches, should be covered by a system of squares whose dimensions are in even inches. As a result, the east or west side of each sheet perforce carries one column of half-squares, or rectangles measuring 2″ x 1″. Why should two-inch squares have been selected in preference to the more logical dimensions of a one-inch square, or, for that matter, a three-inch square? Both of these would have fitted the standard sheet size of 18″ x 27″. It is possible that the first was considered to be too small, and might have obscured the detail of the map, and the second too large.[44] It is a system which the Popular inherited from the Third Edition Large Sheet Series, although the squares were not printed across the face of this map, but were indicated by ticks in the margins. The two-inch square was also used on the half-inch map, to which the same disadvantages applied.

The two-inch square, in the form of marginal indications only, made its first appearance in the regular one-inch series on the coloured military map which was based on the Revised New Series (1897)[45]. Its production was a direct result of the 1892 Baker Committee which had recommended the publication of a coloured one-inch map for military use. Only one of the correspondents suggested a referencing system, but it is notable that the proposal was made in conjunction with the recommendation of a two-inches to the mile map (1:31,680) as the ideal scale for military use in the field, rather than a one-inch map; each two-inch square would therefore represent one square mile. In proposing this scheme, Col. J. Alleyne (Assistant Adjutant General at Aldershot) also recommended that each sheet should cover an exact even number of miles, 20 x 16 miles, say, rather than 20½ x 16½ miles so that (we infer, for it is not overtly stated) the system of two-inch squares would fit the map exactly.

The transposition of a two-inch square to the one-inch map worked perfectly well as long as the sheets of that map were of even dimensions, as was the case with the Small Sheets which measured 12″ x 18″. It was only with the introduction of the 18″ x 27″

42   Close, discussion of Jack, (1924), p.504.

43   PRO OS 1/49. Memorandum dated 10/4/1931.

44   An inconclusive discussion on the optimum size of a grid square appears in 'Ordnance Survey maps: discussion with special reference to the grid system', (1936). See also, Winterbotham, (1925).

45   But Bartholomew had used three-inch alpha-numerically identified squares on his 'Map of the Country round Strathearn House, Crieff. Scale 2 Miles to 1 Inch'. 2200 copies were printed on 4/9/1893. NLS, Bartholomew Printing Archive, vol.20.

sheet in 1906 that the pattern was disrupted, and, for the Third Edition Large Sheet Series, resulted in the north-south column of 'squares' on the eastern side of the sheet measuring 2" x 1". This practice was continued for the Popular Edition sheets, but, as Adams has pointed out,[46] a significant change was made to those sheets which were published from 1920 onwards. From this time, those sheets which formed the eastern continuation of sheets which carried the 1" wide rectangles along the eastern side, now carried the 1" wide rectangles along their western edge, thus forming a complete two-inch square at the junction of sheet edges. This applied to sheets 1-40 and 43-7 (excluding 17, Isle of Man); furthermore, this system carried through to the Scottish Popular sheets and formed, what was, in effect, an embryonic national Cassini grid. This point was recognised in 1924, when, during a discussion on a presentation on the choice of a grid for British maps,[47] it was noted that the two-inch reference squares already formed a skeleton national grid.[48]

The two-inch squares for the sheets of northern England, and of the Popular Edition of Scotland, therefore constitute an un-numbered Cassini grid,[49] but even had the Cassini values been given on the map, instead of letters and numbers, they would have been inordinately difficult to use because they were so cumbersome (see Appendix 7). When a national grid with 5000 yard sides was introduced in 1931 for the Fifth Edition one-inch map and all the small-scale maps, it was welcomed because it provided a universal referencing system for Great Britain. What most users did not realise was that the 5000 yard grid was selected because it gave a square which on the map bore a superficial resemblance to the size of the two-inch square to which the public were already accustomed.[50]

The use of two-inch squares on the Popular Edition for rough locational referencing was one thing but, in 1922, a reorganisation of map policy took place in the Geographical Section, General Staff, during which it was decided to introduce the general use of the one-inch, instead of the half-inch, for military training. In 1923, therefore, 'for the convenience of orders and of artillery surveys',[51] the Popular Edition sheets which were intended for military use began to be overprinted with a grid,[52] similar to that already on the 1:20,000 training maps.[53] Close had been proud to announce in his *Annual*

---

46 Adams, (1990), pp.8-9.

47 Hinks, (1924), pp.491-508.

48 The most useful explanation of the word 'grid' is in *Notes on the making of maps and plans*, (1937), p.124. It is described as a system of graphically true squares which is 'composed of a series of lines drawn parallel to and at equal distances away from the axes of the projection'. The definition is further qualified in this source by an explanatory list of the purposes which a grid fulfills. Winterbotham claimed to have been the first to coin the expression 'map-grid', while translating the German terms 'gitternetz, gradnetz and meldenetz', and commented that 'as the Electrical Commissioners had not yet launched their lighting, we stole no man's thunder'. Winterbotham, (1936a).

49 Adams, (1989b), pp.4-5.

50 PRO OS 1/111. MacLeod to Robinson, 11/3/1937. In fact, the sides of these squares measured 2¾".

51 R.E. Corps Library. 'The history of the formation and work of M.I.4.' Part A, headed '1922'.

52 For the early application, in 1910, of a grid to a one-inch Ordnance map, see Anon, (1985).

53 This grid was constructed on the central meridian of Dunnose, a triangulation station in the south-east of the Isle of Wight, and it therefore lay at an angle to the Popular Edition sheet lines.

Report for 1920 that the Popular Edition had been approved by the War Office as a military map, but three years later great difficulties were encountered in trying to fit the grid to the map because the map had suffered so many distortions as a result of the way in which it had been produced. This kind of inaccuracy was to prompt Hinks to remark that MacLeod had spent nearly all his time from 1916 onwards in 'fudging grids to fit maps.'[54] So, while the Popular Edition was deemed satisfactory as a topographical map it was, after all, 'unsuitable for military requirements'.[55]

Quite apart from considerations of the accuracy of a superimposed grid, the positioning of the two-inch squares themselves was not always consistent from one printing to another, nor, on occasion, between fully coloured and outline versions of the same sheets. The shift may be only of the order of 1 mm in some cases[56] but there are numerous examples where infelicitous breaks in the line for names, or continuations of line across detail, have been corrected on subsequent reprints. While this may be insignificant from a referencing point of view, these small positional changes do set questions about how and when the squaring was put on the map in the first place. These are impossible to answer conclusively, and different methods may well have been used during the lifetime of the Popular. The decision to carry the lines across the map may not have been made until 1918 (when the first sheets were apparently printed) in the first place, for they did not appear on any of the English experimental sheets, referred to in Chapter I, and no instruction for their inclusion is given in the 1913 *General Instructions* for the third revision of England and Wales (Appendix 2).

It might be reasonable to suppose, since the squares should have been identical for standard sized sheets, that two masters might have been made, one for a sheet with rectangles on the west side, and one for an 'east sided' sheet (or, perhaps, one master which could have been reversed as necessary). These could then have been transferred to the outline plate on stone and scraped out where necessary to avoid detail. The minor differences which occur between some printings could then be explained by a possible mismatching of the two elements on reprints. On the other hand, this could have entailed so much making good to the lettering that it might have been quicker to draw the squares straight onto the outline plate, tailoring each line to the detail it encountered as it was drawn. Since the copperplate was regarded as relatively distortion-free,[57] it might be thought that the lines would be engraved on the outline plate, but their absence from the three-colour printing of sheet 85, ca 1919,[58] and particularly from the 1919 black outline sheet, and the Land Utilisation sheets[59] which were based on the Popular, would suggest that this was not so, unless two engraved outline plates were made, one with squaring, and one without. It is always possible that a blue impression of the black plate could have been made, onto which the squaring could have been drawn in order to produce a master from which a combined printing plate - outline and squares - could have

---

54 PRO OS 1/111. Hinks to MacLeod, 3/11/1941.
55 PRO OS 1/9/5. Jack to MAFF, 21/3/1924.
56 For example, the coloured version of sheet 4 compared with the outline sheet.
57 Jack, (1925).
58 RGS OS Specimen no. 57.
59 At least one sheet (sheet 35) had the squaring. See Hellyer, (1999), p.30.

been produced. This too, could account for positional discrepancies.

A somewhat ambiguous clue to the process is provided by two versions of the outline sheets (Part 2, p.282, Outline 7 and 8), which were printed mainly in the 1940s. These are bereft of squaring, but traces of the former lines can easily be seen on some sheets where they have been imperfectly erased. Since we know that from the 1930s the original stones, and even the copperplates, were being photographed in order to supply printing plates for new issues, it could be that the squaring was in fact drawn on the stones, but had been carelessly deleted from the negative. On the other hand, we also know that the copperplates themselves were photographed, where the stones were worn out, and so there may well have existed outline plates where the squaring was engraved on copper. One further option is offered by the list of jobs required for producing the 1940 reprint of the Manchester District sheet.[60] Here, one of the instructions reads: 'make printing plates from original stones and plates, keeping outline plate clean for drawing two inch lines'. The implication of this is that the original outline material, in this instance, never had the squaring, but that it was imposed on some form of a duplicate plate before printing. Of course, different procedures may have been used for standard and district sheets, but the problem well illustrates how difficult it is to pinpoint, retrospectively, the exact methods of production which were in use at any one time.

Map border

The letters and numbers designating the two-inch squares were contained within a border design which, in its simplicity, echoed the style used for the sheets of the coloured map of the Revised New Series, and the Third Edition coloured maps. This was very plain, and comprised a neat line and outer single line, within which were printed the letters and numbers of the two-inch referencing system, contour figures, road directions and county names. The emphasis on function, rather than appearance, which this austerity conveyed, was achieved for these two series at the expense of two features.

The first of these was the purely decorative 'piano key' border which was contained within an outer frame of one thick, and one thin, line. This had been a standard design, with slight variations, for the one-inch map since the publication of Mudge's one-inch map of Kent[61] in 1801. It was retained for two forms of the Revised New Series: outline with contours, and hills in black or brown. The reason for its omission from the coloured maps is not known, but it is easy to see that what enhanced a monochrome, or two-colour map, might have appeared fussy and would have detracted from a map with four or more colours. Its demise was complete with the appearance of the coloured one-inch map. The second omission was not decorative in nature, but strictly functional and therefore less easy to explain. This was the indication of latitude and longitude which had been a standard feature of the later Old Series, and New Series, and which had been shown by an inner black and white banded border graduated at ten second intervals, which in turn

60 CCS Archive, file R.3382.

61 *General Survey of England and Wales. An entirely new & accurate Survey of the County of Kent ... Done by the Surveying Draftsmen of His Majesty's Honourable Board of Ordnance, on the basis of the Trigonometrical Survey ...* Published by W. Faden, January 1st.1801. This in turn copied eighteenth century precedents in border design.

was engraved within another black and white border which was graduated at intervals of one minute, against which the values in degrees and minutes were engraved. Certainly, the deletion of such a fundamental geographical reference system from a map was contrary to contemporary practice, unless, perhaps, the accuracy of the values was in question, but there is no evidence to suggest this.

While the 'piano key' border was never to reappear, the longitude and latitude values were reinstated on the Popular Edition sheets and were not thereafter left off the one-inch maps. They were incorporated into a border whose design was a compromise between the decorative influence of the past and the more practical demands of the twentieth century. A narrow, black and white border, graduated at one minute intervals, with values given at five minute intervals, was drawn just outside the neatline. The outer border comprised three black lines, the central one of which was thickened (fig.17). The space between the inner and outer frames contained the alpha-numeric designations of the two-inch squares, road directions and county names. This style had first been used on a one-inch map with *Killarney District* in 1913. All this information was apparently engraved on the copperplate,[62] although, theoretically, it should have been possible to produce a master border drawing for all the standard-sized sheets. Certainly, the style of the lettering and numbers is reminiscent of a drawn, rather than engraved design. On the other hand, the road directions and latitude and longitude figures are in typical engraved style.

It seems, however, that Jack considered even this improvement on the utilitarian appearance of the Third Edition to be too prosaic, for he himself designed a decorative border for the new Fifth Edition, 'having been swayed by the opinions of Hinks and others in favour of marginal ornament.'[63] It would appear, for the design has not survived, that it incorporated the 'piano-key' or 'dog's tooth' element which was the principal feature of the Old and New Series borders. Jack's border had not reached its final design when Winterbotham succeeded him as Director General in 1930 and scrapped it in favour of one similar in appearance to the Popular, but wider, and with 'enough space to give boldly the destination and transport numbers of the important roads.'[64]

MARGINALIA

Outside the map frame appeared an assemblage of marginalia some of which were unique to the sheet, and others which were common to the series. As a rule, it would seem that the information relating to the individual sheet (sheet name, number, county, adjacent sheet diagram) was engraved on the copperplate, while master images were made for the rest (series title, legend, scale, height and depth information, rights of way note, copyright note, imprint, price note) either on stone or copper - it is not easy to determine which. These were then transferred to stone or zinc before the printing plate was made. Additional illustrations of the variations in each of the marginal data are supplied with the catalogue in Part 2.

---

62 This is evident from RGS OS Specimen no. 58.

63 Winterbotham, (1934b), p.109.

64 PRO OS 1/181. Minute 1 from Winterbotham, 11/4/1931.

Series title and sheet name

The series title 'Ordnance Survey of England and Wales' and 'Popular Edition One-Inch Map' were printed in Upright Egyptian,[65] and appeared in the top margin on the left and right sides of the sheet respectively. This followed the precedent, established with the Third Edition, and which was continued on the Fifth Edition sheets.[66]

Both parts of the series title were evidently transferred from a master original either to the outline on stone, or, perhaps in some instances, straight to the printing plate, rather than to stone. A transfer to the printing plate might explain why, on some later reprints, the positioning of the information is slightly different to that of earlier printings, because on reprint, a new printing plate would have to have been made to incorporate the revisions made to the stone and it could not be guaranteed that marginal information transferred from a source other than the stone, would be in exactly the same position as before. Such small differences can be seen on the reprints of many sheets, such as 123 (*Winchester*, fig.17) and, for example, on the 1932 printing of sheet 65 (*Wisbech*), the statement 'Ordnance Survey of England and Wales' has been shifted to the right, and the 'Popular Edition one-inch map' has also been slightly repositioned in both examples.

When the compilation of the Popular Edition was begun in 1912, the one-inch map of Scotland was still on a separate projection, and no plans had yet been made for a new edition to be based on drawings, rather than engravings, nor had the decision yet been taken to bring the Scottish map onto the Cassini (based on the Delamere meridian), instead of Bonne, projection. Until this occurred (in 1921), there were, essentially, two one-inch surveys of Great Britain, and this was reflected in the titles of the series maps: *'Ordnance Survey of England and Wales'*[67] and *'Ordnance Survey of Scotland'*. However, three sheets of the English survey: 1, 3 and 5, straddled the border with Scotland. By the time they came to be published, in 1925 and 1926, the Scottish Popular Edition map was also appearing, and the cross-border cartographic union between Scotland and England, which had been achieved for the first time in the Ordnance Survey's history on the one-inch map, was marked by designating two of these three sheets (3 and 5) *'Ordnance Survey of Great Britain'*. Sheet 1 remained as the 'Ordnance Survey of England and Wales' even though half of it covered Scotland. Apart from sheet 8, no other sheets of the Popular Edition of either England and Wales or Scotland carried the Great Britain title; and even though it could have been applied to the Scottish maps, most of which were published after these three sheets, it was not to be used for the one-inch map until the Fifth Edition.[68]

---

65 The formal description of typefaces is taken from the pattern book *Ordnance Survey Alphabets*, published in 1934; an example is at BL Maps 7.b.13. In 1934, Ellis Martin, the Ordnance Survey's resident artist, was awarded £5 for designing alphabets for the one-inch map. PRO OS 1/536. f.66A.

66 For folded sheets of the New Popular (Sixth Edition) and Seventh Series sheets, the title, edition statement and sheet names appeared only on the cover of the map. These details were printed high up on the top margins of the flat sheets and were guillotined off so that the sheet would fit a convenient folded size.

67 Although it seems ill-judged, for example, to have labelled the 1925 tourist map of Snowdon simply as 'Ordnance Survey of England', but this followed the example of earlier one-inch series.

68 The first use of the title 'Ordnance Map of Great Britain' seems to have been at the head of an advertisement, dated October 1816, for the first five parts of the Old Series one-inch map. It is illustrated in Margary, (1975), vol.I, and in Owen and Pilbeam, (1992), p.21.

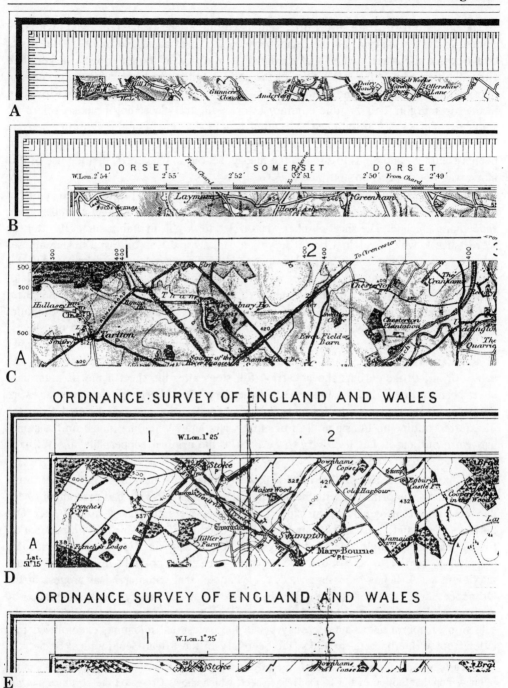

Fig.17 One-inch map borders: **A** Old Series sheet 80 SW (1842) with plain 'piano key' border. **B** New Series sheet 327 (1892) showing the combination of piano key design with latitude and longitude figures and marginal road directions. **C** Third Edition sheet 252 (1905) with plain alpha-numerical border. **D** Popular Edition sheet 123 (1919). **E** Popular Edition sheet 123 (1929) showing the repositioning on reprint of the title. *Private collection.*

The specific part of the series title, 'Popular Edition One-Inch Map', was invariably printed in the top margin, on the right, between the sheet name and number. But it sits oddly beside the other elements of the heading; the size of the lettering is larger than either the first part of the series title, or the sheet number statement, and it is printed on two lines instead of one, and neither of these is level with the other printed information in the top margin. This is quite contrary to preceding or succeeding practice where all elements of the titles are aligned. It is almost as if the title 'Popular Edition' were an afterthought, arrived at after the compilation material for many of the early sheets had been assembled, and tends to support the theory, set out in Chapter I, that the use of this name was not decided on until about 1918.

The most prominent heading was the sheet name, which was printed in the centre of the top margin in a larger size than the other title information, in Roman capitals, open, shaded and hatched. The sheet number was printed top right, in arabic numerals after the word 'sheet', which was in Upright Egyptian capitals and was followed in parentheses by the names of the counties, in stump hand, that appeared on the sheet. All this information was unique to the sheet and was therefore engraved on the copperplate; indeed, the very style of the lettering tends to suggest this, just as the style of the series title lettering might imply that it had been written on stone, or some other medium. Students of these maps will have noticed that in the later reprints of some of the sheets, the sheet name acquires a full stop. This feature is present on the 1919 pull from copper of the Cambridge sheet,[69] and on the 1919 outline sheet and the implication is that some, or all, of the earliest sheets carried full stops after the sheet name. It must then have been decided, before June 1919 (when the first sheets of the Popular were published), that it was an undesirable design characteristic, and was deleted from the transferred outline on the stone. Ten or more years later, when the image on the stones had worn out and it was necessary to go back to the original copperplate, the full stop reappeared and was not erased.

The policy on allocating the individual sheet names must have been governed, in the first place, by the principal settlements covered by the sheet. This had presumably been the most important consideration since sheet names were first used for the later Old Series sheets. But, particularly since the introduction of the Third Edition, 'market forces' had increasingly come into play and, for the Popular Edition, it had become essential to appeal to as wide a geographical market as possible in order to secure maximum sales. It has been suggested, for example, that commercial awareness at the Ordnance Survey in the first three decades of the twentieth century was accompanied by a growing diversity in the titles on a map cover, if not on the sheet itself.[70] But the selection of appropriate names clearly posed the occasional dilemma, exemplified in a letter from Winterbotham to Hinks, the Secretary of the Royal Geographical Society:[71]

> A curious point of nomenclature has recently arisen in connection with one of the sheets of the new Popular Edition of the 1" map. The sheet, which shows Crewe on the northern margin,

69 RGS OS Specimen no. 58.

70 Nicholson, (1994a), illustrates how sheet titles changed between cover and sheet. Messenger, (1988) shows that several Third Edition sheets changed their names during the course of publication.

71 RGS Archives (Winterbotham Correspondence). Winterbotham to Hinks, 27/4/1921.

includes the Pottery area around Stoke on Trent. We had thought of calling this sheet 'The Five Towns', but we are not quite certain whether this is really an accepted expression, or whether it is solely attributable to Mr Arnold Bennett . . . alternatively, the sheet might be called 'The Potteries' or more simply 'Stoke on Trent'.

First published between July and September 1921, sheet 52 was named after the most prominent settlement which appeared on it: *Stoke on Trent*. All other settlements were entirely subordinate to it in size and therefore the choice seems, with the exception of excursions into the literary world (not everyone would have heard of Arnold Bennett's novels whose titles featured the Five Towns), to have been in the end straightforward. But there were other sheets for which the same criteria were not applied. For example, sheet 109, entitled *Pontypridd & Barry*, covers the whole of Cardiff, the capital of Wales, but the title *Cardiff & Mouth of the Severn* is reserved for sheet 110, which includes far less of Cardiff's hinterland than sheet 109. The naming of sheet 109 is an instance where administrative superiority has been subordinated to wider geographical appeal.

The idea that it was the cover title which sold the map must have occurred early on in the history of the Popular Edition (if not already thought of for the coloured Revised New Series and the Third Edition), since sheet 112, published in 1919, was entitled *Marlborough* but, from the first, its cover proclaimed its geographical coverage to be 'Marlborough and Devizes'. This policy of being more descriptive in the cover title - often achieved by adding the words 'and District' to the sheet name - was widespread, and followed the practice established with the Third Edition, and, for that matter, of commercial publishers in the nineteenth century.[72] In this instance the expanded title was actually printed on the cover, but there are numerous examples where printed labels with different location names are stuck over the original title, sometimes by booksellers, in order to promote local sales.[73] In at least one example, a different name was printed directly onto the cover (sheet 135, *Hastings*, became 'Rye'). More rarely, the sheet name was itself more explicit than the cover title, as in the case of sheet 137, where *Dartmoor, Tavistock & Launceston* was abbreviated to 'Tavistock and Dartmoor' on the cover.[74] Occasionally the sheet name was changed on a later printing, thus *Truro* (sheet 143), published in 1919,[75] became *Truro & St. Austell* on the 1925 reprint.[76]

Imprint style

The publishing statement, or imprint, was always printed in the right corner of the bottom margin. It began life as a long account of the survey dates of its constituent large scale sheets, and subsequent one-inch publication and revision history, combined with the name of the current Director General, place and year of printing. This information was

---

72 Virtually all the sheet names of Bartholomew's New Series of half-inch maps carried the suffix 'and district' in the 1880s.

73 All noted examples are given in the catalogue. Nicholson, (1994a), illustrates some Popular Edition cover name changes.

74 One example has been recorded with the full title on the cover (1928, 3500/28).

75 But carrying a printing date of 1918.

76 A copy of this sheet with a 'Perranporth' name sticker on the cover has been recorded in a private collection.

printed from a template, in which the standard components: the words without the dates, were written with sufficient space being left for the insertion of the dates, which were filled in according to the information relevant to the individual sheet. The fact that the same template was used from sheet to sheet can be seen in the early version, where the lettering of the bottom line: 'Printed at the Ordnance Survey Office, Southampton' slopes downwards in an untidy fashion not normally associated with the usually high standards of Ordnance Survey engraving.

By the end of the Popular Edition, the whole statement had been simplified, and omitted not only the historical information, but also the name of the Director General together with his titles and honours. Charles Close, for example, who had been appointed CMG in 1899, received his CB on 3 June 1916, and on 7 June, the order 'for the necessary addition to the imprint on Ordnance Survey plates' was given.[77] Two years later, in 1918, another honour, the KBE, changed the imprint to 'Colonel Sir Charles Close, K.B.E., C.B., C.M.G.' Finally, in 1919, he was elected a Fellow of the Royal Society, and the imprint was changed yet again (from 17 May 1919) to read 'K.B.E., C.B., F.R.S.'[78] This form appears on most sheets which were published in June of that year. Only three of the nine main styles of the imprint (these are described in Part 2) refer to the period before 1930. In August of that year, Winterbotham asked

> Is anyone interested today in the name of the Director General? In the days when an edition was perhaps 50 and maps were few there might have been supposed a personal interest in each sheet. Today it seems to me unnecessary and in doubtful taste.[79]

A month later, on 2 September 1930, the directive was given that 'The Director General of the Ordnance Survey' was to be quoted as the authority for all future maps, and that his personal name would no longer be used.[80] This instruction resulted in altered imprints for all new editions and reprints of Ordnance Survey one-inch maps, but was not immediately followed for reprints of the half-inch map.

Print codes

The earliest states of the Popular Edition carried reprint information in the same form as that for the Third Edition; that is, the month and last two digits of the year of reprint were given in figures in the bottom left corner, either below the border, or beneath the legend. This followed the practice for the large scale-plans which had been established in the nineteenth century, although by the 1920s this routine was being questioned for straight, unrevised reprints for which it was considered that there was no need to alter any marginal printing information.[81]

77 Circulars, C/C 2726/16.

78 Circulars, C/C 6835/19, dated 17/5/1919.

79 PRO OS 1/53. Minute by Winterbotham, 1/8/1930.

80 The Director General's personal name had been used for the imprint of Ordnance Survey maps since 1805, when William Mudge followed the precedent set by the Hydrographer, Captain Hurd, who used his own name instead of that of the Admiralty as authority for the publication of the Admiralty charts, a tradition that continues to this day. PRO WO 44/299 (23/10/1816).

81 PRO OS 1/206. MacLeod (OP) to EO, 17/10/27.

For record-keeping purposes, however, it soon appeared that for both large and small scale maps, the footnotes showing the number printed and the year for each sheet were useful, but only as long as the procedure was consistently followed.[82] Cases were soon noted where copies of large-scale sheets were being received into store with an old print number to which the current print run and year had not been added.[83] Examples of similar inconsistencies are common on the Popular Edition maps; but the print code note seems to have been regarded as a primary record of any sheet's individual publication history: in many instances, the early month and year code is replaced in later printings with retrospective notes on the number printed in the previous years. This information had presumably been taken from the Intermediate Revision Sheet and was given a more permanent place on the published map - we do not know, for example, whether all the Intermediate Sheets were preserved, or whether they were destroyed on being replaced by the next issue. Other examples can be found where previous print notes had been deleted, only to be restored two, or even three, printings later.

From about 1922, the policy of providing only the month and year figures changed, and the month figures were replaced by the number of maps reprinted, thus '2000/23' indicated that 2000 copies were printed in 1923.[84] These figures, combined, from 1922 onwards, with dates for general corrections and alterations to roads and railways, were all originally supplied for the purposes of Ordnance Survey internal record-keeping.[85] But they also gave very specific revision information to the customer, and this policy of including the dates of revision data on the reprint was to cause great difficulties in stock control for firms such as Stanford,[86] who kept large numbers of any given sheet. Since these were not supplied on a sale or return basis, stock was not replaced until it became exhausted, and it sometimes happened that superseded copies of any one sheet were sold as current, when the up-to-date version was available elsewhere. If the revision dates were either omitted, or coded, Stanford suggested, instead of being proclaimed overtly, it would not be possible for the purchaser to discern the difference, in most cases, between the out-of-date map and the current copy. The Ordnance Survey was, in fact, much more open about dating map information than any private map producing firm. Stanford's complaint provoked an immediate reaction by the Survey. Hotine was keen to 'wash out the mass of dates'[87] that appeared on the small-scale maps, on the grounds that there was nothing misleading nor dishonest in such a practice because most of the corrections between one reprint and the next were of very minor significance. But Stanford had a more sophisticated idea which was based on his own methods of dating his London Atlas series of maps. These used a group of four to six digits to express the day, month and year of reprint. His suggestion was that

> Ordnance Survey 1" maps should bear on the corner close up to the bottom line in very small type the following say M33 R34 T31 which being interpreted means, Minor

82 PRO OS 1/260. Minutes 5-7, May 1928.

83 PRO OS 1/206. Minute 6.

84 This practice had been followed for some Revised New Series sheets.

85 PRO OS 1/206. Minute 33, 4/10/1934.

86 PRO OS 1/206. Letter from Edward Stanford to Hotine, 1/8/1934.

87 PRO OS 1/206. Hotine to Stanford, 4/8/1934.

Corrections 1933, Roads 1934, Trains (i.e. Railways) 1931.[88]

This recommendation was well-timed, for the Ordnance Survey was proposing to increase the frequency of reprints of the one-inch maps, and the problems inherent in Stanford's criticism would clearly be exacerbated. In order to avoid the expense of operating a sale or return policy with the agents, Hotine proposed a threefold solution. First, the imprint would be changed to: 'Published by the Director General, Ordnance Survey. First published in 19-- and subject to frequent minor correction on reprint.' Secondly, the following imprint (for example) would be added in small type on the bottom left hand corner: 2000/34M34R33; meaning that 2000 copies were printed in 1934 with minor corrections to 1934 and road revision to 1933. Railways were to be included in minor corrections. Thirdly, no other dates were to appear on the map; Hotine intended that this practice should apply to all the small-scale maps.[89]

Even this procedure was thought by some to be too overt, and in November 1934, Winterbotham approved of the modification to the Publisher imprint, so that it should read: 'First published by the Director General, Ordnance Survey Office, Southampton 19-- with periodical corrected reprints.' A further alteration was made to the print code so that it was contracted to, say, 2034, meaning that 2000 copies were printed in 1934,[90] similarly, '835' would indicate 800 copies printed in 1935. From this documentary evidence, therefore, we may conclude that sheets which carried the bald reference '2034', were printed in November or December of that year (sheet 140, for example). But thereafter, Ordnance Survey practice became markedly inconsistent, with all three systems, that is, the original full references, Stanford's suggested abbreviations, and Winterbotham's approved method, operating simultaneously. This was not all: examples can be found where various elements of old and new systems were combined, probably as a result of failure to duff out the superseded data from the negative.

This multiplicity of imprint and correction date systems must have caused much confusion in the records, and, at best, must equally have confused the customer, although there is no direct evidence to show that he was successfully fooled by these cryptic indications. Retrospectively, however, they are of primary significance in reconstructing the publication history of the sheets for even if the successive Intermediate Revision Sheets were kept at that time for every one-inch map, they do not survive today. The published map is therefore the only record of its printing history, and, even then, the fullest record is provided only by a listing of the published states because it was not uncommon for many of the earlier sheets to be reprinted as many as ten times during their lifetime, and new print codes were added to old ones so that the sequence of printing history was apparent on any one state, thus:

5000/23.1000/26.3000/27.6000/29.6500/31.8000/32.1000/35.

This code appears on a 1935 printing of sheet 124. Not only does it demonstrate the failure to implement the new code, established in 1934, which should simply have read:

88 PRO OS 1/206. Stanford to Hotine, 9/8/1934.
89 PRO OS 1/206. Minute 33, 4/10/1934.
90 PRO OS 1/206. Minute 35.

1035, it also illustrates a common problem which faces the potential user of this record: is it complete? In this case, an earlier state of sheet 124 carries the print code 3000/26. It makes no mention of the previous print run of 5000/23, and the code is different to that of 1000/26 which is cited on later states. Is this to be regarded as an error of transcription, or were there really two printings in 1926? We shall never know for certain unless a state carrying the terminal print code of 1000/26 is found.

Another important point to bear in mind is that the print code alone may not always be sufficient to identify a printing state. Sheet 144, for example, has four states, each of which carries the print code '5000/27', but each one is different. It will be noticed that the print codes of some of the later issues, particularly of the wartime outline sheets, carry the letters 'LR', or 'Ch', or perhaps 'Cr' after the date. These stand for the places where printing was carried out: Ordnance Survey Office London Road, Ordnance Survey Office Crabwood, and Ordnance Survey Office Chessington.[91]

There is no doubt that some of the print codes that appear on the outline sheets refer to the printings of the coloured sheets - the result of leaving the old print code on the outline stone and not changing it - but how far this is a universal truth is difficult to say. It is probable that the print runs for the outline sheets were smaller than for the coloured version, and so, for example, the print code of 300/34 that appears on the outline of sheet 98 is likely to refer to that state, rather than a coloured counterpart.

Magnetic variation

The information given in the magnetic variation diagram was usually printed where it intruded least on the content of the map - often in the right margin, where it might break the border detail, or, more conveniently, in the sea area of coastal sheets. The inclusion of this device on one-inch series maps was only of about twenty-five years standing by the time that the Popular Edition was first published. In his evidence to the Baker Committee in 1892, Col. Alleyne recommended the inclusion of the 'variations of the company for the year'[92] in the margin of the map. That 'company' is an obvious mistranscription for 'compass' is confirmed by the summary table at the end of the report. Since most quick military surveys were made using a compass, and military manoeuvring entailed using map and compass, the lack of information on magnetic variation from any standard military map of the country would have been an unusual omission, and it is surprising that its incorporation was recommended by only one officer.

The diagram showing the difference of magnetic north from true north, which gave the variation for a stated year together with a value for expected annual decrease for the next few years,[93] first appeared on the coloured map of the Revised New Series. Before 1897, a source for data on magnetic variation may have been the Admiralty, on whose charts it appeared as standard information. The military requirement for its inclusion on

---

91 Clark and Mumford, (1982), also: R. Oliver, 'The '1941' style of coded imprint' *Sheetlines* 9:18-19.

92 Baker, (1892), p.38.

93 It was usual for the year only to be given, but there are many examples where January [followed by the year], or 1st January [followed by the year], are also cited. Sheet 142 gives, unusually, the month of September in the 1932 reprint.

the one-inch map was well-timed, for in the years 1885-95, Sir Arthur Rücker and Sir Edward Thorpe had carried out a magnetic survey of the British Isles under the auspices of the Royal Society. The Ordnance Survey had, in fact, assisted in this work by supplying the maps which were needed for the field surveys.

It was known within the Ordnance Survey that the method (used until at least 1915) of arriving at the magnetic declination at any particular spot by taking Rücker and Thorpe's magnetic survey, and applying the amount of the annual decrease as if it were a constant, instead of allowing for secular variation, was not 'strictly correct', even though the error so produced was relatively minor.[94] A far more serious source of error was uncovered in 1907, and revealed genuine confusion about how the values of magnetic variation were to be determined for the one-inch sheets. It was brought to light by an enquiry from a member of the public regarding the accuracy of the magnetic variation given for sheet 128 (Third Edition Small Sheet Series).[95] The value of 18°40' which had been given on the map should have read 16°36'; the incorrect figure was actually the angle that the magnetic meridian formed with the sheet line of the map on its east margin rather than with the true meridian.

It appeared that the officer in charge of the Trigonometrical Section (Capt. W.J. Johnston) had made the mistake of supplying the magnetic variation to the sheet line instead of giving the correct magnetic declination. The source of the misunderstanding was traced to a memorandum from the Director General in 1897,[96] in which he asked how far the east and west lines of each sheet differed from the true north. Having placed the blame for the mistake squarely on Johnston's shoulders, Hellard instructed that in the future (from the end of March 1907), on each new sheet published or reprinted, the correct magnetic declination, 'so far as our present information goes should be given in place of the incorrect values now on the maps.' This meant that erroneous values would have persisted for some years on those sheets which did not come up for reprint for some time, and that the figures on the Third Edition sheets, for example, cannot be regarded necessarily as having been given with any degree of accuracy.

By the time that the Popular Edition came to be devised in 1912, so much time had elapsed since the Rücker and Thorpe survey that the accuracy of the magnetic values for the small-scale maps was increasingly questionable. It was with some alacrity, then, that Close responded to a request from the Royal Society to provide maps for a proposed new magnetic survey, this time to be carried out by George Walker. In his reply, agreeing to supply the required sheets, Close made clear that as far as the Ordnance Survey was concerned, there was one matter of 'special interest, viz. the values of the declination and of the annual change.' He pointed out that the information was needed 'for printing on the small scale maps.'[97] Walker's survey, which included most of the 200 stations observed by Rücker and Thorpe, was finished in 1915, but the results were not immediately published. Meanwhile, more enquiries were being fielded from the public

---

94 PRO OS 1/8. Note from Hellard to EO, 1907.
95 PRO OS 1/8. Letter from Hellard to Edmund Raynes, 20/3/1907.
96 Circulars, C/C 2425/97, dated 31 May 1897; quoted in PRO OS 1/8, but apparently no longer existing.
97 PRO OS 1/8. Letter to Archibald Geikie, President, Royal Society, 28/8/1913.

so that Close wrote in some exasperation to Walker for advice on how to provide information as to the best value of magnetic declination in the United Kingdom. 'Before your survey,' he commented, 'we should have looked up Rücker and Thorpe and approximated to a present value. Now we naturally want to use your results, but they are not yet available.'[98]

Close made a persistent case for early publication of the results, repeating his earlier remarks that it was 'especially desirable that the revised series of small scale maps now being printed should give reliable values for the declination.'[99] The new maps to which Close referred were undoubtedly the first sheets of the Popular Edition, which were being printed in 1918. A further cause of his urgent demands was the 'large issue of Ordnance maps to troops under training in the United Kingdom', which made it an additional reason for 'making use of the most recent values.' Within a few months of this letter, a whole volume of the *Philosophical Transactions* was devoted to Walker's paper, 'The magnetic resurvey of the British Isles for the Epoch January 1, 1915', which gave tables of values, and for which the Ordnance Survey prepared the magnetic charts. Walker's work had long-term consequences for the provision of up-to-date magnetic data, for in his paper he suggested that future surveys should be made the responsibility of the Ordnance Survey. Arguing that this procedure for ensuring periodical revision of the magnetic survey 'would be of real advantage to the state',[100] Close won, in April 1919, the approval of the Board of Agriculture and Fisheries for the revisions to be carried out by the Ordnance Survey under the advice of a Committee of the Royal Society.[101] The next magnetic resurvey began in 1925 and was completed in 1932, and was carried out by the Ordnance Survey's Research Officer, Harold Jolly, and the results were first published in 1927;[102] the data of the completed resurvey were shown on the amended Magnetic Edition (1933) of the Physical Map of England and Wales, and of Scotland, at the scale of one to a million (1:1,000,000).[103]

The first known printed instruction on providing magnetic variation data on the one-inch maps was given in an undated amendment to the 1914 *Instructions* for the future Popular Edition, stating that the magnetic variation was to be corrected if twelve months had elapsed since the last reprint.[104] A more detailed direction was printed in 1924:

> Magnetic variation will be shown on each Popular Edition sheet. The central geographical co-ordinates, to the nearest minute, will be supplied to R.O. who will then furnish the magnetic variation.[105]

98 PRO OS 1/8. Close to Walker, 20/5/1918.

99 PRO OS 1/8. Close to the Assistant Secretary, Royal Society, 22/5/1918.

100 PRO OS 1/8. Close to Walker, 5/11/1918.

101 PRO OS 1/8. Close to the Royal Society, 11/4/1919.

102 *Results of the magnetic observations made by the Ordnance Survey in the Channel Islands ...* , (1927). Further results were published in 1930: *Results of the magnetic observations ...* In addition, the progress of the magnetic survey was written up in the OS *Annual Reports*.

103 The two editions of the Physical Map (1928 and 1933), showing magnetic values, are described in Hellyer, (1992a).

104 Ordnance Survey *Instructions for the revision of the small scale maps ...*, (Jan.1914), p.7, para.29.

105 Ordnance Survey *Instructions to field revisers and draftsmen ...*, (1924), p.8, para.25.

Although these 1924 instructions were doubtless intended more for the Popular Edition of Scotland, this is by no means made clear, and, since so many instructions reflected already established practice, it may be reasonable to assume that this procedure had been in force for the Popular Edition sheets since they began to be printed in 1918. If this were the case, the information would have been provided by the Trigonometrical Division before the appointment of the Research Officer in 1919. We can also assume that, whatever the position on the map of the magnetic variation diagram, its value referred to the centre point of the sheet although this was never stated on the map. Unlike some Third Edition Large Sheets, there were no examples of two different values being printed on the same sheet,[106] although there are instances where values which are written on reprints are earlier than the figures of the previous printing - clearly a drafting error.[107] It has been observed that the values for magnetic variation were changed with every corrected pre-war reprint of the Third Edition Large Sheets.[108] This policy was certainly not followed consistently for the Popular Edition, in spite of the 1914 instructions; often a decade or more, during which time a sheet may have been reprinted two or three times, elapsed before any correction was made to the magnetic variation values.

Legend

When the first sheets of the Popular Edition came to be published in 1919, the inclusion of panels of conventional signs in the bottom margin of the sheets was established practice from the later New Series (1886 and after), and the main additional use of the separate 'characteristics' sheet (Appendix 5) was to explain how the different styles of lettering indicated the size and relative importance of a place. The physical appearance of the legend panel (which was originally known as the 'Tablet of Characteristics') on the Popular Edition sheets was, on the face of it, straightforward. Divided into three sections, it was always printed in the left corner of the bottom margin; it was not engraved on the copperplate, but was prepared from a separate master, either on copper or stone, or zinc, and probably transferred to the outline printing plate. No fewer than twenty-one versions of the first section, twenty-four of the second, and twenty-seven of the third have been identified. Many of the changes were trivial, but the large number of minor differences implies that there was no overall consistent standard of presentation laid down and that the final form may have been in the hands of the draftsman. A similar state of affairs existed for the less complex panels of the Third Edition.[109]

These panels presumably reflected a national specification, and can therefore be taken as an indicator of a constantly mutating map, and there are, therefore, many examples where conventional signs and map are out of step. For example, the symbol for contours might include a reinforced, or strengthened line but this convention would not be

---

106 Messenger, (1988), p.14, records instances in the Large Sheet Series where some sheets carry two diagrams in different positions on the sheet with different values, and this would seem to indicate an intention to provide accurate information.

107 Sheets 118 and 123, for example.

108 Messenger, (1988), p.14.

109 Messenger, (1988), pp.15-17.

followed necessarily on the sheet to which it referred. Since the legend, like the series title, scale, and magnetic information, was prepared separately from the copperplate, it is easy to see how inappropriate variations came to be added to the sheets. Further comparisons can be made with the publication of these panels of symbols in the different editions of the Ordnance Survey *A description of Ordnance Survey small scale maps.*[110] Attention is actually drawn to these changes in the 1937 edition of the *Description* on page 7 where, in a note on the symbols contained in Plate I, it is stated that slight modifications have been made to a few of the conventional signs on the Fifth Edition sheets issued since Sept.1935 and on Popular Edition sheets reprinted since Oct.1934: 'Users of these maps should therefore always refer to the symbols shown on the margin of each sheet'. Further examples can be found in school texts,[111] some showing minor differences which did not appear on the official conventional signs sheet. Where sheets were reprinted more than once in a year, it is sometimes possible to determine the order of reprinting by changes to the legend, such as the addition of the symbol for electricity transmission lines. Similarly, if a print code has been cropped from below the legend (this applies particularly to the very early reprints) a change in the legend may be the only way of identifying the state. A good example of this is seen in the two 1921 printings of sheet 121, where the symbol for heath and moor is present on the first, and absent from the second.

Scale statement

Unlike the magnetic variation diagram, whose design remained unchanged for the Popular Edition, the scale statement, which appears in the centre of the bottom margin of each sheet, was altered both in design and in terms of the information given. This information was usually presented in three forms on each sheet: written statement; representative fraction; and bar scale. These details had been shown consistently in this way for nearly fifty years, since their first systematic inclusion on the one-inch map with the appearance of the New Series (Old Series sheets sometimes showed all three elements of the scale data, but the practice was inconsistent). It had not even altered in style of presentation throughout this whole period.

Now, it was to make at least six variations on the threefold formula during the lifetime of the Popular Edition. Some of these differences were of a very minor nature: an alteration in the position of figures, or the exclusion, in one case, of the written statement and representative fraction. But the major change in the given information appeared at an early stage in the publication of the Popular, and this was the inclusion, for the first time, of a bar scale giving distances in kilometres. This development can be pinpointed to September 1920, when Close, who had studied the Report of the Metric Committee, which had been appointed by the Conjoint Board of Scientific Societies, proposed the

---

110 A post-war *A Description of Ordnance Survey small scale maps* was published in 1947, but included, not unnaturally, no reference to the Popular Edition.

111 Cox, (1924). Lockey, (1942); this includes the symbols for parish boundaries and youth hostels. A second edition of an earlier publication, Bygott, (1938), included only the conventional signs for the Fifth Edition.

following changes to the way in which the scale was shown on the small-scale maps:[112] first, the mile scales to be expressed in miles and tenths, and not in miles and furlongs; secondly, on every new edition of a small-scale map a scale of kilometres and tenths to be printed in addition to the scale of miles. Close intimated that Ministry approval would have to be sought for these changes, and it would seem that this was not fully forthcoming, since the first suggestion was never implemented on any of the small-scale maps, and the Popular continued to show furlongs. In fact, it seems that it was the War Office that was against the proposal to divide the mile scale into tenths, but they were content to allow a kilometre scale on the small-scale maps.[113] Again, the scale information, common to all sheets, was not engraved on the copperplates and it seems that each element may have been drawn, or engraved, as a separate piece because the positioning of each can vary between reprints.

Rights of way statement

The rights of way statement was usually placed in the bottom right hand corner of the map. Ever since the Board of Ordnance had first begun mapping footpaths in the 1780s,[114] their portrayal on printed maps, which were available to the public, must have posed a direct invitation to the would-be explorer of byways. Tucked in the bottom right corner of the sheet, the note 'N.B. The representation on this map of a Road, Track or Footpath, is no evidence of the existence of a right of way.' was first given in this form on the New Series one-inch map from 1889. During the course of the proceedings of the Olivier Committee in 1914, Close stated that the note was put on the maps by 'Government order' to protect Ordnance Survey from any controversy arising out of misinterpretation of the map. This order has not been traced. The note was modified for some sheets of the Revised New Series and Third Edition to exclude 'Track' and 'Footpath'. These terms were reinstated for the Popular Edition, and were retained until the demise of the one-inch map in 1976.

Copyright statement

The copyright statement remained unchanged throughout the life of the Popular Edition, and was invariably printed in the centre of the bottom margin of the sheet. The previous one-inch series had carried the phrase 'All rights of reproduction reserved'. But on 28 June 1912, the Treasury issued a Minute on Crown copyright;[115] this prompted a letter from HMSO to the Ordnance Survey, dated 27 September 1912, instructing that from then on the imprint on Ordnance Survey sheets should read 'Crown Copyright Reserved.'[116] Some of the sheets of the Third Edition Large Sheet Series which were reprinted after this date also carried this revised note.

---

112   RGS Archives (Close Correspondence). Letter from Close to Hinks, 23/9/1920. Close also suggested that contoured issues of the 1:1,000,000 map should have the contours and heights in metres; and that on the six-inch maps the scale of perches and the furlong mark should be omitted.

113   RGS Archives (Close Correspondence). Close to Hinks, 15/11/1920.

114   Hodson, (1991c).

115   Quoted in a copy of Circulars, Copy 6201. 14877/12 A.1931/1912, (27/9/1912). OSL G3964. The original Minute has not been traced.

116   *Ibid.*

Other marginal detail

Every sheet carried a single scale bar along the west and east sides of the map, giving a distance of four miles, with an additional mile divided into furlongs. While this was a standard element, the positions in the margins of other information sometimes changed between states. This was the result of new transfers being laid down in a different place when the sheet came to be reprinted. In practice, the position of the features from sheet to sheet was reasonably standardised, giving a superficial appearance of uniformity of design to the marginalia. No printing has so far been distinguished from another solely on the basis of the difference in position of these marginal data, but such a possibility should not be ruled out. Descriptions of the variations in the format of the corrections and road revisions notes, and other marginal information such as adjoining sheet diagram, price notes, and height and depth data are given in Part 2.

The marginal information supplied on the Popular Edition sheets was undoubtedly fuller, and better designed than that of its predecessors. However, although there was a superficial appearance of standardisation, the number of modifications to which many of the elements were subjected has produced a complex picture of the evolution of map design for the Popular Edition, which is further compounded by the inconsistent application of new rules and revised ideas. The combination of engraved and drawn features meant that the marginal design of the Popular Edition of England and Wales never equalled the elegant simplicity of its drawn Scottish counterpart.

Important though the presentation of marginal data is, the layout of the sheets of a series map is one the most critical aspects of its design, for on it depends not only successful marketing, but also the amount of work needed to maintain the series; for example, more overlaps generate increased revision work. Because the sheet lines of the Popular Edition were tied to the engraved plates of the small sheets of the Third Edition, it was difficult to achieve any real flexibility of layout, and although the number of overlaps was less than for the large sheets of the Third Edition, the corresponding number of special sheets which were needed to compensate for awkward sheet lines had more than doubled. The two-inch squaring which was printed across the face of the Popular Edition was a more easily used reference system than that of its predecessors, where the squaring was indicated only in the margin. Since this squaring could be assigned Cassini values, it also had the merit of forming an embryonic national grid, and although the inaccuracy of its positioning on the map renders it useless for precise purposes, the public had become accustomed to the idea of a reference system superimposed on the map, and the size of squaring on the Popular was to be the determining factor in selecting the 5000 yard grid for the Fifth Edition. While the use of the Delamere meridian, the Cassini projection, and sheet size were carried forward from the Third Edition, the Popular was to make an important break with past tradition in one important respect, and that was the way in which relief was portrayed.

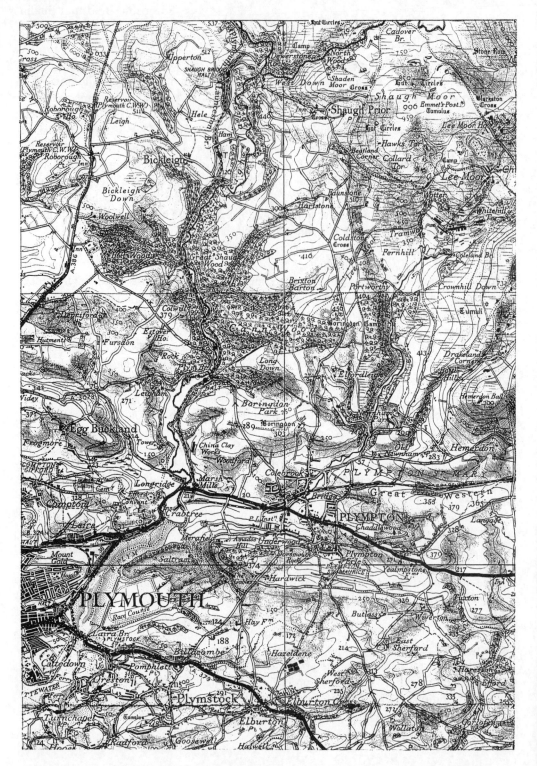

Fig.18 Part of Fifth (Relief) Edition sheet 144 *Plymouth* (1931). This was the first sheet of the Relief Edition to be published. *Private collection.*

Chapter V

THE NATURAL LANDSCAPE: RELIEF

'A contour is a thing perfectly unintelligible to the lay mind.' *Julian C. Rogers*, (1896).[1]

By 1932 it was conceded that to the 'educated eye' hill features came 'naturally and clearly' from the 50ft contours in all but flattish country.[2] It had taken thirty-five years to educate the 'lay mind' and it had been achieved through the Popular Edition, which had introduced a two-fold innovation in relief depiction to the one-inch map of England and Wales. First, the contour interval was decreased from 100ft to 50ft, and secondly, the contours themselves were thickened at 250ft intervals. Overall, the map showed relief by a combination of only two elements: contours, and spot heights.[3] This simplicity was the key to the real popularity of the map with the general public. The marked contrast with its predecessor and successor is typified by the first adverse criticism to be received by Winterbotham about his new Fifth (Relief) Edition. It came from E.B. Shine, Secretary at the Ministry of Agriculture and Fisheries, who, having seen a proof copy of the first sheet, was unimpressed:

> Speaking as one merely interested in maps and in the use of them for walking and motoring as far as possible away from main roads, I am inclined to think that the hachuring makes it more difficult to pick out the indifferent and minor roads and also the footpaths. Your new map is certainly a most artistic and attractive production, and those who like the old Third Edition will presumably find the new shading very pleasing, but to be candid I prefer the less detailed map of the Popular Edition, which is very clear and simple to read.[4]

In effect, this comment was a serious censure of a design for which Winterbotham had claimed the major share of responsibility. The map stood condemned before it was launched in the market place, and he would have done well to have heeded Shine's words for they were representative of the 'ordinary' map purchaser. Winterbotham reacted quickly; clearly taken aback by Shine's lack of enthusiasm, he embarked upon a course of limited consultation which was intended 'not to awaken a critical spirit which may never even arise if I do not definitely call for it.'[5] A period of five years followed in which the final debate on the merits of combining layers, hachures, shading and contours, versus contours and spot heights on the standard one-inch map took place. This

---

1   Hayes Fisher, (1896b), para.816. Mr Rogers was Secretary of the Surveyors' Institution.
2   Winterbotham, (1932a).
3   For the early use of spot heights, see Horner, (1974).
4   PRO OS 1/48. Shine to Winterbotham 19/5/1931.
5   PRO OS 1/48. Winterbotham to F. Debenham, Cambridge, 21/5/1931.

controversy was important because it endorsed, albeit retrospectively, the style of the Popular Edition. As far as hachures on the regular one-inch series were concerned, the nineteenth century ground to a halt only in 1936 with the demise of the Fifth (Relief) Edition.

This search for the most realistic method of representing three dimensions on a two dimensional surface has always provided a great forum for discussion which focuses on the interplay between science and art in cartography, and is often informed by personal opinion. The international literature on relief depiction on maps is vast; the methods vary between country and cartographer, and few ideas are new today. It is merely advanced printing technology and computer graphics which allow the concepts of yesterday to be expressed more realistically on paper than would have been thought possible two hundred years ago. For example, the much cited paper on a 'new method of depicting relief on maps', written in 1932 by Kitiro Tanaka,[6] described an effect which was virtually the same as that achieved by the Ordnance Survey, nearly one hundred years earlier, using the anaglyptograph method, to which many of the digital terrain analysis models of today (although based on more accurate data) bear a striking resemblance.[7] Contemporary ideas and practices of relief representation were, then, familiar territory to Ordnance Survey officers. Like Close before him, Winterbotham was fully aware of the maps and methods of other countries and was equally sure that the techniques appropriate to mountainous areas were not necessarily successful for lower terrain. Both men regarded the depiction of the British physical landscape as a cartographic challenge, which was described eloquently by Winterbotham in a letter to a Swiss cartographer:

> remember that in England we have no Alps, and that perpetual rain and long established agriculture have so smoothed and rounded our small features as to present a variety which is quite unlike anything else I have seen anywhere in the world. To show this homely minor scenery on a map is very difficult.[8]

The sort of country Winterbotham had in mind was, doubtless, the area covered by the Aldershot North sheet; and when the proof of this map, in the Fifth (Relief) style, arrived on his desk in May 1932, he was 'cock-a-hoop' about the results he had achieved in 'that absurdly difficult country'.[9] He maintained that the style was 'singularly expressive' and that the shading 'had broken up, and yet assimilated what was on the Popular Edition a horrible mass of rather unpleasant green.' Yet only eleven days later Winterbotham himself had doubts about the style. Having recognised that the map was 'not a clean one', he made considerable alterations, printing the black plate on top of the physical plates, rather than under them, in an attempt to remove the woolliness of the first impression.[10]

6 Tanaka, (1932).

7 An anaglyptograph was an engraving instrument for copying medallions in lines upon flat surfaces, giving the effect of relief by making the lines furthest apart where light struck the original most strongly. It was first used by the Ordnance Survey in about 1836 when Robert Dawson prepared a small map of North Wales (RGS OS Specimen no. 30), from a topographical model, using this process. Jackson, (1859).

8 PRO OS 1/48. Winterbotham to M. le General Bellot, 21/5/1931.

9 RGS Archives (Winterbotham Correspondence). Winterbotham to Hinks, 31/5/1932.

10 RGS Archives (Winterbotham Correspondence). Winterbotham to Hinks, 11/6/1932.

Winterbotham's obstinate refusal to accept that the simplicity of the Popular Edition was adequate for showing relief on the one-inch map (the Aldershot map was replaced, for military purposes, in 1934 by a plain contoured sheet covering the Aldershot Command), led to his perverse decision to press on with his relief map regardless of his own reservations, and of contrary opinion. He was, in a sense therefore, continuing Close's crusade to produce a map which was a work of art. He was able to do so because advanced printing methods enabled him to produce a similar effect to the Killarney style cheaply, with almost half the number of passes through the press. He did so because he shared the opinion, held by many high ranking Ordnance Survey personnel before him, that

> that curious person, the average man ... understands the idea of contouring, but is quite unable to visualise ground forms from it, especially in undulating or flat country.[11]

This was a typically military comment; the emphasis on acquiring an eye for the lie of the land was always stressed in eighteenth and nineteenth-century military survey manuals,[12] and is no less true today, for no successful manoeuvring is possible without this skill. But to what extent was this a priority with the public? Ironically for Winterbotham, both they and the army (which needed maps that could be clearly read in the gloomy interior of a tank) agreed that the hachures and shading of his one-inch map series obscured other important detail, and it was not continued after 1936. It had already been replaced by a plain contoured map that repeated the successful formula of the Popular Edition. This was devised by Close, who, in 1919, had no option but to fall back on the two bare essentials of relief representation: contours and spot heights. The source data for these features in turn comprised two groups of information: levelling, and contouring and hill sketching. Some of these data were over fifty years old by the time they were incorporated into the Popular map, and had already been used for its one-inch predecessors.

Levelling

The altitudes shown on the Popular Edition, whether by contour or spot height, were derived from a zero point which was determined as about 0.65 feet below mean sea level. This datum was calculated by taking a series of observations of the self-registering tide gauge at Liverpool[13] over one week in 1844; this was then followed by a series of observations of the mean level of the sea at several points around the coast of England. The connection of the levelling network to this datum was, as Close remarked, 'of an inexact character'.[14] The first primary levelling was carried out between 1841 and 1860; all bench marks[15] were shown on the 1:2500 plans, a majority were included on the six-inch map, and many surface altitudes, given to the nearest foot, were shown on both.

---

11 PRO OS 1/48. Winterbotham to Debenham, 21/5/1931.

12 Jones, (1974).

13 Further information and discussion on tidal observations at the beginning of the twentieth century appears in Doodson, (1924).

14 This quote, and a brief history of the Ordnance Survey levelling, are given in Close, (1922). A useful review of Close's report appeared in *The Geographical Journal*, (1923), LXI, 2:131.

15 A description of bench marks and their history is given in Owen and Pilbeam, (1992), pp.42-3.

Secondary lines of levels, based on the initial levelling were also run and the altitudes from these were entered on the manuscript plans.[16]

The first revision of the levelling network was begun simultaneously with the revision of the large-scale plans in 1894, and when the second revision of the plans began in 1904, a further revision of the levels was also started. By this time, the difficulties inherent in the old system were so great that a completely new programme became essential. The second geodetic levelling therefore began in 1912, and was completed in 1921.[17] Owing to postwar financial stringency, however, the fundamental bench marks which had been constructed in anticipation of the geodetic relevelling in Wales were connected only to a network of secondary order levelling.[18] The relevelling of London, for which there was no fundamental bench mark, took place in 1931.[19] Based on a different datum of Mean Sea Level at Newlyn[20] in Cornwall, which was derived from observations taken over seven years, the results of this revised operation do not appear to have been incorporated into the Popular Edition, not least, perhaps, because it would have taken some time for them to have appeared on the six-inch map from which the small-scale height data were derived.

Furthermore, the inclusion of the new data on the large-scale plans was, initially, the subject of some confusion because of carelessness by draftsmen in the Publication Division which resulted in the wrong footnotes being pinned up by the photographer, so that the user was faced with a plan which purported to give the height information according to both systems.[21] Even when this had been corrected (the evidence is given only for one specific sheet,[22] but several others could have been passed, undetected), it was clear that the Ordnance Survey had given no thought to the problems faced by users of adjacent sheets which carried bench marks referring to different data. After complaints by engineers,[23] the Survey eventually decided to insert a note on every new plan giving the approximate difference between the two data,[24] and referred to the new system as the 'Newlyn Datum'.[25]

This term was not used for the small-scale maps. The Popular Edition referred to 'Ordnance Survey Datum', which, on the early sheets, was combined with the qualifier

---

16 Ordnance Survey [*Ordnance Survey of Great Britain*], (1895), p.5.

17 The methods of levelling in the 1920s, together with a description of categories of Bench Mark, are given in Ordnance Survey *Instructions for levellers and contourers*, (1926); amendments are contained in Circular C.C.966. Expected rates of progress for levelling appear in Circular C.C.958.

18 Ordnance Survey *Report on the levelling network of Wales*, (1932).

19 Ordnance Survey *Report on the levelling network of London & Kent*, (1932).

20 The reason for the choice of Newlyn was apparently not recorded, but a letter from G.S.C. Cooke, Executive Officer, to T.C. Skinner, dated 14/5/1929, states that it was 'understood to have been that Newlyn is on the open sea, whereas the other places are in more or less enclosed waters.' PRO OS 1/68. f.107A.

21 PRO OS 1/68. Correspondence on the new Ordnance Survey Datum in *The Times*, 16/7/1928 and 4/8/1928.

22 PRO OS 1/68. Cambridgeshire XIV.4.

23 PRO OS 1/68. For example, letter from J.S. Alford to DGOS, 8/8/1928.

24 PRO OS 1/68. G.S.C.Cooke to Sandford Fawcett, Ministry of Health, 3/5/1929.

25 Ordnance Survey *The Newlyn Datum and Ordnance Survey levels*, (1929).

'0.65 of a foot below the general Mean Level of the Sea' indicating unambiguously the Liverpool origin. Later sheets, and reprints, referred only to 'Ordnance Survey Datum', but this can be taken to mean Liverpool, rather than Newlyn, because even when revised plans with the new datum were available,[26] they seem not to have been generally used for the up-dating of the one-inch map, presumably because spot height information was essentially a low-level priority compared with, for example, road revision. A comparison of spot levels between some Popular Edition and Fifth Edition sheets[27] shows sporadic revision which could indicate that the results of the second geodetic levelling had been used for the later series where the large-scale plans were available with this data, but the marginal note of the Fifth Edition sheets refers only to 'Ordnance Survey Datum'. There is a possibility that the Fifth Edition height information was taken from both data, according to which was readily available, but the map-user is given no overt information that this was so.

Not even the second geodetic levelling appears to have been foolproof, for in 1926, as a result of tidal observations carried out at Hurst and Yarmouth on the Isle of Wight, the Hydrographer of the Navy deduced an apparent error of $+0.745'$ in the Ordnance Survey levelled heights of that island relative to those of the mainland.[28] Concluding that the original 1853 connection was the principal source of error, but not explaining why this had not been corrected subsequently, the Ordnance Survey hurriedly completed a new determination in 1927.[29] The results of this were transferred neither to the Popular Edition nor to the Fifth Edition, and only seem to have been incorporated into the one-inch data with the publication of the Seventh Series.

Contours and hill sketches

The source materials for the surveyed and interpolated contours on the Popular Edition were the six-inch maps and hill sketches at scales of one, two, and six inches to the mile. Contouring on Ordnance Survey maps first took place in Ireland, in 1839-40.[30] There followed a prolonged debate on map scales and height information (the so-called 'Battle of the Scales'[31]) which gave rise to a Committee on Contouring.[32] On reporting in

---

26 For example, a comparison of the levels on the 1920 and 1939 printings was made of sheet 117 (*East Kent*); the revision of the large-scale plans for this area took place between 1929 and 1933.

27 For example, Popular Edition sheet 106 (*Watford*) and Fifth Edition sheet 106 (*N. W. London & Watford*). The relevant Middlesex plans had been revised in 1932-6.

28 Ordnance Survey *Report on the transference of levels to the Isle of Wight, 1927*, (1928).

29 In 1945 Close pressed for the reintroduction of scientific observations connected with the tidal gauges. Unfortunately it was found that the records of the Felixstowe tidal gauge were useless because the gauge had been handed over to the Harwich Harbour Board in 1929. The Board moved the gauge to another jetty and failed to ensure its proper maintenance. In spite of running a line of levels all the way back to Ipswich, in an effort to reconnect with the Geodetic Level Network, serious discrepancies arose between old and new levels, and it became impossible to connect any new tidal records with the old at Felixstowe. RGS Archives (Close Correspondence), H.L.P. Jolly to Lt.-Col. E.H. Thompson, O. Trig. and Levelling, 23/4/1945.

30 Andrews, (1975), pp.111-119.

31 *Correspondence respecting the scale for the Ordnance Survey, and upon contouring and hill delineation.* BPP (1854) [1831] XLI pp. 345-370. The Committee was appointed on 23 May 1854.

32 Many superficial accounts of this episode of the 1850s have been published, particularly in Seymour,

1854, it made five recommendations which were to affect the portrayal of relief on the one-inch map, and which were still relevant to the Popular Edition over sixty years later. They were, briefly summarised:

1   That a map derived from a national survey should show numerous accurate surface levels.

2   That levels, given in feet to two decimal places, should be taken along principal lines and inserted on the maps 'to an extent proportionate to their respective Scales'.

3   That primary levels should be taken along lines of communication (roads, railways and canals) and permanently marked on the ground.

4   That contour lines, instrumentally surveyed, would be a useful addition to the six-inch map.

5   That coloured contour lines, derived from those shown on the six-inch, would be a useful addition to the one-inch map, but not to the 1:2500 plan.

These recommendations were approved by the Treasury on 19 October 1854, and the first published one-inch map of England and Wales with contours derived from the six-inch map appeared in 1857.[33] Contours had first appeared on a one-inch map of England and Wales in 1851,[34] and from 1857, became a standard feature (but not in colour) of the outline edition of the map, from which hachures were omitted. The vertical interval of these contours was 100ft up to 1000ft, and thereafter at 250ft intervals. An initial 50ft contour was first introduced in 1865.

The contouring of England and Wales, which had begun in 1844, was not completed until 1890. The methods by which it was carried out are described in a few contemporary publications;[35] the reliability of the contours shown on the one-inch map depended in the first place on the interval at which they had been surveyed in the field, and then the extent to which intermediate contours had been either sketched in the field or interpolated in the office. A valuable table of surveyed contours is given by Winterbotham[36] and from this it can be seen that the best provided counties were, in order of superiority, two small areas of Durham and Northumberland, Lancashire, Yorkshire and the rest of England, and Wales. The primary publication of the contours was on the six-inch map.

Until the 1820s, relief was sketched and painted, following established eighteenth-century military traditions, on the same sheet of paper which carried the topographical

(1980), pp.129-134; the most comprehensive description is given in Oliver, (1985b).

33   A full account of the introduction of contours to the one-inch map of England and Wales is given by Harley and Oliver, in Margary, (1975-1992) VIII: viii-xvi.

34   The first one-inch sheet published with contours was sheet 91SE; it was produced to the Elcho Committee in 1851, and to the Norreys Committee in 1853. It was unusual in showing contours at a 25ft vertical interval (some of these 25ft contours were used for the Third Edition); it was the forerunner of the outline sheets which were contoured at 100ft intervals, and published from the mid-1850s.

35   *Correspondence ... on hill delineation, op. cit.* and *Account of the Methods and Processes ...*, (1875). Later publications, such as Seymour, (1980), merely repeat these two sources.

36   Winterbotham, (1934a), pp.46-8. A diagram constructed from these data is reproduced in Harley, (1975), p.78.

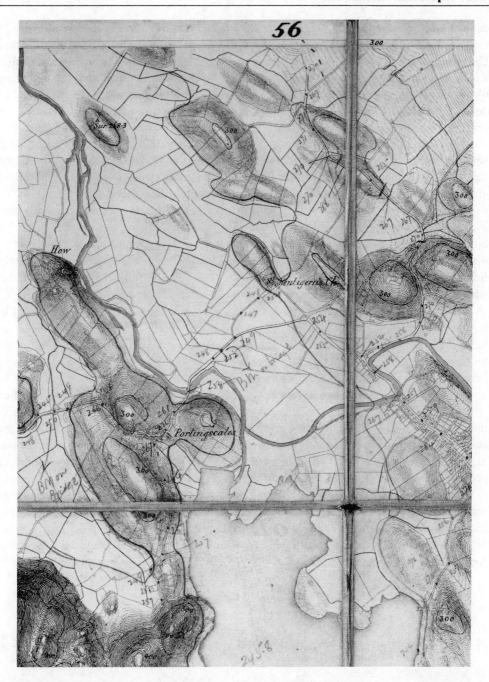

Fig.19 Extract from six-inch hill sketch, OSHS Cumberland LXIV. Hills sketched and penned in by James A. Leslie, 1863. Spot heights, presumably reflecting the primary levelling, are shown at frequent intervals along the roads. Note the depiction of relief in the low lying area of Portinscale, and the interpolated 250ft contour, subsequently drawn in pencil. The horizontally hachured area below the 300ft contour was not transferred by the hill engraver to the one-inch map. *By permission of the British Library.*

detail: the whole map was produced by the same surveyor. This resulted in an image of the third dimension which ranged from the inept to a polished work of art.[37] Uniformity of presentation was completely lacking so that the hill engraver was often at a loss when translating the drawing into hachures on the copperplate, and the engraving of the plate was consequently delayed.[38] The solution was to separate the processes of detail surveying and hill sketching; this policy, which was continued for the rest of the century, was first implemented in the 1820s.[39] The methods of drawing formlines and horizontal hachures,[40] which were established in the early 1820s, were still in use, with some modifications, at the end of the century on the sketches that were used for interpolating contours for the Popular Edition.[41] The hill sketches were made in the field at three scales: six-inch (fig.19); two-inch (photographically reduced from the six-inch), and one-inch, produced either by reduction from the six-inch or by pulls from the one-inch copperplate which contained contours. According to Wilson, the six-inch scale for hill sketches was apparently reserved, at least before 1892, for those parts of the country that were likely to be used for military camps or for operational purposes, such as likely invasion sites.[42] The surviving six-inch hill sketches (now in the British Library[43]), for which the 100ft contours were surveyed, covered south-east and northern England.

These hill sketches were made from the 1850s onwards as part of the final process in the levelling survey, and were the basis of brushwork studies (which do not appear to have survived) on the one-inch scale to guide the engraver who was responsible for the hachure plate. The brushwork studies were used to make the conversion of a horizontally hachured sketch to the vertically hachured engraved map as accurate as possible. The horizontal hachures were not drawn in an arbitrary way, but followed an established 'scale of shade'[44] (fig.20). In practice, the sketcher seems soon to have dispensed with the printed scale, relying on his eye and experience. The result was inevitable, and several examples survive of contiguous sheets, drawn by different sketchers, with serious mismatching in shading. At least one experiment was made to circumvent the laborious process of producing the final brushwork hill study, which could take four to six months to complete for any one sheet. In 1856, the *Annual Report* of the Ordnance Survey stated that a six-inch sheet had been hill-sketched in the vertical style for reduction to the one-inch scale for the engraver, but nothing more appears to have come of it. Thirty years later, the introduction of the air brush[45] produced a saving of half the usual time taken for the final hill drawing.

37 Hodson, (1989).

38 Even with reliable source materials, in 1902 it still took two to three years to engrave the hills for a single small (18″ x 12″) one-inch sheet (*Annual Report* 1902/03).

39 Hodson, (1989), pp.29-30.

40 This technique is fully described in Jones, (1974).

41 The method of hill sketching in the second half of the nineteenth century is given in *Account of the Methods and Processes* ... , (1875), and is paraphrased in Seymour, (1980), p.173.

42 Dorington, (1893c), para.207.

43 Map Library, OS Hill Sketches; arranged in counties.

44 Jones, (1974), and Seymour, (1980), p.173.

45 *Annual Report*, (1886). The process is described in Sankey, (1995).

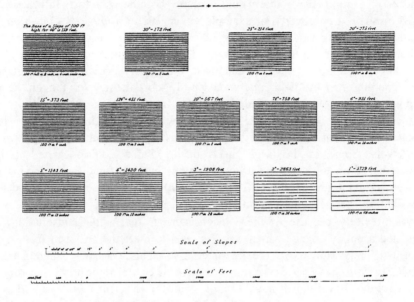

Fig.20 Scale of shade used by hill sketchers in the field, ca 1880. A pencil note at the bottom reads 'Still useful 1923'. NLS Map Library. *Reproduced by permission of the Trustees of the National Library of Scotland.*

The first appearance of contours as part of the specification for the main published one-inch map, rather than just the outline version, was made with the Revised New Series map which was printed with brown or black hachures, when the contours were shown as fine black dotted lines. The recommendation that it would be useful to have the contour lines printed in a different colour had, as noted above, first been made in 1854. The desirability of coloured contours on the six-inch and one-inch maps was discussed further during the Dorington Committee proceedings in 1892, and although experiments in printing contours in colour on the one-inch map had been tried before this time, the Survey had not 'had very much encouragement to go on with them'.[46] The areas of experiment, and the reasons for their apparent lack of success were not given, but eventually coloured contours were introduced to the one-inch on the coloured version of the Revised New Series map, where they were shown in red. This contour colour was carried forward to the Third Edition.

The combination of hachures and contours in the coloured Revised New Series and the Third Edition was not just a palliative for those who preferred the pictorial appearance of the hachure to the clinical precision of the contour. 'For the study of

46 Dorington, (1893c), para.531.

103

physiography' wrote Ogilvie in 1915[47] 'the wideness of the 100-foot contour interval of our maps renders the hachuring of the greatest importance.' Hachures were, it was asserted, essential, while the contour interval remained so large, to give an indication of the nuances of ground shapes that would certainly be otherwise lost. In practice, much depended on the hill engraver. For example, on sheets 8 (*Silloth* and *Cockermouth*) and 12 (*Whitehaven and Keswick*, Plate 8a) of the Third Edition Large Sheet Series, there is no hachured indication, in the Bassenthwaite area, of irregular ground levels below the 300ft contour, in spite of the fact that these are clearly shown on the hill sketches (fig.19). The engraver has deliberately chosen to ignore them, even though the scale of the map was sufficient to have included hachures. In contrast, the Popular Edition of the same area, sheets 9 (*Carlisle*) and 12 (*Keswick & Ambleside*, Plate 8b) show the interpolated 250ft contour which gives, in this instance, a much clearer picture of the surface levels. Some of the large sheets of the Third Edition carried initial 25ft contours,[48] based on the smaller surveyed contour interval for these low lying areas.[49] There were no contours on sheet 17 (*Isle of Man*), which was not contoured until the Popular Edition sheet 17 appeared in 1920.

It was precisely because of these inconsistencies that, after consultation,[50] Close implemented a policy change which was designed to meet the criticism that land levels were insufficiently shown on the one-inch map. This was first announced in the *Geographical Journal* in 1913: 'an improvement of capital importance is promised for the new edition of the English map. *Contours at 50 feet vertical interval will be shown right up to the top of the mountains*'.[51] (Douglas Freshfield, a Secretary of the RGS) had complained in 1892 that 'the stopping of contours at 1000' from a geographer's point of view [was] barbarous'.[52]) It had taken over two decades for the recommendations for a smaller contour interval, made in much of the Dorington Committee evidence, to take effect. The intention in 1913 was that the contours should be shown by brown dotted lines,[53] and indeed, dotted contours were engraved on the separate plates for the first fifty-five sheets, before it was decided, perhaps in 1918, to convert to a solid line.[54] The reason for this change in specification was undoubtedly linked to the decision not to proceed with the full relief version of the one-inch map. Whereas a solid line would have interrupted the imperceptible colour changes between layers, hachures and shading, it became essential, in their absence, to provide a bold coloured line to strengthen the design of the map and to make the relief legible.

---

47 Ogilvie, (1915), p.46.

48 Sheets 24, 26, 27, 29, 32, 33, 34, 37, 38, 39, 47, 48, 55, 56, 64, 65.

49 On Third Edition sheet 7 (*Morpeth and Newcastle*) the 50ft contour line is missing from the Team and Tyne valleys. This was presumably an error, because the contour figures are present. This feature may have been absent from more than one printing of this sheet as it was not noted in the recorded changes to the content of this sheet in Messenger, (1988).

50 Winterbotham, (1934b), p.105.

51 [Hinks], (1913).

52 Dorington, (1893c), para.4785.

53 As shown in the Lake District specimen (Plate 2), and as stipulated in the instructions for the third revision (Appendix 2).

54 PRO OS 1/9/5. '1″ Revision of Great Britain.', [Dec.1922.]

The innovation of the 50ft contour might even have gone one step further but for the fact that the recommendation, in 1918, of the Metric Committee of the Conjoint Board of Scientific Societies that all maps should be contoured in metres as an educative measure,[55] came too late to be considered in the design of the Popular Edition. Doubtless the enormous expense which the conversion would have entailed would have made metrication out of the question in the immediate post-war years. In the meantime, the official introduction of this 'splendid gift' of the interpolated 50ft contour was incorporated into the 1914 provisional instructions for the revision of the small-scale maps. These instructions, together with those issued in 1913 for the third revision (Appendix 2), are significant for they indicate that hill shading was, at that time, to be included as an integral part of the specification of the new one-inch map: draftsmen were to avoid writing the contour figures on the south-east slopes where they 'might be obscured by the hill shading'. Whether this term applied to hachures, or to true shading, is not made clear; it was common, with the engraved map, to refer in the nineteenth century to the hachures as 'shading', whereas shading, from about 1905 onwards, is usually understood as being homogenous in tone. Shading in its true sense had certainly been used, together with hachures, for the experimental maps described in Chapter I, but the interpretation of the term as used in these instructions must remain uncertain.

The 1914 instructions describe the contour and water drawing for the first time. A blue impression was taken, presumably from the copperplate, and on this the 100' contours were inked in; this drawing was also used for reduction to the half-inch scale for the production of the half-inch map. The 50ft contours (that is, those other than the first 50ft contour, which was surveyed) were then added by interpolation which was made by comparing levels on the six-inch map with those on the hill sketches (fig.19). The 1914 instructions also state that the '50ft contours are first plotted on the Hill Sketches', but 'plotted' is too precise a word to describe the interpolation, clearly made by eye, after studying the hachures and the configuration of the 100ft contours, which had been surveyed. On many of these sketches the 50ft interpolated contours have been drawn in either blue or red pencil. They were then transferred by pantograph from the sketch to the contour drawing for the Popular Edition and penned in. On the one-inch map, the 100ft contours were supposed to reproduce all the features shown on the six-inch, and generalisation was to apply only to minor irregularities; the 50ft interpolations were to show as many features as possible which could be identified from the hill sketches, thus making up for the deficiencies, noted on the Keswick sheets above, on the Third Edition. In many instances, the contouring on the sheets of the Popular is interrupted in hilly country, where the lines are broken, as, for example, on sheet 68 (*Aberystwyth*, squares D6,7, fig. 21b), and the policy for this is given in the 1914 instructions which state that

in the case of steep slopes, where there would be undue crowding, the 50' contours may be broken as necessary, and in exceptionally steep ground it may be desirable to break some of the 100' contours.[56]

55 OSL G5186, OSC 56. Referred to in 'Memorandum on re-surveyed maps and plans on a national grid', 12/11/1935.

56 Ordnance Survey *Instructions for the revision of the small-scale maps* ..., (Jan.1914), p.4, para.10.

The contour figures were to be written so that they could be read without turning the map, a practice which was introduced in 1896 (but not fully implemented until the Popular Edition), when it was ruled that

> the contour figures in future to be engraved parallel with the contours, but in all cases so as to read without turning the map upside down. It is immaterial on which side of the contour the figures are engraved as long as it is clear which contour they refer to.[57]

A striking difference in the shape of the contour lines exists between many of the sheets of the Third Edition Large Sheet Series and the Popular, and, in several cases, the Popular contours seem to have been completely redrawn.[58] Although much of the redrawing can be described as merely cosmetic - the smoothing out of rough corners - sometimes there is little reference to the shape of the earlier contour. This tendency to make contours more detailed may have given rise to the 1924 instruction to avoid degeneralising the contours.[59] In 1924, with the introduction of drawings, rather than engraved copperplates, as the basis of the new one-inch map of Scotland, the instructions for drawing the contours became more precise, and apply to sheets 1, 3 and 5 of the Popular Edition of England and Wales. Blue impressions on the two-inch scale, enlarged, presumably photographically, from one-inch pulls from copper, were made on Whatman's 260lb paper (this had equal distortion in all directions), and the contours, now prepared after the water features, were drawn in. The 100ft contours appeared on the blues, and these were drawn in black, and the 50ft contours were interpolated and their position was marked by a series of dashes placed around the spot heights, which were transferred from the six-inch map. Again, the hill drawings were to be used to complete the interpolation; in particular, the temptation to degeneralise the contours was to be avoided. Finally, every 250ft contour was to be shown by a 'thicker line'.[60]

These thicker, or 'reinforced' contours were a standard feature of the Scottish Popular Edition maps, but for England and Wales, their introduction came halfway in the production of the series. Reminiscing in 1934, Winterbotham claimed that the

> genesis of the reinforced contour lies in the American maps which came to me when I was O. Training. I started the reinforced contour not only on the Ordnance Survey, but [also] in France during the War.[61]

Winterbotham was the officer in charge of the Trigonometrical and Training Division at Southampton in 1920, and during this time he conducted a trigonometrical and topographical refresher course for Royal Engineers on the Isle of Man. The main object of this exercise was the contouring of the island, and the resulting work was used to revise the map of the island so that it could be issued in the Popular format.

---

57 Circulars, C/C 659/96. The sheets then in hand were 276 and 358, which were ordered to be altered because the contour figures were 'unsightly.'

58 Compare squares J9 and J10 on Third Edition Large Sheet Series sheet 107 (1908) and Popular Edition sheet 106 (1920). The 100ft contour in the vicinity of Yeading has been redrawn on the Popular Edition.

59 Ordnance Survey *Instructions to field revisers and draftsmen* ... , (1924), p.4.

60 *Ibid.*, p.4.

61 Winterbotham, (1934b), p.105.

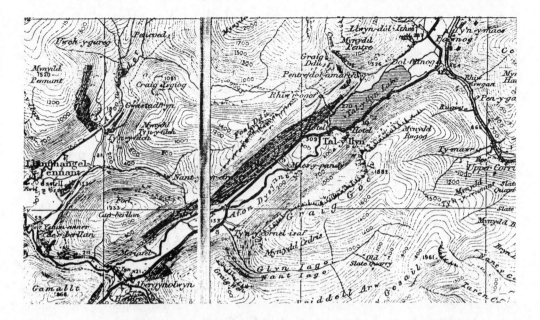

Fig.21a Popular Edition sheet 68 *Aberystwyth* (1922). The drawing of the contour lines is very fine; the engraver has tried to avoid breaking the lines where the slopes are steep, with the result that they appear to have run together in several places. *Private collection.*

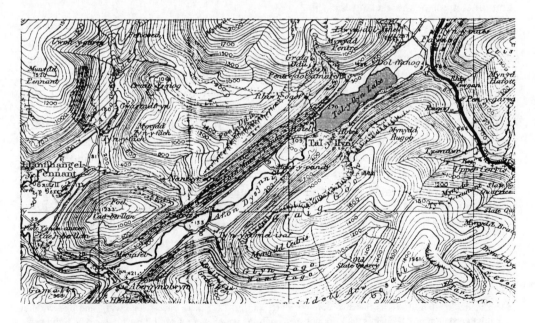

Fig.21b Popular Edition sheet 68 *Aberystwyth* (3000/29) showing contours reinforced at 250ft intervals. The thickening of the lines has left less space for the other contours on steep slopes, particularly on the north-west slopes of Graig Goch, where many of the contours are broken. *Private collection.*

It is clear that the reinforced contour had been used for this exercise, for on examining a proof of sheet 17, Lieut.-Col. W.J. Johnston (Officer in Charge of the Publication Division) noted that he thought 'the emphasising of every 250 [sic] contour to be a great improvement and [I] suggest that it be universally adopted on all the new 1" (Popular)'.[62] Close approved the suggestion three days later, on 9 December 1920, and ordered that the system 'be used for the 1 inch of the Lake Region, Isle of Man, The Yorkshire Hills, the Border Country and the Highlands - in fact for the whole of Scotland.'[63]

The *Isle of Man* sheet (no.17) was published in 1921, and sheets 1-50 of the Popular Edition were published with reinforced contours on their first printing. Thereafter, selected sheets of the remainder appeared with reinforced contours on subsequent reprintings, and even then, the thickened contours did not, in all cases, become a permanent feature and in some instances, such as sheet 134, only appeared on one of several reprints.[64] But inconsistencies abound, and perhaps the oddest case was sheet 115 (*S.E. London & Sevenoaks*), where the reinforced contour was introduced on the 1926 printing, and only partly retained, for the east and south sides, for the 1928 printing. This anomaly, which has no obvious boundaries, is difficult to explain unless somehow an incomplete contour drawing was mistakenly used in preparing the printing plate. On other sheets, for example 106 (*Watford*), otherwise apparently identical states of the 1928 printing are distinguished by one having reinforced contours, while the other is without. This indicates that, in spite of the seemingly comprehensive marginal information on reprints, it was still possible for reprintings to be made without any overt announcement of the fact on the sheet.

The reinforced contour was enthusiastically received by the army, who regarded it as a positive contribution to the overall legibility of the map when read in poor light conditions. Its absence from the Fifth (Relief) Edition of the one-inch was a critical factor in the rejection by the War Office of that style, and in early consultation with military users on the Fifth (Relief) the army stipulated, in their requirements for a special one-inch map, 'that the contour plate would have to be modified so as to show the reinforced contours characteristic of the Popular Edition'.[65] It was Winterbotham who, having pressed for its inclusion on the Popular Edition sheets, conversely decided to exclude it from the Fifth. He did so because a number of experiments designed to find the best solution to the combination of emphasised contours, hill shading and hachures had produced an effect which he pronounced as 'quite definitely ... not good' because the thickened contour introduced a 'jerk into a combination of systems designed to give a smooth sense of relief'.[66] Apart from a brief absence on the Fifth (Relief), the

62 PRO OS 1/208. Remarks on the proof of contours of the 1" Isle of Man, 6/12/1920.

63 PRO OS 1/208. Close to EO 9/12/1920.

64 The implication of this is that two contour plates survived for these sheets, one with, and one without thickened contours. Reprints with unthickened contours which were made following one which did carry reinforced contours, must have been made with the earlier contour plate. Whether this was done by design is not known, but if it were an error, and spotted only at proof, it would probably have been allowed to pass on the grounds of economy.

65 PRO OS 1/72. f.11B. Winterbotham to MacLeod, 30/4/1931.

66 PRO OS 1/48. Winterbotham to MacLeod, 14/3/1931.

reinforced contour has been a feature of the one-inch and 1:50,000 maps ever since.

Published descriptions of the Popular Edition differ in describing the colours of the contours as brown or orange.[67] In fact, there are few cases where a true brown, a perhaps natural colour for a contour, can be identified and these seem to be restricted to a few of the earliest printings, and to some of the last, in the 1940s. The sheets themselves show a variety of hues ranging from yellow, through true orange to red and brown. In view of the variety of colours used for contours in the pre-war trials, it is unsurprising that alterations to the colours should be made during the lifetime of the Popular.[68] The most notable colour change to bright yellowish-orange is apparent in many sheets reprinted from 1938. This was the result of an experiment in printing the contours in the same colour as the second class roads by Lieut.-Col. Geoffrey Cheetham (O/C Publication Division) in January 1938 for sheet 109 (*Pontypridd & Barry*). Four advantages were claimed for this method: 1) it was more pleasing; 2) it saved a printing; 3) it ensured accurate register of the contours with the outline through the fitting of the roads and 4) since the roads, as well as the contours would be on the same negative, all the advantages of using a photoplate for the roads would result.[69] The only objections mounted against the proposal were that the contour figures were not so legible and that there would be a lack of uniformity in mounting sheets of earlier printings with the new.[70] The approval for the new procedure to be followed on the Popular Edition for England and Wales was given on 1 February 1938,[71] and about fifty-four sheets which were reprinted in 1938 to 1940 carried the new contour colour.

In fact the practice of printing contours in the same colour as secondary roads was not new to the Popular Edition in 1938, for many of the earliest sheets (and for some early district sheets, such as the 1920 printing of Salisbury Plain) which had been published in 1919 and 1920, and a few later reprints, used this same device. The 1919 *Description of the Ordnance Survey Small Scale Maps* stated that the 'medium' roads and contours were printed in brown; certainly, a glance at sheet 118, for example, confirms this, although it would be more true to say that the colour was closer to orange. But the 1923 reprint of this sheet has both contours and secondary roads printed in a bright lemon yellow - far more distinctive than the 1938 colour change - and the 1926, and later printings, showed the contours in red, the same colour as the primary roads. Occasionally, otherwise identical states of a sheet can be distinguished by markedly different contour colours which were the result of different printings.[72] These colour

---

67 For example, the different editions of *A description of the small scale Ordnance Survey maps*, published between 1919 and 1935. The 1919 issue describes second class roads and contours as brown, whereas by 1925, the Fifth Edition of the booklet describes the contours as orange.

68 Experiments with contour colours are always being made; dramatic alterations in the colour of the cartographic landscape can be made in this way without employing either hill shading or layering. For instance, trials for the 1:50,000 Landranger map included examples with green and blue contours. Price, (1975), p.24.

69 PRO OS 1/52. OP to EO 26/1/1938.

70 PRO OS 1/52. Capt. C.K. Davies, Map Sales and Issues Division, to EO 31/1/1938.

71 PRO OS 1/52. Minute 10.

72 There are, for example, two versions of the 1921 printing of sheet 50 (*Bala*) in which the contours of one are reddish brown, and those of the other are orange, while for sheet 75 (*Ely*), one of the 1920 printings

changes are not to be explained by different environmental factors during the printing process, and are more likely to reflect deliberate experimenting with colour during the 1920s. There is no doubt that the least successful colour, from the point of view of overall legibility, particularly of the contour figures, was yellow. The contour colours which were tried out for the Popular Edition were no doubt more conservative than the greys, sage greens and maroons of the pre-war experimental maps, some of which were also used for a few of the interwar tourist sheets, but demonstrated a wide variety of possibilities.

The restoration of the combined colouring in 1938, therefore, after a period when many of the Popular Edition sheets had been printed with roads and contours in different colours, was made without reference to the experience of the past, for a different colour would surely have been selected. In spite of this, but again undoubtedly for economic reasons, the first sheets of the New Popular (Sixth) Edition used orange for both contours and second class roads. By the end of 1944 the criticisms, presumably of illegibility of contours and roads where they coincided, received by the Ordnance Survey indicated that it would 'be desirable to print the contours and second roads separately'.[73] The contour colour was changed to brown on later issues of the Sixth Edition, but the whole question of combined colours came full circle with the six-colour printing of the Seventh Series from 1961, when contours and second class roads were both printed in brown.[74]

Spot heights

Hundreds of spot heights were shown on each sheet of the Popular Edition, in addition to contours. Spot heights had been inserted on the one-inch map since the Old Series, for which only some had been trigonometrically ascertained. However, in spite of this long established practice, the earliest known specific reference to any policy governing their selection is given in 1896.[75] One-inch revisers were to note all surface levels or bench marks on the roads which showed the heights of the tops and bottoms of marked ascents; these were to be noted on the six-inch map for insertion on the one-inch. Bench mark heights were to be reduced to surface level by deducting their height above the surface from their value. This policy was to be continued throughout the life of the one-inch series, with occasional modifications. Thus in the 1914 instructions paragraph 45 states that

> levels are written to the nearest foot. On roads, the positions selected for showing levels should preferably be the tops and bottoms of hills. Surface levels should be adopted in preference to bench marks.

By 1924, the ruling on bench marks had become more precise:

> The levels of Bench Marks are not to appear on the 1″ map, but where a Bench Mark is shown on the 6″ map, and it is considered that a Spot Level at these positions would be useful for 1″ purposes, the matter should be reported to Superintendent 1″, who will obtain the Spot Level

has distinct yellow, instead of brownish contours.
73 OSL Minutes of the Director General's Conference no.6, 12/10/1944.
74 Oliver, (1991).
75 Ordnance Survey *Instructions for the revision of the one-inch map in the field*, (16/3/1896), para. 43.

110

value from D.O.1 for insertion on the 1″ map.[76]

The officer responsible for formulating the 1914 ruling may well have been influenced by the evidence submitted by Henry Crook to the Dorington Committee. He had complained that the levels given on roads at the six-inch scale appeared to be 'put down so many to the mile sometimes without regard to indicating the point of change of gradient.'[77] Crook, who was a civil engineer, had, by this time, acquired a reputation for being one of the Survey's sternest critics, but his censures were usually constructive and in this case he remarked that the complaint was not of the inadequacy of the number of levels, for these were ample, but that they were 'not distributed with quite sufficient regard to the form of the ground.' Forty-four years later, in giving evidence to the Davidson Committee, another engineer, W.N. McLean, was more forthright in his criticism, writing that 'OS benchmarks [were] most unreliable' and that it was 'common knowledge that in road works they receive little, if any, consideration.'[78] He was, presumably, referring to those resulting from the second geodetic levelling, but his comments must cast even further doubt, retrospectively, on the standard of accuracy of the levelling that provided the data for the Popular Edition map.

Levels were inserted from the six-inch map, and it might be reasonable to assume that, once the initial selection had been made, say, for the New Series one-inch map, and then engraved on copper for inclusion in the printed map, the expense involved in altering the spot heights on succeeding series derived from the same copperplate would have rendered any change in this respect a low priority. However, a comparison of the Popular and preceding Third Edition Large Sheet Series shows widespread differences. For example, of the 846 spot heights shown on Third Edition sheet 107 (*Watford and High Wycombe*[79]), 180 were erased on the Popular, and 55 were corrected. The remaining 611 spots were carried forward unchanged to the corresponding Popular sheet (106, *Watford*), to which a further 236 new values were added. How far this change was a reflection of the second revision of the large scale plans, which would presumably have incorporated the revised levelling which took place before the second geodetic levelling,[80] could only be determined by a sheet by sheet comparative analysis between Third Edition and Popular Edition and their respective large-scale counterparts.

Although Craster was to say, in 1935, that a contour interpolated in the office was unworthy of the Ordnance Survey,[81] there is no doubt that Close's interpolated 50ft contours were a resounding success. In using a solid coloured contour line at 50ft

76 Ordnance Survey *Instructions to field revisers and draftsmen* ... , (1924), p.7, para.21.

77 Dorington, (1893c), para.1532.

78 OSL Ordnance Survey Committee, G5186. McLean, River-flow records, to Davidson Committee, 14/5/1936.

79 The 6.12 printing; the 1908 printing of sheet 107 of the Third Edition Large Sheet Series was entitled *Rickmansworth*.

80 Buckinghamshire was revised between 1909 and 1912, Hertfordshire between 1912 and 1923, and Middlesex between 1911 and 1913.

81 PRO OS 1/84B. f.45A. Craster to MacLeod, 6/12/1935 in which he asks that, if metric contours are to be adopted by the Ordnance Survey, they should be surveyed on the ground.

intervals, and by emphasising every 250ft contour, the Popular Edition set the standard for the succeeding one-inch maps of Great Britain. With it began the practice of experimentation with the effects of different colours, on the judicious selection of which depended not only the overall appearance of the map from an artistic point of view, but also legibility and economy in map production. The balance of these criteria was not always successful, as the combination of the second class roads with the contour plate demonstrated. The overall extent to which the redrawn contours of the Popular were generalised to the point of inaccuracy, even at the one-inch scale, cannot be assessed without a detailed comparison of each sheet with its large scale source materials. It can be demonstrated, however, that in the process of providing new contour plates, the shape of the contour often changed significantly. The inclusion of the interpolated contours, together with the work of providing new contour drawings and then a new engraved plate, must have been considerable on its own, but it was substantially increased by the change of policy which altered the dotted line of the originally envisaged relief edition to a solid contour. This entailed time-consuming and expensive reworking of the plates which was not confined to the contours, for other aspects of the specification were to experience similar vagaries, particularly the water plates and parish boundaries.

Chapter VI

THE NATURAL LANDSCAPE: WATER AND VEGETATION

Water was shown in a variety of ways which were typified on the early Popular Edition sheets by a lack of consistent policy with regard to style. Either one or two plates were used, depending on the method employed for printing inland water, and whether sea was to be shown. Before the introduction of colour printing for the one-inch map series in 1897, water,[1] like other linear detail such as roads and boundaries, was shown by black lines. The potential confusion between these features, which could easily arise when map reading in a hurry under poor conditions, was pointed out by Colonel Grove in his evidence to the Baker Committee in 1892.[2] He also appears to have been the first to suggest a classification scheme for rivers which would be represented by conventional signs based on military 'goings'[3] requirements. Another witness suggested that the average depth and width of streams should be shown;[4] but nowhere in the printed evidence and correspondence is it clear where the recommendation, made on page 7 of the report, that rivers over fifteen feet wide should be shown by a double line on the one-inch map, originated. This width distinction was to be adopted for the one-inch map.

Instructions for the depiction of rivers and streams

Rivers and streams were shown as solid blue lines on the Popular Edition, and there was no indication, either on the map or on the conventional signs sheet, that the fifteen-foot width classification, which had been introduced for the Revised New Series, was still in force. There was, in fact, little difference between the way in which these features were recorded on the compilation documents for the Popular Edition when compared with those of the Third Edition, and it would indeed be surprising if much costly alteration to the copperplates had been sanctioned. And yet changes were made to the criteria by which watercourses were selected for inclusion at the one-inch scale which would have implied considerable re-engraving had they been enforced.

There appears to be no surviving documentary evidence dated before 1896 to show what policy, if any, governed the engraving of rivers and streams on the Old and New Series. The maps reveal a plethora of signs without a common intent; this is well-

---

1 Man-made waterways are not discussed in this study, but it should be noted that contemporaries regarded their depiction on the Popular Edition as frequently erroneous. See 'Ordnance Survey maps: discussion ...', (1936), p.321.

2 Baker, (1892), para.147.

3 'Goings' is a term meaning the passability of terrain for military purposes: the going over firm open ground for example, would be quicker than over similar ground impeded by obstacles such as woods and hedges, with numerous streams cutting through.

4 Baker, (1892), Col. Elliott Wood, para.131.

demonstrated in the plates of general cartographic signs which have been reconstructed by Rodney Fry for the Margary facsimiles of the Old Series.[5] The general practice seems to have been that the width of the solid engraved line reflected the general width of the stream, so that the thicker the line, the wider the river, until two parallel lines, infilled with waterlining as the width increased, represented rivers in middle and old age.

Since the New Series one-inch maps were based on the large-scale surveys, it is reasonable to suppose that some instruction existed for generalising the measurements of streams and rivers which were reduced from the six-inch map. However, the earliest surviving printed guidelines to specify the width of watercourses to be shown on the one-inch map appeared in 1896[6] and stated that

> No *Streams* with deep well-defined channels should be omitted. Streams *fifteen feet* wide and over are to be distinguished by a continuous coloured line along the stream, and the approximate width in feet shown here and there. [Italics as original.]

The coloured line was to be drawn by the reviser either on the six-inch field sheet, or the one-inch field sheet - the distinction is not made in the instruction. It seems certain that the origins of this ruling lie in the recommendations of the Baker Committee, because the depiction of rivers and streams was neither considered nor brought up during the Dorington Committee. The reason for the selection of fifteen feet, as opposed to any other measurement, is unclear, but it may have been stipulated for military reconnaissance purposes - a supposition which is endorsed by its inclusion in a military textbook of 1893 which is described as 'embodying the latest views of experts on the subject.'[7] The reviser, equipped with the six-inch sheet of his area, the New Series outline sheet and the above instruction, might well have been tempted to correct stream widths on the one-inch outline map where they were wrongly shown according to the new rule. This would, of course, have meant re-engraving the original copperplate, an expensive procedure. Some indication that such corrections may have become common practice is suggested by the 1901 Instructions,[8] where the 1896 rule is repeated together with the following qualifying remark:

> When a field reviser is in doubt whether to show a stream as over or under 15 feet he should see how it is engraved on the 1-inch. If engraved as a double stream, it should be shown as 15 feet, if as a single stream, show it as under 15 feet. The object in each case is to leave the original engraving unaltered.

An implication of this paragraph is that revisers, taking their new instructions literally, had discovered a number of inaccuracies in the portrayal of streams and, as a result, had produced an unacceptable amount of potential re-engraving work which was difficult to justify at the one-inch scale, on which precise representations of such small dimensions

5   Margary, (1975-1992).

6   Ordnance Survey *Instructions for the revision of the one-inch map in the field*, (16/3/1896), para.15, Streams.

7   Verner, (1893), p.11 states that 'streams and rivers are shown by a single line when less than 15 feet wide, and by a double line when over that width.' The 15ft width was also shown by Brunker, (1905), plate facing p.43, although a 12ft width was cited in Anon, (1916), p.15.

8   Ordnance Survey *Instructions to one-inch field revisers*, (1901), para.83.

were not possible. The above qualification therefore negates the 1896 instruction as far as its effect on the printed map is concerned.

By the time that new instructions for the one-inch revision were prepared in 1909, a further refinement had been added:

> Streams with well-defined channels, and, in hilly country, streams which help to define the main hill features, and where the contour shows a marked gully, should be shown. Minor streams which cross contours with no appreciable depression should not be shown. Streams should not be carried too far up a hill side.[9]

We can infer from this that as a result of the original 1896 revision instructions, not only had corrections been made to existing streams on the field documents, but streams which had formerly been omitted from the printed one-inch map were now being drawn on the field sheet for inclusion on the engraved plate, even, perhaps, if they were too minor to merit attention. Thirteen years later, it must have become evident that the only way to prevent the recording of unnecessary detail would be to issue guidelines on the inclusion of streams on the revision sheet. A small clarification was made to the 1909 instructions in 1924, stating that 'streams should not be carried up a hill-side beyond the point where they have well-defined channels.'[10] A further failing of the printed map, brought to light over the years by the revisers, and echoing the military complaint of a confusion of black lines, is reflected in the addition of two sentences:

> Lines sometimes appear on the 1" impressions which are not readily distinguishable as streams. In such cases the Reviser should check them and make clear on the 6" plot.[11]

Little was changed for the 1936 instructions,[12] which added that streams which crossed the contour with a marked bend should be shown. By now the one-inch map was being completely re-drawn; even so, it would have been a waste of resources not to have used existing data, and this is confirmed by the ruling to draftsmen which stipulated that

> unless the reviser has made a note for alteration the Popular Edition Maps should be used as a guide as to whether they [the streams] are to be shown single or double [i.e. under or over 15 feet in width].[13]

The final set of instructions, written in 1961[14] for the Seventh Series, omits all reference to preceding maps, but included the 1909 guidelines, and the 1924 modification to the ruling on including streams too high up on hillsides. The only major difference was that streams now had to be over 8 metres (26.2 feet, but expressed as 25 feet in the specification[15]) in width before they could be shown by a double line. Fluvial features were included in the very abbreviated conventional signs panel in the bottom margin of

9 Ordnance Survey *Instructions for the revision of the 1-inch map*, (1909), paras.73-4.

10 Ordnance Survey *Instructions to field revisers and draftsmen* ... , (1924), para.60.

11 *Ibid.*

12 Ordnance Survey *Instructions for the revision and drawing of the one-inch (Fifth Edition) map*, (1936).

13 *Ibid.*, p.17.

14 Ordnance Survey *Instructions for small scales revision (The Green Book 1961)*, (Sept. 1961).

15 Ordnance Survey *Specification for the production of the one-inch Seventh Series*, (1952).

the Revised New Series, and they were also shown on the characteristic sheet[16] of 1897 (Appendix 5). Here, all streams over 15 feet wide were shown by a double black line, the space between the two lines gradually increasing with the width of the stream or river. Furthermore, the stream was labelled as being 'under 15 feet' or 'over 15 feet'. But by the time that the conventional signs sheet for the Popular Edition was printed in 1924, all mention of the width of streams had been omitted, and henceforth, the map-user was given no indication that such a classification existed.

The one detail that was carried consistently through the Popular specification for all dates, with the exception of six sheets, was that rivers were shown by solid blue lines which tapered in width towards their source. The distinction between streams over or under fifteen feet in width had been dropped so far as the printed map was concerned - hence its absence from the characteristic/conventional signs sheet mentioned above - but was retained in the departmental instructions for internal revision purposes. Double lines for wider streams were restored to the printed map for the Popular Edition of Scotland, and for sheets 1, 3 and 5 of England and Wales, which shared the Scottish Popular specification, but without explanation in the legend or characteristic sheet. Only three other English sheets, 95, 103 and 114, used the Scottish water specification for rivers in later printings,[17] and this was so unusual that a possible explanation may be that the old water plates had become worn out, or perhaps mislaid, so that it was necessary to make new ones. On the other hand, the equivalent Fifth Edition sheets, carrying the same numbers, were very nearly coincident with their Popular counterparts, and material for their production could well have been available in 1932. However, a comparison of the sheets shows that although the style of the Fifth Edition, which included double-lined rivers, was used for the Popular reprints, the configuration of the water plate of the Popular had not been changed to match the later edition.

Lakes and ponds

In contrast to the treatment of rivers and streams in the revisers' and draftsmen's instructions, ponds and lakes received scant attention. When was a pond not a pond? If it was not of a 'large size and of a permanent nature'[18] it was not to be included on the one-inch map. This instruction continued, almost unvaried, until the Seventh Series, without any guide as to what constituted a 'large' size. The idea of including lake depths on the one-inch map had, however, first been introduced by Douglas Freshfield, a Secretary of the Royal Geographical Society in 1892, in his evidence to the Dorington Committee.[19] Comparing the British maps with their Swiss counterparts, he remarked that the Swiss survey showed the depths of all the lakes, 'which for physical geography is very important', and added that some French maps showed the depths of water on the

---

16 Until 1924, the separately issued sheets explaining the conventional signs used on the one-inch map were known as 'Characteristic sheets', after the early examples which were produced to explain the significance of the different lettering, or characters of writing, on the map.

17 These sheets carried the new water specification from the 1932 (95, 114) and 1933 (103) printings onwards. It is possible that later states of other sheets, which have not been seen by the author, exist with this specification.

18 Ordnance Survey *Instructions for the revision of the one-inch map in the field*, (16/3/1896).

19 Dorington, (1893c), para.4827.

sea coast. Freshfield's forlorn comment that he supposed it was 'too much to hope we may be able to come to that some day' was unduly pessimistic so far as the coastline was concerned, for bathymetric contour lines had already been shown around the coast on some sheets, while Dorington recommended that depths be added to important inland waters. The figures which appeared in the lakes themselves on the New Series were merely levels of the surface which had been taken from the larger scale, a practice which, surprisingly, is only confirmed in writing in the 1936 instructions which state that 'the water levels of large Lakes will be shown on the 1-inch maps, where they are shown on the 6-inch scale.'[20]

Dorington also recorded the fact that the Director General of the Ordnance Survey was making enquiries about the possibility of using Mill's surveys of the Lake District for Ordnance Survey purposes. However, it was to be forty-four years before bathymetric contours were included on the one-inch coverage of the Lake District,[21] (Plate 8c) in spite of the fact that the surveys by Dr Hugh Robert Mill, backed by the Royal Geographical Society, were in progress during 1892. The evidence that the Ordnance Survey did indeed receive Mill's information shortly after it was completed is preserved in bathymetric contour traces, with Ordnance Survey stamps dated between 1895 and 1898, (now in the British Library).[22] Some of these bear the annotation 'contours in red only to be engraved'. Wilson had stated in 1892 that the provision of lake soundings had always been regarded as the responsibility of the Hydrographic Department. The only lake in England to be the subject of an Admiralty survey was Windermere, which was sounded in 1937; the freshwater lochs of Scotland were surveyed privately between 1897-1909 by Sir John Murray and Lawrence Pullar. The data from these surveys were used by Bartholomew before being passed to the Ordnance Survey from about 1906.[23]

The portrayal of water on the Third Edition - streams under fifteen feet as a single blue line, those over fifteen feet as a double blue line with waterlining infill where wide enough, and larger bodies of water shown with waterlining infill and blue casing - was abandoned with the Popular Edition. Sheets published in 1920 or earlier lack a consistent specification, reflecting an unformed policy on water depiction at this time, and shows the extent to which the design of the Popular may have been interrupted by wartime duties. Three main methods of showing inland water were used for this early period:

a) stippled, with a thick blue, or thickly stippled edge and black casing, or occasionally a flat blue with blue stippled edging; smaller bodies of water were solid blue with black casing.

b) solid blue with black casing throughout.

c) horizontally ruled blue lines with a broad blue edge and black casing.

---

20 Ordnance Survey *Instructions for the revision and drawing of the one-inch (Fifth Edition) map*, (1936), p.30, para.74.

21 Bathymetric contours first appeared on the 1936 printings of the Popular Edition regular series sheets, and were inserted on the M.37R.36.10038 printing of the Lake District Tourist sheet.

22 Map Library, Maps cc.2.g.12. Traces for the following lakes, together with date stamps, where present, are preserved: Bassenthwaite 9/6/1898; Buttermere; Coniston Water; Crummock Water 9/6/1898; Derwent Water 9/6/1898; Ennerdale Water 9/6/1898; Ullswater 5/3/1895; Wastwater; Windermere.

23 These traces are now in the BL, Map Library, Maps C.21.f.13. See also Murray and Pullar, (1910).

Several of these early sheets included minor variations in style which add to the visual interest of many of the southern maps.

The transition from an indeterminate to a standard specification for inland water on the Popular Edition appears to have taken place in 1921. There is a close correlation between publication date and method of water portrayal; within the area of the south of England covered by sheets first published in 1920 or earlier.[24] From now on, all sheets (except for 1, 3 and 5) were to show open inland water by horizontal ruled blue lines with blue casing, which was thickened, or shaded on the north and west sides. This method had been adopted for the half-inch scale by 1911, but first appears to have been used by the Ordnance Survey for the one-inch scale on the tourist map of Killarney, and for the Lake District specimen (Plate 2), both published in 1913. These two examples also showed rivers as single, solid blue lines. The two blues were the same, and if used as a solid colour for lakes, would have been excessively heavy; the use of fine lines, closely spaced, gave a paler effect without the need for two blue plates on sheets which covered inland areas. However, the fineness of the lines on the 1913 maps was not matched for most of the Popular Edition, where a larger gauge seems to have been used.

Between 1938 and 1940, the reprints of at least 27 sheets[25] showed both inland water and sea in the same manner as the blue stipple adopted for the Fifth Edition. This was, in fact, following the design selected by Winterbotham in 1932:

> I have gone back in the one-inch to the old Scotch stipple for the sea which is not so pleasant in deep water, but allows you on the same plate to get a darker single line and therefore to bring up the inland waters sufficiently.[26]

By 1938, the reproduction material for the Popular Edition was deteriorating, and it may have been cheaper to produce a new water plate than to patch up the old one. Also, it would have been clear by then that the progress of the Fifth Edition was too slow to be able to envisage coverage of the north of England within the near future, and so it would have been logical to have incorporated the new specification in reprints of the old material wherever this was possible.

The sea coast

Ever since the publication of Mudge's map of Kent in 1801, the Ordnance Survey one-inch map had always shown the foreshore; but the terms High Water Mark and Low Water Mark seem to have been first used for the Revised New Series. However, the 1896 instructions for this revision say only that 'the character of the coast line is to be corrected where necessary and distinguished as cliff, sand dunes &c.' Although it can be assumed that the low water mark would have been taken from the six-inch map, this is not explicitly stated until 1901, when paragraph 82 of the revision instructions states that

> the low water mark for the 1-inch map will be taken from the 6-inch plots, unless extensive alterations to it have occurred since the 6-inch survey.

24 See the calendar of first printings in Part 2, p.377-8.
25 These were: 4, 6, 11, 12, 14, 17, 18, 20, 22, 26-30, 40-2, 47, 53, 57, 61, 67, 71, 76, 77, 79, 88.
26 PRO OS 1/181. f.18A. Winterbotham to MacLeod 18/7/1932.

By 1909, it would seem that some revisers had been going to great lengths to include many of the frequent fluctuations in the shape of the foreshore. Just as it had been necessary to issue guidelines to restrict the scope for stream revision, now the reviser was told to take no notice

> where the low water mark is continually altering, e.g. mud flats or sand banks in estuaries, the shape and position of which are liable to constant change.[27]

Only with the 1924 instructions is the inclusion of the high water mark from the six-inch map actually specified, although it is probable that these two lines had always been taken off the larger scale for the derived one-inch maps. What, then, did the two lines actually represent on the ground, and how were they measured in the first place? For England, Wales and Ireland the surveyed lines were those of the high and low water of ordinary tides, that is, tides halfway between neaps and springs, whereas for Scotland, the lines were those of ordinary spring tides. The difference between the requirements for Scotland and England reflected the disparity in the law governing the definition of foreshore for legal purposes.[28]

The surveys of both lines were made by the Ordnance Survey, and the earliest surviving detailed instructions date from about 1882.[29] They give a vivid impression of the meticulous planning needed to capture on paper the line of low water before the tide came in. Occasionally, and under special circumstances, the original surveys for the Admiralty charts were used to correct areas where great changes took place, as in Morecambe Bay, where the sands were constantly shifting, and 'it was not worth their while to re-survey these sands . . . when the latest maps in two or three years would be all altered again'.[30] Clearly, under these kinds of conditions, it made economic sense to use the hydrographic data, but it was not 'the regular thing', especially as the Admiralty surveyed their own low water mark, and the two sources rarely agreed because they were based on different premises: the Admiralty surveyed the low water mark of Spring Tides.

The coastal sheets of the Popular Edition, and those of their predecessors, the Third Edition and Revised New Series, carried the standard note that the submarine contours, which were drawn at five and ten fathoms, were taken from the soundings of Admiralty surveys. The first mention of how this was done appears in the 1914 instructions to the draftsmen of what was to be the Popular Edition, from which it appears that the contours were first constructed on the Admiralty charts 'by an inspection of the soundings', and were then transferred by pantograph to the water drawing and penned in. The contour figures were then to be written in blue on the seaward side of the lines so that they could be read without turning the map - it was decided in 1896 that the former practice of

27 Ordnance Survey *Instructions for the revision of the 1-inch map*, (1909), para.72.

28 Winterbotham, (1934a); a brief history of the depiction of HWM and LWM on Ordnance Survey plans is given on p.25. See also Ordnance Survey *High and Low water marks as shown on Ordnance Survey plans*, [1940].

29 Winterbotham, (1934a), p.25, cites instructions of 1851; these have not been found. The earliest so far traced is a 1908 reprint of Circular O.S.307 [1882].

30 Dorington, (1893c), para. 4950.

engraving sea contour figures upside down on the one-inch map was not to be continued.[31] By 1924, and possibly earlier, the sea contours (at 5 fathom intervals) for the Popular of both England and Wales and Scotland were derived at one remove from the Admiralty chart. This was because they were actually enlarged from the contours that had been taken directly from the charts for the half-inch drawings from which the New Series Quarter-Inch map was compiled. Printed in blue, the bathymetric contours were either stippled, as on the early sheets, or were printed as a solid line.

The earliest printed description available on survey methods (1875)[32] does not include the instructions to surveyors of the coastline which were in force at the time. The only mention of littoral description is in a reference to the examiner's duties:

> in examining a coast he is careful to give an accurate representation of the foreshore and to sketch the stratified rocks so as to give a correct idea of their "strike" and "dip". In tidal rivers he has also to ascertain the highest point to which ordinary tides flow.[33]

This distinction of the boundary between fresh and salt water in rivers was first made overtly on the one-inch map with the Popular Edition. Previously, it had been possible to infer the tidal reach, at least in large rivers, by examining the high water mark line. Now, with the use of two different blues, one for the sea, and one for inland water,[34] combined with the black high water line, the change was obvious.[35] Gone was the delicate blue waterlining which rippled away from the coasts of the Third Edition map - it had been deleted, at considerable expense, from the copperplates - and in its place was a solid, greenish blue. For the first time, a conventional signs sheet, that of the Popular Edition, marked the 'highest point to which Tides flow', a convention that was carried forward to the Seventh Series, and which has become, with the 1:50,000 map, the 'normal tidal limit'.

This specification had already been used for the experimental Bridgwater sheet (sheet 120) in 1916, which resembled what was to become the standard Popular style. But when the standard sheet 120 was first printed only two years later it was markedly different in appearance. One of four sheets to be printed in 1918 (the others were 119, 128 and 143), it showed two bathymetric layers: below and above 5 fathoms. Only one other sheet, 119 (*Exmoor*), showed sea in the same way, but this was discontinued with the 1928 printing, and bathymetric layers were omitted from sheet 120 after the 1929 printing. These two sheets also show an attractive convention of portraying mud or sand flats by printing black stipple on top of a brownish stipple, giving a 'sandy' image. The brownish stipple, common to many 1920s printings of coastal sheets, was omitted from some of the later reprints.

---

31 Circulars, C/C 659/96.

32 *Account of the Methods and Processes ...* , (1875).

33 *Ibid.*, p.46.

34 On some of the early sheets (printed 1920 or before), open inland water was shown in the same blue as the sea, and one sheet, 89, showed the tidal waters of the Towy by horizontal ruled lines.

35 The transition from sea to inland water in rivers is well demonstrated, for example, in the estuary of the River Tyne, sheet 7. However, on some other sheets the transition between tidal and inland water is far from precise. Notable examples are sheets 38 and 39 (River Trent) and 114 and 115 (River Thames).

The Bridgwater sheet also introduced another convention which was common on the early block of southern coastal sheets. This was the use of blue stippling for estuaries; in many cases this undoubtedly enhanced the appearance of the map,[36] but its use for inland water was often messy and unattractive, and the method was discontinued when the standard water specification was adopted in 1921, although it was retained on some of the later printings of the early sheets. Thereafter, the only major change took place when the Fifth Edition style of using the 'old Scotch stipple' was used for the reprints of some sheets from 1938-40.

VEGETATION

The full conventional signs sheet (Plate 12) for the Popular Edition shows six categories of vegetation: deciduous, coniferous, and mixed woods, rough pasture, marsh, and dangerous bog. The first five were, as would be expected from the map's origin, carried over from the preceding Third Edition; but 'dangerous bog' was a new symbol, peculiar to the Popular Edition because it was dropped from the Fifth, even though revisers were instructed to differentiate between 'marsh' and 'bog' on the revision documents.[37]

Woods

Although separate symbols for coniferous and deciduous trees had been used on the eighteenth-century Ordnance Surveyor's drawings,[38] a firm policy of distinguishing between different types of woodland only became apparent for the first time with the Revised New Series. Certainly, by 1896, the area of a distinct patch of deciduous or coniferous trees judged to be large enough to be shown separately on the one-inch map was set at 400 square yards, and this distinction was carried through until the first issues of the Fifth (non Relief) Edition, when woodland was shown only by a green fill without symbols.

The practice of colouring the six-inch field sheets with light green for deciduous trees and dark green for coniferous, and stripes of each colour for mixed woods, was abandoned by 1924 in favour of delineating the area by a green band and writing 'Con', 'Dec' or 'Mix'. The engraving of woodland symbols must have been an extremely labour-intensive process, for whereas 'stamps', or punches, with the appropriate tree symbols were used for the large scales, there is no direct evidence to suggest that this was so for the small scales. Slight irregularities in the tree symbols, and the lack of repeat patterns, all tend to suggest that each 'tree' was individually engraved. The tree symbols in the large areas of new plantations which burgeoned across sheets such as *Thetford* (sheet 76) in the 1930s, were presumably drawn either on the stone, or on a negative; they are inelegant and clumsy compared with the almost etched appearance of the symbol on the copperplate. Scattered and isolated trees were shown with the appropriate symbol, usually in parkland, but also in heathland areas. So fine was the

---

36 Attractive blue stippling in the estuarine areas is well shown on sheet 141, *Bournemouth & Swanage*, and sheet 103, *Stroud & Chepstow*.

37 Ordnance Survey *Instructions for the revision and drawing of the one-inch (Fifth Edition) Map*, (1936), para.31.

38 Hodson, (1989), p.28.

engraved tree that it was possible to show the tree-lined rural roads during the period of the Popular Edition; only a few examples of their deletion from the map have been found.[39]

Woods had first been printed in green on the later issues of some of the coloured sheets of the Revised New Series; on these, an interesting experiment seems to have been carried out in which the tree symbols were printed in the same brown as the hachures.[40] This reduced their legibility, and it may have been for this reason (as well as the fact that, unless the wood symbols plate was combined with the hachure plate, an extra run through the press would have been necessary) that black was restored for the symbols for the Third and Popular Editions.[41] The dark green colour used for the early Popular printings was very similar to that of the Third Edition. In most cases the woodland areas were enclosed by a black line, which presumably reflected an enclosure boundary on the ground; contemporary drawing instructions give no guidance, unlike those for the Seventh Series,[42] about how to show unenclosed woodland. It can only be assumed, therefore, that open woods were to be implied by the lack of an enclosing black line. For many of the first issues of the Popular Edition, the black tree symbol was reasonably clean and clear, but became increasingly faint on reprinting as the stones wore out. A major change in colour took place in about 1936, when a light yellow-green was introduced; this is particularly characteristic of the printings of 1938 and later. The specification for woodlands on the Popular was identical to that of the Revised New Series, and had not been altered on the copper; the shape of the woodland boundaries was largely inherited from the Third Edition. However, two national revisions had intervened, and by the time the Popular Edition came to be published, significant changes in national woodland management were taking place with the formation in 1919 of the Forestry Commission.

How, if at all, was this reflected at the one-inch scale? For most of the country there was very little change to woodland boundaries on the one-inch map within the lifetime of the Popular Edition, and any alterations were mainly of the order of up-grading former scrubland to full woodland status, or the reverse. While a comparison with the Third Edition shows striking deforestation for parts of central Wales, the Forestry Commission's programme of afforestation in the north west of England, North Wales and Brecon, East Anglia and Cannock Chase, is reflected in the large tracts of new coniferous plantations which have been added to the later printings. However, it cannot be assumed that the portrayal of new plantings is accurate, as any comparison with the Land

---

39 An example is on sheet 21, *Ripon & Northallerton*, squares 8E, and F. Trees are deleted on the 3000/29 printing.

40 Experiments in portraying woodland on hill-shaded and/or layered Ordnance Survey maps were made with the early half-inch series, which used open green symbols. Half a century later, open green trees were used for the 1964 Cairngorms 1″ tourist sheet because the usual convention of a flat green wash would have detracted from the stereoscopic effect of the trichromatic printing and hill shading. The symbols themselves were drawn so that the trees appeared to be viewed from the south at a low oblique angle - very similar to seventeenth and eighteenth-century military practice. Griffith, (1964).

41 Black tree symbols were also used for some of the 1905-7 reprints of the coloured Revised New Series.

42 Ordnance Survey *Specification for the production of the one-inch Seventh Series*, (1952), p. 10: 'The limits [of woods] will be shown by firm lines if enclosed, or by pecked lines if open'.

Utilisation Survey (LUS) will show. For example, LUS sheet 12 (Cumberland surveyed 1931, printed 1933), based on Popular Edition sheet 12, shows a more up-to-date forestry pattern than the 1936 and 1938 printings of the standard topographical sheet (Plates 8c, d).

Using the one-inch map as evidence of wood clearance is also unreliable. For example, when large areas of woodland are shown to have disappeared between the Third and Popular Editions, we can assume, on the one hand, that trees had been felled; but on the other, the status of the cleared land is uncertain: was it planned to replant it? By the time that revisions came to be made to the sheets in the 1920s, the reviser was instructed not to delete a felled wood unless it had been completely cleared and the roots grubbed up. A published cartographic record of temporary clearance would not, therefore, be made, even though a new planting might not happen for some time. This decision was modified, probably in the late twenties, when the reviser was instructed to cancel (i.e., delete) all coniferous woods which had been cut down and not replanted, unless he had been able to ascertain that it was to be restored in the immediate future.[43] If a mixed or deciduous wood had been felled, and seemed to be regenerating, he was to 'use his judgement as to whether the area should be shown as wood, or scattered trees and R.P [rough pasture]'.

Heath and moor

The symbols for woods had first been shown in the conventional signs panels at the foot of the one-inch sheets of the Revised New Series. By 1919, these panels had been expanded to include marsh and 'heath and moor'. In a way, this expansion of the explanation of the symbols was ironical, for while it was made in response to public demand, the map on which it appeared was so far removed, in most cases, from the crispness of the engraved image, that the signs themselves could often hardly be made out. As a result, only the very early printings, and the last, where the image was touched up on the negative, show recognisable areas of rough pasture and marsh.

Although 'heath and moor' was the terminology which appeared in the map legend, the same symbol was called 'rough pasture' on the full conventional signs sheet, and the only source which confirms the interchangeability of the two terms is the 1896 instruction which is headed 'heath or rough pasture'. This same paragraph also gives the fullest explanation of what this category was supposed to cover:

> moors, commons, and uncultivated ground covering large areas which are not cut up by fences; small areas through which public roads run; sides of valleys or ravines; summits of hills, and along tops of cliffs.

However, it would appear that a definite distinction was made between the type of rough pasture which was eligible for depiction, for in 1901 it was laid down for the Second Revision that rough pasture which was shown on the six-inch map was not to be included on the one-inch unless the area so added was 'Heath, Moorland, or covered with Furze'.[44] Ground which, in the reviser's opinion was merely 'rough grass, rushes, etc.'

43 Ordnance Survey *Instructions to field revisers and draftsmen* ... , (1924), undated replacement for para.63.
44 Ordnance Survey *Instructions to one-inch field revisers*, (1901), para.26. Furze is another name for gorse.

was not to be marked for insertion on the one-inch. So, the curious anomaly arose that vegetation, such as gorse, which was not normally grazed by animals, was referred to as rough pasture, and rough grass was excluded from the category unless it was mixed in with heath and furze.

A further complication in the interpretation of this symbol, where it can be seen on the Popular Edition, is that it imported from the Third Edition a symbol for furze, whose existence at this scale[45] is confirmed only by the instruction given in 1909 that it was no longer to be shown on the one-inch map, 'but that where it exists it will not be removed unless badly engraved and likely to be mistaken for marsh.'[46] Another move towards the generalisation of the moorland symbol came in 1914, when the printed instructions for the preparation of the Popular Edition laid down that the boundary of heath and moor areas, formerly shown by a dotted line, was to be erased. The absence of this edge, which was restored for the Scottish Popular Edition, sheets 1, 3 and 5 of the Popular Edition, and for the Fifth Edition, makes it even more difficult to read the printed map where the image is faint. But a boundary might have implied a surveyed line; at this time, the cost of providing an accurate demarcation of vegetation type, even at a larger scale may not have been justified. So, in 1911, it had been decided that the removal of the dotted line would 'obviate the necessity for such accuracy in detail as has hitherto obtained.'[47] An early decision to remove the symbol from the legend on the map, perhaps because of its overall illegibility, seems to have been taken in 1920, for it appeared only on the sheets printed up to, and including this date, and was erased on 1921 reprints.

The instruction, given in 1924, that small alterations in the extent of rough ground were not to be made, is irrelevant to the interpretation of the map, because, unless the plate were touched up, even large alterations would be impossible to discern. In some of the later printings of the Popular Edition, the Fifth Edition rough pasture symbol has been printed over the area originally covered by the Revised New Series signs.[48]

Marsh and bog

The conventional signs sheet of the Popular Edition carries a symbol which has not been found on any of the map sheets, and which appears on no other map or conventional signs sheet for England and Wales. This is the symbol for 'dangerous bog'. Unlike the symbol for rough pasture, which it resembled, it shows a firm, dotted boundary. It is not to be found where it might be expected, such as at Borth Bog, south of Aberdovey (sheet 68, square 4K), and the only clue to its origin is hidden in the drawing instructions of 1914, which say that the boundaries of 'marshes, and of dangerous bogs in Ireland, will be indicated by a blue band [on the drawing sheet]', and a dangerous bog was to be marked by the letters D.B. It would seem, then, that a symbol intended for the one-inch map of Ireland found its way, unchecked, onto the conventional signs sheet of the Popular Edition of England and Wales, and remained there, through its revision of 1937.

45 Its use for the large scales is described in Harley, (1979).
46 Ordnance Survey *Instructions for the revision of the 1-inch map*, (1909), para.97.
47 Circulars, C/C 460/11.
48 For example, sheet 13 (1939).

Marshland, by comparison, was straightforward, and its depiction did not vary. It was a standard inclusion on the sheet legends, but no differentiation was made between fresh, brackish, or salt marsh,[49] and osiers (willow shoots) were also included in the definition of marsh.

So far as the representation of natural features on the Popular Edition was concerned, then, it could hardly be said of the water and vegetation symbols that they added to its lucidity. Unlike the clear conventions used for relief, the changing specification for water, in particular, perhaps reflected a preoccupation with the use of colour as a symbol at the expense of a simple, legible and intelligible image. The Popular was the only one-inch map to distinguish, by colour, salt from fresh water; the ruled blue lines which were the predominant specification for inland water were a fussy way of using colour, and echoed sixteenth-century traditions of showing bodies of water on engraved black and white maps by engraved horizontal lines. The coarse blue stipple used in the early printings could sometimes be attractive, but again, the object seems to have been not so much to convey information as to add to the pictorial quality of the map.

Of the six categories of vegetation, only the green-printed woodland areas are immediately recognisable for what they represent; any further interpretation of the three woodland categories requires a closer scrutiny of the tiny unstandardised symbols. In this, of course, the map was entirely the child of its engraved parent, and no improvement in legibility could be made until drawing, rather than engraving, became the basis for reproduction, but even here, the drawn Scottish Popular Edition closely imitated its engraved predecessor. The drawn symbols on the early Fifth Edition maps were hardly better, resembling their eighteenth-century predecessors, and were, again, an attempt to present an image which conformed as closely to the mind's eye view of a wood as possible. Only with the Seventh Series one-inch map did unequivocal, standard tree symbols replace the more artistic impression. And yet, this very standardisation, while contributing to the clarity of the map, at the same time removed from it the essence of the English landscape. Individual trees were not to be shown outside woods.[50] The symbol was too large to permit the depiction of tree-lined roads, or scattered trees in parkland. Gone too, from the face of the map, were the avenues of trees which characterised the eighteenth- and nineteenth-century plantings in country estates. As a mirror of the arboreal landscape, then, the modern map is measurably poorer than its pre-Second World War counterparts.

49 Ordnance Survey *Instructions for the revision of the small scale maps ...*, (Jan. 1914), para.46.
50 Ordnance Survey *Specification for the production of the one-inch Seventh Series*, (1952), para.19.

Ordnance Survey Leaflets: No.2.

Ordnance Survey Maps
F O R
CHAR·A·BANC TOURS.

Ordnance Survey Office,
Southampton.

Fig.22 The front of a leaflet printed by the Ordnance Survey in March 1926 to advertise the value of the quarter-inch, half-inch and one-inch maps for leisure travel. *Private collection.*

Chapter VII

COMMUNICATIONS: ROADS AND RAILWAYS

I have broken a good many pony carriage springs by trusting to the Ordnance maps in regard to roads. *D.W. Freshfield, 1893*[1]

It is probably true to say that the primary purpose of the one-inch map was to enable the user to select the best route, according to his method of transport, from one point to another. Ideally, the user required clear representation of the different categories of route which would allow unequivocal interpretation of the map. From 1886, the user could assume that first class roads were public, and most second class roads were also public, just as today we can be more or less confident that a coloured road on an Ordnance Survey map is public, even though the rights of way disclaimer implies that this may not always be so. Major problems of interpretation have always arisen where the minor routes were concerned, for here the question of status - whether public or private - was not readily, if at all, apparent. These less frequented ways have always drawn the eye of the leisurely traveller, either with vehicle, horse, or on foot, in search of the quiet scenic route away from the bustle of the nation at work. Of course, it is well known that the representation of roads and footpaths on Ordnance Survey maps and plans is no evidence of public rights of way,[2] except, on current mapping, where the information is taken from the definitive maps of rights of way prepared by County Councils under the provisions of the National Parks and Access to the Countryside Act of 1949 and its successors.[3] Such information was not available to the map user before 1950. All the same, the classification schemes used for the one-inch map would have enabled him to form a reasonable assessment of the function of different routes, and the use to which they were subject. This became much easier after the introduction of colour to the map in 1897.

Coloured roads were first used to maximum effect on the one-inch map with the Popular Edition, and a striking feature of the map is the changing colour of many of the roads between reprints. These alterations, which first resulted in a plethora of red roads, followed by a change to a preponderance of yellow roads, were the consequences of shifts in road classifications which mirrored the changing ideas of the Ordnance Survey as it tried to bring its own criteria into line with those of the Ministry of Transport. The classifications used for the Popular were complex because they sought to provide the road user with almost minute detail about the quality of the surface, and how 'fast' it was for the motorist, as well as attempting to identify the importance of routes between

1   Dorington, (1893c), para.4796.
2   Sauvain, (1997), p.46; Oliver, (1993), p.67.
3   The Countryside Act (1968), and the Wildlife and Countryside Act (1981).

settlements. These intricacies were a reflection of the widely differing road conditions which prevailed before the First World War, when the system used for the Popular was first devised.

Within two decades these discrepancies had largely disappeared as a result of improvements in road construction and maintenance. The problems that were encountered by the Ordnance Survey in their depiction of roads on the small-scale maps in the inter-war period were compounded by a Ministry of Transport classification scheme, whose purpose was to provide the basis for grants from the Road Fund, and which anticipated road maintenance and construction.[4] The Survey refused to adopt this scheme at first, since it did not reflect what was actually on the ground at the time; but its attempts to find workable compromises were to result in confusion on the map. The underlying principal concepts of road classification, as they applied to the Popular Edition, had their origins in the discussions relating to the Baker and Dorington Committees of 1892.

In 1890, the one-inch map was described baldly as a 'general map';[5] by 1913 the map had become 'the general road map of the country';[6] in 1919 it was 'unsurpassed' as a road map,[7] but only eleven years later the Director General was to ask 'does anyone nowadays consult a one inch for a motor route?'[8] Winterbotham's rhetorical question was prompted partly by his dislike of the colour red for first class roads which dominated the Popular Edition map,[9] but also, perhaps, by the formal abolition in 1930 of the 20 m.p.h. speed limit for private cars. Untrammelled by speed restrictions, the motorist soon travelled off the one-inch sheet, in the same way that his nineteenth-century cycling counterpart had ridden off the small sheets of the New and Revised New Series, and apparently the motoring public came to prefer the quarter-inch map.[10] Although it was undoubtedly true that for long distance route planning purposes a smaller scale map was essential, the one-inch nonetheless remained the key cartographic tool for local navigation at the end of the journey, and an increasingly elaborate road classification was devised for it. In this respect, the Ordnance Survey was faced with commercial competition, for Bartholomew's contoured road maps and Gall and Inglis's maps, both of the 1890s and early 1900s, already used colour to distinguish different categories of roads. In particular, Gall and Inglis's 'graded road maps' were innovative in showing four classes of road in colour: 'superior roads' in yellow, 'good roads' in orange, 'inferior roads' in red and 'rough roads' in blue.[11]

4 Barker and Savage, (1974), p.188.
5 *Ordnance Survey maps ... A description of their scales ...*, (1890).
6 *Ordnance Survey maps ... A description of their scales ...*, (1913).
7 Ordnance Survey *A description of the small scale Ordnance Survey maps ...*, [1919].
8 PRO OS 1/53. Winterbotham to EO, 1/8/1930.
9 According to Winterbotham (1934b), red was selected by the 1912 War Office committee on road classification. Interestingly, the cartography of the International Map of the World was criticised when the specification for principal roads was changed in 1913 (perhaps influenced by the War Office committee) from fine double black lines to a solid red line. The visual effect was unflattering; MacLeod, (1925a, b).
10 Board, (1981).
11 Contemporary road maps are described in Nicholson, (1983a), and Oliver, (1996).

Classification

In the twenty years between 1919 and 1939, the road classification used for the Popular Edition was modified so that it conformed more to civilian requirements (specifically, those of the Ministry of Transport) than to the military criteria which were first promulgated in the 1890s.[12] This was, quite simply, because there was scarcely a road in the country which, by the 1930s, was impassable by army vehicles, and therefore any classification which emphasised the importance of the road according to its surface quality, was now of relatively small consequence. Writing in 1934, Winterbotham was to remark that

> Our classification has been based on rigid rules of width and surface ... A fellow now upon the road is faced with a whole variety of widths, but mainly of a surface which to the map makers of fifteen years ago would have been of the first class. Indeed the classification is beginning to depend much more upon whether that is the best road of the neighbourhood than upon whether it is 17 feet wide or under 14.[13]

The distinctions between width, surfacing, and route function, and which of these should have priority in any classification, were to be contentious subjects in discussions between the Ordnance Survey and Ministry of Transport in the 1920s and 1930s.

The vexed question of road classification was aired publicly in 1892. At that time, three categories of road were distinguished on the New Series map: turnpike or main roads, ordinary metalled, and minor roads (including carriage drives and cart roads; fig.23a). This threefold classification was designed specifically in response to requests from the driving public for improvements in the ways that roads were shown at the one-inch scale.[14] It appeared on New Series maps from 1886, when, for the first time, a legend was printed in the bottom margin of the one-inch sheets of England and Wales. The depiction of these different road categories followed directly from a change, in 1885, in the way that roads were shown on the published 1:2500 plans: between 1885 and 1912, the south and east sides of first and second class roads that were metalled[15] and kept in good repair were shaded, that is, drawn with a thicker line. The purpose of this new specification was to enable the one-inch draughtsman more easily to select primary and secondary routes from the large-scale plans for transfer to the one-inch map on which they were also shown with a shaded line.[16]

12 PRO OS 1/2/5. Wilson specified, in 1893, that one-inch road classification should agree with military requirements.

13 Winterbotham, (1934b), p.122.

14 Pilkington White, (1886), p.103.

15 Metalling was a term used to described any hard surface made up of broken stones.

16 OSL G3962. A series of circulars, entitled 'Roads, Carriage Drives, &c.' and dated 28/4/1884, 25/6/1884, 30/11/1885, and 8/7/1886 relate to the use of the shaded line on the 1:2500 plans to distinguish roads 'kept in proper repair and under the Supervision of district Surveyors'. The shaded line was also to be used for carriage drives (i.e. private roads) that were metalled and kept in good repair; in this case, the shading for the private roads was to be 'less prominent' than the shading for second class roads. In practice, it is not possible to distinguish, on the printed plans, any universal systematic difference in the gauge of the shaded line between known public and private roads, nor between first and second class roads. These circulars, and their effect on the large-scale plans, are discussed in detail in Y. Hodson, 'Roads on OS 1:2500 plans 1884-1912' *Rights of Way Law Review*, (1999) Section 9.3: 107-118.

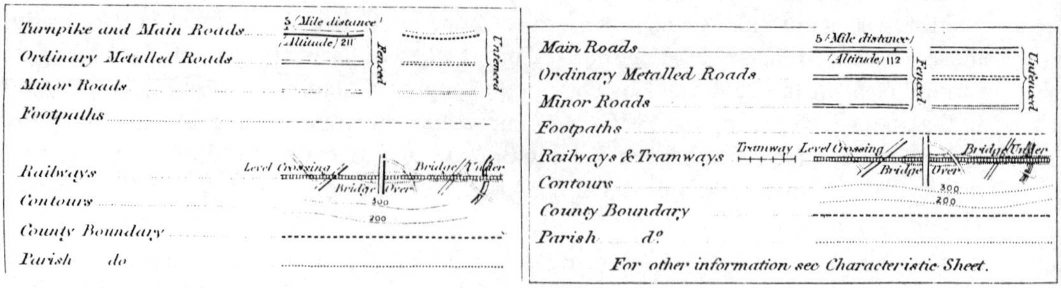

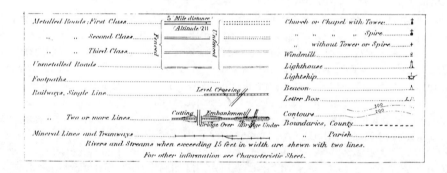

Fig.23a New Series legends from sheet 85 (1886) and sheet 328 (1892) showing the three-fold classification of roads. The category of turnpike road was dropped from legends from 1892.

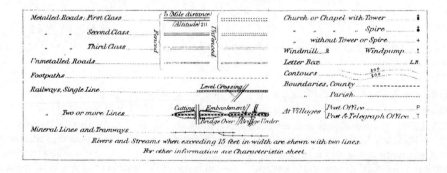

Fig.23b Revised New Series legend from sheet 225 (1895) showing the fourfold classification. First and second class roads were printed in yellow for the coloured Revised New Series.

Fig.23c Third Edition legend from sheet 297 (1906). The fourfold classification is the same as the Revised New Series; first and second class roads were printed in orange for the coloured versions of the Third Edition. All *private collection.*

Even so, the consensus of opinion among those giving evidence to the Dorington Committee in 1892 was that it was still not easily possible to tell the difference between classes of route on the map either at the large or the small scale unless one were acquainted with the area; and impossible altogether if the key were not present in the bottom margin (it might have been cropped in the process of mounting and folding). There was no doubt, as Wilson had stated, that there had been 'so many complaints' about the way roads were shown on Ordnance Survey maps.[17] Similar views had been expressed by officers giving evidence to the Baker Committee which had sat just a few months earlier. Their main concern was that roads passable by military vehicles should be clearly shown, perhaps by being printed in brown, and that a distinction ought to be made between metalled and unmetalled roads. However, one officer was more specific and suggested that surface conditions should be linked to width. Lieut.-Col. John Farquharson, who was to become Director General from 1894 to 1899 (and under whom Close served), recommended a fourfold scheme which included metalled roads of 18ft, 12ft, and 9ft widths and unmetalled tracks. This suggestion of classification by width and surface was taken up at the Dorington Committee where 14ft became the accepted measurement for first class roads; this width was still current for the Popular Edition nearly thirty years later. These changes were introduced specifically with the aim of 'adding to the value of the map for military purposes'.[18]

The proposals made in 1892 that turnpike and main roads should be amalgamated[19] were, in fact, carried out on some sheets of the New Series (fig.23a), but classification based on width and surface only came into force consistently with the Revised New Series, and continued, with minor modifications, onto the copperplates of the Third Edition Small Sheets on which the Popular Edition was based. In this way, the Popular inherited, for example, the mile figures between towns along the roads.[20] Before the publication of the Popular Edition, neither the legend on the one-inch map nor the characteristic sheet informed the user that width was a factor in classifying the roads. The precise description was confined to internal revisers' instructions which, for the Revised New Series, were brief:

> First class roads ... are main trunk roads, generally leading from town to town. They must be metalled and kept in good repair; and the *minimum* width of metalled roadway exclusive of edges or footway must be *fourteen feet*.[21]

17 Dorington, (1893c), para.5909.

18 *Annual Report*, (1904-5), p.11.

19 Dorington, (1893c), para.4495.

20 But the figures on the Popular Edition did not always correspond with those on the Third; towns from which the distance was measured were varied, for example on sheet 12, the distance on one of the roads from Keswick to Cockermouth was counted from Keswick on the Third Edition; this was reversed on the Popular. No instruction appears to survive which gives the criteria for selecting points of departure. According to the 1914 drawing instructions, mile marks were supposed, as a rule, 'to correspond with milestones on the ground.' Distances were otherwise to be measured. Mileages appeared only on 'main routes between towns, over 14ft of metalling'.

21 Ordnance Survey *Instructions for the revision of the one-inch map in the field*, (16/3/1896).

The same instructions described second class roads as

metalled roads in good repair, and fit for fast traffic at all seasons i.e., it should be possible to drive carriages and light carts over them at a trot. They are inferior to first class roads in width, but should be sufficiently wide, in all parts, to allow two carts to pass each other without difficulty.

Third class roads were

all other metalled roads suitable for wheeled traffic. This class will include all metalled roads which are not wide enough to allow two carts to pass each other; or which from want of repair are not fit for fast traffic.

Fourth class roads were all unmetalled. Private roads were similarly classified on the printed map.[22]

A further expansion on what was meant by the terms first and second class is contained in a circular dated December 1896,[23] in which it was stated that

roads should be classed as 1st & 2nd class according as they are returned by the Surveyor to each Rural District Council as Main or District roads. It will be necessary to distinguish metalled roads from unmetalled roads & drives, and to show Occupation Roads, Bridle Paths &c.

In order to implement this directive, the revising Superintendent was to be provided with a one-inch map showing the area of each Rural District Council (RDC). The Superintendent was then to ask the RDC Surveyor to indicate which were the Main and District roads; the two categories of roads were to be marked on the one-inch map in different colours. To complete the process, the RDC Surveyor was then to sign and date the map to confirm that 'All roads shown in Red on this map are Main Roads. Those in Blue are District Roads.' in the top right hand margin. None of these maps seems to have survived.

Even this circular seems to have left some doubt in the minds of revisers about the meaning of the classification system, for within six months, another circular on roads[24] stated that first class roads were defined as 'all roads classed by the County Surveyor as Main Roads. There are no other 1st Class Roads.' Second class roads were 'other good roads, whether public district roads or not' that were metalled and kept in good repair. These second class roads were to be distinguished on the field revision cards according to whether they were public or parish roads, metalled occupation roads, or main carriage drives. For the most part, these second class roads were taken to be lines of communication between villages and towns and railways stations, or between one main road and another, but, 'Their condition as fit for wheeled traffic is the chief point to be noted.' Third class roads included public roads, occupation roads and 'old metalled roads not kept in repair or roughly metalled or not metalled &c'.

The inclusion in the third class category of unmetalled roads is something of a conundrum, in view of the statement in the one-inch instructions of 16 March 1896 that

---

22 *Annual Report*, (1904/5), p.12.

23 Photocopy of a manuscript notebook 'the property of Mr Cawsey, Boundary Department, Ordnance Survey', made by the late J.B. Harley, and very kindly made available to the author by Richard Oliver.

24 Cawsey, *op.cit.,* 'Circular Roads 31/5/97'.

these constituted fourth class roads. Since fourth class roads were definitely included in the conventional signs for the one-inch series relevant to this date - the Revised New Series - it may be that these two circulars applied to the 1:2500 plans; unfortunately, the circulars make no mention of the scales to which they refer. However, they may well have been relevant to the large-scale plans, for the descriptions of the three classes of road match the 1885 specification to show metalled roads kept in good repair by a shaded line (in force until 1912), and unmetalled roads, or unrepaired roads without the shaded line (see p.129, footnote 16). If this is indeed the case, it underlines the point that it is not possible to distinguish public roads on the large-scale plans solely by the use of the shaded line.

Requests had been made in both of the 1892 committees for a distinction to be made between public and private roads - it had formerly been too easy to plan a route only to find that one was unable to pursue it because it crossed private land. Bartholomew, in his evidence to the Dorington Committee, had pressed for a distinction to be made between private and public roads on the Ordnance map, but had to admit that when his firm had tried to do the same, it had involved them in legal proceedings.[25] Bartholomew's one-inch map *Environs of Keswick, Grasmere, &c.*, published in the 1880s, had amplified the rather brief legend by actually describing routes on the face of the map as 'pony track', 'cart track', 'footpath' and, in at least one instance, 'private road'.

Routes on Ordnance Survey maps were not to be given such overt identification. It was stated in the 1896 one-inch instructions that private roads were classified in the same way as ordinary public roads on Ordnance Survey maps; there was therefore no means of distinguishing between the two. Only on the field sheet was the identification to be made clear by the addition of the letters 'P.R.' which did not, however, appear on the printed map, so that the manuscript record was useless for public purposes. These field sheets do not survive. No distinction between public and private roads was made either in the legend of the published map, or on the characteristic sheet until the publication of the Popular Edition on which it was stated that private roads were uncoloured. Even here, it was impossible to identify, on the map, the difference between a minor road and a private road, both of which were uncoloured; all that could be said was that all private roads were uncoloured, but not all uncoloured roads were private.

The anomaly was only realised in 1934, when Winterbotham gave instructions on 12 February that the statement 'Private roads are uncoloured', which had always appeared on the Popular Edition sheets, and on the early issues of the Fifth Edition, was to be deleted from the legend on all future Fifth Edition sheets.[26] From some point in 1935, the statement was also omitted from some reprints of the Popular Edition (Plate 10e). It is arguable that the statement should never have been included in the first place because it contradicted the Ordnance Survey's strongly made assertions that no distinction was

25 Dorington, (1893c), paras 1767-72.

26 PRO OS 1/312. Minute 104, 15/2/1934. However, it may be possible to use Fifth Edition one-inch sheets as supporting evidence for the identification of a road as private if a gate is shown at each end of the road, and it can be demonstrated that gates existed in between at the time of survey; see Ordnance Survey *Instructions for the revision and drawing of the one-inch (Fifth Edition) map*, (1936), p.7., para.18.

made in the status of the routes on their maps. In this case it would surely be reasonable for the user to infer that, if private roads were uncoloured, all coloured roads were public. The rights of way disclaimer might have been more accurately worded to read that 'an uncoloured Road, or Track or Footpath, is no evidence of the existence of a right of way.'

The warning, issued in 1896, that roads were to be classed according to their general character overall, and not on their 'best or worst portions', was reinforced with a caution that no classification was to be altered unless 'clearly necessary'. Revisers worked in all weathers, at all times of year; what, in winter, appeared to be an impassable quagmire, would in summer be rated more highly. Clearly, matters of opinion were obstructing the course of true classification, hence 'the condition of minor roads is apt to vary from year to year'. When framing his rules in 1909 for the third revision of the one-inch (that is, the first, abortive, third revision), Grant made no additions to a now well-established formula. The care that had been taken to allow as little room as possible for misinterpretation of the classification had a greater significance than merely lessening the burden of unnecessary alterations for the engraver. For in this one instance of road classification the basic large-scale plans now relied upon the small scale-map, and had done so for at least eight years.

In 1901 a new procedure had been introduced which was to remain current during the lifetime of the Popular Edition. In a circular entitled 'Classification of roads on the 1/2500 and 6-inch scales',[27] it was laid down that the categories represented on the one-inch map were 'in future [to] apply also to the larger scales'. Since the one-inch revisers dealt with a larger area of country than the large-scale reviser, they were more likely to 'arrive at a uniform classification', and therefore one-inch data were to be used as far as possible for the large scales. It was, of course, inevitable that differences of opinion would occur, and that discrepancies would 'also arise owing to the revision on the 1-inch and on the larger scales not being of the same date'. In these cases, no alterations were to be made on the large-scale sheets until they came up for revision. The same principle was to apply to one-inch sheets. The result was that different classifications existed side by side, even on adjacent sheets, until revision had worked its way through the series. This was exactly the case with the Popular Edition, whose sheets went through several minor classification changes in twenty years. The system of uniform criteria for all scales had great merit because it provided a valuable cross-check on accuracy, for 'should in the course of large-scale revision serious and palpable errors of classification be found on the 1-inch scale, they should be reported ... with a view to their correction on the 1-inch map.' This principle was to pass down, virtually unaltered, until after 1945.[28]

The fourfold classification (five, if footpaths were included) of the Revised New Series and the Third Edition was to be replaced in the Popular Edition by a new concept that Close and his colleagues may well have derived from commercial practice, for Bartholomew was already producing his half-inch maps with a similar tenfold

27 Circular C.C.146. (16/9/1901).
28 Ordnance Survey *Instructions to field revisers 1/2500 scale*, (1932). Amended issue April 1936, with pasted in printed amendments dating post-1945.

classification.[29] This revised structure contained no less than thirteen categories, which had first been used for the 1914 experimental maps of *Torquay & Dartmouth* and *Aldershot District (North)* and *(South)*. It was first announced by Close during the proceedings of the Olivier Committee[30] where he referred to its use on an outline map of Dartmouth. In fact, the thirteen categories are only made up by including bridle/footpaths and unfenced roads, and when they are grouped together, it can be seen that they still fall within a fourfold hierarchy (Plate 10a):

I **Main routes between towns, over 14ft of metalling** [gauge[31]:0.5mm]

   1 good and fit for fast traffic [2 thick lines, red infill]

   2 fit for ordinary traffic [2 thick lines, yellow infill]

   3 indifferent or winding [2 thick lines, yellow dashed infill]

II **Other roads, over 14ft of metalling** [gauge: 0.4mm]

   4 good and fit for fast traffic [1 thick line, 1 thin line, red infill]

   5 fit for ordinary traffic [1 thick line, 1 thin line, yellow infill]

   6 indifferent or winding [1 thick line, 1 thin line, yellow dashed infill]

III **Roads under 14ft wide [presumably metalled]** [gauge: 0.3mm]

   7 fit for ordinary traffic [2 thin lines, yellow infill]

   8 indifferent or winding [2 thin lines, yellow dashed infill]

   9 bad [2 thin lines, uncoloured]

IV **[other categories]**

   10 minor roads [uncoloured; gauge: 0.1mm]

   11 private roads [uncoloured, therefore equal to either **9** or **10**]

   12 bridle and footpaths [dashed lines]

   13 unfenced roads [any category, dotted lines]

In essence, however, this new one-inch scheme was merely the old classification dressed up in colours on the printed map to give the extra information on surface quality: the private roads, although mentioned in the map legend and on the conventional signs sheet, were indistinguishable from bad roads under 14ft wide or minor roads and therefore constituted either the old third class metalled roads or the fourth class unmetalled roads of the Revised New Series and Third Edition. By using colour, rather than line, as the dominant distinguishing feature between the first eight categories, the need for excessive re-engraving of the copperplate, or alteration on the stones, for the first three classes

---

29 'First class' [3 divisions]; 'Through routes'; 'Secondary (good)' [3 widths]; 'Indifferent (passable)'; 'Footpaths'; 'Inferior'. This classification appeared on printings from at least August 1901. NLS, Bartholomew Printing Archive.

30 Olivier, (1914a), para.432.

31 The space between the double lines of the road, measured with a x15 loupe, with a scale graduated in tenths of a millimetre.

could be avoided. Nevertheless, it is clear that a considerable amount of re-engraving - either thinning or thickening of the lines - was carried out on the Third Edition copperplates that came to make up the Popular Edition. These alterations to the line-work of the roads must have taken a huge number of man-hours to achieve.[32]

Even so, it was no easy matter to distinguish, at a glance, between categories 2, 5 and 7, which were printed in yellow (Plate 10a). It seems that at some point it was realised that the yellow roads[33] in category 7 - that is, roads shown by thin double lines under 14ft wide fit for ordinary traffic - could also be main (in the sense of most important in a local context) routes between settlements, but could not be identified as such from the map legend. In order to make this clear to the map user, the word 'main'[34] was added to category 7 in the legend from about 1924.[35] Since this word did not appear alongside the appropriate road on the map itself, it was still possible to confuse all three solid yellow roads, especially in a bad light. In any case, it seems odd that the word 'main' should not also have been added to category 4 roads in the legend, and the occasional addition of the qualifier 'other roads' to category 8 only served to confuse the message further. Added to this, the gauge of the roads on the face of the map did not always match that in the legend: an example of this can be seen on sheet 96, squares H9, 10, 11 and J10, 11, where the road from Hatfield Heath to Chipping Ongar is shown in yellow on the 1919 and 1923 printings. The thin lines and yellow colour would seem to indicate a road under 14ft wide, but the width of the engraved road suggests a category II route (in later reprints, much of this road was printed in red). Clearly, the map user would not be able to interpret such features unequivocally.

The scheme for the Popular Edition was a modified form of one which was devised by a committee which assembled at the War Office at Close's instigation in February 1912.[36] Its chairman was Sir Aylmer Hunter Weston, and evidence was taken from,

---

32 The 1914 instructions refer, on page 12, para.69, to the alteration of the gauge, and the thinning of shaded [i.e. thickened] lines, as a result of reclassification. A comparison of, for example, Third Edition Small Sheet Series sheet 221 (*Hitchin*) with Popular Edition sheet 96 (*Hertford & Bishop's Stortford*) shows a considerable amount of revision to the line-work of the roads.

33 For some reason, unexplained, the official Ordnance Survey *Descriptions* of the small-scale maps always referred to the colour of the 'medium' roads - a phrase never used on the map or conventional signs sheet - as brown. This colour does not appear to have been used much for secondary roads on the regular sheets of the Popular Edition, and seems to have been confined to some of the very early printings (e.g. sheet 119), and to the 1940s printings (e.g. sheet 135). Colours could vary considerably on otherwise identical states, e.g. sheet 75 (1920). True brown was used for main roads on the Fifth Edition-based *Aldershot (North)*, 1932, sheet, and was criticised for being indistinct against the shaded relief background; the same criticism was made of the brown primary roads on the early issues of the Fifth (Relief) Edition.

34 The use of the word 'main' on the one-inch map was objected to in 1928 by the Ministry of Transport (PRO OS 1/312. Minute 27, 30/11/1928) on the grounds that it denoted a legal obligation on the part of the County Councils to maintain the road. In 1914 the Ordnance Survey claimed that their classification was made irrespective of who was responsible for maintenance (Olivier, (1914a), para.925) in spite of the circulars of 1895-6 (see p.134); however, the word 'main' remained on the Popular Edition maps until it began to be replaced by MOT classification in 1935.

35 Only one sheet, 30 (published in the last quarter of 1924), has been recorded for 1924 with this convention. All other known examples were printed from 1925 onwards.

36 Ordnance Survey *Instructions to field revisers and draftsmen ...*, (1924), p.13.

among others, the Secretary of the Royal Automobile Club and Lord Montagu of Beaulieu, who was Chairman of the Road Board.[37] One of the duties of this Board, which had been set up in 1910, was to design a suitable road classification system for motorists; and so the War Office Committee represented the major interests of the day. The full details of the scheme, as adopted by the Ordnance Survey, were apparently not set out in print until the 1924 instructions for field revision of the small scale maps. Entitled 'Principles of road classification' (transcribed in Appendix 6), it gave the three main considerations in classifying roads: width, quality, and importance. Width and importance were to be shown by the drawn symbol (thickness and spacing of the lines), while quality was indicated by colour. The rule was that colour was not to be used for private or minor roads, or for a road that was not easily passable by wheeled traffic; the map user would then realise that 'if he takes an uncoloured road, he does so at his own risk'.

In 1920, the newly formed Ministry of Transport took on, as one of its main tasks, the completion of the road classification which had been begun by its predecessor, the Road Board.[38] There followed a decade of discussions in which the Ministry endeavoured to persuade the Ordnance Survey to follow their system. The primary obstacle to an amicable union between the two was the Survey's insistence on showing the roads as they physically were; this conflicted with the Ministry's criterion of importance of the route, regardless of surface. In fact, the differences were not critical, for virtually all Ordnance Survey 'main' routes corresponded with Ministry 'A' roads; the conflict arose when an 'A' road fell below the exacting standards of an Ordnance Survey 'main route' with over fourteen feet of metalling. By 1932, improvements in roads and vehicles had 'rendered the road classification ... used for the Popular Edition very much out of date',[39] and it was proposed to restrict the definition of primary roads to those of twenty feet and over.[40] However, a width of eighteen feet had been adopted for the new Fifth Edition,[41] and so it was decided to conform to the new specification and simplify the classification of the Popular by using a threefold system based on 'principal' roads of eighteen feet and over, secondary roads of fourteen to eighteen feet and other metalled roads.

The point of this plan, which was approved by Winterbotham, was that it would avoid the necessity of altering widths of roads on the stones.[42] In appearance, the roads legend which reflected this policy on the Popular Edition closely resembled that used for some of the early 1920s tourist sheets, on which the surface distinctions had been omitted, so that the old four classes of roads, now shown in colour, were easily apparent. The width of eighteen feet (Plate 10c) appears to have been used for only five sheets of the Popular Edition,[43] four of which were reprinted in 1933 and one in 1934. As far as the Popular

---

37 Olivier, (1914b), p.30.

38 Barker and Savage, (1974), p.188.

39 PRO OS 1/312. Minute 54, 14/7/1932.

40 *Ibid.*

41 Oliver, (1989a), p.16.

42 PRO OS 1/312. Minute 56, 18/7/1932.

43 Sheets 20, 30, 82, 96 (all 1933), 45 (1934).

was concerned, this width definition was cancelled by January 1934,[44] and all sheets, including reprints of the above five 1933-4 maps, were to retain the road classification which was in force when the Popular Edition first appeared 'i.e. with a great many first class roads'. With hindsight, it is easy to see that this short-lived scheme was, without doubt, the least complex and most practical of the classifications which predated the adoption of the Ministry of Transport system.

The description of roads on the Fifth Edition was also reviewed.[45] It had already been acknowledged that too many classes of roads were shown on the Popular, and that the distinction between them was too small to be of any practical value. Now it was suggested that any mention of width should be dropped from the legends of small-scale maps because it made the classification too rigid and served no real civil purpose. This suggestion was implemented for the Fifth Edition, but here the Ministry of Transport road numbers were drawn on the map, whereas they never seem to have appeared on Popular Edition sheets, whose road classification was already out of sympathy with modern road construction in the north of England by 1934. As more and more roads were improved and brought up to what warranted an Ordnance Survey first class description, so the one-inch map became covered with an increasing number of red roads. Nevertheless, a ruling was made in 1934 that

> The Popular Edition England and Wales will be left on the classification which it already shows ... The only alterations in editions will be those of colour and insertion perhaps of new roads.[46]

This situation was not to persist. The three categories of roads under fourteen feet on the Popular Edition: fit for ordinary traffic, indifferent or winding, and bad, were represented on the Fifth Edition by good, indifferent, and bad. But what, asked Winterbotham, would the average motorist do when faced with an indifferent road on the map? 'It is better to tell him flatly good or bad. Indifferent will be eliminated.'[47] The note about indifferent and private roads was to be dropped from the legend of the Popular,[48] but only after a change in the specification which brought the classification of roads into line with the Ministry of Transport system. For the Fifth Edition, the new classification, embracing 'A' and 'B' roads, together with their numbers, was adopted in full in 1934, but to do so for the Popular Edition would have resulted in more alteration to the stones. In order to avoid this problem, the 'B' roads were all grouped into the Popular classification of secondary ('Other Motor Roads') and minor roads, without this being stated either in the legend (Plate 10d) on the map, or on the conventional signs sheet, even when this was revised in 1937. Another advantage claimed for this scheme

---

44 PRO OS 1/312. Minute 101, 5/1/1934.

45 PRO OS 1/312. Minute 71, 24/10/1932.

46 PRO OS 1/312. Minute 102, 9/1/1934.

47 *Ibid.* The three Fifth Edition categories were shown on the 1932 conventional signs sheet, and in the legends on some of the sheets themselves. The category of 'indifferent' was omitted from the 1935 Fifth Edition conventional signs sheet.

48 On some War Revision sheets indifferent roads were distinguished by a chequered pattern in the same colour as that of the main and secondary roads (e.g. sheet 17, 1940-2). This compromise was clearly thought worthwhile for military purposes, but was not adopted for the civil version of the map.

was that the number of red roads on the Popular would be reduced; this is borne out by the later states of many of the sheets in the series.

It is small wonder, in view of the constantly changing road conditions, that Winterbotham was to suggest, in 1934, that the Ordnance Survey should 'give up and announce that we are giving up the road classification in favour of a quick production of the classification of another government department.'[49] Because the roads were classified by width (line) and surface (colour), both, in theory, should have been altered to keep pace with improvement. In practice, the expense of revising the width on the stone or negative was prohibitive, and usually only the colour would be changed.[50] The Survey's rigid rules had been overtaken by the better road construction of the day, which meant that the surfaces of an increasing number of roads were fast meeting the Ordnance Survey's first class criteria. But even the simpler Ministry of Transport based scheme, announced in the *Annual Report* for 1934/5, and which was introduced on the Popular Edition from 1935[51] was not easy to interpret on the map, because the legend gave two distinct symbols for 'A' roads and two for 'other motor roads', without explaining the difference (Plate 10c, d). Even though the variation was only a matter of line thickness in the casing, it was clearly visible on, for example, the drawn maps covering the borders of England and Scotland. No description has been found which defines the differences, and the contemporary user might have inferred that the distinction was one of width or surface, or both. The new classification was as confusing as those it sought to simplify.[52]

Road revision

The development of road classification, then, as it emerges on the Popular Edition sheets, is not a straightforward story, and any historian of transport using this map as a tool would have to make judgements which could only be subjective in nature. On the other hand, the map is a valuable aid in plotting, at a reasonable scale for England and Wales as a whole, the improvement in road conditions and the construction of new roads in the period after 1925. In that year, the problem of representing the state of the roads on the one-inch and smaller scales had become so acute, that a special road revision exercise was carried out for the one-inch map,[53] but the publication of the information was not soon enough to prevent a question being asked in Parliament about when the Ordnance Survey maps would begin to show the new trunk roads which had been completed in the

---

49 Winterbotham, (1934b), p.122.

50 PRO OS 1/54. Minute 100, 22/6/1934. Although this Minute is on a file dealing with quarter-inch maps, it may be reasonable to assume that this practice was common to the small scales.

51 This date is based on an analysis of the different printings of the sheets. No sheet printed before 1935 has been seen with the MOT classification.

52 In addition to the road classification system, a common feature of many sheets is that minor roads are named; thus 'Flamborough Road' (sheet 23 squares J12-13), 'Bluestone Heath Road' (sheet 40 square J5), and 'Bury Lane' (sheet 76 squares G-H9). No written rule governing this practice has been found, but the names were presumably taken from the large-scale plans; they also appeared on previous one-inch series.

53 *Annual Report,* (1925/6), p.1. Some Popular Edition sheets were road-revised in 1924: 124, 133, 134, 138-140, 143, 146.

previous three years.[54] A continuous programme of road revision developed, so that all sheets, as they came up for reprinting included, hypothetically, up to date classification (insofar as that could be ascertained) and new roads. Whilst it is obvious that new arterial roads were shown, and upgrading of coloured roads was made, it is not yet clear how comprehensive this road revision was. The implication of the map evidence so far studied is that revision was focused on roads over fourteen feet wide.

In theory, therefore, it should be possible to determine how frequently roads were kept up to date simply by looking at the overall picture of the reprinting programme for England and Wales. In practice, according to the marginal statements on road revision which appeared on many reprints, and which can be corroborated by examination of the maps themselves, many sheets were reprinted once or twice without change. The omission of road revision notes in the bottom margin should not be construed to mean that none took place, as study of these sheets will show.[55] On the other hand, several of these revision notes conflict with the dates given in the annual reports and also contradict themselves between states (e.g. sheets 119, 120 and 143).

The first indexes to show the state of road revision of the one-inch map subsequent to the third revision appeared in the annual reports for 1926/7[56] and 1927/8. They need to be interpreted carefully, for not all the revision shown on the indexes was available in published form: sheets 61 and 62, for example were first printed in 1921, and were not reprinted until 1933, by which time the first unpublished road revision was out of date and a new one had to be made. Another similarly misleading index was given in the Annual Report for 1931/2; the dates of road revision shown there bore little relation to the dates of publication of the one-inch map. The only point, for example, in revising the roads for sheet 66, which was never reprinted, would be to provide information for the large scales, and it could be that these revisions become more significant if they are studied in conjunction with the large-scale plans which took road classification information from the smaller scale. However, at the beginning of 1934, another parliamentary questioner suggested that few Ordnance Survey large-scale maps showed arterial or bypass roads,[57] he received no answer; and when the question was repeated ten months later it elicited the response that 90% of the arterial roads were shown on the one-inch scale, and that 'no such roads are shown on the 25" or 6" maps except those in the close proximity of some of the larger towns.'[58]

The accuracy of some of the dates for road revision is therefore in doubt. Even so, many of the one-inch sheets showed road information which was in advance of publication of the large scales, and the development of ring roads is demonstrated especially well when reprints were frequent. The case of Norwich (sheet 67) is an

---

54 Parliamentary Debates. H.C.Deb.5s.198, 3/8/1926.

55 None of the reprints of sheet 19, for example, indicate that road revision has taken place, but reclassifications are apparent on each state. Similarly, those sheets printed in or after 1935, and which carry no road note, usually show road revision in urban areas.

56 Road revision had actually begun in 1924 (see footnote 53, p.139).

57 Parliamentary Reports. H.C.Deb.5s.285, 1/2/1934.

58 Parliamentary Reports. H.C.Deb.5s.296, 17/12/1934.

excellent example of this (Plate 9a-d).[59] Although Winterbotham had decried the use of the one-inch as a motoring map, it was quite evident that failure to keep up to date with the construction of new roads had had an adverse affect on sales, particularly in tourist areas. In 1934 the omission of the new Blackgang road on the Isle of Wight sheet was said to be 'killing sales',[60] and Hotine[61] made a strong case for including all new roads on reprint, even if a sheet were to be replaced by the Fifth Edition within two years. This policy was certainly applied to the London sheets where new symbols of dashed parallel lines for roads under construction, which were shown neither on map legend nor conventional signs sheet, appeared from 1926 allowing, for example, the course of the new Kingston bypass on sheet 114 (1927) to be plotted. Rapid road revisers had been appointed in the 1930s whose rate of progress in the London area was eighteen square miles a month - not so rapid compared with the monthly rate of forty square miles expected from a normal reviser in the same decade, but reflecting the priority given to keeping communications mapping up to date, at least on the small scales.[62]

Gradients

A new symbol to appear on the Popular Edition - for gradients - was an innovation on the Ordnance Survey one-inch map. It was not, however, a concept which was new to British cartography, for Bacon's maps showing 'danger hills', by colour-printed symbols which distinguished 'hills to be ridden with caution' from 'hills dangerous', had been popular with cyclists at the end of the nineteenth century.[63] So, too, had the graded road maps of Gall and Inglis, whose triangular symbols for bad and steep hills, fairly cluttered their tourist map of the Lake District; the same firm's contoured road books were also popular.[64] The Michelin maps at 1:200,000 had shown three gradients[65] by one, two, or three arrows which pointed up the direction of the slope. For a short period at the end of the nineteenth century, Bartholomew's half-inch maps had also shown hills dangerous for cyclists by arrows pointing downhill. However, this was abandoned in the early 1900s because there were, among those of the Cyclists' Touring Club who carried out the revision of the sheets, 'so many differences of opinion as to what constituted a "dangerous hill"' that it was decided to delete the symbol.[66] The technique using arrows pointing downhill was adopted by the Ordnance Survey for the Popular Edition.

---

59 Perhaps the best sheet for showing the proliferation of bypasses is 110 (1000/24.2000/32), on which no less than seven new constructions are recorded, while on the 1931 printing of 143, the St Austell bypass is hurriedly included without any black casing.

60 PRO OS 1/312. Memorandum 107 by Martin Hotine, 31/10/1934.

61 Captain Martin Hotine, Head of the Trigonometrical Division, and of the Map Sales and Issues Branch.

62 Langstaff and Sainsbury, (1974). In the 1960s an 'intelligence system' was established with the MOT and Local Divisional Road Engineers to keep road representation on the one-inch up to date, (OS *Technical Bulletin* no.2, Dec.1960).

63 Nicholson, (1983a).

64 The word 'contour' was used in the sense of 'shape'; only the profiles of the hills, together with gradients were shown, contours in the cartographic sense were not. The Michelin maps also used the word contour in this way.

65 1 in 20 to 1 in 14; 1 in 14 to 1 in 10, and over 1 in 10.

66 NLS, Bartholomew Archive: Acc 10222 III B25 f.118. Bartholomew to Robert Redhead, 21/7/1910.

The first Ordnance Survey one-inch maps to show gradients were the 1914 *Torquay & Dartmouth*, and *Aldershot (North)* and *(South)* sheets (Chapter I).[67] The cheap contoured version of the Torquay map (which does not appear to have survived) had been printed before 17 June 1914, for on that day it was shown, complete with gradient symbols, to a witness to the Olivier Committee in response to his request for steep inclines to be marked on Ordnance Survey maps. In common with the Aldershot sheets, two gradients were indicated: 'slopes 1/10 to 1/7', indicated by one arrow-head, and 'steeper than 1/7', which were shown by two arrows. It is doubtless more than a coincidence that these gradients were exactly the same as those described in the 1912 *Manual of map reading and field sketching* which was produced by the General Staff of the War Office. On page 25 of this book it is stated that a slope of 1/7 was practicable for artillery over short distances, and that a gradient of 1/10 was passable for transport animals. Steeper than 1/10 was 'inconvenient for animals or wheeled traffic.'

The precise date at which the decision to include slope values on the one-inch map was taken is not known, because the key document, the revisers' instructions for 1914, does not appear to have survived. It would seem that at some point in 1914, it was decided to show only one gradient value, for slopes steeper than 1/7. This was the form in which it was given on the Popular Edition, but the explicit reasons for restricting the information to one set of values have not been found. A clue to the explanation is provided by the Aldershot 1914 maps. On only one state of these are the two values given; the other two states show only those slopes steeper than 1/7. A census of the symbols shows that for 45 single arrows indicating the gentler slope, only six marked the steeper inclines. In view of the emphatic statement at the Olivier Committee by the representative of the Automobile Association that 'to a man with a powerful car a hill is of no moment ... practically, the car does not exist today which will avoid a hill ... bar such as those in the Lynton district',[68] it may well have been decided that it was unnecessary to show the gentler slopes.

Two values for slopes (steeper than 1/5, and over 1/7 but under 1/5) were to be reintroduced for the Fifth Edition.[69] The first surviving instructions to include gradients are those for 1924, which answer the question 'how were gradients measured?':

> three observations with the curved bicycle level should be taken at the steepest part of the hill at say 5 yards interval, and the average taken as the maximum gradient. Arrows are inserted in blue on the road sheets, at the steepest point of the gradient.[70]

Gradients were only shown, pointing down the slope,[71] on the first three classes of road, and this was equivalent, on the Fifth Edition, to Ministry of Transport classified roads

67 GSGS 3036, *Map of East Anglia,* (1914), scale 2½ inches to 1 mile, showed slopes of 6° and over by an arrow, which pointed downhill: illustrated in Clark, (1983), p.3.

68 Olivier, (1914a), para.894.

69 OS *Instructions for the revision and drawing of the one-inch (Fifth Edition) map*, (1936), p.8, para.22.

70 Ordnance Survey *Instructions to field revisers and draftsmen ...*, (1924), p.22, para.55.

71 The explanation that the arrows were to point downhill was given only in the instructions; it was taken for granted that the map user could read contours, but during the Davidson Committee proceedings, a request was made for the direction to be explained on the map (this was never done) because 'most people take it for granted that the arrows point up hills'. OSL G5186, OSC 72, 13/2/1936.

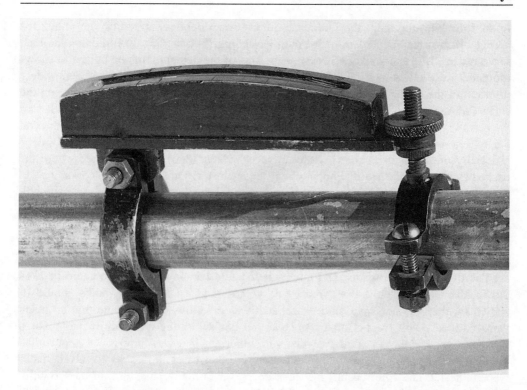

Fig.24 Curved bicycle level, [1930s]. This example was possibly used for the Fifth Edition. *Private collection.*

and tarred roads.[72] The bicycle level (fig.24) must have been developed specifically for this purpose, for F.J. Mortlock, in the Stores Department, was awarded £4 in February 1915 for inventing a 'curved level for fixing to top bar of 1" reviser's bicycle frame'.[73] The level was still in use in the 1960s.[74] The word 'slope' was replaced in the map legend by 'gradient' for the Scottish Popular and the Fifth (Relief) and succeeding one-inch editions; this convention has so far only been found on Popular Edition sheet 1, on the 15/37.M.36.R.32. printing.

Footpaths

By the 1930s, the emphasis on the one-inch as a road map in Ordnance Survey advertising material had shifted away from the motorist towards the pedestrian:

> For walking in particular "One-Inch" maps are essential, as it is impossible to delineate on any smaller scale the footpaths, byways, antiquities and many other details which give charm to the countryside.[75]

---

72 Ordnance Survey *Instructions for the revision and drawing of the one-inch (Fifth Edition) map,* (1936), p.25, para.32.

73 Circular C.C.520.

74 Ordnance Survey *Instructions for small scales revision (The Green Book 1961),* (Sept.1961); with amendments to 1963. Appendix A: representation of detail.

75 Ordnance Survey *Abridged List ...* [1938], OS Leaflet No.**6**/38.

In so describing the map, the Ordnance Survey was doubtless targeting the vogue for hiking which spread in tandem with Youth Hostelling. But just how well did the one-inch serve the needs of the walker? Several criticisms of the depiction of, or failure to show, footpaths were made to the Dorington Committee in 1892. Footpaths had been widely inserted on the eighteenth-century three-inch and and six-inch drawings from which the early Old Series one-inch sheets had been compiled, but very few had been included on the resulting printed maps.[76] This is not to say that no footpaths were marked on the Old Series one-inch map, for several can be found, shown by a single dashed line,[77] especially on the Welsh sheets, while on sheet 79NE (1840), is an example where the dashed symbol has the word 'Footway' written against it. On some of the Yorkshire Old Series sheets, footpaths, bridleways and minor roads are all shown with the same symbol, and are indistinguishable. Footpaths appear to have been first shown unambiguously, again, by a single dashed line, on the New Series from 1886; even so, complaints were made that many of the cart tracks, which were shown by a double dotted line, were also merely footpaths and not passable for wheeled traffic.

The question of footpaths, and how many should be shown, came up again in 1914 during the Olivier Committee, where one witness had asked that all paths should be shown on the one-inch map, and said that it was a serious disadvantage that so many were omitted. Close replied that there was no doubt that the question of paths was a difficult one, and that in areas crowded with other detail it was impossible to put in all the paths without the map becoming confused. In other cases, it was stated, all the paths were indicated and 'the recent practice is to put in as many paths as can be shown'.[78] The witness was able to demonstrate that not only were all paths not shown on certain maps, they were not all shown on the relevant six-inch maps either.

The criteria for the selection of paths for the first revision of the one-inch map in 1896 confirmed that not all paths were shown. Important footpaths and bridlepaths, which were to be distinguished by the initials F.P. and B.P. on the six-inch field sheets, were described as

> footpaths that are habitually used by the public. Unimportant footpaths such as short paths or those only used by farm occupants, &., are to be crossed out on the six-inch impressions ... Unimportant paths need not be remarked upon on the six-inch impressions, unless such a path be already shown on the one-inch, when it should be erased on the six-inch impressions. The same should be done should any path shown on the one-inch map have ceased to exist.[79]

An implication of the above instruction is that if a footpath disappears from the one-inch map of this period, or is not included on it, but is shown at the larger scale, it could be interpreted as of doubtful status, and could be used as supporting evidence for the possibility of a path being private or, at the very least, one that was not habitually used by the wider public at that time. The instructions for the inclusion of footpaths on the large-scale plans were explicit, and some of these are recorded by Oliver.[80] However,

---

76 Hodson, (1989), p.30.

77 However, the possibility that these might also be bridleways has not been investigated.

78 Olivier, (1914a), para.750.

79 Ordnance Survey *Instructions for the revision of the one-inch map in the field*, (16/3/1896), para.8.

80 Oliver, (1993), p.57.

an important change was made in 1915 to the way in which footpaths whose routes had changed were to be shown on the large-scale plans. From now on, when the alignment of a path was altered, it was to be shown as a straight line, unless there were a permanent obstacle, in which case a deviation would be indicated,[81] regardless, one infers, of whether this actually represented the new route or not. In practice, this seems to have had little effect on the Popular Edition sheets and there was little change between their first printing and the previous Third Edition, and in any case, the generalisation of the route at the one-inch scale was relatively minor in importance; but clearly, care is needed in interpreting path alignments at the larger scale.

Another point that arises out of this instruction is the use of the word 'public'. It is not entirely clear how precisely the Ordnance Survey defined this term since we have no unambiguous documentary sources to explain this point. It is, perhaps, something of a contradiction that, on the one hand, the Ordnance Survey should insist that no route marked on the map is evidence of a right of way, while on the other, the internal unpublished instructions for surveyors and field revisers frequently use the term 'public' in this context, and direct that private routes were to be distinguished, on the field sheet, by the initials 'P.R.'. Had these field documents survived, the identification of the status of routes on unpublished Ordnance Survey maps would have been valuable evidence in the numerous litigations of the 1990s.

However, the policy of the Ordnance Survey, as far as its published plans were concerned, was made abundantly clear in 1886, when Lieut.-Col. Pilkington White, Executive Officer (i.e. Deputy Director General) wrote at some length on the subject of footpaths:

> Another point is the representation of footpaths across fields, &c, in the large-scale maps, and of the roads in the one-inch map. Following the consistent rule of the Survey as applied generally, our practice is to mark down on the cadastral plans all footpaths which are palpable physical features on the ground - e.g., made or gravelled paths, and paths provided with stiles or foot-gates, without regard to whether they are or are not public rights-of-way. To these objects are written the letters 'F.P.' denoting 'footpath,' in every case except when the path is very short, and there is no room for them. Yet these innocent initials are not unfrequently misunderstood, and many are the letters of inquiry addressed to Southampton on this subject by proprietors. In some cases it may be that the footpaths are private rights-of-way only; and then the sight of the path on the Ordnance map with these two obnoxious letters seems to have quite a perturbing influence on the owners. There appears to be an idea among them that the calling a footpath a footpath on our maps may hereafter be deemed to establish a title to claim it as a *public* thoroughfare. It cannot be too widely known that 'F.P.' means nothing more than to record the existence at the date of survey of the thing so described (to distinguish it from bridle or cart roads), of which these letters are an abbreviation; and that it is not, nor I trust ever will be, the business of the Survey to discern as to private proprietary rights, either in respect of roads and pathways, or of property boundaries as such.[82]

It is unsurprising, in view of the apparently widespread consternation of landowners at the identification of footpaths on their property, that the rights of way disclaimer was

81 Ordnance Survey *Instructions to field examiners and revisers*, (Jul. 1912), amendment noted as transcribed from Circular C/C4582/15 (not found).
82 Pilkington White, (1886), pp. 101-2.

published on Ordnance Survey maps within a couple of years of Pilkington White's views being made public. His statement, on the face of it, seems unambivalent: physical features alone were marked on the large-scale plans and it was up to the user to ascertain the status of any route. And yet we come back to the point that when selecting information for the one-inch map, the principle, between 1896 and 1936, was that only footpaths 'that are habitually used by the public' were to be shown. A remark made by Pilkington White himself seems to suggest that this might have been the case ten years earlier, in 1886, for he says that

> On the one-inch map, also, when the space admits, are shown the footpaths as cross-cuts between roads; and any pedestrian who has travelled the country much will know the value of this information.[83]

This seems to convey the message that, in general, the footpaths included on the one-inch map were chosen because they would be of use to the general, wider public, in other words, to '*any* pedestrian'. There does seem to have been a marked difference of intention between the policies of showing paths on the large scales and the small scales. The principal purpose of the first was as an all embracing record of the physical landscape regardless of ownership, while the second was selective, with a specific user - the traveller - in mind. The choice of which paths to include at the one-inch scale must have been based, at least in part, on the surveyors' and revisers' annotated field sheets. Apart from user requirements - and there is no doubt that the Ordnance Survey was very alive to these considerations in the 1880s - there is another, more practical aspect to the criteria for the selection of paths for the one-inch scale. From the Ordnance Survey's point of view, much effort and trouble would be saved in revision, and all the cartographic actions consequent upon it (drawing, engraving, etc) if it were possible to identify permanent routes rather than the more ephemeral paths so typical of the agricultural working environment. 'Public' routes were likely to be of a more permanent nature, hence the emphasis on them for the purposes of the small-scale maps. On balance, then, it would seem that the intention was that the most frequently used footpaths were to be marked on the one-inch map, regardless, in the end, of status. It follows that some caution needs to be exercised in attempting any firm interpretation of the status of a path on the map, for any private regularly used path would also have the appearance of permanence to a surveyor.

This brings us to the question of how the surveyor or reviser identified whether a route was public or not. In 1909, the one-inch reviser was again instructed that 'only footpaths habitually used by the public are to be shown',[84] but this was now followed by an important qualification which was to be included in the 1936 instructions for the Fifth Edition of the one-inch:

> but no question as to footpaths being public should be raised, as the O.S. does not concern itself with rights of way.[85]

This might mean, therefore, that the surveyor was simply supposed to use his judgement,

---

83 Pilkington White, (1886), p.102.

84 Ordnance Survey *Instructions for the revision of the 1-inch map*, (1909), p.16, para.67.

85 *Instructions for the revision and drawing of the one-inch (Fifth Edition) map*, (1936), p.7, para.16.

and mark what seemed to be well-trodden routes. Little is written about the methods to be used by surveyors and revisers in establishing the status of a minor (i.e., third class and below) road, track, or path. A clue is given in a circular dated 28 April 1884[86] where it is stated that the classifications of roads inserted on the reviser's Road Map were to be verified by the District Surveyors if practicable.[87] This implies that it was not always possible for the surveyor to provide an independent check on the accuracy of his identification of a route's status, especially if it were not first or second class.

Since there is no surviving record of what was, or was not checked, no absolute reliance can be placed on the total accuracy of the way in which any route was portrayed on the plans and maps, even though we know that one-inch road maps were supposed to be verified, in the 1890s, by the Rural District Council Surveyor. As we have no means of knowing what systematic consultation of local authorities may have taken place in order to verify the status of minor roads or footpaths, it is probably safest to say, especially in view of the 1909 instructions quoted above, that footpaths marked on Ordnance Survey maps and plans represented routes that were well-used by an indeterminate group of people at the time of survey or revision. These people might be the 'general public' in the widest meaning of the term; equally, they might be a more narrowly defined group with restricted rights. It is not possible to identify this difference from the map alone.

From 1886 to 1914, the known symbol for a footpath was a single black, dashed line. There was no separate symbol, on the one-inch maps for this period, for a bridleway, even though these were marked on the field sheets. Although bridleways are mentioned in the same paragraphs as footpaths, there seems to be no specific text, before 1924,[88] that describes the combination of both features in the same symbol. The amalgamation of the two features in a single dashed line first seems to have appeared on the 1914 *Torquay & Dartmouth* and Aldershot maps (Chapter I), and this was the symbol used on the Popular Edition and its one-inch successors until the Seventh Series, when the term 'bridle path' was replaced by 'track' in the legend.

The growth in the leisure activities of rambling and hiking from the 1920s onwards is reflected in the change of attitude from restricting the number of 'new' paths to be put on the one-inch map, to actively encouraging the incorporation of more paths. In 1909, for example, the cases where footpaths were to be added to the one-inch map were to be deemed rare,[89] but this advice was dropped from the 1924 instructions, which added that coastguards' coastal paths should be shown, no matter how indistinct on the ground. By the 1930s, the Ordnance Survey's concern to sell the one-inch map to the pedestrian

86 OSL G3962. Circular entitled 'Roads, Carriage Drives. &c.'

87 A useful source of evidence for the status of minor routes such as named green lanes, etc is contained in the Object Names Books (PRO OS 35). Dating from the last quarter of the nineteenth century, they contain the authority - usually a prominent member of the local community - for every name on the 1:2500 plans. The columns headed 'Descriptive remarks, or other general observations which may be considered of interest' in these books contain much fascinating information, and lanes may be described, for example, as an occupation road, or, sometimes, as a public road. Footpaths, unless they are named, will not be covered.

88 Ordnance Survey *Instructions to field revisers and draftsmen ...*, (1924), p.22, para.57.

89 Ordnance Survey *Instructions for the revision of the 1-inch map*, (1909), para.68.

public was made exceptionally clear in its policy for the Fifth Edition. The difference between the number of footpaths shown on the Popular Edition compared with the Fifth Edition is so marked - there are considerably more on the later map - that some explanation must be sought. The 1932 instructions for the revision of the 1:2500 plans, current into the 1940s, repeat the previous rules for the large scales, but the one-inch revision rules of 1936 contained an important addition. Now, not only were paths 'habitually used by the public' to be shown, but also 'mountain tracks and less important paths used by hikers and tourists', although the caveat that the Ordnance Survey should not concern itself with rights of way was retained.[90] A comparison between the one-inch map and the large-scale plans would be necessary in any attempt to establish how many of these apparently new paths on the Fifth Edition were actually new, or were just cartographic revivals of already existing paths.

There is some evidence to show that rules on footpaths for the Fifth Edition were put into practice for the Popular Edition on some of the sheets which came up for reprint after 1935. On sheet 21 (*Ripon and Northallerton*) many more paths have been added, alignments changed, and a few paths have been deleted.[91] Other sheets show less spectacular changes, while some, such as 103 (*Stroud*) have clearly been updated from Fourth Revision (Fifth Edition) material. The implementation on the Popular Edition of the wider interpretation of footpaths does not seem to have been very widespread, and, far from including more mountain tracks, the 1938 reprint of sheet 12 (*Keswick & Ambleside*) actually omitted the well-known path over Catbells which was present on the previous printing.[92]

Railways

While the policy of showing more footpaths was implemented on the Popular Edition, principally from 1936 onwards, and serious attempts were made to keep road information up to date, the revision of railway information was made to keep pace not with growth, but rather with decline. The data which the Popular had inherited from the Third Edition portrayed the railways at the height of their development. Their dwindling importance in the inter-war period as a result of the increasing significance of road transport in the economy, is reflected in the Popular Edition map.

To begin with, though, the railway information on the first printings of the Popular sheets originated in the nineteenth century. Although railway information had been shown on the one-inch map from the outset, the earliest instructions so far found for the inclusion of railways at this scale are dated 11 October 1897.[93] While the amount of detail which was put in as an aid to interpretation of the data by the draftsman was considerable, the surveyor was, nevertheless, not to 'waste time on features which are

---

90 Ordnance Survey *Instructions for the revision and drawing of the one-inch (Fifth Edition) map*, (1936), para.16.
91 Other sheets which have been noted with footpath revision are: 29(1939), 33(1936), 39(1935), 54(1938), 60(1936), 71(1936), 72(1938), 73(1939), 74(1936), 75(1939), 76(1937), 77(1937), 80(1938), 81(1938), 82(1937), 83(1927- this is an isolated early example of footpath revision, no other has been found pre-dating 1935; and 1935), 84(1938), 85(1939), 87(1936), 91(1937), 92(1936).
92 This path was reinstated on the 1948 tourist map of the Lake District.
93 Circular O.S.463.

not shown' on the one-inch map. The details which were not required for one-inch purposes were, for example, mile posts and signal posts, signal boxes, short sidings, and railways in course of construction. Most of the railways which appeared on the Popular Edition had been included on the copperplates according to these principles; succeeding one-inch revision instructions tended to reduce the information required for railways, while expanding that needed for roads.

The way in which double railway lines were shown on the Popular Edition - a solid black line[94] - differed from the Third Edition which used a chequered line symbol. The decision to reverse the symbols was contained in circular C/C 7052/13, dated 7 November 1913, and was referred to in another circular dated 5 December 1913.[95] The attempts to fill up the chequered line on the copperplates of the Third Edition to convert it to a solid line had not been successful, and so the order was given to scrape off all railways from the matrix and re-engrave them (the single lines were converted from an open double line crossed by single strokes to a chequered line).[96] Not only were the lines themselves deleted, but so also were station and junction names; when both lines and names came to be re-engraved, stations were much easier to identify because they were given a legible symbol.[97] Large stations in towns were shown by a black rectangle,[98] and country stations by an unfilled black circle. Although these were a great improvement on the Third Edition, which merely indicated stations by name or description, this convention was still not easily legible, and from 1921 the symbols were filled with red on reprints and on new sheets.[99] Station names were usually omitted where the identity was thought to be obvious from the surrounding place-names, but where in doubt, the name was combined with the abbreviation 'STA.' There was no symbol for a level crossing - the railway was simply shown crossing a road. A separate symbol was suggested in 1928;[100] it was incorporated in the specification for the Fifth Edition, but it does not seem to have appeared on the Popular sheets.

Two events were to have a major effect on the portrayal of railways on the Popular Edition sheets. The first of these was the passing of the Railway Act[101] on 19 August 1921, under which about one hundred companies were amalgamated into four main

---

94   Baker, (1892), had recommended a red line for railways, but this was overruled by Dorington, (1893c), p.14.

95   Circular C/C 7677/13. A specimen of the new symbol had been prepared on the Killarney sheet, but since the tourist Killarney sheet had already been published, this note probably referred to a standard one-inch Irish sheet.

96   The portrayal of electric tramways in towns was not attempted at the one-inch scale, and the only indication of their presence was the name 'Electric Tramway', or the abbreviation 'Elec. Tram.' written along a stretch of road where space allowed.

97   Station symbols appeared from late 1909 on engraved one-inch small sheets (Oliver, (1982b), pp.4, 6) and from mid 1910 on the Third Edition Large Sheets, but they were very small and somewhat illegible.

98   At least four sheets showed large stations by unfilled rectangles on their first printings: 119, 120, 136 and 143.

99   Exceptions were sheets 139 and 144 (both 1922 states), which show the main station in solid black, while the circular symbol is filled with red.

100 PRO OS 1/312. Conventional signs dated ca Aug.1928.

101 *Railway Act*, 1921, 11 & 12 Geo.V, c.55.

groups: London, Midland & Scottish; London & North-Eastern; the Southern; and Great Western. These companies had all come into being on 1 January 1923 and the resulting change in nomenclature meant that all railway names were to be revised on Popular Edition sheets as they came up for reprint in, or after, 1923.[102] The renaming of the main railways and deletion of old pre-grouping names was straightforward, but the many inconsistencies in the treatment of the names of branch lines would seem to indicate either the lack of an overall policy or disparity of information in the compilation materials (Bradshaw's guides, for example). The 1924 instructions that the name of the owning company was to be given at intervals along the line, and that names of branch lines were to be given only when their destination was not obviously apparent, had not changed since the printing of the 1914 rules (the sentences referring to names were omitted from the Fifth Edition instructions). Many of the sheets show minor name changes, but the most frequent alteration was to delete the word 'Branch', or its abbreviation, 'Br.'. In 1926 a new ruling was made about railway names.[103] Although it does not specify whether it was to refer to large or small scales, or both, it does explain some of the changes on the Popular Edition. In future, only the main trunk routes of the grouped railway companies were to have the group name written in full, and the practice of retaining as named main lines, the main routes of former small or joint companies, which were now amalgamated and renamed within a group company, was to cease. In order to make the work of the Drawing Office staff easier, the four groups were asked to supply lists of their main trunk routes. The main routes of companies outside the grouping of the 1921 Railway Act were to continue to have their names shown in full; the word 'Branch' was not normally to be added to a subsidiary name unless the line ran to a terminus.

The second event became apparent from 1932, when the majority of reprints of Popular Edition sheets added a new symbol, an unfilled black circle, for closed stations. This anticipated the use of the same symbol on the Fifth Edition by one year,[104] and reflected the check to railway traffic which was in part due to the expansion and upgrading of the road network. The closure of passenger lines,[105] which, as one officer remarked, 'is nowadays a very frequent occurrence and involves a lot of searching'[106] entailed considerable extra work, not in drawing, but in the selection of information. Over one thousand miles of unprofitable lines were closed in the 1930s, and this is reflected in the successive reprints of the Popular during this period. This trend was particularly noticeable in the North, Midlands and South Wales. Certainly, the maps show many more closures than constructions, and while new railway bypasses such as those around Frome and Westbury,[107] or new lines on Dungeness[108] were permanent,

---

102   Sheet 124 was an exception; no change was made on the 1923 reprint, but the railways were renamed on the 1926 state.

103   Circular C.C.913. This refers back to a previous circular, which has not been found: C.C.639 dated 8/8/1919.

104   Oliver, (1989a), p.17.

105   These can be checked against the Popular Edition sheets by using Clinker, (1978).

106   PRO OS 1/312. Minute 61, 9/9/1932.

107   Sheet 121, state 2037 M36 R32.

the Welsh Highland & Ffestiniog Railway (i.e. the Welsh Highland Light Railway), which first appeared on the 1927 reprint of sheet 49, was closed on the 1936 state. But the reliability of the portrayal of the railways on the map must often be questioned. For example, on the 1939 state of sheet 29, the line from Preston to Longridge is shown as open, whereas, on the overlap section of sheet 30 (1938), it is shown as closed.

The independent revision for the one-inch map ensured that the portrayal of the transport systems of England and Wales in the inter-war period was more up to date than that of the large scales. Precise dating of the closures of railways and stations can only be derived from written sources, and if used in conjunction with these, the Popular Edition gives, overall, a reasonably representative picture of the decline of the railways at that time. The introduction of a formal road classification system was first made, in 1886, on the one-inch map. In this respect, the one-inch map is a classic example of one of Andrews's 'map history rules', which states that 'small maps sometimes contain information not to be found on the larger maps from which they purport to derive.'[109] The large-scale plans were not regarded as road maps; their primary function was to depict physical features and administrative boundaries as accurately as the scale would allow. In contrast, the smaller scale showed a range of road classification, first, by line-work, and then by line and colour. These conventions allowed the user to make an intelligent deduction of the suitability of routes for different purposes that would have been impossible at the larger scale. In this respect, the one-inch maps are an invaluable aid to the interpretation of roads on the large-scale plans.

Another demonstration of the map history rule is that the Popular Edition, rather than the 1:2500 plans, was, unquestionably, the largest scale at which road development was most faithfully portrayed, although its road classification system was unnecessarily complex as a result of inheriting principles which had been established in the days of more leisurely traffic; but most sheets had been 'road-revised' at least twice at about a seven- or eight-year interval. The advance in the development of motor transport had led to the building of these new roads, and the upgrading of old routes. This in turn was one of the causes of major locational shifts in industry, and house-building on an unprecedented scale, but the depiction of this new urban landscape was not to be so regularly revised as the transport network had been.

108   Sheet 135, states 3500/26.5000/28 and M39 R38 3041LR.
109   Andrews, (1997), p.142.

Chapter VIII

BUILDINGS, SECURITY DELETIONS, UTILITIES, PARISHES AND PARKS

One of the features which served to emphasise the identity of the Popular Edition as a map for the age of motor transport was the great decline in the appearance of the word 'Smithy' on the later states of its sheets.[1] Other elements to disappear were the garden symbol, parish boundaries, and the abbreviation for letter boxes. But new ones took their place: electricity transmission lines, telephones, and youth hostels, for example. The changing human landscape was marked by other features, for which there were written descriptions rather than symbols: aerodromes began to proliferate,[2] and the increase in leisure activities, such as golf, became evident from the spread of golf courses on the map - although the wider social significance of this game only really became apparent on the Fifth Edition when clubhouse buildings (C.H.) were specified.[3]

Just as the cartographic policy for showing lines of communication had reflected the social policies and practice of inter-war Britain, so too, did the addition of these new conventional signs and features. In this way the impact of modern society on the physical landscape became imprinted on the map; but the heritage of older societies was not ignored, and some revision to the detail of antiquities which resulted from the vigorous activities of O.G.S.Crawford, the Archaeology Officer, made its way onto the Popular Edition.[4] Less obvious, for it was not a matter for public announcement, were the numerous deletions of detail made as a result of security measures taken in anticipation of a European war. Some of these major changes are considered here.

Buildings

The symbols for settlement - the *raison d'être* of communications and the other man-made features and concepts which appeared on the map - were explained neither in the

---

1   The depiction of facilities for mechanised horsepower was provided for in the 1924 instructions under the heading 'motor garages', but does not seem to have been implemented for the post-1924 printings of the Popular Edition.

2   In 1919 the Air Ministry was unable to give authoritative information to the Ordnance Survey about the numbers and positions of aerodromes; the word 'aerodrome' was therefore not to be included on maps (OSL, Southampton Circulars, G3964, Webster, Air Ministry to OS, 25/10/1919); but by 1921 the position had altered and 'all aerodromes of a permanent nature' were to be shown on both large and small-scale maps on revision (Circular, C.C.775, 28/11/1921); at the same time, a symbol of a black circle round a black dot was devised for the quarter-inch map (OSL, Southampton Circulars, G3964, Close to EO, 29/11/1921).

3   The flag symbol for a golf course was not used on the one-inch maps until the Seventh Series. It had been used by Michelin since about 1914.

4   For example, sheet 70, revision to the NE corner on the 1935 reprint. However, for the south of England, the bulk of the revision of archaeological detail was incorporated in the Fifth Edition sheets.

legend nor on the conventional signs sheet. It seems to have been taken for granted that all would understand the signs used; this point is underlined by the fact that no reference to buildings was contained in the 1896 instructions, and only one sentence: 'All are shown and where convenient are blocked' appeared in those for 1901. It was only with the Seventh Series, when a clear distinction was made between groups of buildings, public buildings and small isolated structures, that the symbols were included on the conventional signs sheet.

No such distinctions were shown on the Popular Edition sheets, which inherited from the Third Edition the convention of showing groups of buildings either by a black ruled infill, or by a solid black block. A difference between the two seems to have been intended, but it is only with the 1936 instructions for the Fifth Edition that a clue is given:

> The close districts in towns, where houses are contiguous, or practically so, are shown by solid blocks; care must be exercised in this judgement as it is not intended that suburban areas should be so represented.[5]

The second half of this paragraph had been added after 1924, since when the patterns of inter-war municipal suburbia,[6] designed for the first time to provide space for the motor car, had begun to be recorded on the large-scale plans. Their distinctive geometrical configuration at the one-inch scale (figs 26b-d) provides, in many cases, an instantly identifiable location of new building sites. These modern suburban developments possessed a greater percentage of open space than the housing in inner cities, or in large towns, and it is easy to see that if such areas had been blocked in, the map would have been disproportionately heavy with solid black in any urban location. One other aspect of the space surrounding domestic buildings deserves mention here, and that is the portrayal of gardens. In general, these symbols were erased from the Third Edition Small Sheet copperplates when they were being made up for the Popular Edition; but some areas escaped the total deletion of this ornament, and vestiges remain which are especially marked on sheet 35, at Huyton (square H11) and south-east Liverpool.[7] Where these do appear, they serve as a reminder of how much detail was removed from the engraved map in order to simplify the coloured edition.

Unlike the Seventh Series for which specific instructions were given for the way buildings were to be treated,[8] those for the preceding one-inch series were vague but could be found, at various dates, under the headings of, for example, churches and chapels, greenhouses, hotels and inns, houses, mills, and schools. Of these the most important were churches, and it was undoubtedly their value as prominent landmarks of a permanent and easily recognisable nature which led to the recommendation by the army in 1892 that churches should be shown more clearly than had been the custom on the Old and New Series. The symbols for churches with spires, towers, or neither, which have

5   Ordnance Survey *Instructions for the revision and drawing of the one-inch (Fifth Edition) map*, (1936), p.29, para.66.

6   Edwards, (1981), chap.3.

7   The garden symbol persisted through different states, or printings, of the sheet. Other sheets which retain garden symbols include: 11, 34, 38, 40, 45, 58, 64.

8   Harley, (1975), pp.113-114; Ordnance Survey *Specification ... one-inch Seventh Series*, (1957), p.6.

persisted, unchanged, to the present Landranger Series,[9] were first printed in the Baker report (1892) and were initially adopted for the Revised New Series in 1895. The circle and square denoting a spire or tower were left unfilled in the diagrams in the instructions for 1896, 1901 and 1909, but were always filled in in black on the published map.[10]

The instructions for the selection of churches to be shown on the map varied from series to series. In towns, for example, only the most conspicuous churches were shown for the Revised New Series, but for the Third, Fourth, and Popular Editions no selection criteria for urban churches were given. By 1924, all churches and chapels on newly-drawn one-inch maps were to be shown 'invariably', with the additional proviso that in towns, all those that were important and conspicuous were to be numbered in order of importance on the six-inch plots to provide data for the half-inch maps.[11] In practice, there is no evidence that this last ruling had applied to the Popular Edition. The first written indication that the selection of churches shown on the one-inch map was not comprehensive appeared with the Seventh Series,[12] where, in cases where detail was too crowded to allow the inclusion of all structures, preference was given to churches with spires, then towers - the priority following a clear order of visibility on the ground.

One feature was peculiar to the instructions for the Second Revision (1901), and that was the inclusion beside the church symbol of the abbreviation 'Ch' for church, or 'Chap' for chapel. This is an excellent example of the inclusion in new instructions of procedures that had been implemented for some time before being confirmed in print, for this particular practice appears to have been first used with the New Series from 1887 (the 1896 revision instructions for the Revised New Series did not specify, incidentally, that the earlier New Series custom of naming parish churches, rectories and vicarages was to be dropped, although this omission was carried out on the map). However, the number of chapels identified on the map was so few compared with churches, that the ubiquitous 'Ch' abbreviation was, to say the least, superfluous and it was discontinued by Grant's instructions of 1909. There is another aspect to this differentiation between church and chapel which lends to the one-inch maps of this period the air of social, even political, rather than topographical comment. Churches played an important political role in the years up to 1914, and the rivalry between Church (Conservative) and Chapel (Liberal) is well documented, and both played a significant part in 'maintaining and shaping the allegiance of a broad swathe of the community'.[13] With the advent of the Labour Party and the rise of trade unions before 1914 the traditional church-chapel rivalry began to disappear, just as the cartographic distinction between them vanished in 1909.

---

9   However, since 1991, these symbols have been described as 'Places of worship' ('PW' on the map) with tower; with spire, minaret or dome; without such additions: King, (1995).

10 A useful illustrated summary of church symbols on the one-inch map is Oliver, (1990).

11 Ordnance Survey *Instructions to field revisers and draftsmen* ..., (1924), para. 18. This rule was repeated for the Fifth Edition (Ordnance Survey *Instructions* ..., (1936), para.7), but was dropped from the small scales revision instructions (*The Green Book 1961*) in 1961.

12 Harley, (1975), p.113. The selection procedure is not recorded in *The Green Book* (1961), and must have been incorporated as an amendment at a later date. The same procedure which is described by Harley is in force with the current 1:50,000 specification.

13 Stevenson, (1984), pp.356-62.

Individual buildings and structures were, however, relatively static components of the landscape and less liable to great change than urban areas. Since this was a period of unprecedented urban development it is relevant to ask here, first, to what extent the Popular Edition sheets recorded the spread of built-up areas, and secondly, how quickly was revised detail incorporated? In the face of a stated revision interval of fifteen years for the one-inch map, there is no reason to suppose that any alterations would be made to the sheets of middle and northern England until at least the mid-1930s, and in the main this is, indeed, the case. But building expansion, which had already been referred to in 1914,[14] had been recorded on the Third Edition in an incipient form which was to be inherited by the Popular Edition. It would appear that what was inserted on the map were the road systems of future developments which had been laid out by speculators in the first two decades of the twentieth century. Thus Peacehaven, the archetypal inter-war shanty town development,[15] had already been laid out by 1916 and its empty streets were collectively labelled 'New Anzac on Sea' on the first printing of Popular Edition sheet 134 in 1920 (it was changed to 'Peacehaven' on the 1920 [published 1921] printing of the outline edition).

The insertion of these dotted 'building roads' was first mentioned in the 1901 instructions for the Second Revision, which stated that roads that 'had been laid out for building purposes' (para. 70) were to be given third-class status even though their present condition might not meet the standard; such a policy would have been unacceptable twenty years later. These skeleton developments are to be found on some Third Edition sheets - particularly marked are those in the vicinity of Whitstable, Herne Bay, Margate and Deal in 1904[16] - and on many Popular Edition sheets. Building, then, was already well underway in the 1920s to the extent that in 1931 a Capt. Bourne pointed out in the House of Commons that

> there are quite large areas on the outskirts of our cities which a year or two ago were open fields but are now covered with houses. These ... are not marked on any map whatever. There is a complete absence of any record on the maps of these building programmes and I suggest that one of the things which will be necessary ... is to get accurate maps showing recent developments.[17]

This was one of the first public rumblings indicating that the Ordnance Survey was beginning to be unable to cope with the amount of revision necessary to bring the large-scale plans up to date. In 1934, in response to yet another question on the failure of Ordnance Survey maps to record new developments, the Secretary of the Ministry of Agriculture and Fisheries was forced to admit that 'the new housing estates in Hertfordshire and Essex are not shown on the 25 inch or 6 inch ... but will be shown on

14 Olivier, (1914a), para. 865, refers to 'the constant expansion of the towns'. This is borne out by the revised detail which appeared on some sheets at the turn of the century; see Nicholson, (1994b), p. 126.

15 Edwards, (1981), pp. 123-4.

16 Third Edition, East Kent (North), a composite of Small Sheets 273, 274, and parts of 289, 290. Revised 1903-4, published 1906.

17 Parliamentary Debates. H.C.Deb.5s.255, 28/7/1931.

the new edition of the 1 inch [i.e. the Fifth Edition]'.[18]

Those Popular Edition sheets which were to be replaced, in southern England, by the Fifth Edition were, with minor exceptions, not revised for urban development.[19] They became markedly out of date in the late 1920s, by which time they were mostly at the end of the stipulated fifteen-year revision cycle. The extent to which the Popular Edition of 1934 in the south reflected, as far as housing was concerned, the state of twenty years earlier, is well demonstrated by sheet 115 (*S.E. London & Sevenoaks*). It was reprinted in 1934 and was on sale at the same time as sheet 115 of the Fifth Edition.[20] The difference between the urban representation of the two sheets is enormous. On the Popular Edition sheet, only the roads had been revised, railway names changed, and security deletions made. The Popular sheets for this area therefore present virtually no intermediate detail as far as settlement is concerned; such development can only be inferred by the sudden appearance of an unnamed new railway station in the middle, seemingly, of nowhere, as on sheet 114 (*Windsor*, 1933, square E13) which on the Fifth Edition sheet 114 (1934) is Stoneleigh Station, surrounded by new housing. Other sheets of southern England showed similar discrepancies (figs 28f,g).

Elsewhere in England and Wales the picture was different. From 1934 onwards, several sheets were revised for urban detail as they came up for reprint.[21] This followed a statement that information from sheets of the large-scale plans which had been published since the current printing of the Popular sheet whose revision was in hand, was to be incorporated in the new reprint of that sheet.[22] Between 1935 and 1938, the annual reports gave a total of 165 one-inch sheets which had been revised in this way.[23] During this period, a maximum of 208 reprints of Popular Edition sheets had been made, but only about thirty-six sheets actually showed any urban change and this tended not to be revised on subsequent reprints.

Most of the revision to urban detail appeared on the Popular Edition after the publication of the relevant six-inch sheets and, in some examples, was linked to road development. But there are instances where information appeared on the one-inch map in advance of large-scale publication, and, in at least one case, detail was shown on the

18 Parliamentary Debates. H.C.Deb.5s.296, 17/12/1934. The Dagenham estates appeared on sheet 107, Fifth Edition, first published 1935.

19 The exceptions were sheets 92, 95-8, 104-6, 130, 141. The revisions to urban detail were minor in extent, and in some instances were confined to the inclusion of new major buildings, such as Wembley Stadium on the 1924 printing of sheet 106.

20 It may have been published some months before the Fifth Edition sheet was issued; but, in any case, the sheet lines of the two series were not coincident.

21 The following sheets have been noted as revised from 1935: 14(1935), 16(1935), 21(1935), 23(1936), 24(1935), 26(1936), 27(1935), 29(1938), 30(1938), 31(1935), 32(1938), 33(1936), 34(1939), 36(1937), 37(1936), 38(1935), 39(1935), 40(1935), 45(1936), 46(1936), 47(1938), 48(1939), 60(1935), 61(1936), 64(1935), 67(1935), 72(1938), 73(1939), 74(1938), 77(1937), 81(1938), 82(1937), 83(1936), 84(1938), 85(1936), 92(1936). There were a few earlier exceptions to the 1935 date, for example, sheets 15(1931), 37(1931), 87(1933), 95(1929, 1932), 97(1932), 105(1926: insertion of Cowley motor works only), 106(1924: insertion of Wembley Stadium only), 130(1930), 141(1933).

22 *Annual Report*, (1934/5), p.15.

23 This specifically excluded road revisions; sheet numbers were not specified, some sheets were presumably revised more than once.

one-inch where it did not appear at all on the six-inch (figs 25-27). In this example, at Billingham near Middlesbrough, new housing is first shown on the one-inch map (fig.26a) thirteen years in advance of its publication at the larger scale (fig.27), which, although dated 1938, does not appear to have been published until ten years later.[24] This is, however, a relatively rare instance of this kind and with a few exceptions (the early development of Welwyn Garden City, for example, appears on Popular Edition sheet 95 at least ten years in advance of its large-scale counterpart), the states of the standard sheets tend to reflect the previous publication of information at a larger scale. Nevertheless, these anomalies are an important indication that for this period the Popular Edition should be consulted in conjunction with the large-scales when dating topographical change.

In this context, four other one-inch versions of the Popular Edition provide invaluable intermediate cartographic evidence of urban development for the period 1938-42, which is not to be found on the standard coloured sheets. These are first, the outline edition (see Part 2, p.282); secondly, the War Revision and Second War Revision of the military version of the Popular, GSGS 3907; thirdly, the later printings of the special district sheets; and lastly the sheets of the Land Utilisation Survey of Britain, which recorded new building by a purple wash. The data for the LUS sheets were gathered independently of Ordnance Survey revisions, but the others appear to have incorporated revision information from the Special Emergency Edition of the six-inch map which was revised in 1938-9 for Air Raid Precaution planning for areas with a population of over 2000. Few of these printed six-inch sheets appear to have survived,[25] and therefore the generalised data which appear on these one-inch maps provide the only readily accessible contemporary cartographic coverage of urban development at a national level for this period.

Security deletions

While, on the one hand, new housing was gradually being added to the map in the 1930s, details of other buildings and structures were being deleted. Some of the erasures were startlingly obvious: the area of Woolwich Arsenal, for example; others were barely noticable, such as small wireless telegraph stations.[26] These alterations, which took place on reprints from 1925[27] onwards, have been found on at least twenty-six sheets of the Popular Edition,[28] and were made as the result of security regulations which came into force in 1924.[29]

---

24 County series six-inch sheets carried the national grid from about 1945. Oliver, (1993), p.32, gives ca 1948 as the beginning of the publication of the six-inch map with National Grid on National Grid sheet lines.

25 Oliver, (1993), p.31.

26 These were radio stations which initially communicated using morse code.

27 On the 1925 printing of sheet 132 the words 'HM Dockyard', for example, are deleted.

28 Sheets 33, 34, 40, 43, 47, 55, 57, 77, 86, 98, 99, 101, 106, 108, 111, 114-17, 126, 132, 134-5, 140, 142, 144.

29 Circulars, C.C.844, 15/3/1924; C.C.846, 24/4/1924; C.C.882, 13/6/1925; C.C.926, 16/2/1927. Much of the information in the earlier circulars was included in security regulations for 1928, whose content and implementation is discussed in Board, (1991).

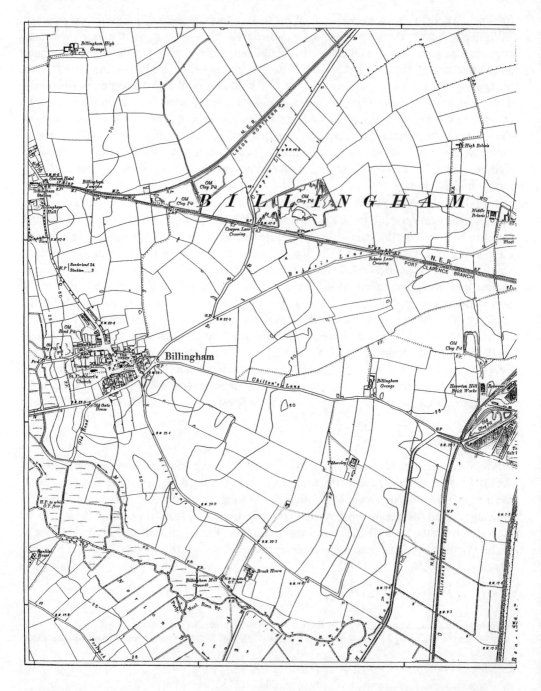

Fig.25 Part of six-inch sheet Durham LINW (reduced), revised 1913; Edition of 1923. This was the most up-to-date published six-inch map which would, theoretically, have been used for the compilation of part of Popular Edition sheet 15, first published in 1925. By this time the six-inch sheet was already twelve years out of date, and had been superseded for urban detail by the one-inch map (fig.26a). *Royal Geographical Society (with IBG).*

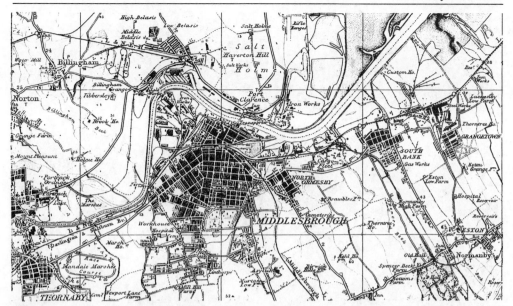

Fig.26a Popular Edition sheet 15, *Middlesbrough* (1925); reduced. Although based on fig.25, it shows new housing at Middle and Low Belasis, as well as the development of the light railways and buildings of the chemical works of J.W. House and B. Fullerton, east of Billingham. Manufacture of nitrogen fertiliser began at this site in 1923. Dotted building roads are shown at Grangetown. *Private collection.*

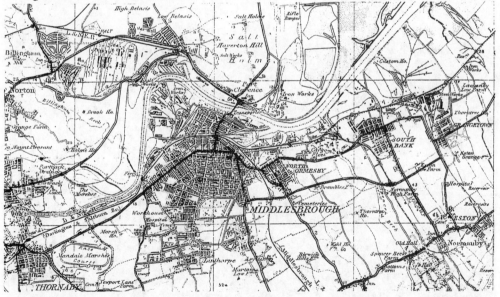

Fig.26b Popular Edition Sheet 15 (1931 reprint 3750/31); reduced. Showing further development at Middle Belasis (no longer named) and Billingham; none of this information was published at either the 25-inch or six-inch scales at this time. This new housing was undoubtedly associated with the expansion of the chemical works which occurred in 1925, and which is shown on this map; ICI Billingham Division was formed on this site in 1926. The data for this revision may have been derived from updated but unpublished six-inch material. *Private collection.*

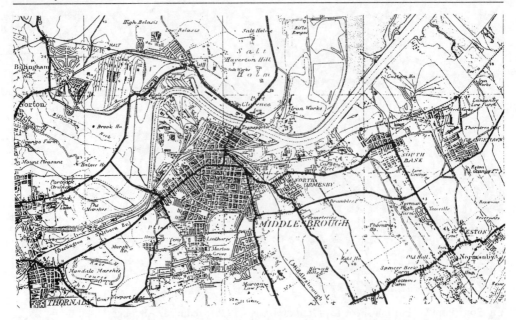

Fig.26c Popular Edition Sheet 15 (1938 reprint 2538.M37.R36.); reduced. Shows suburban development around Grangetown (along the old dotted building roads), at Normanby High Farm (the settlement is newly named 'Teesville'), and south of Middlesbrough. Note the addition of electricity transmission lines south of Billingham Beck. *Private collection.*

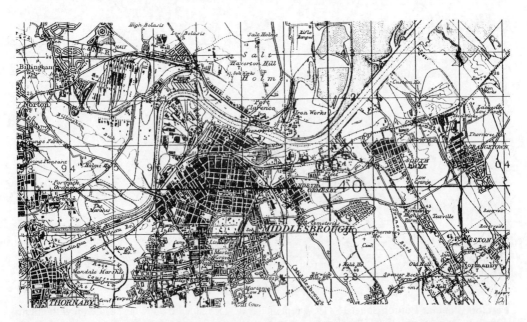

Fig.26d Second War Revision, Popular Edition Style sheet 15 (1942 printing 70,000/2/42 L.R.); reduced. More urban revision to Middlesbrough, Grangetown and Billingham has been incorporated from the six-inch map, which was not published until about six years later. The ICI chemical works remains on the one-inch map despite its absence from the larger scale (fig.27). *Private collection.*

160

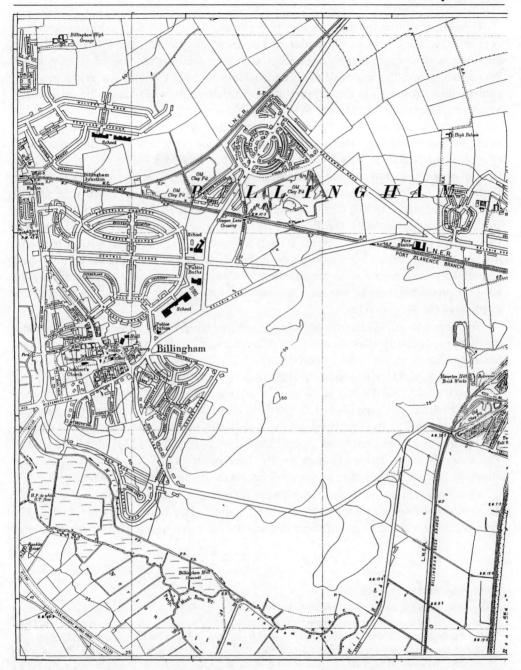

Fig.27 Part of six-inch sheet Durham LINW (reduced), Provisional Edition with National Grid, with additions to 1938, but probably not published until the late 1940s. Note the further expansion of residential development around Billingham, which was incorporated in fig.26d in advance of the publication of this six-inch sheet. The ICI chemical works has not been included (even though it still appears on the one-inch map), presumably on security grounds; all the detail such as field boundaries has been omitted (compare with fig.25); only the contours remain. *Royal Geographical Society (with IBG).*

These instructions for deleting sensitive information on the national maps were not new in 1924. They were a continuation of a defence policy which, as far as the Ordnance Survey was concerned, had its beginnings with the prohibition of the sale of Ordnance Survey maps towards the end of the Napoleonic wars in 1811.[30] To what extent mapping security measures were in force during the nineteenth century remains to be researched. Much retrospective information is available in old Air Force files, but the majority of the old instructions and circulars have not survived the vagaries of time and the bombings of the Second World War. However, the evidence of the maps implies the implementation of a standard policy, at least by the 1890s, and possibly back as far as the 1870s.[31] It is also possible to infer, from a memorandum dated 1908 on the depiction of War Department property on the one-inch map,[32] that from some unspecified time (but at least from the early 1890s) until 1907, the practice had been for special editions of the small-scale maps, on which fortifications had been shown in full, to be printed 'for War Department purposes only'.[33] From 1908, fortifications were to be treated in the same way as any other detail, and were to be included on the one-inch sheets.[34] This would undoubtedly have been a welcome economy to Grant, who was already streamlining the revision procedures of the one-inch, because separate copperplates had been necessary to produce the two versions.

The new policy, which was reflected in paragraph 77 of the 1909 one-inch revision instructions, is nicely illustrated by the differences in detail between the Third Edition Small and Large sheets. Small Sheets 316 and 331, and the coloured combined version, 316 and part of 331, published in 1904, lack spot heights, contours, coastal defence works and all dockyard detail in the neighbourhood of Portsmouth and Gosport, but they were all inserted on Large Sheet 135, published in 1908, after the new directive had been introduced (figs 28a,b). Similarly, all the details of Chatham Dockyard and Sheerness, having previously been left blank, were included on Large Sheet 117, published in 1909. The state of affairs which obtained for the later issues of the Large Sheet Series was inherited for the first printing of the southern sheets of the Popular Edition.

More stringent security rules, which were set out in the 1924 revision instructions for the depiction of sensitive information on the one-inch map, were a response to the 1924 War Office regulations. One of these forbade the inclusion of the written description of

30 Margary, (1975-1992), vol.III, p.xxxiv.

31 Some sheets of the New Series carry no defence detail, or contours and spot heights, in areas such as naval dockyards. Public attention was actually drawn, albeit unwittingly, to this policy by Bartholomew in 1895, for a printed note on his half-inch map of South Devon reads: 'The contours around Plymouth are only shown approximately on this map, as they are not published in the Ordnance Survey'. NLS, Bartholomew Printing Archive, 20/5/1895. Complaints were made about the absence of contours in the vicinity of fortified places in the evidence given to the Dorington Committee: Dorington, (1893c), paras 756-61.

32 OSL, Southampton Circulars, G3964, 'Revision of the one-inch map. W.D. Information'. Memorandum by A.J. Savage, OSO Southampton 18/6/1908.

33 The methods outlined in the various circulars quoted above for producing the separate plates were essentially the same as those quoted from PRO OS 1/250 by Board, (1991).

34 The 1908 memorandum (footnote 32) refers to a War Office decision A/2608/1907, which has not been traced. By inference, though, security information was still not allowed on sales editions of the large scales; c.f. Ilkeston, (1911b), para.1886. where the removal of such information is described.

explosives factories, which can be found on numerous Popular Edition sheets published before 1924, like those on the 1921 printing of sheet 98 (*Clacton on Sea & Harwich*, square D10). The descriptive names were removed on the 1929 reprint.[35] In the same category were included chemical factories (deleted from, for example, square C12 of the 1938 reprint of sheet 86). How, therefore, the ICI chemical complex at Billingham[36] came to be inserted on the 1931 reprint of sheet 15 (Middlesbrough fig.26b), and retained on the reprints, especially in view of government interest in the plant at the time (it was producing nitrogen fertiliser, nitric acid and ammonium nitrate) remains a complete mystery which is further compounded by its absence from the corresponding six-inch sheet (fig.27).

The many apparent inconsistencies in the deletions are partly explained by the interpretations allowed of the security rules,[37] for the emphasis was on safeguarding government, rather than civilian, property. For example, the detail of private explosive works was allowed to remain, as long as it was not described; similarly, provided that the configuration of buildings, and the layout of roads within defence works did not suggest 'any definite association with measures of national defence', they could be allowed if the identifying nomenclature was removed. Thus, for instance, the whole of Catterick Camp (sheet 21, *Ripon & Northallerton*) was shown, and even updated, on successive reprints, but the words 'Military Rail·' were removed from the 1929 reprint and did not reappear. In the same way, aerodromes and wireless telegraph stations (W.T.S.) were not erased if they were purely civilian in nature, but where they were described as 'military' or 'admiralty', they were removed.

The reluctance of the Ordnance Survey to compromise on the intellectual content of their maps in the face of demands by, for example the Air Ministry, who preferred the insertion of fictitious information to a blank space when it came to deleting large complexes of buildings, has been well illustrated by Board.[38] But whereas such areas could easily be falsified by a colour wash on land use maps, for example, it was not so simple to camouflage an obviously white space on the standard topographical map. The 1928 circular over which there was access other than by the landowner (C.C.944) was quite specific in its recommendation on this point:

> Where detail is omitted from sales editions … any natural features, ornament, etc., will be shown in the blank space as nearly practicable to what they were prior to the construction of the works of defence…

Why then, were the areas of Chatham Dockyard, Sheerness, Devonport and Woolwich Arsenal, for example, shown on Popular Edition reprints after this date as white spaces? It would have been a simple matter to have disguised these areas by a mud stipple, in exactly the same way that Pembroke Dock had been treated on sheet 99. Indeed, this very question was brought up by the War Office, who asked whether there were any political

---

35 These instructions were printed for Ordnance Survey use in Circular C.C.944. At least three copies are known, in PRO OS 1/250, another in a small book of circulars in OSL (G2795), and the other in OSL (G7096).

36 The full history of the Billingham site is given in House and Fullerton, (1960).

37 Separate rules governed the handling of secret documents: Circular, C.C.1087, 3/10/1935.

38 Board, (1991).

or technical reasons why blank spaces should not be filled in.[39]

The dilemma is encapsulated in MacLeod's reply.[40] Resisting the suggestion that deleted detail should be replaced by symbols or words which could be interpreted as giving erroneous information, he remarked that even using less definite symbols such as rough pasture, was objectionable. Woolwich, for example, had been shown as a blank space on the twenty-five-inch and six-inch maps (although the generalised details appeared on the one-inch Third Edition Large Sheet Series, 116, published in 1909) for many years. In these circumstances, the filling in of a blank by fictitious symbols would always contrast strongly with the adjacent houses, and would, MacLeod contended, arouse even more curiosity and comment from every user of the map than would a blank space. He suggested that concealment, 'if map concealment is considered practicable, desirable or necessary', would be best achieved if the deletions were confined only to such few buildings and objects that would clearly betray their purpose. After considering the enemy's possible methods of bombing and sabotage, he concluded that 'no advantage from the point of view of secrecy is gained by inserting fictitious matter in the blank spaces'.[41] Perhaps the real reason for his reluctance to indulge in cartographic deception was the extra time and expense that it would entail in the drawing office. All the same, the blanks were not always unidentified on the map: the 1929 reprint of Chatham (sheet 116) omitted all the detail of the naval base, down to the eighteenth-century lines of fortifications, but retained the label 'Royal Dockyard'. This was hurriedly removed from the next reprint.

The treatment of sheet 132 (*Portsmouth & Southampton*) exemplifies the inherent difficulties of attempting to conceal detail systematically on a long-established map series for which consistent security policies had not been laid down in the past, since there were probably more defence installations within an area of 48 square miles than could be found on any other sheet. It was also the first Popular Edition sheet to be edited for defence data following the implementation of the 1924 regulations. On its first three printings, between 1919 and 1923, the sheet was replete with potentially 'sensitive' information. This included the outlines and internal layouts of seventeen forts, two redoubts, together with their names; eight batteries (one disused); five barracks (one named as 'Artillery Barracks'); a torpedo range; four rifle ranges; an Admiralty wireless telegraph station; two coastguard stations; one lifeboat station; a gas works; an oil storage depot; and the name 'H.M. Dockyard'. The ensuing reprints, between 1925 and 1938, were an exercise in the gradual removal of information, beginning with the erasure of the words 'H.M. Dockyard', the names of all the forts, the word 'Admiralty' from wireless telegraph stations and all the batteries. But, conversely, a wireless telegraph station was inserted where formerly there had been Fort Blockhouse - surely implying a defence connection - and an aerodrome and wireless station were placed between two military installations.[42]

When the Committee of Imperial Defence regulations were introduced in 1928, the 1928 printing of the Portsmouth sheet made further concessions to the new rules: the

39 PRO OS 1/250. Letter dated 23/12/1937 from the War Office to MacLeod.
40 PRO OS 1/250. MacLeod to the Director of Military Operations and Intelligence, 11/1/1938.
41 PRO OS 1/250. MacLeod to the Director of Military Operations and Intelligence, 11/1/1938.
42 Hodson, (1995), p.164, fig.39.

internal detail of the forts was removed, but the outlines remained. This was clearly not going far enough, however, for by 1932, all the oil storage tanks were deleted, together with the words 'barracks', 'torpedo range' (although the basin was still shown), and 'wireless telegraph station' from Horsea Island, and 'gas works' (but the buildings remained) from Portsea. This was following the 1928 instructions to the letter, but the picture became confused on the 1935 printing with the restoration of the wireless telegraph station on Horsea Island - an obviously military base - and the erasure of that from the aerodrome.

This apparently inexplicable discrepancy was present on the 1938 printing of the sheet and was further compounded by the publication in the same year of the Fifth Edition sheet (141) for the area. On this, the paradox was completed: the words 'Royal Dockyard' and 'Barracks' (or the abbreviation 'Bks') were restored, but the torpedo range basin was deleted together with the outlines of all the forts. Two one-inch sheets were therefore available simultaneously, but with different security treatments, in spite of the fact that in 1934 it was stated that full precautions had been taken to ensure that all information of a secret character was to be deleted from the sales edition of the new Fifth Edition one-inch map,[43] and that at the same time, care should be taken to make the same deletions of information on reprints of the Popular Edition.

In 1931 Winterbotham had written that as far as the Fifth Edition was concerned, authority was given to insert forts of historical interest so long as they were not used by the services as dumps or magazines; he commented that the Popular Edition had raised 'serious objections' because it went so far as to say 'Battery, unused'.[44] This precise description has not been found on the Popular Edition, but there are examples of 'Battery (Dis^d)' on sheet 132. Even more unacceptable, one would have thought, was the description 'Battery (Dummy)', which occurs on sheet 116 square B7. The Officers in charge of the one-inch and printing departments of the Ordnance Survey were exhorted to ensure that between them all steps were taken 'to prevent the reprinting from any Popular sheet until it is certain that it contains no information which ought not to be on the Sales Edition'.[45]

A comparison of the states of sheet 132 with the editions of its constituent six-inch sheets[46] shows discrepancies in cartographic editing between the large and small scales which are difficult to explain. On none of the larger scale sheets, for example, is the torpedo range on Horsea Island shown, whereas it remained on all the reprints of the Popular Edition. Conversely, on some of the six-inch sheets which were revised in the early 1930s, the full internal layouts of the fortifications are shown, while they are absent from the one-inch map. This astonishing inconsistency in cartographic policy may have been caused simply by a lack of communication between the large scales and small scales drawing departments. Whatever the cause, the result was that a pointless exercise had produced a profound confusion of cartographic confidentiality which would hardly have

43 PRO OS 1/250. Minute 102, 5/7/1934.

44 RGS Archives (Winterbotham Correspondence). Winterbotham to Hinks, 25/8/1931.

45 PRO OS 1/250. Minute 102, 5/7/1934.

46 Six-inch county series Hampshire LXXV, LXXVI, LXXXIII, LXXXIV. Fifty-five quarter sheets, dated 1856 to 1938 were examined for this purpose.

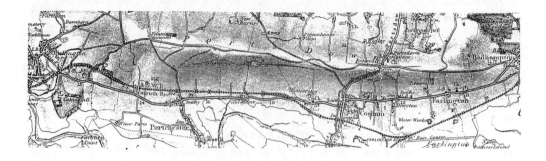

Fig.28a Portsdown Hill: security deletions All extracts reduced. Third Edition Small Sheet Series, sheet 316 & part of 331 (coloured; 1905, 4-05 printing). All contours and spot heights, which are present on all but the Portsmouth area of the sheet, have been deleted together with the names and outlines of the Portsdown Hill forts. *Private collection.*

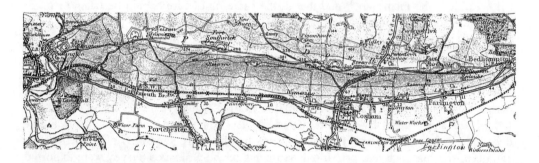

Fig.28b Third Edition Large Sheet Series, sheet 135 (1914). Contours, spot heights and fortifications have been restored following the 1908 ruling that fortifications could be shown on the one-inch map. *Private collection.*

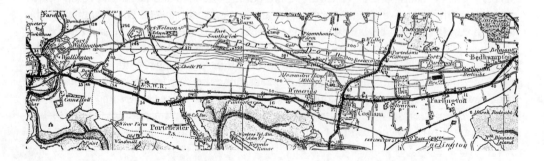

Fig.28c Popular Edition, sheet 132 (1919). Contours have been redrawn, and contour figures are now readable without turning the map; some spot heights have been revised; the internal details of the fortifications appear to be more precise. Note the disappearance of smithies along the Fareham-Bedhampton road, and the deletion both of 'L.B.'s and the abbreviation 'Ch.'. Parish boundaries have also been deleted. *Private collection.*

166

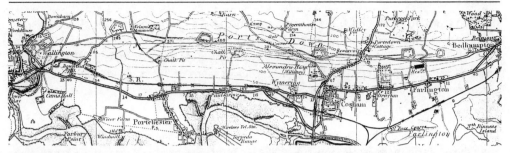

Fig.28d Popular Edition, sheet 132 (1925 reprint 2000/25). Fort names have been erased. *Private collection.*

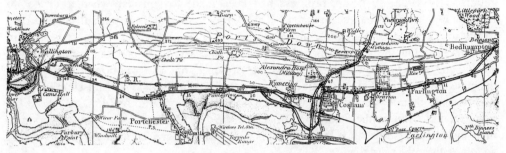

Fig.28e Popular Edition, sheet 132 (1928 reprint 2000/25.3000/28.) The internal details of the forts have been deleted. *Private collection.*

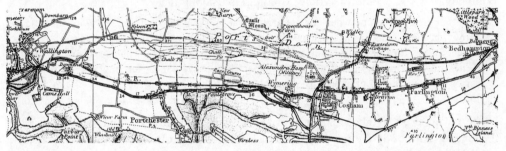

Fig.28f Popular Edition, sheet 132 (1938 reprint 2538). Defence information remains the same as fig.28e; electricity transmission lines have been added. Note the difference in settlement depiction between this extract and fig.28g which was on sale at the same time. *Private collection.*

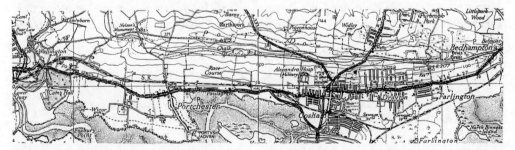

Fig.28g Fifth Edition, sheet 141 (1938 reprint 10038.M38.R37.). All fortification details have been deleted except for Fort Purbrook and Farlington Redoubt (just west of Bedhampton); the lettering of Nelson's Monument has been moved so that it occupies the space of Fort Nelson, whose outline is still shown on fig.28f. Parish boundaries have been restored. *Private collection.*

deluded German Intelligence, who were probably as well prepared for the Second World War[47] as they had been for the First. When the Ordnance Survey agent, Fisher Unwin, was asked in June 1914 if he sold Ordnance Survey maps abroad, the significance of his answer, which was that of late the highest sales of maps on the continent had been to the Germans, could hardly have escaped Close.[48]

Utilities

One of the features which it was decided not to treat as a candidate for security deletion was the electricity transmission line. The Central Electricity Board (CEB) had been formed in 1926, and in the following year began to lay a grid of power lines across the country. By 1928, sufficient progress had been made to consider whether or not to include them on the small-scale maps.[49] They were 'undoubtedly important' and seemed likely to 'become land marks', and their portrayal on maps was to be requested in Parliament.[50] On the other hand, they were of the same national importance as gas works and electric power stations, whose presence on sales editions of maps was disguised by omitting the descriptive words. The problem with the transmission lines was that to show them by any symbol would be to betray their identity without any need for nomenclature. But neither the War Office nor the Air Ministry raised any objection to their inclusion, asserting that they did not pose the same degree of vulnerability to enemy action as the other installations.[51]

It was to be another five years before the subject was raised again. On this occasion, Withycombe wrote to the Electricity Commission saying that

> The time has now come when the electricity transmission lines carried on pylons should be shown on the 1" maps, and perhaps also on some of the smaller scales. As the 4th revision proceeds, we are, of course, surveying the lines and putting them on the sheets of the 5th Relief Edition, but it will be at least ten years before we can cover England with the new series, and in the meantime it is desirable to put the lines on the sheets of the Popular Edition.[52]

In the meantime, a symbol for the lines had already been devised, and had appeared in the legend (but not on the map) of the first Fifth (Relief) Edition sheet (144, *Plymouth*), published in 1931. In fact, at the beginning of the fourth revision of the one-inch map in 1928, the revisers had been instructed to show the transmission lines, and several sheets were revised, but not published, showing primary, secondary and low pressure lines, but there was no symbol to distinguish between the different grades on the printed map. These instructions were altered in February 1932 so that only the main grid (in other

---

47 On 19/7/1937 it was reported in the House of Commons (Parliamentary Debates. H.C.Deb.5s.326.) that an 'exceptionally heavy rush of orders recently placed from a foreign country [Germany] for large scale British Ordnance maps of the environs of London and other large towns' had been noted in the press.

48 Olivier, (1914a), para.45.

49 PRO OS 1/250. f.44A, 29/11/1928.

50 Parliamentary Debates. H.C.Deb.5s.241, 10/7/1930.

51 PRO OS 1/250. ff.46A, 13/12/1928 and 47A, 15/12/1928.

52 PRO OS 1/541. Withycombe to R.T.G. French, Electricity Commission, 4/9/1933.

words, those lines carried on pylons) should be shown.[53] The point of Withycombe's writing to the Electricity Commission was to ask if they kept record sets of six-inch maps marked up with the routes of the lines; for these, the Ordnance Survey was referred to the CEB, and in writing, Withycombe confirmed the policy of making corrections on reprints: 'opportunity is taken of reprints to insert such major changes as roads, railways, etc., and it would be convenient to add also the grid lines at such times'.[54] In view of Clough's statement that it was only proposed to show 'tower positions[55] and power lines' on the one-inch Fifth Edition, the six-inch and the twenty-five inch scales,[56] it might be inferred that they were not to be included on the Popular Edition. It was, in fact, to be some time before the lines actually appeared on the Popular Edition - sheets 22 and 87 appear to have been the first to carry the symbol in the legend, in 1937 - and even then, only about thirty sheets showed the lines on the face of the map.

In order to speed up data capture, an arrangement was made whereby Ordnance Survey staff took six-inch maps to the Electricity Board, and copied onto them the details from the Board's own maps. It was soon found that the CEB plotting was not accurate enough to transfer, unaltered, to the large scales, but the use of the information was authorised for the one-inch map.[57] Although this was a considerable effort of data collection, it had the merit, at least, of ensuring that the information was given to the public faster than had the usual procedure of waiting for the revised six-inch publications been adhered to. The first area to be covered, in October 1933, was south-east England; this was followed, in July 1934, by the rest of southern England. As might be expected, most of the Popular Edition sheets showing the power lines were on reprints dating from 1937 of the areas not covered by the Fifth Edition: the midlands and north of England.

Two other utilities made their appearance for the first time on a one-inch series with the Popular Edition. The first was the wireless telegraph station; following from Marconi's patent in 1896, wireless telegraphy came under the wing of the Post Office and was increasingly used for public service from about 1909 onwards. Wireless telegraph stations were first shown on the one-inch map after 5 September 1910,[58] and were indicated on the Popular either by the abbreviation 'W.T.S.' or by words; if it was operated by the Admiralty, this word was added. The second utility was the telephone, which was available for public use in village post offices (it was understood that 'all towns have offices, so they need not be shown in towns'[59]). This, together with the inclusion of wireless telegraph stations, was a significant change between the Third and Popular Editions. Until 1910, only public telegraph services, also available at post offices were shown; telephones were first mentioned in revision instructions in 1913:

53 This résumé is given in PRO OS 1/541. Letter from Clough to Hedderwick, 19/2/1937.

54 PRO OS 1/541. 21/9/1933.

55 Tower positions were not shown on either the Popular Edition or the Fifth Edition.

56 PRO OS 1/541. A.B. Clough (Executive Officer, i.e. Deputy Director General), to the CEB, 10/12/1935.

57 PRO OS 1/541. The use of the six-inch plots for the compilation of the small scales was approved by the Director General on 11/10/1933.

58 Ordnance Survey *Instructions for the revision of the 1-inch map*, (1909), MS amendments.

59 *Ibid.*, p.13, para.43.

Examiners & Draftsmen will in future insert on the L.S.Sheets 1" Drawings P.t. for telephone offices when situated at Country post offices from which Telegrams can be sent by telephone for transmission.[60]

Although this information may have been incorporated in the Third Edition Large Sheet Series drawing sheets, neither its use nor that of the wireless telegraph station, on the post-1913 reprints of that series has been noted;[61] it seems likely therefore that the 'L.S. Sheets 1" Drawings' referred to compilation material for the Popular Edition. The earliest appearance of the telephone symbol occurs in the legends of the *Torquay & Dartmouth*, and Aldershot sheets, which were all printed in 1914.

Within a short time of the completion of the publication of the Popular Edition in 1926, discussions were under way to include the telephone kiosks of the General Post Office, the Automobile Association, and the Royal Automobile Club.[62] In an effort to show everything, the original specification for Post Office, telegraph and telephone facilities on the pre-1935 sheets of the Fifth Edition expanded to include five symbols which attempted to distinguish by letters, for example, between public and private telephones. These were rationalised from 1935;[63] unlike other symbols which appeared on the Fifth Edition, they did not find their way onto the Popular. This was probably because the different use of the letters to denote types of post, telegraph and telephone services would have entailed an inordinate amount of revision of small detail to the stones and the operation would not have justified the expense. The spread of telephone facilities marked, on the one hand, the upgrading of equipment in post offices; on the other, their inclusion on the map reflected their value to an ever more mobile map user, who had more leisure to explore the countryside. Writing in 1928, Winterbotham commented that

At the date at which the characteristic sheet for the Popular Edition was made, the telegraph was no doubt the great standby throughout the country in cases of emergency; it is not so today ... it is believed that the first re-action in case of trouble would be to look on the ... map for the nearest Post Office.[64]

By then, almost all post offices had telephones, supplying one of the benefits, which, like the introduction of bus services, was symptomatic of the general improvement in the 1920s in amenities for the countryman. His town cousin, too, was drawn to the country in increasing numbers in the following decade, and for the walker, the one-inch map was a graphic representation of the available facilities.

Parks and parish boundaries

Hikers generally walked the wide open spaces, but their paths occasionally crossed parklands. The predominant green ruling which was used for this category on most sheets was responsible for lending to the Popular Edition an air of lightness which was especially marked on sheets with large areas of grey and black urban sprawl. The green

---

60 Ordnance Survey *Instructions for the revision of the 1-inch map*, (1909), MS annotation, dated 30/6/1913.

61 It is not referred to in Messenger, (1988).

62 PRO OS 1/312. Correspondence between OS and the War Office in 1928.

63 Three categories: post office with telegraph and telephone; other post offices; telephone kiosk (GPO, AA, RAC).

64 PRO OS 1/312.f.16A. Winterbotham to Jack, 22/10/1928.

ruling (Plate 11c) was one of four methods used to show parks; the other three were different types of stippling. The first of these was the old hand-engraved stipple that had appeared on all the one-inch sheets from the Old Series to the Third Edition (Plate 11a); the second stipple was new to the one-inch map series, and was made with a dotting wheel or roulette[65] which produced dots in straight lines (Plate 11b); the third stipple was newly drawn, and was used on some reprints of the Popular Edition. As with other specification changes, two questions need to be asked: first, when did the alteration take place, and secondly, why was it necessary? The first is easily answered simply by looking at all the states of the sheets and recording the dates: a predominant specification of green ruled lines emerges in early 1920.

To begin with, however, the thirty-one sheets that were published in June 1919[66] showed parks by a regular rouletted black stipple (sheet 132, unusually, showed both Third Edition and rouletted stipple for different parks on the same sheet, Plate 11b). Four sheets published in September and October of 1919 reproduced the old Third Edition stipple; two sheets published in January 1920 carried the rouletted stippling once again, but sheet 85, published in February 1920, was the first to employ the characteristic green ruling which was used for the first printing of all sheets published after this date, apart from sheets 1, 3 and 5, which employed the Scottish Popular specification. Later reprints of some sheets were again to use stippling in place of the green ruling, and the reason for this will be explained below. This muddle of early changes in specification for parklands, which all occurred within a few months, poses a conundrum. Why, in the first place, if it were decided to use a stipple as the conventional sign, was the Third Edition stipple not taken straight from the old Small Sheet copperplates? The trouble of erasing it must have been considerable. The answer would appear to be inextricably bound up with the original specification for the Killarney-style relief map and with the decision about whether or not to include parish boundaries on the one-inch map.

As with so many other aspects of the Popular Edition specification, the omission of parish boundaries was suggested in the recommendations of the 1892 Dorington committee. This was not followed for the Revised New Series sheets because, first, it would have been expensive to remove them, and secondly because the Local Government Board had asked for their retention.[67] The combination of a rouletted stipple and the lack of parish boundaries first seems to have occurred on the *Torquay & Dartmouth* map, and the earliest *Aldershot (North)* and *(South)* sheets of 1914. These three sheets had one further common denominator not present on any of the other one-inch maps of 1914 which, in any case, were based on the Second Revision (1901-12) and retained the specification for the Third Edition. This was that contours were shown by black dotted

---

65 A description of the dotting wheel, or roulette, which was supposed to produce the same effect as an Indian ink wash on the copperplate, is described in *Account of the methods and processes ...*, (1902), pp.195-6. This method of representing parks had been used for some years by Bartholomew for his half-inch layered maps. It may be that Close studied the ingredients of his rival's cartographic success, and copied them, initially for his projected layered relief map.

66 See calendar of first publication in Part 2, p.377.

67 PRO OS 1/9/2. Minute from Johnston, 24/3/1899.

lines that were very similar to the parish boundary symbol,[68] and, where they crossed the irregular Third Edition stipple of parks would have created a confused dotted image where all three symbols coincided, were the parish boundaries to be retained. The main problem here would have been with the contours - far more of these crossed parks than did boundaries.[69]

A solution, if the retention of dotted contours was considered preferable, would have been to have changed the park symbol; indeed, dotted contours on a rouletted stipple for parks, rather than the random stipple of the Third Edition, stood out perfectly - especially if the contours were to be printed in brown, as originally envisaged. But why not use a colour for parks, as was to be done for the later Popular Edition printings? The answer to that question probably is that at that time, Close was contemplating a fully layered, hachured and hill shaded map: a further colour for parks would have been just as confusing as the convergence of three dotted symbols. This point is well illustrated by comparing the tourist map of Lands End (whose sheet lines were coincident with those of the standard coloured series) first published in 1922, with its sister sheet 146 in the Popular Edition. The layered tourist map has used the rouletted stippling which distinguishes parks more clearly than the green ruling would have done.

Why, then, did the first few sheets of the Popular Edition retain the rouletted parks when, by 1919, it was probably clear that Close's cherished de luxe relief version would not be published? It may be that these were the sheets to which Close referred in his *Annual Report* for 1913/14 as being in an advanced state of preparation, and likely to be published later in 1914. At this stage, two versions of the map were still being contemplated, and it would have been uneconomic to have had a different convention for parks for each style of map, even though, on the unlayered sheets contours were to be shown as coloured continuous lines. Here again, though, we face the question of parish boundaries, and when the final decision to omit them was taken. Their absence from the Lake District specimen and Torquay and Aldershot maps may have been experimental because in fact, Close, having sought ministerial approval first, had recommended their deletion in about 1912-13 on the grounds that they would confuse the detail of the Killarney-style map.[70]

No instruction to delete the parish boundaries has been found, and the relevant rulings of 1914 imply their intended retention by the absence of any reference to their withdrawal. Indeed, an undated amendment to paragraph 35 on boundaries reads that while administrative counties and county boroughs were to be defined by the county symbol, parish boundaries 'are not shown within the area of a County Borough, and where appearing will be marked for erasure'. It can be inferred, therefore, that parish boundaries were to be shown outside county boroughs. That parish boundaries actually were included on those sheets of the Popular Edition which were in preparation in 1914,

---

68 The Lake District specimen (Plate 2) of 1913 also lacked parish boundaries, but parks were shown in the old Third Edition stipple and contour lines were printed with brown dots.

69 Johnston, (1920), wrote that the parish boundaries were easily confused with footpaths; in practice, it could hardly be said that dotted parish boundaries were difficult to distinguish from the dashed lines of the footpaths.

70 Olivier, (1914a), p.30.

is confirmed by linear gaps, indicating the former presence of the boundaries, in the rouletted parkland stipple of sheets published in June 1919. One last piece of evidence points to early 1919 as the time when parish boundaries were finally removed from the map. The erasure sheet (fig.10, p.47) which is dated 22 January 1919, did not have the boundaries marked for erasure. In order to be able to delete the boundaries from the stones or copperplates in time for the first sheets to be published in June, it is probable that the decision must have been made at the end of January 1919, or soon after.[71]

The last minute nature of the decision seems to be confirmed by the extract of sheet 118 in the first edition of the *Description of the small scale Ordnance Survey maps*, published in December 1919, which also showed the symbol for parish boundaries both on the map extract and in the conventional signs for the Popular Edition. Sheet 118 was first published in June 1919 and carried a 1919 print date, but this printing date was changed on subsequent reprints to 1918. It may well be that the other sheets with a 1918 print date (119, 120, 128, 143) were originally printed in 1918 with parish boundaries. They may then have been reprinted, without boundaries, for publication in 1919, without the original printing date being altered.

It is difficult to imagine that the poor quality image generated by these deletions in the park stipple would have gone unnoticed, and some thought must have been given to the problem, because four sheets published in September and October 1919 (93, 94, 105, 113) used the copperplates of the Third Edition for the park stipple. On sheet 94 (*Bicester*) in particular, some attempt to patch up the gaps had been made in the parkland surrounding Waddesdon Manor (square H12), but by trying to make good the deletions, had produced only a messy compromise. The Great and Lower Parks of Blenheim Palace not only showed the white lines of the erased parish boundaries, but also had unsightly gaps where the name of the parish had been deleted - no attempt had been made to fill these. On coastal and estuarine sheets it was also possible to see where the parish boundary symbol had been erased from the stipple of the mudflats. What was the solution to this defacement? Sheets 93 and 105 received no remedial treatment; but the broken stippling on sheet 113 was so carefully repaired on the 1927 printing that it is difficult to spot the mends, while sheet 94 received star attention. For the 1928 printing of this sheet the Third Edition parish boundaries and parish names were restored; one might speculate, albeit with no other evidence than that of the map, that the Duke of Marlborough may have played a part in the cartographic restoration of his parklands.

The next phase in this muddled handling of the parks symbols came with the publication of sheets 82-84 (Oct. and Dec. 1919), and 95 and 96 (Jan. 1920). These five sheets used the rouletted stipple, which was kept, unaltered, for sheet 82 throughout its life.[72] However, an interesting development took place on sheets 95 and 96. The first printing of 95 (*Luton*), which was undated in the margin, but announced as published in

71 The question was clearly debated throughout the war years because the symbol for the boundaries is retained in the legend of the 1916 experimental Bridgwater sheet, but none appears on this map except for one small area, in square J11, where the boundary appears to have been overlooked. It was incompletely deleted on the first printing of Popular Edition sheet 120.

72 Careful restoration of the stippling can be seen in some areas, indicating the former presence of parish boundaries.

January 1920, showed parks by rouletted stipple. Furthermore, because none of the park areas show signs of repair after the deletion of parish boundaries (particularly evident, for example in the pristine stipple of Ashridge Park, square J6), it seems that the compilation material was prepared after the decision to omit the boundaries had been taken. On the printings of sheet 95 made between and including 1921 and 1929 no park symbol was used, and parklands were simply blank areas;[73] then, on the 1932 state, not only did the Third Edition stipple reappear, but with it the parish boundaries and names.[74] The sheet retained these features, in the same way as sheet 94, until it was replaced by the Fifth Edition.

This was not quite the end of the stippled park on the Popular Edition, however, for a few sheets, printed mainly in the late 1930s, reverted from green ruling to the stipple of the Third Edition copperplates.[75] The undoubted explanation for this change was that the stones for these sheets had become so worn out that it had been necessary to go back to the original copperplates in order to produce new reprints. An exceptional variation occurred on the 1938 reprint of sheet 30 (*Blackburn*) where the original parks were printed in green rouletted stipple, but new parks were added in hand-drawn black stipple. The impression given, in the absence of explanation on the sheet, is that the two conventions might have implied a distinction between public and private parks, such as that adopted for the Fifth Edition, but this proves not to be the case, and merely reflects revision to the plate; parkland additions had also been made to other sheets in the past.[76] The case of sheet 120 (*Bridgwater & Quantock Hills*) was slightly different, for here the sequence was rouletted stipple, followed, on the 1926-9 reprints by green fill, and returning to the rouletted stipple, together with parish boundaries for the remaining reprints.

The reason for using green ruling instead of a rouletted stipple is not recorded. It might well have been a conscious effort to improve the design of the map, in the same way that blue ruling had replaced the early muddle of water specifications. Parish boundaries did not disappear completely, for, apart from the two instances mentioned above (94 and 95), and sheet 115 (*S.E. London & Sevenoaks*) which sported both green parks and the usual parish boundary dotted lines between 1930 and 1934, the Third Edition parish boundary symbol of a dotted line was shown in the legends of some thirty standard Popular Edition sheets. A different parish boundary symbol was printed on at least nine sheets[77] in the 1930s. This was a dotted line with every fourth dot enlarged.

---

73 Sheet 96 (*Hertford & Bishop's Stortford*) similarly lacked any park symbol of the 1921 printing, but green ruling was used for its 1923 reprint.

74 The Parish name was written across the parish in sloping hair-line Egyptian letters for those parishes which did not have a village of the same name; Ordnance Survey *Instructions for the revision of the small scale maps* ..., (Jan.1914), para.54.

75 Those noted are: 11, 12, 13, 22, 25, 26, 27, 38, 42, 47, 77, 95, 109, 114.

76 Notably 91 (1937), 93 (1936), 102 (1936). Many new additions stand out because they are in a different stipple.

77 Sheets 91, 102, 103, 112, 120, 121, 122, 130, 140. Theoretically, since fifty-five sheets were engraved with this convention, it is possible that more states of the later reprints exist with this symbol; even if they do not occur on the Popular Edition, they can be found on some tourist and district sheets where the original copperplates, rather than revised electrotype copies, have been used in the production of the maps

The genesis of this convention was formerly unknown, but it now appears that fifty-five sheets (not identified, but presumably the first fifty-five to be printed) were treated in this way, and the plates underwent substantial reworking by removing the water detail and at the same time strengthening every fourth dot of the parish boundary (in order to distinguish it from dotted contours), before the policy was reversed and the water was put back and the boundaries erased.[78] The earliest appearance in print of this new symbol seems to have been on an Officers' Training Course examination extract dated November 1920.[79] It was also used for some of the military special sheets which were based on Popular material, but was not used as the symbol for parish boundaries when these were restored to the Fifth Edition sheets.[80]

It would seem, then, that the complex relationship between the parkland symbol, contours and parish boundaries caused radical rethinking of the specification in the first few months of the Popular Edition's public life, and added to the labour of producing an outline edition which, because it carried no green plate, still required the black stippled parks. In deciding to leave parish boundaries off the one-inch map, Close made a fundamental misjudgement which was to cost the Ordnance Survey dearly. In five years alone, between 1927 and 1932, over 140,000 impressions were taken from the Third Edition Small Sheet copperplates which, although out of date, supplied the missing boundaries which were so much in demand.[81] This was about 20% of the number of impressions of the Popular Edition printed for this period,[82] and overall may have had some influence on the sales of the regular sheets. Selling the map was to be one of the Ordnance Survey's major preoccupations after 1918. It was not enough constantly to be trying to improve the appearance of the sheets by altering the specification so that water, for example, was more consistently shown, and new forestry added, or contours made easier to read; even keeping up to date with road classifications and the insertion of new utilities would have been in vain if, in the end, the maps did not reach enough retail outlets. Packaging, presentation, pricing and advertising were all to play a more significant role in marketing the Popular Edition than for any previous one-inch map.

in the later 1930s, and on some sheets of GSGS 3907, e.g. 122 (*Salisbury & Bulford*, 25,000/40).

78 PRO OS 1/9/5. Undated memo [ca Dec.1922], '1″ revision of Great Britain'.

79 Officers Training Course. Examination for Certificate 'A.'. Tactics, first paper (Parts I and II). Index No. (Popular Edition). Part of sheet 121. November 1920. *Private collection*. This extract has contours and first class roads in red, secondary roads in yellow; there is no green, and the contours are augmented by brown hachures. The legend in the bottom margin, which is in the same format as the standard Popular Edition sheets, includes the new symbol for parish boundaries.

80 Only one example of a Popular sheet legend to carry the modified parish boundary has been noted: sheet 130 (1535. and 1535.2535. printings).

81 The annual reports for these years are the only ones to refer to the number of outline small sheets printed for this purpose; the overall figure would have been much greater.

82 Calculations based on print-run figures on the maps.

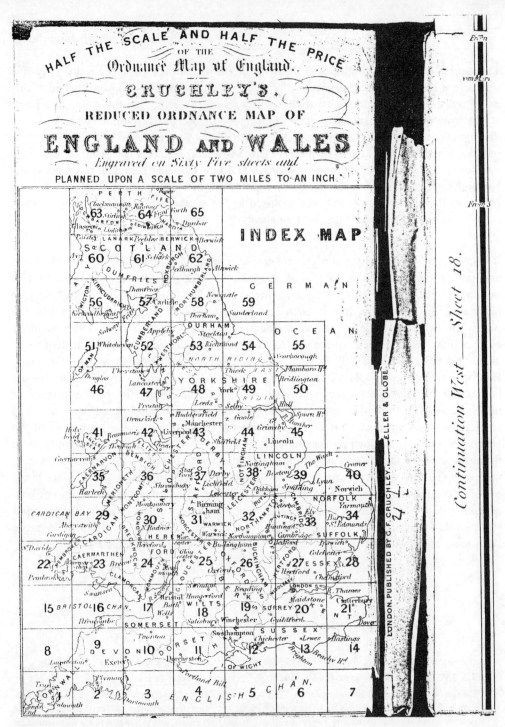

Fig.29 Part of sheet 19 (1865) of Cruchley's half-inch series of England and Wales, dissected and mounted on linen, showing the inside of the 'book' cover. This type of reinforced cover, which had been used by Cruchley since at least the 1850s, was commonly used by commercial publishers in the nineteenth century. The Ordnance Survey referred to it as a 'wrapper' or 'wrap round' cover, and first used it in the 1890s. The concept of placing a series index on the cover was not adopted by the Survey until about 1902. *Private collection.*

Chapter IX

MARKETING THE MAP

I suppose the Ordnance maps supply the raw material out of which private enterprise often supplies the finished article? - Yes, ... for the mass of the travelling public, private enterprise supplies a more serviceable map. *Hayes Fisher Committee*, (1896).[1]

The Popular Edition one-inch map had been designed to retrieve for the Ordnance Survey the market in small-scale mapping which had been firmly cornered by the commercial sector since the beginning of the nineteenth century. The Survey was, in the inter-war years, to claim a notable success in selling the one-inch map; this was achieved principally by more aggressive marketing tactics. But what was the nature of the competition? Who were the users, and was any attempt made to promote the national mapping in education? Did commercial practice really have any direct influence on Ordnance Survey selling methods? How did the Survey price its products and decide its print runs? Lastly, did the Popular Edition make a profit? These questions are discussed here.

The 'mother of all maps'

Almost as soon as the early one-inch maps were published, commercial map makers seized what must have seemed a golden opportunity and began to issue derived mapping based on the government survey. The relationship of the Ordnance Survey with these map-sellers has been discussed elsewhere,[2] and it is significant to note the magnanimous attitude of the Board of Ordnance in those early days towards allowing private individuals to construct 'more correct maps of the counties' from the trigonometrical data. However, the potential harm to government map sales of a privately produced national series, by John Cary, gave rise in 1817 to the first public pronouncement on copyright infringement.[3] In spite of the prohibition of 'copying, reducing or incorporating into other Works, and publishing all or any part of the Trigonometrical Survey,'[4] private map sales based on the Ordnance Survey one-inch maps proliferated, largely unchecked, for the second half of the nineteenth century.[5]

Foremost among the 'cheap and cheerful' products of the 1850s were those by G.F.

---

1   Hayes Fisher, (1896b), para.1320. The Hayes Fisher Committee was appointed to inquire into the sale of Ordnance Survey maps. It sat in 1895, but the proceedings were not published until 1896.

2   Seymour, (1980), pp.73-7.

3   *Ibid.*, p.76.

4   *London Gazette*, 28 Feb.1817.

5   The few rulings made on copyright for this period are given in PRO OS 1/233.

Cruchley, whose 'Reduced Ordnance Map of England and Wales' in sixty-five sheets was marketed under the slogan 'Half the scale and half the price of the Ordnance Map' (fig.29). No action was taken by the Ordnance Survey against this blatant pirating of their name. Other map publishers imitated the example, but none more successfully than Bartholomew, who, in the last quarter of the century, began to issue his now celebrated layered half-inch series. Here, at last, was serious competition, for not only were his products attractively coloured, they purported to be as accurate as those of the Ordnance Survey, on whose maps they were firmly based and whose name figured prominently in the titles, following the common custom of nineteenth-century map publishers.[6] So prevalent was the practice of using the national maps for private enterprise that discussions of the procedures were entirely open; thus Bartholomew writes about 'the revision of our older plates from the sheets of the Revised 1in [sic] Ordnance Survey now being issued'.[7] Indeed, Bartholomew fielded complaints about the inaccuracy of his own maps by blaming it on the obsolescence of the Ordnance Survey![8] A full assessment of the true extent to which Bartholomew derived any real financial gain from using Ordnance Survey material has yet to be made; it would be especially worthwhile in view of his policy of appealing to the public by producing a superior, rather than cheap product.[9]

Much has been made by the Ordnance Survey, both at the beginning of this century and in recent accounts, of the damage done by the infringement of their copyright by others. However, as early as the 1840s, the Treasury (doubtless acting as the mouthpiece of the Ordnance Survey) suggested that small-scale derivatives of the large-scale surveys in Ireland should be left to private enterprise.[10] This principle was reiterated by the Dorington Committee which actually recommended that 'great freedom be allowed to private publishers'[11] who were to be supplied with transfers from the one-inch and smaller scales on favourable terms for the purpose of producing derived commercial cartographic products. The position was further clarified by Wilson in 1894, when he stated that the Ordnance Survey did not disagree with this recommendation, but added that the only objection was to facsimiles of Ordnance Survey maps.[12] Only four years earlier, Wilson had stated that the construction of 'special maps for popular use was designedly left to private enterprise, and any attempt [by the Ordnance Survey] to compete with private firms in "catering for the public" has been discouraged'.[13] In 1890, of course, Bartholomew's half-inch of England and Wales had not yet been published - it was only when this heartland of Ordnance Survey map production was

6 Gardiner, (1976), p.32.

7 NLS, Bartholomew Archive: Acc.10222 III B10 Letter dated 15/3/1898.

8 NLS, Bartholomew Archive: Acc.10222 III B11 Letter dated 20/4/1898.

9 NLS, Bartholomew Archive: Acc.10222 III B11 Letter dated 3/6/1898, in which Bartholomew claims to spend more on the correction and elaboration of his plates than any other publisher, and that his profits were therefore proportionately small. He cites the cost of the corrections to the new Surrey half-inch sheet as having absorbed all the profits of more than one edition [of one sheet, presumably].

10 Oliver, (1985b), p.126.

11 Dorington, (1893a), p.xxxix, recommendation 23.

12 Dorington, (1894), p.10.

13 *The Manchester Geographical Journal*, (1890), pp.520-2.

assailed (beginning in 1891) that the balloon went up. Even so, there was a tacit understanding in the Ordnance Survey, which persisted into the 1930s, that although map sales could be increased if they were advertised more, the Survey deliberately held back because 'it would cut at private firms' who had interests which went back 'a long way in machinery and so on'.[14]

The point perhaps needs to be made that the Ordnance Survey's copyright problems were entirely self-inflicted, for by not implementing the 1816 threats of prosecution under copyright laws, nor systematically enforcing the Copyright Act of 1842, the Ordnance Survey had allowed, by default, a substantial number of 'formidable competitors'[15] to develop. In 1891, for example, Stanford, the Ordnance Survey agent, railed against their total neglect in protecting their copyright.[16] Although the question of royalty payments was discussed in the Dorington Committee in 1892, it was recommended that outside the national topographical scales of twenty-five inches and six inches to the mile, private enterprise should be allowed to produce maps for special purposes at the one-inch scale or smaller,[17] and Wilson was in favour of combined sheets being produced privately.[18] No suggestion was made by the Hayes Fisher Committee in 1895 that royalties should be charged, even when it was noted that it was particularly the one-inch map which suffered as a consequence of so many provincial agents who made 'large profits', having produced maps of their own districts by joining Ordnance Survey sheets together, photographing them, and producing a smaller scale derivative which suited local needs better than those of the national survey.[19] This kind of commercial competition was to flourish in the 1930s, when the rapid growth of cheap photographic copying methods 'enormously stimulated' private competition.[20]

The moves to prevent the Ordnance Survey's name from being overtly used on private publications began in 1901.[21] It elicited an understandably astonished response from Bartholomew who retorted that he had used the name for thirty years 'without objection having been raised', and that he had made no more use of Ordnance Survey maps than any 'other private Map Maker necessarily does'.[22] The correspondence between Bartholomew and HMSO and Ordnance Survey became ominously polite, but feelings of justifiably righteous indignation on the part of the private publisher underscored the courteous interchange of letters. Bartholomew felt obliged to explain how his maps were produced:

> our method hitherto in the matter of revision has been to get new roads, railways, docks,

14 PRO OS 1/338. Minute 80, 3/11/1934.

15 Hayes Fisher, (1896b), para.656.

16 Stanford, (1891). See also, Aylward, (1971).

17 Dorington, (1893a), p.10.

18 PRO OS 1/2/5.

19 Hayes Fisher, (1896b), paras.653-60.

20 PRO OS 1/20. Winterbotham to the Under Secretary of State, War Office, 6/4/1932.

21 *London Gazette*, 30/8/1901, a notice inserted by the Board of Agriculture, objecting to maps produced by Bartholomew. A fuller background, but by no means the whole story, is given in Seymour, (1980), pp.198, 207, and in Owen and Pilbeam, (1992), pp.96-8.

22 NLS, Bartholomew Archive: Acc.10222 III B15, Letter dated 28/4/1902.

buildings and other features from the engineers, surveyors and local authorities. When the revised Survey sheet appears, usually some years later, we naturally compare our mapping with the Survey and as the latter is the standard authority we make any modification necessary. In doing so we fail to see that we are infinging the copyright of the survey.[23]

Bartholomew, getting well into his stride in tackling what he plainly regarded as the intransigence of the official survey authority, then passed a comment which, although written nearly ninety years ago, has an undoubtedly modern ring to it:

> Surely it [the Survey] does not contend that the correct topographic outline of the British Isles is its private property and copyright, and that all maps and atlases of the British Isles are to be prepared without reference to the survey? Such an idea has never been advanced before, and as far as we are aware it exists in no other state. Among geographers the Survey is looked on and referred to as the mother of all maps![24]

In the next few years Bartholomew was unrelentingly pursued by the Ordnance Survey on the copyright of even the most trivial maps, such as those in Baddeley's guides. These had been printed about twenty years before stringent restrictions on the use of Ordnance Survey material came into force after the Copyright Act of 1911. The reprint of the little Snowdon map in 1913 for the guide to North Wales occasioned yet another copyright skirmish, illustrating that the new attitude of Ordnance Survey towards protecting its own products was beginning to have the desired effect, for Bartholomew replied:

> I may say that since the restrictions came into force we have practically ceased producing new maps of this country. In the few cases when we have done so the payment of royalty has made it financially prohibitive and resulted in a loss, so we are not doing it any more. In conclusion I would like to add that if the aim of the Ordnance Survey is to put a stop to all private enterprise in cartography it is ... hard that it should penalise British firms and allow German firms to do what they like in copying survey maps.[25]

Bartholomew was referring to German publishing firms who produced large-scale town plans based on the six-inch plans; these would then be copied and reduced by local publishing firms who thus escaped copyright penalties. In spite of the initial success of the Ordnance Survey's new aggression in the market place, Bartholomew's grip on the market for small-scale maps was so firmly established that the map-buying public were described in 1914 as having the 'Bartholomew habit'.[26]

It was against this background that the Popular Edition was published. The Select Committee on National Expenditure (Geddes) of 1918 had recommended that greater revenues should be obtained from royalties in respect of the use of the national maps by private map-making firms[27] and Close became the first Director General to carry out a consistent policy of enforcing royalty payments. In 1921 he wrote to the Stationery Office stating that his principles in assessing royalties were to impose substantial fees on maps which were likely to compete with Ordnance Survey products.[28] The direct implication

23 NLS, Bartholomew Archive: Acc.10222 III B26 f.905, Bartholomew to HMSO, 5/10/1911.

24 NLS, Bartholomew Archive: Acc.10222 III B26 f.905, Bartholomew to HMSO, 5/10/1911.

25 NLS, Bartholomew Archive: Acc.10222 III B30 f.378, J.G. Bartholomew to Close, 26/1/1914.

26 Olivier, (1914a), para.97, quoted in Seymour, (1980), p.225.

27 Parliamentary Debates. H.C.deb.5s.160, 1/3/23.

28 PRO OS 1/233. f.16.

is that the heaviest charges would be made for the use of small-scale mapping, but this cannot be confirmed by examining the royalty revenues[29] since the figures for large and small scales are combined. These figures do reveal that the receipts in these early days were small - usually no more than about 4% of the total sales income - but the important principle of copyright payment had been established during the life of the Popular Edition and has been maintained ever since.[30] It was not always easy to establish copyright transgression, but infringements were pursued with zeal. For example, Bartholomew's six-inch map of Jersey erred in copying an Ordnance Survey mistake, and his publication was examined 'square by square' by the Survey's 'expert nosey parker' in copyright questions with the intention of having him 'nicely nailed down in his coffin'.[31] However, by 1936, new regulations[32] had come into force which phased out the concessions to the established commercial map productions of thirty years earlier, and the scale at which new compilations, based on Ordnance Survey data, were allowed was reduced to one inch to six miles (1:380,160), effectively ruling out any serious competition to the one-inch map.

Educating the customer

For whose custom were state and private map publishers competing, and how many were cartographically literate? In 1914 the potential market was not greatly different to that of twenty years earlier. Although cheaper cars were being mass produced in Britain between 1910 and 1914, there were still only about 132,000 private cars in circulation,[33] but all publishers were aware of the potential sales target of the motorised road user. This was reflected in the Ordnance Survey's preoccupation with road classification - a reaction to the claim that trade in the one-inch had gone 'very much into the hands of the London publishers' such as Bacon, who issued simple maps with the roads coloured.[34] The possible one-inch map user was less easy to identify in 1914 than he was in 1940. Cyclists seemed to prefer the half-inch scale, motorists required the quarter-inch maps. And although walking was becoming popular - enough for the Federation of Rambling Clubs to have been asked to give evidence to the Olivier Committee - hiking was not then the major public pastime that it was to become in the 1930s.

As yet, few government concerns, apart from the ubiquitous use of the one-inch for setting out the railways for parliamentary purposes, are recorded as employing the one-inch map for official purposes. Within twenty years there was to be a dramatic change. In the 1930s the one-inch was to become a primary cartographic tool for broad planning purposes for local government and the Department of Health; the Town Planning Institute used the one-inch to create a 'Resolution Map' for defining the boundaries of the areas to which planning schemes were to apply. The Air Ministry selected aerodrome sites with

29 These were given in the annual reports.
30 Today, copyright revenue is in excess of £25.5 million, a useful contribution to a total turnover of £74,825,000. *Annual Report* (1997/8).
31 PRO OS 1/125. P.K. Boulnois to C.S.V. Cooke, 13/7/1932.
32 Ordnance Survey *Regulations governing the reproduction of Ordnance Survey maps*, (1936).
33 Nowell-Smith, (1964), p.241.
34 Hayes Fisher, (1896b), para.1198.

the aid of the one-inch; on it were indicated by the Forestry Commission the relative positions of forest blocks. The War Office, Hydrographic Department and Electricity Commission were also customers for the one-inch map. In the private market place the one-inch map appeared to have succeeded at last in establishing an 'Ordnance Survey habit' at least among walkers.[35]

It was recognised, certainly from the mid-1890s, that what nowadays would be termed 'brand loyalty' was best established in the cradle. It is significant that throughout the documentation for the fifty years from 1892 to 1942, there are repeated references to the concept that the ordinary layman was insufficiently educated to appreciate Ordnance Survey maps. That thousands bought commercial products, and seemed to have no trouble in using them was explained by the comparative simplicity of the privately produced map. Were comments such as '[metric measurement] will prove almost beyond the intelligence of the average person' and 'the smaller topographical scales, such as the one-inch ... are frequently used by people of less education'[36] patronising, or were they a realistic assessment? In writing to the Davidson Committee in about 1935, Lord Sandon was to observe

> We tell our citizens to be air conscious, we indulge in a somewhat wistful conceit that they are sea conscious, yet no one has ever thought of adding 'map conscious' to the vernacular ... it suggests a very practical variation of illiteracy.[37]

This remark seems to have been somewhat out of touch with reality, for by 1943 it was possible to tell the junior army map instructor that most of his men 'will already have a fair knowledge of maps, for they have grown up in an age of maps'.[38] There may well have been some truth in the belief that the general public was not taught mapwork in school at the beginning of the century. But there is evidence that much was done to improve the situation between 1895, when it was stated that 'teachers don't understand how to teach geography from the one-inch - which little boys cannot be got to understand',[39] and 1939, when Margaret Wood's *Map-reading for schools*, replete with nine full-page colour extracts from Ordnance Survey maps, appeared.

Her book was the latest in a line of school-oriented texts on reading and interpreting the Ordnance Survey maps, which had embraced such classics as Bygott's *An introduction to mapwork and practical geography* (1934), and especially C.H. Cox's *Exercises on Ordnance maps*.[40] This went through five editions and eleven reprints between its first publication in March 1924 and 1939. Cox's book was a masterpiece in public relations, for not only was it the same size as the Ordnance Survey's booklet *A description of the small scale Ordnance Survey maps*, but it also used the same map extracts and was the first to be able to make use of the appearance of the Popular Edition. Adult and child were therefore simultaneously exposed to the same map information.

---

35 This list of use of the one-inch has been compiled from the Davidson Committee files in OSL.
36 OSL G5186, OSC 72, 13/2/1936; OSC.56, 12/11/1935.
37 OSL G5186 OSC 28. Undated memorandum by Lord Sandon asking if it were too late to appoint a representative of the Board of Education to the Committee.
38 War Office, (1943), p.3.
39 *Hayes Fisher*, (1896b), para.1610.
40 See also Lockey, (1942).

What a contrast Cox's colourful presentation was to Marion Newbigin's *Ordnance Survey maps: their meaning and use*. Its second edition was published in 1920, only four years before Cox's work. Drab in appearance, and with only one small black and white reproduction of a map, its text, which aimed 'to show in detail how the 1-inch sheets of the Ordnance Survey maps can be used with profit by student and teacher alike', was rather negative about the very maps whose object it was to promote. The Ordnance Survey one-inch map was 'a document whose interpretation presents considerable difficulties, except to the trained eye'. This book was written as a guide to the use of the Third Edition, and one of the principal reasons given for the unpopularity of that map was that its contour interval was too great, and the colouring was not the equal to that of commercial products.

In spite of this, it is apparent that the Ordnance Survey did a brisk trade in supplying maps to schools. After all, some of the very difficulties of interpretation cited by Newbigin arose from the plethora of symbols which conveyed essential geographical information which was lacking in the commercial counterparts. In 1914 it was stated that selling maps to schools was 'an old policy';[41] it seems to have been begun in 1903 at the request of the Geographical Association.[42] In fact the sales of maps to schools had previously been pushed for years by Stanford, the Ordnance Survey Agent, who in his 1890 catalogue referred to the Education Code, which gave 'especial prominence to the teaching of the geography of the district in which the pupil resides', for which purpose 'no other maps published can be so full and useful ... as those of the Ordnance Survey'.[43] No wonder, then, that nearly twenty-five years later, in 1914, it was noted that 'all the Board schools now buy Ordnance maps' and that 50,000 or 60,000 maps a year were sold in this way.[44] In 1912, more than 54,000 maps were printed for educational purposes; this compared, for example, with only 69,000 one-inch maps printed during the year for the whole of Great Britain.[45] Special terms were arranged for minimum orders of 200; most of the maps were either the six-inch scale, or the outline Third Edition, which was printed on thin paper.[46] It seems that the coloured Third Edition was not so popular - perhaps the hachures confused the detail - but some examples of school printings can still be found. The market for the standard black and white sales edition was protected by printing on the schools version a licence assigning the use of the map to a specified scholar of a named school (fig.30).

Instruction in using the Popular Edition was made available not just in schools, but also to adults through the publication of 6d. booklets such as Thompson's *Map reading for ramblers: how to use the 1-inch Ordnance map*. Published by Stanford in 1927, it briefly

---

41 Olivier, (1914a), para.500.

42 *Annual Report*, (1903/4), p.7.

43 Stanford, (1890).

44 Olivier, (1914a), paras.419-420. The concessional rates for educational use are given on Circular, [form:] O.S. 318, (1913) and on PRO OS 1/15/2. f.46A, 11/4/1928.

45 *Annual Report*, (1911/12), p.19.

46 Not everyone approved of the quality of the cheap product: see Carter, (1915), where he complains of 'inferior printing' and 'shoddy paper' so that they were 'next to impossible to use'. Close replied (1915) that sheets of the coloured one-inch could be obtained for 3d. a copy, and that he was 'not aware of any country where coloured official maps could be obtained by schools so cheaply'.

covered aspects such as how to set the map and read contours, the conventional signs and magnetic variation. With a red cover, on which the pictorial design, modified from the covers of the Popular Edition sheets was emblazoned, the consumer was in no doubt of the identity of the booklet with its subject matter; it was instantly apparent at a distance

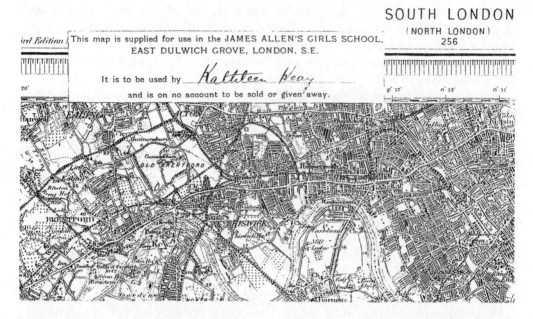

SOUTH LONDON

(NORTH LONDON)
256

ird Edition | This map is supplied for use in the JAMES ALLEN'S GIRLS SCHOOL, EAST DULWICH GROVE, LONDON. S.E.

It is to be used by *Kathleen Hoay*

and is on no account to be sold or given away.

Fig.30 Part of a 'school edition' of sheet 270 (South London) of the Third Edition outline Small Sheet Series, showing the label which was printed on the map identifying the school and the student who was entitled to use it. O.S.318 (1913) stated that 'the scholar's name should be written in the place left for the purpose on the Map issued to him'. Schools would combine to make up the minimum order of 200 copies (200 copies of one Third Edition outline sheet would cost £1.5s.0d.). *Private collection.*

of several paces from the shop counter.[47] Thompson's booklet had referred those readers who wanted further details of the maps to the War Office map reading manual that had been published in 1921 and which could be bought for 3s. at Stanford's. Education in the use of maps received a great boost during the First World War, and as Close commented in his *Annual Report* for 1919/20, the Popular Edition was launched at a time that was unusually favourable for the reception of a new map, because soldiers, who were now returning to civilian life, had been trained in map reading. The difference in scope between the little military *Manual of map reading and field sketching*, published by the War Office in 1912, and its 1921 successor, which for the first time included information

47 Nearly twenty years later, a more ambitious booklet, *Map reading for the countrygoer* by S.F. Marriott, was published by the Ramblers' Association in 1946. This had colour extracts from the New Popular Edition and the Popular Edition of Scotland (with National Grid), together with a foreword by the Director General of the Ordnance Survey.

on squaring, gridding and air photographs, reflected a significant development in the role of the military map.[48] To all its usual functions was now added that of predicted shooting, or artillery firing by the map, which in turn required a grid system. This 1921 manual included an extract of the Popular Edition, referred to in this context as the 'military version'. It was this version of the Popular, to be known from 1931 as GSGS 3907, which carried an overprinted military grid from 1923.[49] It was the first one-inch map series to do so.

The approval by the War Office of the Popular Edition as a military map (it had, after all, embodied virtually all the recommendations of the 1892 Baker Committee), which replaced the half-inch as the standard tactical map for the British army, might have improved its cost effectiveness if the copies needed for military purposes were printed at the same time as the civil sheets. Although there is no indication, as yet, that this was so, the demand for the Popular sheets was increased as a result of military requirements. By 1932, Winterbotham was able to say that the demand for maps from the educational establishment was satisfactory and that 'the use of the National Maps in schools and colleges is increasing steadily'.[50] This would have been a further boost to the demand for the one-inch map. Of course, the Popular Edition was not the only Ordnance Survey map used in education, but the number of teaching sets that have survived in university colleges, and the many examination and schools extracts which can still be found in 'map boxes' in secondhand bookshops, all indicate that it played a central role in geography teaching in the inter-war years.[51]

Packaging the product

When first published, the Popular Edition therefore had a more cartographically literate potential audience than any previous one-inch map. However, the stimulation of the passive interest of the student into an actively map-purchasing adult required careful presentation. All aspects of the packaging - paper, mounting, folding and covers - were geared to attract and satisfy the consumer. No previous one-inch map had been so successfully market oriented.

The quality of the paper[52] on which the one-inch maps were printed was the subject of discussion in all four committees which sat between 1892 and 1914. In 1922, Close claimed that the Ordnance Survey was the largest government printing department in the world, capable of printing 100,000 maps a day,[53] and in 1927, the paper purchasing

---

48 The role of the map and of topographical training in war is discussed in MacLeod, (1923).

49 R.E. Corps Library. L.355.486. R.L. Brown to Winterbotham, 14/8/1933.

50 *Annual Report*, (1931/2), p.18.

51 A short list of Popular Edition extracts is given in Hodson, (1995), Appendix 9. These extracts were not restricted to the Popular, but included the Third Edition, e.g. *Aldershot*, done for the Public School Provisional Brigade (black detail plus brown hachures, red contours, blue water; no date); half-inch extracts such as *Winchcombe Area*, 13000/34; *Scarborough Area*, 9000/36.C.R.3281/1.; *Burnley Area* 'Oxford School Certificate Examination. Geography 1. Map required for question 1. July 1938', C.R.3281/1.12500/38.; and *Portion of the Land Utilisation Map No.37 Barnsley & Sheffield* [no date].

52 Paper standards and quality are set out on 'Tender for the supply of lithographic and other papers' [O.S. printed form, 1913], on PRO OS 1/4/3.

53 PRO OS 1/2/5. Memorandum by Close on the military organisation of the Ordnance Survey, 29/6/1922.

power of the Ordnance Survey was greater than that of the Stationery Office. Quality control was strictly monitored by the Ordnance Survey[54] (poor paper generated an inferior image); on the other hand, the thick papers used for the copper-printed impressions produced maps which were stiff and awkward to handle. The late 1890s saw the coloured edition of the Revised New Series being printed mainly on linen-backed paper, but a plea had been made for maps to be printed on thin paper and folded for the pocket.[55] With the Third Edition Large Sheet Series, the customer was able to acquire his map in one of four formats: paper flat; paper folded; mounted on linen (i.e. printed on linen-backed paper) and folded; and printed on paper, dissected, mounted on linen and folded. (A fifth style - flat, on cloth - is also found, but this was not advertised, and may have been produced to special order, for educational purposes, etc.)

These four formats were adopted for the Popular Edition (again, the cloth flat version can be found, but this was not advertised as a standard option). They were not without their problems; printing on linen-backed paper had its own disadvantages while mounting by hand was labour-intensive. To avoid these troubles, a map-mounting machine was devised to Ordnance Survey specifications and was first brought into operation in 1928,[56] and the new position of 'Map Mounting Machine Minder' was introduced in May 1928.[57] Within four years it was joined by another machine, 'believed to be the first of its kind' which, while not completing the whole of the section mounting task, enabled the section mounters to increase their individual output by 50%.[58] It had been built specifically for the standard sheets of the Popular Edition which at that time comprised about half of the section mounting work in the Department. Until that time, this had been done entirely by hand, usually by women (fig.31) of whom there were twenty-seven performing map mounting and folding duties in 1923.[59] A folding machine was introduced in 1931; this folded the map in one direction and scored it for the remaining folds - no machine had yet been devised which was capable of folding the entire map.[60]

---

54 The duties of the Paper Tester included the examination and mechanical testing, tensile weighing, examination of texture, ultra violet ray action, of all papers purchased by the Ordnance Survey. He was also responsible for selecting the actual paper for issue for each printing service, and for having it cut to correct size and issue to the printers, and was an expert on lithographic printing papers. The chemical and microscopic examination of the paper was carried out on payment by Southampton University. PRO OS 1/24B. C.R. Williams to P.G. Inch, 18/1/1935.

55 Hayes Fisher, (1896b), para.1326.

56 *Annual Report*, 1927/8. A full description of the machine is given by Martin, (1931).

57 Circular, C.C.953, 14/5/1928.

58 *Annual Report*, (1930/31), p.13. A rate of three maps per man hour for section mounting is quoted in Ordnance Survey *Notes on map reproduction*, (1927). Hand folding was done at the rate of 50-60 maps per man hour, and twenty maps could be mounted on cloth per man hour. A higher grade of skill was required by section mounters who had to achieve the correct alignment of sections on the cloth backing, and distance between the sections, so that the map could fold neatly, while making allowances for the expansion and contraction of paper when coated with paste.

59 PRO OS 1/7/4. Table of distribution of technical staff.

60 *Annual Report,* (1931/2), p.7. A concertina folding machine was acquired in 1960, and in 1962 it was proposed to purchase a machine which would combine cross and concertina folding in a single operation. *OS Technical Bulletin*, no.4, (Jan.1962).

To the four formats was added from 1929 the map on waterproof paper.[61] Unsuccessful attempts had been made by private map publishers to print maps on such paper, and there had been a succession of Pegamoid, Celluloid and Jernoid[62] since the 1890s; none had sold well. What seems to be the first mention of the Ordnance Survey process is given in a leaflet dated 17 July 1929 and entitled 'A revolution in map making: Ordnance Survey maps on Place's waterproof paper' (named after its inventor, Col. C.O. Place, R.E.).[63]

Fig.31 Women mounting dissected maps at Ordnance House, Southampton, ca 1914-16; a section mounting machine was bought in 1930-1 in order to increase output. *Ordnance Survey.*

It was not merely ordinary paper coated with a waterproof solution, but was 'specially manufactured and impregnated after printing by a process which renders it absolutely waterproof and washable and gives it a parchment-like toughness and durability'.[64] The first Popular Edition maps to be printed on this paper were sheets 26, 72, 83, 101, 114, and 117 at a price of 3s.6d. They were available to the public in July 1929.

---

61 Nicholson, (1985).

62 Bartholomew tried Pegamoid in 1898 but sales were insufficient to justify using the process (NLS, Bartholomew Archive: Acc.10222 III B11, 21/6/1898); celluloid is referred to as a 'secret' process in Olivier, (1914a), para.84, and Fisher Unwin had prepared a quarter-inch map on Jernoid, *ibid.* para.381.

63 This leaflet is in a private collection.

64 'The Ordnance Survey maps of Great Britain on the scale of one-inch to the mile', OS Leaflet, (1932).

The new material was enthusiastically received, at least by the scouts, who accepted the invitation to 'give it hard usage'[65] and rolled up their map, used it for hockey and cricket, left it out in the dew and the rain and used it as a doormat. The map was finally scrubbed and found to be 'quite usable'.[66] In the meantime, the problems of printing on such a tough medium had not been resolved. For example, by 1933, it had been found that if the map were waterproofed when flat, it had a tendency to crack when folded; this weakness seemed to be overcome by folding the map first, then opening it up and waterproofing it before refolding it.[67] Even this was unsatisfactory and in 1935 over 18,000 Popular Edition waterproof maps alone had to be cancelled (i.e. destroyed).[68] In June that year, O.S. Leaflet No.49/35 was published; it listed all the maps then available on Place's waterproof paper and remaindered at reduced prices - sixty sheets of the Popular were included at 2s.6d - a reduction of 6d.[69] In the following year it was announced that 'after careful consideration' it had been decided to discontinue the publication of Ordnance Survey maps on waterproof paper.[70]

Folding the map

Once the map had been printed and mounted or dissected, and before it acquired a cover, it had to be folded. This critical aspect of presentation has recently received some attention,[71] but no detailed study of folding has previously been made of any Ordnance Survey map series. In the same way that the selection of sheet lines was crucial to the commercial success of the map, so too was the method of folding, which required meticulous precision. The aim was that the one-inch should fit neatly into the pocket when folded, and the search for the most 'user friendly' fold was a 'totally distinct problem bristling with difficulties'.[72] Twenty-two[73] different methods of map folding have been recorded for the sheets of the Popular Edition; all but eight of them were

---

65 Early examples of waterproofed maps bore a label asking the user to treat it roughly and to forward their comments to the Director General. Dean, (1983), p.14.

66 *The Scouter*, July 1931, p.306.

67 PRO OS 1/148. Minute 34, 19/12/1933.

68 PRO OS 1/256. Minute 148, 7/5/1938. More waterproofed military maps seem to have survived, perhaps because they were issued flat, rather than folded.

69 The list is in a private collection; the Popular Edition sheets which were remaindered were: 2, 3, 5-15, 23, 24, 26, 28, 29, 32, 35, 37, 40, 43, 45, 48-52, 55, 56, 61, 62, 64, 65, 67, 69-71, 73, 82, 87, 90, 91, 93, 97, 100-2, 113, 116-120, 122, 125, 129, 131, 136.

70 Ordnance Survey *Important Notice relating to Ordnance Survey maps on Place's waterproof paper*. O.S. Leaflet No.48/36. Private Collection.

71 The best overall description of Ordnance Survey folding methods, which includes a diagram of Ansell folding (not used on the Popular Edition), is given by Cruickshank and Archer, (1987); the fullest account of Ansell folding is in Hellyer, (1992b), pp.98-9; Stanford-Bridges mounting method is explained, with diagrams, in Board, (1993); Messenger and Oliver, (1992), have given brief accounts of the Ansell, Michelin and Bender folds.

72 *Annual Report*, (1930/31), p.13.

73 Until recently, the Ordnance Survey Cartographic Library had a collection of fifty different folds which had been devised for the First Series 1:50,000 map. The aim of the exercise had been to try to invent a system with the most convenient folds. I owe this information to John Paddy Browne.

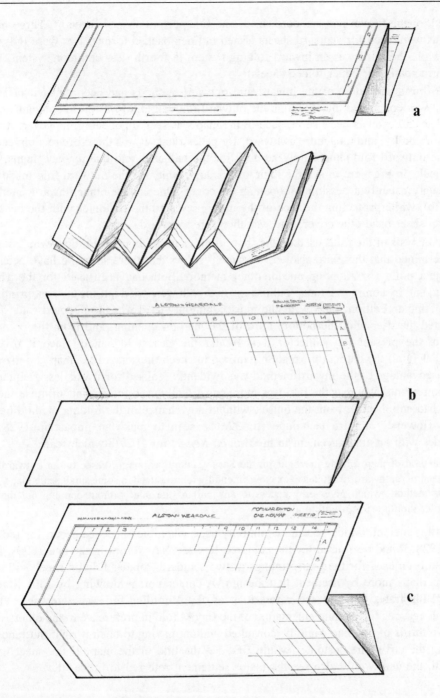

Figs 32a Outward fold. **32b** Inward fold. **32c** 'Book' fold; it was common for maps with this fold to be re-folded by the user according to fold 'a'. That 'c' was the original fold is indicated by the height of the bottom section of the fold, which was made slightly shorter than the height of the other two sections to enable it to be tucked under the top third of the map more neatly when folded.

189

devised for the fifteen non-standard sized, and five portrait-shaped sheets.[74] Three main methods were used for standard sheets issued in linen-backed format; two were outward folds while the third was an inward folding system (a fourth, less common system, was used principally for paper folded sheets).

The 'pros and cons' of the inward and outward methods had been debated in 1914 when it was concluded that although the outward fold (fig.32a) was more convenient for motorists and cyclists because the face of the map was seen on opening; however, it was also more bulky, and thus more awkward, for pedestrians. It was therefore recommended that the outward fold should only be used for the half-inch and quarter-inch maps.[75] It is difficult, in practice, to see the logic of this argument, for the outward fold made the map detail instantly accessible on opening the cover, whereas the other, inward, method (fig.32b), while protecting the face of the map, presented the customer with the back of the map sheet inside the cover, and was therefore awkward to use.

An analysis of the folds used on the first printings of the Popular Edition, where it can be determined that these are also early issues,[76] shows that there seems to have been no consistent policy of adopting one or other method. Both had been used for the Third Edition, and by commercial map publishers, and both were tried out for the first printings of the Popular Edition, but by far the most commonly used was the outward fold. This presented the user with the bottom third of the map on opening, and from the point of view of the present day collector it is by far the easiest to handle since it reveals immediately all the dating information required to check the state of the map at a glance. The disadvantage of the inward method was evidently realised for it was less frequently used on reprints, whereas the first was more consistently used for reprints of those sheets which had employed it from the outset, without any change in the folding method being made. However, a third technique (fig.32c) is seen to make an impact in 1928. It coincides with an announcement in the *Annual Report* for 1927/8 which read

> A method of map folding in vogue on the Survey many years ago, based on an outward instead of an inward, fold, has been experimentally reintroduced in some small scale maps. This method, which gives easy access to any part of the map without opening out the whole, should prove useful to all users.

It was this method which became commonly used when the sheets came up for reprint from 1928; it had been used for the coloured Revised New Series in the late 1890s, and had also been used for the first printings of two standard Popular Edition sheets (13 and 130), perhaps more by accident than design. A contemporary drawing by Ellis Martin (fig.33) illustrates the fold and refers to it as 'Book-folding for easy reference.' The probable reasons for the implementation of the 'book' fold in preference to the others was that two thirds of the map could be consulted without having to open it right out, and on opening the cover the customer would first see the title of the map. If the sheet lines allowed, the user would also see the major settlement referred to in the title.

74 Full details are given in Hodson, (1995), Appendix 10.
75 Olivier, (1914b), p.15, para.69.
76 The folds of examples with the earliest cover styles were analysed.

Fig.33 Design by Ellis Martin, ca 1928, to promote the 'new' easy to use, bookfold. The map in the advertisement is Popular Edition sheet 72, Birmingham. This design was also incorporated in advertising cards. *Private collection*.

More often, the principal town did not fall so conveniently; however, in most cases it could be found without unfolding the map but simply by turning it over. The Ordnance Survey advertisements for the 'new' book-fold came about five years after Michelin advertised on their maps 'Do not unfold this map, it opens like a book'. (label fixed to Michelin 1:200,000 sheet 3, Perth, print code 235-17). It may be that Ordnance Survey was copying this commercial example. Later, in the 1940s, Bartholomew was to draw attention to their own book-folding method: printed on the back cover of Great Britain half-inch sheet 35 (print code A42), for example, is a note on the 'Utility Map Fold', with advice on how to use it 'as a book'.

Fig.34 'Study of Alec Bender'. Signed and dated, Ellis Martin, Southampton 1932. Copy of an original, present location unknown. A.R.E. Bender was the inventor of the 'Bender' fold, first used on the New Forest one-inch map in 1938. He became Superintendent of the Map Sales and Issues Branch in about 1929. *Private collection.*

The other types of fold used by the Ordnance Survey for the regular sheets are versions of the Bender fold (figs 35a-c) so named after Alexander R.E. Bender (fig.34) who had been appointed Superintendent of the Map Sales and Issues Branch in about 1929. He first developed the fold in 1937, and the decision to adopt the method for the small scales, including the one-inch, was taken in November 1937.[77]

---

77 The date of 4/11/1937 for the policy of using the Bender fold on one-inch, half-inch and quarter-inch maps is given in PRO OS 1/96, Director General's Conference minutes. The introduction of the fold is summarised by Messenger and Oliver, (1992). In practice, the Bender fold was implemented from February 1939; PRO OS 1/460, Minute 9, 1/2/1939.

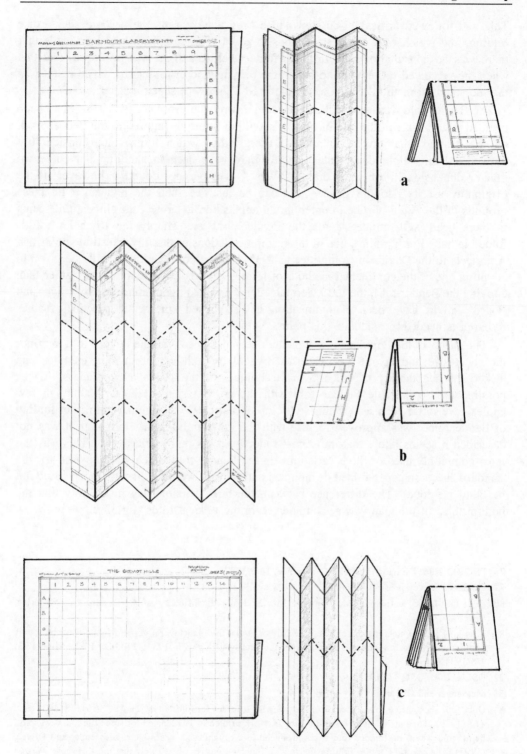

Fig.35a-c Three versions of the Bender fold used for the Popular Edition.

This had followed critical discussions since May that year on the need to standardise folding, and which were the best methods to adopt. The complaint had been made that there was no consultation with the map folders before a sheet was produced, and that when they received it they 'had to invent the best method of folding it'.[78] The result was that no standard method, which accommodated all sizes of sheet, existed.

The Bender fold was seen as the panacea to a perennial problem. By 1938, it had been decided that the size of the one-inch sheet should in future be tailored to the Bender fold, on the grounds that the advantages of accessibility which it provided considerably outweighed any slight disadvantage there might have been in handling flat copies of greater dimensions north-south than east-west.[79] It is perhaps doubtful, however, if the originality ascribed to the Bender fold can be justified, and the reluctance on these grounds of the Patent Office to entertain an application to protect the 'invention' seems to have been well-founded,[80] for the Bender fold was simply the Michelin fold,[81] folded in half. Furthermore, one of the recommendations of the Royal Institute of British Architects to the Davidson Committee in 1935 was that consideration should be given to adopting one of the continental methods of folding.[82] It is just possible, that, rather than copying the Bender fold, the 1939 German 'Bender-folded' map referred to by Oliver and Board[83] might have been a continuation of established continental practice; further research is needed to elucidate this point.

The sheets of the Popular Edition had not been designed with the Bender fold in mind; the sheet size and layout was governed by old, inflexible reproduction methods and lacked the adaptability of the drawing techniques of the 1930s. Nevertheless, it was possible to use the true Bender fold with the portrait shaped sheets,[84] although few copies have so far been seen in this style. In February 1939 an 'improved form of folding of Bender type' was approved for use with the Popular Edition;[85] although it was not described it seems likely that the semi-Bender fold was being referred to. This was the most commonly used of three variations on the Bender fold which were devised for the standard sheets in paper-folded or mounted and folded form (the dissected map could not be Bender folded). The difference between the three versions lay in the way that the bottom third of the map was accommodated in the vertical folds (fig.35c).

---

78 PRO OS 1/96. Director General's Conference, 18/5/1937.

79 Ordnance Survey [Research Bulletin no.3, ca May 1938], p.33.

80 PRO OS 1/460, correspondence between MacLeod and the Ministry of Agriculture and Fisheries, Dec.1937.

81 This long fold, which comprised one outward horizontal fold and several vertical folds, was apparently popular with motorists, and was proposed for the quarter-inch map in 1934. PRO OS 1/54. Minute 93, 4/6/1934.

82 OSL G5186, OSC 34 [1935].

83 Messenger and Oliver, (1992); Board, (1993).

84 Only four sheets have so far been recorded using the true Bender fold: 8 (1932), 41 (1939), 68 (1939) and 117 (1939). The date of sheet 8 implies that the stock printed in 1932 lasted for some time, and was still being sold when the Bender fold was introduced to the public six years later. Messenger and Oliver, (1992), lists several Popular Edition sheets with Bender folds, but it is likely that most of these were in one of the variants of the true Bender fold.

85 PRO OS 1/460, minute 9, 1/2/1939.

One further method of mounting and folding deserves mention here, although it was not devised by the Ordnance Survey, but was patented by Edward Stanford in the 1920s. Known as 'Stanford-Bridges Patent Mounting' method,[86] it allowed sections of the map to be turned north to south, east to west, and vice versa.[87] Popular Edition sheets mounted in this way were advertised by Stanford, but are uncommonly found today; this may be because the system allowed only a small expanse of the map to be seen at any one time, which might not have been popular with many customers; collectors who are lucky enough to acquire examples will usually find that the covers are badly cracked as a consequence of the inevitable wear and tear resulting from this ingenious folding system. At 4s.6d. a sheet, it was also a shilling dearer than the most expensive form of the Popular available in conventional formats.

Covers

The consequence of introducing the Bender fold, and its variations, and the book fold before that, was that a different method of attaching the cover to the map became necessary. The story of the development of map covers and their role in the marketing of the small-scale maps has been comprehensively told by Browne,[88] and will be expanded here only in so far as it affects the Popular Edition. The covers of the early Populars were attached in a similar way to those used for the Third Edition; they were either 'slapped on,' that is, the front and back covers were stuck to the reverse of the top left and top right folded panels of the map, or they were 'wrapped round.' In this last case the cover opened like a book; the back was stuck down to the reverse of the top or bottom (depending on the method of folding) left panel, and the front wrapped round and was free of the map. This method had been used by commercial publishers for over seventy years and, from the Ordnance Survey's point of view, had the advantage of allowing for advertising matter to be printed on the inside of the front cover, giving information about the other map scales available. The disadvantage must soon have become apparent. The thin paper card, by no means as robust as its predecessors, was apt to wear quickly, and the map soon lost its front cover; it is rare to find these intact and in good condition today. The wrap-round method was used again in the 1930s in spite of the vulnerability of the 'spine' to wear and tear. It appears to have been most commonly used for the paper folded issues, although these were also issued in other cover styles.

When the book-folded map was re-introduced in 1928, the Popular Edition covers underwent a facelift and the front and back panels were each designed to be attached by a card hinge to the map. It was a more expensive article to produce because of the extra work of scoring and cutting the card to produce the hinge. The same applied to the cover for the Bender-folded map, which, although in one piece, was attached by two hinges to the left centre and top left map panels. When cost accounting was introduced to the Ordnance Survey in 1932[89] it was remarked, when suggesting ways of cutting

---

86 Described and illustrated in Thompson, (1927), p.9.
87 A full diagram of Bridges Patent Mounting system is given in Board, (1993).
88 Browne, (1991).
89 The background to this is given Seymour, (1980), pp.244-5.

expenditure, that the cheapest covers to produce were the wrapper style, and that while it was agreed that the new style of folding was so convenient that it 'would be inadvisable to revert to the old style' it was recommended that the wrapper cover, although more awkward, could be used and would be cheaper.[90] This advice was not taken for the majority of Popular sheets, and the hinged covers continued to be used to the end of the Popular Edition's life. The development of the cover for the Popular ended with the style used for the Bender-folded maps. It was, in effect, a hinged wrap-wround device used vertically instead of horizontally; it had the great advantage of providing space on the 'spine' for the series title, sheet name and number to be written, although this system of spine notation was not adopted immediately. Exactly when the first Bender-folded map was produced with spine titles is not known - it was not used for the early Bender covers for either the Popular Edition or the Fifth Edition, but a handful of Popular covers with series title, sheet name, and sheet number on the spine is known.[91]

Fig.36 Cover design by Ellis Martin for the Popular Edition. The first covers were printed in buff with black lettering, except for the sheet name which was printed in orange. A cyclist, pipe in mouth, map in hand, contemplates his route.

The design of the cover (which until 1919 was 'evidently produced with a minimum of mental effort'[92]) with its pictorial front, and series index on the back, was among the earliest of the tasks assigned to Ellis Martin, a commercial artist who joined the Ordnance Survey on 9 May 1919.[93] Since the Popular Edition went on sale in the following

---

90 PRO OS 1/22. Document 3A. 8/4/1932.

91 See Check-list 8, p.382.

92 Close, referring to the covers of earlier series, (1928), p.49.

93 Browne, (1991), p.66. The production of Martin's, and others' coloured tourist covers in the 1920s was a new departure for the Ordnance Survey, and the use of panchromatic plates and the preparation of three-colour half tone negatives from a water colour featured in the tests for photographers in the 1930s. Circulars, C.C.1051.

month, it seems improbable that he would have had sufficient time for the completion of the design and letterpress work of the new covers unless he had been given the work on a free-lance basis: he had already produced a Christmas card for 1918, and it may be that he was given the designing of the covers for the new one-inch map at the same time. One of the cover prototypes which he had produced, possibly in late 1918 or early 1919 (fig.6, p.31) was now adapted for the Popular Edition and outclassed, for the first time in the history of the one-inch map, the products of its commercial rivals. The design included three elements which were to remain unchanged on all the standard covers.

First, and most eye-catching was the cyclist, seated on a hillside with map spread before him; second was a rectangular location map, neatly enclosed in a narrow border of 'ranging pole' design around which was an ornate baroque border; the third element, the royal coat of arms and swags of oak leaves and acorns, linked the first two. A fourth factor, colour, completed the livery. The first maps were issued in a buff cover with the design, series title, price and scale in black, while the sheet name was in orange. In view of the criticisms made in 1914 that the white covers of the Edwardian maps soiled easily, it seems a retrograde step to have introduced a light coloured background for the new product. Although the combination of buff, orange and black is aesthetically pleasing, it must have been decided that the visual impact was too subtle, for within months the cover sported a vermilion border and sheet name.

The dating of the introduction of new covers must always, in the absence of documentary confirmation, be an imprecise science, especially when it was common practice to put old stock into new clothing. Four broad categories of cover can be discerned for the Popular Edition; they are, in chronological order of issue: buff, red, buff and red, and Bender. In this instance it is possible to infer that the buff covers were applied to all maps on sale to the public in June 1919, and on some which were published in October.[94] Other October publications were issued in red covers, but it seems reasonable to state that the changeover in style occurred at this time, although buff covers, with revised price stickers, continued to be in circulation for some months after October 1919, until old buff stock had been exhausted. Even a 1921 printing of sheet 123 has been seen in a buff cover with a revised price sticker. Occasional errors have been spotted, such as a 1919 printing of sheet 103 in a buff cover for sheet 93. All covers produced between June 1919 and January 1920 had the price of 1s.6d. printed directly on the cover; the price was increased to 2s.6d. on 26 January 1920.

The third type can be dated to 1928 with the reintroduction of the book fold. It gave to the folded maps a slightly larger format, similar, and in many cases identical to the dissected maps, so that, for the first time, all three folded formats could be a standard size. This was achieved for the standard sheets by enlarging the top and bottom margins of the map and reducing the number of vertical folds from seven to six. The small extra height and width was catered for by surrounding the red printed area by a buff border, which became the hallmark of the Popular covers from this period[95] (fig.46d, p.270). No figures survive for the stock levels of covers for individual sheets, and the extent to

94 Sheet 113, for example.
95 The design of the covers of Bartholomew's half-inch maps was also changed in the early 1940s after the introduction of the Great Britain series, so that the blue was surrounded by a buff border.

which old covers were cancelled in favour of new designs cannot be gauged accurately. There is evidence to show, however, that some economy was exercised, for some of the earliest 'buff border' covers are merely buff card with the old small red cover pasted on.

The fourth main category of cover was the Bender fold type, generally the same size as its predecessor but usually with different lettering, absence for the first time of the subtitle 'contoured road map,' and lack of buff border (fig.46e, p.270). It should be noted, however, that at least one example of a Bender style red cover has been seen on a dissected map (the 1940 printing of sheet 20) which was not issued with a Bender fold. The Bender cover appears to have been used for the first time for the Popular Edition in 1939. A fifth cover type was that used for the waterproofed maps. In colour - buff, black and orange - they echoed the earliest design from 1919 (fig.46g, p.271).

The relevance of a minute study of cover details is that they can occasionally provide some indication of the length of currency of individual map states, and can be used to assign an approximate date of issue. The back cover carried an index to the rest of the sheets in the series, and this, too, underwent changes in design (these are dealt with in Part 2, pp.277-281). Covers for the same print run could vary enormously, presumably because only a limited number of sheets were folded and mounted at first, the remainder being stored flat, to be folded and mounted in batches to meet demand. This would have been the cheapest method because covers would then not be wasted in the event of cancellations of unwanted stock, and flat sheets would have been easier to store. This system is well illustrated by those sheets which had a long gap between reprints, such as 57 (*Fakenham*). The case of sheet 66 (*Swaffham & East Dereham*), which seems never to have been reprinted, is an excellent example of old stock being marketed under fresh colours during the twenty odd years that the original printing was sold as current stock.

Finally, the Ordnance Survey printed covers for use by their agent, Stanford. Nothing is known, as yet, of the background to this arrangement. The covers retained the main element of design: colour, royal coat of arms, oak leaf and acorn swags, and picture of the cyclist. The difference lay in the omission of the series title and sheet name - the space was left blank - and, in place of the location diagram, was inserted Stanford's address. The form of this address changed at least four times, and is helpful in dating issues of stock.

Selling the map

It was not enough, however, to have produced an attractive product; it now had to be available in as many retail outlets as possible. A quarter of a century before the publication of the Popular Edition it had been recognised that 'in these days you cannot promote the sale of anything, unless you put it under the nose of the Public'.[96] At the same time it had been asserted that no Ordnance Survey officer was interested in developing sales.[97] Matters were left in the hands of the agent, of whom there had been several in the nineteenth century.[98] The significant move, from the point of view of the

96   Hayes Fisher, (1896b), para.852.

97   *Ibid.*, para.356.

98   The background to the relationships between the Ordnance Survey and their agents has been described in Seymour, (1980), and Owen and Pilbeam, (1992).

Popular Edition, came in the very month that the map was first published, June 1919, when the contract with the wholesale agent was terminated, and the sale of small-scale maps was carried on directly from Southampton.[99]

This clean break with tradition was made at the insistence of Capt. J.G. Withycombe,[100] whose artistic skills had been used in the designing of the Popular Edition. Close had remarked that although Withycombe was an 'excellent artist' he was a 'still better man of business'.[101] Within a short time 2370 accounts had been opened with retailers and railway bookstalls and sales were considerably increased.[102] The employment of travellers to sell products across the counter to small retail outlets had been strongly recommended by the commercial witnesses to the Olivier Committee in 1914. Close acted on this advice and appointed the first map traveller in February 1919;[103] a Ford car was provided and a 'smart appearance and good manner' were essential.[104]

The Ordnance Survey's advertising, in the form of leaflets, showcards, descriptive booklets and posters (Plate 13), the importance of all of which had been emphasised by the 1896 and 1914 committees, now appeared.[105] Aimed at promoting the small-scale maps, they were colourful and eye-catching; the format of the leaflets was a virtual copy of the successful formula established by Bartholomew in the 1880s, as were the trade cards. When, in 1926, it was asked in the Commons if the Ordnance Survey tried to increase its sales by advertising, the questioner was told that advertisements were put in the daily press, educational, motoring and other technical publications, and that booksellers and stationers displayed leaflets and showcards.[106] The occasional radio broadcast by the Director General also had an immediate effect on demand;[107] as a trading concern, the Ordnance Survey had never seemed so healthy, and appeared finally to have turned the tables on its principal rival. A London map depot was set up in 1920[108] and sales went up 'by leaps and bounds',[109] in spite of general trade depressions, to the extent that by 1931 the value of the wholesale business conducted had

---

99   This lasted until the Second World War, when Stanford again took over the distribution of small-scale maps. The Ordnance Survey resumed control of small-scale distribution in 1971. Chapman, (1971).

100   Withycombe was the Officer in charge of the Map Sales and Issues Department in 1919.

101   RGS Archives (Close Correspondence). Close to Jack, 3/2/1934.

102   *Report from the Select Committee of Public Accounts*, (1923). BPP.1923.iv.

103   PRO OS 1/289. f.19B.

104   OSL, G7095, C.C.833, 26/9/1923. An internal advertisement for the replacement of a map traveller. An account of the work of OS sales representatives fifty years later appears in O'Donoghue, (1972).

105   Their development has been described by Nicholson, (1991b), and by Browne, (1991). A list of some of the leaflets is provided in Nicholson, (1983b); OS attempts at advertising before 1918 are described by Mumford and Clark, (1986).

106   Parliamentary Debates. H.C.Deb.5s.192, 25/2/1926.

107   PRO OS 1/96. Director General's Conference, 27/8/1935.

108   PRO OS 1/24A. There had previously been an Ordnance Survey map depot in St Martin's Place in the 1880s; it was discontinued apparently because it was too expensive to maintain, Hayes Fisher, (1896b), paras.193 and 1286.

109   RGS Archives. (Close Correspondence). Close to Jack, 3/2/1934.

risen from £3077 in 1920 to £10,860.[110] But, while selling techniques had clearly been studied closely, there is no evidence to show that systematic attempts at market research were made until 1970.[111]

When the Popular Edition came on to the market, it was cheaper in price than the Third Edition which it replaced. In fixing the selling price, the Ordnance Survey had followed the principles laid down in a Treasury letter of 1866 which indicated that pricing was arrived at by ascertaining

> the average cost of producing each description of map, in paper, printing, office and incidental expenses, and then to fix as the selling price such even sum of money as (after deducting the 33⅓% allowed to publishers) will leave a moderate margin of profit.[112]

In other words, the cost of basic survey or revision was not to be charged on the grounds that this had already been paid by the public in taxes. There appear to be no figures for the cost of the Popular Edition sheets in the 1920s,[113] but in giving evidence to the Select Committee on Publications and Debates in 1913,[114] Close estimated that the unit cost of the 2s. mounted one-inch map (i.e. the Third Edition Large Sheet Series) was 8d. or 9d., but the Agent, Fisher Unwin, received a disproportionate discount of 53%, leaving the Survey with a slender profit margin of 2d. per sheet. Nothing had changed in the eighteen years since it had been stated that there was 'little or no profit to the Exchequer on the publication of the one-inch maps in England and Wales'.[115] It has always been axiomatic that the specification of the Killarney style map was dropped because it was too expensive for a national series, but what exactly were the costs involved? From the printing stage, that is from the preparation of the plates to printed map, and for which the public was charged through the purchase price, the cost of the Large Sheet Series in 1914 was £53 per sheet, while for the stones and plates of the Killarney style sheet it was £60;[116] and on top of this, a print run of 1000 for one sheet would have cost about 15s. Unfortunately, there are no post-war figures for the costings of a Killarney style map, and so direct comparisons cannot be made, although we can note that the overall cost for a Fifth Edition sheet with a print run of 4000 was £138.8s.0d. in 1937.[117]

Before the introduction of cost accounting in 1932,[118] the Ordnance Survey was not considered to be a trading concern, and its accounts were not arranged so that profit and

110 PRO OS 1/24A. C.J.H. Thomas to the Treasury, 8/6/1932.

111 Drewitt, (1973).

112 PRO OS 1/283. Quoted on f.2.A.

113 The figures given in PRO OS 1/22 and T161.1184, file S37751/1 relate to the Scottish Popular Edition, which was based on drawings rather than copperplates, and was therefore more representative of future methods than the outmoded Popular Edition of England and Wales.

114 *Report from the Select Committee on Publications and Debates' Reports...*, (1913), paras.449-50.

115 Hayes Fisher, (1896b), p.73. Letter from T.H. Elliott, Board of Agriculture, to the Treasury, 9/4/1894.

116 Olivier, (1914a), para.702.

117 PRO OS 1/113. Cost accounting office 19/5/1937. The figures for the Fifth (Relief) edition, which would have given a more direct comparison with the Killarney style, were not used since this series had gone out of production by this time.

118 The implementation of cost accounting is described in Seymour, (1980), pp.244-5.

loss for any one series could be readily identified.[119] After 1932, attempts were made to establish the profitability of the different series. The practice was to base the cost of maps on a year's production, so that in 1935 the unit cost per Popular Edition sheet, from the printing stage, was given as 2.26d. while that for 1937 was 2.36d.[120] These costs correspond with production figures of 102,900 copies in 1935, and only 61,200[121] in 1937. The schedule of costs for the Popular Edition, calculated in May 1938 (taken from PRO OS 1/256) was:

	Cost	Retail price	Wholesale price	Profit
Paper flat	6.00d	1s.6d.	1s.0d.	6.00d.
Paper folded	9.40d	1s.9d.	1s.2d.	4.60d.
Mounted and folded	11.37d	2s.6d.	1s.8d.	8.63d.
Sections	1s.9.18d	4s.0d.	2s.8d.	10.82d.
Outline	7.84d	1s.6d.	1s.0d.	4.16p.

Fig.37 Schedule of costs for the Popular Edition, May 1938.

The wholesale price was based on a discount on the retail price of 33⅓%, but this was sometimes considered inadequate by mapsellers in the face of strong competition from Michelin, who offered 45% on their smaller scale road maps.[122] However, the price for the Popular Edition when it was first published in 1919 had been 1s.0d. for a flat sheet and paper folded map, 1s.6d. for a mounted and folded sheet, and 2s.6d. for a map in sections. This was increased on 26 January 1920[123] to 1s.6d., 2s.6d. and 3s.6d. The price for the flat, and mounted and folded, versions remained unchanged thereafter,[124] but in 1934 the price of the sectioned maps was raised to 4s.0d.[125] In 1938 (calendar year) the total print run of the Popular Edition standard series sheets was about 144,000, but the percentage of the total that was allocated to each category of format (excluding outline) is not known and so the overall retail value and profit (deducting 4.5% to

119   Parliamentary Debates. H.C.Deb.5s.184, 26/5/1925.

120   PRO OS 1/256. Minute 154.

121   These figures are the print runs for the calendar years 1935 and 1937 (totals are derived from the print codes on the sheets for those years), but accounting years ran from 1 April to 31 March. Nevertheless, the figures are still indicative of the relative print runs for those financial years.

122   *Select Committee of Public Accounts*, (1930-31), para.1979.

123   *Annual Report*, (1919/20), and a notice, 'Revised prices of small-scale maps' in *Publications issued 1st-31st January 1920.*

124   But the cost of sheet 5, (1932 printing) was 2/- flat, the same as the Scottish Popular whose specification it shared. Sheets 1 and 3, also on the Scottish specification, either bore the 1/6 price note, or no note at all.

125   Ordnance Survey *Price list of Ordnance Survey small scale maps revised 1st January, 1934.*

represent cancellations[126]) cannot be accurately calculated. The factors which determined the cost of a map, and therefore its price, were all intimately linked, and were common to all other manufacturing industries; much depended on a nice judgement of print runs, because the overall profit depended on selling as much as possible of the stock before it was superseded by a revised issue. There was not always a great profit at the end of the day, in spite of increased sales. In 1921-2 for example, the costs of producing, promoting and distributing the small scale maps came to £19,135, while the income from sales amounted to only £20,508.[127]

Stock control was not straightforward for the one-inch map. In the days of copper-printed maps, the one-inch sheets were not printed in large batches, but only on demand;[128] in 1895 the number printed of each sheet was given as 'at least 50' and sometimes as many as 200.[129] These totals must have altered with the introduction of the litho-printed coloured map, but no precise figures of print runs appear to be available,[130] although they could have been accessible to Close if the system of recording every map which left Southampton, in force in 1895,[131] had been implemented during the lifetime of the Third Edition Large Sheet Series.[132] The average print run for this series, with exceptions (not stated) for better selling areas, was 1,000.[133] This was expected to last for three years,[134] but as the only corrections to be made to the sheets were principally to roads and railways, it was suggested that enough stock should be printed to last five years.

In his *Annual Report* for 1919/20 (p.7), Close announced a plan which would have produced a radical change in the policy of stock retention for the one-inch map. New storehouses had been built during the war to hold future larger, and more economical, editions of each series sheet. In time, fifteen years' supply, corresponding to the fifteen-year revision interval, was to be kept for the small scale maps. The implications for the revision policy for the one-inch need hardly be spelled out. It seems extraordinary, not just with hindsight, but in the contemporary view, that it should have been considered acceptable, as a matter of policy, not to correct the sheets of the urban and industrial areas, at least, periodically. Clearly, this plan was not implemented for all the sheets of the Popular Edition for which, however, there are no sales figures; therefore a study of the print runs, as recorded on the map, is important because it is the only source of information on production statistics. The interpretation of the print codes has been explained (pp.84-7); the figures themselves can only be taken at face value, for there is

126   The figure of 4.5% is given in PRO OS 1/256, f.146.A, 27/4/1938.

127   Parliamentary Debates. H.C.Deb.5s.164, 29/5/1923.

128   Dorington, (1893c), para.681.

129   Hayes Fisher, (1896b), para.10.

130   Messenger, (1988), p.6.

131   Hayes Fisher, (1896b), para.162.

132   In 1914 the figures for map issues were described as only having been 'recently kept by the Map Branch'; whether this included data for the Third Edition Large Sheet Series is open to speculation. Olivier, (1914a), para.693.

133   Only one Popular Edition sheet (115) had a print run of over 10,000, the average was 2,500 (PRO OS 1/256. f.146A).

134   Olivier, (1914a), para.694.

no independent check on their accuracy. The area of least reliability lies in estimating the size of the issues for the first printings, and for many of the first reprints of individual sheets for which few print codes exist. Any calculation of total printing figures for single sheets cannot be accurate, therefore, since it must embody an approximate figure for these early issues. It is suggested, for the present purposes, that an average figure of 1,000, based on the information cited above from the Olivier Committee, might be assigned to those sheets published in 1919, (however, 3,500 copies are recorded retrospectively for sheet 143 in a later imprint), and for 1920 (except sheet 107, which had a known print run of 500 copies). It seems reasonable that 1,500 could be taken as a conservative average for the remaining initial print runs to 1926; it could be argued that this figure is too low in view of the evidence that reprint figures were gradually increasing in size from 1923 onwards, but, generally speaking, these referred to sheets in more popular areas, while those which were printed for the first time in 1926, for example, were in the far north of England in territory which never claimed significant sales. Enough information is available from the maps to be able to indicate which sheets were potentially most profitable.

Figure 38 shows up quite clearly what Winterbotham liked to call the 'nation's playgrounds'; the Isle of Man: destination of the Lancashire cotton workers, the Pennines, the North Wales coast, and the coasts of north Devon, Somerset, Cornwall and the Torbay area, the south-east coast, and the Vale of Evesham with the Malvern Hills. More subtle distinctions can be seen in the north, where the predominance of sheets 16 and 22 over the Scarborough coastal area presages the introduction of the North York Moors tourist map in 1958. Print run figures were discontinued for the New Popular and Seventh Series, perhaps because they revealed too much to competitors: Lieut.-Col. Brooker had remarked, even in 1914, that he did not think that the incidence of those sheets which sold well should be published in case they called 'the attention of map makers to particular districts'[135] - but a set of figures for issues of the Seventh Series between 1961 and 1971 shows not only the enormous increase in the size of total print runs (the largest total issue for a Popular Edition map was for sheet 115 (*S.E. London & Sevenoaks*), with about 63,500 copies; the equivalent for the Seventh Series was sheet 170 (*London S.W.*), with 317,479 copies being issued between 1961 and 1971), but also the similarity in the regional distribution of the 'best selling' areas.[136]

The average print run of a Popular Edition sheet for any calendar year, based on recorded figures, did not exceed 3,788 (for 1932), and by 1941, the last year in which a standard sheet is recorded as having been printed, the average fell back to that of 1919, that is, 1,000 copies. The lowest single print run was 100 (for sheet 103 in 1935) and the highest was 10,000 (sheet 115 in 1933). This was probably not significantly higher than for the Third Edition, and was not greatly exceeded for the Fifth Edition, but it does not compare favourably with Bartholomew's half-inch maps which already had an average

135   Olivier, (1914a), para.711.
136   See fig.51 in Hodson, (1995). The figures for Seventh Series issues of standard and tourist sheets are taken from *Publication Division one-inch issues 1961-1971*. Copy in private collection.

print run of over 10,000 for the southern English sheets in 1911-12.[137] In judging the size of any issue when a sheet came up for reprint, several factors would have been taken into account. For example, the estimates for the print runs for the 1:50,000 First Series were based on six factors: on the historical sales of the one-inch, the calculated effect on the market of the introduction of the new series, the scale of advertising allowed, the economic situation, the increased ownership of cars and the increasing use of outdoor leisure facilities.[138] Similarly, for the Popular Edition, the past performance of the Third Edition sheets under normal selling conditions would give a reasonable basis for calculation; secondly, prompt notice would have to be taken of important trends in public behaviour which could affect the potential use of maps in order to maximise their sales. In this respect it may perhaps be significant that the highest average print run was reached in 1932, the year after the Youth Hostel movement was inaugurated. It supported Winterbotham's contention that the Ordnance Survey had seen the hiking trend coming and had advertised in the relevant journals.[139] Thirdly, educational demands, which have been discussed above, may have been influential in increasing the print runs for selected sheets; finally, the effect of the tourist and district sheets would have to be gauged.

The production of 'special' sheets, variously named 'tourist', 'district', or 'tourist district' was well established by 1919; their early background and genesis has been examined by Nicholson,[140] and those based on the Third Edition have been described by Messenger, (1988). The tourist maps were visually more eye-catching than their standard siblings because relief was shown by coloured layers and unusual contour colours, and sometimes hachures were added; in contrast, the district maps tended to be based on the standard Popular format. Between 1922 and 1941, forty-six special maps, or 31% of the number of standard series sheets, were published for England and Wales, based on Popular Edition material.[141] This was more than twice the total of fully coloured district sheets which had been prepared from Third Edition material.[142] The policy of increasing the number of coloured district maps was pushed by Close in order to meet the competition from private firms which had been actively encouraged by the Ordnance Survey in the 1890s. However, the selection of special areas, which was made not just by Close, but also by Jack and Winterbotham, was not entirely judicious, and the Ordnance Survey found themselves generating self-made competition which might have been justified on the grounds of excluding commercial products, but which was less easy to defend in purely financial terms.

137 Data taken from the record maps in the Bartholomew Printing Archive in the National Library of Scotland.
138 Chapman, (1974).
139 *Annual Report*, (1930/31), p.26.
140 Nicholson, (1991a) and (1994b).
141 Graphic indexes to the tourist and district maps are described in Appendix 4; see also fig.52 in Hodson, (1995).
142 There had been, of course, fifty-nine black outline with coloured roads district maps based on Revised New Series and Third Edition material; Nicholson, (1994b).

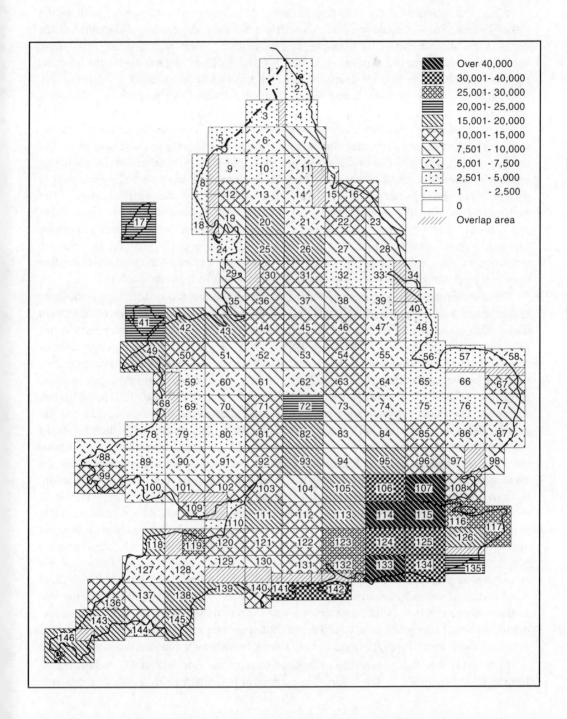

Fig.38 Index showing the number of copies reprinted of each sheet of the Popular Edition between 1921 and 1941. Data are based on the print codes of the individual states of each sheet.

While the reasons for the selection for special treatment of some areas, such as the Lake District, Snowdon and the Peak District are obvious, the choice of Barnsley as the centre for a district map, for example, is less clear.[143] What effect, if any, did these special maps have on the production of the Popular Edition? Again, there are no sales figures, and therefore the only evidence is in the form of the figures for print runs. No fewer than seventeen standard sheets were completely covered by the special productions, and therefore some straight comparisons can be made. Two of the tourist maps, the *Isle of Wight* and *Land's End*, were actually on the same sheet lines as the standard Popular sheet; in each case, the print runs for the tourist maps were less than those for sheets 142 (*Isle of Wight*) and 146 (*Land's End*) in the same period, and neither special map was reprinted after 1928. In contrast, their standard counterparts went on to be reprinted in greater than average quantities before being replaced by the Fifth Edition. The implication is that the normal series map, especially where the sheet lines were sympathetic, was preferred to the more colourful and elaborate, and more expensive tourist version, notwithstanding the latter's more attractive cover. It was, in effect, a repetition of the consumer preference in the nineteenth century for the simpler outline one-inch map, unadorned or, some might say, less confused, by the hachures.

The case of the Lake District and Peak District tourist maps was different. Both these tourist maps had been deliberately designed with more accommodating sheet lines than those of the standard series in what were prime tourist areas. The average print run for the Lake District tourist map between 1925 and 1939 was about 8,000, while that of standard sheet 12 (*Keswick & Ambleside*, first published 1925) which was almost entirely covered by the tourist map, was only 2,440 for the same period. Similarly, the average print run for the Peak District tourist map between 1924 and 1940 was 6,833, while that for sheet 45, which fell entirely within the tourist sheet lines, was only 2,125 for the period 1923-36. The 'top ten' tourist (T) and district (D) maps, with their dates of production and total print runs are shown in fig.39. Of the remainder, the Exmoor (20,500 total print run) and Cheltenham (20,000 total print run) tourist maps were the most successful; others, mainly the district maps in the straight Popular specification, seemed hardly worth producing as separate maps, with combined print runs falling as much as 50% short of those of their constituent standard sheets. A comparison of the print runs for standard sheets and the special maps which covered them shows that some areas, such as the south coast from Bournemouth to Hastings, which were densely populated, or were consistently popular with tourists, could successfully support simultaneous production of different cartographic publications. On the other hand, there were instances where it seemed that it was possible to saturate the market, and the two London district maps, North and South, were discontinued after the 1928 printings, having suffered competition, it would seem, not from commercial sources, but from the standard sheets and other Ordnance Survey tourist maps which covered the same ground.

How profitable then, were the different forms of the one-inch map? According to figures issued in 1938,[144] the theoretical maximum potential profit of 10.99d. for any

---

143   It is possible that maps of such locations may have been commissioned by local sources who would have guaranteed an acceptable minimum sales figure; Nicholson, (1994b).

144   PRO OS 1/256. f.152A, May 1938.

1	Lake District (T)	1925-39	97,000
2	Peak District (T)	1924-40	82,000
3	Snowdon (T)	1919-38	39,500
4	Dorking (T)	1929-39	38,500
5	Brighton (T)	1922-38	33,000

6	Manchester (D)	1924-40	31,750
7 =	Middle Thames (T)	1923-35	25,000
7 =	New Forest (T)	1920-35	25,000
8	Liverpool (D)	1924-38	24,000
9	Dartmoor (T)	1922-36	23,600

Fig.39 Table showing the top ten best-selling tourist and district maps based on the Popular Edition. The figures in the final column are the number of copies printed for each sheet according to the print codes which appear on printings issued during the known years of publication shown in the third column.

one-inch sheet was to be made on a mounted and folded district sheet (with a dissected standard Popular sheet coming a close second at 10.82d.). The tourist maps, with their more complex specification, were appreciably more expensive to produce and made less profit on all formats than the district sheets which were simply reassembled extracts from the standard Popular Edition. But apart from the exceptions listed above, both categories of special maps appear to have sold poorly, to the extent that Winterbotham, writing to Close, commented that 'the fact is that we are losing rather heavily on many of the tourist maps'.[145] He continued that Close's policy of giving the public a cheap map, while providing the wealthier tourist with a more expensive article, 'had rather fallen through'.

Winterbotham was making the point that his policy in opting for the design of the Fifth (Relief) Edition, which resembled the specification of the more elaborate tourist maps of the early 1920s, was 'gradually to let the tourist editions die'. In this context it is instructive to note the experience of Bartholomew whose policy in 1900 was not to 'issue any "special" maps' on the half-inch scale because they were apt to clash with the regular series.[146] Winterbotham's policy of dropping the tourist maps was never enforced, but in 1938 a review of the viability of the special maps[147] resulted in several of the less profitable district maps being discontinued, and in 1945, the idea of discontinuing the tourist maps may have been kept in mind, for priority was given to the production of those Sixth Edition sheets which could replace the tourist and district sheets.[148]

The introduction of the Fifth Edition in 1931 might have been expected to have an immediately terminal effect on those sheets of the Popular which it replaced.[149] This

---

145   PRO OS 1/48. Winterbotham to Close, 25/4/31.

146   NLS, Bartholomew Archive: Acc.10222 III B12, f.843, 8/2/1900.

147   PRO OS 1/375.

148   OSL Director General's Conference no.19, 26/4/1945. The first sheets it was planned to replace were the Peak District and Manchester, both among the top ten best-sellers.

149   The combined index to the Popular and Fifth Editions is described in Appendix 4, and is illustrated in Hodson, (1995), fig.54, p.205.

was certainly so in areas such as Devon and Cornwall, where the sheet lines of the two series were almost identical. The situation was, however, more ambiguous in the London region, and examples have already been noted where the two series co-existed. The competition between Fifth Relief and non-Relief sheets has been noted by Oliver,[150] and the confusion that must have existed in having two versions of one map on sale may well have been a critical factor in prolonging the life of the familiar, and preferred, Popular Edition in some localities, especially where the sheet lines of the two series did not quite coincide.

The Ordnance Survey had presumably worked out a running stock control policy for the Popular Edition, and by 1934 it would have been based on the three and two-year reprint schedule;[151] for example, it can be deduced that when the 3000 sheets of the Popular Edition *Isle of Wight* (sheet 142) were printed in 1935, it was known that the Fifth Edition was expected within two years, and that that amount of stock would be sufficient. However, sheets 139 (*Bridport & Lyme Regis*) and 141 (*Bournemouth*) were both reprinted in the same year that the corresponding Fifth Edition sheets appeared. In this case the new map was published at the end of the year, and it may well be that the reprints of the Popular Edition were made at the beginning of the year in order to anticipate the holiday season, and therefore to avoid losing sales. In this instance, selling an out-of-date map would have been less important than losing the market to private firms. The print run ought have been calculated to have been sufficient for one season, so it can be assumed that the 3,000 copies of sheet 141, for example, were expected to sell in one year. However, as the Officer in charge of the Map Sales and Issues Division noted, 'it would be quite impossible to trace the exact influence of the new edition on the old'.[152]

But what of overall profits? There appear to be no figures for sales of individual map series and the only indication of yearly income from overall sales is given in the printed annual reports. There is no possibility, therefore, of making any other than theoretical calculations of profits for the Popular Edition. However, if from the total print run of 1,978,750[153] for the Popular sheets, 4.5%[154] is deducted to allow for unsold copies, and the result, 1,889,706 is multiplied by the average profit of 7.5d. per sheet of the four formats,[155] a total hypothetical profit of £59,053 is produced for the Popular Edition between 1919 and 1942, representing 4.75% of the total income from sales of all scales for this period[156] and giving an annual average profit of £2,460.1s.10d.[157]

150   Oliver, (1989a), p.9.

151   PRO OS 1/312. Minute 105, 29/10/1934.

152   PRO OS 1/256. Minute 146, 27/4/1938.

153   The sum of all the different print codes on all the states of the 146 sheets. The total print run is only approximate because it includes estimated figures for the early issues, and does not allow for undiscovered states.

154   The estimated costs of the Popular Edition sheets allowed for 4.5% being unsold; see p.203.

155   See figures on p.201. There are no figures to show the relative sales of the different formats of the sheets, and the total number of sheets seen in folded format is too small to provide a significant value for statistical purposes; the average profit of all four formats was therefore taken as the only useful, if unsatisfactory, figure for this purpose.

156   Sales income is derived from the annual reports.

At no time, between 1920 and 1939, would this have amounted to more than 1% of the annual gross cost to the state of the Ordnance Survey.[158] On the other hand, as a proportion of the total net sales income it varied from 4.9% in 1920 to 2.8% in 1939, and, in 1936-7, amounted to 8.3% of the income from small scale maps.[159] The income from the sale of the Popular Edition was therefore a reasonable contribution towards cost recovery, if the charge for survey and revision is ignored. (As an aside, it can be noted that the profits made on the engraved outline sheets of the Third Edition Small Sheet Series, which were only printed to supply the parish boundaries which were lacking on the Popular, amounted to over £6,000 between 1927 and 1932.[160]) In the end, it was all very well for Winterbotham to say that the production of the small scales practically paid for itself;[161] the pronouncement of the accountants, who had access to more data than currently survives, was that 'taken as a whole, there is a net loss on the one-inch and smaller scale maps.'[162]

Was the Popular Edition the success it was claimed to be? Certainly the annual reports of the late 1920s record increased demand for the map, and there are numerous references in the files to increased sales, but a precise answer cannot be given without comparative figures for the Third Edition, many of whose sheets were reprinted just as frequently as those of the Popular. In fact, just at the time when sales of the one-inch were allegedly booming, the Ordnance Survey was operating under great stress from undermanning. The increased sales, which were achieved without any increase in manpower, were ascribed solely to improved marketing techniques, and masked the decrease in the sale of the large scales which were now so out of date.[163] The availability of the Popular Edition also coincided with an upturn in the use of the one-inch map in schools and by the army, and it was able to benefit from the noticeable improvement in trade because Close responded vigorously to the advice, given in the 1890s, that 'Government would be wise to take a lesson from the experience of private publishers',[164] by doing precisely that. Almost every aspect of the small scales presentation and promotion had been copied from commercial practice, from folding and covers to advertising and selling. Indeed, such careful note was taken of the private mapsellers that when it was proposed to drop the traffic diagrams from the Fourth Edition of the quarter-inch map, it was suggested that 'a feature which is worth Bartholomew's

---

157   No account has been taken of the change in price which occurred in 1920, since relatively few maps were probably sold before this date at the old prices. The 1934 price change only affected the dissected maps which were not sold in such great numbers as the mounted and folded versions.

158   Calculated from figures provided in the annual reports.

159   Separate figures for the income from sales of small and large scales were given in annual reports from 1937.

160   The profit on a single engraved sheet was 10.5d.; PRO OS 1/256. May 1935.

161   OSL G5186, Appendix I to OSC 9, 5/12/1934.

162   PRO OS 1/22. Cost accounting for Ordnance Survey. Enclosure 1G. C.R.8338. 7/3/1932.

163   PRO OS 1/94. French to Trickett, 29/12/1933.

164   Hayes Fisher, (1896b), para.1368.

while to copy is probably worth our while to perpetuate'.[165] It is possibly true to say that the Popular Edition, bolstered by the new commercial selling tactics of the Ordnance Survey, and protected by an aggressive copyright policy, was more of a public relations achievement than it was a financial success.

165 PRO OS 1/54. Minute 29, 16/9/1937.

AFTERWORD

The Popular Edition was obviously a great disappointment to Close, who was always to regret the demise of his cherished Killarney-style coloured relief one-inch map. Indeed, his cartographic achievements in 1913 and 1914 could be regarded as the zenith in Ordnance Survey colour-printing at this scale, and they have not been matched to the present day. At that time, experimenting with colour was an expensive process, because the map had to be taken to the final printing stage before its success or failure could be assessed. The trials which were undertaken before the First World War were, in effect, the cartographic equivalent of the lavish style of living and high standards enjoyed by the Edwardian upper classes; it was never to be regained in post-war Britain.

The importance of the one-inch map - the Ordnance Survey's premier small-scale product - can be measured by the direct involvement in those days of the Director General in its design, specification and production. We associate Close with the Popular Edition, Winterbotham with the Fifth (Relief) Edition and Cheetham and Brown with the Seventh Series. In fact, the influence of Close can also be seen in the Fifth (Relief) Edition, which was modelled on his pre-war experiments, and in the Seventh Series, which in clarity of design took as its model the Popular. Unwittingly, and against his own aesthetic judgement, Close had therefore, by force of circumstances, provided in the Popular Edition the prototype for the preferred one-inch style, and, later, the 1:50,000 series. In this respect, its title was aptly chosen. In turn, Close was undoubtedly inspired by Wilson, whose handling of the Baker and Dorington committees in 1892 was to have a lasting impact on the appearance of the one-inch map, from the determination of widths of rivers, church symbols, road classification, the incorporation of magnetic variation diagrams, and reference squaring, to printing the map in colour. The New Series of the 1870s and 1880s had been criticised in the Dorington Committee as being far from the best cartography in the world - its only merit was in the skill of its engraving.

Wilson's contribution to the shaping of the specification, particularly of the conventional signs, of the one-inch map is of lasting importance. However, his insistence that engraving should be the preferred method of production lacked any element of forward thinking which, even in 1892, should have included a rigorous examination of the disadvantages of producing a coloured map - which had been requested in that year by the army - from an engraved base. Of course, the privilege of hindsight allows such harsh judgement; that there would be inherent inaccuracies in a coloured one-inch map produced from an engraved base was recognised by Dorington, who recommended that the demand for coloured detail at this scale could be met by the proposed military map 'for which such strict accuracy is not required'; at the time when the Popular Edition was conceived, this opinion was probably still valid. Close had made a great effort to ensure that the Popular fulfilled the military requirements laid down by the Baker Committee, and was rewarded by the approval of the map for military purposes in 1919. However, by adhering to engraving as the basis, he had produced a map which, when printed in colour, was distorted so that when, in 1923, it was decided to use the Popular Edition as a gridded training map, it was found to be unsuitable for the accurate superimposition of a military grid. Although it is doubtful whether the need for such a grid could have been envisaged when the Popular was first devised, before the First World War, it could be argued that Close, with his profound knowledge of, and interest in, projections and mathematical cartography in general, might have foreseen this eventuality and ensured the accuracy of the base map.

In taking up Wilson's mantle and by maintaining the superiority of the engraved image, Close was to leave a legacy of production difficulties for the Popular Edition whose financial cost, although not now quantifiable, may well not have been offset, overall, by sales income. In making the decision to continue with engraving, Close's judgement was flawed on two counts. The first concerned the retention of hachuring. It could not be disputed that engraved hachures were unequalled - the error was in believing that this was what the public wanted. An examination of the Popular Edition in the context of its predecessors and successors strongly indicates that, provided the sheet lines are convenient, the public preferred for use (as opposed to armchair browsing) a map which showed relief by contours only. Hachures and shading, even layering, served only to obscure detail. This was as true of the New Series, Revised New Series, and Third Edition as it is, for example, of the Lake District Tourist map today. The fact that the last sold more than its standard series constituents in the 1920s and 1930s undoubtedly owes more to its sheet lines than to its relief depiction. Although Close was never to discover if his proposed relief series would have been well received, it is significant that the Fifth (Relief) was not critically acclaimed and was abandoned. The principal interface between art and science in cartography - the depiction of relief - has probably, since the eighteenth century, been the most significant contributor to controversy in cartographic design, and to high production costs. And yet, all the evidence points to public preference for a map untrammelled by artistic licence. This was the key to the popularity of the Popular Edition.

Close's second misjudgement was to underestimate the amount of correction which would be needed to the sheets for intermediate printings - indeed, at one point he clearly anticipated that one print run would last for the whole of the fifteen year revision cycle. This might well have been the case for rural areas, but if more thought had been given to the need for correction and revision, the Popular might have been a drawn map from the outset. As it was, the use of the Third Edition copperplates was not straightforward, for, quite apart from the labour of duplicating, cutting and rivetting them into new sheet lines and making good the joins, numerous changes were made to the symbols, and placing and lettering of names, which involved extensive re-engraving. Further expense resulted from the indecision over the new specification, and also from actual reversals of policy halfway through the re-engraving of the Popular. Three prime examples of this were first, the separation of water and outline on the engraved plate, followed by the decision to incorporate water with detail once more. Secondly, having decided to retain parish boundaries, and to emphasise their distinction from the dotted contours by strengthening every fourth dot, it was then decided to erase the parish boundaries altogether. Lastly, having originally specified dotted contours, which meant replacing the Third Edition symbol of a combination of dot and dash, these then had to be converted to solid lines. The substantial work which all this involved for fifty-five sheets - more than a third of the total number of Popular Edition sheets - was, as Jack remarked, a total waste of money. The technical headaches of matching an engraved base to a coloured overprint, together with the resulting dithering over specification, were the direct cause of the decision to produce the Popular Edition of Scotland from drawings, rather than from an engraved base. As it was, the outmoded production methods of the Popular Edition made it expensive to maintain and revise.

When this study was begun, the casual examination of a few sheets of the later printings of the Popular Edition, which chanced to show building developments, new roads under construction and new symbols for electricity transmission lines and youth hostels, had led to the expectation that the series would be shown to be an important graphic source in any research into the geography of inter-war Britain, especially during a period when the large-scale plans were becoming obsolete. The results have been disappointing in this respect for several reasons, which are principally concerned with the production and revision methods which were consequent on Close's decision to continue with engraving. Although the production of the map spanned the entire inter-war period, it had come to the end of its useful life even before the completion of its first publication in 1926. In 1928, when work on its replacement, the Fifth (Relief) Edition was started, the southern sheets were at the end of their fifteen-year revision cycle. In that year, the famous Liberal 'yellow book', *Britain's industrial future*, was published by the Liberal Industrial Inquiry; its recommendations included a vast programme of national development - more roads, houses, garden cities, electricity and afforestation. Some of this had already begun, and it is true that the Ordnance Survey had responded swiftly to the rapid road construction, which had begun soon after the First World War, by establishing a separate road revision programme specifically tailored to the one-inch map and in this respect, at least, the Popular Edition is a more faithful representation of development than its large-scale counterparts.

However, the incorporation of housing expansion on reprints of the one-inch map depended on this information first being present on the published six-inch map from which the intermediate revisions of the one-inch sheets were partly compiled. Since the six-inch and twenty-five-inch plans were hopelessly out of date by 1928, the material for revising urban detail on the Popular Edition was largely non-existent. The need to extend the life of the Popular beyond its original expectancy had arisen from the failure to complete the Fifth Edition, of which only 38 sheets, covering southern England, had been published by 1939. The Popular Edition sheets for northern England continued to be issued in the late 1930s and, by partly incorporating Fifth Edition conventions, paid lip service to those social and industrial changes, such as hiking and national electrification, which were to change Britain's way of life. As far as urban revision was concerned, the situation only changed significantly with the emergency six-inch revision of the late 1930s. Following this, great tracts of urban landscape appeared on the map, principally on the outline sheets of the Popular Edition, and on the northern sheets of the War Revisions. By recording urban spread in an overprinted purple, the Popular-based sheets of the Land Utilisation Survey (whose data were collected independently of the Ordnance Survey) also allowed a comparative assessment of town development to be made, which could not be done using the states of the topographical base alone. The standard sheets of the Popular Edition did include piecemeal revision to urban detail, but very little of this preceded publication at the six-inch scale, although there are notable exceptions, such as the development of the industrial complex at Middlesbrough.

In looking, then, at the cartography and content of the Popular Edition, it can be said that it certainly failed to reflect the cartographic possibilities of its time, principally because its production methods tied it firmly to the past. From a design point of view it ended up as an ungainly compromise between old and new techniques. Its great success was the simplicity of the 50ft contours, ungarnished by artistic aids to relief interpretation. As far as content is concerned, its primary usefulness is the portrayal of the expanding road network, most of which is not to be found on the large-scale plans of the inter-war period. Because the Popular Edition was based on essentially nineteenth-century cartographic design, and on the Third Revision, which mostly took place before 1921, it is more redolent of leisurely pre-First World War Britain than of the economically depressed, inter-war period of the 1920s and 1930s.

Although the Popular Edition was therefore in most respects a map behind the times, the way in which it was marketed broke new ground on the Ordnance Survey. When Close began designing the new one-inch map in 1911, the main competition was Bartholomew's half-inch series, for which the Ordnance Survey's equivalent in scale was no match either in colour or in sheet lines. Not only did Close copy Bartholomew's layer interval for the proposed relief map, but also, the road classification of the Popular Edition bore an uncanny resemblance to that used on the commercial map. Even the sub-title of the Popular Edition: 'Contoured Road Map' was taken from Bartholomew's products. Close also copied Bartholomew's ideas in marketing: the leaflets, counter cards, posters and travellers had all been used by the Scottish firm in the nineteenth century; folding methods and types of cover had already been derived from commercial practice. In one respect, the Ordnance Survey could claim originality, and that was in the production of pictorial covers, which soon began to be copied by others. However, it would seem that the firm of Bartholomew was a major catalyst in the development at the beginning of this century of the Ordnance Survey's small-scale cartography, and especially of its commercial practice. Bartholomew's aesthetically pleasing maps, produced at a popular scale, and, more significantly, on far more sympathetic sheet lines than those of the Ordnance Survey, played a major role in the development of 'map awareness' in the general public during the nineteenth and early twentieth centuries. The public National Survey therefore owed much to the private national map.

In the inter-war years, the Ordnance Survey achieved pre-eminence in the market place for small-scale maps, of which the Popular Edition was a leading component, by copying commercial selling practice on the one hand, and, on the other, by establishing for the first time a firm copyright policy which gradually squeezed out effective competition for the one-inch map from private firms. There is no question that, in reversing their publicly acknowledged policy of allowing firms to make free use of their small-scale maps for the production of derived mapping, the Ordnance Survey treated Bartholomew, in particular, in an ungentlemanly manner. In vigorously pursuing an effective copyright policy, and in encouraging the use of the national maps in schools, the Ordnance Survey succeeded in establishing a ready market for the Popular Edition. And yet, one of the conclusions to be drawn from a study of the print runs of its sheets is that map-buying was still by no means as developed as it was to be with the Seventh Series. Although it was constantly stated that revenue was increasing, this may have had more to do with the direct control of sales being in the hands of the Ordnance Survey, so that the agents' discounts - previously as much as 53% for sole agents - was saved. On the other hand, the cost of promoting the maps could not have been insignificant; travellers' salaries and expenses, designers' salaries, and the cost of printing advertising matter would all have to be set against the revenue of the Popular Edition, so that at the end of the day the profit margin would not have been great. The Popular Edition certainly seems to have been a successful public relations exercise, but it did not match up to the expectations of a one-inch map expressed in 1935 by the British Association for the Advancement of Science (quoted on p.1) for it could not be regarded as a 'complete and authoritative record of the country', even at the time it was first produced.

THE ONE-INCH MAPS OF ENGLAND AND WALES

A chronological outline

The information given in this brief synopsis is taken from Hellyer (1999), the guides published by the Charles Close Society, Ordnance Survey catalogues, publications lists, annual reports, library catalogues, and from the maps themselves. The dates in parentheses refer to the dates of initial publication of the series.

The phrase 'with hills' is the term used by the Ordnance Survey to describe the representation of relief by hachures. A map 'without hills' lacked hachures; relief, if shown at all, would be indicated by contours and/or spot heights.

I OLD SERIES (1805-69, 1873) 110 sheets

Most sources cite the four-sheet map of Kent, published on 1 January 1801, as the first Ordnance Survey one-inch map. Although it was based on the Trigonometrical Survey, and the detail was surveyed and drawn by the Board of Ordnance's military surveying draftsmen from the Tower of London, it was engraved and published by a private publisher, William Faden. Since these four sheets were replaced in 1818 by revised maps which were entirely produced by the Board of Ordnance, and which carried the sheet numbering of the national series, which did not appear on the original Kent maps, it has been decided, in this listing, to treat the map of Essex, published in 1805, as the first true Ordnance Survey one-inch map (see Hodson (1991d)). A comprehensive account and cartobibliography of the Old Series is given in the eight volumes of the Margary facsimiles (1975-1992).

Sheets 1, 42-6, 48-57, 59-63, 66-8, 71-82, 87-99, and 101-110 were issued in quarter sheets. The Old Series was withdrawn from sale in May 1903 (*Publications issued ... 1st to 30th May 1903*), but even before this, in 1899, it was available only on special request (*Ordnance Survey maps of the United Kingdom. A description of their scales, characteristics, ...*, 1899). Lithographed facsimiles of some of the southern sheets were printed by the Ordnance Survey in the 1920s and 1930s.

1 Sheets 1-90. Derived mainly from two-inch surveys. (1805-44) Hills only. Complete.

2 Sheets 91-110. Derived from large-scale surveys. (1842-74).

  2a Outline with contours. Incomplete.

  2b With hills (on same plate as detail). Complete.

II NEW SERIES (1872-97) Nominally 360 sheets

No published cartobibliographical studies have yet been made of the New Series. Sheets 1-73 were merely Old Series sheets 91-110 re-numbered. Sheets 243 and 260 were never published, and the total of sheets was reduced by means of combined sheets. The maximum number of copperplates was 348. The *Isle of Man* sheet had no contours until the Popular Edition. Derived from large-scale surveys.

1 Outline with contours. 343 sheets in 336. Incomplete. (1874-96).

2 With hills in black, engraved on same plate as detail. Incomplete. (1878-92).

2a Without contours. 72 sheets in 68. Incomplete.
2b With contours. 13 sheets. Incomplete.

3 With hills in black or brown, engraved from separate plate. 61 sheets in 60. Incomplete. (1892-8).

4 Outline Advance Edition published by photozincography. 87 sheets in 86. Incomplete. (1891-2).

5 Temporary Advance Edition with hills. 73 sheets. Incomplete. (1892-7).

III REVISED NEW SERIES (1895-1904) 346 sheets (First Revision 1893-8)

No detailed study has been made of the whole of the Revised New Series; a cartobibliography of the coloured Revised New Series is in preparation by Dr Tim Nicholson, on whose work the entry for **III 4** is based. The information for the remaining sections may need revision. Not based on new large-scale surveys, but on a special revision for the one-inch scale, using the six-inch maps as field sheets.

1 Outline with contours. 356 sheets in 346. Incomplete. (1895-9). The first sheets to be published were 274, 306, 315, and 321 (*Publications issued ...* 1st to 31st Mar. 1895).

2,3 With hills in black (**2**) or brown (**3**). 344 sheets in 338 recorded. Incomplete. (1895-1904).

4 In colour. 351 sheets in 290 reducing to 289 as sheet combinations were rearranged. (1897-1904). Roads in burnt sienna, brown hachures, water in blue and contours in red. Sheets numbered in the range 1 to 73 also had woods in green. The first announcement of the publication of the 'One Inch Map, New Series (Revised). Printed in colours and folded in cover' appeared in *Publications issued ... 1st to 30th Sep.1897*. The first sheets published were: 268-70, 284, 285, 299, 300 and 316.

IV THIRD EDITION (1903-13) 346 sheets (Second Revision 1901-12)

1 Small Sheet series (1903-13) No detailed study has been made of this Small Sheet Series. The name 'Third Edition' was not used in the Publication lists until the issue for 1st to 31st Jan.1904. It was first referred to as the 'One Inch Map - (Second revision)' in July 1903. See Hellyer, (1999), pp.18-19

1a Outline with contours. 357 sheets in 346. (1903-13). The first sheets to be published, as indicated in *Publications issued ... 1st to 31st July 1903*, were 1, 4, 5, 317, 331-3, 344 and 345. This series was still being printed into the 1930s because it showed parish boundaries which were omitted from the Popular.

1b,c With hills in black (**b**) or brown (**c**). 332 sheets in 325. Incomplete. (1904-11). A printed sticker, pasted over the entry for this series in the Ordnance Survey *Catalogue ... to 1st April 1912* announced that 'The printing of One-Inch Maps of the United Kingdom ... With hills shaded in brown ... With hills shaded in black, has been discontinued.'

1d In colour. 118 sheets in 96. Incomplete. (1903-7). The first sheet published was 300 (*Publications issued ... 1st to 31st Dec. 1903*). Superseded by **2**.

2 Large Sheet Series (1906-13) The standard reference work on this series is Messenger (1988), which lists the states of the coloured and outline sheets. One sheet, no.85, was still available for issue in 1933 (PRO OS 1/70, Cooke to Grundy, 15/2/1933).

    2a In colour. 152 sheets. Complete. (1906-13). The first sheet to be published was 17 (*Isle of Man*), (*Publications issued ... 1st to 31st Dec. 1906*).

    2b Black Outline. 58 sheets. Incomplete. (1907-17; published 1918-19).

V   FOURTH EDITION (1911-12) 7 sheets (Third Revision 1909-10, abandoned)

1 Outline with contours. 7 sheets (273, 274, 289, 290 [the RGS copy of 290 has railways and minor corrections inserted to October 1914], 305, 306, 321). Incomplete. (1911-12).

2,3 With hills in black (**2**) or brown (**3**). 4 sheets (273, 274, 289, 290). Incomplete. (1911).

VI   POPULAR EDITION (1919-26) 146 sheets (Third Revision 1912-23)

This series is sometimes referred to as the Fourth Edition, or '4th Popular Edition' (*Annual Report* for 1934/5, p.15). Full details of this series are given in Part 2.

1 Coloured. Complete. (1919-26).

2 Outline with contours in red, or contours in red and water in blue. Complete. (1921-6).

3 Outline edition, with water in blue. Probably 124 sheets. Incomplete. (1941-2).

Variations of these outline maps are described in Part 2, p.282.

VII   FIFTH EDITION (1931-9) 38 sheets (Fourth Revision 1928-36)

A listing and description of this series is given in Oliver (1989)a.

1 Fifth (RELIEF) Edition. 22 sheets. (1931-6). Incomplete.

2 Fifth Edition. 38 sheets. (1934-9). Incomplete, without hachures and hill shading. *London* and *St Albans* were published as Special District Maps, but have been included in the total because they were constructed on series sheetlines.

3 Fifth (BLACK) Edition. 38 sheets. (1931-9; published 1932-9). Incomplete.

4 Physical Features only. 22 sheets. (1931-6; published 1932-6). Incomplete.

5 Outline edition, with water in blue. 27 sheets recorded. (1942). Incomplete.

VIII WAR REVISION 1940 (Issued For Official Use 1940-1, published 1943-5) 137 sheets recorded

Some War Revision sheets (107, 118-9, 127-8, 136-8, 143-6) were based on the Fifth Edition; others were based on the Popular Edition. They were prepared in the first instance for military purposes, but the decision to place the military version on sale to the public was taken 'in the summer' of 1942, because it was then the only way to supply the public with a reasonably up-to-date one-inch map. (*Annual Report* 1942/3). No full listing or study has been made of this complex series, and although the publication reports list very few that were placed on sale to the public, examples of most sheets can be found with the red sticker denoting 'sales edition'. Most map collections hold incomplete sets of both the War Revision Series; the most comprehensive is kept by the Map Library of the Ministry of Defence. The numbers of sheets available for each version are not known.

1 With grid, on Popular Edition sheet lines. 126 sheets recorded.

2 Without grid, on Popular Edition sheet lines. 12 sheets recorded.

3 With grid, on Fifth Edition sheet lines. 11 sheets recorded.

4 Without grid, on Fifth Edition sheet lines. 3 sheets recorded.

5 Outline editions, on Fifth Edition sheet lines. 4 sheets recorded.

IX SECOND WAR REVISION 1940 (Issued For Official Use 1940-1; published 1943-5) 129 sheets

1 Coloured edition on Popular edition base. 72 sheets recorded.
2 Coloured edition on Fifth Edition base. 46 sheets recorded.
3 Outline edition on Popular Edition base. 33 sheets recorded.
4 Outline edition on Fifth Edition base. 19 sheets recorded.

X NEW POPULAR EDITION MAP OF GREAT BRITAIN (1945-7) 114 sheets Incomplete

Also known as the *New Popular (Sixth) Edition* or the *Sixth (New Popular) Edition*. A listing of the sheets of this series is provided in Oliver (1989b).
1 [Final Fifth Edition style], coloured. 50 sheets.
2 [Final Fifth Edition style], outline. 50 sheets.
3 Provisional (Popular Edition) style, coloured. 64 sheets.
4 Provisional (Popular Edition) style, outline. 64 sheets.

XI SEVENTH SERIES MAP OF GREAT BRITAIN (1952-62) 190 sheets [revised 1947-58]

The best account of this series is Oliver (1991).

1 Coloured edition. (1952-61). Complete.

2 Outline edition. (1952-62). Complete.

GENERAL INSTRUCTIONS
FOR THE 3rd REVISION OF THE ONE-INCH MAP, 1913

These instructions, dated 6 March 1913, are printed on three pages. Only one copy is known, in PRO OS 1/4/3. It is transcribed here, as far as possible, according to the layout of the original except that the typed annotations in the right hand margins, headed 'Departments Concerned', indicating which department was responsible for what action, are given in parentheses in **bold** at the end of the relevant paragraphs, or within the text where this is more appropriate. The reference in these instructions to L.S.S (i.e. Large Sheet Series) does not refer to the Third Edition Large Sheet Series, but to its successor, the Popular Edition, which was also devised on a Large Sheet layout.

ENGLAND & WALES, 3RD REVISION 1-INCH MAPS.

GENERAL INSTRUCTIONS

FOR

GUIDANCE OF DEPARTMENTS.

----

1 The general policy in respect of Small Scale O.S. Maps is described in D.G. Circular, 30-9-12. C/C 6342/12. [*This document has not been found.*]

2 The 3rd Revision 1″ Map will be published in two forms.

    (a)   Outline Map - 3 printings. Outline black, Water blue, Contours red.

    (b)   Fully coloured with Hills - probably 11 printings. 1. Outline. 2. Water, blue. 3, Contours, brown. 4 & 5, Roads, brown and yellow. 6, Hachures, brown. 7, 8, 9, Ground Tints, green, light buff, darker buff; but in sheets of small features only two former. 10, 11, Hill shade.

3 A new Sheet-line Diagram is approved. District or special sheets will be produced according to demand.

4 Outline. The existing 18″ x 12″ copper plates (matrices) to be joined up to new L.S.S. sheets, and receive 1st scraping to remove or clear **(Electro-typing)**-

(i) Contours. (ii) Water and water lining and sea bed contours. (iii) Woods, clear crowded detail. (iv) Stipple, remove where it obscures detail and slopes. (v) Badly engraved or placed names. **(Engraving)**

As regards (iv) and (v), Superintendent 1″ draftsmen will submit first through A.O.P. to O.P. models showing proposed erasures. When approved, these will guide Superintendent Engravers. In most cases (iv) will be dealt with on the stones only. **(1″ Drawing)**

When the Field Revision documents are completed for a whole L.S.S. sheet, the 2nd scraping will be done, and Electro will make a new plate. **(Electro-typing)**

The F.R. Additions sheets to have added by the draftsmen the names in (v) above (to be replaced by the engraver). **(1″ Drawing)**

5 On the new plate, the Engraver adds:- **(Engraving)**

   (i)   The sheet lines first, and a proof is taken for Photo., and one for Z.P.

   (ii)   The matter in the F.R. additions sheets.

   (iii) Continuous line for railways, and also the word (single) where required, and which should be shown by draftsmen on the drawings.

   (iv)   The margins with latitudes and longitudes and reference numbers as for the new sheets ½″ Ireland.

6 Contours. New drawings on 1″ blues from 18″ x 12″ plates, with L.S.S. sheet lines scored in blue.
   Intervals. To be 50′ except where such would be crowded over a considerable area, when 100′ to be used.

   The draftsmen to interpolate, with hill sketch maps and 6″ plots as [*the rest of the word is torn and not legible*]. They are to refer all doubtful cases of intervals for A.O.P. to see before penning in. They are to insert contour numbers where they should appear on the map in blue, as these numbers are to be engraved and not photo-etched. Where contours are close together, the places selected for numbering should not be on the South and East slopes, since the shading will be there to obscure it. The West slope will generally be best for convenience in reading. **(1″ Drawing)**

   An imprint note will appear as to change of interval. It is desirable that if the interval has to be changed from 50′ to 100′ at a certain level, it shall continue at 100′ to the end, and not revert to 50′ because features flatten out again on top. But if a 50′ ring contour on a summit would aid to define its shape, the draftsmen should make a note and refer it to A.O.P. **(Zinc Printing)**

7 Water. New drawings as for contours. The sea-bed contours will also be drawn; but their numbers will be entered in blue (to be engraved). **(1″ Drawing)**

8   The success of photo-etching depends on the quality of the drawing. Superintendents will bring to notice such draftsmen as excel. It is unlikely that 1″ draftsmen unable to attain such proficiency will be recommended for a higher classification. **(1″ Drawing. Photo.)**

9   Hachures. To avoid delay, the plates will not at present be joined up. They will be improved. Any strengthening necessary should be chiefly on the S. and E. sides, as the hills will be printed for a map shaded to a N.W. light. The Superintendent H.E. to arrange with Superintendent Z.P. for such pulls off stone as will assist his engravers in selecting work to do.

    Pulls of improved plates to go to Z.P. when a new L.S. is completed.   **(Hill Engraving. Zinc Printing)**

10 Photo-etching. When they are all ready, Superintendent Draftsmen 1″ will forward for each L.S. to Photo. together -

    (a)   Outline impression of new plate (see para.5 (i)). This will be the register guide. **(1″ Drawing)**

    (b)   Contour drawings. **(Photo.)**

    (c)   Water drawings. **(Zinc Printing)**

    To secure eventual register on the copper plates, the procedure will be as follows:-

    (i)   Photo. makes three helio-plates for Z.P. **(Photo.)**

    (ii) Z.P. supplies to 1″ draftsmen three tracing paper impressions, a,b, & c. Also three combined proofs, a & b & c, a & c, b & c. **(Zinc Printing)**

    (iv)[sic] The 1″ draftsmen enter corrections on tracing and pass to Photo. **(1″ Drawing)**

    (v)   Photo. corrects negatives, and produces etched plates of b and c. Combined proof to O.P. after examination by 1″ draftsmen. **(Photo.)**

11 The approved contour and water plates to engravers to add numbers, after pulls have been taken for Z.P. **(Engraving)**

12 Shade drawings will be commenced by Superintendent Z.P. immediately he has received pulls from the plates - Hachures, Contours and Water. **(Litho-draftsmen)**

    Experiments to be commenced to see if a satisfactory shade plate can be produced on copper or zinc in order that there may be a permanent record. **(Photo.)**

13 [As] soon as the engravers have completed the outline plate, except for names and [margins,] the Superintendent will send an impression to Z.P. in order that the road plates or stones may be prepared. **(Engraving. Zinc Printing)**

14 Superintendent 1″ draftsmen will supply road models for Z.P. to be ready with the

completed F.R. documents. **(1″ Drawing)**

15 The 1″ draftsmen to prepare all documents necessary for the engravers without engravers having to compile or pick out scattered information themselves. **(1″ Drawing. Engraving)**

16 Field Revision. A programme has been drawn up to produce about 2½ L.S. per month.

(i) On the 1st of each month, a statement will be submitted to O.P. showing the average square miles each day of each revision, and final revision, and the month's total.

(ii) A history sheet for each sheet will be kept by the Superintendent draftsmen and Superintendent engravers, and will be submitted weekly to A.O.P. **(Field Revision)**

17 Progress diagrams. The Superintendent in each department concerned (5) will keep up diagrams showing the detailed stages within the Department. The passing of work to other departments, and the field (with dates) will also be shown on this or on a separate diagram, if preferred.

A generalised diagram of the principal stages will be kept by A.O.P for O.P's use.

Superintendents of the 5 departments will meet once a month in A.O.P.'s office to compare diagrams and progress. **(1″ Drawing. Outline engrving [sic]. Hill Engraving. Photo. Zinc Printing.)**

E.P. BROOKER,
Lt. Colonel, R.E.
O.P.
6-3-13.

Abbreviations used in these instructions:

AOP   Assistant Officer in charge of the printing department

FR   Field revision

HE   Hill engraving

OP   Officer in charge of the printing department

ZP   Zinc printing department

APPENDIX 3

STAGES IN THE PRODUCTION OF A POPULAR EDITION SHEET FOR THE ENGRAVER 1914

The principal source for the reconstruction of this series of actions is *Instructions for the revision of the small scale maps (Provisional)*, which was issued in January 1914. This document refers to 'revisers' instructions' which have not been traced. Only one copy of the 1914 instructions is known, in the Ordnance Survey Library, G2973.

The information has been represented here in a more logical arrangement for the purposes of reconstructing the sequence of actions necessary to prepare the sheet for the engraver; added explanations are given where necessary. OS original documents are written in **bold**, and the personnel involved are highlighted in **UPPER CASE BOLD**. Supplied information appears in square brackets: [ ].

1   Receive **FIELD REVISERS'** documents:

    (i)   **6″ plots**

2   **DRAFTSMAN prepares:**

    A) **Erasure sheet** [a blue impression taken from the 3rd Edition Small Sheets]

        (i)   show all detail for erasure in red

3   **DRAFTSMAN**, using field documents and sources mentioned below, prepares:

    B) **Drawing sheet** for black detail [a blue impression taken from the 3rd Edition Small Sheets]

        (i)   Mark 6″ sheet lines on drawing sheet

        (ii) Show in red all detail to be added

SOURCES:

        (i)   **6″ plots**

        (ii)   **Intermediate revision sheets**

        (iii)   **Record book of changes**

        (iv)   **1″ boundary sheets**

        (v)   **Road sheet**

        (vi)   Local guide books (antiquities)

        (vii)   Bradshaw's Guide (railway stations)

        (viii) Postal Guide (post and telegraph offices)

        (ix)   Admiralty List of Lights (lighthouses & -ships)

        (x)   Lifeboat Journal 'wreck chart' (lifeboat stations)

        (xi)   **Names sheets**

4 **DRAFTSMAN** prepares:

C) **Contour and water drawing:** a blue impression [taken from the 3rd Edition Small Sheets]

  (i) 100′ contours penned in [i.e. inked over existing contours]. These then checked against 6″ to ensure maximum similarity; only minor irregularities to be generalised

  (ii) 100′ contoured drawing then reduced for use on the half-inch map

  (iii) 50′ contours interpolated:

   a) levels on **6″ plots** and **hill sketches** compared

   b) 50′ contours plotted on **hill sketches**

   c) 50′ contours transferred to **contour drawing** by pantograph and penned in

  (iv) contour figures written in blue

  (v) water penned in:

   a) outline of lakes and ponds not shown

   b) double streams not shaded

   c) selected submarine contours plotted on admiralty charts

   d) submarine contours transferred to drawing by pantograph

[**5** **DRAFTSMAN** prepares:

D) **Road sheet**: a blue impression taken from 3rd Edition Small Sheets

  (i) all changes marked from field revisers' documents

  (ii) classification marked in different colours

*The existence of this sheet is inferred from para.16 in the 1914 instructions. The Road sheet, which was prepared for the purpose of correcting the copperplate, would appear to be different from the **road model**, which was prepared to guide the litho-draftsman in preparing the road stone for printing. The road sheet would have to have been available for the preparation of the drawing sheet.*]

6 **EXAMINER**

  (i) compares **drawing** and **erasure sheets** with all sources in 3B

  (ii) checks road classification on **field sheets** which have been prepared by more than one field reviser

  (iii) checks authentication of name changes

  (iv) **Name sheets** then pasted into **object name book**, for reference at next large-scale revision

  (v) **DRAFTSMAN** attends to any queries

  (vi) **EXAMINER** prepares form **OS 513** which describes points to be settled by examination on the ground

7 FINAL REVISER

(i)   checks disputed points

[8 DRAFTSMAN

(i)   deals with points arising from 7]

9 EXAMINER

[(i)   checks 8]

(ii)   checks **contour** and **water drawings**, and edges thereof

10 SUPERINTENDENT

(i) prepares **cost return**

11 DIRECTOR GENERAL

(i)   approves 2A, 3B and 10(i)

12 ENGRAVER

(i)   receives **drawing and erasure sheets**

(ii)   prepares matrix from joined copperplates

(iii)   scrapes matrix according to erasure sheet

(iv)   engraves new detail according to drawing sheet on new duplicate

13 [PRINTER]

(i)   prints **proof impression**

14 PROOF EXAMINER

(i)   notes any imperfections on proof and makes list on **proof revision sheet**

(ii)   engraver produces **2nd, amended proof** (and a 3rd, if necessary)

15 Proof is taken with return of engraving cost to Director General for final approval

16 DRAFTSMAN prepares:

E) **road model**: black impression of outline, taken when engraving was complete
  (i)   roads coloured as they would appear on printed map
  (ii)   symbols for gradients and dangerous turnings added [it is not known what the symbol for dangerous turnings was; none was used for the Popular Edition]

[The draftsmen and litho-draftsmen would also have prepared other models for the other colours, but these were then not the engraver's concern.]

APPENDIX 4

INDEXES TO THE POPULAR EDITION
at the scale of thirty miles to one inch (1:1,900,800)

There are four principal sources of graphic indexes to the Popular Edition maps: 1) those appearing in annual reports from 1921/22 to 1931/32 at a scale of 1:4,835,360; 2) indexes printed in the Ordnance Survey catalogues at a scale of about 1:3,750,000; 3) sections of indexes, also at the scale of about 1:3,750,000 that were printed on the back of the map covers, and 4) the separately published indexes.

This last category was the most important, and the most accurate in showing the sheet lines as they actually were. They were printed at a scale of 1:1,900,800 (or one inch to thirty miles) and were obtainable from 'any Agent or from the Ordnance Survey Office at Southampton' and sold for 2d. These indexes to the Popular Edition of England and Wales were printed in black and white from at least 1923 to 1941. Later printings carried an index to the Popular Edition of Scotland on the reverse, and some versions showed the sheet lines of the special, or tourist and district maps overprinted in red. In the same way that the index to the Third Edition Large Sheet Series had been combined with that of the Popular, so, in the 1930s, the index to the Popular was combined with that of the Fifth Edition, whose sheet lines were shown by red and blue overprints.

The entries are arranged in chronological order; the list is not complete, and, doubtless, many more states remain to be found. Line endings in the transcriptions are expressed: | . Supplied information is given in square brackets: [ ]. All the following indexes bear a scale statement, representative fraction, and a bar scale at the bottom of each index. All measure approximately 390 x 320 mm (printed area), height x width.

1919   Index | To The | Ordnance Survey Of England And Wales | Published in Colours on the Scale of One Inch to a Mile = 1/63360 | Large Sheet Series | The cross hatching represents those overlapping portions | which are published on two or more Sheets. | Price of each 1-inch Sheet; flat or folded in cover, unmounted 1s.6d., | mounted 2s., or folded in sections 3s. net. | Price of this Index 2d. | 1" Old Large Sheet Series - [in blue printed lettering] Blue numbers and Blue sheet lines. | 1" Popular Edition - [in red printed lettering] Red numbers and red sheet lines. [1919]. **Plate 7**

RGS Eng & Wales G80 (received 12/12/1919); CUL Maps. 34.013.147. [the price note of the one-inch maps on this example has been crossed out in manuscript, probably following the price increases which came into effect in January 1920.]

Showing Popular Edition, printed and published, in green: sheets 91, 92, 102-5, 110-113, 118-123, 127-132, 136-146; Popular Edition promised by January 1st, 1920, in half green and half yellow (coloured diagonally within each sheet): sheets 81, 82, 84, 85, 93-5; Popular Edition promised by April 1st 1920, all yellow: sheets 70, 74-6, 80, 83, 96, 106, 107, 115, 124, 133, 134. The index, and all associated information, is contained within an inner neatline which is surrounded by a border comprising a central thick line and an inner and outer fine line.

1920   Ordnance Survey | of | England and Wales | Published in Colours on the Scale of One Inch to a Mile. 1920

BL Maps 207.f.

Published in *Catalogue of the 6-inch and 25-inch county maps and town plans of England and Wales and The Isle of Man ... to 1st. April 1920.* Shows the following sheets of the Popular Edition as published: 80-5, 91-6; 102-5; 110-113; 118-123; 127-132; 136-146. This index has neither border, nor price, and does not appear to have been published separately.

1923   Index | To The | Ordnance Survey Of England And Wales | Published in Colours on the Scale of One Inch to a Mile = 1/63360 | Popular Edition | The crosshatching represents those portions | which are published on two or more Sheets. | Crown Copyright Reserved [below scale bar, bottom centre] | Price of Index 2.^{d} | Ordnance Survey, 1923. [outside border, bottom right.]

CUL Map Library, CCS Archive (Indexes).

This example is annotated in manuscript: Sheets 1 to 21 (except 17) are still to be published. 26.5.25.

The following indexes are completely redrawn and do not have a border; they all have the title: 'Index | To The | Popular Edition Sheets | of | England & Wales' and carry the statements 'Crown Copyright Reserved' and 'Price 2d.' below the scale, bottom centre. Illustrated at fig.15, p.72.

1925   [Not seen; inferred from 1926 printing.]

1926   Ordnance Survey, 1925. Reprint 500/26.

BL Maps 1175.(259.); CUL Map Library, CCS Archive (Indexes).

1927a   [Print code:] 500/27.

PC

1927b   [Print code:] 500.27.1000/27.1000/27.4000/27.

RGS Eng & Wales G.82.

1932   [Print code:] 500/27.1000/27.4000/27.3000/30.6000/32.

OS Box TL23. (OS Departmental Records)

1933   [Not seen; inferred from 1933 Special sheet index.]

1941   [Bottom right:] An Index of the Scotland 1" to 1 mile Popular | Edition appears on the back of this sheet. [Print code:] 9000/41.Cr.

PC

1940s [Print code:] 3206. As for 1941, but the price has been increased to 3d.
OSRML W415

Index to Special sheets

1925 Index | To The | Popular Edition Sheets | Of | England & Wales | Special
Sheets in Red. [1925].

BL Maps 1175.(157.) [received 29/10/1925]. Bod C17(29). CUL Map Library,
CCS Archive (Indexes).

Supp. to Cat. 1 Apr./30 June 1925. The following Special Sheets are shown: Aldershot;
Bristol; Liverpool; London (North); London (South); Manchester; Salisbury Plain;
Oxford; Worcester.

1933 [Print code:] 500/27.1000/27.1000/27.4000/27.3000/30.6000/32.5000/33.

CUL Map Library, CCS Archive (Indexes).

The print code probably refers to the printing of the black and white base index; see entry
for 1932 state above. The following Special Sheets are shown: Aldershot; Barnsley;
Bexhill; Chilterns; Birmingham; Bolton; Bristol; Huddersfield; Leeds; Liverpool; London
(North); London (South); Maidstone; Manchester; Norfolk Broads; North East Wales;
North Staffordshire; Oxford; Salisbury Plain; Sidmouth; Southampton; Weston super
Mare; Worcester; Wye Valley.

Index to Tourist District sheets

[1925] Index | To The | Popular Edition Sheets | Of | England & Wales | [in red
printed lettering:] Tourist District Maps in Red

BL 1175.(149) [received 1/4/1926].

Supp. to Cat. 1 July/30 Sept.1925. The following Tourist District maps are shown:
Brighton; Cheltenham; Chichester; Dartmoor; Exmoor; Hertford; Ilkley; Isle of Wight;
Lake District; Land's End; London; Middle Thames; New Forest; Peak District;
Snowdon.

1931 Index | To The | Popular Edition Sheets | Of | England & Wales | [in red
printed lettering:] Tourist District Maps in Red [print code:]
W.O.750/31.10.000/31.

CUL Map Library, CCS Archive (Indexes).

The following Tourist District maps are shown: Brighton; Cheltenham; Chichester;
Dartmoor; Dorking & Leith Hill; Exmoor; Hertford; Ilkley; Isle of Wight; Lake District;
Land's End; London; Middle Thames; New Forest; Peak District; Snowdon.

Combined index to Special and Tourist District sheets

1935 Index | To The | Popular Edition Sheets | Of | England & Wales | [in red
printed lettering:] Special Sheets in Red | [in blue printed lettering:] Tourist
District Maps in Blue   [Print code:] 10000/35.

CUL Map Library, CCS Archive (Indexes).

The following Special sheets are shown: Aldershot; Barnsley; Bexhill & Hastings;

Birmingham & Wolverhampton; Bristol; Bury & Bolton; Chilterns; Derby; Forest of Bowland; Huddersfield; Leeds; Liverpool; London (North); London (South); Manchester; Maidstone; North East Wales; North Staffordshire; Oxford; Salisbury Plain; Sidmouth & Exmouth; Southampton; Weston super Mare; Worcester; Wye Valley.

The following Tourist District maps are shown: Brighton; Cheltenham; Chichester; Dartmoor; Dorking & Leith Hill; Exmoor; Hertford; Ilkley; Isle of Wight; Lake District; Land's End; Middle Thames; New Forest; Norfolk Broads; Peak District; Snowdon.

Combined index to the Popular and Fifth Editions

1937 Index | To The Popular Edition Sheets | Of | England & Wales [print code probably refers to the black base index:] 500/27.1000/27.4000/27.3000/30. 6000/32.5000/33, 10,000/35, 4000/37.

PC

With published Fifth Edition small sheets overprinted in blue, and Fifth Edition large sheets, published or about to be published, overprinted in red.

1941 - Another issue of the 9000/41.Cr. printing of the standard index with the same red and blue overprint as for **1937** above, showing the Fifth Edition sheet lines. The note on the Scottish index is struck out. An oval, purple rubber stamp, bottom right, reads 'Crabwood Ho.Reproduction Sect. Ordnance Survey, Southampton. C.R. 11 OCT 1941. Proof.' The word 'Proof' has been struck out.

OS Cartographic Library, G-8. Another copy, without the OS proof stamp: CUL Map Library, CCS Archive (Indexes).

Miscellaneous

The following indexes, although not at the same scale, are included for the sake of completeness.

[1949] Index showing sheets of the New Popular | 5th Edition and Popular Edition | one inch maps of Great Britain | for compiling sheets to be drawn, reconstituted | and Provisional Edition [brown base map] 1946. [print code in red:] 3393. Scale 1:1,250,000; one inch to twenty miles.

PC; OSRML

The sheet lines of the Popular Edition are printed in yellow; those of the New Popular in red, and those of the Fifth Edition are printed in blue. See Hellyer (1992b), p.140.

[1952] Index showing sheets of the Popular, | New Popular, and 7th Series | One Inch Maps of Great Britain | As approved by D.G. 20.11.52. Scale 1,1,250,000; one inch to twenty miles. Print code: 3794. 840 x 529 mm. See Hellyer (1992b):140.

CUL Map Library, CCS Archive (Indexes).

Popular Edition sheet lines are printed in green, New Popular and Seventh Series in red. The only English Popular Edition sheet to be shown is sheet 17, *Isle of Man*.

APPENDIX 5

CHARACTERISTIC AND CONVENTIONAL SIGNS SHEETS
FOR THE ONE-INCH MAP TO 1937

With one exception (Seventh Series sheet 87, *Isle of Man*), the one-inch map of England and Wales has never carried an explanation of the different characters, that is, styles of lettering, associated with various geographical features, in its margins. The legend explaining the conventional signs, which we all take for granted today, did not appear in the margins of the one-inch map until 1886,[1] and, even then, the symbols it contained were limited in number. In order to be able to interpret the map fully, the user was referred to the separate 'characteristic sheet' which he could purchase for 6d. - a price which did not vary for over eighty years.[2] Like graphic indexes, characteristic sheets and sheets of conventional signs tend to be an ephemeral adjunct to any map series; their study, in relation to the one-inch map, has been neglected. The earliest example of a one-inch characteristic sheet (fig.40, p.233) appears to be consistent with some Old Series sheets, although it does not state to which scale of map it refers.[3] The corresponding characteristic sheets for Scotland and Ireland have no dating evidence, and could have been produced between the 1850s and the 1890s.

Except for the three drawn northern sheets, the Popular Edition style of writing for England and Wales was directly inherited from the copperplate traditions of the eighteenth century. The main changes, made to names on the Third Edition small copperplates in preparation for the Popular Edition, were the numerous repositioning of names which had been badly engraved, or were awkwardly placed, and the up-grading of the status of some settlements according to population figures.[4] The history of modern lettering on the Ordnance Survey really began when the one-inch Popular Edition of Scotland became a drawn, rather than transferred map. It was the first opportunity to design an alphabet without the fine hair lines which took so much time to repair when damaged in the transfer from copper to stone. The trials, which included the Perth

---

1   Hodson, (1991b), p.15.

2   The earliest listing of the price of a characteristic sheet so far seen is in *Catalogue of the maps and plans and other publications of the Ordnance Survey of England and Wales, to 1st March 1863*, p.31.

3   The earliest characteristic sheet for the six-inch maps appears to be: *Examples for the characters of the writing to the Ordnance map of Great Britain on the scale of six inches to a mile*. Ordnance Map Office Southampton 1st March 1847. The boundaries section of this sheet followed 'Major General Colby's order of the 9th. February 1847.' NLS, Map Library.

4   The principal change to the lettering of settlements between the 1880 and 1897 characteristic sheets was that on the latter, settlements were categorised not only according to administrative status, but also according to population. The principles behind the revision of the engraving of names for the Popular Edition are set out in Ordnance Survey, *Instructions for the revision of the small scale maps ...* (Jan.1914) p.10, paras.48-56, but it should be noted that rules for the writing of names of parishes (which stated that the parish names should be inserted where no church or village of that name existed), were superseded when it was decided, in 1919, to omit parish boundaries.

sample, described by Winterbotham as a 'matter famous in our annals',[5] and results, were described at length by Withycombe in 1929. The new style of lettering can be seen on sheets 1, 3 and 5 of the Popular Edition.

The first characteristic sheet to identify itself unequivocally with the one-inch map of England and Wales was issued in about 1880 for use with the New Series (fig.41); except for county and parish boundaries, it shows no conventional signs and simply illustrates the different styles of lettering to be found on the map. The style of writing on the next known example of a characteristic sheet, dated nearly twenty years later, 1897, also shows the conventional signs for the 'Revised one-inch map of Great Britain' (fig.42). This sheet was revised in 1906, and then cancelled in 1908. Another revised sheet was issued on 1st July 1908 (fig.43) to incorporate the changes which were made as a result of a review of the conventional signs used for the Irish one-inch map.[6] At this time, it was realised that while one characteristic sheet applied to both England and Wales and Scotland, none existed for Ireland. Five additions were suggested in order to make the sheet applicable to Ireland,[7] but only one of these was adopted, and followed through to the Popular Edition. This was the addition of 'Celtic' to the 'Roman, British or Subsequent' antiquities. The title was changed for the first time to 'Ordnance Survey Characteristic Sheet for the Revised One-Inch Map of Great Britain, and Ireland'; none of the symbols was changed between the 1906 and 1908 versions, but alterations to the notes are given in the appropriate entries below.

By the time the separate explanatory sheet came to be issued for the Popular Edition map, in 1924, its title had been changed to the more user-friendly twentieth-century language 'Conventional Signs and Writing', and, apart from the advent of colour, its principal differences were in the depiction of roads and railways and in the lettering for the Scottish maps. The earliest known example is dated 1924, which is surprisingly late considering that the publication of the Popular of England and Wales was almost complete by this time. Lacking all reference to Great Britain and Ireland, and applying, in its title, only to England and Wales (in spite of the references to Scottish lettering), it was advertised in the Ordnance Survey's catalogue for 1924[8] and it continued to be reprinted, without change, until 1931. Yet it is possible that an earlier version of the sheet was printed before 1924. The slender evidence for this is contained in the 1918

5   PRO OS 1/334. Winterbotham to McCaw, 8/8/1934. The original Perth sample has not been found, but one copy of a printed black and white extract of a drawing of the Perth area has been located at OSL in G7094 (Southampton Circulars). This accompanied Circular C.C.885, dated 5/8/1925, which laid down that the style and gauge of the writing for draftsmen's tests should be 'similar to that on the Perth drawing'.

6   OSL. Southampton Circulars, G3962. Memoranda by Capt. A.J. Savage and Major R.U.H. Buckland, March 1908.

7   An extra lighthouse with the words 'Irish maps' in brackets; the addition of 'and Ireland' to the notes on low water marks, submarine contours, land contours, a note to state that the sheet also applied to Irish maps, and lastly, the addition of the word 'Celtic' to antiquities.

8   Ordnance Survey *Catalogue of Maps and other Publications of the Ordnance Survey*, (1924), p.18. A useful reprint of this catalogue was issued by David Archer in 1991, with a short introduction by Richard Oliver.

EXAMPLES FOR THE
SIZE and CHARACTERS
of the NAMES in the
ORDNANCE MAP.

Cities and County Towns	CANTERBURY
Market Towns	TEWKESBURY
Parishes	Rockingham
Hamlets	Lampton
Royal Parks, Forests &c.	*RICHMOND PARK
Other Parks	*Wimbledon Park
Small Parks and Mansions	Strawberry Hill
Woods, Commons, Heaths, Marshes	*Wimbledon Common
Moors, Fens, Small Rivers &c.	*Barnes Common
Large Farms	Melburn
Bridges, Sluices, Lodges, Cottages	
Small detached houses, Obelisks	Obelisk
Beacons, Toll houses &c. &c.	
Roman Remains	SVLLONICÆ
Old English and Druidical Ditto	Stonehenge
County Boundaries	-------------
Hundreds & Counties of Cities	----------
Borough Boundaries & Minor Divisions	....

1 T.P.Road passing under
2 Embankment
3 River and Viaduct
4 Road crossing on a level
5 Stream passing under
6 Canal passing over
7 Cutting
8 Tunnel
9 D.º and Shaft
10 T.P.Road passing over

* These Examples must vary in size and extent according to the importance of the Districts they refer to. And when the Districts are very extensive, the ITALIC CAPITAL, must be used, as also for the names of large Rivers Bays &c.

Fig.40 Characteristic sheet, 1840s, for use with the Old Series. *Reproduced by permission of the Trustees of the National Library of Scotland.*

catalogue[9] where, on the page devoted to the one-inch map, a 'Sheet of Conventional Signs and Lettering' is referred to, while in the same publication, the 'Characteristic Sheet for the 1-inch map of Great Britain and Ireland' is also included on another page. The implication of the different titles is that there were indeed two separate publications, as might be expected since the printing, if not publication, of the first Popular Edition sheets had taken place in 1918. However, no example of this early state has yet been

9   *Catalogue of the 6-inch and 25-inch county maps ... to 1st. July 1918*, (1918), p.9.

found; it may well have had a short life, for the 1920 *Catalogue* (no catalogue appears
to have been published for 1919) mentioned only the Great Britain and Ireland sheet, and
no further catalogue appears to have been issued until 1924. A new sheet was published
in 1925 (Plate 12) and twelve years later, when it was realised that the Popular Edition
would be continuing in production for much longer than anticipated, because of the slow
progress of the Fifth Edition, it was decided to issue a revised version (January 1937),
of the conventional signs sheet. This incorporated the Ministry of Transport road classification, the inclusion of 'closed' railway stations, Youth Hostels, and other minor
changes. This state was reprinted as late as 1946. The following entries are arranged in
chronological order. Line endings are denoted: |. Supplied information is given in square
brackets: [ ]. Measurements are height x width.

OLD SERIES

[ca 1840s] Examples For The | Size and Characters | of the Names in the | Ordnance
Map. 145 x 98mm [printed area.]

BL Maps Ref.C.7a.1 (received 25/2/1854); NLS Map Library (fig.40)

Asterisks against the lettering for Royal Parks, Forests &c; Other Parks; Woods,
Commons, Heaths, Marshes; Moors, Fens, Small Rivers &c, are explained in a note
at the bottom of the sheet: 'These examples must vary in size and extent according to
the importance of the Districts they refer to. And when the Districts | are very
extensive the Capital Italic must be used as also for the names of large Rivers Bays
&c.' The size and style of the lettering indicates that this refers to the one-inch map,
and the lack of parish boundaries, which were first introduced on the New Series,
suggests that this example was prepared for the Old Series. Since this characteristic
sheet was certainly available by 1854, it pre-dated the publication of the one-inch
maps of Ireland and Scotland by at least two or three years - there would, therefore,
have been no need to specify, in the title, the country of the mapping to which it
referred for all, presumably, would have known at that time that it could only have
been England and Wales. No other examples are known.

[1850s?] Characteristic Sheet For The One Inch Engraving | Of | Scotland and
Ireland. 335 x 240mm [approx.]

NLS Map Library

Engraved. A note at the foot of the sheet reads: 'N.B. These examples must vary in
size and extent according to their importance.' This example shows only the style of
lettering that was to be used for the two one-inch series; it is impossible to date
accurately, and could have been printed at any time from the 1850s to the 1890s.

NEW SERIES

[ca 1880] Characteristic Sheet For The One Inch Map | Of | England & Wales. [ca
1880.] 320 x 270mm [approx.]

NLS Map Library (fig.41)

Engraved. Two printed notes at the foot of the sheet read: 'These examples must vary
in size and extent according to their importance.' and 'The distinction between Parish
and other Churches discontinued from 1879.' Shows styles of lettering only.

CHARACTERISTIC SHEET FOR THE ONE INCH MAP

OF

ENGLAND & WALES.

County Names	**C**
District D.º	*ROCKINGHAM*
Parish D.º	HINTON
Extra Parochial places	DUNKIRK(E.P.)
Cities and County Towns	CANTERBURY
Market Towns & other Important Towns	*RINGWOOD*
Villages	Bishopstoke
Hamlets, Mansions, Farms, &c	Burton
Woods	Kings Wood
* Parish Churches	Church
* Other D.º	Church
Royal Parks, Forests, Moors, &c	*RICHMOND PARK*
Minor D.º	Letley Common
Principal Lakes, Bays, and Rivers	*WINDERMERE*
Minor D.º D.º	Malham Tarn
Canals	Liverpool Canal
Principal Headlands, Islands, &c	*START POINT*
Secondary D.º	Heatherwood Point
Small D.º	Colhost Point
Ranges of Hills	*MENDIP HILLS*
Valleys of large extent	*TAFF VALE*
Separate Parts of Hills	Norton Top
Small Valleys	Painswick Valley
Bridges	High Bridge
Railways	Furness Railway
Principal Stations	DUNMOW STA.
Secondary D.º	FELSTED STA.
Antiquities	ROMAN Druidical and Saxon and others
County Boundaries	··
Parish D.º	

These examples must vary in size and extent according to their importance.

* *The distinction between Parish and other Churches discontinued from 1879.*

Fig.41 Characteristic sheet for the New Series one-inch map, ca 1880. *Reproduced by permission of the Trustees of the National Library of Scotland.*

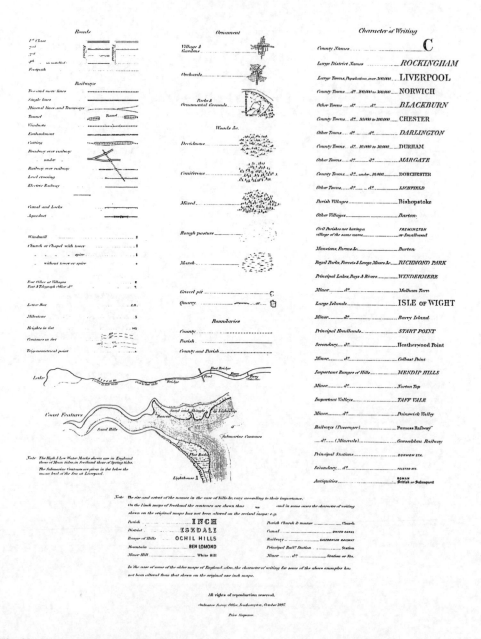

Fig.42 Characteristic sheet for the Revised New Series, 1897. *Reproduced by permission of the Trustees of the National Library of Scotland.*

REVISED NEW SERIES

1897   Ordnance Survey | Characteristic Sheet | for the | Revised One-Inch Map
| of | Great Britain. [Centre of bottom margin:] All rights of reproduction
reserved. | Ordnance Survey Office, Southampton, October 1897. | Price
Sixpence. 420 x 290mm.

NLS Map Library (fig.42)

Engraved. Later printings, still dated October 1897, lack the 'Village & Gardens'
ornament.

THIRD EDITION

[ca 1903] Ordnance Survey | Characteristic Sheet | for the | Revised One-Inch Map
| of | Great Britain. [Centre of bottom margin:] All rights of reproduction
reserved. | Ordnance Survey Office, Southampton, October 1897. [i.e. ca
1903.] | Price Sixpence. 420 x 290mm.

OS Cartographic Library

Engraved. A manuscript note at the top of the sheet reads: 'To be used for 2nd
revision only'. This sheet was prepared for the Third Edition. The only difference
between this example and the later printings of the Revised New Series characteristic
sheet is the insertion of a symbol for 'Ontario Pump' above the windmill symbol. This
appears to have been the only symbol to have distinguished the Third Edition from the
Revised New Series, and was soon renamed 'Wind Pump'.

1906   Ordnance Survey | Characteristic Sheet | for the | Revised One-Inch Map
| of | Great Britain. [Centre of bottom margin:] All rights of reproduction
reserved. | Revised to the 1st. July 1906. | Ordnance Survey Office,
Southampton, July 1906. | Price Sixpence. 420 x 290mm

PC

Engraved. A pencilled note across the face of the sheet reads: 'Cancelled 10th Sept
/08'. Three changes differentiate this example from the 1903 example: 1) '5 (Mile
distance)' appears above the first class fenced road; 2) the Ontario Pump is renamed
'Wind Pump,' and 3) the symbol for electric railway is deleted and the note 'Electric
Railway_ to be treated as ordinary Railways' is substituted.

1908   Ordnance Survey | Characteristic Sheet | for the | Revised One-Inch Map
| of | Great Britain, | and | Ireland [Centre, bottom margin:] All rights of
reproduction reserved. | Revised to the 1st. July, 1908. | Ordnance Survey
Office, Southampton, July 1908. | Price 6^{d}. net. 420 x 290mm.

CUL (fig.43)

'Celtic' has been added to the lettering denoting Antiquities; the High and Low Water
Mark and submarine contours notes have been changed to incorporate Ireland, and the
note 'The One Inch Maps of Ireland do not agree in all respects with the characteristic
sheet, e.g. County boundaries only are shewn, and important villages are written in
parish village character, | the character of writing differs also in other minor
particulars.' has been added above the imprint.

Fig.43 Characteristic sheet for the Third Edition, 1908. *Reproduced by permission of the Syndics of Cambridge University.*

POPULAR EDITION

1924   Ordnance Survey | Conventional Signs And Writing | for the | Revised One-Inch Map | of | Great Britain. | (Popular Edition) [Centre, bottom margin:] Published by Colonel E.M. Jack, C.M.G., D.S.O., Director General, Ordnance Survey, Southampton 1924. | Crown Copyright Reserved. | Price 6^d. net. 428 x 320mm

NLS Map Library

Engraved and hand-coloured. This sheet is completely recast for the Popular Edition, and while retaining many of the features of the preceding example, such as 'Character of Writing,' it also incorporates many changes such as the new road classification and the new lettering devised for the Popular Edition of Scotland. It would seem, from the spacing of the lettering, and some of the symbols, that the copperplate for this sheet was derived from an electrotype of the 1897-1908 conventional signs and characteristics. This would explain why the words 'Popular Edition' appear in parentheses in the title, to clarify the fact that 'revised one-inch', which had previously denoted first the Revised New Series, and then the Third Edition, now applied to yet another new revision. It is possible that an earlier example was published for England alone, before 1924 (perhaps showing parish boundaries), but no copy has been located.

1925   Ordnance Survey | Conventional Signs And Writing | for the | Revised One-Inch Map | of | Great Britain. | (Popular Edition) [Centre, bottom margin:] Published by Colonel Commandant E.M. Jack, C.M.G., D.S.O., Director General, Ordnance Survey, Southampton, 1925. | Crown Copyright Reserved. | Price 6^d. net. 428 x 320mm.
CUL Map Library, CCS Archive (Indexes).
Lithographed and colour printed.

1930   [Not seen; inferred from 1931 reprint.]

1931   -- Another issue [print code:] 250-30. 1500-31.

PC **Plate 12**

Lithographed, colour-printed. Except for the method of printing, and the detail of the imprint, this copy is identical to the 1924 example.

1937   [Not seen; inferred from 1946 reprint.]

1946   Ordnance Survey | Conventional Signs And Writing | for the | One-Inch Map | of | Great Britain. | (Popular Edition) [Centre, bottom margin:] Published by Colonel Commandant E.M. Jack, C.M.G., D.S.O., Director General, Ordnance Survey, Southampton, 1924 [sic]. | Crown Copyright Reserved. | Revised, January 1937. | Price 6^d. net. [print code:] 1046. 428 x 320mm.
OSCL BPC 8.

Lithographed, colour-printed. The word 'revised' has been omitted from the title because, by now, the Fifth Edition was the 'revised' one-inch map. The most important of several changes made to the sheet is the alteration of the road classification to show Ministry of

Transport 'A' roads; other changes include a symbol for closed railway stations, the replacement of the symbol for underground waterpipes by a new one for 'waterpipes and conduits', and the inclusion of symbols for Youth Hostels and national boundaries. It does not include the symbol for Electricity Transmission Lines, which appeared on later printings of the Popular Edition.

FIFTH EDITION

[8/1928]i Ordnance Survey | Conventional Signs And Writing | for the | Revised One-Inch Map | of | England & Wales [ca August 1928.] 355 x 278mm.

PRO OS 1/312.

Lithographed, uncoloured. The first of four unpublished trial sheets for what was to become the Fifth Edition of the one-inch map. It followed the design of its predecessors, with conventional signs on the left side, and character of writing on the right. The principal difference between this completely redrawn sheet and its 1924 predecessor, is the new alphabet, new classification for roads, and new symbols for railways. Other changes include a new symbol for public parks, the inclusion of telephone call boxes, National Trust areas, parish boundaries and the transference of waterway symbols to a redrawn freshwater diagram at the foot of the sheet.

[8/1928]ii Ordnance Survey | Conventional Signs And Writing | for the | Revised One-Inch Map | of | England & Wales [ca August 1928.] 345 x 282mm.

PRO OS 1/312.

Lithographed, colour-printed; unpublished. The black base is identical to **[8/1928]i** except that the Ministry of transport road numbers are in a smaller typeface. A red stippled band is printed over the county boundary symbol. The sheet is annotated in at least three different hands, principally by Jack (Director general), in pencil.

5/9/1928 Ordnance Survey | Conventional Signs And Writing | for the | Revised One-Inch Map | of | England & Wales [dated 5/9/1928.] 339 x 280mm.

PRO OS 1/312; CUL Map Library, CCS Archive (Indexes) [annotated in manuscript: ? only in suggestion form ... 10-12 28.]

Lithographed, colour-printed; unpublished. Many changes were made to this sheet, mostly as a result of Jack's pencilled suggestions on **[8/1928]ii**. The road classification was considerably simplified, the symbol for dangerous bog was deleted, a symbol for the intersection of latitude and longitude, a simple cross, was included and the sign for a site of antiquity, which had been a similar cross, was redrawn to avoid confusion. A pencilled note, bottom right, states:'Appd [approved] by DG at Min 9'. The Minute, dated 4/10/28, reads: 'Appd. including the new signs for L.C. [level crossing] and Toll gate. When complete, a copy to be sent to M.I.4. calling attention to the chief points in which alterations have been made, & inviting comments; and to M. of T., for their information ...'

12/10/28 Ordnance Survey | Conventional Signs And Writing | for the | Revised One-Inch Map | of | England & Wales [12/10/1928.] 328 x 270mm.

PRO OS 1/312.

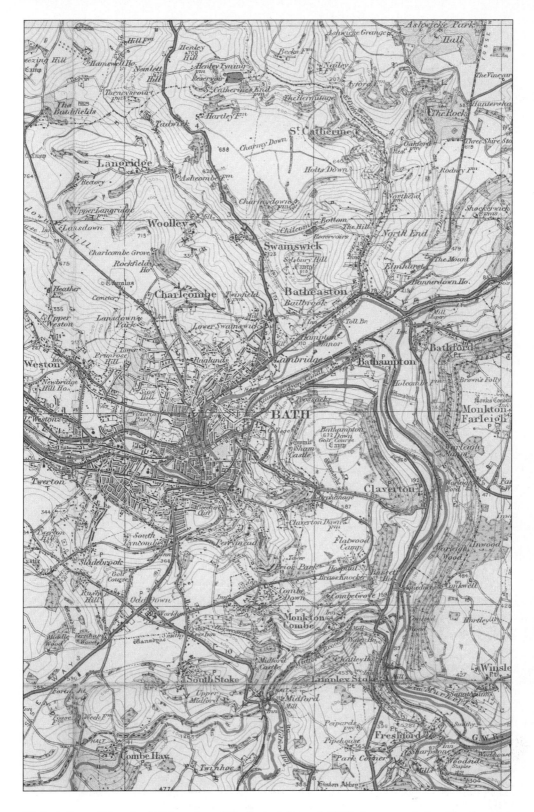

Plate 1 Part of Popular Edition sheet 111, *Bath & Bristol*, 1919. A new road classification and the simplicity of 50ft contours combine to make a legible map even in urban areas of high relief. *Private collection.*

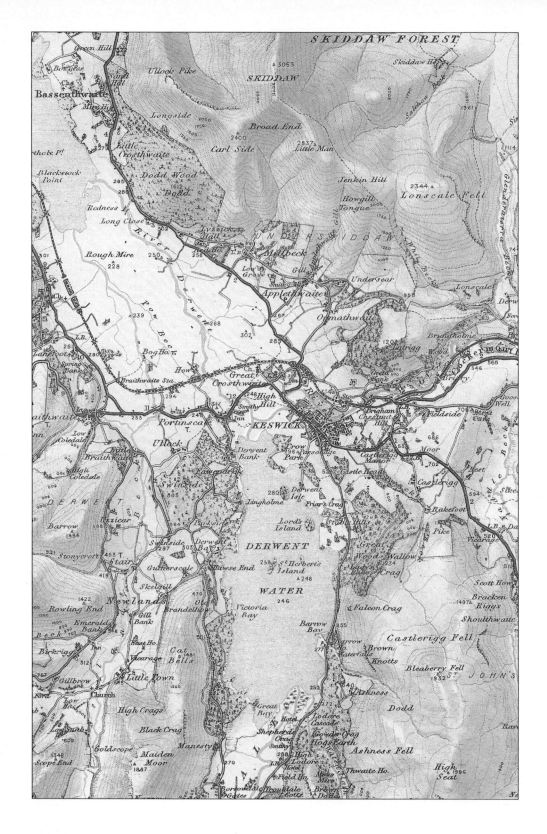

Plate 2 The 'Lake District specimen'; extract from Plate XXIV, *Text book of topographical and geographical surveying*, (1913). *Private collection.*

Plate 3 Part of the *Torquay & Dartmouth* sheet (1914). Unusual grey/brown colours distinguish the layers on this map from the other experimental maps of this period. *Royal Geographical Society (with IBG)*

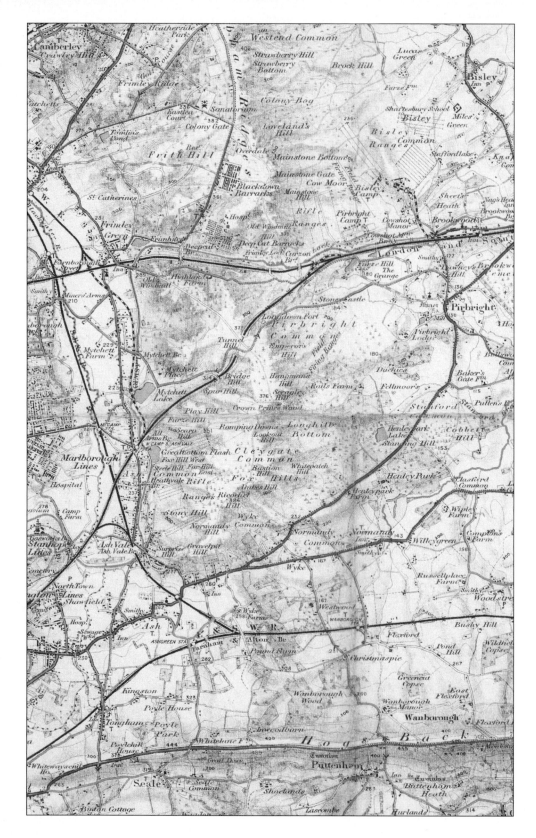

Plate 4 *Aldershot District (North)*, 'relief' style (1914). *Private collection*

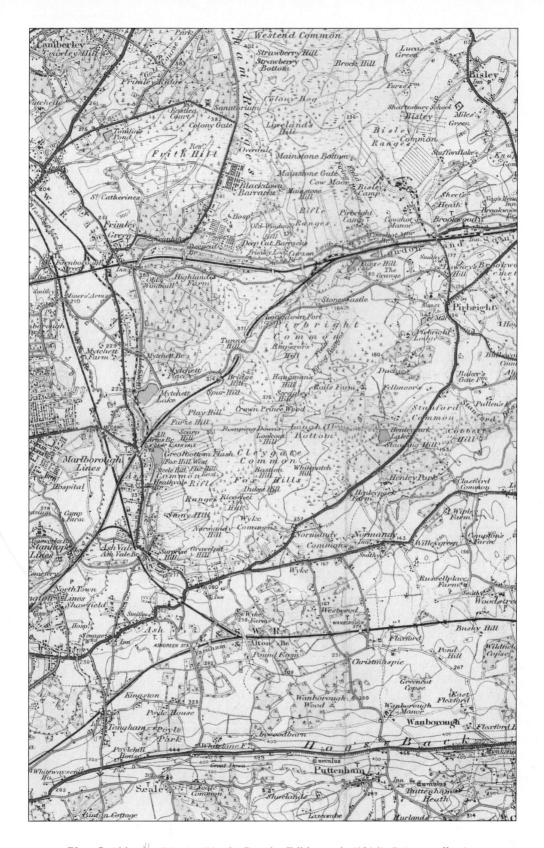

Plate 5 *Aldershot District (North)*, Popular Edition style (1914). *Private collection*

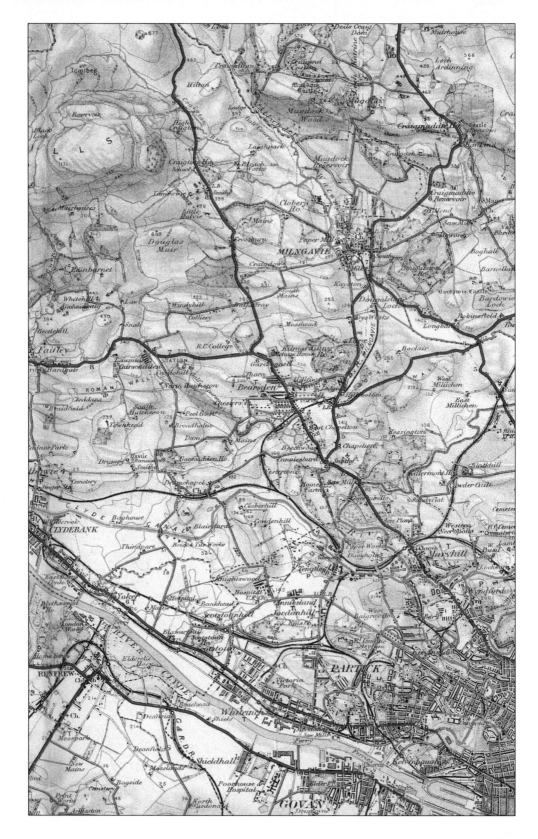

Plate 6 *Glasgow District* (1914). *Private collection*

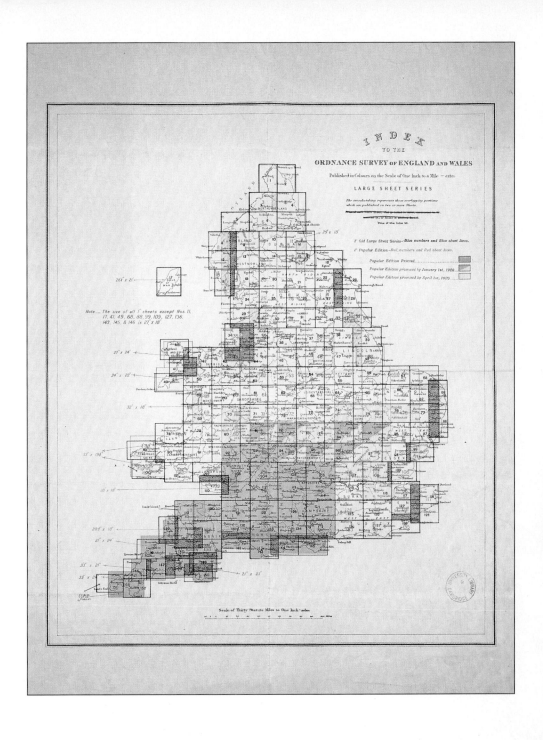

Plate 7 Combined index for the Third Edition Large Sheet Series and the Popular Edition, ca 1919.
Reproduced by permission of the Syndics of Cambridge University.

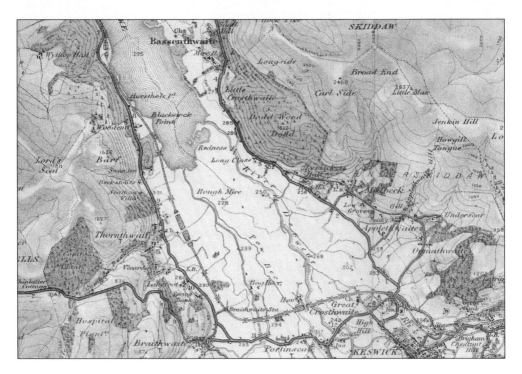

Plate 8a Third Edition Large Sheet Series sheet 12 *Whitehaven* (1914 printing); waterlining fills Bassenthwaite; the River Derwent is shown by a double blue line, west and north sides shaded. The lack of contours below 300ft makes the Derwent valley seem wider and flatter than it actually is. **8a-d:** *Private collection.*

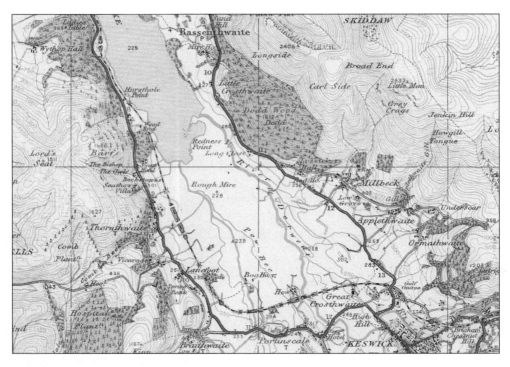

Plate 8b Popular Edition sheet 12 *Keswick & Ambleside* (1929). Inland water is shown by ruled blue lines; all fluvial features are shown by solid blue lines. The interpolation of the 250ft contour around Portinscale and Keswick and along the east bank of the Derwent gives a more realistic impression of height in this area. Forestry coverage has changed.

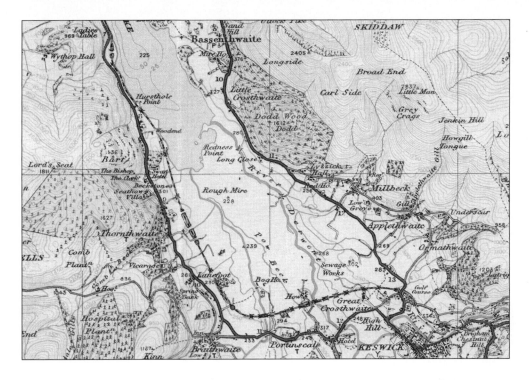

Plate 8c Popular Edition sheet 12 (1938). The depth of Bassenthwaite is now shown by bathymetric contours. Although considerable revision has been made to forestry cover, it does not reflect the true extent of new plantations as shown by the earlier Land Utilisation Survey of 1931.

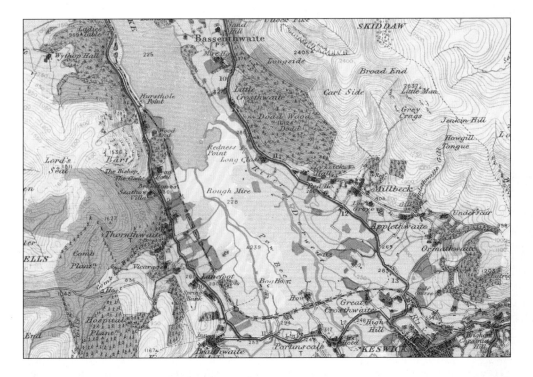

Plate 8d Land Utilisation map of Britain sheet 12 *Keswick & Ambleside* (Cumberland surveyed in 1931, printed 1933). This map pre-dates **8c**, but is more up to date in its portrayal of forestry.

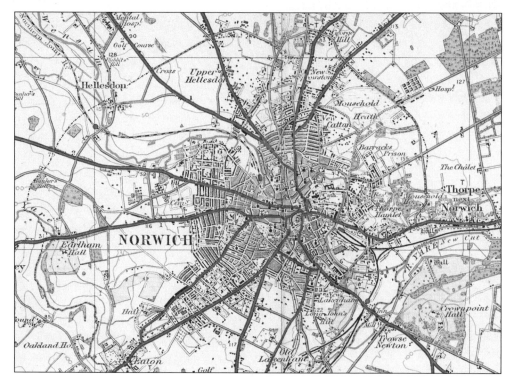

Plate 9a Sheet 67 *Norwich* (1921), The city is shown as it was before the beginning of urban development in the early 1920s. **9a-d:** *Private collection.*

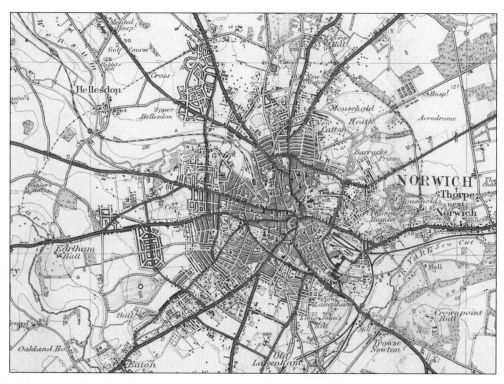

Plate 9b Sheet 67 (1931 reprint 3750/31). Urban development, to the north and west of the city, has been generalised from the large-scale plans. The classification of some existing roads has been upgraded; new roads, linking the recently built-up areas, have been constructed.

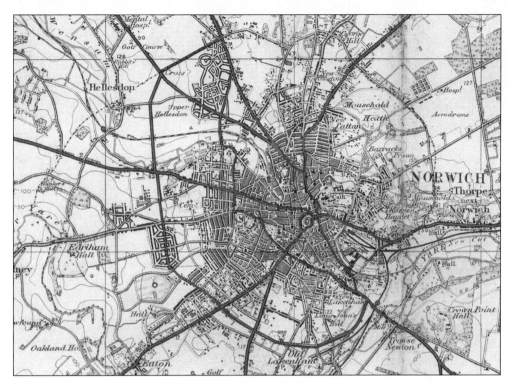

Plate 9c Sheet 67 (1935 reprint 2535). The construction of more new roads, and the further upgrading of existing roads, results in the completion of the western half of the Norwich ring road.

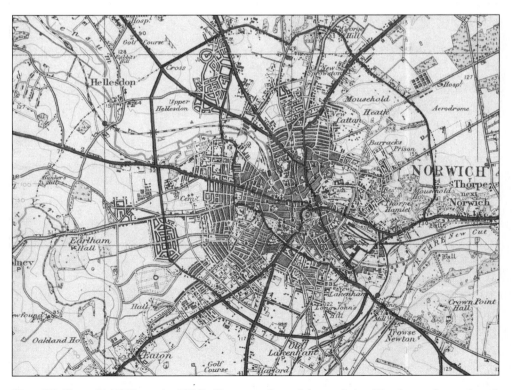

Plate 9d Sheet 67 (1939 reprint 2539). The upgrading of the road classification to the north and east of the city completes the ring road.

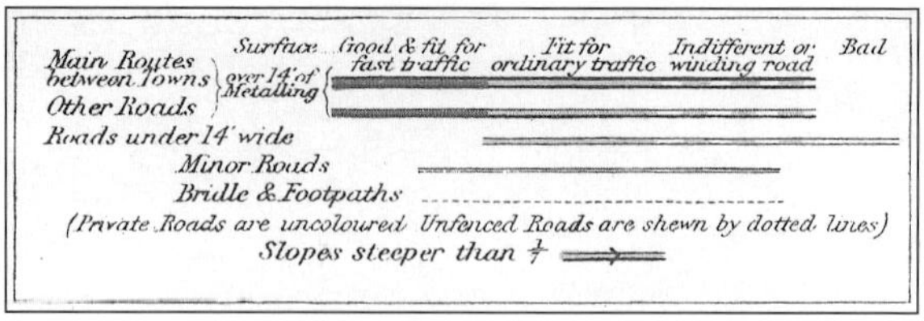

Plate 10a Popular Edition sheet 20 *Kirkby Lonsdale & Hawes* (1925). Earliest road classification used on the Popular Edition. Main routes are indicated by thick double black lines; other roads are shown by a double line, one of which is thickened; roads under 14' wide are shown by thin double lines; surface quality is indicated by colour. **10a-e:** *Private collection.*

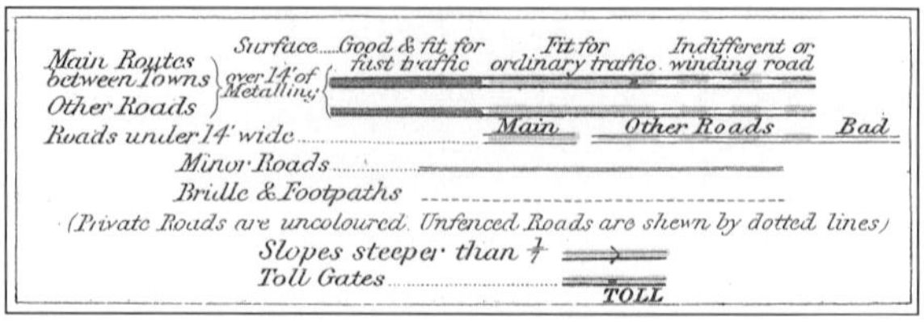

Plate 10b Sheet 20 (1929 reprint 4000/29). From 1926: the addition of qualifying descriptions, 'Main', and 'Other Roads' to roads under 14' wide, ('Main' was not always accompanied by 'Other Roads'). A symbol for tolls, unnamed, in the 'Main Routes' over 14ft is also added.

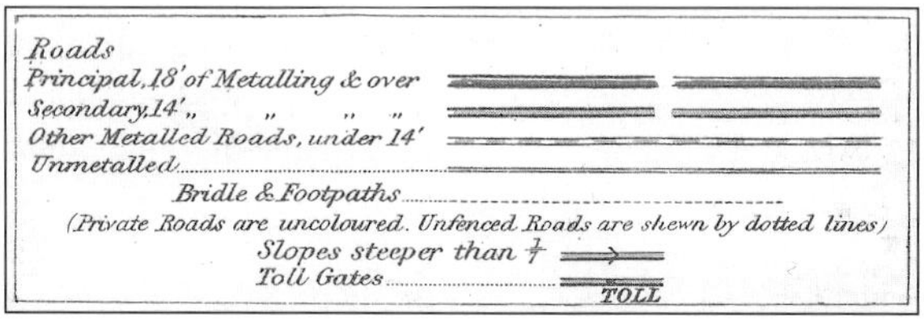

Plate 10c Sheet 20 (1933 reprint 3,000/33). A rare example of the classification which used a width of 18ft and over for 'Principal' roads. This appeared on only five sheets reprinted 1933-4. The significance of the second group of principal and secondary roads which are drawn with different line guages is not explained.

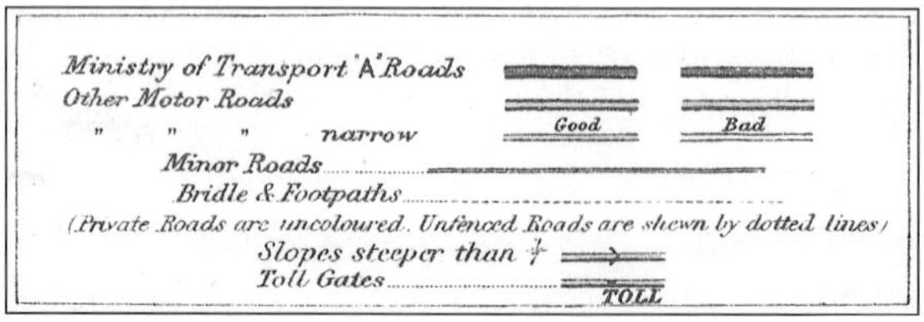

Plate 10d Sheet 20 (1935 reprint 1535). Classification showing MOT 'A' roads, with no reference to specific width, and with no explanation of the significance of the different line guages used for the second group of 'A' roads and 'Other motor roads'.

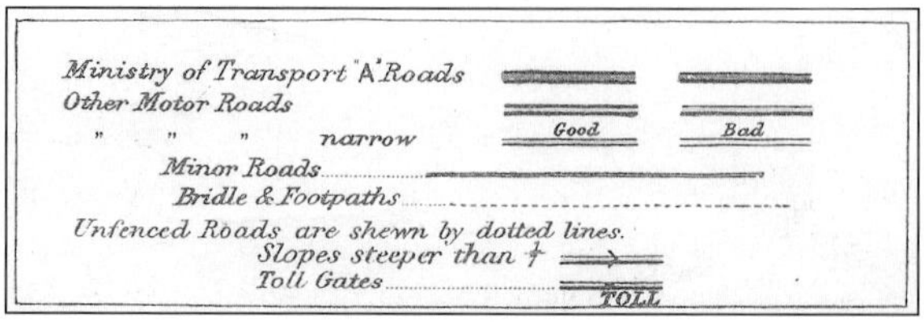

Plate 10e Sheet 20 (1936 reprint 2536). The same classification as **10d**, but omitting, from 1935, the reference to private roads.

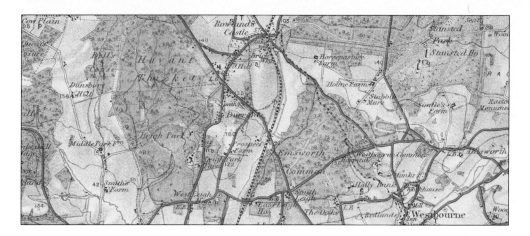

Plate 11a Third Edition Large Sheet Series, sheet 135 (1914 reprint); parklands are shown in black stipple, note the dotted parish boundary crossing Stansted Park. **11a-c:** *Private collection.*

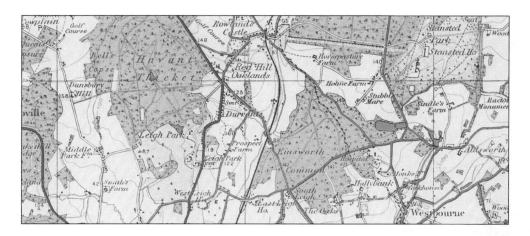

Plate 11b Popular Edition, sheet 132 (1919); three parkland areas have been deleted in the vicinity of Eastleigh House and Westleigh House; note the linear gap in the stipple of Stansted Park where the parish boundary has been erased. This sheet is unusual in showing two methods of depicting parks: Leigh Park is shown with rouletted stipple, while Stansted Park retains the Third Edition stipple.

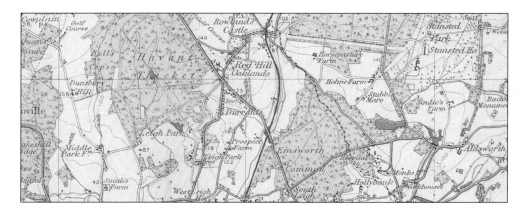

Plate 11c Popular Edition, sheet 132 (1925 reprint 2000/25); parkland is now shown by green ruled lines.

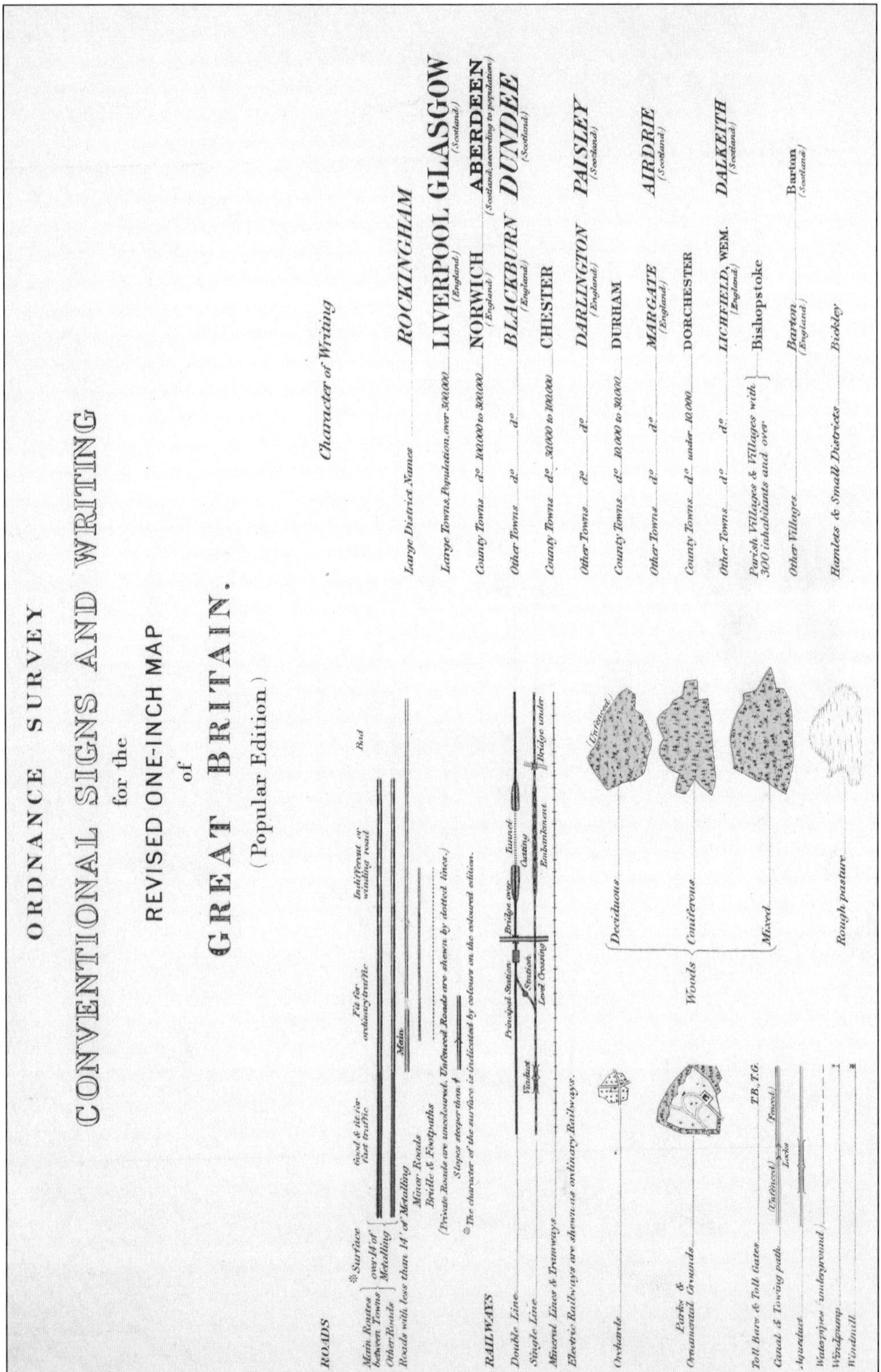

Plate 12 Conventional signs for the Popular Edition, 1925 (1931 reprint). *Private collection.*

Church or Chapel with tower
spire
without either

Sites of Antiquities
do. Roman Roads

Post & Telegraph Office

Post Office
with Telephone

Mile distances

Heights in feet above Mean Sea Level

Contours at 50 intervals

Trigonometrical point

Lake

Marsh

Dangerous Bog

Gravel pit

Quarry

Boundaries

County
County & Parish
Parish
County
(Parish Boundaries are not shewn in England)
Scotland
England

Note. The High & Low Water Marks shown are in England; those of Mean tides; in Scotland those of Spring tides.

The Submarine Contours are given in Fathoms and are taken from the Soundings of Admiralty Surveys.

Mansions, Farms &c.	Burton
Royal Parks, Forests & Large Moors &c.	RICHMOND PARK (England) / MAR FOREST (Glenavon Forest) (Moor) (Scotland)
Principal Lakes, Bays & Rivers	WINDERMERE
Minor do.	Malham Tarn
Large Islands	ISLE of WIGHT
Secondary do.	HOLY ISLAND
Minor do.	Barry Island
Principal Headlands	START POINT
Secondary do.	Heatherwood Point (England) / Spur Ness (Scotland)
Minor do.	Colbost Point
Important Ranges of Hills	MENDIP HILLS (England) / OCHIL HILLS (Scotland)
Minor Hills	Norton Top (England) / White Hill (Scotland)
Important Valleys	TAFF VALE
Minor do.	Polnassick Valley
Railways (Passenger)	L & N.E.R. (London & Southend) (England) / L.M & S.R. (Scotland)
do. (Minerals)	Gorseddau Railway (England) / FORDELL RAILWAY (Scotland)
Railway Stations	DUNMOW STA.
Antiquities	ROMAN &c. / British or Subsequent
Parish	INCE (Scotland)

Bridge
Highest point to which Tides flow
Ford
High Water Mark
Low Water Mark
Sand & Mud
Sand & Shingle
Earth Slopes
Lighthouse
Beacon
Fort
Flat Rocks
Cliffs
Sand Hills
Ferry for Vehicles
Ferry for Foot Passengers
Lightship
Submarine Contours

Published by Colonel Commandant E.M.Jack, C.M.G., D.S.O. Director General, Ordnance Survey, Southampton, 1925.

Crown Copyright Reserved.

Price 6d net.

Reprint 250-30. 1600-31.

Plate 13 Poster advertising the one-inch map [1930s]. It employs a familiar theme of the hand holding the book-folded map; in this case the map appears to be on fictional sheet lines which match neither those of the standard series nor those of a district map. However, it shows National Trust property which did not appear on the standard Popular sheets; it would seem that artistic licence has been used with the Chilterns Special District map (1932). *Private collection.*

Lithographed, colour-printed; unpublished. This sheet is identical to **[8/1928]ii** with two exceptions: 1) A symbol for level crossing is added and the letters 'L.C.' deleted; 2) the phrase '(5' intervals)' is added to the intersection of latitude and longitude.

1932   Ordnance Survey | Conventional Signs And Writing | for the | Revised One-Inch Map | of | Great Britain | Fifth (Relief) Edition | [centre, bottom margin:] Published by the Director General, Ordnance Survey, Southampton, 1932. | Crown Copyright Reserved. | Price 6^d. net [Print code:] 1000/32.

OSCL

The road classification incorporates the 18ft principal metalled roads which were a feature of the conventional signs panel of the Popular Edition for some reprints made in 1933.

1935   Ordnance Survey | Conventional Signs And Writing | for the | Revised One-Inch Map | of | Great Britain | Fifth Edition [centre, bottom margin:] Published by the Director General, Ordnance Survey, Southampton, 1935. | Crown Copyright Reserved. | Price 6^d net. [Print code:] 1035. 420 x 290mm.

CUL Map Library, CCS Archive (Indexes).

Three main changes have been made: 1) the road classification omits the 18' width, and the note on classification is omitted; 2) the post office and telephone symbols have been rationalised and 3) only one symbol for woodland, instead of three, is shown.

1937   -- Another issue. Revised January, 1937. [Print code:] 5037.

CUL Map Library, CCS Archive (Indexes).

APPENDIX 6

PRINCIPLES OF ROAD CLASSIFICATION

The documents relating to the 1912 War Office Committee on the classification of roads have not been traced. The following is transcribed from Ordnance Survey *Instructions to field revisers and draftsmen for the revision and preparation of the small scale maps for reproduction by heliozincography*, (1924), 'Sections dealing with field revision', Section 1, pp.13-14.

1 The former system of road classification in use on the Ordnance Survey having been found somewhat inadequate to the requirements of modern traffic, both civil and military, a committee was assembled at the War Office in February, 1912, and the scheme now approved is based on their recommendations.

2 In classing roads the three main considerations are:-

   a) WIDTH, a clear distinction is to be made between roads of 14' and over of metalling, and those of less than that width, the former being capable of taking 2 lines of traffic, and the latter only one.
   A road should not be shown as over 14' wide unless that width is practically continuous throughout the section. To show small alternating portions of over and under 14' would be unsightly and would serve no useful purpose. If two continuous lines of transport cannot pass each other the section should not be shown as over 14'.

   b) QUALITY, which includes condition of surface, straightness, gradients, safety and general suitability for fast traffic. *Foundations*, though of great importance from a military point of view, as affecting the durability of roads, cannot in practice be considered by the Ordnance Survey.
   Gradients steeper than 1/7th are to be shown by an arrow head pointing downhill.

   c) IMPORTANCE. The main routes between important towns are emphasised by a distinguishing symbol.
   Roads are, as a rule, classed in sections. A section may be defined as a portion of road lying between two principal road-junctions at which traffic can be diverted to another route.

3 The class of road having been decided upon in accordance with the above considerations, it now remains to show it in a suitable manner on the map.
   The principles are that:-
   a)   Width and importance are shown by the drawn symbol.
   b)   Quality is shown by the added colour.

4 WIDTH (*Drawn symbol*)
    i)   Roads with less than 14' of metalling are shown by two fine lines.
    ii) Roads with over 14' of metalling are emphasised by thickening one of these lines.
    iii) Main roads over 14' connecting important towns are further emphasised by thickening both lines.
    iv) Minor roads, such as those leading to farms, etc., are shown by two fine parallel lines close together. They are not classed, or their width indicated.
    v)   Bridle-paths and footpaths are shown by a single pecked line.
No road should be shown by a double line which is not passable for wheeled traffic.

5 QUALITY (*Colour on printed edition*)
    i)   Roads with over 14' of metalling which have a good surface, and are fit for fast traffic, are coloured Red.
    ii) Those with fair surfaces, and fit for ordinary traffic, of whatever width, are coloured Yellow.
    iii) Bad roads, and also minor roads, are left uncoloured.

No road should have any colour on it which is not easily practicable for horse drawn vehicles, or passable for ordinary touring motor cars. The user of the map will then understand that if he takes an uncoloured road, he does so at his own risk.

Private roads, and roads which have been laid out for building purposes, are not coloured, even though their surface may be up to the standard.

APPENDIX 7

GEOGRAPHICAL & CASSINI CO-ORDINATES

The latitudes and longitudes of the sheet corners are given for each sheet. These are derived from values that are written in manuscript in a volume entitled 'Cassini coords of one-inch. Quarter Inch. Half Inch.' currently held in Ordnance Survey, Departmental Records, Box TL23. Similarly, the Cassini co-ordinates for the sheet lines are derived from a graphic index (scale 1:1,900,800) to the Popular Edition, also in this volume, that has been marked up in ink with the Cassini values. It has to be presumed that the geographical co-ordinates had been calculated by laborious inter-war methods using logarithms and unidentified tables. The author subsequently requested Brian Adams to check her transcriptions, and, out of curiosity, to check the values of the co-ordinates. In order to do this, Adams had no option but to recalculate them using more recent machine-calculation tables and his HP-32S computer, giving results accurate to a few ten-thousandths of a second. These showed a fair number of small differences from the old figures, rising in a few cases to 0.05 second. The new, more accurate, figures are given below; anyone familiar with Adams's work will know that they have been rigorously double-checked.

1 Geographical co-ordinates

1	NW 55°49'40"00/2°28'16"07W	NE 55°49'33"99/2°00'31"93W
	SW 55°26'14"86/2°28'23"66W	SE 55°26'08"94/2°00'55"98W
2	NW 55°49'33"99/2°00'31"93W	NE 55°49'21"73/1°32'48"00W
	SW 55°26'08"94/2°00'55"98W	SE 55°25'56"85/1°33'28"50W
3	NW 55°26'15"51/2°42'07"54W	NE 55°26'08"94/2°00'55"98W
	SW 55°10'38"69/2°42'07"12W	SE 55°10'32"18/2°01'11"68W
4	NW 55°26'11"20/2°08'33"65W	NE 55°25'53"33/1°27'22"43W
	SW 55°10'34"42/2°08'46"37W	SE 55°10'16"72/1°27'51"28W
5	NW 55°10'31"47/3°23'02"54W	NE 55°10'38"69/2°42'07"12W
	SW 54°54'54"68/3°22'46"27W	SE 54°55'01"83/2°42'06"71W
6	NW 55°10'38"69/2°42'07"12W	NE 55°10'32"18/2°01'11"68W
	SW 54°55'01"83/2°42'06"71W	SE 54°54'55"39/2°01'27"14W
7	NW 55°10'32"18/2°01'11"68W	NE 55°10'11"94/1°20'16"71W
	SW 54°54'55"39/2°01'27"14W	SE 54°54'35"34/1°20'48"02W
8	NW 54°54'47"87/3°39'20"05W	NE 54°54'57"84/3°12'13"81W
	SW 54°31'22"71/3°38'46"62W	SE 54°31'32"54/3°11'55"93W

| 9 | NW 54°54'54"68/3°22'46"27W | NE 54°55'01"83/2°42'06"71W |
| | SW 54°39'17"85/3°22'30"25W | SE 54°39'24"94/2°42'06"30W |

| 10 | NW 54°55'01"83/2°42'06"71W | NE 54°54'55"39/2°01'27"14W |
| | SW 54°39'24"94/2°42'06"30W | SE 54°39'18"55/2°01'42"35W |

| 11 | NW 54°54'55"39/2°01'27"14W | NE 54°54'33"31/1°17'47"37W |
| | SW 54°39'18"55/2°01'42"35W | SE 54°38'56"69/1°18'19"34W |

| 12 | NW 54°39'17"85/3°22'30"25W | NE 54°39'24"94/2°42'06"30W |
| | SW 54°23'40"98/3°22'14"48W | SE 54°23'48"00/2°42'05"91W |

| 13 | NW 54°39'24"94/2°42'06"30W | NE 54°39'18"55/2°01'42"35W |
| | SW 54°23'48"00/2°42'05"91W | SE 54°23'41"67/2°01'57"32W |

| 14 | NW 54°39'18"55/2°01'42"35W | NE 54°38'58"69/1°21'18"83W |
| | SW 54°23'41"67/2°01'57"32W | SE 54°23'22"00/1°21'49"16W |

| 15 | NW 54°46'55"17/1°34'33"84W | NE 54°46'36"20/1°06'03"21W |
| | SW 54°23'30"04/1°35'11"80W | SE 54°23'11"33/1°06'57"44W |

| 16 | NW 54°38'47"92/1°06'21"43W | NE 54°38'09"62/0°25'59"23W |
| | SW 54°23'11"33/1°06'57"44W | SE 54°22'33"39/0°26'50"56W |

| 17 | NW 54°25'13"68/4°51'32"90W | NE 54°25'46"97/4°15'51"15W |
| | SW 54°01'49"20/4°50'19"39W | SE 54°02'22"03/4°14'57"73W |

| 18 | NW 54°31'22"71/3°38'46"62W | NE 54°31'32"54/3°11'55"93W |
| | SW 54°07'57"45/3°38'13"98W | SE 54°08'07"14/3°11'38"47W |

| 19 | NW 54°23'40"98/3°22'14"48W | NE 54°23'48"00/2°42'05"91W |
| | SW 54°08'04"07/3°21'58"97W | SE 54°08'11"02/2°42'05"52W |

| 20 | NW 54°23'48"00/2°42'05"91W | NE 54°23'41"67/2°01'57"32W |
| | SW 54°08'11"02/2°42'05"52W | SE 54°08'04"75/2°02'12"05W |

| 21 | NW 54°23'41"67/2°01'57"32W | NE 54°23'22"00/1°21'49"16W |
| | SW 54°08'04"75/2°02'12"05W | SE 54°07'45"27/1°22'19"00W |

| 22 | NW 54°23'22"00/1°21'49"16W | NE 54°22'49"00/0°41'41"85W |
| | SW 54°07'45"27/1°22'19"00W | SE 54°07'12"58/0°42'26"79W |

| 23 | NW 54°22'49"00/0°41'41"85W | NE 54°22'02"67/0°01'35"83W |
| | SW 54°07'12"58/0°42'26"79W | SE 54°06'26"69/0°02'35"83W |

| 24 | NW 54°08'04"07/3°21'58"97W | NE 54°08'11"02/2°42'05"52W |
| | SW 53°52'27"11/3°21'43"70W | SE 53°52'34"00/2°42'05"13W |

| 25 | NW 54°08'11"02/2°42'05"52W | NE 54°08'04"75/2°02'12"05W |
| | SW 53°52'34"00/2°42'05"13W | SE 53°52'27"79/2°02'26"55W |

| 26 | NW 54°08'04"75/2°02'12"05W | NE 54°07'45"27/1°22'19"00W |
| | SW 53°52'27"79/2°02'26"55W | SE 53°52'08"49/1°22'48"38W |

27	**NW** 54°07'45"27/1°22'19"00W		**NE** 54°07'12"58/0°42'26"79W	
	SW 53°52'08"49/1°22'48"38W		**SE** 53°51'36"11/0°43'11"02W	
28	**NW** 54°07'12"58/0°42'26"79W		**NE** 54°06'26"69/0°02'35"83W	
	SW 53°51'36"11/0°43'11"02W		**SE** 53°50'50"66/0°03'34"88W	
29	**NW** 53°52'30"86/3°08'30"87W		**NE** 53°52'33"38/2°28'52"25W	
	SW 53°36'53"83/3°08'20"72W		**SE** 53°36'56"33/2°28'56"76W	
30	**NW** 53°52'34"00/2°42'05"13W		**NE** 53°52'27"79/2°02'26"55W	
	SW 53°36'56"94/2°42'04"75W		**SE** 53°36'50"79/2°02'40"83W	
31	**NW** 53°52'27"79/2°02'26"55W		**NE** 53°52'08"49/1°22'48"38W	
	SW 53°36'50"79/2°02'40"83W		**SE** 53°36'31"67/1°23'17"30W	
32	**NW** 53°52'08"49/1°22'48"38W		**NE** 53°51'36"11/0°43'11"02W	
	SW 53°36'31"67/1°23'17"30W		**SE** 53°35'59"60/0°43'54"56W	
33	**NW** 53°51'36"11/0°43'11"02W		**NE** 53°50'50"66/0°03'34"88W	
	SW 53°35'59"60/0°43'54"56W		**SE** 53°35'14"57/0°04'33"02W	
34	**NW** 53°51'07"26/0°16'46"77W		**NE** 53°50'30"50/0°11'04"77E	
	SW 53°27'42"88/0°18'06"37W		**SE** 53°27'06"64/0°09'29"85E	
35	**NW** 53°36'50"12/3°21'28"66W		**NE** 53°36'56"94/2°42'04"75W	
	SW 53°21'13"08/3°21'13"86W		**SE** 53°21'19"84/2°42'04"38W	
36	**NW** 53°36'56"94/2°42'04"75W		**NE** 53°36'50"79/2°02'40"83W	
	SW 53°21'19"84/2°42'04"38W		**SE** 53°21'13"75/2°02'54"88W	
37	**NW** 53°36'50"79/2°02'40"83W		**NE** 53°36'31"67/1°23'17"30W	
	SW 53°21'13"75/2°02'54"88W		**SE** 53°20'54"81/1°23'45"77W	
38	**NW** 53°36'31"67/1°23'17"30W		**NE** 53°35'59"60/0°43'54"56W	
	SW 53°20'54"81/1°23'45"77W		**SE** 53°20'23"03/0°44'37"43W	
39	**NW** 53°35'59"60/0°43'54"56W		**NE** 53°35'14"57/0°04'33"02W	
	SW 53°20'23"03/0°44'37"43W		**SE** 53°19'38"43/0°05'30"26W	
40	**NW** 53°35'31"02/0°17'40"04W		**NE** 53°34'37"36/0°21'40"48E	
	SW 53°19'54"72/0°18'32"49W		**SE** 53°19'01"57/0°20'33"69E	
41	**NW** 53°25'30"30/4°42'39"95W		**NE** 53°26'05"77/4°00'32"63W	
	SW 53°04'41"56/4°41'41"15W		**SE** 53°05'16"59/3°59'54"18W	
42	**NW** 53°24'21"67/4°00'29"40W		**NE** 53°24'41"32/3°21'17"13W	
	SW 53°05'16"59/3°59'54"18W		**SE** 53°05'36"00/3°20'59"29W	
43	**NW** 53°21'13"08/3°21'13"86W		**NE** 53°21'19"84/2°42'04"38W	
	SW 53°05'36"00/3°20'59"29W		**SE** 53°05'42"70/2°42'04"01W	
44	**NW** 53°21'19"84/2°42'04"38W		**NE** 53°21'13"75/2°02'54"88W	
	SW 53°05'42"70/2°42'04"01W		**SE** 53°05'36"66/2°03'08"72W	

45	**NW** 53°21'13"75/2°02'54"88W		**NE** 53°20'54"81/1°23'45"77W	
	SW 53°05'36"66/2°03'08"72W		**SE** 53°05'17"90/1°24'13"80W	
46	**NW** 53°20'54"81/1°23'45"77W		**NE** 53°20'23"03/0°44'37"43W	
	SW 53°05'17"90/1°24'13"80W		**SE** 53°04'46"42/0°45'19"64W	
47	**NW** 53°20'23"03/0°44'37"43W		**NE** 53°19'38"43/0°05'30"26W	
	SW 53°04'46"42/0°45'19"64W		**SE** 53°04'02"24/0°06'26"61W	
48	**NW** 53°19'49"45/0°14'11"73W		**NE** 53°18'54"87/0°24'54"27E	
	SW 53°04'13"15/0°15'04"94W		**SE** 53°03'19"09/0°23'46"94E	
49	**NW** 53°04'34"04/4°48'53"26W		**NE** 53°05'16"59/3°59'54"18W	
	SW 52°45'29"37/4°47'57"27W		**SE** 52°46'11"43/3°59'19"62W	
50	**NW** 53°05'16"59/3°59'54"18W		**NE** 53°05'36"00/3°20'59"29W	
	SW 52°49'39"65/3°59'25"86W		**SE** 52°49'58"88/3°20'44"94W	
51	**NW** 53°05'36"00/3°20'59"29W		**NE** 53°05'42"70/2°42'04"01W	
	SW 52°49'58"88/3°20'44"94W		**SE** 52°50'05"51/2°42'03"65W	
52	**NW** 53°05'42"70/2°42'04"01W		**NE** 53°05'36"66/2°03'08"72W	
	SW 52°50'05"51/2°42'03"65W		**SE** 52°49'59"53/2°03'22"34W	
53	**NW** 53°05'36"66/2°03'08"72W		**NE** 53°05'17"90/1°24'13"80W	
	SW 52°49'59"53/2°03'22"34W		**SE** 52°49'40"95/1°24'41"40W	
54	**NW** 53°05'17"90/1°24'13"80W		**NE** 53°04'46"42/0°45'19"64W	
	SW 52°49'40"95/1°24'41"40W		**SE** 52°49'09"77/0°46'01"19W	
55	**NW** 53°04'46"42/0°45'19"64W		**NE** 53°04'02"24/0°06'26"61W	
	SW 52°49'09"77/0°46'01"19W		**SE** 52°48'25"99/0°07'22"10W	
56	**NW** 53°04'02"24/0°06'26"61W		**NE** 53°03'05"35/0°32'24"90E	
	SW 52°48'25"99/0°07'22"10W		**SE** 52°47'29"64/0°31'15"52E	
57	**NW** 53°00'29"40/0°32'13"26E		**NE** 52°59'19"94/1°11'00"56E	
	SW 52°44'53"68/0°31'04"06E		**SE** 52°43'44"87/1°09'37"54E	
58	**NW** 52°58'02"02/1°10'53"59E		**NE** 52°56'39"99/1°49'37"47E	
	SW 52°42'26"94/1°09'30"68E		**SE** 52°41'05"67/1°48'00"82E	
59	**NW** 52°49'39"65/3°59'25"86W		**NE** 52°49'58"88/3°20'44"94W	
	SW 52°34'02"66/3°58'57"97W		**SE** 52°34'21"72/3°20'30"82W	
60	**NW** 52°49'58"88/3°20'44"94W		**NE** 52°50'05"51/2°42'03"65W	
	SW 52°34'21"72/3°20'30"82W		**SE** 52°34'28"29/2°42'03"29W	
61	**NW** 52°50'05"51/2°42'03"65W		**NE** 52°49'59"53/2°03'22"34W	
	SW 52°34'28"29/2°42'03"29W		**SE** 52°34'22"37/2°03'35"76W	
62	**NW** 52°49'59"53/2°03'22"34W		**NE** 52°49'40"95/1°24'41"40W	
	SW 52°34'22"37/2°03'35"76W		**SE** 52°34'03"96/1°25'08"58W	

63	NW	52°49'40"95/1°24'41"40W	NE	52°49'09"77/0°46'01"19W
	SW	52°34'03"96/1°25'08"58W	SE	52°33'33"06/0°46'42"12W

64	NW	52°49'09"77/0°46'01"19W	NE	52°48'25"99/0°07'22"10W
	SW	52°33'33"06/0°46'42"12W	SE	52°32'49"69/0°08'16"74W

65	NW	52°48'25"99/0°07'22"10W	NE	52°47'29"64/0°31'15"52E
	SW	52°32'49"69/0°08'16"74W	SE	52°31'53"86/0°30'07"20E

66	NW	52°47'29"64/0°31'15"52E	NE	52°46'20"72/1°09'51"29E
	SW	52°31'53"86/0°30'07"20E	SE	52°30'45"59/1°08'29"33E

67	NW	52°46'20"72/1°09'51"29E	NE	52°44'59"26/1°48'24"84E
	SW	52°30'45"59/1°08'29"33E	SE	52°29'24"88/1°46'49"30E

68	NW	52°46'02"24/4°12'12"09W	NE	52°46'19"23/3°46'27"08W
	SW	52°18'16"59/4°11'14"89W	SE	52°18'33"30/3°45'46"03W

69	NW	52°34'02"66/3°58'57"97W	NE	52°34'21"72/3°20'30"82W
	SW	52°18'25"64/3°58'30"50W	SE	52°18'44"51/3°20'16"90W

70	NW	52°34'21"72/3°20'30"82W	NE	52°34'28"29/2°42'03"29W
	SW	52°18'44"51/3°20'16"90W	SE	52°18'51"02/2°42'02"94W

71	NW	52°34'28"29/2°42'03"29W	NE	52°34'22"37/2°03'35"76W
	SW	52°18'51"02/2°42'02"94W	SE	52°18'45"16/2°03'48"97W

72	NW	52°34'22"37/2°03'35"76W	NE	52°34'03"96/1°25'08"58W
	SW	52°18'45"16/2°03'48"97W	SE	52°18'26"92/1°25'35"34W

73	NW	52°34'03"96/1°25'08"58W	NE	52°33'33"06/0°46'42"12W
	SW	52°18'26"92/1°25'35"34W	SE	52°17'56"31/0°47'22"42W

74	NW	52°33'33"06/0°46'42"12W	NE	52°32'49"69/0°08'16"74W
	SW	52°17'56"31/0°47'22"42W	SE	52°17'13"35/0°09'10"55W

75	NW	52°32'49"69/0°08'16"74W	NE	52°31'53"86/0°30'07"20E
	SW	52°17'13"35/0°09'10"55W	SE	52°16'18"03/0°28'59"91E

76	NW	52°31'53"86/0°30'07"20E	NE	52°30'45"59/1°08'29"33E
	SW	52°16'18"03/0°28'59"91E	SE	52°15'10"39/1°07'08"61E

77	NW	52°30'45"59/1°08'29"33E	NE	52°29'24"88/1°46'49"30E
	SW	52°15'10"39/1°07'08"61E	SE	52°13'50"43/1°45'15"21E

78	NW	52°17'54"39/4°36'43"38W	NE	52°18'25"64/3°58'30"50W
	SW	52°02'17"61/4°36'03"00W	SE	52°02'48"56/3°58'03"45W

79	NW	52°18'25"64/3°58'30"50W	NE	52°18'44"51/3°20'16"90W
	SW	52°02'48"56/3°58'03"45W	SE	52°03'07"27/3°20'03"20W

80	NW	52°18'44"51/3°20'16"90W	NE	52°18'51"02/2°42'02"94W
	SW	52°03'07"27/3°20'03"20W	SE	52°03'13"72/2°42'02"59W

81	**NW** 52°18'51"02/2°42'02"94W	**NE** 52°18'45"16/2°03'48"97W
	SW 52°03'13"72/2°42'02"59W	**SE** 52°03'07"90/2°04'01"98W

82	**NW** 52°18'45"16/2°03'48"97W	**NE** 52°18'26"92/1°25'35"34W
	SW 52°03'07"90/2°04'01"98W	**SE** 52°02'49"83/1°26'01"70W

83	**NW** 52°18'26"92/1°25'35"34W	**NE** 52°17'56"31/0°47'22"42W
	SW 52°02'49"83/1°26'01"70W	**SE** 52°02'19"51/0°48'02"11W

84	**NW** 52°17'56"31/0°47'22"42W	**NE** 52°17'13"35/0°09'10"55W
	SW 52°02'19"51/0°48'02"11W	**SE** 52°01'36"94/0°10'03"55W

85	**NW** 52°17'13"35/0°09'10"55W	**NE** 52°16'18"03/0°28'59"91E
	SW 52°01'36"94/0°10'03"55W	**SE** 52°00'42"14/0°27'53"64E

86	**NW** 52°16'18"03/0°28'59"91E	**NE** 52°15'10"39/1°07'08"61E
	SW 52°00'42"14/0°27'53"64E	**SE** 51°59'35"13/1°05'49"11E

87	**NW** 52°15'10"39/1°07'08"61E	**NE** 52°13'50"43/1°45'15"21E
	SW 51°59'35"13/1°05'49"11E	**SE** 51°58'15"91/1°43'42"53E

88	**NW** 52°07'53"27/5°22'51"15W	**NE** 52°08'47"94/4°36'19"75W
	SW 51°50'58"93/5°21'50"37W	**SE** 51°51'53"06/4°35'36"41W

89	**NW** 52°02'17"61/4°36'03"00W	**NE** 52°02'48"56/3°58'03"45W
	SW 51°46'40"78/4°35'23"22W	**SE** 51°47'11"45/3°57'36"81W

90	**NW** 52°02'48"56/3°58'03"45W	**NE** 52°03'07"27/3°20'03"20W
	SW 51°47'11"45/3°57'36"81W	**SE** 51°47'29"98/3°19'49"70W

91	**NW** 52°03'07"27/3°20'03"20W	**NE** 52°03'13"72/2°42'02"59W
	SW 51°47'29"98/3°19'49"70W	**SE** 51°47'36"37/2°42'02"25W

92	**NW** 52°03'13"72/2°42'02"59W	**NE** 52°03'07"90/2°04'01"98W
	SW 51°47'36"37/2°42'02"25W	**SE** 51°47'30"61/2°04'14"80W

93	**NW** 52°03'07"90/2°04'01"98W	**NE** 52°02'49"83/1°26'01"70W
	SW 51°47'30"61/2°04'14"80W	**SE** 51°47'12"71/1°26'27"67W

94	**NW** 52°02'49"83/1°26'01"70W	**NE** 52°02'19"51/0°48'02"11W
	SW 51°47'12"71/1°26'27"67W	**SE** 51°46'42"66/0°48'41"21W

95	**NW** 52°02'19"51/0°48'02"11W	**NE** 52°01'36"94/0°10'03"55W
	SW 51°46'42"66/0°48'41"21W	**SE** 51°46'00"49/0°10'55"75W

96	**NW** 52°01'36"94/0°10'03"55W	**NE** 52°00'42"14/0°27'53"64E
	SW 51°46'00"49/0°10'55"75W	**SE** 51°45'06"20/0°26'48"37E

97	**NW** 52°00'42"14/0°27'53"64E	**NE** 51°59'35"13/1°05'49"11E
	SW 51°45'06"20/0°26'48"37E	**SE** 51°43'59"80/1°04'30"81E

98	**NW** 52°00'10"16/0°46'51"61E	**NE** 51°58'57"04/1°24'46"10E
	SW 51°44'34"51/0°45'39"82E	**SE** 51°43'22"07/1°23'21"29E

99	NW 51°50'58"93/5°21'50"37W	NE 51°51'53"06/4°35'36"41W
	SW 51°34'04"54/5°20'50"57W	SE 51°34'58"13/4°34'53"78W

100	NW 51°46'40"78/4°35'23"22W	NE 51°47'11"45/3°57'36"81W
	SW 51°31'03"90/4°34'44"04W	SE 51°31'34"29/3°57'10"56W

101	NW 51°47'11"45/3°57'36"81W	NE 51°47'29"98/3°19'49"70W
	SW 51°31'34"29/3°57'10"56W	SE 51°31'52"65/3°19'36"41W

102	NW 51°47'29"98/3°19'49"70W	NE 51°47'36"37/2°42'02"25W
	SW 51°31'52"65/3°19'36"41W	SE 51°31'58"98/2°42'01"92W

103	NW 51°47'36"37/2°42'02"25W	NE 51°47'30"61/2°04'14"80W
	SW 51°31'58"98/2°42'01"92W	SE 51°31'53"27/2°04'27"42W

104	NW 51°47'30"61/2°04'14"80W	NE 51°47'12"71/1°26'27"67W
	SW 51°31'53"27/2°04'27"42W	SE 51°31'35"53/1°26'53"24W

105	NW 51°47'12"71/1°26'27"67W	NE 51°46'42"66/0°48'41"21W
	SW 51°31'35"53/1°26'53"24W	SE 51°31'05"77/0°49'19"72W

106	NW 51°46'42"66/0°48'41"21W	NE 51°46'00"49/0°10'55"75W
	SW 51°31'05"77/0°49'19"72W	SE 51°30'23"99/0°11'47"17W

107	NW 51°46'00"49/0°10'55"75W	NE 51°45'06"20/0°26'48"37E
	SW 51°30'23"99/0°11'47"17W	SE 51°29'30"19/0°25'44"07E

108	NW 51°45'06"20/0°26'48"37E	NE 51°43'59"80/1°04'30"81E
	SW 51°29'30"19/0°25'44"07E	SE 51°28'24"41/1°03'13"67E

109	NW 51°36'53"39/3°46'10"15W	NE 51°37'10"11/2°58'45"96W
	SW 51°21'16"14/3°45'47"97W	SE 51°21'32"71/2°58'39"92W

110	NW 51°31'52"65/3°19'36"41W	NE 51°31'58"98/2°42'01"92W
	SW 51°16'15"27/3°19'23"31W	SE 51°16'21"54/2°42'01"59W

111	NW 51°31'58"98/2°42'01"92W	NE 51°31'53"27/2°04'27"42W
	SW 51°16'21"54/2°42'01"59W	SE 51°16'15"89/2°04'39"85W

112	NW 51°31'53"27/2°04'27"42W	NE 51°31'35"53/1°26'53"24W
	SW 51°16'15"89/2°04'39"85W	SE 51°15'58"32/1°27'18"44W

113	NW 51°31'35"53/1°26'53"24W	NE 51°31'05"77/0°49'19"72W
	SW 51°15'58"32/1°27'18"44W	SE 51°15'28"83/0°49'57"65W

114	NW 51°31'05"77/0°49'19"72W	NE 51°30'23"99/0°11'47"17W
	SW 51°15'28"83/0°49'57"65W	SE 51°14'47"43/0°12'37"83W

115	NW 51°30'23"99/0°11'47"17W	NE 51°29'30"19/0°25'44"07E
	SW 51°14'47"43/0°12'37"83W	SE 51°13'54"13/0°24'40"72E

116	NW 51°29'30"19/0°25'44"07E	NE 51°28'24"41/1°03'13"67E
	SW 51°13'54"13/0°24'40"72E	SE 51°12'48"95/1°01'57"68E

117	**NW** 51°25′48″50/1°03′00″92E	**NE** 51°24′58″07/1°27′58″18E
	SW 51°02′25″28/1°01′07″64E	**SE** 51°01′35″54/1°25′52″36E

118	**NW** 51°15′40″68/4°18′52″65W	**NE** 51°16′05″93/3°41′31″61W
	SW 51°00′03″58/4°18′19″74W	**SE** 51°00′28″60/3°41′11″26W

119	**NW** 51°15′57″08/3°56′44″71W	**NE** 51°16′15″27/3°19′23″31W
	SW 51°00′19″84/3°56′19″24W	**SE** 51°00′37″86/3°19′10″41W

120	**NW** 51°16′15″27/3°19′23″31W	**NE** 51°16′21″54/2°42′01″59W
	SW 51°00′37″86/3°19′10″41W	**SE** 51°00′44″07/2°42′01″26W

121	**NW** 51°16′21″54/2°42′01″59W	**NE** 51°16′15″89/2°04′39″85W
	SW 51°00′44″07/2°42′01″26W	**SE** 51°00′38″47/2°04′52″11W

122	**NW** 51°16′15″89/2°04′39″85W	**NE** 51°15′58″32/1°27′18″44W
	SW 51°00′38″47/2°04′52″11W	**SE** 51°00′21″06/1°27′43″26W

123	**NW** 51°15′58″32/1°27′18″44W	**NE** 51°15′28″83/0°49′57″65W
	SW 51°00′21″06/1°27′43″26W	**SE** 50°59′51″84/0°50′35″03W

124	**NW** 51°15′28″83/0°49′57″65W	**NE** 51°14′47″43/0°12′37″83W
	SW 50°59′51″84/0°50′35″03W	**SE** 50°59′10″82/0°13′27″73W

125	**NW** 51°14′47″43/0°12′37″83W	**NE** 51°13′54″13/0°24′40″72E
	SW 50°59′10″82/0°13′27″73W	**SE** 50°58′18″01/0°23′38″32E

126	**NW** 51°13′54″13/0°24′40″72E	**NE** 51°12′48″95/1°01′57″68E
	SW 50°58′18″01/0°23′38″32E	**SE** 50°57′13″43/1°00′42″81E

127	**NW** 50°59′48″00/4°35′31″19W	**NE** 51°00′19″84/3°56′19″24W
	SW 50°44′11″00/4°34′53″04W	**SE** 50°44′42″54/3°55′54″14W

128	**NW** 51°00′19″84/3°56′19″24W	**NE** 51°00′37″86/3°19′10″41W
	SW 50°44′42″54/3°55′54″14W	**SE** 50°45′00″40/3°18′57″70W

129	**NW** 51°00′37″86/3°19′10″41W	**NE** 51°00′44″07/2°42′01″26W
	SW 50°45′00″40/3°18′57″70W	**SE** 50°45′06″56/2°42′00″94W

130	**NW** 51°00′44″07/2°42′01″26W	**NE** 51°00′38″47/2°04′52″11W
	SW 50°45′06″56/2°42′00″94W	**SE** 50°45′01″01/2°05′04″18W

131	**NW** 51°00′38″47/2°04′52″11W	**NE** 51°00′21″06/1°27′43″26W
	SW 50°45′01″01/2°05′04″18W	**SE** 50°44′43″75/1°28′07″71W

132	**NW** 51°00′21″06/1°27′43″26W	**NE** 50°59′51″84/0°50′35″03W
	SW 50°44′43″75/1°28′07″71W	**SE** 50°44′14″80/0°51′11″85W

133	**NW** 50°59′51″84/0°50′35″03W	**NE** 50°59′10″82/0°13′27″73W
	SW 50°44′14″80/0°51′11″85W	**SE** 50°43′34″16/0°14′16″90W

134	**NW** 50°59′10″82/0°13′27″73W	**NE** 50°58′18″01/0°23′38″32E
	SW 50°43′34″16/0°14′16″90W	**SE** 50°42′41″84/0°22′36″83E

| 135 | NW | 51°03'30"06/0°23'59"02E | NE | 51°02'25"28/1°01'07"64E |
| | SW | 50°47'53"90/0°22'57"23E | SE | 50°46'49"72/0°59'53"51E |

| 136 | NW | 50°46'13"02/5°05'46"84W | NE | 50°46'49"16/4°32'56"17W |
| | SW | 50°28'00"16/5°04'51"09W | SE | 50°28'35"92/4°32'13"05W |

| 137 | NW | 50°44'12"99/4°32'49"96W | NE | 50°44'42"54/3°55'54"14W |
| | SW | 50°28'35"92/4°32'13"05W | SE | 50°29'05"20/3°55'29"42W |

| 138 | NW | 50°44'42"54/3°55'54"14W | NE | 50°45'00"40/3°18'57"70W |
| | SW | 50°29'05"20/3°55'29"42W | SE | 50°29'22"90/3°18'45"17W |

| 139 | NW | 50°52'49"13/3°19'04"03W | NE | 50°52'55"32/2°42'01"10W |
| | SW | 50°37'11"65/3°18'51"41W | SE | 50°37'17"78/2°42'00"78W |

| 140 | NW | 50°52'55"32/2°42'01"10W | NE | 50°52'52"91/2°17'19"12W |
| | SW | 50°29'29"00/2°42'00"63W | SE | 50°29'26"62/2°17'30"90W |

| 141 | NW | 50°50'16"66/2°17'20"45W | NE | 50°50'03"27/1°40'19"74W |
| | SW | 50°34'39"14/2°17'28"31W | SE | 50°34'25"87/1°40'39"86W |

| 142 | NW | 50°50'03"27/1°40'19"74W | NE | 50°49'38"14/1°03'19"54W |
| | SW | 50°34'25"87/1°40'39"86W | SE | 50°34'00"97/1°03'51"92W |

| 143 | NW | 50°27'44"40/5°17'05"12W | NE | 50°28'35"92/4°32'13"05W |
| | SW | 50°09'31"64/5°16'05"67W | SE | 50°10'22"62/4°31'30"67W |

| 144 | NW | 50°28'35"92/4°32'13"05W | NE | 50°29'05"20/3°55'29"42W |
| | SW | 50°12'58"81/4°31'36"68W | SE | 50°13'27"82/3°55'05"05W |

| 145 | NW | 50°29'05"20/3°55'29"42W | NE | 50°29'19"97/3°26'55"04W |
| | SW | 50°10'51"59/3°55'01"03W | SE | 50°11'06"19/3°26'37"55W |

| 146 | NW | 50°16'38"44/5°44'57"00W | NE | 50°17'40"58/5°00'15"84W |
| | SW | 49°55'50"03/5°43'37"55W | SE | 49°56'51"42/4°59'15"65W |

2 Cassini co-ordinates

1	N+951820	S+809260	W+43830	E+138870
2	N+951820	S+809260	W+138870	E+233910
3	N+809260	S+714220	W-3690	E+138870
4	N+809260	S+714220	W+112470	E+255030
5	N+714220	S+619180	W-146250	E-3690
6	N+714220	S+619180	W-3690	E+138870
7	N+714220	S+619180	W+138870	E+281430
8	N+619180	S+476620	W-204330	E-109290
9	N+619180	S+524140	W-146250	E-3690
10	N+619180	S+524140	W-3690	E+138870
11	N+619180	S+524140	W+138870	E+291990
12	N+524140	S+429100	W-146250	E-3690
13	N+524140	S+429100	W-3690	E+138870
14	N+524140	S+429100	W+138870	E+281430

15	N+571660	S+429100	W+233910	E+334230
16	N+524140	S+429100	W+334230	E+476790
17	N+444940	S+302380	W-463050	E-336330
18	N+476620	S+334060	W-204330	E-109290
19	N+429100	S+334060	W-146250	E-3690
20	N+429100	S+334060	W-3690	E+138870
21	N+429100	S+334060	W+138870	E+281430
22	N+429100	S+334060	W+281430	E+423990
23	N+429100	S+334060	W+423990	E+566550
24	N+334060	S+239020	W-146250	E-3690
25	N+334060	S+239020	W-3690	E+138870
26	N+334060	S+239020	W+138870	E+281430
27	N+334060	S+239020	W+281430	E+423990
28	N+334060	S+239020	W+423990	E+566550
29	N+239020	S+143980	W-98730	E+43830
30	N+239020	S+143980	W-3690	E+138870
31	N+239020	S+143980	W+138870	E+281430
32	N+239020	S+143980	W+281430	E+423990
33	N+239020	S+143980	W+423990	E+566550
34	N+239020	S+96460	W+519030	E+619350
35	N+143980	S+48940	W-146250	E-3690
36	N+143980	S+48940	W-3690	E+138870
37	N+143980	S+48940	W+138870	E+281430
38	N+143980	S+48940	W+281430	E+423990
39	N+143980	S+48940	W+423990	E+566550
40	N+143980	S+48940	W+519030	E+661590
41	N+80620	S-46100	W-441930	E-288810
42	N+70060	S-46100	W-288810	E-146250
43	N+48940	S-46100	W-146250	E-3690
44	N+48940	S-46100	W-3690	E+138870
45	N+48940	S-46100	W+138870	E+281430
46	N+48940	S-46100	W+281430	E+423990
47	N+48940	S-46100	W+423990	E+566550
48	N+48940	S-46100	W+534870	E+677430
49	N-46100	S-162260	W-468330	E-288810
50	N-46100	S-141140	W-288810	E-146250
51	N-46100	S-141140	W-146250	E-3690
52	N-46100	S-141140	W-3690	E+138870
53	N-46100	S-141140	W+138870	E+281430
54	N-46100	S-141140	W+281430	E+423990
55	N-46100	S-141140	W+423990	E+566550
56	N-46100	S-141140	W+566550	E+709110
57	N-61940	S-156980	W+709110	E+851670
58	N-69860	S-164900	W+851670	E+994230
59	N-141140	S-236180	W-288810	E-146250
60	N-141140	S-236180	W-146250	E-3690
61	N-141140	S-236180	W-3690	E+138870
62	N-141140	S-236180	W+138870	E+281430
63	N-141140	S-236180	W+281430	E+423990

64	N-141140	S-236180	W+423990	E+566550
65	N-141140	S-236180	W+566550	E+709110
66	N-141140	S-236180	W+709110	E+851670
67	N-141140	S-236180	W+851670	E+994230
68	N-162260	S-331220	W-336330	E-241290
69	N-236180	S-331220	W-288810	E-146250
70	N-236180	S-331220	W-146250	E-3690
71	N-236180	S-331220	W-3690	E+138870
72	N-236180	S-331220	W+138870	E+281430
73	N-236180	S-331220	W+281430	E+423990
74	N-236180	S-331220	W+423990	E+566550
75	N-236180	S-331220	W+566550	E+709110
76	N-236180	S-331220	W+709110	E+851670
77	N-236180	S-331220	W+851670	E+994230
78	N-331220	S-426260	W-431370	E-288810
79	N-331220	S-426260	W-288810	E-146250
80	N-331220	S-426260	W-146250	E-3690
81	N-331220	S-426260	W-3690	E+138870
82	N-331220	S-426260	W+138870	E+281430
83	N-331220	S-426260	W+281430	E+423990
84	N-331220	S-426260	W+423990	E+566550
85	N-331220	S-426260	W+566550	E+709110
86	N-331220	S-426260	W+709110	E+851670
87	N-331220	S-426260	W+851670	E+994230
88	N-386660	S-489620	W-605610	E-431370
89	N-426260	S-521300	W-431370	E-288810
90	N-426260	S-521300	W-288810	E-146250
91	N-426260	S-521300	W-146250	E-3690
92	N-426260	S-521300	W-3690	E+138870
93	N-426260	S-521300	W+138870	E+281430
94	N-426260	S-521300	W+281430	E+423990
95	N-426260	S-521300	W+423990	E+566550
96	N-426260	S-521300	W+566550	E+709110
97	N-426260	S-521300	W+709110	E+851670
98	N-426260	S-521300	W+780390	E+922950
99	N-489620	S-592580	W-605610	E-431370
100	N-521300	S-616340	W-431370	E-288810
101	N-521300	S-616340	W-288810	E-146250
102	N-521300	S-616340	W-146250	E-3690
103	N-521300	S-616340	W-3690	E+138870
104	N-521300	S-616340	W+138870	E+281430
105	N-521300	S-616340	W+281430	E+423990
106	N-521300	S-616340	W+423990	E+566550
107	N-521300	S-616340	W+566550	E+709110
108	N-521300	S-616340	W+709110	E+851670
109	N-584660	S-679700	W-246570	E-67050
110	N-616340	S-711380	W-146250	E-3690
111	N-616340	S-711380	W-3690	E+138870
112	N-616340	S-711380	W+138870	E+281430

113	N-616340	S-711380	W+281430	E+423990
114	N-616340	S-711380	W+423990	E+566550
115	N-616340	S-711380	W+566550	E+709110
116	N-616340	S-711380	W+709110	E+851670
117	N-632180	S-774740	W+851670	E+946710
118	N-711380	S-806420	W-373290	E-230730
119	N-711380	S-806420	W-288810	E-146250
120	N-711380	S-806420	W-146250	E-3690
121	N-711380	S-806420	W-3690	E+138870
122	N-711380	S-806420	W+138870	E+281430
123	N-711380	S-806420	W+281430	E+423990
124	N-711380	S-806420	W+423990	E+566550
125	N-711380	S-806420	W+566550	E+709110
126	N-711380	S-806420	W+709110	E+851670
127	N-806420	S-901460	W-439290	E-288810
128	N-806420	S-901460	W-288810	E-146250
129	N-806420	S-901460	W-146250	E-3690
130	N-806420	S-901460	W-3690	E+138870
131	N-806420	S-901460	W+138870	E+281430
132	N-806420	S-901460	W+281430	E+423990
133	N-806420	S-901460	W+423990	E+566550
134	N-806420	S-901460	W+566550	E+709110
135	N-774740	S-869780	W+709110	E+851670
136	N-885620	S-996500	W-558090	E-431370
137	N-901460	S-996500	W-431370	E-288810
138	N-901460	S-996500	W-288810	E-146250
139	N-853940	S-948980	W-146250	E-3690
140	N-853940	S-996500	W-3690	E+91350
141	N-869780	S-964820	W+91350	E+233910
142	N-869780	S-964820	W+233910	E+376470
143	N-996500	S-1107380	W-605610	E-431370
144	N-996500	S-1091540	W-431370	E-288810
145	N-996500	S-1107380	W-288810	E-177930
146	N-1059860	S-1186580	W-716490	E-542250

Contructional Elements

Horizontal Datum	OSGBI 1858
All latitudes are	North
Projection	Cassini's
Spheroid	Airy
Unit	Foot (Ordnance Survey Foot of O_1)
True origin	Delamere (53°13'17"274N/2°41'03"562W)
False co-ordinates	None
Scale factor	Unity

(1 Foot of O_1 = 0.304 800 749 1 international Metre)

PART 2

CATALOGUING THE POPULAR EDITION

Introduction

In setting out to make a catalogue of a series map, whose many component sheets have lived separate lives and undergone several reprints over more than two decades, the student begins with some sort of idea of how things should be arranged. As acquaintanceship with the subject deepens into a closer relationship, however, the original formula inevitably undergoes several changes until the point is reached where he must begin again, hoping, at last, that all the elements of description are in the right order. So it was with the making of the full catalogue of the Popular Edition, but even so, perfection has undoubtedly eluded its compiler. The same could be said of the Popular Edition of England and Wales itself: the original design precepts had to be continually modified as the difficulties of printing in colour from an engraved plate were experienced. Near perfection was only achieved with the last three sheets of the series. In between came a gradual shifting of the formula from engraving to drawing as the basis for the printed map. The resulting changes to the map have provided numerous little cartographic (one might say, almost philatelic) conundrums which give such joy to the collector. Along the way, they also supply some enlightenment as to how the map was made.

The Popular Edition is a major challenge to the serious collector; its 146 standard coloured sheets underwent a total of 783 known printings (original printings and reprints); each of these was, theoretically, issued in four main formats: paper flat; paper folded; mounted on linen and folded, and, dissected and mounted and folded. In the 1930s, many sheets were printed on Place's waterproof paper; a special cover was designed for these sheets, but not all waterproofed maps were issued in the special cover: some were sold in the standard cover with an explanatory sticker fixed to the map inside - examples of these are rarities today. In the 1920s, Stanford sold the Popular Edition in the Bridge's Patent folding format, again, with a special cover; no complete set is known, and survivors are scarce indeed. The Bender fold was introduced for the Popular Edition in 1939, so, theoretically, it should be possible to track down a copy of all those sheets printed in and after that year in the Bender format with its specific Bender cover (in practice, though, some of these late printings retained the old covers while stocks of these lasted). Then there are the covers themselves: outwardly similar, but teeming with minor variations in detail. The collector will often find the same state, or printing, of a sheet in different covers: these differences supply a clue to the approximate date of issue. Some enjoy simply collecting as many different covers as possible for one sheet throughout its lifetime. For the Ordnance Survey map collector, then, the Popular Edition offers something for everyone.

The purpose of this part of the book, therefore, is to introduce the reader to the complexities of the design of the marginal data of the Popular Edition, and to set out a method of cataloguing the standard and outline sheets of the series so that most of the variations on a common theme can be taken account of. The technique outlined here, while not claiming to be comprehensive, does provide for most of the vagaries encountered on the published sheets. The different states of the Popular Edition sheets are identified principally by changes in the marginalia. Some examples have been recorded where states with identical marginalia can be shown to be different printings because, for example, the contour plates vary, either in colour or in emphasis of the contours at 250ft intervals. The ability to distinguish between printings in this way depends on the number of copies of any one state which can be examined side by side. It is therefore quite probable that some such printing differences have been overlooked simply because insufficient numbers of examples have been to hand for comparative purposes at any one time. No attempt is made to describe the change in topographical content between states, unless it is noticed that such change is the only means of identifying one printing from another. Topographical differences are considered more properly to be the province of the local historian, or the geographer, perhaps studying changes in settlement pattern.

Explanation of the catalogue

Each catalogue entry for the coloured sheets comprises twelve basic sections; the first two elements are given for the first entry for each sheet, and are not repeated for reprints unless there is a change in the information, such as a different sheet name:

1   Sheet number, name and print date
2   The survey, publication and revision history of the sheet
3   Imprint style
4   Minor corrections dates, etc
5   Print codes
6   Magnetic variation date
7   Legend description
8   Scale
9   Other marginal data: price note, etc
10 Cover
11 Location
12 Notes

In order to compress the descriptions of the variations in marginalia into as small a space as possible, each section has been coded, so that the differences between states can be seen at a glance on the page. The amount of information for each entry is complex and substantial, and could not have been contained in a columnar layout (as, for example, has been the practice with many Charles Close Society guides) without sacrificing the ease with which the data could be accessed by the user. When the first data capture was complete, Elements 1, and 3-9, were entered on a database (dBase IV) so as to facilitate the analysis and dating of changes in the marginal data. The database has been of particular value in illustrating how elements were originally recorded in the wrong chronological order. This was a natural consequence, when dealing with a large group of maps in different locations, of having to record complex data, such as variations in the legend, in the sequence in which they were observed. The catalogue has therefore been restructured, wherever possible, so that each feature within a section appears approximately in its correct chronological order. It therefore now bears little relationship to the information on the database. The historical background to many of the marginal features has been described in Chapter IV. The different forms of the outline map are described on page 282. Supplied information is given in square brackets [ ].

1 SERIES TITLE AND SHEET NAME

In the catalogue, the sheet name appears in upper case bold at the beginning of the entry in the form in which it is printed on the map. New sheet names are given against the entries to which they apply. When a sheet name acquires a full stop at the end, the whole name, plus stop, is written against the appropriate entry. If the stop is then absent on subsequent printings, the whole name without the stop is given. The sheet name is only indicated for reprints if this has changed in any way from the previous printing. The date which follows the survey and revision history details in the first entry is the print date of that state. The entries for subsequent reprints are identified by the printing date, underlined, in bold, followed by the print code, if present, also in bold. Where a sheet has been reprinted more than once in one year, it is distinguished by a lower case letter after the date, thus: **1927a**; **1927b**; **1927c**; etc., in chronological order, where this can be determined.

A name in bold in parentheses indicates the name which appears on the cover of the example described, if it is different from that of the sheet. A name not in bold in parentheses indicates a cover title which is stuck on.

2 SURVEY, PUBLICATION AND REVISION DATA

This information is only given for the first entry for each sheet; the survey date refers to the original large-scale survey, and the publication and revision dates refer to the subsequent one-inch maps. Only the dates are transcribed, the wording is paraphrased.

3 IMPRINT STYLE

Nine principal forms of imprint have been recorded for the Popular Edition, some of which have minor variants, recorded below. The form of imprint is expressed in the catalogue by a number, representing one of the styles listed below, followed by a slash, followed by the printing date or publication date.

1   *Engraved at the* ORDNANCE SURVEY OFFICE, *Southampton.*
    Surveyed in [date] *and Published in* [date].
    Revised in [date] *and in* [date].
    Revised (3ʳᵈ. Revision) in [date]. *and Published by* [Director General's name].
    Printed at the Ordnance Survey Office, Southampton. [date].

2   *Engraved at the* ORDNANCE SURVEY OFFICE, *Southampton.*
    Surveyed in [date] *and Published in* [date].
    Revised in [date] *and in* [date].
    Revised (3ʳᵈ. Revision) in [date].
    Published by [Director General's name] *Director General.*
    Printed at the Ordnance Survey Office, Southampton [date].

Note: One example of Imprint **2** has been noted without the words 'Director General' (sheet 143/1927). Sometimes the printing date in **2** is lacking; this is noted in the entry where it occurs. The initials after Close's name may change between states from 'K.B.E.,C.B.,C.M.G.' to 'K.B.E.,C.B.,F.R.S.'. (See p.84.) No state has yet been found which can be identified solely by this difference. The substitution of F.R.S. for C.M.G., instead of adding F.R.S. after C.M.G., may have been easier to make in the limited space within the imprint template on the stone that constituted the outline plate, otherwise the whole template would have to have been remade to accommodate the extra letters; Close clearly valued the designation of F.R.S. above that of C.M.G. When Jack became Director General in 1922, his name was sometimes substituted for Close's in reprints of sheets which had been first published before he succeeded Close. Occasionally, the imprint would revert to Close on subsequent printings (e.g. sheet 115); this is noted in the catalogue where it occurs. Similarly, where an outline state was first published during Jack's Director Generalship, Jack's name would appear in the imprint, although Close's name would be kept for later reprints of the coloured sheet. The name of Colonel E.M. Jack., C.M.G., D.S.O. appeared on sheets which were printed from the end of 1922; he was appointed Colonel Commandant in 1924, and the new rank was abbreviated to 'Cmdt.' in the imprint. In the present catalogue it is assumed that all sheets first printed from the beginning of 1923 will include Jack's name in the imprint. No state has been recorded where the distinction between Colonel and Colonel Commandant is the only difference between the states.

3   *Surveyed in* [date]
3rd. Revision [date]
Drawn, Heliozincographed, and Printed at the
ORDNANCE SURVEY OFFICE. *Southampton.*
Published by Colonel Commandant E.M. Jack. C.M.G.,D.S.O., Director General [date].

4   *Published by* The Director General, at the Ordnance
       Survey Office, Southampton, [date].

    Revision of [date].
    Roads [etc.] *to* [dates]

5   *First published by* The Director General, at the Ordnance Survey Office,
       Southampton, [date], with periodical corrected reprint.

Note: Used from Nov.1934. The comma after the date is often lacking. The last word of **5** is occasionally expressed in the plural; where this occurs, it is noted in the catalogue.

6   *First published by* The Director General, at the ORDNANCE SURVEY OFFICE.
       SOUTHAMPTON, [date], with periodical corrected reprints.

Note: Occasionally a comma instead of a stop has been used after 'OFFICE', or punctuation is lacking altogether at this point; a comma is not always present after the date. These punctuation differences have not been noted in the catalogue. Rarely, the word 'imprints' is substituted for 'reprints'; this is noted where it occurs.

7   *First published by* The Director General *at the*
ORDNANCE SURVEY OFFICE, SOUTHAMPTON, [date]
with periodical corrected reprints.

8   *First published by* The Director General, at the
Ordnance Survey Office, Southampton, [date], with
periodical corrected reprint[s].

9   *First published by* The Director General, at the
ORDNANCE SURVEY OFFICE, SOUTHAMPTON,
[date], with periodical corrected reprints.

Note: The comma is sometimes lacking after the date; the comma after the date is
sometimes replaced by a full stop.

4 MINOR CORRECTIONS, REPRINT NOTE, ROADS, AND RAILWAYS

Because certain elements of the map content, such as roads and railways, were subject
to frequent revision, it became necessary to issue reprints of most of the sheets. The
record of each reprint was preserved in two forms: first, the Intermediate Revision Sheet,
which carried all correction and reprint data, was kept by the officer in charge of the
One-Inch Department, and secondly, the dates of corrections, the number of the print run
and the year of reprint were printed on the map itself, although a record copy of the
reprinted map does not appear to have been kept in the map store.[1] The reprint
information was given in four categories: Minor Corrections, Roads, Railways, and
reprint code. These sometimes appeared singly, or in various combinations, and their
position in the bottom margin was not consistent from one sheet, or even reprint of one
sheet, to another. The data normally appear below the imprint, bottom right, and may
include some, or all, of the following details:

(1) Minor Corrections [date]/Minor corrections [date]/Minor Corrections to
[date]/Minor corrections to [date].

(2) Roads to [date]/Road Corrections to [date].

(3) Railways inserted to [date]/Railways to [date]/Railways revised to [date].

(4) Reprint [followed by up to ten different sets of figures, each giving print run and
year].

(5) [Reprint figures without the word 'reprint'.]

(6) Railways and Minor Corrections to [date].

(7) Roads, Railways and Minor Corrections to [date].

These items may be given in different sequences, on one or more lines, all varying from
sheet to sheet and between different states of any one sheet. The position of each element
in relation to the others is important as it may, rarely, be the only factor to distinguish
one state from another, where otherwise the marginal information is identical. The
approximate relative positions of each item below the imprint text are expressed as:

1   PRO OS 1/260. Minute 36 by the Executive Officer, Clough, dated 14/11/1934.

a	b	c
d	e	f
g	h	i

[Rights of way statement]

j

k = bottom left, between border and legend; l = bottom left, below roads panel of legend.

The information in the above categories is given in the catalogue after the imprint style code and date (from which it is separated by a semicolon) by a number in parentheses that identifies the type of note according to the scheme numbered 1 - 7 above, followed by two digits which are the final digits of the year of printing, followed by a lower case letter which gives the position of the information in the margin. Thus:

(1)31a; (3)30b; (5)31d.

indicates:

Minor Corrections 1931. Railways inserted to 1930.
2000/25.1500/29.2000/31.

Roads revised note

In addition to the above correction and revision dates, where these do not include details of road revision dates, a separate road revision note is usually given in the following form:

Roads revised to [date] / Roads partially revised to [date]

The date is usually given in the form '9.28' (month and year may be separated either by a dot, a slash, or a dash). This note is usually located in the bottom margin between the scale and the imprint. The different approximate positions of the note are shown in the following diagram:

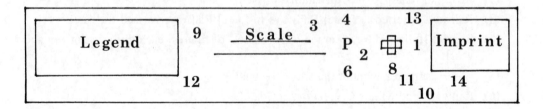

Fig.44 Positions of road revision notes. P = price note; 5 = location when no price note is present in this position.

Catalogue entry: This form of road revision note is distinguished from the preceding road information (from which it is separated by a semicolon) by being prefaced with the word 'roads', followed by a number in parentheses that indicates the position of the note in the bottom margin, followed by a transcription of the date in the form in which it appears on the map. Thus: ; roads (4) 7-29.

5 PRINT CODES

The print code for the coloured sheets is transcribed in full, including punctuation, from the map. All print codes of the type '2036', etc., are in position **k** (see p.262) unless otherwise stated.

6 MAGNETIC VARIATION

Following the initial 'M', the date is transcribed in the form in which it appears on the map.

7 LEGEND

In order to simplify the description of the different legends, each has been divided into three, following the three-fold division into panels on the map, and the features within each have been individually coded so as to provide a 'key' to the identification of each variant. The text within each division may show slight differences in writing and in positioning of the information. This reflects the number of times each legend may have been redrawn or altered, particularly in the 1930s, when the legends to the Popular were sometimes completely redrawn and lettered in Scottish Popular style. To take account of these minor variations would have increased the complexity of the description, and no notice has been taken of them in this catalogue. The legend is described in the catalogue in arabic numerals followed by lower case letters according to the scheme below:

(1) 'Road' legend

- **a** Classification of 'Main Routes between Towns' etc., with road widths of over 14′ of metalling, and under 14′, together with surface conditions.
- **b** The addition of the word 'Main' (from 1924) to the category of roads under 14′ wide which are 'Fit for ordinary traffic'.
- **c** The addition of the words 'Other Roads' to the category of roads under 14′ wide which are either 'Fit for ordinary traffic' or an 'Indifferent or winding road'. This is occasionally accompanied by the dropping into this line of the word 'Bad' which had formerly been written on the top line.
- **d** 'Other Roads' under 14′ wide lacking in colour.
- **e** 'Other Roads' under 14′ wide in solid colour.
- **f** 'Bad Roads' printed in yellow and white dashes instead of colourless with black casing.
- **g** With 'Toll Gates' and symbol. (From 1925).
- **h** Classification change to 'Roads, Principal, 18′ of metalling & over'. (Only in 1933-4).
- **i** Classification change to 'MOT 'A' Roads', etc. (From 1934).
- **j** Omission of the statement 'Private Roads are uncoloured'. (From 1935).
- **k** Substitution of the word 'Gradient' for slope.

(2) 'Railway' legend

a Two railway stations: one rectangular, uncoloured; one circular, uncoloured.

b Two railway stations: one rectangular, black; one circular, uncoloured.

c Two railway stations: rectangular, red with black casing; circular, red with black casing.

d Two railway stations: one rectangular, black; one circular, red with black casing. (This appears to pre-date c, and may even pre-date b; it has been left in reverse order to avoid excessive changes to the record.)

e Three railway stations: as for c, and a circular uncoloured, closed station. (From 1932).

f Rectangular red station now designated 'Principal station'.

g Viaduct symbol moved from 'Double Line' to 'Single Line'.

h,i [Left blank].

j Addition of 'Electricity Transmission Lines'. (From 1937).

k Outline of orchards and woods redrawn.

l Marsh symbol added.

m Rough pasture symbol added.

n River and canal solid blue.

o Canal, and river beneath 'Bridge under', in blue, with blue casing, estuary in same blue.

Note: in a few instances the river under the 'bridge' has black casing.

p Estuary in different solid blue to n.

q Estuary stippled blue.

r Estuary in blue ruled lines (horizontal).

s Estuary not coloured.

t Sand coloured.

u Sand not coloured.

(3) 'Parks' legend

a Parks and ornamental ground in black stipple.

b [Left blank]

c Parks and ornamental ground in green ruled lines (horizontal).

d [Left blank]

e 'Boundaries, National' symbol added. (From 1933. The 1932 printing of sheet 5 has 'International boundaries'.)

f 'Boundaries, County' the only boundary symbol present.

g 'Boundaries, Parish only' added.

h 'Boundaries, Parish' added. (From 1930, mainly from 1934.)

i Youth Hostel symbol added. (From 1934.)

j [Left blank]

k   Heath and Moor symbol present.

l   [Left blank]

m   Marsh symbol omitted.

n   No contour line/s.

o   Single contour with value of 50/100/200/250 or 300ft.

p   [Left blank]

q   Two or more contours, one emphasised with a value of 250ft or 500ft.

r   [Left blank]

s   No blue depth contour.

t   [Left blank]

u   Solid blue depth contour, with or without a value.

v   [Left blank]

w   Stippled blue depth contour, with or without a value.

The 'roads panel' has been omitted from the following three illustrations of legends (all reduced). Five versions of the road legend are shown in Plate 10.

Fig.45a Legend sheet 143 (1918): (2) a, n, p, q, t; (3) a, k, o, w.

Fig.45b Legend sheet 120 (1931): (2) c, n, p, u; (3) a, h, o, w.

Fig.45c Legend sheet 68 (1939): (2) e, j, n, p, t; (3) c, i, q, m.

8 SCALE STATEMENT

The word 'Scale' is followed by an arabic number according to one of the following styles:

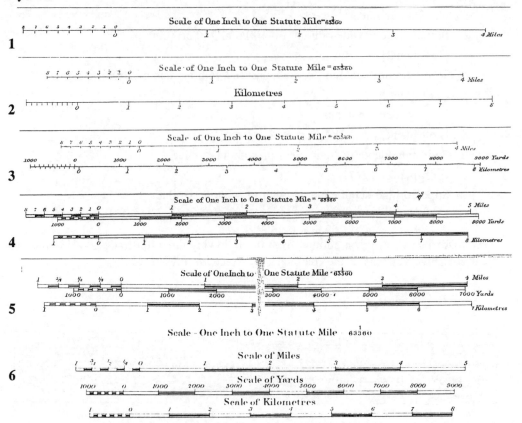

9 OTHER MARGINAL DETAIL

The positions on the sheet of the features given in this section were sometimes changed between states. This was the result of new transfers being laid down in a different place when the sheet came to be reprinted. In practice, the position of the features from sheet to sheet was reasonably standardised, giving a superficial appearance of uniformity of design to the marginalia. No state has so far been distinguished from another solely on the basis of the difference in position of these marginal data, but such a possibility should not be ruled out.

The description of Other Marginal Data in the sheet entry comprises the initial **O**, followed by arabic numerals and lower case letters according to the following designations:

1   **Adjoining sheet diagram**   It was uncommon for sheets to carry no indication of adjacent sheet numbers. A local sheet index, which usually showed up to four neighbouring maps, was printed in the bottom right margin, to the left of the imprint.

Its configuration varied according to the regularity of the sheets it portrayed, and, because it was unique to the sheet, was the only item in the bottom margin to be engraved on the outline copperplate.

1a '*N^{os}. of the adjoining Sheets of the* One *Inch Map.*' This is usually placed between the scale and the imprint. The form of the regular five-sheet diagram is standard to the inland sheets of the series; that is, the sheet in question, is in a central position and the adjoining north, south, east and west sheets are shown.

1b '*N^{os}. of the adjoining Sheets of the* One *Inch Map.*' An irregular sheet diagram is standard to coastal areas.

1c No adjoining sheet diagram present.

2 **Price statement** (cover prices are described in section **10**, pp.274-5) Prices had been printed in the margins of Ordnance Survey maps since the early days of the Old Series one-inch maps at the beginning of the nineteenth century.[2] The price of the Popular Edition varied according to the form in which it was sold. The deluxe version - dissected, mounted on linen and folded in covers - was the most expensive. The price of the folded maps appeared only on the cover; only the cheapest price (for the flat and unmounted version) appeared on the map itself. Some sheets of the Popular Edition gave no indication of cost. The earliest price note, 'Price: [or :-] unmounted 1/- net', was printed in the centre of the bottom margin, between the contour note and the copyright statement; in this, it followed the pattern of the Third Edition. The 1919 prices of 1/- for unmounted sheets, 1/6 for mounted and folded, and 2/6 for mounted and dissected maps, had been fixed by the Olivier Committee in August 1914.[3] These prices were increased in January 1920 to 1/6 and the price note on the map was accompanied by the qualifier 'For Prices mounted and folded see Lists & Catalogue'. This was the most common form of the price statement.

2a '*Price: unmounted 1/- net.*' This is usually placed between the contour and copyright statements. The word 'net' was not always present.

2b '*Price flat and unmounted 1/6 net.* | *For Prices mounted and folded see Lists & Catalogue.*' The position of this statement varied from sheet to sheet, and between reprints. It is usually found between the scale statement and the adjoining sheet diagram. The word 'net' was not always present; no state has been seen where the presence or absence of this word marks the only difference. Prices were increased in January 1920.

2c No price statement. The absence of the price statement is sometimes valuable in identifying the earliest reprint, where the reprint date, expressed as month and year, may have been cropped. A tell-tale gap would often be left between the contour and copyright statements where the price had formerly been printed. This is indicated by

2   These are recorded in Margary, (1975-1992).
3   *Olivier*, (1914b), p.15, para.65.

the word 'gap', in square brackets following the designation **2c** in the **O** section; the gap was usually closed up on subsequent reprints. Occasionally, the lack of the price note is the only clue, in the absence of a reprint code (especially on sheets where the margins have not been trimmed), to the fact that the sheet has been reprinted. However, some sheets which were ready for printing in January 1920 may have had the price erased from the plate at the last minute, following the price rise in that month. It is possible that the presence of a gap in these cases may simply reflect this late change rather than a reprint. This can be verified by looking at the publication lists.

2d *Price flat and unmounted 2/- net | For Prices mounted and folded see Lists & Catalogue.* This has been recorded for sheet 5 only; it also appears on some tourist and district maps from 1928.

3 **Altitude statement** As well as including spot heights and contours in the legend, a separate statement on the origin of the height information was printed in the centre of the bottom margin. It was given in two parts, and the first of these, relating to the datum at Liverpool (see p.97), had originally appeared in a similar form on the New Series sheets and continued, with little change, through to the Third Edition Large Sheet Series. The only salient difference in the earliest Popular statement was the omission of any reference to Liverpool; only three versions have been recorded:

3a *'The Altitudes are given in Feet above Ordnance Survey Datum, which is about 0.65 of a Foot below the general Mean Level of the Sea, and are indicated thus, (326).'* [This is printed on one line, usually below the scale bar.]

3b *'The Altitudes and Contours are given in Feet above Ordnance Survey Datum. (Mean Sea Level.)'*

3c *'The Altitudes and Contours are given in Feet above Mean Sea Level.'*

4 **Contour statement** The second part of the height information was an innovation which was introduced with the Popular Edition; it referred to the contour data and was usually printed below the altitude note. The contours of the earlier one-inch maps were shown at 100ft intervals, and had all been instrumentally surveyed, but the Popular embodied interpolated contours at 50ft intervals and, clearly, some explanation of the relative accuracy of the values was deemed essential.

4a *'The Contours are spaced at intervals of 50 Feet, reckoning from Ordnance Survey Datum.'* [This usually appears below **3**.]

4b *'Contours surveyed on the ground, 50', 100', 200',* [in 100s up to 1000ft, then at 250ft intervals according to the topography] *Other Contours interpolated and only approximately correct.'*

4c As for **4b**, but specifying counties. This occasionally made such a long note that it was printed below the level of the legend; this was usually altered on reprint so that the note was written on two lines, instead of one.

4d *'All contours surveyed on the ground.'*

4e *'Contours surveyed on the ground,'* [Followed by a list.]

Note: In the catalogue the absence of a contour statement is implied by the lack of the figure **4** in the area for **O**. The surveyed and interpolated contour reference (i.e. 4b or 4c) was to be deleted from sheets when they came to be transferred to negatives as from 14/5/1938.[4]

5 Marine information

5a *'The Submarine Contours are given in Fathoms, and are taken from the Soundings of Admiralty Surveys.'* This is usually printed on one line below the contour statement; it can also appear below **4**, or below **5c**.

5b *'The Submarine Contours are given in Fathoms.'*

5c *'Sandbanks surrounded by water and submarine contours are based upon Admiralty Surveys, the datum of which is approximately Mean Low Water Springs.'*

5d *'Contours in Lakes sketched from Soundings by Hugh Robert Mill, D.Sc., and Edward Heawood, M.A.'*

10 COVERS

The following eight illustrations show the principal types of cover used for the Popular Edition:

ORDNANCE SURVEY.

The following are the principal small scale Maps published by this Department:—

1.—Map on the scale of One Inch to One Mile, in colour or in black outline. The size of each sheet, for England and Wales, is 27 inches by 18 inches, and for Scotland 24 inches by 18 inches. The price of the coloured edition is 1s. 6d. unmounted, 2s. mounted. A popular edition in coloured outline is also in course of publication, price unmounted, 1s. per sheet.

2.—Map on the scale of Half Inch to One Mile with the hills shown by hypsometrical colouring (layers), or by shading. The size of each sheet is 27 inches by 18 inches and the price unmounted 1s. 6d., mounted 2s. Very suitable for motoring.

3.—Map on the scale of Quarter Inch to One Mile, in colour or outline. Ten sheets cover the whole of England and Wales. Price per sheet of the coloured edition, 1s. 6d., unmounted, 2s. mounted.

4.—Map on the scale of Ten Miles to One Inch. Suitable for a wall map.

5.—General Map of the United Kingdom on the scale of One to One Million, or about 16 Miles to One Inch, in two sheets 25 inches by 35 inches, coloured. Price, each sheet, unmounted 2s. 6d.

The following are the principal large-scale Maps published by this Department:—

6.—Cadastral Maps on the scale of ¹⁄₂₅₀₀ or about 25 inches to One Mile. These maps show boundaries and areas of fields and enclosures, levels and bench marks. The size of each sheet is 38 inches by 25 inches and the price 5s. Available for the whole of the United Kingdom except mountainous and waste areas.

7.—Maps on the scale of Six Inches to One Mile, in black with contours in colour. The size of each quarter-sheets is 18 inches by 12 inches and the price 1s. 6d. Available for the whole of the United Kingdom.

Geological Maps on scales of Six Inches (for certain Districts), One Inch to One Mile, and Quarter Inch to One Mile, are also published.

Complete information can be obtained by application to the

DIRECTOR-GENERAL,
ORDNANCE SURVEY,
SOUTHAMPTON.

Fig.46a Buff cover design, 1919.   Fig.46b Inside buff cover, 1919.

4   PRO OS 1/52. Minute 12.

Fig.46c Red cover, 1919.

Fig.46d Red and Buff cover, 1928.

Fig.46e Red Bender cover, 1939.

Fig.46f Stanford cover, 1919.

Fig.46g Waterproof map cover, (1931).   **Fig.46h** Stanford Bridges cover.

Catalogue entry: No attempt has been made to record all the variations in cover design for any one printing; only one example is given for each entry. The covers are described in seven sections, six of which are numbered. Words, letters and arabic numerals, after the word 'Cover' are used as follows:

Front cover:

Buff   Buff background with black and orange lettering.

Red   Red background with black and red lettering.

B&Ra   Red cover stuck on buff card to leave a buff border. In these cases the index on the back cover is, as a rule, also stuck onto card.

B&Rb   Red cover with a buff border printed as one.

WP   Waterproof. Covers of waterproofed maps were usually buff with black and orange lettering.

The tone of the red which was used for the covers could vary considerably; the early reds were a vermilion, but later printings took on an orange cast. No record has been made of colour changes in the catalogue, but it should be noted that it is possible to find covers which are identical in all but colour for any one state of a sheet; this may indicate a different issue of the map, or, that the covers had been used up and new stock had to be printed.

The following abbreviations, where applicable, are placed in front of the cover colour description:

B   Bender. The front and back cover is printed in one piece, and hinged at the top.

Ba   Bender cover with title on the spine.

P   Pictorial. Only one pictorial cover has been noted, for sheet 17, *Isle of Man*.

The abbreviations listed below are given in parentheses after the cover colour description to indicate the method by which the cover is attached:

(h) Hinged. The cover is printed on a wider piece of card, which was scored to leave a hinge which was stuck to the reverse of one of the panels of the map. Occasionally, this hinge would be much larger, almost the size of one of the folded panels of the map. This last feature is not noted in the catalogue. In practice, virtually all **B&R** covers were hinged, and this is not therefore noted against a **B&R** description; any other method of attaching a **B&R** cover is noted.

(s) Slap on. The cover is pasted straight down onto the reverse of one of the map panels. In practice this applied to all red covers (except Bender-folded red covers), and this description is not, therefore noted against a **Red** description in the catalogue; any other method of attaching a **Red** cover is noted.

(wr) Wrap round. Front and back cover are printed in one piece, allowing for a narrow spine. The back cover is pasted to the reverse of one of the map panels; the front cover then wraps round the folded map, giving the appearance of a book, but it is not necessarily used with the book fold (see pp.189-90). This cover was common on paper folded maps.

1 Series title and sheet number

1a 'ORDNANCE SURVEY | *Contoured Road Map of*. This is the standard wording of the title which appears on the front cover. The title 'Popular Edition' appears lower down and is combined with the price note. This is common to all sheets issued in Ordnance Survey sales covers (except for Bender covers) and is not therefore entered in the catalogue in these instances.

1b 'ORDNANCE SURVEY | *Contoured Road Map*'. This form was usually combined with a Stanford address cover.

1c 'ORDNANCE SURVEY | "ONE-INCH" MAP | *POPULAR EDITION*'. This form invariably appeared on a Bender cover.

1d No sheet number. All early buff covers lack a sheet number, top right. Some early red covers also lack a sheet number, top right; the absence of a sheet number is noted where it occurs. The sheet number on Stanford covers is sometimes stamped top right, or below the series title; if the number has been written in manuscript, the cover is recorded as lacking a number. Stanford covers have only been seen on dissected maps.

2 Sheet name lettering styles

The sheer diversity of different lettering styles used for the cover sheet titles, and the use of several styles at any one time (although usually for different sheets) makes it impossible to create anything other than an approximate order of appearance. Early styles could remain current for the entire life of some sheets, while others changed several times. No attempt to standardise styles seems to have been made at the outset, and many of the lettering designs used for the Popular were also used for the other small-scale maps. The apparent leap-frogging of styles is probably explained by the fact that a batch of any one cover could be prepared, but not all would be used immediately, leaving a residual pile for later use. The old covers, overlooked when a new batch with different lettering was made up, could then be rediscovered and used at a later date. Stanford covers were printed with a blank space in place of the sheet name, which could then be written in by the purchaser, or, sometimes, was used for a stamped sheet number.

HASTINGS *Tunbridge Wells*

2a First used between 1919 and 1926. This category is characterised by seemingly idiosyncratic styles of lettering, all having the appearance of having been hand-written.

HEXHAM

2b Used from about 1922. The characters are sometimes slimmer.

RIBBLESDALE

2c Used from about 1922; also used for the half-inch, and Scottish Popular Edition maps.

Peterborough

2d Used from about 1922.

Bishop's Castle

2e Used from about 1922. The size of this lettering could vary from sheet to sheet.

CHESTER

2f Used from about 1922. The capital letters were usually equal in size; an exception is sheet 60 where the initial 'S' of Shrewsbury is larger than the rest of the name. Where sheet titles comprised two or more names, each name was printed the same size on the early versions of this style; on later printings the subordinate name would be shown in smaller letters, and the 'and' would often be printed in lower case letters: sometimes this would be the only difference in otherwise identical covers. This was the most commonly used style overall for the Popular Edition, appearing first in about 1922, and was also used for the Bender Covers. This lettering was also used for the Scottish Popular Edition and Fifth Edition.

WEALD OF KENT

2g Used from about 1929. This style, a compressed form of **2f**, was also printed in black for Bender covered sheets, and was used for the Fifth Edition.

SHREWSBURY and WELSHPOOL

2h First used from about 1933.

The Cheviot Hills

2i First used from about 1938. It appears on a 1935 printing of sheet 111, issued in a buff and red cover, but otherwise was mainly used for Bender covers and also for the Fifth Edition covers.

3 Prices

Some Stanford covers have no price note; this is recorded where relevant.

3(1/-) Theoretically possible for the first issues of paper folded sheets. Not yet found; it is possible that no paper folded sheets were issued before January 1920. Following the precedent of the Third Edition Large Sheet Series, the price of 1/-, quoted in the bottom margin of the first printings of the Popular Edition sheets, applied to both paper flat and paper folded forms, though this is not overtly stated for the Popular Edition. The fact that sheets were available in paper folded form appears to have been advertised only from about 1933.

3(1/6) This was the price for folded and mounted sheets from July 1919 to 26 January 1920. Thereafter, 1/6 was the price for paper folded maps (as well as flat, and unmounted versions) until at least 1929.

3(1/6)a Popular Edition Price 1/6   **3(1/6)b** Popular Edition Price ⅙

3(1/6)c Popular Edition Price 1/6   **3(1/6)d** Popular Edition Price ⅙ Net.

3(1/9) The price of paper folded maps increased in about 1929 so that, for the first time, there was a difference in price between paper flat and paper folded forms of the one-inch map.

3(1/9)a Popular Edition Price 1/9 Net.   **3(1/9)b** Popular Edition Price 1/9 Net.

3(1/9)c Popular Edition Price 1/9   **3(1/9)d** Price (paper) 1s. 9d.

3(2/-) This was a sticker on a waterproof cover. Waterproof maps were reduced from 3/6 to 2/6 in June 1935 (O.S.Leaflet No.49/35), and this price was still current in September 1936 (the print code of the leaflet is 9-36). It may be that the sheets were further reduced to 2/- in order to clear the stock; it is also possible that the wrong price was stuck to the map.

3(2/6) This was the price for dissected maps from July 1919 to 26 January 1920. From January 1920, it became the price for mounted and folded maps. This was the most commonly bought form of the Popular Edition, and its price did not vary from 1920 to 1939.

3(2/6)a Popular Edition Price 2/6   **3(2/6)b** Popular Edition Price 2/6
Scale One Inch to One Mile

3(2/6)c Popular Edition Price 2/6   **3(2/6)d** Popular Edition Price 2/6   2/6

3(2/6)e Popular Edition Price 2/6 net.   **3(2/6)f** Popular Edition Price 2/6 Net.

3(2/6)g Popular Edition Price 2/6 Net.   **3(2/6)h** Popular Edition Price 2/6.

3(2/6)i Price ...on cloth... 2s. 6d.   **3(2/6)j** Popular Edition Price 2/6 Net.
¶ *Scale: One Inch to O.*

3(2/6)k 'Mounted in Sections ... Price 2/6'

3(3/-) Sticker on WP map; the tourist sheets were reduced to 3/- in June 1935, and it is possible that the wrong price sticker was fixed to the example on which this is recorded.

3(3/-)a Popular Edition *Price* 3/- *Net.*

3(3/6) This was the price for dissected, mounted and folded maps from 26 January 1920 until about 1 January 1934.

3(3/6)a *Popular Edition, Mounted in Sections* Scale: 1 INCH to 1 MILE. Price 3/6   **3(3/6)b** As for **3(3/6)a**, on a sticker

3(3/6)c *Popular Edition, Mounted in Sections* Scale: 1 INCH to 1 MILE. Price 3/6 net.   **3(3/6)d** *Popular Edition, Mounted in Sections* Scale: 1 INCH to 1 MILE. Price 3/6 Net.

3(3/6)e PRICE 3/6 NET sticker   **3(3/6)f** **Popular Edition Price 3/6**

3(4/-) The price of dissected maps was increased to 4/- by 1 January 1934 (O.S. Leaflet **18**/33). No earlier note of this price rise has so far been found.

3(4/-)a *Popular Edition, Mounted in Sections* Scale: 1 INCH to 1 MILE. Price 4/-   **3(4/-)b** *Popular Edition, Mounted in Sections* Scale: 1 INCH to 1 MILE. Price 4/- Net.

3(4/-)c *Mounted in Sections Price* 4/- *Net.*   **3(4/-)d** Sticker: '4/- NET'

3(4/-)e *Popular Edition. Mounted in Se.* Scale: 1 INCH to 1 MILE. Price 4/-   **3(4/-)f** 'PRICE 4/- NET'

3(4/-)g *Popular Edition, Mounted in Sections* Scale : 1 Inch to 1 Mile. Price 4/- Net.   **3(4/-)h** *Popular Edition, Mounted in Sections* Scale : 1 Inch to 1 Mile. Price 4/-

3(4/-)i 'Popular Edition: Price 4/-'   **3(4/-)j** 'Mounted in Sections - Price 4s.0d.'

Isle of Man prices

The prices for the Isle of Man sheets were the same as those for the other sheets of the Popular Edition, but appeared within a scroll at the bottom of the pictorial cover, and are transcribed in the catalogue entries.

4 Scale statement

None of the following scale statements appeared on Bender covers, which included the scale in the map series title.

4a Variable lettering, particularly of the 'n' and 'h'. ¶ *Scale: One Inch to One Mile*

4b¹ ¶*Scale One Inch to One Mile* **4b²** ¶*Scale: One Inch to One Mile*

4c¹ ¶ *Scale One Inch to One Mile* **4c²** ¶ *Scale: One Inch to One Mile*

4d ¶ *Scale: One Inch to One Mile* **4e** ¶ *Scale One Inch to One Mile*

5 Location diagram

Illustrated below are the eighteen principal versions of the location diagram. Even within these, minor variations will be spotted by the keen eye: the inner border was not always in the 'stave' design, it was sometimes simply a plain line; the compass point on the cover of sheet 120 was drawn differently to the others; the diagram for sheet 145 has an inner decorative border to compensate for the smaller size of the map. No distinction has been made between such features. In practice, the most significant changes were those relating to the differences in Stanford's address; these allow the date of issue to be established with some precision.

5a¹ Sheet number in 'art nouveau' cartouche   **5a²** Sheet no. in scroll.   **5b** Sheet no. in box.

5c Sheet number unenclosed.   **5d** With compass rose.   **5e** No compass rose.

5f Dolphin 1.

5g Dolphin 2.

5h Diagram sideways on.

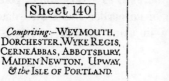

5i List of names instead of map.

5j Ship 1.

5k Ship 2.

5l Ship 3.

5m Ship 4.

EDWARD STANFORD L⁰ᵈ
Agents for
Ordnance Survey Maps.
LONDON
12.13 & 14.Long Acre.W.C.2.

5n Stanford 1 (to 12/1925).

EDWARD STANFORD L⁰ᵈ
Agents for
Ordnance Survey Maps.
LONDON
12.13 & 14.Long Acre.W.C.2.

5o Stanford 2 (From 12/1925).

EDWARD STANFORD L⁰ᵈ
Agents for
Ordnance Survey Maps.
LONDON
12,13,14,Long Acre,W.C.2 &
29 & 30, Charing Cross, S.W.1.

5p Stanford 3 (From 1926).

EDWARD STANFORD L⁰ᵈ
Agents for
Ordnance Survey Maps.
LONDON
12,13,14,Long Acre,W.C.2 &
43,Whitehall,S.W.1.

5q Stanford 4 (From 1/1931).

Note: The author is indebted to Francis Herbert for providing the dates for Stanford's address changes.

6 Back cover index

Until 1937, the sheet line diagram which appeared on the back cover took one of three basic forms, corresponding to the division of England and Wales into north, central, and south regions; the appropriate index was printed on the reverse of the cover. Each of these categories was in turn derived from one of two basic indexes to the whole of

England and Wales. The earliest of these showed the incorrect alignment of sheets 34 and 42 (see p.73), and the second, which seems to have been introduced in about 1928, not only corrected these mistakes but also altered the positioning of some county names, and place-names other than county towns were rewritten in italic lettering.

Many examples of the covers of those sheets which fell in the north or south of the central region can be found with north or south indexes respectively. In 1937, an index showing the Popular Edition sheet lines for the whole of Great Britain was designed,[5] and was used for many of the Popular Edition covers that were printed from this time on. This index invariably appeared on Bender covers. With the exception of the 1937 diagram, the presence of any particular indexes can only be used as a very rough guide to chronological order; inconsistencies, such as the use of an earlier index on a later reprint, have been recorded and may reflect economy in using up old, previously overlooked, stock.

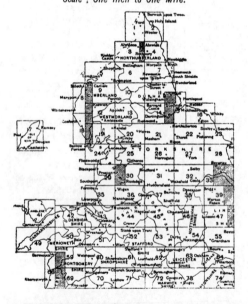

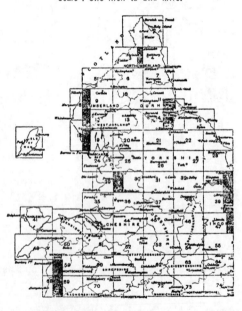

6a North England and Wales, showing sheets 34 and 42 incorrectly aligned.

6c Redrawn; revised sheet lines.

6b As for 6a, but with 'Published by the Ministry of Agriculture and Fisheries.' printed above the index.

5   The author saw the manuscript design of this index in the Ordnance Survey's Cartographic Library on 11/3/1988. The Manuscript Store stamp was dated '24 APR 37'.

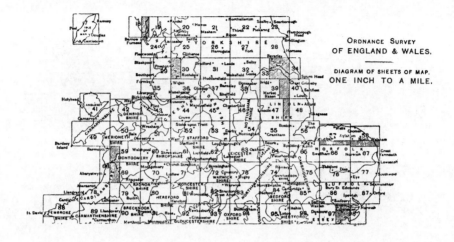

6d Central England. Taken from the same base as **6a,b**, showing the incorrect positions of sheets 34 and 42.

6e As for **6d**, but *'Published by the Ministry of Agriculture and Fisheries'* printed above the index.

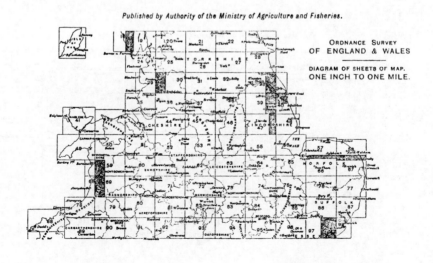

6f Redrawn; revised sheet lines.

279

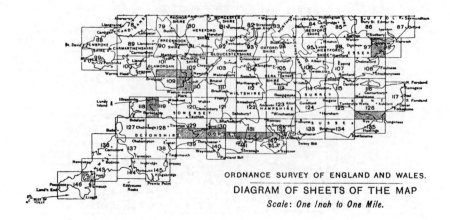

ORDNANCE SURVEY OF ENGLAND AND WALES.

DIAGRAM OF SHEETS OF THE MAP

Scale: One Inch to One Mile.

6g Southern England and Wales. First index.

6h As for **6g**, with '*Published by the Ministry of Agriculture and Fisheries*' printed above the index.

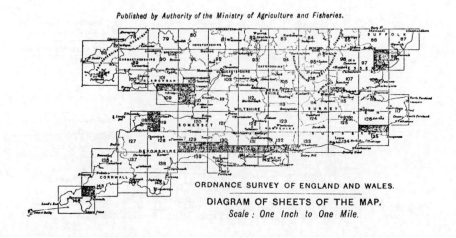

Published by Authority of the Ministry of Agriculture and Fisheries.

ORDNANCE SURVEY OF ENGLAND AND WALES.

DIAGRAM OF SHEETS OF THE MAP.

Scale : One Inch to One Mile.

6i Southern England and Wales. Redrawn index.

Published by Authority of the Ministry of Agriculture and Fisheries

"ONE-INCH" ORDNANCE MAPS OF GREAT BRITAIN.

6j Index to the Popular Edition of the whole of Great Britain; used from 1938.

11 LOCATION

One or more locations may be cited according to the abbreviations found on p.iv. The cover description given in the catalogue applies to the first given location only; any other locations apply solely to the sheet description. Public collections have been cited wherever possible, but they are often not the primary source of information because their holdings do not reflect the full range of printing states of the Popular Edition. Reprints were rarely deposited in the copyright libraries which, in any case, tended to receive flat sheets without covers. Any contemporary library accessions date that might be stamped on the sheet is recorded in parentheses following the location. Library accessions dates need to be treated with caution because of the practice, followed in some collections, of waiting, perhaps up to a month or more, for a batch of accessions to accumulate before date-stamping them.

12 NOTES

This section is used primarily to record the published source in which the announcement of the publication of any state is given. Any comments on specification change, and other general remarks are also given here.

THE OUTLINE MAPS

The entry for an outline sheet is given in the catalogue within the chronological order of the standard sheets and is headed by: latest date and the word 'outline' followed by an arabic numeral denoting one of the styles described below. The print code, where present, is also entered. The absence of a style number indicates that the author has relied on supplied information, and has not seen the map herself. Any further details follow the descriptive formula of the standard sheets, where relevant.

1   **Black only [1919]**. Outline, contours and water. Title, top right, instead of 'Popular Edition One-Inch Map': 'BLACK OUTLINE EDITION | ONE-INCH MAP'. The statement *'Note _ An edition of this map | is published in colours'* is printed top left, between 'Ordnance Survey of England and Wales' and the sheet name. Alphanumerical squaring is indicated in the margins only. The marginalia are in their earliest forms, the legend shows parish boundaries which are also on the map. The price is given as 1/-. Contours are shown as solid lines, parks are in rouletted stipple.

2   **Black and brown [1921-23]**. Outline and water, black; contours, brown. Title, top right, replacing Popular Edition title: 'ONE-INCH | OUTLINE EDITION'. The coloured edition note is printed in black in the bottom right margin. With alpha-numerical squaring.

3   **Black and blue [1924]**. Outline and contours black; water blue. Other details as for Outline **2**.

4   **Black, blue and brown [1923-4]**. Outline, black; water, blue; contours, brown. Other details as for Outline **2**.

5   **Black, blue and brown [1923-1939]**. Outline, black; water blue; contours, brown or orange. The title: '(OUTLINE)' is printed in the same colour as the contour plate, to the right, or left, of the standard black-printed Popular Edition title. The coloured edition note is also printed in the same colour as the contour plate, usually in the bottom right margin. With alpha-numerical squaring.

6   **Black only [1932-5]**. Black plate only, no water, no contours. Lacks any outline title and coloured edition note. With alpha-numerical squaring, and usual marginalia.

7   **Black and blue [1941-43]**. Outline, black; water blue (occasionally, wider rivers are shown with blue casing and no blue infill, e.g. sheet 103:1942); no contours. Lacks any outline title and coloured edition note. All, or part, of the imprint may be deleted, presumably for wartime security purposes. This version, and Outline **8**, are useful for showing building developments as hatched areas on the map. Alphanumerical squaring is indicated in the map frame only, although traces of the former squaring can be seen on some sheets where it has been imperfectly removed from the reproduction material.

8   **Black and blue [1941-43]**. As for Outline **7**, but with no indication of alphanumerical squaring in the map frame.

1 RIVER TWEED
Surveyed 1855-62; 3rd Rev.1921-3.

1926

I 3/1926. **M** 1ˢᵗ Janʸ 1926.
L (1)a,b,c; (2)c,k,l,m,o,u; (3)a,g,q,u.
S 2. **O** 1b,2c,3b,4b,5a.
C Red,2b,3(1/6)b,4c² 5bdh,6c.
CUL(9/9/27); BLa(12/9/27); BLb;
Bod(26/9/27); RGS(24/7/26)
Supp. to Cat.1 Jul./30 Sep.1926.

   1926 Outline 5
   BLd(12/9/27); BLe(GSGS 23/7/26);
   Bod(26/9/27)
   Supp. to Cat.1 Jul./30 Sep.1926.

1937 15/37.M.36.R.32.
I 9/1926. **M** 1ˢᵗ Janʸ 1926.
L (1)g,i,j; (2)e,f,g,k,l,m,o,t; (3)a,e,g,i,q,u.
S 5. **O** 1b,2b,3b,4b,5a.
C B&Rb,2e,3(2/6)h,4d,5bdh,6j.
BLc; Bod
*AR 1936/7. The figure '1' in the price note
appears to have been altered from a '2'.*

   1941 Outline 8 **1000/10/41.L.R.**
   BLf
   AR 1941/2

2 HOLY ISLAND
Surveyed 1859-60; published 1864-7; revised
1894 and 1901; 3rd revision 1922.

1925

I 2/1925. **M** Jan.1925.
L (1)a,b,c,g; (2)c,n,p,u; (3)c,q,u.
S 2. **O** 1b,2c,3b,4b,5bc.
C Red,2b,3(2/6)e,4b²,5bdh,6b.
BLa(30/10/26); BLb; Bod; CUL(30/10/26);
RGS(16/3/26)
Supp. to Cat.1 Jan./31 Mar.1926.

   1925 Outline 5
   BLd(30/10/1926); BLe; Bod(24/12/26)
   Supp. to Cat.1 Jan./31 Mar.1926.

1932 3000/32.
I 2/1925; (1)31a; (5)32d; roads (10) 8-29.
M Jan.1925.
L (1)a,b,c,g; (2)c,n,p,t; (3)c,q,u.
S 4. **O** 1c,2b,3b,4b,5bc.
C B&Rb,2e,3(2/6)h,4d,5bdh,6j.
CUL; BLc; RGS

1937 1537.M.36.R29.
I 9/1925. **M** Jan.1937.
L (1)g,i,j; (2)e,n,p,t; (3)c,i,q,u.
S 4. **O** 1b,2b,3b,4b,5bc.
C B&Rb,2e,3(2/6)h,4d,5bdh,6j.
PC; BLb; Bod; KGM

   1941 Outline 8 1000/11/41 L.R.
   BLf
   AR 1949/2

3 THE CHEVIOT HILLS (Sheet 86 Scotland)
Surveyed 1857-63; 3rd revision 1921-2.

1926
I 3/1926. **M** 1ˢᵗ Janʸ 1925.
L (1)a,b,c; (2)c,k,l,m,o,u; (3)a,g,q,s.
S 2. **O** 1b,2c,3b,4b,5a.
C Red,2c,3(2/6)d,4b²,5cd,6a.
PC; BLa; BLb; KGM; RGS(16/3/26)
*Supp. to Cat.1 Jan./31 Mar.1926; the Supp.
to Cat. for 1 Jul./30 Sept.1925 includes the
note: 'The 1-inch scale Popular Edition
sheets 3 and 5 England & Wales are common
to England and Wales and to Scotland ... It
has been decided that these two maps shall be
issued in both the Scottish and English covers
... in order to make the series of each
country complete.' Parish boundaries are
shown for Scotland only.*

   1926 Outline 5
   PC; BLe; Bod
   Supp. to Cat.1 Jan./31 Mar.1926.

1934 2150/34.
I 3/1925 [note change of date]; (1)30d; roads
(10)10/32.
M 1ˢᵗ Janʸ 1925.
L (1)a,b,c; (2)e,k,l,m,o,u; (3) a,e,g,q,s.
S 6. **O** 1b,2d,3b,4e,[no 6].
PC

1938 3038.M.38.R.37.
I 7/1925. **M** 1ˢᵗ Janʸ 1925.
L (1)g,i,j; (2)e,k,l,m,o,t; (3)a,e,g,q,s.
S 6. **O** 1b,2b,3b,4b,5a.
C BaRed,1c,2i,3(2/6)i,5cd,6j.
PC; BLb; Bod
AR 1939/40.

1942 Outline 7 (k)**3038.M.38.R.37.**
(l)**1000/8/42 L.R.** [in blue]
BLf

4   ALNWICK & ROTHBURY
Surveyed 1858-65; published 1866-7; revised
1894-5 and 1901-2; 3rd revision 1921-2.

1925
I 2/1925. M Jan.1925.
L (1)a,b,c; (2)c,n,p,u; (3)c,q,u.
S 2. O 1b,2c,3b,4b,5a.
C Red,2f,3(2/6)a,4b^2,5bd,6b.
RGS(21/1/26); BLa(28/8/26); BLb;
Bod(2/9/26); CUL(31/8/26)
Supp. to Cat.1 Oct./31 Dec.1925.

  1925 Outline 5
Parks in rouletted stipple, except squares
J12 and J13, where two parks are hand-
stippled.
BLd(28/8/26); BLe; Bod(2/9/26)
Supp.to Cat.1 Oct./31 Dec.1925.

1934 2,500/34.
I 4/1925. (1) 34b; (2) 29a; (5) 34c.
M Jan.1925.
L (1)a,b,c; (2)e,n,p,u; (3)c,i,q,u.
S 4. O 1b,2b,3b,4b,5a.
C B&Rb,2h,3(4/-)h,5bd,6j.
BLc; KGM; RGS

1938 M.38.R.37.2038.
I 6/1925. M 1937.
L (1)g,i,j; (2)e,j,n,q,t; (3)a,h,i,q,u.
S 4. O 1b,2b,3b,4b,5a. Flat.
BLb
*AR 1938/9. Specification changes: inland
water blue stipple; contours printed in the
same colour as 2nd class roads.*

  1941 Outline 8 **1000/11/41.L.R.**
Date erased from imprint.
BLf
AR 1941/2

5   SOLWAY FIRTH & RIVER ESK Sheet 89
Scotland
Surveyed 1849-64; 3rd revision 1921-2.

1925
I 3/1925. M 1st Jany 1925.
L (1)a,b,c; (2)c,k,l,m,o,p,u; (3)a,g,q,s.
S 2. O 1b,2c,3b,4c,5a.

C Red,2f,3(2/6)d,4b^2,5cd,6c.
CUL; BLa(1/4/26); BLb; KGM; RGS
*Supp. to Cat.1 Jul./30 Sept.1925; parish
boundaries are shown only in Scotland.*

  1925 Outline 5
BLd(1/4/26); BLe; Bod(16/3/40)
Supp. to Cat.1 Jul./30 Sept.1925.

1932 3000/32.
I 3/1925. (1)31d; (2)in England 29a; (5)32j.
M 1st Jany 1925.
L (1)a,b,c; (2)c,k,l,m,o,t; (3)a,e,g,q,s.
S (see note). O 1b,2d,3b,4c,5a.
C B&Rb,2f,3(4/-)g,4d,5cd,6c.
PC; BLb; Bod
*The roads revised note reads: 'Roads in
England revised to September 1929.' The
scale bar is similar to Scale 4, but the
kilometre figures are written above the scale.
No other example of this scale version has
been found. Parish boundaries are shown
only in Scotland.*

  1942 Outline 7 **1000/8/42 LR.** [in blue]
BLf

6   HEXHAM
Surveyed 1856-64; published 1866-7; revised
1895 and 1902-3; 3rd revision 1921.

1925
I 2/1925. M Jan.1925.
L (1)a,b,c; (2)c,n,s,u; (3)c,q,s.
S 2. O 1b,2c,3b,4b.
C Red,2c,3(2/6)a,4b^2,6b.
PC; BLa(30/10/26); BLb; Bod(24/12/26);
CUL(30/10/26); RGS(13/2/26)
Supp. to Cat.1 Jan./31 Mar.1926.

  1925 Outline 5
BLd(30/10/26); BLe; Bod(24/12/26)
Supp. to Cat.1 Jan./31 Mar.1926.

1932 3500/32.
I 2/1925; (1)30a; (5)32d; roads (5)9.29.
M Jan.1925.
L (1)a,b,c; (2)c,n,s,u; (3)c,q,s.
S 4. O 1b,2b,3b,4b.
C B&Rb,2f,3(2/6)g,4d,5bd,6c.
BLc; Bod; KGM; RGS

C cover: 271-81; I imprint: 259-62; L legend: 263-5; M magnetic variation; O other marginal data: 266-9;
S scale: 266; (k) left, between legend and map border; (l) left, below legend; location abbreviations: xii;
outline: 282; print codes: 84-7. *AR:* annual report; *Supp. to Cat.* see OS *Catalogues*: 394.

1938 **2538 M.37.R.37.**
I 6/1925. M 1st Jan.1937.
L (1)g,i,j; (2)e,n,q,t; (3)c,i,h,q,s.
S 4. O 1b,2b,3b,4b. Flat.
Bod
AR 1938/9. Specification changes: inland water blue stipple with dark blue casing; contours printed in the same colour as second class roads.

1941 Outline 7 **1000/11/41.L.R.**
Date deleted from imprint.
BLf

7 NEWCASTLE UPON TYNE
Surveyed 1854-63; published 1865-6; revised 1895-6 and 1902-3; 3rd revision 1922.

1925
I 2/1925. M Jan.1925.
L (1)a,b,c,g; (2)c,n,p,t; (3)c,q,u.
S 2. O 1b,2c,3b,4c,5a.
C Red,1b,[no price],5p,6a.
PC; BLa(30/10/26); BLb; Bod(24/12/26); CUL(30/10/26); RGS(13/2/26)
Supp. to Cat.1 Jan./31 Mar.1926.

1925 Outline 5
BLd(10/10/26); BLb; Bod(24/12/26)
Supp. to Cat.1 Oct./31 Dec.1926.

1929 **500/29.**
I 2/1925; (1)27a; (5)29d. M Jan.1925.
L (1)a,b,c,g; (2)c,n,p,t; (3)c,q,w.
S 2. O 1b,2b,3b,4c,5a.
C Red,2c,3(3/6)a,5bd,6c.
PC

[1930 **1000/30.** not seen; inferred from 1932]

1932 **500/29.1000/30.3500/32.**
I 2/1925;(1)29a; (5)32d; roads (5)8.29.
M Jan.1925.
L (1)a,b,c,g; (2)c,n,p,u; (3)c,q,u.
S 4. O 1b,2b,3b,4c,5a.
C B&Rb,2i,3(2/6)f,4c[1],5bd,6c.
PC; CUL; KGM; RGS

1935 **2035.**
I 6/1925. M Jan.1925.
L (1)g,i; (2)e,n,p,t; (3)c,i,q,u.
S 4. O 1b,2b,3b,4c,5a. Flat.
BLb

1936 **3036.M.36.R.29.**
I 6/1925. M Jan.1925.
L (1)g,i,j; (2)e,n,p,t; (3)c,i,q,u.
S 4. O 1b,2b,3b,4c,5a.
C B&Rb,2i,3(2/6)h,4d,5bd,6c.
PC

1941 Outline 8 (l)**1,000/11/41 L.R.**
Date erased from imprint. M Jan.1937.
PC
AR 1941/2.

1946 Outline 7 (k)**M.40.R.40** (l)**846/Cr.**
BLf

8 WORKINGTON & COCKERMOUTH
Surveyed 1859-64; published 1866-8; revised 1895 and 1903; 3rd revision 1920-1.

1925
I 2/1925. M Jan.1925.
L (1)a,b,c,i; (2)c,n,p,t; (3)c,q,u.
S 2. O 1b,2c,3b,4b,5a.
C Red,2f,3(3/6)a,5bdh,6a.
KGM; BLa(30/10/26); BLb; Bod(24/12/26); CUL(30/10/26); RGS(13/2/26)
Supp. to Cat.1 Jan./31 Mar.1926.

1925 Outline 5
BLd(30/10/26); BLb; Bod(24/12/26)
Supp. to Cat. 1 Jan./31 Mar.1926.

1932 **3000/32.**
I 2/1925; (1)31a; (4)32d; roads (10)7/31.
M Jan.1925.
L (1)a,b,c,g; (2)c,n,p,t; (3)c,q,u.
S 4. O 1c,2b,3b,4b,5a.
C BRed,1c,2f,3(1/9)d,5bdh,6j.
BLc; BLb; Bod; KGM

1941 Outline 8 (l)**1000/11/41 LR** M 1937.
PC *AR 1941/2.*

9 CARLISLE
Surveyed 1859-64; published 1867-8; revised 1895 and 1903; 3rd revision 1920-1.

1925
I 2/1925. M Jan.1925.
L (1)a; (2)c,n,p,t; (3)c,q,s.
S 2. O 1b,2c,3b,4b.
C Red,2b,3(1/6)b,4b[2],5bd,6c.
PC; BLa(1/4/26); BLb; Bod(13/4/26); CUL(16/4/26); RGS(20/8/25)
Supp. to Cat.1 Jul./30 Sep.1925.

<u>1925</u> Outline 5
BLd(1/4/26); BLe; Bod(13/4/26)
Supp. to Cat.1 Jul./30 Sep.1925.

1935 1035.
I 5/1925. M Jan.1925.
L (1)g,i; (2)e,n,p,t; (3)c,i,q,s.
S 4. O 1b,2b,3b,4b.
C B&Rb,2h,3(2/6)h,4d,5bd,6c.
BLc

1936 [1937?] 1536.M.36.R.31.
I 5/1925. M Jan.1937.
L (1)g,i,j; (2)e,n,p,t; (3)c,h,i,q,s.
S 4. O 1b,2b,3b,4b,5e.
C B&Rb(wr),2h,3(1/9)c,4e,5bd,6c.
BLc; BLb; Bod; KGM
AR 1936/7. Although the print code indicates that the sheet was printed in 1936, the magnetic variation date is 1937.

<u>1942</u> Outline 7 **1000/1/42 L.R.** [in blue]
BLf   *AR 1941/2.*

10 ALSTON & WEARDALE
Surveyed 1855-64; published 1864-7; revised 1895 and 1902-5; 3rd revision 1921-2.

1925
I 2/1925. M Jan.1925.
L (1)a,b,c; (2)c,n,s,t; (3)c,q,s.
S 2. O 1a,2c,3b,4c.
C Red,2f,3(2/6)d,4b^2,5bd,6a.
PC; BLa(30/10/26); BLb; Bod(24/12/26); CUL(30/10/26); RGS(16/3/26)
Supp. to Cat.1 Jan./31 Mar.1926.

<u>1925</u> Outline 5
BLd(30/10/26); BLe; Bod(24/12/26)
Supp. to Cat.1 Jan./31 Mar.1926.

1934 2,200/34.
I 4/1925; (1)33b; (2)31a; (5)34c.
M Jan.1925.
L (1)a,b,c; (2)e,n,s,t; (3)c,q,s.
S 4. O 1a,2b,3b,4c.
C B&Rb(wr),2h,3(1/9)c,4e,5bd,6c.
BLc; KGM

1938 2038.M37,R36.
I 6/1925. M 1937.
L (1)g,i,j; (2)e,n,s,t; (3)c,i,q,s.
S 4. O 1a,2b,3b,4c.

C B&Rb,2h,3(2/6)h,4d,5bd,6j.
PC; BLb
AR 1938/9.

<u>1941</u> Outline 8 (l)**1,000/11/41 L.R.**
BLf

11 DURHAM & SUNDERLAND
Surveyed 1854-60; published 1865; revised 1895-6 and 1902-3; 3rd revision 1922.

1925
I 2/1925. M Jan.1925.
L (1)a,b,c,g; (2)c,n,p,t; (3)c,q,u.
S 2. O 1b,2c,3b,4c,5b.
C Red,2f,3(1/9)b,4c^2,5bd,6c.
PC; BLa(30/10/26); BLb; Bod; CUL(30/10/26); RGS(16/3/26)
Supp. to Cat.1 Jan./31 Mar.1926.

<u>1925</u> Outline 5
BLd(20/10/26); BLe; Bod(24/12/26)
Supp. to Cat.1 Jan./31 Mar.1926.

1932 3000/32.
I 2/1925; (1)31a; (5)32d; roads (4)7-29.
M Jan.1925.
L (1)a,b,c,g; (2)c,n,p,t; (3)c,q,u.
S 4. O 1b,2b,3b,4c,5b.
C B&Rb,2f,3(2/6)g,4d,5bd,6c.
KGM

1937 537.
I 6/1925. M Jan.1925.
L (1)a,b,c,g; (2)c,n,p,t; (3)c,q,u.
S 4. O1b,2b,3b,4b,5b.
C B&Rb,2h,3(2/6)h,4d,5bd,6j.
PC

1938 2038.M.37.R.37.
I 9/1925. M Jan.1937.
L (1)g,i,j; (2)e,j,k,n,q,t; (3)a,i,q,u.
S 4. O 1b,2b,3b,4c,5c.
C B&Rb,2h,3(2/6)h,4d,5bd,6j.
KGM; BLb; Bod
AR 1937/8. Specification change: inland water blue stipple; contour colour is similar to 2nd class roads; parks in black stipple.

[**1938** or **1939** not seen]
AR 1938/9.

C cover: 271-81; I imprint: 259-62; L legend: 263-5; M magnetic variation; O other marginal data: 266-9; S scale: 266; (k) left, between legend and map border; (l) left, below legend; location abbreviations: xii; outline: 282; print codes: 84-7. *AR*: annual report; *Supp. to Cat.* see OS *Catalogues*: 394.

<u>1941</u> Outline 8 **1,000/11/41 L.R.**
'SOUTHAMPTON' erased from imprint.
BLf

AR 1941/2.

[<u>1944</u> or <u>1945</u> Outline; not seen]
AR 1944/5.

12 KESWICK & AMBLESIDE

Surveyed 1845-63; published 1864-6; revised
1895 and 1903; 3rd revision 1920-1.

<u>1925</u>

I 2/1925. M 1925.
L (1)a,b,c,g; (2)c,n,s,u; (3)c,q,s.
S 2. O 1b,2c,3b,4c.
C Red,2f,3(2/6)d,4b²,5bd,6b.
PC; BLa(28/8/26); BLb; Bod(2/9/26); CUL
(31/8/26); RGS(21/1/26)
Supp. to Cat.1 Oct./31 Dec.1925

<u>1925</u> Outline 5
BLd(28/8/26); BLe; Bod(2/9/26)
Supp. to Cat.1 Oct./31 Dec.1925.

<u>1929</u> **2500/29.**

I 2/1925; (4)29a. M Jan.1926.
L (1)a,b,c,g;(2)c,n,s,u; (3)c,o,s.
S 3. O 1b,2b,3b,4c.
C Red,1b,3(3/6)a,5o,6c.
RGS; BLc; KGM

<u>1934</u> **2,200/34.**

I 4/1925; (1)33b; (9)31a; (4)34c.
M Jan.1926.
L (1)a,b,c,g; (2)e,n,s,u; (3)c,i,o,s.
S 4. O 1b,2b,3b,4c.
C B&Rb,2h,3(2/6)h,4d,5bd,6c.
PC

<u>1936</u> **3036.M36.R31.**

I 6/1925. M Jan.1926.
L (1)g,i,j; (2)e,n,s,u; (3)c,i,o,s.
S 4. O 1b,2b,3b,4c,5d.
C B&Rb,2h,3(2/6)h,4d,5bd,6c.
BLc; KGM
AR 1936/7.

<u>1936</u> Outline 5 (l)**336.**
PC *AR 1936/7 'reprinted'.*

<u>1938</u> **M37.R37.3038.**

I 6/1925. M 1937.
L (1)g,i,j; (2)e,n,q,t; (3)a,h,i,q,s.
S 4. O 1b,2b,3b,4c,5d.

C BRed,1c,2f,3(2/6)i,5bd,6j.
PC; BLb
*AR 1938/9. Specification change: inland
water in blue stipple; contours are printed in
the same colour as 2nd class roads; parks in
black stipple.*

<u>1941</u> Outline 8 (l)**1,000/11/41 LR**
'SOUTHAMPTON' has been erased from
the imprint. BLf *AR 1941/2.*

13 KIRKBY STEPHEN & APPLEBY

Surveyed 1845-60; published 1864-5; revised
1895 and1903-4; 3rd revision 1920-1.

<u>1925</u>

I 2/1925. M Jan.1925.
L (1)a; (2)c,n,s,u; (3)c,q,s.
S 2. O 1a,2c,3b,4c.
C Red,2f,3(2/6)a,4b²,5bd,6b.
PC; BLa(1/4/26); BLb; Bod(13/4/26);
CUL(16/4/26); RGS(20/8/25)
Supp. to Cat.1 Jul./30 Sep.1925.

<u>1925</u> Outline 5
BLd(1/4/26); BLe; Bod(13/4/26)
Supp. to Cat.1 Jul./30 Sep.1925.

<u>1930</u> **3300/30.**

I 2/1925; (1)30a; (4)30d. M Jan.1925.
L (1)a; (2)c,n,s,u; (3)c,q,s.
S 4. O 1a,2b,3b,4c.
C B&Rb,2f,3(2/6)f,4c²,5bd,6c.
PC; BLc; CUL; KGM

<u>1937</u> **1537.M.35.R.31.**

I 6/1924[sic]. M Jan.1937.
L (1)g,i,j; (2)e,n,s,u; (3)c,i,q,s.
S 4. O 1a,2b,3b,4c.
C B&Rb,2h,3(1/9)c,4e,5bd,6c.
BLc; KGM
AR 1937/8.

<u>1939</u> **2039. M.38.R.38.**

I 6/1924. M 1939.
L (1)g,i,j; (2)e,j,l,o,q,t; (3)a,e,i,m,q,s.
S 4. O 1a,2b,3b.
C BRed,1b,2f,3(2/6)i,5bd,6j.
PC; BLb; KGM
*AR 1939/40. Specification changes: inland
water blue stipple; contours printed in the
same colour as 2nd class roads; parks in
black stipple.*

<u>1941</u> Outline **1,000/11/41 L.R.**
BLf *AR 1941/2.*

14 DARLINGTON

Surveyed 1853-7; published 1865; revised 1895-6 and 1904; 3rd revision 1921-2.

1925
I 2/1925. M Jan.1924.
L (1)a; (2)c,n,s,t; (3)c,q,s.
S 2. O 1b,2c,3b,4b.
C Red,2b,3(2/6)c,4b^2,5bd,6a.
KGM; BLa(29/10/25); BLb; Bod;
CUL(29/10/25); RGS(24/7/25)
Supp. to Cat.1 Apr./30 Jun.1925.

   1925 Outline 5
   BLd(29/10/25); BLe; Bod
   Supp. to Cat.1 Apr./30 Jun.1925.

1930 3,300/30.
I 2/1925; (1)30a; (4)30d. M Jan.1924.
L (1)a,b,g; (2)c,n,s,u; (3)c,q,s.
S 4. O 1b,2b,3b,4c.
C B&Rb,2g,3(2/6)g,4d,5bd,6c.
KGM; BLc; RGS

1935 1535
I 6/1925. M Jan.1924.
L (1)g,i; (2)c,n,s,u; (3)c,i,q,s.
S 4. O 1b,2b,3b,4c.
C B&Rb,2e,3(2/6)h,4d,5bd,6c.
PC; KGM

1938 2038 M.38 R.37
I 6/1925. M Jan.1937.
L (1)g,i,j; (2)e,j,n,q,t;(3)c,i,m,q,s.
S 4. O 1b,2b,3b,4c.
C B&Rb,2e,3(2/6)h,4d,5bd,6j.
CUL; BLb
AR 1938/9.

   1941 Outline 8 **1,000/11/41 L.R.**
   BLf   *AR 1941/2.*

15 MIDDLESBROUGH & HARTLEPOOL

Surveyed 1847-57; published 1865; revised 1895-6 and 1904; 3rd revision 1921-2.

1925
I 2/1925. M Jan.1924.
L (1)a; (2)c,n,p,t; (3)c,q,u.
S 2. O 1b,2c,3b,4c,5bc.
C Red,2f,3(2/6)a,4b^2,5bdh,6a.
RGS(21/1/26); BLa(28/8/26); BLb; Bod;
CUL(31/8/26)
Supp. to Cat.1 Oct./31 Dec.1925.

   1925 Outline 5
   BLd(30/10/26); BLe; Bod(24/12/26)
   Supp. to Cat.1 Jan./31 Mar.1926.

   [1930 Outline; not seen]
   Supp. to Cat.1 Oct./31 Dec.1930.

1931 3750/31.
I 2/1925; (1)31a; (5)31e; roads (8)5·29.
M Jan.1924.
L (1)a,b,g; (2)c,n,p,u; (3)c,q,u.
S 3. O 1b,2b,3b,4c,5bc.
C B&Ra,2f,3(2/6)g,4e,5bdh,6c.
PC; BLc

1938 2538.M37.R36.
I 9/1925. M Jan.1937.
L (1)g,i,j; (2)e,j,l,q,u; (3)c,h,i,m,q,u.
S 4. O 1b,2b,3b,4c,5bc.
C B&Rb,2h,3(2/6)h,4d,5bdh,6j.
PC; BLb; Bod
A/R 1938/9. Specification change: the sea is now in blue stipple; contours are very orange, but are not quite the same as 2nd class roads.

   1941 Outline 8 **1,000/11/41 L.R.**
   BLf
   AR 1941/2.

16 WHITBY & SALTBURN

Surveyed 1847-53; published 1859-65; revised 1895-6, 1904; 3rd revision 1921-2.

1925
I 2/1925. M Jan.1925.
L (1)a,g; (2)c,n,p,t; (3)c,q,u.
S 2. O 1b,2c,3b,4b,5b.
C Red,2f,3(3/6)a,5bd,6b.
PC; BLa(16/4/26); BLb; Bod(13/4/26);
CUL(16/4/26); RGS(21/9/25)
Supp. to Cat.1 Jul./30 Sep.1925.

   1925 Outline 5
   BLd(1/4/26); BLe; Bod(13/4/26)
   Supp. to Cat.1 Jul./30 Sep.1925.

1929 3000/29.
I 2/1925; (1)29a; (5)29d; roads (1)4·29.
M Jan.1925.
L (1)a,b,g; (2)c,n,p,t; (3)c,q,u.
S 3. O 1b,2b,3b,4b,5b.
C Red,2f,3(3/6)a,5bd,6c.
PC; BLc; KGM

C cover: 271-81; I imprint: 259-62; L legend: 263-5; M magnetic variation; O other marginal data: 266-9;
S scale: 266; (k) left, between legend and map border; (l) left, below legend; location abbreviations: xii;
outline: 282; print codes: 84-7; *AR*: annual report; *Supp. to Cat.* see OS *Catalogues*: 394.

1932 3000/29.3000/32.
I 2/1925; (1)31a; (5)32d; roads (1)4.29.
M Jan.1925.
L (1)a,b,g; (2)e,n,p,t; (3)c,q,u.
S 4. O 1b,2b,3b,4b,5b.
C B&Rb,2f,3(2/6)g,4d,5bd,6c.
PC; BLc; CUL; RGS

1935 3035
I 6/1925. M Jan.1935.
L (1)g,i; (2)e,n,p,u; (3)c,i,q,s.
S 4. O 1b,2b,3b,4b,5b.
C B&Rb(wr),2h,3(1/9)c,4e,5bd,6c.
PC; BLc; KGM

1937 3035.537.
I 6/1925. M Jan.1935.
L (1)g,i,j; (2)e,n,p,t; (3)c,i,q,u.
S 4. O 1b,2b,3b,4b,5c.
C B&Rb,2h,3(2/6)h,4d,5bd,6j.
PC

1938 3038.M.37.R.36.
I 6/1925. M Jan.1935.
L (1)g,i,j; (2)e,n,q,t; (3)c,h,i,q,s.
S 4. O 1b,2b,3b,4b,5c.
C B&Rb,2h,3(2/6)h,4d,5bd,6c.
Bod; BLb; KGM
AR 1937/8. Specification change: sea in blue
stipple.

1941 Outline 8 **1000/11/41.L.R.**
Date and 'SOUTHAMPTON' deleted from
imprint.
BLf   *AR 1941/2.*

17 ISLE OF MAN
Surveyed 1866-9; published 1873; revised
1896 and 1905; 3rd revision 1920.

1921
I 2/1921. M 1st Jany 1921.
L (1)a; (2)c,n,p,t; (3)c,o,w.
S 1. O 1c,2b,3a,4d,5a.
C P. 'PRICE 2/6 Mounted.', 6d.
PC; BLa(1/3/22); BLb; Bod; CUL(27/2/22);
RGS(15/4/21)
Supp. to Cat.1 Jan./31 Mar.1921. The
pictorial cover by Edward John Hoy is
illustrated in Browne (1991) p.51, and in
fig.76 in the Hellyer listings at the end of the
book. This was the only standard sheet to
carry a pictorial cover, and was the first to
show reinforced, or emphasised, contours at
intervals of 250ft. It was also the only sheet

with all contours surveyed on the ground, as
a result of a contouring exercise in 1919
(except for those fenland sheets where only
the 50ft and 100ft contours appeared).

1921 Outline 2 **ISLE OF MAN.**
BLd(17/6/22); BLe; Bod
Supp. to Cat.1 Oct./31 Dec.1921.

1924 6000/24. ISLE OF MAN
I 2/1921; (1)24a; (4)24d.
M 1st Jany 1921.
L (1)a; (2)c,n,p,t; (3)c,o,w.
S 1. O 1c,2c,3a,4d,5a.
C P, 'PRICE 1/6 Paper', 6d.
KGM

1927 6000/24.5000/27.
I 2/1921; (1)24a; (4)27d.
M 1st Jany 1921.
L (1)a; (2)c,n,p,t; (3)c,o,w.
S 1. O 1c,2b,3a,4d,5a.
C P,'PRICE 1/6 Paper',6e.
KGM; BLb; BLc; RGS

1931 6000/24.5000/27.5500/31.
I 2/1921; (1)31a; (4)31d.
M 1st Jany 1921.
L (1)a,b,g; (2)c,n,p,t; (3)c,n,w.
S 4. O 1b,2b,3b,5a. Library cover.
PC

1934 4000/34.
I 4/1921; (1)31a; (5)34b.
M 1st Jany 1921.
L (1)a,b,g; (2)e,n,p,t; (3)c,o,w.
S 4. O 1c,2b,3b,5a.
C P,'Price (mounted) 2/6',6j.
PC; KGM

1938 4038 M37.
I 9/1921. M 1st Jany 1938.
L (1)a,b,c,g,j; (2)e,n,q,t; (3)c,h,i,o,u.
S 4. O 1b,2c,3b,5a.
C P,'Price 2/6',6j.
PC; KGM
Specification change: both inland water and
sea in blue stipple; contours are printed in the
same colour as 2nd class roads.

1941 Outline 8 **1,000/11/41 L.R. ISLE**
OF MAN.   BLf

[1942 or 1943 Outline; not seen]
AR 1942/3.

18 WASDALE

Surveyed 1843-63; published 1865-6; revised 1895-6 and 1903-4; 3rd revision 1920-1.

1925

I 2/1925. M Jan.1925.

L (1)b,c; (2)c,n,p,t; (3)c,q,u.

S 2. O 1b,2c,3b,4c,5bc.

C Red,2c,3(2/6)a,4b^2,5bdh,6a.

CUL(31/8/26); BLa(28/8/26); BLb; Bod; RGS(26/1/26)

Supp. to Cat.1 Oct./31 Dec.1925.

   1925 Outline 5

   BLd(28/8/26); BLe

   Supp. to Cat.1 Oct./31 Dec.1925.

1935 1035.

I 9/1925. M Jan.1925.

L (1)g,i; (2)e,n,p,t; (3)c,i,q,u.

S 4. O 1b,2b,3b,4b,5bc.

C B&Rb,2e,3(2/6)h,4d,5bdh,6c.

PC

1938 538.

I 6/1925. M Jan. 1925.

L (1)g,i,j; (2)e,n,p,t; (3)c,i,q,u.

S 4. O 1b,2b,3b,4c,5bc.

C B&Rb,2e,3(2/6h),4d,5bdh,6j.

PC

AR 1937/8.

1939 2039 M.38.R.37.

I 9/1925. M Jan.1937.

L (1)g,i,j; (2)e,j,n,q,t; (3)c,i,q,u.

S 4. O 1b,2b,3b,4c,5bcd. Flat.

BLb; Bod

AR 1939/40.

   1941 Outline 8 **1000/11/41 L.R.**

   BLf   *AR 1941/2.*

19 WINDERMERE & ULVERSTON

Surveyed 1843-61; published 1865; revised 1895-6 and 1903-4; 3rd revision 1920-1.

1925

I 2/1925. M Jan.1925.

L (1)a,b,c; (2)c,n,p,t; (3)c,q,u.

S 2. O 1b,2c,3b,4c,5bc.

C Red,2f,3(2/6)d,4b^2,5bd,6c.

KGM; BLa(28/8/26); BLb; Bod(2/9/26); CUL(31/8/26); RGS(21/1/26)

Supp. to Cat.1 Oct./31 Dec.1925.

1925 Outline 5

BLd(28/8/26); BLe; Bod(2/9/26)

Supp. to Cat.1 Oct./31 Dec.1925.

1928 2500/28.

I 2/1925; (1)27a; (4)28b.

M Jan.1925.

L (1)a,b,c; (2)c,n,p,t; (3)c,q,u.

S 2. O 1b,2b,3b,4c,5bc.

C B&Rb,2f,3(2/6)f,4c^2,6bd,6c.

PC; BLc; KGM

1934 2,250/34.

I 4/1925; (2)32a; (5)34c; (6)33b.

M Jan.1925.

L (1)a,b,c; (2)e,n,p,t; (3)c,q,u.

S 4. O 1b,2b,3b,4c,5bc.

C B&Rb,2f,3(2/6)g,4d,5bd,6f.

PC; BL; KGM

1936 3036

I 9/1933. M Jan.1925.

L (1)g,i,j; (2)e,n,p,t; (3)c,i,q,u.

S 4. O 1b,2b,3b,4c,5bcd.

C B&Rb,2h,3(2/6)h,4d,5bd,6c.

PC; BLc; KGM

AR 1936/7.

   1941 Outline 7 **1000/12/41 L.R.** [in blue]

   I 5/1925. M 1937.   BLf

   [1944 or 1945 Outline; not seen]

   AR 1944/5.

20 KIRKBY LONSDALE & HAWES

Surveyed 1843-58; published 1865; revised 1895-6 and 1903-4; 3rd revision 1920.

1925

I 2/1925. M Jan.1924.

L (1)a; (2)c,n,s,u; (3)c,q,s.

S 2. O 1a,2c,3b,4c.

C Red,2f,3(2/6)d,4b^2,5bd,6c.

PC; BLa(29/10/25); BLb; Bod; CUL(29/10/25); RGS(18/6/25)

Supp. to Cat.1 Apr./30 Jun.1925.

1925 Outline 5

BLd(29/10/25); BLb; Bod

Supp. to Cat.1 Apr./30 Jun.1925.

1929 4000/29.

I 2/1928 [sic]; (1)27a; (4)29d; roads (1)9-28.

M Jan.1929.

C cover: 271-81; I imprint: 259-62; L legend: 263-5; M magnetic variation; O other marginal data: 266-9; S scale: 266; (k) left, between legend and map border; (l) left, below legend; location abbreviations: xii; outline: 282; print codes: 84-7; *AR*: annual report; *Supp. to Cat.* see OS *Catalogues*: 394.

290

L (1)a,b,c,g; (2)c,n,s,u; (3)c,o,s.
S 3. **O** 1a,2b,3b,4c.
C Red,2f,3(2/6)d,4b²,5bd,6c.
KGM; BLc; RGS

1933 3,000/33.
I 4/1928; (5)33c; (7)32a.
M Jan.1929.
L (1)h,g; (2)e,n,s,t; (3)c,o,s.
S 4. **O** 1a,2b,3b,4c.
C B&Rb,2f,3(2/6)g,4d,5bd,6c.
PC; BLc; KGM

1935 1535
I 5(reprints)/1928. **M** Jan.1929.
L (1)g,i; (2)e,n,s,t; (3)c,i,o,s.
S 4. **O** 1a,2b,3b,4c.
C B&Rb,2f,3(4/-)g,5bd,6c.
PC; KGM

1936 1535.2536.
I 5/1928. **M** Jan.1929.
L (1)g,i,j; (2)e,n,s,u; (3)c,i,o,s.
S 4. **O** 1a,2b,3b,4c.
C B&Rb,2h,3(2/6)h,4d,5bd,6c.
PC; BLc; KGM
AR 1936/7.

1938a 1535.2536.838.
I 5/1928. **M** Jan.1929.
L (1)g,i,j; (2)e,n,s,t; (3)c,i,o,s.
S 4. **O** 1a,2b,3b,4c.
C B&Rb,2h,3(2/6)h,4d,5bd,6j.
PC; KGM
AR 1937/8.

1938b 2538.M.38.R.37.
I 5/1928. **M** 1937.
L (1)g,i,j; (2)e,j,l,n,q,t; (3)c,e,i,m,q,s.
S 4. **O** 1a,2b,3b,4c. Flat.
PC; BLb
*AR 1938/9. Specification change: inland
water in blue stipple; contours resemble 2nd
class roads in colour.*

1940 1040.
I 5/1928. **M** Jan.1929.
L (1)g,i,j; (2)e,[no j],n,s,t; (3)c,i,o,s.
S 4. **O** 1a,2b,3b,4c.
C Red,1c,2g,3(4/-)i,5bd,6j.
PC

1941 Outline 8 **1000/11/41 L.R.**
OSG
AR 1941/2.

1942 Outline **1000/12/42 LR**
PC
AR 1942/3.

21 RIPON & NORTHALLERTON
Surveyed 1847-55; published 1865; revised
1895-6 and 1904; 3rd revision 1920-1.

1925
I 2/1925. **M** Jan.1925.
L (1)a,b,c; (2)c,n,s,u; (3)c,q,s.
S 2. **O** 1a,2c,3b,4b.
C Red,2f,3(2/6)a,4b²,5bd,6a.
PC; BLa(1/4/26); BLb; Bod(13/4/26);
CUL(16/4/26); RGS(20/8/25);
Supp. to Cat.1 Jul./30 Sep.1925.

1925 Outline 5
BLd(1/4/26); BLe; Bod(13/4/26)
Supp.to Cat.1 Jul./31 Dec.1925.

1929 3000/29.
I 2/1925; (1)27-9a; (4)29b; roads (4)3/27.
M Jan.1925.
L (1)a,b,c; (2)c,n,s,u; (3)c,q,s.
S 2. **O** 1a,2b,3b,4b.
C B&Rb,2f,3(2/6)f,4c¹,5bd,6c.
PC; BLc; KGM

1935 1535.
I 5/1925. **M** Jan.1925.
L (1)g,i; (2)c,n,s,t; (3)c,i,q,s.
S 4. **O** 1a,2b,3b,4b.
C B&Rb,2h,3(2/6)h,4d,5bd,6c.
PC; BLc; KGM; RGS

1936 25/36.M36.R33.
I 5/1925. **M** Jan.1925.
L (1)g,i,j; (2)e,n,s,u; (3)c,i,q,s.
S 4. **O** 1a,2b,3b,4b.
C B&Rb,2h,3(4/-)h,5bd,6c.
PC; KGM
AR 1936/7.

1941 Outline **1000/12/41 LR**
PC *AR 1941/2.*

1946 Outline 7 **2040.M.39.R.39. 846Cr.**
BLf

22 PICKERING & THIRSK
Surveyed 1847-55; published 1865; revised
1895-6 and 1904; 3rd revision 1921.

1925
I 2/1925. **M** Jan.1924.
L (1)1a; (2)c,n,s,t; (3)c,q,s.

S 2. O 1b,2c,3b,4b.
C Red,2f,3(2/6)a,4b²,5bd,6a.
PC; BLa(29/10/25); BLb; Bod;
CUL(29/10/25); RGS(16/5/25)
Supp. to Cat.1 Apr./30 Jun.1925. GSGS
accession stamp 15 MAY 1925 on PC copy.

1925 Outline 5
BLd(29/10/25); BLe; Bod
Supp. to Cat.1 Apr./30 Jun.1925.

1930 3800/30.
I 1/1924 [sic]; (1)30a; (5)30d; roads (5)3·27.
M Jan.1924.
L (1)a,b,c; (2)c,n,s,u; (3)c,q,s.
S 4. O 1b,2b,3b,4b.
C B&Rb,2f,3(2/6)g,4d,5bd,6c.
PC; BLc; KGM
The words 'main', 'other roads' and 'bad'
which describe the roads under 14' wide in
the legend, are faintly written in all examples
seen.

1934 3,000/34.
I 4/1924; (1)33b; (2)32a; (5)34c.
M Jan.1924.
L (1)a,b,c; (2)e,n,s,u; (3)c,q,s.
S 4. O 1b,2b,3b,4b.
C B&Rb,2h,3(2/6)j,4d,5bd,6b.
PC; BLc; KGM

1937 737.M.37.R.36.
I 5/1924. M Jan.1937.
L (1)g,i,j; (2)e,j,n,s,u; (3)c,i,q,s.
S 4. O 1b,2b,3b,4b.
C B&Rb,2h,3(2/6)h,4d,5bd,6j.
PC; RGS
AR 1937/8. Specification change: contours are
printed in the same colour as 2nd class roads.

1939 3039.M.39.R38.
I 6/1924. M Jan.1937.
L (1)g,i,j; (2)e,j,l,n,q,u; (3)a,e,i,m,q,s.
S 4. O 1b,2b,3b.
C BaRed,1c,2f,3(2/6)i,5bd,6j.
PC; BLc; Bod
AR 1938/9. Specification change: inland water
in blue stipple; contours as for 1937; parks in
black stipple.

[1939 or 1940]
AR 1939/40. If this sheet were reprinted in

1939 [other than the 1939 printing above], the
stocks may have been destroyed in the
bombing of OS in November 1939.

1942 Outline 7 **1000/1/42 L.R.** [in blue]
BLf
AR 1941/2.

23 SCARBOROUGH
Surveyed 1847-50; published 1857; revised
1895-6 and 1904-5; 3rd revision 1920-1.

1925
I 2/1925. M Jan.1924.
L (1)a; (2)c,n,p,t; (3)c,q,u.
S 2. O 1b,2c,3b,4b,5a.
C Red,2c,3(2/6)a,4b²,5bd,6a.
PC; BLa(11/9/25); BLb; Bod(27/10/25);
CUL(9/9/25); RGS(17/4/25)
Supp. to Cat.1 Jan./31 Mar.1925.

1925 Outline 5
BLd(11/9/25); BLe; Bod(27/10/25)
Supp. to Cat.1 Jan./31 Mar.1925.

1932 3000/32.
I 2/1925; (1)31a; (5)32d; roads (5)3.29.
M Jan.1924.
L (1)a,b,g; (2)c,n,p,t; (3)c,q,u.
S 4. O 1b,2b,3b,4b,5a.
C B&Rb,2a,3(2/6)f,4c²,5bd,6c.
PC; KGM

1935 2035.
I 5/1925. M Jan.1924.
L (1)a,b,g; (2)e,n,p,t; (3)c,i,q,u.
S 4. O 1b,2b,3b,4b,5a.
C B&Rb,2e,3(2/6)h,4d,5bd,6c.
PC; KGM

1936 2035.3036.M.36.R.29.
I 5/1925. M Jan.1937.
L (1)g,i,j; (2)e,n,p,t; (3)c,h,i,q,s.
S 4. O 1b,2b,3b,4b,5a.
C B&Rb,2e,3(4/-)h,5bd,6j.
PC; BLc; KGM
AR 1936/7.

1942 Outline 7 **1000/1/42 L.R.** [in blue]
BLf
AR 1941/2.

C cover: 271-81; I imprint: 259-62; L legend: 263-5; M magnetic variation; O other marginal data: 266-9;
S scale: 266: (k) left, between legend and map border; (l) left, below legend; Location abbreviations: xii;
outline: 282; print codes: 84-7; *AR*: annual report; *Supp. to Cat.* see OS *Catalogues*: 394.

24 LANCASTER & BARROW

Surveyed 1842-8; published 1847-52; revised 1896 and 1903-12; 3rd revision 1920-1.

1924

I 2/1924; (1)24a. M 1923.
L (1)a; (2)c,n,p,t; (3)c,o,u.
S 2. O 1b,2c,3b,4b,5bc.
C Red,2f,3(2/6)d,4b^2,6g.
BLb(GSGS 21/10/24); BLa(15/12/24); BLc;
Bod(16/1/25); CUL(2/12/24); RGS(21/10/24)
Supp. to Cat.1 Jul./30 Sep.1924.

  1924 Outline 4
BLd(15/12/24); BLe; Bod
Supp. to Cat.1 Jul./30 Sep.1924.

1930 3030/30.

I 2/1924; (1)30a; (4)30d; roads (1)3.27.
M 1923.
L (1)a,b,g; (2)c,n,p,t; (3)c,o,u.
S 4. O 1b,2b,3b,4b,5bc. Library cover.
PC

  [1930 Outline; not seen]
Supp. to Cat.1 Oct./31 Dec.1930.

1935 1535

I 6/1925. M 1923.
L (1)g,i; (2)e,n,p,t; (3)c,i,o,u.
S 4. O 1b,2b,3b,4b,5bc.
C B&Rb,2h,3(2/6)h,4d,5bd,6f.
PC; KGM

  1942 Outline 7 **1000/8/42 L.R.** [in blue]
No imprint. M 1939.
BLf

25 RIBBLESDALE

Surveyed 1842-9; published 1852-8; revised 1896 and 1910-2; 3rd revision 1920.

1924

I 2 1924; (1)24a. M Jan.1924.
L (1)a; (2)c,n,s,t; (3)c,o,s.
S 2. O 1a,2c,3b,4c.
C Red,2c,3(3/6)c,5bd,6d.
PC; BLa(15/12/24); BLb; BLc(GSGS
21/10/24); Bod; CUL(2/12/24);
RGS(12/11/28)
Supp. to Cat.1 Jul./30 Sep.1924.

  1924 Outline 4
BLd(7/8/25); BLe; Bod;
Supp. to Cat.1 Oct./31 Dec.1924.

1928 3500/28.

I 2/1924; (1)27a; (4)28d; roads (1)4.27.

M Jan.1924.
L (1)a,g; (2)c,n,s,u; (3)c,o,s.
S 3. O 1a,2b,3b,4c.
C B&Rb,2g,3(2/6)f,4c^2,5bd,6f.
PC; BLc; KGM

1932 3500/28.3500/32.

I 2/1924; (1)30a; (4)32d; roads (1)4.27.
M Jan.1924.
L (1)a,b,c,g; (2)c,n,s,t; (3)c,o,s.
S 4. O 1a,2b,3b,4c.
C B&Rb,2g,3(2/6)g,4d,5bd,6f.
PC; BLc; KGM; RGS

1934 3,500/34.

I 4/1924; (1)33b; (2)33a; (5)34c.
M Jan.1924.
L (1)a,b,c,g; (2)e,n,s,u; (3)c,i,o,s.
S 4. O 1a,2b,3b,4c.
C B&Rb,2e,3(2/6)h,4d,5bd,6f.
PC; BLc; KGM

1937 3037.M37.R36.

I 6/1924. M Jan.1924.
L (1)g,i,j; (2)e,n,s,u; (3)c,i,o,s.
S 4. O 1a,2b,3b,4c.
C B&Rb,2e,3(2/6)h,4d,5bd,6j.
PC; KGM
AR 1937/8.

[**1940a** 3040.M.39.R.38. not seen, inferred
from 1940b; this was mentioned in *Sheetlines*
32:57, but does not now appear to be in the
KGM collection.]

1940b 3040.M.39.R.38. 3,500/40.

I 6/1924. M Jan.1939.
L (1)g,i,j; (2)e,j,l,n,s,t; (3)a,e,i,m,q,s.
S 4. O 1a,2b,3b.
C BRed,1c,2g,3(2/6)i,5bd,6j.
PC; KGM
*Specification change: parks stippled black.
Some printings of this sheet have fainter reds
and more yellowish contours, although not
quite the same as 2nd class roads.*

  1941 Outline **1000/11/41 LR**
OSG   *AR 1941/2.*

26 HARROGATE

Surveyed 1843-52; published 1858-9; revised 1896 and 1910-11; 3rd revision 1920-1.

1925

I 2/1925. M Jan.1924.
L (1)a; (2)c,n,s,u; (3)c,q,s.

S 2. **O** 1a,2c,3b,4b.
C Red,2b,3(2/6)d,4b²,5bd,6d.
KGM; BLa(11/9/25); BLb; Bod(27/10/25);
CUL(9/9/25); PC(GSGS 16/3/25);
RGS(13/3/25)
Supp. to *Cat.1 Jan./31 Mar.1925.*

1925 Outline 5
BLd(11/9/25); BLe; Bod(27/10/25)
Supp. to *Cat.1 Jan./31 Mar.1925.*

1927 3000/27.
I 2/1924 [sic]; (4)27a; roads (5)4/27.
M Jan.1924.
L (1)a,g; (2)c,n,s,u; (3)c,q,s.
S 2. **O** 1a,2b,3b,4b.
C Red,2f,3(2/6)d,4b²,5bd,6f.
PC; BLb
Supp. to *Cat.1 Oct./31 Dec.1927 'With
special Road Revision.'*

[1929 3000/29 not seen; inferred from 1931]

[1930 500/30 not seen; inferred from 1931]

1931 3000/27.3000/29.500/30.4500/31.
I 2/1924; (1)30d; (4)31a; roads (5)4/30.
M Jan.1924.
L (1)a,b,g; (2)c,n,s,u; (3)c,q,s.
S 4. **O** 1a,2b,3b,4b.
C B&Ra,2g,3(4/-)b,5bd,6f.
PC; BLc; KGM; RGS

1935 2035.
I 5/1924. **M** Jan.1924.
L (1)g,i; (2)e,n,s,u; (3)c,i,q,s.
S 4. **O** 1a,2b,3b,4b.
C B&Rb,2e,3(2/6)h,4d,5bd,6f.
PC; KGM; RGS

1936 3036.M36.R33.
I 5/1924. **M** Jan.1924.
L (1)g,i,j; (2)c,n,s,u; (3)c,i,q,s.
S 4. **O** 1a,2b,3b,4b.
C B&Rb,2e,3(2/6)h,4d,5bd,6f.
PC; BLc
AR 1936/7.

1939 3039.M.38.R.38.
I 6/1924. **M** 1939.
L (1)g,i,j; (2)e,j,l,o,q,u; (3)a,e,i,q,s.
S 4. **O** 1a,2b,3b.
C BRed,1c,2g,3(2/6)i,5bd,6j.

PC; BLc; KGM
*AR 1938/9. Specification change: inland water
in blue stipple; contours in same colour as
2nd class roads; parks in black stipple.*

[1939 or **1940** *A/R 1939/40. If this does not
refer to the above entry, stocks of this reprint
may have been destroyed in the bombing of
OS in November 1940.*]

1942 Outline 7 **1000/1/42 L.R.** [in blue]
PC   *AR 1941/2.*

1942 Outline **1000/10/42 LR**
PC   *AR 1942/3.*

27 YORK
Surveyed 1843-52; published 1858-9; revised
1893-6 and 1904-11; 3rd revision 1920-1.
1924
I 2/1924. **M** Jan.1924.
L (1)a; (2)c,n,s,u; (3)c,o,s.
S 2. **O** 1a,2c,3b,4b.
C Red,2f,3(2/6)c,4b²,5bd,6d.
PC; BLa(15/12/24); BLb; Bod;
CUL(2/12/24); PC(GSGS 29/10/24); RGS
*Supp.to Cat.1 Jul./30 Sep.1924. The station
at Easingwold, squares A4-5, and at North
Grimston, A14, have inadvertently been left
uncoloured.*

1924 Outline 4
BLd(15/12/24); BLe; Bod(16/1/25)
Supp. to *Cat.1 Jul./30 Sep.1924.*

1929 3000/29.
I 2/1924; (1)27-9b; (3)26a; (4)29d;
roads(4)4/27. **M** Jan.1924.
L (1)a,g; (2)c,n,s,u; (3)c,o,s.
S 3. **O** 1a,2b,3b,4b.
C B&Rb,2h,3(2/6)h,4d,5bd,6f.
PC; BLc; KGM

1935 2035.
I 6/1924. **M** Jan.1935.
L (1)g,i; (2)e,n,s,u; (3)c,i,o,s.
S 4. **O** 1a,2b,3b,4b.
C B&Rb,2h,3(2/6)h,4d,5bd,6j.
KGM; RGS

1938 638.
I 6/1924. **M** Jan.1935.
L (1)g,i; (2)e,n,s,u; (3)c,i,o,s.

C cover: 271-81; **I** imprint: 259-62; **L** legend: 263-5; **M** magnetic variation; **O** other marginal data: 266-9;
S scale: 266: (k) left, between legend and map border; (l) left, below legend; Location abbreviations: xii;
outline: 282; print codes: 84-7; *AR*: annual report; *Supp. to Cat.* see OS *Catalogues*: 394.

294

S 4. **O** 1a,2b,3b,4b.
C B&Rb,2h,3(2/6)h,4d,5bd,6j.
PC
AR 1938/9.

1939 2539.M.37.R.37.
I 6/1924. **M** 1ˢᵗ Jan.1937.
L (1)g,i,j; (2)e,j,n,q,u; (3)a,h,i,q,s.
S 4. **O** 1a,2b,3b,4b.
C BRed,1c,2f,3(2/6)i,5bd,6j.
BLc
AR 1939/40. Specification change: inland water in blue stipple; parks in black stipple.

  1941 Outline 7 [in blue:] **1000/12/41.L.R.**
  [in black:] **M.37.R.37.**
  BLf
  AR 1941/2.

  [1942 or 1943 Outline; not seen]
  AR 1942/3.

28 GREAT DRIFFIELD & BRIDLINGTON
Surveyed 1848-52; published 1857-9; revised 1893-6 and 1904-5; 3rd revision 1920.

1924
I 2/1924. (1)24a. **M** 1924.
L (1)a; (2)c,n,p,u; (3)c,o,u.
S 2. **O** 1b,2c,3b,4b,5a.
C Red,2f,3(2/6)d,4b²,5bd,6e.
KGM; BLa(15/12/24); BLb; Bod;
CUL(2/12/24); RGS(12/11/28)
Supp. to Cat.1 Jul./30 Sep.1924.

  1924 Outline 4
  BLd(15/12/24); BLe; Bod(16/1/25)
  Supp. to Cat.1 Jul./30 Sep.1924.

1930 2500/30.
I 2/1924; (1)29a; (4)30d; roads (4)3·29.
M 1924.
L (1)a,b; (2)c,n,p,t; (3)c,o,u.
S 3. **O** 1b,2b,3b,4b,5a.
C B&Rb,2f,3(2/6)g,4d,5bd,6f.
PC

1931 2500/30.3000/31.
I 2/1924; (1)30a; (4)31d; roads (4)3·29.
M 1924.
L (1)a,b; (2)c,n,p,t; (3)c,o,u.
S 4. **O** 1b,2b,3b,4b,5a.
C B&Rb,2h,3(2/6)h,4d,5bd,6f.
KGM; BLc; Bod

1939 3039.M.38.R.37.
I 6/1924. **M** 1938.
L (1)g,i,j; (2)e,j,l,n,q,t; (3)c,e,i,q,u.
S 4. **O** 1b,2b,3b,5a.
C BRed,1c,2f,3(1/9)d,5bd,6j.
BLc; RGS
AR 1939/40.

  1941 Outline 8 **1000/11/41.L.R.**
  BLf   *AR 1941/2.*

29 PRESTON, SOUTHPORT & BLACKPOOL
Surveyed 1842-93; published 1847-96; revised 1894-6 and 1911-12; 3rd revision 1920.

1924
I 2/1924. **M** 1923.
L (1)a; (2)c,n,p,t; (3)c,o,u.
S 2. **O** 1b,2c,3b,4b,5bc.
C Red,2c,3(2/6)c,4b²,5bd,6d.
PC; BLa(28/5/24); BLb; Bod(9/10/24);
CUL(4/6/24); RGS(20/5/24)
Supp. to Cat.1 Jan./31 Mar.1924.

  1924 Outline 4
  BLd(16/9/24); BLe; Bod(9/10/24)
  Supp. to Cat.1 Apr./30 Jun.1924.

1928 3500/28.
I 2/1923[sic]; (1)24-7a; (4)28d; roads (5)3/27.
M 1923.
L (1)a,g; (2)c,n,p,t; (3)c,o,u.
S 2. **O** 1b,2b,3b,4b,5bc.
C B&Rb,2f,3(3/6)d,5bd,6f.
PC; KGM; RGS

1930 3500/28.2250/30.
I 2/1923; (1)30a; 4(30)d; roads (5)3/27.
M 1923.
L (1)a,b,g; (2)c,n,p,t; (3)c,o,u.
S 2. **O** 1b,2b,4b,4b,5bc.
C B&Rb,2f,3(2/6)h,4d,5bd,[lacks back cover].
PC

  [1930 Outline; not seen]
  Supp. to Cat.1 Oct./31 Dec.1930.

  1931 Outline **3500/28.2250/30.500/31**
  SG

1938 638.
I 5/1923. Roads (5)3/27.
M 1923
L (1)a,b,g; (2)c,n,p,t; (3)c,n,u.

S 4. **O** 1b,2b,3b,4b,5b.
C B&Rb,2f,3(2/6)h,4d,5bd,6j.
KGM
AR 1938/9.

1939 3039. M.37.R.37.
I 6/1924. **M** 1937.
L (1)g,i,j; (2)e,n,q,t; (3)a,h,i,q,u.
S 4. **O** 1b,2b,3b,4b,5bc.
C B&Rb,2f,3(2/6)h,4d,5bd,6j.
PC; BLc
AR 1939/40. Specification change: inland water and sea in blue stipple; contours: similar colour to 2nd class roads; parks in black stipple.

1941 Outline 8 **1,000/11/41 L.R.**
BLf
AR 1941/2.

30 BLACKBURN
Surveyed 1842-93; published 1852-96; revised 1894-6 and 1911-2; 3rd revision 1920.

1924
I 2/1924. **M** Jan.1924.
L (1)a,b,c; (2)c,n,s,u; (3)c,o,s.
S 2. **O** 1a,2c,3b,4c.
C Red,2f,3(2/6)c,4b²,5bd,6d.
PC; BLa(7/8/25); BLb; Bod; CUL(22/7/25); PC(GSGS 21/25); RGS(29/7/27)
Supp. to Cat.1 Oct./31 Dec.1924.

1924 Outline 5
BLd(7/8/25); BLe; Bod
Supp. to Cat.1 Oct./31 Dec.1924.

1929 6000/29.
I 2/1924; (1)29a; (4)29d; roads (5)3/27.
M Jan.1928.
L (1)a,b,c,g; (2)c,n,r,t; (3)c,q,s.
S 3. **O** 1a,2b,3b,4c.
C B&Rb,2g,3(2/6)g,4d,5bd,6f.
PC; BLc; KGM

1933 5,000/33.
I 4/1924; (5)33c; (7)33a.
M Jan.1928.
L (1)h,g; (2)e,n,r,u; (3)c,q,s.
S 4. **O** 1a,2b,3b,4c.
C B&Rb,2g,3(2/6)g,4d,5bd,6f.
PC; RGS

1938 3038.M.37.R.37.
I 9/1924. **M** Jan.1928.
L (1)g,i,j; (2)e,j,n,q,u; (3)a,h,i,o,s.
S 4. **O** 1a,2b,3b,4c. Flat.
BLb
AR 1938/9.

1941 Outline **1000/11/41 LR**
OSG
AR 1941/2.

1942 Outline 7 **1,000/10/42 L.R.** [in blue]
BLf
AR 1942/3.

31 LEEDS & BRADFORD
Surveyed 1843-93; published 1858-96; revised 1894-6 and 1908-10; 3rd revision 1920-1.

1925
I 2/1925. **M** Jan.1924.
L (1)a; (2)c,n,s,u; (3)c,q,s.
S 2. **O** 1a,2c,3b,4b.
C Red,2f,3(2/6)c,4b²,5bd,6d.
PC; BLa(11/9/25); BLb; Bod; CUL(9/9/25); RGS(13/3/25)
Supp. to Cat.1 Jan./31 Mar.1925.

1925 Outline 5
BLd(11/9/25); BLe; Bod(27/10/25)
Supp. to Cat.1 Jan./31 Mar.1925.

1929a 500/29 not seen; inferred from 1929c]

1929 Outline **500/29**   PC

1929b 500/29.3000/29.
I 2/1924; (1)27-9a; (4)30d; roads (2)3.27.
M Jan.1924.
L (1)a,g; (2)c,n,s,u; (3)c,q,s.
S 3. **O** 1a,2b,3b,4b. Flat.
MCL

[**1930** not seen; unspecified straight line overprint. *See* Hellyer (1999, p.30, para.9.)

1932 500/29.3000/29.3500/32.
I 2/1925. (1)31a; (4)32d; roads (5)3·27.
M Jan.1924.
L (1)a,b,g; (2)c,n,s,u; (3)c,q,s.
S 4. **O** 1a,2b,3b,4b.
C B&Rb,2f,3(2/6)g,4d,5bd,6f.
KGM; RGS

C cover: 271-81; I imprint: 259-62; L legend: 263-5; M magnetic variation; O other marginal data: 266-9; S scale: 266: (k) left, between legend and map border; (l) left, below legend; Location abbreviations: xii; outline: 282; print codes: 84-7; *AR*: annual report; *Supp. to Cat.* see OS *Catalogues*: 394.

296

1935 2035.
I 6/1925. M 1ˢᵗ Jan.1935.
L (1)g,i; (2)e,n,s,u; (3)c,h,i,q,s.
S 4. O 1a,2b,3b,4b.
C B&Rb,2i,3(2/6)h,4d,5bd,6f.
BLc

1936 3036.M36.R33.
I 6/1925. M 1ˢᵗ Jan.1935.
L (1)g,i,j; (2)e,n,s,u; (3)c,h,i,q,s.
S 4. O 1a,2b,3b,4b.
C B&Rb,2i,3(2/6)h,4d,5bd,6f.
BLc
AR 1936/7.

  1938 Outline 5 **538.**
  PC   *AR 1938/9.*

  [1942 or 1943 Outline; not seen]
  AR 1942/3.

  1943 Outline **600/8/43 Wa**
  PC
  AR 1943/4.

  [1944 or 1945 Outline; not seen]
  AR 1944/5.

  1946 Outline 7 **446**
  BLf

32 GOOLE & PONTEFRACT
Surveyed 1843-92; published 1858-96; revised
1893-6 and 1903-10; 3rd revision 1920.
1924
I 2/1924. (1)24a.
M 1924.
L (1)a; (2)c,n,p,t; (3)c,o,s.
S 2. O 1a,2c,3b,4b.
C Red,2f,3(2/6)c,4b²,5bd,6d.
PC; BLa(15/12/24); BLb; BLc(GSGS
15/9/24); Bod; CUL(2/12/24); RGS(3/9/24)
*Supp. to Cat.1 Jul./30 Sep.1924. The railway
station symbol at square D14 (near Ashtree
House) appears to have been left unfilled in
error; it was not filled in red until the 1938
printing.*

  1924 Outline 4
  BLd(15/12/24); BLe; Bod(16/1/24)
  Supp. to Cat.1 Jul./30 Sep.1924.

1934 2,000/34.
I 4/1924; (1)33b; (2)32a; (5)34c. M 1924.
L (1)a,b,g; (2)e,n,p,t; (3)c,o,s.
S 4. O 1a,2b,3b,4b.

C B&Rb,2h,3(2/6)h,4d,5bd,6f.
PC; BLc; RGS

  [1936 or 1937 Outline; not seen]
  AR 1936/7.

1938 2038.M37.R37.
I 9/1924. M 1ˢᵗ Jan.1937.
L (1)g,i,j; (2)e,j,n,q,t; (3)c,i,q,s.
S 4. O 1a,2b,3b,4b.
C B&Rb,2h,3(2/6)h,4d,6bd,6j.
PC
AR 1938/9.

  1941 Outline **1000/11/41 LR**
  PC   *AR 1941/2.*

  1946 Outline 7 (k)**M.40.R.40.** (l)**846/Cr**
  BLf

33 HULL
Surveyed   1850-90;   published   1857-90;
revised 1893-4 and 1905; 3rd rev. 1920-1.

1924
I 2/1924. (1)24a.
M 1923.
L (1)a; (2)c,n,p,u; (3)c,o,w.
S 2. O 1b,2c,3b,4c,5bc.
C Red,2f,3(2/6)c,4b²,5bd,6d.
PC(GSGS 3/9/24); BLa(15/12/24); BLb;
Bod(16/1/25); CUL(2/12/24); RGS(3/9/24)
Supp. to Cat.1 Jul./30 Sep.1924.

  1924 Outline 4
  BLd(15/12/24); BLe; Bod(16/1/25)
  Supp. to Cat.1 Jul./30 Sep.1924.

1931 3000/31.
I 2/1924; (1)30a; (5)31d; roads (1)2.29.
M 1923.
L (1)a,b,g; (2)c,n,p,t; (3)c,o,w.
S 4. O 1b,2c,3b,4c,5bc.
C B&Rb,2f,3(2/6)f,4c²,5bd,6f.
PC; KGM

1936 1536.
I 6/1924. M JAN.1936.
L (1)g,i,j; (2)e,n,p,t; (3)c,i,o,w.
S 4. O 1b,2b,3b,4b,5ac.
C B&Rb,2h,3(2/6)h,4d,5bd,6j.
KGM   *AR 1936/7.*

  1941 Outline 7 [in black:] **M.38.R.37.** [in
  blue:] **1000/12/41.L.R.**   BLf
  AR 1941/2.

34 MOUTH OF THE HUMBER

Surveyed 1850-88; published 1857-90; revised 1893-7 and 1905-6; 3rd revision 1920-1.

1924

I 2/1923; (1)24a. M 1923.
L (1)a; (2)c,n,p,t; (3)c,o,u.
S 2. O 1b,2c,3b,4b,5bc.
C Red,2f,3(2/6)c,4b^2,5bdh,6d.
PC(GSGS 15/9/24); BLa(15/12/24); BLb; Bod(16/1/25); CUL(2/12/24); RGS(12/11/28)
Supp. to Cat.1 Jul./30 Sep.1924.

   1924 Outline 4
   BLd(7/8/25); BLe; Bod
   Supp. to Cat.1 Oct./31 Dec.1924.

   1924 Outline 4 **W.O.8 24.**
   OSRML

   [1930 Outline; not seen]
   Supp. to Cat.1 Oct./31 Dec.1930.

1939 2039,M.38,R.37.

I 9/1923. M 1923.
L (1)g,i,j; (2)e,j,l,n,p,t; (3)c,e,i,o,u.
S 4. O 1b,2b,3b,4b,5bc.
C B&Rb,2h,3(2/6)h,4d,5bdh,6j.
PC; BLb; Bod
AR 1939/40.

   1941 Outline 7 **1000/12/41.L.R.**
   BLf

   [1942 or 1943 Outline; not seen]
   AR 1942/3.

35 LIVERPOOL & BIRKENHEAD

Surveyed 1845-75; published 1847-87; revised 1895 and 1904-10; 3rd revision 1920.

1923

I 2/1923. M 1923.
L (1)a; (2)c,n,p,t; (3)c,o,u.
S 2. O 1b,2c,3b,4c,5bc.
C Red,3(3/6)a,5bd,6e.
KGM; BLa(1/2/24); BLb; Bod(8/2/24); CUL(8/2/24); RGS(8/1/24)
Supp. to Cat.1 Oct./31 Dec.1923.

   1923 Outline 4
   BLd(1/2/24); BLe; Bod(8/2/24)
   Supp. to Cat.1 Oct./31 Dec.1923.

1927 3500/27. (Liverpool)

I 2/1923; (1)27a; (4)27b; roads (5)3-27.
M 1923.
L (1)a; (2)c,n,p,t; (3)c,o,u.
S 2. O 1b,2b,3b,4c,5bc.
C Red,2b,3(4/-)b,5bd,6f.
PC; BLb; KGM

Supp. to Cat.1 July/30 Sept.1927. 'With special Road Revision.'

1935 2535.

I 5/1923. M 1923.
L (1)a,b,g; (2)e,n,p,t; (3)c,e,i,o,u.
S 4. O 1b,2b,3b,4b,5bc.
C B&Rb,2h,3(2/6)h,4d,5bd,6f.
PC; BLc

1937 2537.M.36.R.34.

I 5/1923. M 1937.
L (1)g,i,j; (2)e,n,p,t; (3)c,e,i,o,u.
S 4. O 1b,2b,3b,4c,5bc.
C B&Rb,2h,3(4/-)h,6j.
PC; BLb
AR 1937/8. The Mersey road tunnel has been inserted in red.

   1941 Outline **1000/12/41 LR**
   PC
   AR 1941/2.

   [1942 or 1943 Outline; not seen]
   AR 1942/3.

   1946 Outline 7 **446**
   BLf

36 BOLTON & MANCHESTER

Surveyed 1870-93; published 1886-96; revised 1895 and 1904-11; 3rd rev. 1920-21.

1924

I 2/1924. M 1923.
L (1)a; (2)c,n,s,t; (3)c,o,s.
S 2. O 1b,2c,3b,4c.
C Red,2f,3(3/6)a,5bd,6d.
PC; BLa(16/9/24); Bod(9/10/24); CUL(11/9/24); RGS(11/7/24)
Supp. to Cat.1 Apr./30 Jun.1924.

   1924 Outline 4
   BLd(16/9/24); BLe; Bod(9/10/24)
   Supp. to Cat.1 Apr./30 Jun.1924.

C cover: 271-81; I imprint: 259-62; L legend: 263-5; M magnetic variation; O other marginal data: 266-9; S scale: 266; (k), left, between legend and map border; (l) left, below legend; location abbreviations: xii; outline: 282; print codes: 84-7. AR: annual report; *Supp. to Cat.* see OS *Catalogues*: 394.

298

1928 500/28.
I 2/1924; (1)28a; (4)28d; roads (6) 3/27.
M Jan.1927.
L (1)a,b,c,g; (2)c,n,s,t; (3)c,o,s.
S 3. O 1a,2b,3b,4c.
C Red,2f,3(3/6)a,5bd,6f.
KGM; BLc

1929 500/28.2000/29.
I 2/1924; (1)28a; (4)29d; roads (6) 3/27.
M Jan.1927.
L (1)a,b,c,g; (2)c,n,s,t; (3)c,o,s.
S 3. O 1a,2b,3b,4c. Library cover.
PC

1930 Outline **500/28.2000/29.500/30.**
SG

1931 500/28.2000/29.2500/31.
I 2/1924; (1)30a; (4)31d; roads (6)3/27.
M Jan.1927.
L (1)a,b,c,g; (2)c,n,s,t; (3)c,o,s.
S 4. O 1a,2b,3b,4c.
C B&Rb,2f,3(2/6)g,4d,5bd,6f.
PC

1934 3,000/34.
I 4/1924; (1)34b; (2)32a; (5)34c.
M Jan.1927.
L (1)a,b,c,g; (2)e,n,s,t; (3)c,o,s.
S 4. O 1a,2b,3b,4c.
C R&Bb,2h,3(2/6)h,4d,5bd [no back cover]
PC

1937 4037.M36.R34.
I 6/1924. M Jan.1936.
L (1)g,i,j; (2)e,n,s,t; (3)c,i,o,s.
S 4. O 1a,2b,3b,4c.
C B&Rb,2h,3(2/6)h,4d,5bd,6f.
PC; BLb; Bod; KGM
AR 1937/8.

1941 Outline 8 **1,000/11/41 L.R**
BLf
AR 1941/2.

[1944 or 1945 Outline; not seen]
AR 1944/5.

1946 Outline 7 **446** BLf

37 BARNSLEY & SHEFFIELD
Surveyed 1871-91; published 1887-96; rev.
1894 and 1906-8; 3rd revision 1920-1.
1924
I 2/1924. M 1923.

L (1)a; (2)c,n,s,u; (3)c,o,s.
S 2. O 1a,2c,3b,4c.
C Red,2f,3(2/6)c,4b^2,5bd,6d.
PC; BL(16/9/24); BLa(16/9/24); BLb;
Bod(9/10/24); CUL(11/9/24); RGS(11/7/24)
Supp. to Cat.1 Apr./30 Jun.1924.

1924 Outline 4
BLd(16/9/24); BLe(GSGS 9/7/24);
Bod(9/10/24)
Supp. to Cat.1 Apr./30 Jun.1924.

1927 Outline 4 **500/27**
I 2/1924; (1)24-6a; (4)27d
BLe

1929 500/29.
I 2/1924; (1)24-8a; (4)29d; roads (1)3·28.
M Jan.1928.
L (1)a,b,c,g; (2)c,n,s,u; (3)c,q,s.
S 3. O 1a,2b,3b,4c. Flat.
BLb

1931 500/29.4000/31.
I 2/1924; (1)31a; (4)31d; roads partially
revised to (1)29.
M Jan.1928.
L (1)a,b,c,g; (2)c,n,s,u; (3)c,q,s.
S 4. O 1a,2b,3b,4c.
C B&Rb,2f,3(3/6)d,5bd,6f.
KGM

1936 2536.M36.R35.
I 6/1924.
M Jan.1928.
L (1)g,i,j; (2)e,n,s,u; (3)c,i,q,s.
S 4. O 1a,2b,3b,4c.
C B&Rb,2h,3(2/6)h,4d,5bd,6j.
BLc
AR 1936/7.

1939 3039.M.39.R.38.
I 6/1924.
M Jan.1928.
L (1)g,i,j; (2)e,j,n,s,u; (3)c,i,q,s.
S 4. O 1a,2b,3b,4c.
C BRed,2f,3(2/6)i,5bd,6j.
KGM

1942 Outline 7 **1000/8/42 LR**
BLf
AR 1942/3.

[1944 or 1945 Outline; not seen]
AR 1944/5.

38 DONCASTER

Surveyed 1874-91; published 1887-96; revised 1894-7, 1905-8; 3rd revision 1920.

1923
I 2/1923. **M** 1923.
L (1)a; (2)c,n,s,t; (3)c,o,s.
S 2. **O** 1a,2c,3b,4c.
C Red,2f,3(2/6)c,4b^2,5bd,6d,
PC(GSGS 14/12/23); BLa(1/2/24); BLb;
Bod(8/2/24); CUL(8/2/24); RGS(12/12/23)
Supp. to Cat.1 Oct./31 Dec.1923.

> 1923 Outline 4
> BLd(1/2/24); BLe; Bod(8/2/24)
> *Supp. to Cat.1 Oct./31 Dec.1923.*

1929 3000/29.
I 2/1923; (1)29a; (4)29d; roads (5) 5·28.
M 1923.
L (1)a,b,g; (2)c,n,s,t; (3)c,o,s.
S 3. **O** 1a,2b,3b,4c.
C B&Rb,2g,3(2/6)g,4d,6f.
PC; BLc; Bod; KGM

1935 2035.
I 6/1923. **M** Jan.1935.
L (1)g,i; (2)e,n,s,u; (3)c,h,i,o,s
S 4. **O** 1a,2b,3b,4c.
C B&Rb,2e,3(2/6)h,4d,5bd,6j.
PC; KGM; RGS

1939 539.
I 6/1923. **M** 1923.
L (1)g,i; (2)e,n,s,u; (3)c,i,o,s.
S 4. **O** 1a,2b,3b,4c.
C B&Rb(wr),2e,3(1/9)c,4e,5bd,6j.
PC.
AR 1938/9. In the legend, the roads with the slope and toll symbols lack any colour fill.

> 1939 Outline 5 **539.**
> PC   *AR 1938/9.*

[**1940** 2040.M.38.R.37. not seen; inferred from 1940.]

1940 2040.M.38.R.37.2,000/40.
I 6/1923. **M** 1938.
L (1)g,i,j; (2)e,j,n,q,u; (3)a,h,i,q,s.
S 4. **O** 1a,2b,3b.
C B&Rb,2e,3(2/6)h,4d,5bd,6j.
PC
Specification change: inland water in blue

stipple; contours very orange; parks in black stipple.

> 1941 Outline 8 **1,000/11/41 L.R.**
> BLf
> *AR 1941/2.*

39 SCUNTHORPE & MARKET RASEN

Surveyed 1883-8; published 1890-1; revised 1897 and 1905-6; 3rd revision 1920.

1923
I 2/1923. **M** 1922.
L (1)a; (2)c,n,s,t; (3)c,o,s.
S 2. **O** 1a,2c,3b,4b.
C Red,2f,3(2/6)c,4b^2,5bd,6d.
PC; BLa(19/10/23); BLb; Bod(13/12/23);
CUL(18/10/23); RGS(16/10/23)
Supp. to Cat.1 Jul./30 Sep.1923.

> 1923 Outline 4
> BLd(1/2/24); BLe; Bod(8/2/24)
> *Supp. to Cat.1 Oct./31 Dec.1923.*

1935 1535.
I 6/1923. **M** Jan.1935.
L (1)g,i,j; (2)e,n,s,t; (3)c,i,o,s.
S 4. **O** 1a,2b,3b,4b.
C B&RB,1a,2h,3(2/6)h,4d,5bd.
PC

1937 1537.M37.R36.
I 6/1923. **M** Jan.1935.
L (1)g,i,j; (2)e,n,q,t; (3)c,h,i,o,s.
S 4. **O** 1a,2b,3b,4b.
C B&Rb,2h,3(2/6)h,4d,5bd,6j.
PC; BLb
AR 1937/8.

> [1939 or 1940 Outline; not seen]
> *AR 1939/40.*

> 1942 Outline 7 **1000/4/42 LR** [in blue]
> Imprint erased.   BLf

40 GRIMSBY & LOUTH

Surveyed 1885-8; published 1890-1; revised 1897 and 1905-6; 3rd revision 1920.

1923
I 2/1923. **M** 1923.
L (1)a; (2)c,n,p,t; (3)c,o,u.
S 2. **O** 1b,2c,3b,4b,5a.
C Red,2c,3(2/6)c,4b^2,5bd,6d.

C cover: 271-81; **I** imprint: 259-62; **L** legend: 263-5; **M** magnetic variation; **O** other marginal data: 266-9; **S** scale: 266; (k), left, between legend and map border; (l) left, below legend; location abbreviations: xii; outline: 282; print codes: 84-7. *AR*: annual report; *Supp. to Cat.* see OS *Catalogues*: 394.

300

KGM; BLa(1/2/24); BLb; Bod(8/2/24); CUL(8/2/24)
Supp. to Cat.1 Oct./31 Dec.1923.

> 1923 Outline 4
> BLd(1/2/24); BLe; Bod(8/2/24)
> *Supp. to Cat.1 Oct./31 Dec.1923.*

1935 1035.
I 5/1923. M 1923.
L (1)g; (2)e,n,p,t; (3)c,i,o,u.
S 4. O 1b,2b,3b,4b,5a.
C B&Rb,2i,3(2/6)h,4d,5bd,6e.
PC; KGM; RGS

1938 M.37.R.37.2038.
I 5/1923. M 1938.
L (1)g,i,j; (2)e,j,o,q,t; (3)c,h,i,o,u.
S 4. O 1b,2b,3b,4b,5a.
C B&Rb,2i,3(2/6)h,4d,5bd,6j.
KGM; BLb
AR 1938/9.

> 1942 Outline 7 **1,000/1/42 L.R.**
> BLf
> *AR 1941/2.*

41 ANGLESEY
Surveyed 1871-88; published 1895; revised 1898 and 1908; 3rd revision 1918-9.

1922
I 2/1922. M 1922.
L (1)a; (2)c,n,p,t; (3)c,o,u.
S 2. O 1b,2c,3b,5bc.
C Red,2f,3(2/6)d,4b^2,5bd,6e.
PC; BLa(26/7/23); BLb; Bod; CUL(24/7/23); RGS(12/2/23)
Supp. to Cat.1 Jan./31 Mar.1923.

> 1922 Outline 2
> BLd(26/7/23); BLe; Bod
> *Supp. to Cat.1 Jan./31 Mar.1923.*

1927 3500/27.
I 2/1922; (1)24-7a; (4)27b.
M 1922.
L (1)a; (2)c,n,p,t; (3)c,o,u.
S 2. O 1b,2b,3b,4b,5bc.
C Red,2f,3(1/6)b,4a,5bd,6e.
PC; BLb

[1929 500/29 not seen; inferred from 1931b]

[1931a 500/29.6500/31 not seen; inferred from 1931b]

1931b 3500/27.3750/31.
I 2/1922; (1)31a; (4)31b; roads (1)10.29.
M 1922.
L (1)a,b,g; (2)c,n,p,t; (3)a,o,u.
S 4. O 1b,2b,3b,4b,5bc.
C B&Rb,2f,3(2/6)f,4c^2,5bd,6f.
KGM; BLc
Faint traces can be seen of a partially erased print code: 500/29.6500/31 to the right of the print code on this state.

1934 3,000/34.
I 4/1922; (1)34b; (2)34a; (5)34c.
M 1922.
L (1)a,b,g; (2)e,n,p,t; (3)c,i,o,u.
S 4. O 1b,2b,3b,4b,5bc.
C B&Rb(wr),2f,3(1/9)c,4e,5bd,6f.
PC; BLc; Bod

[1936 overprinted with the sites of ancient monuments. In *An Inventory of the Ancient Monuments in Anglesey* (The Royal Commission on Ancient & Historical Monuments in Wales & Monmouthsire), London, HMSO, 1937. *See* Hellyer (1999), p.30, para.11.

1936 3,000/34 (k)3036.
I 4/1922; (1)34a; (2)34b; (5)34c; 36k.
M 1922.
L (1)a,b,g; (2)e,n,p,t; (3)c,i,o,u.
S 4. O 1b,2b,3b,4b,5bc.
C B&Rb,2f,3(2/6)h,4d,5bd,6f.
PC
AR 1936/7.

1938 3,000/34 (k)538.
I 4/1922; (1)34b; (2)34a; (5)34c; 38k.
M 1922.
L (1)a,b,g; (2)e,n,p,t; (3)c,i,o,u.
S 4. O 1b,2b,3b,4b,5bc.
C B&Rb(wr),2e,3(1/9)c,4e,5bd,6j.
PC
AR 1938/9.

1939 M.37.R.37.3039.
I 6/1922. M 1st Jan.1938.
L (1)g,i,j; (2)e,j,l,n,q,t; (3)a,e,i,m,q,u.
S 4. O 1b,2b,3b,5ac.
C B&Rb,2e,3(2/6)h,4d,5bd,6j.
KGM; BLb
AR 1939/40. Specification change: inland water and sea in blue stipple; parks in black

stipple. Welsh glossary note is printed to the right of the scale bar.

<u>1941</u> Outline 8 **1,000/11/41 L.R.**
BLf
AR 1941/2.

<u>1942</u> Outline **1000/9/42 LR**
PC
AR 1942/3.

42 LLANDUDNO & DENBIGH
Surveyed 1870-88; published 1887-95; revised 1895-8 and 1903-4; 3rd revision 1918-19.

1922
I 2/1922. M 1922.
L (1)a; (2)c,n,p,t; (3)c,o,u.
S 2. O 1b,2c,3b,5bc.
C Red,2f,3(2/6)c,4b^2,5bd,6d.
PC; BLa(8/5/23); BLb; Bod; CUL(16/5/23); RGS(12/11/28)
Supp. to Cat.1 Oct./31 Dec.1922. Cover name sticker (Colwyn Bay) is known.

<u>1922</u> Outline 2
BLd(8/5/23); BLe(GSGS 16/12/22); Bod
Supp. to Cat.1 Oct./31 Dec.1922.

1928 3500/28.
I 2/1922; (1)24-7a; (4)28d.
M 1922.
L (1)a; (2)c,n,p,t; (3)c,q,u.
S 2. O 1b,2b,3b,4b,5bc.
C Red,2a,3(1/6)b,5a,5bd,6f.
PC; BLc; KGM; RGS

On some examples the final digit of the year of printing is very faint and resembles a '3' instead of an '8'; on others, the '8' is clear.

[<u>1930</u> 2500/30 not seen; inferred from 1931]

<u>1931</u> 2500/30.2300/31. (Prestatyn to Bangor)
I 2/1922; (1)30a;(4)31d; roads (1)10·29.
M 1922.
L (1)a,b,g; (2)c,n,p,t; (3)c,q,u.
S 4. O 1b,2b,3b,4b,5bc.
C B&Rb,2f,3(2/6)f,4d,5bd,6f.
PC; KGM
Another variant sticker name is 'Prestatyn'.

1933 3,000/33.
I 4/1922; (2)29a; (5)33c; (7)33b.
M 1922.
L (1)a,b,c,g; (2)e,n,p,t; (3)c,q,u.
S 4. O 1b,2b,3b,4b,5bc.
C B&Rb,2h,3(2/6)h,4d,5bd,6f.
PC; BLc; KGM
Some examples of this state have the cover sticker 'Prestatyn to Bangor'.

1936 3036.
I 6/1922. M 1936.
L (1)g,i,j; (2)e,n,p,t; (3)c,h,i,q,w.
S 4. O 1b,2b,3b,4b,5bc.
C B&Rb,2h,3(2/6)h,4d,5bd,6j.
KGM; BLc
AR 1936/7.

[<u>1937</u> or <u>1938</u> Outline; not seen]
AR 1937/8.

1938 3538 M.37.R.37.
I 6/1922. M 1937.
L (1)g,i,j; (2)e,n,q,t; (3)a,h,i,q,u.
S 4. O 1b,2b,3b,4b,5bc.
C B&Rb,2h,3(2/6)h,4d,5bd,6j.
PC; BLb; Bod; KGM
AR 1938/9. Specification change: inland water and sea in blue stipple; contours similar to 2nd class roads; parks in black stipple. Welsh glossary note is printed between the scale bar and sheet diagram.

<u>1941</u> Outline 8 **1,000/11/41 L.R.**
PC
AR 1941/2.

[<u>1944</u> or <u>1945</u> Outline; not seen]
AR 1944/5.

43 CHESTER
Surveyed 1869-75; published 1887; revised 1895 and 1904-5; 3rd revision 1919-20.

1924
I 2/1924. M 1923.
L (1)a; (2)c,n,p,t; (3)c,o,s.
S 2. O 1b,2c,3b,4c,5bc.
C Red,2f,3(2/6)c,4b^2,5bd,6d.
PC; BLa(28/5/24); BLb; Bod; CUL(4/6/24); RGS(20/5/24)
Supp. to Cat.1 Jan./31 Mar.1924.

C cover: 271-81; I imprint: 259-62; L legend: 263-5; M magnetic variation; O other marginal data: 266-9; S scale: 266; (k) left, between legend and map border; (l) left, below legend; location abbreviations: xii; outline: 282; print codes: 84-7. *AR*: annual report; *Supp. to Cat.* see OS *Catalogues*: 394.

1924 Outline 4
BLd(16/9/24); BLe; Bod(9/10/24)
Supp. to Cat.1 Apr./30 June 1924.

1927 6000/27.
I 2/1924; (1)27a; (4)27d; roads (5)3·27.
M 1923.
L (1)a; (2)c,n,p,t; (3)c,o,s.
S 2. O 1b,2b,3b,4c,5bc.
C Red,2f,3(2/6)d,4b²,5bd,6f.
PC; BL; KGM; RGS
Supp. to Cat.1 July/30 Sept.1927. 'With special Road Revision.'

1934 3,200/34.
I 4/1924; (1)33b; (2)32a; (5)34c. M 1923.
L (1)a,b; (2)e,n,p,t; (3)c,e,i,o,s.
S 4. O 1b,2b,3b,4c,5bc.
C B&Rb,2h,3(2/6)h,4d,5bd,6f.
PC; BLc; KGM; RGS

1936 3036.M36.R32.
I 6/1924. M 1936.
L (1)g,i,j; (2)e,n,p,t; (3)c,e,i,o,s.
S 4. O 1b,2b,3b,4c,5bc.
C B&Rb,2h,3(2/6)h,4d,5bd,6j.
PC; BLc; KGM
AR 1936/7. Welsh glossary note is printed to the right of the scale bar.

[1939 3039.M38R38 not seen; inferred from 1940]

1940 M.38.R.38.3039.3,400/40.
I 6/1924. M 1936.
L (1)g,i,j; (2)e,j,n,p,t; (3)c,e,i,o,s.
S 4. O 1b,2b,3b,4c,5bc.
C BRed,1c,2f,3(2/6)i,5bd,6j.
PC; KGM

[1941 or 1942 Outline; not seen]
AR 1941/2.

44 NORTHWICH & MACCLESFIELD
Surveyed 1870-7; published 1887; revised 1895 and 1904-5; 3rd revision 1919-20.
1923
I 2/1923. M 1923.
L (1)a; (2)c,n,s,u; (3)c,o,s.
S 2. O 1a,2c,3b,4c.
C Red,2f,3(2/6)c,4b²,5bd,6d.
PC; BLa(1/2/24); Bod(8/2/24); CUL(8/2/24);
PC(GSGS 1/4/24); RGS(3/1/24)
Supp. to Cat.1 Oct./31 Dec.1923.

1923 Outline 4
BLd(16/9/24); BLe; Bod(9/10/24)
Supp. to Cat.1 Apr./30 Jun.1924.

1927 500/27.
I 2/1925 [sic]; (4)27a.
M Jan.1927.
L (1)a,b,c; (2)c,n,s,u; (3)c,o,s.
S 2. O 1a,2b,3b,4c.
C Red,2f,3(2/6)d,4b²,5bd,6d.
PC; BLb

1930 3000/30.
I 2/1925; (1)30a; (4)30d; roads (6)2·27.
M 1ˢᵗ Janʸ 1928.
L (1)a,b,c,g; (2)c,n,s,u; (3)c,q,s.
S 3. O 1a,2b,3b,4c.
C B&Rb,2f,3(2/6)f,4c¹,5bd,6f.
PC; BLc; KGM

1930 Outline **3000/30.500/30**
SG

1934 3,000/34.
I 4/1925; (1)33b; (2)32a; (5)34c.
M 1ˢᵗ Janʸ1928.
L (1)a,b,c,i; (2)e,n,s,u; (3)c,q,s.
S 4. O 1a,2b,3b,4c.
C B&Rb,2f,3(2/6)h,4d,5bd,6f.
BLc; KGM; RGS

1936 3036.
I 6/1925.
M 1st Janʸ 1928.
L (1)g,i,j; (2)e,n,s,u; (3)c,i,q,s.
S 4. O 1a,2b,3b,4c.
C B&Rb,2h,3(2/6)h,4d,5bd,6f.
KGM; BLc; RGS
AR 1936/7.

1939 3039.M38.R37.
I 6/1925.
M 1ˢᵗ Janʸ 1928.
L (1)g,i,j; (2)e,j,n,s,u; (3)c,i,q,s.
S 4. O 1a,2b,3b,4c.
C B&Rb,2h,3(2/6)h,4d,5bd,6j.
KGM; BLb

1941 Outline **1000/11/41 LR**
PC *AR 1941/2.*

[1943 or 1944 Outline; not seen]
AR 1943/4.

1946 Outline 7 **846 Cr**
BLf

45 BUXTON & MATLOCK

Surveyed 1870-85; published 1887-9; revised 1894-5 and 1905-7; 3rd revision 1919-20.

1923
I 2/1923.
M 1923.
L (1)a; (2)c,n,s,u; (3)c,o,s.
S 2. O 1a,2c,3b,4c.
C Red,2c,3(2/6)a,4b^2,5bd,6d.
PC; BLa(19/10/23); BLb; Bod(13/12/23);
CUL(18/10/23); RGS(16/10/23)
Supp. to Cat.1 Jul./30 Sep.1923.

1923 Outline 4
BLd(1/2/1924); BLe; Bod(8/2/24)
Supp. to Cat.1 Oct./31 Dec.1923.

1927 1000/27.
I 2/1923; (1)24a; (4)27d.
M 1923.
L (1)a; (2)c,n,s,u; (3)c,o,s.
S 2. O 1a,2b,3b,4c.
C Red,[no price],5p,6d.
PC

1928 see [1936]

1930 3000/30.
I 2/1923; (1)28a; (4)30d; roads (1)2/28.
M Jan.1928.
L (1)a,b,c,g; (2)c,n,s,u; (3)c,q,s.
S 3. O 1a,2b,3b,4c.
C B&Ra,2c,3(2/6)f,4c^2,5bd,6d.
PC; BLc; KGM; RGS

1934 3,200/34.
I 4/1923; (1)33b; (2)33a; (5)34c.
M Jan.1928.
L (1)h,g; (2)e,n,s,u; (3)c,h,q,s.
S 4. O 1a,2b,3b,4c.
C B&Rb,2i,3(2/6)h,4d,5bd,6f.
PC

[1936a] No print code
I 9/1928 [sic]. [No corrections notes, or reprint code.]
M Jan.1928.
L (1)g,i,j; (2)e,n,s,u; (3)c,h,i,q,s.
S 4. O 1a,2b,3b,4c.
C B&Rb,2i,3(2/6)h,4d,5bd,6f.
KGM
This appears to be the same as the 1936

printing below, but lacks the print code; the road classification would indicate that this state dates from at least 1934.

1936b 3036
I 9/1928. M Jan.1928.
L (1)g,i,j; (2)e,n,s,u; (3)c,h,i,q,s.
S 4. O 1a,2b,3b,4c.
C B&Rb,2i,3(2/6)h,4d,5bd,6j.
PC; BLb; BLc

1940 3040.M.39.R.39.
I 9/1928.
M Jan.1928.
L (1)g,i,j; (2)e,j,n,s,u; (3)c,h,i,q,s.
S 4. O 1a,2b,3b,4c.
C BRed,1c,2i,2(2/6)i,5bd,6j.
KGM
An example of this sheet has been seen with a faint print code and lacking the green plate (PC).

1942 Outline 1000/8/42 LR
PC   *AR 1942/3.*

[1944 or 1945 Outline; not seen]
AR 1944/5.

46 THE DUKERIES

Surveyed 1874-88; published 1887-90; revised 1894-8 and 1906-7; 3rd revision 1920.

1923
I 2/1923. M 1923.
L (1)a; (2)c,n,s,u; (3)c,o,s.
S 2. O 1a,2c,3b,4c.
C Red,2c,3(2/6)c,4b^2,5bd,6d.
PC; BLa(19/10/23); BLb; Bod(13/12/23);
CUL(18/10/23); RGS(16/10/28)
Supp. to Cat. 1 Jul./30 Sep.1923.

1923 Outline 4
BLd(1/2/24); BLe; Bod(8/2/24)
Supp. to Cat.1 Oct./31 Dec.1923.

1930a 3000/30.
I 2/1923; (1)26/9a; (4)30d; roads (2)6.28.
M 1923.
L (1)a,b,g; (2)c,n,s,u; (3)c,o,s.
S 4. O 1a,2b,3b,4c.
C B&Rb,2g,3(2/6)f,4c^2,5bd,6f.
KGM; RGS

C cover: 271-81; I imprint: 259-62; L legend: 263-5; M magnetic variation; O other marginal data: 266-9;
S scale: 266; (k) left, between legend and map border; (l) left, below legend; location abbreviations: xii;
304   outline: 282; print codes: 84-7. *AR*: annual report; *Supp. to Cat.* see OS *Catalogues*: 394.

[**1930b** 500/30 not seen, inferred from 1932; may refer to outline state.]

1930 Outline **3000/30.500/30.** SG

1932 3000/30.500/30.4000/32.
I 2/1923; (1)26-8a; (4)32d; roads (4)6.28.
M 1923.
L (1)a,b,g; (2)c,n,s,u; (3)c,q,s.
S 4. O 1a,2b,3b,4c.
C B&Rb,2g,3(2/6)h,4d,5bd,6f.
BLc

1936 3036,M.36,R.33.
I 9/1923. M 1st Jan.1936.
L (1)g,i,j; (2)e,n,s,u; (3)c,i,o,s.
S 4. O 1a,2b,3b,4c.
C B&Rb,2g,3(2/6)h,4d,5bd,6j.
PC; BLc
AR 1936/7.

[**1938** or **1939** not seen]
AR 1938/9.

[**1938** or 1939 Outline; not seen]
AR 1938/9.

1940 3040 M.39.R.39.
I 9/1923. M 1st Jan.1936.
L (1)g,i,j; (2)e,j,n,s,u; (3)c,i,q,s.
S 4. O 1a,2b,3b,4c.
C BRed,2g,3(2/6)i,5bd,6j.
KGM; BLb

[**1941** or **1942** Outline; not seen]
AR 1941/2.

1946 Outline 7 **446**
BLf

47 LINCOLN
Surveyed 1883-8; published 1890-1; revised 1897-8 and 1906; 3rd revision 1920.

1923
I 2/1923. M 1922.
L (1)a; (2)c,n,s,u; (3)c,o,s.
S 2. O 1b,2c,3b,4b.
C Red,2f,3(2/6)c,4b^2,5bd,6d.
PC(GSGS 21/11/24); BLa(19/10/23); BLb; Bod(12/12/23); CUL(18/10/23); RGS(16/10/23)
Supp. to Cat.1 Jul./30 Sep.1923.

1923 Outline 4
BLd(1/2/1924); BLb; Bod(8/2/24)
Supp. to Cat.1 Oct./31 Dec.1923.

1930 2250/30.
I 2/1923; (1)28a; (4)30d; roads(5)12/28.
M 1922.
L (1)a,b,c,g; (2)c,n,s,u; (3)c,o,s.
S 3. O 1b,2b,3b,4b.
C B&Rb,2f,3(2/6)f,4c^2,5bd,6e.
PC

1934 2,500/34.
I 4/1923; (1)34b; (2)34a; (5)34c. M 1922.
L (1)a,b,c,g; (2)e,n,s,u; (3)c,i,o,s.
S 4. O 1b,2b,3b,4b.
C B&Rb(wr),2h,3(1/9)c,4e,5bd,6e.
PC

1938 2538,M38,R37.
I 6/1923. M Jan 1938.
L (1)g,i,j; (2)e,j,l,n,o,q,u; (3)a,e,i,o,s.
S 4. O 1b,2b,3b.
C B&Rb,2h,3(2/6)h,4d,5bd,6j.
BLc; BLb; RGS
AR 1937/8. Specification change: inland water in blue stipple; parks in black stipple.

1942 Outline 7 **1,000/1/42 L.R.** [in blue]
I 6/1924 [sic]. BLf *AR 1941/2.*

48 HORNCASTLE & SKEGNESS
Surveyed 1885-8; published 1891; revised 1897 and 1906; 3rd revision 1919-20.

1923
I 2/1923. M 1922.
L (1)a; (2)c,n,p,t; (3)c,o,u.
S 2. O 1b,2c,3b,4b,5bc.
C Red,2f[&],3(2/6)c,4b^2,5bd,6d.
PC; BLa(19/10/23); BLb; Bod(13/12/23); CUL(18/10/23); RGS(16/10/23)
Supp. to Cat.1 Jul./30 Sep.1923.

1923 Outline 4
BLd(26/7/1923); BLe; Bod(8/2/24)
Supp. to Cat.1 Oct./31 Dec.1923.

1934 2,200/34.
I 4/1923; (1)34b; (2)34a; (5)34c. M 1922.
L (1)a,b,g; (2)e,n,p,t; (3)c,o,u.
S 4. O 1b,2b,3b,4b,5bc.
C B&Rb,2h,3(2/6)h,4d,5bd,6f.
PC; BLc; KGM

1939 2039.M38,R37.
I 6/1923. M 1922.
L (1)g,i,j; (2)e,j,n,p,t; (3)c,i,o,u.
S 4. O 1b,2b,3b,4b,5bc. Flat.
BLb *AR 1939/40.*

<u>1941</u> Outline 8 **1000/11/41.L.R.**
BLf   *AR 1941/2.*

49 PORTMADOC & CRICCIETH
Surveyed 1874-88; published 1895; revised
1898 and 1903; 3rd revision 1918-9.

1922
I 2/1922. **M** 1922.
L (1)a; (2)c,n,p,u; (3)c,o,w.
S 2. **O** 1b,2c,3b,5bc.
C Red,2c,3(3/6)a,5bd,6d.
PC; BLa(14/9/22); BLb; Bod(21/9/22);
CUL(13/9/22)
Supp. to Cat.1 Apr./30 June 1923.

   <u>1922</u> Outline 2
   BLd(26/7/1923); BLe; Bod
   Supp. to Cat.1 Jan./31 Mar.1923.

1927 **3000/27.**
I 2/1922; (1)24-7d; (3)24a; (4)27g.
M 1927.
L (1)a,b,c,g; (2)c,n,p,t; (3)c,o,u.
S 3. **O** 1b,2b,3b,4b,5c.
C Red,2f,3(1/6)b,4a,5bd,6e.
PC; BLb; BLc; RGS

1930 **3000/27.3500/30.**
I 2/1922; (1)29d; (3)28a; (4)30g; rds(1)11-29.
M 1927.
L (1)a,b,c,g; (2)c,n,p,t; (3)c,o,u.
S 3. **O** 1b,2b,3b,4b,5a.
C B&Rb,2f,3(2/6)f,4c^2,5bd,6f.
PC; BLc

1933 **3,700/33:** (PWLLHELI)
I 4/1922; (1)33b; (2)29a; (5)33c.
M 1927.
L (1)a,b,c,g; (2)e,n,p,u; (3)c,o,u.
S 4. **O** 1b,2b,3b,4b,5a.
C B&Rb(wr),2h,3(1/9)a,5bd,6f.
PC

1936 **3,700/33:4000/36.**
I 4/1922; (1)33b; (2)29a; (5)36c.
M 1927.
L (1)a,b,c,g; (2)e,n,p,u; (3)c,o,u.
S 4. **O** 1b,2b,3b,4b,5a.
C B&Rb,2h,3(2/6)h,4d,5bd,6f.
PC; BLc
AR 1936/7.

1938 **4038.M33.R37.**
I 9/1922. **M** 1927.
L (1)g,i,j; (2)e,j,n,p,t; (3)c,h,i,o,w.
S 4. **O** 1b,2b,3b,4b,5a.
C BRed,1c,2f,3(2/6)i,5bd,6j.
BLc; BLb; RGS
AR 1938/9.

   <u>1942</u> Outline **1000/6/42 LR**
   PC   *AR 1942/3.*

50 BALA
Surveyed 1873-88; published 1895; revised
1895-8 and 1903-4; 3rd revision 1918-9.

1921
I 2/1921. **M** 1921.
L (1)a; (2)c,n,s,u; (3)c,o,s.
S 2. **O** 1a,2c,3a,4a.
C Red,2f,3(3/6)a,5bd,6d.
PC; BLa(31/7/22); BLb; Bod; CUL(27/7/22);
RGS(24/3/22)
Supp. to Cat.1 Jan./31 Mar.1922.

   <u>1921</u> Outline 2
   BLd(31/7/22); BLb; Bod
   Supp. to Cat.1 Jan./31 Mar.1922.

1934 **2,700/34.**
I 4/1921; (1)33b; (2)29a; (5)34c. **M** 1921.
L (1)a,b; (2)e,n,s,u; (3)c,i,o,s.
S 4. **O** 1a,2b,3a,4b.
C B&Rb,2h,3(2/6)h,4d,5bd,6f.
PC; BLc; KGM

1937 **3037 M36.R.34.**
I 6/1921. **M** Jan.1st 1937.
L (1)g,i,j; (2)e,n,s,u; (3)c,i,o,s.
S 4. **O** 1a,2b,3a,4b.
C B&Rb,2h,3(2/6)h,4d,5bd,6j.
PC; BLb; BLc; Bod; KGM
*AR 1936/7. Welsh glossary note is printed
below the price note.*

[**1939**   **2539.M38.R37.** not seen; inferred
from 1940]

1940 **2539.M38.R37. 2,500/40.**
I 6/1921. **M** Jan.1st 1937.
L (1)g,i,j; (2)e,j,n,s,u; (3)c,i,o,s.
S 4. **O** 1a,2b,3a,4b.
C BRed,1c,2f,3(2/6)i,5bd,6j.
PC; BLc

C cover: 271-81; I imprint: 259-62; L legend: 263-5; M magnetic variation; O other marginal data: 266-9;
S scale: 266; (k) left, between legend and map border; (l) left, below legend; location abbreviations: xii;
outline: 282; print codes: 84-7. *AR*: annual report; *Supp. to Cat.* see OS **Catalogues**: 394.

1941 Outline 8 **1,000/11/41 L.R.**
BLf

51 **WREXHAM & OSWESTRY**
Surveyed 1870-85; published 1882-92; revised 1895-8 and 1904-5; 3rd revision 1916.

1921
I 2/1921. M 1921.
L (1)a; (2)c,n,s,u; (3)c,o,s.
S 2. O 1a,2c,3a,4a.
C Red,2c,3(2/6)c,4b^2,5bd,6d.
PC; BLa(17/6/22); BLb; Bod; CUL(3/7/22); PC(GSGS 19/7/22); RGS(8/12/21)
Supp. to Cat.1 Oct./31 Dec.1921.

 1921 Outline 2
 BLd(17/6/1922); BLe; Bod(5/7/22)
 Supp. to Cat.1 Oct./31 Dec.1921.

1932 3000/32.
I 2/1921; (1)31a; (5)32d; roads (1)12-29.
M 1921.
L (1)a,b,g; (2)c,n,s,t; (3)c,o,s.
S 4. O 1a,2b,3a,4b.
C B&Rb,2f,3(2/6)f,4d,5bd,6f.
KGM; BLc

1935 2035.
I 6/1921. M Jan.1935.
L (1)g,i; (2)e,n,s,u; (3)c,e,i,o,s.
S 4. O 1a,2b,3a,4b.
C B&Rb,2h,3(2/6)h,4d,5bd,6f.
PC; KGM; BLc

1937 2037.M37.R29.
I 6/1921. M 1935.
L (1)g,i,j; (2)e,n,s,t; (3)c,e,i,o,s.
S 4. O 1a,2b,3a,4b.
C B&Rb,2h,3(2/6)h,4d,5bd,6j.
PC; BLc; KGM
AR 1937/8.

1939 3039.M38.R37.
I 6/1921. M 1935.
L (1)g,i,j; (2)e,j,n,s,u; (3)c,e,i,o,s.
S 4. O 1a,2b,3a,4b. Flat.
BLb
AR 1939/40. Contours printed in the same colour as 2nd class roads.

 1941 Outline **1000/11/41 LR**
 PC   *AR 1941/2.*

 1943 Outline 8 **800/2/43 LR.** BLf

[1943 or 1944 Outline; not seen]
AR 1943/4

52 **STOKE ON TRENT**
Surveyed 1871-81; published 1887-9; revised 1895-8 and 1904-5; 3rd revision 1916-8.
1921
I 2/1921. M 1921.
L (1)a; (2)c,n,s,u; (3)c,o,s.
S 2. O 1a,2c,3a,4a.
C Red,2c,3(2/6)a,4b^1,5bd,6d.
PC; BLa(20/5/22); BLb; Bod; CUL(18/5/22); RGS(20/9/21)
Supp. to Cat.1 Jul./30 Sep.1921.

 1921 Outline 2
 BLd(17/6/22); BLe; Bod(5/7/22)
 Supp. to Cat.1 Oct./31 Dec.1921.

1933 3,200/33.
I 4/1921; (5)33b; (7)32a.
M 1921.
L (1)a,b,g; (2)e,n,s,u; (3)c,o,s.
S 4. O 1a,2b,3b,4b.
C B&Rb,2g,3(2/6)h,4d,5bd,6f.
PC; BLc; KGM

1939 3039.M38,R37.
I 6/1921. M 1921.
L (1)g,i,j; (2)e,j,n,s,u; (3)c,i,o,s.
S 4. O 1a,2b,3b,4b.
C B&Rb,2g,3(4/-)h,5bd,6j.
Bod; BLb
AR 1939/40.

 1941 Outline **1000/11/41 LR**
 KGM   *AR 1941/2.*

53 **DERBY**
Surveyed 1876-83; published 1889-90; revised 1895-6 and 1905-6; 3rd revision 1916-8.

1921
I 2/1921. M 1921.
L (1)a; (2)c,n,s,u; (3)c,o,s.
S 2. O 1a,2c,3a,4a.
C Red,2f,3(2/6)a,4b^1,5bd,6d.
PC; BLa(20/5/22); BLb; Bod; CUL(18/5/22); PC(GSGS 19/7/22); RGS(12/10/21)
Supp. to Cat.1 Jul./30 Sep.1921.

1921 Outline 2
BLd(20/5/22); BLe; Bod
Supp.to Cat.1 Jul./30 Sep.1921.

1932 3500/32.
I 2/1921; (1)31a; (5)32d; roads (1)5.28.
M 1921.
L (1)a,b,g; (2)c,n,s,u; (3)c,o,s.
S 4. **O** 1a,2b,3a,4b.
C B&Rb,2f,3(2/6)g,4d,5bd,6f.
PC; BLb; BLc; KGM

1935 2535
I 5/1921. **M** 1921.
L (1)g,i; (2)e,n,s,u; (3)c,i,o,s.
S 4. **O** 1a,2b,3b,4b.
C B&Rb,2h,3(2/6)h,4d,5bd,6f.
PC; BLc; KGM

[1936 or 1937 Outline; not seen]
AR 1936/7.

1938 638.
I 5/1921. **M** 1921.
L (1)g,i,j; (2)e,n,s,u; (3)c,i,o,s.
S 4. **O** 1a,2b,3b,4b. Flat.
BLb

1939 3039. M38.R37.
I 6/1921. **M** 1938.
L (1)g,i,j; (2)e,j,k,l,n,s,t; (3)c,e,i,m,q,s.
S 4. **O** 1a,2b,3b.
C BRed,1c,2f,3(2/6)i,4d,5bd,6j.
KGM; RGS
Specification change: inland water in blue stipple with heavy blue casing.

1941 Outline **1000/11/41 LR**
PC   *AR 1941/2.*

1946 Outline 7 (k)**638.** (l)**846Cr.**
BLf

54 NOTTINGHAM
Surveyed 1876-87; published 1889-90; revised 1895-8 and 1905-6; 3rd revision 1916-8.
1921
I 2/1921. **M** 1921.
L (1)a; (2)c,n,s,u; (3)c,o,s.
S 2. **O** 1a,2c,3a,4a.
C Red,2c,3(2/6)d,4b²,5bd,6f.
KGM; BLa(17/6/22); BLb; Bod;

CUL(3/7/22); RGS(12/11/21)
Supp. to Cat.1 Oct./31 Dec.1921.

1921 Outline 2
BLd(17/6/22); Bod(5/7/22)
Supp. to Cat.1 Oct./31 Dec.1921

1931 3000/31
I 2/1921; (1)30b; (3)28a; (5)31d; roads (5)4.28. **M** 1921.
L (1)a,b,g; (2)c,n,s,u; (3)c,o,s.
S 4. **O** 1a,2b,3b,4b.
C B&Rb,2g,3(2/6)g,4d,5bd,6f.
PC

1931 Outline 5 **3000/31**   PC

1933 3,000/33.
I 4/1921; (1)33c; (2)33a; (3)28b; (5)33l.
M 1921.
L (1)a,b,g; (2)e,n,s,u; (3)c,o,s.
S 4. **O** 1a,2b,3b,4b.
C B&Rb,2e,3(2/6)h,4d,5bd,6f.
BLc

1936 3036.
I 6/1921. **M** 1936.
L (1)g,i,j; (2)e,n,s,u; (3)c,i,o,s.
S 4. **O** 1a,2b,3b,4b.
C B&Rb,2e,3(2/6)h,4d,5bd,6f.
PC; BLc; KGM; RGS
AR 1936/7.

1938 3038.M.38,R.37.
I 6/1921. **M** 1936.
L (1)g,i,j; (2)e,j,k,n,s,u; (3)c,i,o,s.
S 4. **O** 1a,2b,3b,4b.
C BRed,1c,2g,3(2/6)i,4d,5bd,6j.
KGM; BLb; RGS
AR 1938/9.

1941 Outline **1000/11/41 LR**
PC   *AR 1941/2.*

1942 Outline **1000/9/42 LR**
PC *AR 1942/3.*

[1944 or 1945 Outline; not seen]
AR 1944/5.

1946 Outline 7 **446**
BLf

C cover: 271-81; **I** imprint: 259-62; **L** legend: 263-5; **M** magnetic variation; **O** other marginal data: 266-9;
S scale: 266; (k) left, between legend and map border; (l) left, below legend; location abbreviations: xii;
outline: 282; print codes: 84-7. *AR*: annual report; *Supp. to Cat.* see OS *Catalogues*: 394.

55 GRANTHAM
Surveyed 1883-8; published 1891; revised
1897-8 and 1906-7; 3rd revision 1919-20.

1922
I 2/1922. M 1922.
L (1)a; (2)c,n,s,u; (3)c,o,s.
S 2. O 1a,2c,3b.
C Red,2f,3(2/6)a,4b^2,5bd,6d.
PC(GSGS 13/9/22); BLa(26/1/23); BLb;
Bod; CUL(18/1/23); RGS(13/9/22)
Supp. to Cat.1 Jul./30 Sep.1922.

    [1922] Outline 2
    I lacks date.
    BLd(26/1/23); BLe; Bod
    Supp. to Cat.1 Jul./30 Sep.1922.

1930 3800/30.
I 2/1922; (1)30a; (4)30d; roads (1)11/28.
M 1922.
L (1)a; (2)c,n,s,u; (3)c,o,s.
S 4. O 1a,2b,3b,4b.
C B&Rb,2e,3(2/6)h,4d,5bd,6f.
PC; BLc; KGM; RGS

    [1936 or 1937 Outline; not seen]
    AR 1936/7.

1938 2038.M38.R38.
I 6/1922. M 1922.
L (1)g,i,j; (2)e,j,n,s,u; (3)c,i,o,s.
S 4. O 1a,2b,3b,4b.
C B&Rb,2e,3(2/6)h,4d,5bd,6j.
PC
AR 1938/9.

    1941 Outline 8 **1000/10/41 L.R.**
    BLf   *AR 1941/2.*

56 BOSTON
Surveyed 1883-8; published 1891; revised
1897 and 1906-7; 3rd revision 1919-20.

1922
I 2/1922. M 1922.
L (1)a; (2)c,n,p,t; (3)c,o,w.
S 2. O 1b,2c,3b,5bc.
C Red,2b,3(2/6)d,4b^2,5bd,6e.
PC; BLa(26/1/23); BLb; Bod;
CUL(18/1/23); RGS(13/9/22)
Supp. to Cat.1 Jul./30 Sep.1922.

    1922 Outline 2
    BLd(8/5/1923); BLe; Bod
    Supp. to Cat.1 Oct./31 Dec.1922.

1934 2,200/34.
I 4/1922; (1)34b; (5)34c.
M 1922.
L (1)a,b; (2)e,n,p,t; (3)c,o,w.
S 4. O 1b,2b,3b,4b,5bc.
C B&Rb,2h,3(2/6)h,4d,5bd,6f.
KGM; BLb; Bod

1939 1539.M38.R38.
I 6/1939. M 1922.
L (1)g,i,j; (2)e,j,n,p,t; (3)c,i,o,w.
S 4. O 1b,2b,3b,[no 4],5bc.
C BRed,1c,2f,3(1/9)d,5bd,6j.
PC
AR 1939/40.

    1941 Outline 7 **1,000/3/42.L.R.**
    BLf
    AR 1941/2.

57 FAKENHAM
Surveyed 1880-5; published 1890; revised
1897 and 1906-8; 3rd revision 1919-20.

1921
I 2/1921. M 1921.
L (1)a; (2)c,n,p,t; (3)c,o,w.
S 2. O 1b,2c,3a,4a,5c.
C Red,2c,3(2/6)a,4b^1,5bd,6d.
PC; BLa(17/6/22); BLb; Bod; CUL(3/7/22);
RGS(12/1/22)
Supp. to Cat.1 Oct./31 Dec.1921.

    1921 Outline 2
    BLd(26/1/23); BLe; Bod
    Supp. to Cat.1 Jul./30 Sep.1922.

1935 1535.
I 6/1921. M 1935.
L (1)g,i; (2)e,n,p,t; (3)c,i,o,w.
S 4. O 1b,2b,3a,4b,5c.
C B&Rb,2e,3(2/6)h,4d,5bd,6f.
PC; BLc; RGS

1938 2038.M.37 R36
I 6/1921. M 1.st Jan.1937.
L (1)g,i,j; (2)e,j,n,q,t; (3)c,i,o,u.
S 4. O 1b,2b,3b,4b,5c.
C B&Rb,2e,3(2/6)h,4d,5bd,6j.
PC; BLb; KGM
*AR 1938/9. Specification change: inland
water and sea in blue stipple.*

    1942 Outline 7 **1,000/1/42 LR**
    BLf
    AR 1941/2.

58 CROMER
Surveyed 1879-85; published 1888-90; revised 1897 and 1906-8; 3rd rev. 1919-20.

1922
I 2/1922. M 1921.
L (1)a; (2)c,n,p,t; (3)c,o,w.
S 2. O 1b,2c,3a,4a,5c.
C Red,2f,3(2/6)c,4b^2,5bd,6d.
PC(GSGS 22/8/22); BLa(14/9/22); BLb; Bod(21/9/22); CUL(13/9/22); RGS(8/6/22)
Supp.to Cat.1 Apr./30 June 1922.

   1922 Outline 2
   BLd(14/9/1922); BLe; Bod(21/9/22)
   Supp. to Cat.1 Apr./30 June 1922.

1929 3500/29.
I 2/1922; (1)28a; (4)29d; roads (1)11/28.
M 1921.
L (1)a; (2)c,n,p,t; (3)c,o,w.
S 3. O 1b,2b,3b,4b,5c.
C B&Rb,2f,3(2/6)f,4c^2,5bd,6f.
PC; BLc; KGM

1936 1536.
I 6/1922. M 1921.
L (1)g,i,j; (2)e,n,p,u; (3)c,i,q,w.
S 4. O 1b,2b,3b,4b,5c.
C B&Rb,2f,3(1/9)a,4e,5bd,6f.
KGM; BLc
AR 1936/7.

1938 M37.R37.2038.
I 6/1922. M 1921.
L (1)g,i,j; (2)e,n,p,t; (3)c,i,o,w.
S 4. O 1b,2b,3b,4b,5c.
C B&Rb,2h,3(2/6)h,4d,5bd,6j.
PC; BLb; BLc; Bod; RGS

   1942 Outline 7 **1000/4/42 LR** [in blue]
   Imprint erased.
   BLf
   AR 1942/3.

59 DOLGELLY & LAKE VYRNWY
Surveyed 1874-87; published 1894-5; revised 1898 and 1903-4; 3rd revision 1918-9.

1921
I 2/1921. M 1921.
L (1)a; (2)c,n,s,t; (3)c,o,s.
S 2. O 1b,2c,3a,4a.

C Red,2f,3(2/6)a,4b^1,5bd,6d.
PC; BLa(17/6/22); BLb; Bod; CUL(3/7/22); RGS(12/11/21)
Supp. to Cat.1 Oct./31 Dec.1921.

   1921 Outline 2
   BLd(17/6/22); BLe; Bod(5/7/22)
   Supp. to Cat.1 Oct./31 Dec.1921.

1936 2036.M.36.R.29.
I 6/1921. M 1936.
L (1)g,i,j; (2)e,n,s,t; (3)c,i,o,s.
S 4. O 1b,2b,3b,4b.
C B&Rb,2h,3(2/6)h,4d,5bd,6f.
KGM; BLc
AR 1936/7. Welsh glossary note printed below the price statement.

1940 2040.M38.R38.
I 6/1921. M 1936.
L (1)g,i,j; (2)e,j,n,s,t; (3)c,i,o,s.
S 4. O 1b,2b,3b,4b.
C BRed,1c,2f,3(2/6)i,5bd,6j.
PC

   1941 Outline 8 **1000/11/41 L.R.**
   BLf
   AR 1941/2.

60 SHREWSBURY
Surveyed 1872-85; published 1889-94; revised 1895-8 and 1904; 3rd revision 1916.

1921
I 2/1921. M 1921.
L (1)a; (2)c,n,s,u; (3)c,o,s.
S 2. O 1a,2c,3a,4a.
C Red,2f,3(2/6)a,4b^1,5bd,6d.
PC; BLa(20/5/22); BLb; Bod; CUL(18/5/22); RGS(20/9/21)
Supp. to Cat.1 Jul./30 Sep.1921.

   1921 Outline 2
   BLd(20/5/1922); BLe; Bod
   Supp. to Cat.1 Jul./30 Sep.1921.

1935 1535
I 6/1921. M 1.st Jan.1935.
L (1)g,i; (2)e,n,s,u; (3)c,e,i,o,s.
S 4. O 1a,2b,3a,4b.
C B&Rb,2h,3(2/6)h,4d,5bd,6f.
PC; BLc

C cover: 271-81; I imprint: 259-62; L legend: 263-5; M magnetic variation; O other marginal data: 266-9; S scale: 266; (k) left, between legend and map border; (l) left, below legend; location abbreviations: xii; outline: 282; print codes: 84-7. AR: annual report; *Supp. to Cat.* see OS *Catalogues*: 394.

310

1936 2036,M.36,R.29.
I 6/1921. M 1.ˢᵗ Jan.1935.
L (1)g,i,j; (2)e,n,s,u; (3)c,e,i,o,s.
S 4. O 1a,2b,3a,4b.
C B&Rb,2h,3(2/6)h,4d,5bd,6j.
KGM; BLc
AR 1936/7. Welsh glossary note printed below the scale statement.

1939 2039.M38.R38.
I 6/1921. M 1.ˢᵗ Jan.1935.
L (1)g,i,j; (2)e,j,n,s,u; (3)c,e,i,o,s.
S 4. O 1a,2b,3a,4b.
C BRed,1c,2f,3(2/6)i,5bd,6j.
KGM; BLb
AR 1939/40.

   1939 Outline 5 **2039.M38.R38.**
   BLe

   1941 Outline 8 **1000/11/41 LR**
   PC

   AR 1941/2.

61 WOLVERHAMPTON
Surveyed 1872-85; published 1889-95; revised 1898 and 1904-5; 3rd rev. 1916-7.

1921
I 2/1921. M 1921.
L (1)a; (2)c,n,s,u; (3)c,o,s.
S 2. O 1a,2c,3a,4a.
C Red,2f,3(2/6)a,4b¹,5bd,6d.
PC; BLa(20/5/22); BLb; Bod;
CUL(18/5/22); RGS
Supp. to Cat.1 Jul./30 Sep.1921.

   1921 Outline 2
   BLd(17/6/22); BLe; Bod(5/7/22)
   Supp. to Cat.1 Oct./31 Dec.1921.

1933 2,700/33.
I 4/1921; (2)31a; (5)33c; (6)33b. M 1921.
L (1)a,b,g; (2)e,n,s,u; (3)c,o,s.
S 4. O 1a,2b,3a,4b.
C B&Rb,2i,3(2/6)g,4d,5bd,6f.
BLc; KGM

1936 2036.
I 6/1921. M 1921.
L (1)g,i,j; (2)e,n,s,u; (3)c,i,o,s.
S 4. O 1a,2b,3a,4b.
C B&Rb,2i,3(4/-)h,5bd,6f.
KGM; BLc
AR 1936/7.

1938 538.
I 6/1921. M 1921.
L (1)g,i,j; (2)e,n,s,u; (3)c,i,o,s.
S 4. O 1a,2b,3a,4b.
C B&Rb, 2i,3(2/6)h,4d,5bd,6j.
PC
AR 1938/9.

1939 2539.M38.R37.
I 6/1921. M 1938.
L (1)g,i,j; (2)e,j,l,n,q,u; (3)c,e,i,m,o,s.
S 4. O 1a,2b,3b.
C BRed,1c,2d,3(2/6)i,5bd,6j.
PC; BLb; Bod; KGM
AR 1939/40. Specification change: inland water in blue stipple.

   1941 Outline **1000/12/41 LR**
   PC

   [**1942** or **1942** Outline; not seen]
   AR 1941/2.

   [**1944** or **1945** Outline; not seen]
   AR 1944/5.

62 BURTON & WALSALL
Surveyed 1878-86; published 1890-5; revised 1895-8 and 1905-6; 3rd revision 1916-7.

1921
I 2/1921. M 1921.
L (1)a; (2)c,n,s,u; (3)c,o,s.
S 2. O 1a,2c,3a,4a.
C Red,2f,3(2/6)a,4b¹,5bd,6d.
PC; BLa(20/5/22); BLb; Bod;
CUL(18/5/22); RGS(25/8/21)
Supp. to Cat.1 Jul./30 Sep.1921.

   1921 Outline 2
   BLd(31/7/22); BLe; Bod
   Supp. to Cat.1 Oct./31 Dec.1921.

1933 2,700/33.
I 4/1921; (2)31a; (5)33c; (6)32b. M 1921.
L (1)a,b; (2)e,n,s,u; (3)c,q,s.
S 4. O 1a,2b,3b,4b.
C B&Rb,2h,3(2/6)h,4d,5bd,6f.
BLc
Specification change: contours reinforced.

1936 2036.
I 6/1921. M 1921.
L (1)g,i,j; (2)e,n,s,u; (3)c,i,q,s.
S 4. O 1a,2b,3b,4b.
C B&Rb,2h,3(2/6)h,4d,5bd,6f.
KGM *AR 1936/7.*

[<u>1937</u> or <u>1938</u> Outline; not seen]
AR 1937/8.

1939 2539.M.38.R.37.
I 6/1921. M 1937.
L (1)g,i,j; (2)e,j,n,q,t; (3)c,h,i,q,s.
S 4. O 1a,2b,3b,4b.
C B&Rb,2h,3(4/-)g,5bd,6j.
PC; KGM
AR 1939/40. Specification change: inland water in blue stipple.

   <u>1941</u> Outline **1000/11/41 LR**
PC
AR 1941/2.

   [<u>1944</u> or <u>1945</u> Outline; not seen]
AR 1944/5.

63 LEICESTER
Surveyed 1879-86; published 1889-92; revised 1895-8 and 1905-6; 3rd revision 1916-18.

1921

I 2/1921. M 1921.
L (1)a; (2)c,n,s,u; (3)c,o,s.
S 2. O 1a,2c,3a,4a.
C Red,2f,3(2/6)a,4b[1],5bd,6d.
PC; BLa(20/5/22); BLb; Bod;
CUL(18/5/22); PC(GSGS 25/8/22);
RGS(20/9/21)
Supp. to Cat.1 Jul./30 Sep.1921.

   <u>1921</u> Outline 2
BLd(17/6/22); BLe; Bod(5/7/22)
Supp. to Cat.1 Oct./31 Dec.1921.

1930 3000/30.
I 1/1921; (1)30a; (4)30d; roads (2)8.28.
M 1921.
L (1)a,b; (2)c,n,s,u; (3)c,o,s.
S 4. O 1a,2b,3b,4b.
C B&Rb,2f,3(2/6)f,4c[2],5bd,6f.
KGM

1933 2,500/33.
I 4/1921; (1)33c; (2)33a; (3)32b; (5)33[to the right of c]. M 1921.
L (1)a,b; (2)e,n,s,u; (3)c,o,s.
S 4. O 1a,2b,3b,4b.
C B&Rb,2e,3(2/6)h,4d,5bd,6f.
KGM; BLc

1936 3036.
I 6/1921. M 1921.
L (1)g,i,j; (2)e,n,s,u; (3)c,i,o,s.
S 4. O 1a,2b,3b,4b.
C B&Rb,2h,3(2/6)h,4d,5bd,6j.
KGM; BLc

1938 3038.M38.R37.
I 6/1921. M 1921.
L (1)g,i,j; (2)e,j,n,s,u; (3)c,i,o,s.
S 4. O 1a,2b,3b,4b.
C BaRed,1c,2f,3(2/6)i,5bd,6j.
BLc; BLb; Bod; KGM
AR 1938/9.

   <u>1941</u> Outline **1000/12/41 LR**
PC *AR 1941/2.*

   <u>1942</u> Outline 8 **1,000/12/42.L.R.** [in blue] Imprint erased.
BLf
AR 1942/3.

   [<u>1943</u> or <u>1944</u> Outline; not seen]
AR 1943/4.

64 PETERBOROUGH
Surveyed 1883-7; published 1891-2; revised 1897-8 and 1906; 3rd revision 1916-9.

1922
I 2/1922. M 1922.
L (1)a; (2)c,n,s,u; (3)c,o,s.
S 2. O 1a,2c,3c.
C Red,2e,3(2/6)a,4b[2],5bd,6d.
PC(GSGS 25/8/22); BLa(31/7/22); BLb;
Bod; CUL(27/7/22); RGS(20/4/22)
Supp. to Cat.1 Jan./31 Mar.1922.

   <u>1922</u> Outline 2
BLd(14/9/22); BLe; Bod(21/9/22)
Supp. to Cat.1 Apr./30 June 1922.

1930 2500/30.
I 2/1922; (1)28-9a; (4)30d; roads (2)11.28.
M 1922.
L (1)a,b,g; (2)c,n,s,u; (3)c,o,s.
S 2. O 1a,2b,3c,4b.
C B&Rb,2e,3(2/6)h,4d,5bd,6f.
BLc; KGM; RGS

1935 1035.
I 5/1922. M 1922.

C cover: 271-81; I imprint: 259-62; L legend: 263-5; M magnetic variation; O other marginal data: 266-9;
S scale: 266; (k) left, between legend and map border; (l) left, below legend; location abbreviations: xii;
outline: 282; print codes: 84-7. *AR:* annual report; *Supp.to Cat.* see OS *Catalogues:* 394.

L (1)g,i; (2)e,n,s,u; (3)c,i,o,s.
S 4. O 1a,2b,3b,4b.
C B&Rb,2e,3(2/6)h,4d,5bd,6f.
RGS

1937 2037.M.36.R34.
I 5/1922. M Jan.1937.
L (1)g,i,j; (2)e,n,s,u; (3)c,i,o,s.
S 4. O 1a,2b,3c,4b.
C B&Rb,2e,3(2/6)h,4d,5bd,6j.
BLc; KGM
AR 1936/7.

1940 2040.M38.R37.
I 5/1922. M Jan.1937.
L (1)g,i,j; (2)e,j,n,s,u; (3)c,i,o,s.
S 4. O 1a,2b,3b,4b.
C BRed,2d,3(1/9)d,5bd,6j.
PC; BLb; KGM
AR 1939/40.

> 1941 Outline 8 **1000/11/41L.R.**
> BLf
> *AR 1941/2.*

65 **WISBECH & KING'S LYNN**
Surveyed 1883-7; published 1891-2; revised 1897-8 and 1906-7; 3rd revision 1919-20.
1922
I 2/1922. M 1922.
L (1)a; (2)c,n,s,t; (3)c,o,s.
S 2. O 1a,2c,3b.
C Red,2f,3(2/6)c,4b^2,5bd,6d.
PC(GSGS 29/8/22); BLa(26/1/23); BLb; Bod; CUL(18/1/23); RGS(20/7/22)
Supp. to Cat.1 Jul./30 Sep.1922.

> 1922 Outline 2
> BLd(14/9/22); BLe; Bod(21/9/22)
> *Supp. to Cat.1 Apr./30 June 1922.*

1932 3500/32.
I 2/1922; (1)30a; (5)32d; roads (9)10.28. M 1922.
L (1)a,b,g; (2)c,n,s,u; (3)c,o,s.
S 4. O 1a,2b,3b,4d.
C B&Rb,2h,3(2/6)h,4d,5bd,6f.
BLc; BLb; Bod; RGS

> 1941 Outline 8 (l)**1,000/11/41 L.R.**
> I 5/1922.
> BLf
> *AR 1941/2.*

66 **SWAFFHAM & EAST DEREHAM**
Surveyed 1880-5; published 1890; revised 1897 and 1907-8; 3rd revision 1919-20.
1921
I 2/1921. M 1921.
L (1)a; (2)c,n,s,u; (3)c,o,s.
S 2. O 1b,2c,3a,4a.
C Red,2f,3(1/6)b,4b^2,5bd,6d.
PC; BLa(31/7/22); BLb; Bod; CUL(27/7/22); RGS(21/2/22)
Supp. to Cat.1 Jan./31 Mar.1922.

> 1921 Outline 2
> BLd(31/7/22); BLb; Bod
> *Supp. to Cat.1 Jan./31 Mar.1922.*

> 1942 Outline 7 **1000/3/42LR.** [in blue]
> I 2/1921; (1)28a; roads (5)10.28.
> BLf
> *Although the revision dates for this state might indicate that there had been a reprint of the standard sheet at some date in or after 1928, no such reprint has yet been recorded. However, were an example of the 1921 printing to be found in a B&R cover (i.e. issued 1928, or later), it would be worth making a careful comparison of the topographical content of the map to determine whether or not minor revisions had been made.*

> [1942 or 1943 Outline; not seen]
> *AR 1942/3.*

67 **NORWICH & GREAT YARMOUTH**
Surveyed 1879-85; published 1889-90; revised 1897 and 1908; 3rd revision 1919-20.
1921
I 2/1921. M 1921.
L (1)a; (2)c,n,p,t; (3)c,o,w.
S 2. O 1b,2b,3a,4a,5c.
C Red,2f,3(2/6)d,4b^2,5bd,6e.
PC; BLa(31/7/22); BLb; Bod; CUL(27/7/22); RGS
Supp. to Cat.1 Jan./31 Mar.1922.

> 1921 Outline 2
> BLd(31/7/22); BLe; Bod
> *Supp. to Cat.1 Jan./31 Mar.1922.*

1924 1000/24.
I 2/1921; (1)24d; (4)24-5a. M 1921
L (1)a; (2)c,n,p,t; (3)c,o,w.

S 2. O 1b,2c,3a,4b,5c.
C Red,2f,3(2/6)d,4b^2,5bd,6f.
PC

[**1924-5 1000/24-5** not seen; inferred from 1931; possibly a misprint]

[**1929 500/29** not seen; inferred from 1931]

1931 1000/24-5.500/29.3750/31.
I 2/1921; (1)30d; (4)31a; roads (4)11.28.
M 1921.
L (1)a,b; (2)c,n,p,u; (3)c,o,w.
S 4. O 1b,2b,3a,4b,5c.
C B&Rb,2f,3(2/6)f,4c^2,5bd,6f.
PC; KGM; RGS

1935 2535.
I 6/1921. M 1921.
L (1)g,i; (2)e,n,p,t; (3)c,i,o,w.
S 4. O 1b,2b,3a,4b,5c.
C B&Rb(wr),2h,3(1/9)c,4e,5bd,6f.
BLc; KGM

1939 2539.M.37.R.37.
I 6/1921. M 1937.
L (1)g,i,j; (2)e,j,n,q,t; (3)c,i,o,u.
S 4. O 1b,2b,3b,4b,5c.
C B&Rb,2h,3(1/9)c,4e,5bd,6j.
PC; BLb; KGM; RGS
AR 1939/40. Specification change: inland water in blue stipple.

> 1942 Outline 7 **1000/8/42 L.R.** [in blue]
> No imprint. M 1st.Jan.1940.
> BLf   *AR 1942/3.*

68   BARMOUTH & ABERYSTWYTH
Surveyed 1884-7; published 1894-5; revised 1897-8 and 1903-9; 3rd revision 1918-9.

1922
I 2/1922. M 1922.
L (1)a; (2)c,n,p,t; (3)c,o,s.
S 2. O 1b,2c,3b,5a.
C Red,2f,3(3/6)a,4b^2,5bdh,6d.
PC; BLa(8/5/23); BLb; Bod;
CUL(16/5/23); RGS(15/12/22)
Supp. to Cat.1 Oct./31 Dec.1922. A statement below the adjoining sheets diagram reads: 'Note - The Cambrian and Vale of Rheidol Railways should read Great Western Railway.'

1922 Outline 2
BLd(26/7/23); BLe; Bod
Supp. to Cat.1 Jan./31 Mar.1923.

1929 3000/29.
I 2/1922; (1)23-5a; (4)29d.
M Jan.1929.
L (1)a,b,c,g; (2)c,n,p,t; (3)c,q,u.
S 3. O 1b,2b,3b,4b,5a.
C Red,2f,3(2/6)e,4b^2,5bdh,6f.
PC; BLc; KGM
Specification change: contours reinforced. Railway note omitted.

1932 3000/29.3000/32.
I 2/1922; (1)31a; (4)32d; roads (1) 9·29.
M Jan.1929.
L (1)a,b,c,g; (2)e,n,p,t; (3)c,q,u.
S 4. O 1b,2b,3b,4b,5a.
C B&Rb,2h,3(2/6)h,4d,5bdh,6f.
PC; BLc; RGS

1935 2035.
I 9/1922. M Jan.1929.
L (1)g,i; (2)e,n,p,t; (3)c,i,q,u.
S 4. O 1b,2b,3b,4b,5a.
C B&Rb,2h,3(2/6)h,4d,5bdh,6f.
PC; RGS

1936 4036.M36.R29.
I 9/1922. M Jan.1929.
L (1)g,i,j; (2)e,n,p,t; (3)c,i,q,u.
S 4. O 1b,2b,3b,4b,5a.
C B&Rb,2h,3(2/6)h,4d,5bdh,6f.
PC; BLb; BLc; RGS
AR 1936/7. Welsh glossary note is printed below the imprint.

1939 4039.M39.R39.
I 9/1922.
M Jan.1929.
L (1)g,i,j; (2)e,j,n,p,t; (3)c,i,q,u.
S 4. O 1b,2b,3b,4b,5a.
C BRed,1c,2f,3(2/6)i,4d,5bdh,6j.
PC; KGM; RGS
AR 1939/40.

> 1941 Outline 8 **1,000/11/41 L.R.**
> Imprint erased.
> BLf
> *AR 1941/2.*

C cover: 271-81; I imprint: 259-62; L legend: 263-5; M magnetic variation; O other marginal data: 266-9; S scale: 266; (k) left, between legend and map border; (l) left, below legend; location abbreviations: xii; outline: 282; print codes: 84-7. *AR*: annual report; *Supp.to Cat.* see OS *Catalogues*: 394.

69 LLANIDLOES

Surveyed 1884-8; published 1894-5; revised 1897 and 1908-9; 3rd revision 1919.

1922

I 2/1922. M 1922.
L (1)a; (2)c,n,s,t; (3)c,o,s.
S 2. O 1b,2c,3b.
C Red,2f,3(3/6)a,5bd,6d.
PC; BLa(8/5/23); BLb; Bod;
CUL(16/5/23); PC(GSGS 17/1/23); RGS
Supp. to Cat.1 Oct./31 Dec.1922. 'Note - The Cambrian & Vale of Rheidol Railways should read Great Western Railway' is printed to the right of the scale statement.

1922 Outline 2
BLd(8/5/23); BLe; Bod
Supp. to Cat.1 Oct./31 Dec.1922.

1934 2,700/34.

I 4/1922; (1)33b; (2)29a; (5)34c. M 1922.
L (1)a,b; (2)e,n,s,t; (3)c,o,s.
S 4. O 1b,2b,3b,4b.
C B&Rb,2h,3(2/6)h,4d,5cd,6j.
PC; BLc

1939 2039.M.38.R.37.

I 6/1922. M 1938.
L (1)g,i,j; (2)e,n,s,t; (3)c,i,o,s.
S 4. O 1b,2b,3b,4b.
C B&Rb,2h,3(2/6)h,4d,5bd,6j.
BLc; BLb; Bod
AR 1939/40. Contours are very orange, but not quite the colour of 2nd class roads. Welsh glossary note is printed to the right of the scale statement.

1942 Outline 7 (l)**1,000/6/42.L.R.** [in blue] Imprint erased. M 1936.
BLf   *AR 1942/3.*

70 BISHOP'S CASTLE

Surveyed 1881-8; published 1889-94; revised 1897-8 and 1906-8; 3rd revision 1915-6.

1920

I 2/1920. M 1920.
L (1)a; (2)b,n,s,u; (3)c,k,o,s.
S 1. O 1a,2c,3a,4a.
C Red,2d,3(2/6)a,4b^1,5bd,6d.
PC(GSGS 19/7/22); BLa(23/12/21); BLb;
Bod; CUL(21/12/21); RGS(22/10/20)
Supp. to Cat.1 Jul./30 Sep.1920.

1924 Outline 4
I 2/1924; (1)23a.
BLd(15/12/24); BLe; Bod(16/1/25)
Supp. to Cat.1 Jul./30 Sep.1924.

1932 3000/32.

I 2/1920; (1)31a; (5)32d; roads (4)9-29.
M 1920.
L (1)a,b,c; (2)c,n,s,u; (3)c,q,s.
S 4. O 1a,2b,3b,4b.
C B&Rb,2d,3(2/6)g,4d,5bd,6f.
PC; BLc; RGS
Specification change: contours reinforced.

1935 [1936] 2000/35.

I 6/1920; (5)35k. M 1.ˢᵗ Jan.1936.
L (1)g,i,j; (2)e,n,s,u; (3)c,e,i,o,s.
S 4. O 1a,2b,3b,4b.
C B&Rb,2e,3(2/6)h,4d,5bd,6f.
BLc; KGM
The later date in the heading is derived from the magnetic variation date.

1938a 538.

I 6/1920. M 1.ˢᵗ Jan.1936.
L (1)g,i,j; (2)e,n,s,u; (3)c,e,i,o,s.
S 4. O 1a,2b,3b,4b.
C B&Rb,2e,3(2/6)h,4d,5bd,6j.
PC
The print code is indented so that it is directly under the W.Long.3°20'. The black plate is faint. The 'Other Motor roads' in the legend are drawn as one straight line, rather than being divided into two.

1938b 538.

I 6/1920. M 1.ˢᵗ Jan.1936.
L (1)g,i,j. (2)e,n,s,u; (3)c,e,i,o,s.
S 4. O 1a,2b,3b,4b.
C B&Rb,2e,3(2/6)h,4d,5bd,6j.
PC; KGM
AR 1937/8. The print code is lined up with the left edge of the legend; 'Much Wenlock Branch' in square C13 is erased, and relettered, mostly in C12. The black plate is fresh and crisply printed.

1938c 2538.M.38.R.37.

I 6/1920. M 1.ˢᵗ Jan.1936.
L (1)g,i,j; (2)e,j,n,s,u; (3)c,e,i,o,s.
S 4. O 1a,2b,3b,4b.
C B&Rb,2e,3(2/6)h,4d,5bd,6j.
PC; BLb; BLc; KGM; RGS
AR 1938/9, reprinted. Welsh glossary note

is printed below the scale statement. The 'Much Wenlock Branch' is reinstated in square C13.

> 1942 Outline **1000/4/42 LR**
> PC
> *AR 1942/3.*

> 1943 Outline 7 **600/7/43.Ch.** [in blue]
> BLf
> *AR 1943/4. Traces of erased squaring visible.*

> [1944 or 1945 Outline; not seen]
> *AR 1944/5.*

71 KIDDERMINSTER

Surveyed 1881-5; published 1889-95; revised 1897-8 and 1906-7; 3rd revision 1915-6.

1921

I 2/1921. **M** 1921.
L (1)a; (2)c,n,s,u; (3)c,o,s.
S 1. **O** 1b,2c,3a,4a.
C Red,2a,3(2/6)a,4b^1,5bd,6d.
PC; BLa(23/3/22); BLb; Bod;
CUL(20/3/22); RGS(24/5/21)
Supp. to Cat.1 Apr./30 Jun.1921.

> 1921 Outline 2
> BLd(20/5/22); BLe; Bod
> *Supp. to Cat.1 July/30 Sept.1921.*

1929 3000/29.

I 2/1921; (1)28d; (3)24-6a; (5)29b; roads (5)11·26.
M 1921.
L (1)a; (2)c,n,s,u; (3)c,q,s.
S 3. **O** 1a,2b,3b,4b.
C B&Rb,2g,3(4/-)g,5bd,6f.
BLc; BLb; KGM

1934 3,200/34.

I 4/1921; (1)33b; (2)31a; (5)34c.
M 1921.
L (1)a,b; (2)e,n,s,u; (3)c,q,s.
S 4. **O** 1b,2b,3b,4b.
C B&Rb,2g,3(2/6)h,4d,5bd,6f.
PC; BLc; KGM

1936 3036.

I 6/1921. **M** 1st Jan.1936.
L (1)g,i,j; (2)e,n,s,u; (3)c,i,q,s.
S 4. **O** 1a,2b,3b,4b.

C B&Rb,2g,3(2/6)h,4d,5bd,6j.
BLc
AR 1936/7.

1938 538.

I 6/1921. **M** 1st Jan.1936.
L (1)g,i,j; (2)e,n,s,u; (3)c,i,q,s.
S 4. **O** 1a,2b,3b,4b.
C B&Rb,2g,3(2/6)h,4d,5bd,6f.
PC
AR 1938/9.

1939 2539.M.37.R.37.

I 6/1921. **M** 1938.
L (1)g,i,j; (2)e,j,l,n,q,t; (3)c,e,i,q,s.
S 4. **O** 1a,2b,3b.
C B&Rb,2c,3(4/-)h,5bd,6j.
PC; BLb; Bod
AR 1939/40. Specification change: inland water in blue stipple; contours printed in the same colour as 2nd class roads.

> [1939 or 1940 Outline; not seen]
> *AR 1939/40.*

> [1941 or 1942 Outline; not seen]
> *AR 1941/2.*

> [1942 or 1943 Outline; not seen]
> *AR 1942/3.*

72 BIRMINGHAM

Surveyed 1881-8; published 1892-5; revised 1897-8 and 1906-7; 3rd revision 1915-6.

1921

I 2/1921. **M** 1921.
L (1)a; (2)c,n,s,u; (3)c,o,s.
S 2. **O** 1a,2c,3a,4a.
C Red,2a,3(2/6)d,4b^2,5bd,6d.
PC; BLa(23/3/22); BLb; Bod;
CUL(20/3/22); RGS(12/11/28)
Supp. to Cat.1 Apr./30 Jun.1921.

> 1921 Outline 2
> BLd(20/5/22); BLe; Bod
> *Supp. to Cat.1 July/30 Sept.1921.*

1927 3500/27.

I 2/1921; (1)24-6a; (4)27d; roads (6)11/26.
M 1921.
L (1)a,g; (2)c,n,s,u; (3)c,o,s.
S 2. **O** 1a,2b,3b,4b.
C Red,2a,3(2/6)d,4b^2,5bd,6e.

C cover: 271-81; I imprint: 259-62; L legend: 263-5: **M** magnetic variation; **O** other marginal data: 266-9; S scale: 266; (k) left, between legend and map border; (l) left, below legend; location abbreviations: xii; outlines: 282; print codes: 84-7. *AR*: annual report; *Supp. to Cat.* see OS *Catalogues*: 394.

316

BLc; RGS

Supp. to Cat. 1 Oct./30 Sept. 1927. 'With special Road Revision.'

<u>1928</u> Outline 5 **500/28.**
I 2/1921; (1)24-8a; (4)28b; roads (3)11/26.
PC

1931 3500/31.
I 2/1921; (1)31a; (4)31d; roads (2)11/26.
M 1921.
L (1)a,b,g; (2)c,n,s,u; (3)c,o,s.
S 4. O 1a,2b,3b,4b.
C B&Rb,2g,3(2/6)f,4c¹,5bd,6f.
PC; BLb

1934 4,500/34.
I 4/1921; (1)33b; (2)31a; (5)34c.
M 1921.
L (1)a,b,c,g; (2)e,n,s,u; (3)c,o,s.
S 4. O 1a,2b,3b,4b.
C B&Rb,2e,3(2/6)h,4d,5bd,6f.
KGM

1936 4036.M36.R31.
I 6/1921. M 1936.
L (1)g,i,j; (2)e,n,s,u; (3)c,i,o,s.
S 4. O 1a,2b,3b,4b.
C B&Rb,2e,3(2/6)h,4d,5bd,6f.
RGS
AR 1936/7.

1938 5038.M36.R37.
I 6/1921. M 1936.
L (1)g,i,j; (2)e,j,n,s,u; (3)c,i,o,s.
S 4. O 1a,2b,3b,4b.
C B&Rb,2e,3(2/6)h,4d,5bd,6j.
PC; BLb
AR 1938/9.

<u>1941</u> Outline 8 **1,000/11/41 L.R.**
Imprint erased.
PC
AR 1941/2.

[<u>1942</u> or <u>1943</u> Outline; not seen]
AR 1942/3.

[<u>1943</u> or <u>1944</u> Outline; not seen]
AR 1943/4.

<u>1946</u> Outline 7 **846 Cr.**
BLf

---

73 RUGBY
Surveyed 1883-6; published by 1890-2; revised 1897 and 1904-7; 3rd revision 1915.

1920
I 2/1920.
M 1920.
L (1)a; (2)b,n,s,u; (3)c,k,o,s.
S 1. O 1a,2c,3a,4a.
C Red,2a,3(2/6)a,4b¹,5bd,6d.
PC; BLa(23/12/21); BLb; Bod;
CUL(21/12/21); RGS(22/10/20)
Supp. to Cat.1 Jul./30 Sep.1920.

<u>1924</u> Outline 4
I 2/1924; (1)24a.
BLd(15/12/24); BLe; Bod

Supp. to Cat.1 July/30 Sept. 1924

[<u>1931a</u> **3300/31** not seen; inferred from 1931b]

1931b 3300/31.800/31.
I 2/1920; (1)24-8a; (5)31d; roads (5)8.28.
M 1920.
L (1)a; (2)c,n,s,u; (3)c,o,s.
S 4. O 1a,2b,3b,4b.
C B&Rb,2a,3(2/6)f,4c²,5bd,6f.
BLc

1936 2036.
I 6/1920.
M Jan.1935.
L (1)g,i,j; (2)e,n,s,u; (3)c,i,o,s.
S 4. O 1a,2b,3b,4b.
C B&Rb,2h,3(4/-)h,5bd,6j.
PC; RGS

1939 2039.M.38.R.37.
I 6/1920.
M Jan.1935.
L (1)g,i,j; (2)e,j,n,s,t; (3)c,h,i,o,s.
S 4. O 1a,2b,3b,4b.
C B&Rb,2h,3(2/6)h,4d,5bd,6j.
PC; BLb
AR 1939/40.

<u>1941</u> Outline **1000/10/41 LR**
PC
AR 1941/2.

<u>1943</u> Outline 8 (l)**1000/2/43.L.R.** [in blue]
Imprint erased.
BLf

74 KETTERING & HUNTINGDON
Surveyed 1881-7; published 1890-1; revised 1895-7 and 1904-5; 3rd revision 1915.

1920
I 2/1920. M 1920.
L (1)a; (2)b,n,s,u; (3)c,k,o,s.
S 1. O 1a,2c,3a,4a.
C Red,2a,3(2/6)a,4b^1,5be,6d.
PC; BLa(21/1/22); BLb; Bod;
CUL(17/1/22); RGS(22/10/20)
Supp. to Cat.1 Oct./31 Dec.1920.

   1923 Outline 4
   I 2/1923.
   BLd(13/9/1923); BLe; Bod
   Supp. to Cat.1 Apr./30 Jun.1923.

1930 2500/30.
I 2/1923; (1)24-30a; (4)30d; roads (4)9-28.
M 1920.
L (1)a,b; (2)c,n,s,u; (3)c,q,s.
S 2. O 1a,2b,3b,4b.
C B&Ra,2a,3(2/6)f,4c^2,5be,6f.
PC; BLb; BLc
Specification change: contours reinforced.

1936 2036.
I 9/1923. M Jan.1936.
L (1)g,i,j; (2)e,n,s,u; (3)c,i,q,s.
S 4. O 1a,2b,3b,4b.
C B&Rb,2h,3(2/6)h,4d,5bd,6f.
KGM

1938 2038.M.38.R.37.
I 9/1923. M Jan.1936.
L (1)g,i,j; (2)e,j,n,s,u; (3)c,h,i,q,s.
S 4. O 1a,2b,3b,4b.
C B&Rb,2h,3(2/6)h,4d,5be,6j.
PC; BLc; RGS
AR 1938/9.

   1941 Outline 8 (l)**1000/10/41.L.R.**
   BLf
   AR 1941/2.

75 ELY
Surveyed 1880-7; published 1891; revised 1897 and 1905-7; 3rd revision 1914-5.

1920
I 2/1920. M 1920.
L (1)a; (2)b,n,s,u; (3)c,k,o,s.

S 1. O 1a,2c,3a,4a.
C Red,2a,3(2/6)a,4b^2,5bd,6d.
PC; BLa(23/12/21); BLb; Bod;
CUL(21/12/21); RGS(22/10/20)
Supp. to Cat.1 Jul./30 Sep.1920. A version of this printing has been seen with yellow, rather than orange contours (PC).

   1923 Outline 4
   I 2/1923.
   BLd(13/9/23); BLe; Bod
   Supp. to Cat.1 Apr./30 Jun.1923.

1937 1537.M36.R34.
I 6/1920. M Jan.1926.
L (1)g,i,j; (2)e,n,s,u; (3)c,i,o,s.
S 4. O 1a,2b,3b,4b.
C B&Rb,2h,3(2/6)h,4d,5bd,6j.
PC; BLb; BLc; Bod
AR 1936/7.

1939 2039.M.38.R37.
I 6/1920. M Jan.1926.
L (1)g,i,j; (2)e,j,n,s,u; (3)c,i,o,s.
S 4. O 1a,2b,3b,4b.
C B&Rb,2h,3(2/6)h,4d,5bd,6j.
PC; KGM
AR 1938/9.

   1941 Outline 8 (l)**1000/10/41.L.R.**
   BLf
   AR 1941/2.

76 THETFORD
Surveyed 1880-5; published 1899; revised 1897 and 1905-7; 3rd revision 1914.

1920
I 2/1920. M 1920.
L (1)a; (2)b,n,s,u; (3)c,o,s.
S 1. O 1a,2c,3a,4a.
C Red,2a,3(2/6)a,4b^1,5bd,6d.
PC; BLa(21/1/22); BLb; Bod;
CUL(17/1/22); RGS(11/11/20)
Supp. to Cat.1 Oct./31 Dec.1920.

   1920 Outline 2
   BLd(20/5/22); BLe; Bod
   Supp. to Cat.1 Jul./30 Sep.1921.

1937 1537.M36.R34.
I 6/1920. M 1937.
L (1)g,i,j; (2)e,n,s,u; (3)c,i,o,s.

C cover: 271-81; I imprint: 259-62; L legend: 263-5: M magnetic variation; O other marginal data: 266-9; S scale: 266;   (k) left, between legend and map border;   (l) left, below legend;   location abbreviations: xii; outlines: 282;   print codes: 84-7. *AR*: annual report; *Supp. to Cat.* see OS *Catalogues*: 394.

S 4. O 1a,2b,3b,4b.
C B&Rb,2h,3(2/6)h,4d,5bd,6j.
PC
AR 1936/7.

1940 2040.M.38.R.37.
I 6/1920. M 1937.
L (1)g,i,j; (2)e,j,n,s,t; (3)c,h,i,o,s.
S 4. O 1a,2b,3b,4b.
C BRed,1c,2g,3(2/6)i,5bd,6j.
PC; BLc; KGM
Specification change: inland water in blue stipple.

   1941 Outline 8 **1,000/11/41 L.R.**
BLf   *AR 1941/2.*

77 LOWESTOFT & WAVENEY VALLEY
Surveyed 1880-5; published 1889; revised 1897 and 1905-7; 3rd revision 1914-9.

1921
I 2/1921. M 1921.
L (1)a; (2)c,n,p,u; (3)c,o,w.
S 2. O 1a,2c,3a,4a,5c.
C Red,2f,3(2/6)c,4b^2,5bd,6d.
PC; BLa(31/7/22); BLb; Bod;
CUL(27/7/22); RGS(21/2/22)
Supp. to Cat.1 Jan./31 Mar.1922.

   1921 Outline 2
BLd(17/6/22); BLb; Bod(5/7/22)
Supp. to Cat.1 Oct./31 Dec.1921.

1933 2,500/33.
I 4/1921; (2)28a; (5)33c; (6)33b.
M 1921.
L (1)a,b; (2)e,n,p,t; (3)c,o,w.
S 4. O 1a,2b,3b,4b,5a.
C B&Rb,2h,3(2/6)h,4d,5bd,6f.
BLc; KGM; RGS

1937a 2037.M36.R34.
I 6/1921. M Jan.1937.
L (1)g,i,j; (2)e,n,p,t; (3)c,i,o,w.
S 4. O 1a,2b,3b,4b,5a.
C B&Rb,2h,3(2/6)h,4d,5bd,6f.
PC   *AR 1936/7.*

1937b 1537,M.36,R.36.
I 6/1921. M Jan 1st 1937.
L (1)g,i,j; (2)e,n,q,u; (3)a,h,i,o,w.
S 4. O 1a,2b,3b,4b,5a.
C B&Rb,2h,3(2/6)h,4d,5bd,6j.
PC
AR 1937/8. Specification change: inland

water and sea in blue stipple; parks in black stipple.

   [1937 or 1938 Outline; not seen]
AR 1937/8.

1938 2538.M.38.R.37.
I 6/1921. M Jan.1st 1938.
L (1)g,i,j; (2)e,j,l,n,q,u; (3)a,e,i,m,q,s.
S 4. O 1a,2b,3b,4b,5a.
C B&Rb,2h,3(2/6)h,4d,5bd,6j.
PC
AR 1938/9.

   1941 Outline 8 **1,000/11/41 L.R.**
Date erased from imprint.
BLf
AR 1941/2.

78 LAMPETER
Surveyed 1885-8; published 1894; revised 1897 and 1908-9; 3rd revision 1919.

1923
I 2/1923. M 1922.
L (1)a; (2)c,n,p,t; (3)c,o,u.
S 2. O 1b,2c,3b,4b,5a.
C Red,2f,3(2/6)c,4b^2,5bd,6d.
PC; BLa(19/10/23); BLb; Bod(13/12/23);
CUL (18/10/23); RGS(16/10/23)
Supp. to Cat.1 Jul./30 Sep.1923.

   1923 Outline 4
BLd(1/2/24); BLe; Bod(8/2/24)
Supp. to Cat.1 Oct./31 Dec.1923.

1935 1535.
I 6/1923. M 1922.
L (1)g,i; (2)e,n,p,t; (3)c,i,o,u.
S 4. O 1b,2b,3b,4b,5a.
C B&Rb,2g,3(2/6)h,4d,6j.
PC; KGM

1938 2038.M.37.R.37.
I 6/1923. M 1938.
L (1)g,i,j; (2)e,n,p,t; (3)c,i,o,s.
S 4. O 1b,2b,3b,4b,5a.
C BRed,2g,3(2/6)i,5bd,6j.
KGM; BLb; Bod
AR 1938/9. Welsh glossary note is printed below the price statement.

   1942 Outline 7 **1,000/3/42 L.R.** [in blue]
Imprint erased.
BLf
Lacks the Welsh glossary note.

[1942 or 1943 Outline; not seen]
AR 1942/3.

79 LLANDRINDOD WELLS
Surveyed 1884-8; published 1894; revised 1897 and 1908-9; 3rd revision 1919.

1923
I 2/1923. M 1922.
L (1)a; (2)c,n,s,u; (3)c,o,s.
S 2. O 1a,2c,3b,4b.
C Red,2a,3(2/6)d,4b^2,5bd,6d.
PC; BLa(10/10/23); BLb; Bod;
CUL(18/10/23); RGS(25/8/23)
Supp. to Cat.1 Jul./30 Sep.1923.

1923 Outline 4
BLd(1/2/24); BLe; Bod(8/2/24)
Supp. to Cat.1 Oct./31 Dec.1923.

1933 2,500/33.
I 4/1922; (2)31a; (5)33c; (6)32b.
M 1922.
L (1)a,b; (2)e,n,s,u; (3)c,o,s.
S 4. O 1a,2b,3b,4b.
C B&Rb,2i,3(2/6)h,4d,5bd,6f.
PC; BLc; Bod; KGM

[1937 or 1938 Outline; not seen]
AR 1937/8.

1938 M37.R37.2538.
I 6/1922. M 1937.
L (1)g,i,j; (2)e,n,q,u; (3)c,h,i,o,s.
S 4. O 1a,2b,3b,4b.
C B&Rb,2i,3(2/6)h,4d,5bd,6j.
BLc; BLb; Bod; KGM
AR 1938/9. Specification change: inland water in blue stipple. Welsh glossary note is printed below the price statement.

1941 Outline 8 **1,000/11/41 L.R.**
Date erased from imprint.
BLf
AR 1941/2. Lacks the Welsh glossary note.

80 KINGTON
Surveyed 1883-8; published 1893-4; revised 1897 and 1907-8; 3rd revision 1915-6.

1920a
I 2/1920. M 1920.
L (1)a; (2)b,n,s,u; (3)c,k,o,s.

S 1. O 1a,2c[gap],3a,4a.
C Red,2a,3(2/6)a,4b^1,5bd,6d.
PC; BLa(23/12/21); BLb; Bod;
CUL(21/12/21); RGS
Supp.to Cat.1 Jul./30 Sep.1920. There is sufficient space between the contour and copyright notes for the 1/- price note to have been present. There may be an earlier state with the price note; it is more likely that the price was removed from the black outline plate, which may have been ready before January 1920 (when the price increased to 1/6), before printing.

1920b
Identical to **1920a** *except that the circular railway stations have a red fill - i.e.* L (2)d - *on the face of the map and in the legend. The only example of this sheet so far seen is printed on the reverse of a 1:25,000 map of Gallipoli. It may pre-date* **1920a** *because it is cased in the earliest of the red cover styles, whereas examples of* **1920a** *are known in later cover styles, including one inscribed with the date of purchase in 1931.* PC

1924 Outline 4
I 1/1924.
BLd(16/9/24); BLe; Bod(9/10/24)
Supp. to Cat.1 Apr./30 June 1924.

1932 3000/32.
I 2/1920; (1)31a; (4)32d; roads (6)8.31.
M 1920.
L (1)a,b,g; (2)c,n,s,u; (3)c,o,s.
S 4. O 1a,2b,3b,4b.
C B&Rb,2e,3(2/6)g,4d,5bd,6f.
BLc; KGM; RGS

1938 20/38.M37.R37.
I 6/1920. M 1920.
L (1)g,i,j; (2)e,n,s,u; (3)c,e,i,o,s.
S 4. O 1a,2b,3b,4b.
C B&Rb,2h,3(2/6)h,4d,5bd,6j.
BLc; BLb; Bod; KGM
AR 1938/9. Contours printed in same colour as 2nd class roads. Welsh glossary note is printed below the price statement.

1941 Outline 8 **1,000/11/41 L.R.**
I 5/1920 Southampton erased.
PC *AR 1941/2. Lacks Welsh glossary note.*

C cover: 271-81; I imprint: 259-62; L legend: 263-5: M magnetic variation; O other marginal data: 266-9;
S scale: 266; (k) left, between legend and map border; (l) left, below legend; location abbreviations: xii;
outlines: 282; print codes: 84-7. *AR:* annual report; *Supp. to Cat.* see OS *Catalogues*: 394.

81 WORCESTER

Surveyed 1882-6; published 1893-5; revised 1897 and 1907; 3rd revision 1915.

1920

I 2/1920. M 1920.
L (1)a; (2)b,n,s,u; (3)c,k,o,s.
S 1. O 1a,2c,3a,4a.
C Red,2a,3(2/6)d,4b^2,5bd,6f.
PC; BLa(21/1/22); BLb; Bod;
CUL(17/1/22); RGS(29/7/27)
Supp. to Cat.1 Oct./31 Dec.1920.

  1924 Outline 4
  I 2/1924; (1)24a.
  BLd(7/8/25); BLe; Bod
  Supp. to Cat.1 Oct./31 Dec.1924.

1928 5000/28.

I 2/1920; (1)28a; (4)28d; roads (9)6.28.
M 1920.
L (1)a; (2)c,n,s,u; (3)c,q,s.
S 2. O 1a,2b,3b,4b.
C B&Rb,2a,3(2/6)f,4c^2,6f.
PC; BLb; BLc; KGM; RGS
Specification change: contours reinforced.

1936 3036.

I 9/1920. M 1ˢᵗ Jan.1936.
L (1)g,i,j; (2)e,n,s,u; (3)c,i,q,s.
S 4. O 1a,2b,3b,4b.
C B&Rb,2e,3(2/6)h,4d,5bd,6f.
PC; BLc; KGM; RGS

1938 3038.M38.R37.

I 7/1920. M 1ˢᵗ Jan.1936.
L (1)g,i,j; (2)e,j,n,s,u; (3)c,i,q,s.
S 4. O 1a,2b,3b,4b.
C B&Rb,2e,3(2/6)h,4d,5bd,6j.
PC; BLb; BLc; Bod; KGM
AR 1938/9.

  [1942 or 1943 Outline; not seen]
  AR 1942/3.

82 STRATFORD ON AVON (STRATFORD-on-AVON and DISTRICT)

Surveyed 1880-6; published 1891-5; revised 1893-7 and 1906-7; 3rd revision 1915.

1919

I 2/1919. M 1919.
L (1)a; (2)b,n,q,u; (3)a,k,o,s.
S 1. O 1a,2a,3a,4a.
C Red,2a,3(3/6)a,5bd,6g.
PC; BLa(3/12/20); BLb; Bod;

CUL(30/11/20); RGS(16/2/20)
Supp. to Cat.Oct.1919.

  1923 Outline 5
  I 2/1919; (1)23b.
  BLd(11/9/25); BLe; Bod(27/10/25)
  Supp. to Cat.1 Jan./31 Mar. 1925.
  Specification change: contours reinforced.

1923 1000/23.

I 2/1923; (1)23c; (4)23a. M 1919.
L (1)a; (2)c,n,q,u; (3)a,o,s.
S 1. O 1a,2c,3a,4b.
C Red,2a,3(1/6)b,4a,5bd,6d.
PC; BLc
Specification change: contours not reinforced.

1930 3500/30.

I 2/1919; (1)29c; (4)30f; roads (5)7/28.
M 1919.
L (1)a; (2)c,n,q,u; (3)a,q,s.
S 3. O 1a,2b,3b,4b.
C B&Rb,2a,3(2/6)f,4c^2,5bd,6f.
PC; BLc
Specification change: contours reinforced.

1933 3,000/33.

I 4/1919; (5)33c; (7)33a.
M 1919.
L (1)h,g; (2)e,n,q,u; (3)a,h,q,s.
S 4. O 1a,2b,3b,4b.
C B&Rb,2g,3(2/6)h,4d,5bd,6f.
PC; BLc; RGS

1935 2535.

I 6/1919.
M Jan.1935.
L (1)g,i,j; (2)e,n,q,u; (3)a,i,q,s.
S 4. O 1a,2b,3b,4b.
C B&Rb,2g,3(2/6)h,4d,5bd,6i.
PC; BLc; RGS

1937 4037.M.36.R.33.

I 6/1919.
M Jan.1935.
L (1)g,i,j; (2)e,n,q,u; (3)a,i,q,s.
S 4. O 1a,2b,3b,4b.
C B&Rb,2g,3(2/6)h,4d,5bd,6j.
PC; BLc
AR 1937/8.

  [1939 or 1940 Outline; not seen]
  AR 1939/40.

1940 4040.M39.R39.
I 6/1919. M Jan.1935.
L (1)g,i,j; (2)e,j,n,q,u; (3)a,i,q,s.
S 4. O 1a,2b,3b,4b.
C BRed,1c,2g,3(2/6)i,5bd,6j.
PC; BLb; Bod
AR 1939/40. Specification change: contours printed in the same colour as 2nd class roads.

1941 Outline 8 **1,000/11/41 L.R.**
Imprint erased.
PC
AR 1941/2.

1943 Outline 2 **800/2/43.L.R.** [in blue, traces of 1940 print code are visible underneath]
Imprint erased.
PC

83 NORTHAMPTON (NORTHAMPTON AND DISTRICT)
Surveyed 1880-86; published 1888-92; revised 1893-7 and 1904-7; 3rd rev. 1915.

1919
I 2/1919. M 1919.
L (1)a; (2)b,n,q,u; (3)a,k,o,s.
S 1. O 1a,2a,3a,4a.
C Red,2a,3(3/6)a,5bd,6d.
PC; BLa(3/12/20); BLb; Bod;
CUL(30/11/20); PC(GSGS 25/4/25); RGS
Supp. to Cat.Dec.1919.

1924 Outline 5
I 2/1919; (1)24a.
BLd(11/9/25); BLe; Bod(27/10/25)
Supp. to Cat.1 Jan./31 Mar.1925.
Specification change: contours reinforced.

1925 500/25.
I 2/1919; (1)24a; (4)25b. M 1919.
L (1)a; (2)c,n,s,u; (3)c,q,s.
S 2. O 1a,2c,3b,4b.
C Red,1b,[no price],5p,6d.
BLc
Specification change: parks in green ruling.

1930 3000/30.
I 2/1919; (1)28a; (4)30d; roads (5)8-28.
M 1919.
L (1)a,b; (2)c,n,s,u; (3)c,q,s.

S 4. O 1a,2b,3b,4b.
C Red,1b,[no price],5p,6d.
PC; BLc

1931 Outline 5 **3000/30.500/31.** PC

1935a 1535. (NORTHAMPTON)
I 5/1919. M 1919.
L (1)g,i; (2)e,n,s,u; (3)c,i,q,s.
S 4. O 1a,2b,3b,4b.
C B&Rb,2e,3(/6)h,4d,5bd,6f.
PC; BLc

1935b 1535,435.
I 5/1919. M 1919.
L (1)g,i; (2)e,n,s,u; (3)c,i,q,s.
S 4. O 1a,2b,3b,4b.
C B&Rb,2e,3(2/6)h,4d,5bd,6f.
BLc

1936 3036.M.36.R.33.
I 5/1919. M 1st Jan.1937.
L (1)g,i,j; (2)e,n,s,u; (3)c,i,q,s.
S 4. O 1a,2b,3b,4b.
C BRed,1c,2d,3(2/6)i,4d,5bd,6j.
BLc; BLb; KGM
AR 1936/7.

1941 Outline 8 (l)**1000/10/41.L.R.**
I 4/Southampton and date erased.
PC
AR 1941/2. The print code is written over a partially deleted and mostly illegible previous print code; last two digits '/39'?.

84 BEDFORD
Surveyed 1880-7; published 1887-91; revised 1893-7 and 1904-5; 3rd revision 1914-5.

1919
I 2/1919. M 1919.
L (1)a; (2)b,n,q,t; (3)a,k,o,s.
S 1. O 1a,2a,3a,4a.
C Red,2a,3(2/6)b,5bd,6d.
PC; BLa(3/12/20); BLb; Bod;
CUL(30/11/20); RGS(12/12/19)
Supp. to cat. Oct.1919.

1923 Outline 4
I 2/1923.
BLd(13/9/23); BLe; Bod
Supp. to Cat.1 Apr./30 Jun.1923.

C cover: 271-81; I imprint: 259-62; L legend: 263-5; M magnetic variation; O other marginal data: 266-9; S scale: 266; (k) left, between legend and map border; (l) left, below legend; location abbreviations: xii; outline: 282; print codes: 84-7. *AR*: annual report; *Supp. to Cat.* see OS *Catalogues*: 394.

1924 750/24.
I 2/1919; (4)24a. M 1919.
L (1)a; (2)c,n,q,t; (3)c,o,s.
S 2. O 1a,2c,3b,4b. Flat.
PC
Specification change: parks in green ruling.

1930 750/24.2500/30.
I 2/1919; (1)30d; (4)30a; roads (1)9·28.
M 1919.
L (1)a,b; (2)c,n,q,u; (3)c,q,s.
S 3. O 1a,2b,3b,4b.
C B&Rb,2f,3(2/6)f,4c^2,5bd,6f.
KGM; BLb; BLc
Specification change: contours reinforced.

1935 1535.
I 6/1919. M 1919.
L (1)i; (2)e,n,q,u; (3)c,i,q,s.
S 4. O 1a,2b,3b,4b.
C B&Rb,2h,3(2/6)h,4d,5bd,6f.
PC; BLb; BLc; RGS

1936a 1535.2036.
I 6/1919. M 1st Jan.1936.
L (1)g,i,j; (2)e,n,q,t; (3)c,i,q,s.
S 4. O 1a,2b,3b,4b.
C B&Rb,2h,3(2/6)h,4d,5bd,6j.
PC; KGM
AR 1936/7.

  1936b Outline 5 **1535.436.**
  BLf *AR 1936/7.*

1938 2038.M38.R37.
I 6/1919. M 1st Jan.1936.
L (1)g,i,j; (2)e,j,n,q,u; (3)c,i,q,s.
S 4. O 1a,2b,3b,4b.
C B&Rb(wr),2h,3(1/9)c,4e,5bd,6j.
PC; BLc
AR 1938/9.

  1941 Outline 8 **1000/10/41.L.R.**
  Southampton and date erased from
  imprint.
  PC *AR 1941/2.*

85 CAMBRIDGE
Surveyed 1875-87; published 'by' 1890-1;
revised 1893-7 and 1904-5; 3rd revision
1914-5.

1920
I 2/1920. M 1920.
L (1)a; (2)b,n,q,u; (3)c,k,o,s.
S 1. O 1a,2c[gap],3a,4a.

C Red,2a,3(2/6)a,4b^2,5bd,6d.
PC; BLa; BLb; Bod; CUL(27/9/21);
RGS(2/7/20)
Supp. to Cat.Feb.1920. There is enough
space for a 1/- price note to have been
present; it was probably erased from the
outline plate just before printing, after the
price rise in January 1920.

  1923 Outline 4
  I 2/1923.
  BLd(13/9/23); BLe; Bod
  Supp. to Cat.1 Apr./30 Jun.1923.

1929 3000/29.
I 2/1923 [sic]; (1)29a; (5)29d; roads (4)9-
28. M 1920.
L (1)a,i; (2)c,n,q,u; (3)c,o,s.
S 2. O 1a,2b,3b,4b.
C B&Rb,2a,3(2/6)f,4c^2,5bd,6f.
BLc; BLb; KGM; RGS

1932 3500/32.
I 2/1923; (1)29a; (4)32d; roads (4)9-28.
M 1920.
L (1)a,b,g; (2)c,n,q,u; (3)c,o,s.
S 4. O 1a,2b,3b,4b.
C B&Rb,2f,3(2/6)g,4d,5bd,6f.
PC; Bod; KGM; RGS
The RGS example, now placed at England
and Wales Gen.80, was formerly OS
Specimen 56: 'Ordnance Survey 56' is
written in blue ink in Ian Mumford's hand,
and has subsequently been crossed out in
black ballpoint pen [by Francis Herbert].

1936 3036.
I 6/1923. M 1st Jan.1936.
L (1)g,i,j; (2)e,n,q,u; (3)c,i,o,s.
S 4. O 1a,2b,3b,4b.
C B&Rb,2e,3(2/6)h,4d,5bd,6f.
PC; Bod

1939 3039.M.38.R.37.
I 6/1923. M 1st Jan.1936.
L (1)g,i,j; (2)e,j,n,q,t; (3)c,h,i,o,s.
S 4. O 1a,2b,3b,4b.
C BRed,1c,2g,3(2/6)i,5bd,6j.
PC; BLb; BLc
AR 1938/9.

  1941 Outline **1000/10/41 LR**
  PC *AR 1941/2.*

  1942 Outline 7 **1,000/10/42 L.R.**
  BLf *AR 1942/3.*

86 BURY ST.EDMUNDS & SUDBURY
Surveyed 1875-85; published 1889-90;
revised 1893-7 and 1905-6; 3rd revision
1914-19.

1921
I 2/1921. M 1ˢᵗ Janʸ 1921.
L (1)a; (2)c,n,s,u; (3)c,f,o,s.
S 1. O 1a,2c,3a,4a.
C Red,2a,3(3/6)a,5bd,6d.
PC; BLa(23/3/22); BLb; Bod;
CUL(20/3/22); PC(GSGS 19/7/22);
RGS(24/5/21)
Supp. to Cat.1 Apr./30 Jun.1921.

  1921 Outline 2
BLd(20/5/22); BLe; Bod
Supp. to Cat.1 Jul./30 Sep.1921

1935 2735.
I 5/1921. M 1ˢᵗ Janʸ 1935.
L (1)a,b,c,g; (2)e,n,s,u; (3)a,i,o,s.
S 4. O 1a,2b,3b,4b.
C B&Rb,2h,3(2/6)h,4d,6f.
PC; BLc; KGM
Specification change: parks in black stipple.

1938 2538.M38.R37.
I 5/1921. M 1ˢᵗ Janʸ 1935.
L (1)g,i,j; (2)e,j,n,s,u; (3)a,i,o,s.
S 4. O 1a,2b,3b,4b.
C B&Rb,2h,3(2/6)h,4d,6j.
PC; BLb; KGM
AR 1938/9.

  1941 Outline 8 **1000/10/41.L.R.**
Southampton and date erased from
imprint.
BLf *AR 1941/2.*

87 IPSWICH
Surveyed 1879-85; published 1889-90;
revised 1893-7 and 1905-6; 3rd revision
1914-19.
1921
I 2/1921. M 1921.
L (1)a; (2)c,n,p,t; (3)c,f,o,w.
S 1. O 1b,2c,3a,4a,5a.
C Red,2a,3(3/6)a,5bd,6d.
PC; BLa(23/3/22); BLb; Bod;
CUL(20/3/22); RGS(22/7/21)
Supp. to Cat.1 Apr./30 Jun.1921.

  1921 Outline 2
BLd(20/5/22); BLe; Bod
Supp. to Cat.1 Jul./30 Sep.1921

1933 2,700/33.
I 4/1921; (1)33b; (2)33a; (5)33c.
M 1921.
L (1)a,b; (2)e,n,p,t; (3)c,o,w.
S 4. O 1b,2b,3a,4b,5a.
C B&Rb,2h,3(2/6)g,4d,5bd,6f.
PC; BLc

1936 2036,M.36,R.33.
I 6/1921.
M 1936.
L (1)g,i,j; (2)e,n,p,t; (3)c,i,o,w.
S 4. O 1b,2b,3b,4b,5a.
C B&Rb,2h,3(2/6)h,4e,5bd,6f.
PC

1937 25/37.M37.R36.
I 6/1921.
M 1936.
L (1)g,i,j; (2)e,j,n,p,t; (3)c,i,o,w.
S 4. O 1b,2b,3b,4b,5a.
C B&Rb,2h,3(2/6)h,4d,5bd,6j.
PC; BLb; Bod; KGM
AR 1936/7.

[1937 or **1938** not seen]
AR 1937/8.

  1941 Outline 8 **1,000/11/41 L.R.**
BLf
AR 1941/2.

88 ST.DAVID'S & CARDIGAN
Surveyed 1886-8; published 1894; revised
1896-7 and 1909; 3rd revision 1919.

1923
I 2/1923. M 1922.
L (1)a; (2)c,n,p,t; (3)c,o,u.
S 2. O 1b,2c,3b,4b,5a.
C Red,2f,3(3/6)a,5bd,6g.
PC; BLa(13/9/23); BLb; Bod;
CUL(13/9/23); PC(GSGS 30/7/23); RGS
Supp. to Cat.1 Apr./30 Jun.1923.

  1923 Outline 2
BLd(7/8/25); BLe; Bod
Supp. to Cat.1 Oct./31 Dec.1923.

C cover: 271-81; I imprint: 259-62; L legend: 263-5; M magnetic variation; O other marginal data: 266-9;
S scale: 266; (k) left, between legend and map border; (l) left, below legend; location abbreviations: xii;
324   outline: 282; print codes: 84-7. *AR*: annual report; *Supp. to Cat.* see OS *Catalogues*: 394.

1935 1535.
I 5/1923. M 1922.
L (1)g,i; (2)e,n,p,t; (3)c,i,o,u.
S 4. **O** 1b,2b,3b,4b,5a.
C B&Rb(wr),2h,3(1/9)c,4e,5bd,6i.
PC; BLc; KGM; RGS

1937 2037.M.36.R.31.
I 5/1923. M 1922.
L (1)g,i,j; (2)e,n,p,t; (3)c,i,o,u.
S 4. **O** 1b,2b,3b,4b,5a.
C B&Rb,2h,3(2/6)h,4d,5bd,6i.
PC; BLc; KGM
AR 1937/8.

1939 3039.M.39.R.38.
I 5/1923. M 1922.
L (1)g,i,j; (2)e,j,n,q,t; (3)c,i,o,u.
S 4. **O** 1b,2b,3b,4b,5a.
C B&Rb,2h,3(2/6)h,4d,5bd,6j.
BLc; BLb; KGM
AR 1939/40. Specification change: sea and inland water in blue stipple.

   1941 Outline 8 **1,000/11/41 L.R.**
Southampton and date erased from imprint. BLf *AR 1941/2.*

89 CARMARTHEN
Surveyed 1875-88; published 1892-4; revised 1894-7 and 1908-9; 3rd revision 1919-20.

1923
I 2/1923. M 1922.
L (1)a; (2)c,n,r[vertical ruled lines],t; (3)c,o,s.
S 2. **O** 1b,2c,3b,4b.
C Red,2f,3(3/6)a,5bd,6g.
PC; BLa(13/9/23); BLb; Bod;
CUL(13/9/23); RGS(29/7/27)
Supp. to Cat.1 Apr./30 Jun.1923. The estuaries of the rivers Taf and Towy are shown by horizontal ruled blue lines.

   1923 Outline 2
BLd(26/7/23); BLe; Bod
Supp. to Cat.1 Jan./31 Mar.1923

1936 2036.
I 6/1923. M 1922.
L (1)g,i,j; (2)e,n,r,t; (3)c,i,o,s.
S 4. **O** 1b,2b,3b,4b.
C B&Rb,2e,3(2/6)h,4d,5bd,6i.
PC; BLb; BLc; KGM
AR 1936/7.

1940 2540.M39.R39.
I 6/1923. M 1922.
L (1)g,i,j; (2)e,j,n,s,t; (3)c,i,o,s.
S 4. **O** 1b,2b,3b,4b.
C BRed,1c,2f,3(2/6)i,5bd,6j.
PC

   1941 Outline 8 **1,000/11/41 L.R.**
Imprint erased.
BLf   *AR 1941/2.*

   [**1942** or **1943** Outline; not seen]
AR 1942/3.

90 BRECON & LLANDOVERY
Surveyed 1867-88; published 1894; revised 1893-7 and 1907-9; 3rd revision 1919-20.

1923
I 2/1923. M 1922.
L (1)a; (2)c,n,s,t; (3)c,o,s.
S 2. **O** 1a,2c,3b,4b.
C Red,2f,3(2/6)c,4b^2,5bd,6g.
RGS(29/7/27); BLa(19/10/23); BLb; Bod;
CUL(18/10/23)
Supp. to Cat.1 Jul./30 Sep.1923.

   1923 Outline 4
BLd(1/2/24); BLe; Bod(8/2/24)
Supp. to Cat.1 Oct./31 Dec.1923.

1931 3500/31.
I 2/1923; (1)31a; (4)31d; roads (1)8/31.
M 1922.
L (1)a,b; (2)c,n,s,u; (3)c,o,s.
S 4. **O** 1a,2c,3b,4b.
C B&Rb,2f,3(2/6)f,4c^1,5bd,6i.
PC; BLc; RGS

1938 2038.M.37.R.37.
I 6/1925[sic]. M 1937.
L (1)g,i,j; (2)e,n,s,u; (3)c,i,o,s.
S 4. **O** 1a,2b,3b,4b.
C B&Rb,2h,3(2/6)h,4d,5bd,6j.
PC; BLc; KGM
AR 1937/8. Welsh glossary note is printed to the right of the scale statement.

1940 2040.M.39.R.39.
I 6/1925. M 1937.
L (1)g,i,j; (2)e,n,s,u; (3)c,i,o,s.
S 4. **O** 1a,2b,3b,4b.
C B&Rb,2h,3(2/6)h,4d,5bd,6j.
PC; BLb; Bod
AR 1939/40.

1941 Outline 8 **1,000/11/41 L.R.**
Southampton erased from imprint.
BLf *AR 1941/2. No Welsh glossary note.*

91 ABERGAVENNY (Abergavenny & District)

Surveyed 1872-87; published 1893; revised
1893-4 and 1904-8; 3rd revision 1913.

1919a
I 2/1919. M 1919.
L (1)a; (2)b,n,q,r,t; (3)a,k,o,s.
S 1. O 1a,2a,3a,4a.
C Buff,2a,3(2/6)b,5a¹d,6g.
PC; BLa(13/10/19); Bod; CUL(28/9/19);
RGS
Supp. to Cat.Jun.1919.

[1919b]
This example is identical to **1919a** *except for
the circular railway stations which are red on
the map and in the legend (i.e.* **L** *(2)d).*
PC

1921 (l)7·21.
I 2/1919. M 1919.
L (1)a; (2)b,n,q,r,t; (3)a,k,o,s.
S 1. O 1a,2c[gap],3a,4a. Flat.
BLb; RGS(29/7/27)
*Close's honours include the C.M.G., rather
than F.R.S of the first printing; this imprint
may have been taken in error from an earlier
version of the template.*

1923 Outline 5
I (1)23a.
BLd(29/10/25); BLe; Bod
Supp. to Cat.1 Apr./30 Jun.1925.
Specification change: contours reinforced.

1924 1000/24.
I 2/1919; (1)23a; (4)24d.
M 1919.
L (1)a; (2)c,n,q,t; (3)a,o,s.
S 1. O 1a,2c,3a,4b.
C Red,2a,3(3/6)a,5bd,6i.
BLc

1934 2,000/34. ABERGAVENNEY.
I 4/1919; (1)32b; (2)32a; (5)34c.
M Jan.1931.
L (1)a,b,c,g; (2)e,n,q,u; (3)a,e,i,k,o,s.
S 4. O 1a,2b,3b,4b.

C B&Rb,2h,3(2/6)h,4d,5bd,6i.
PC; BLc
*Specification change: parish boundaries are
shown.*

1937 2537.M.37.R.32.
I 6 ['imprints']/1919. M Jan.1937.
L (1)g,i,j; (2)e,n,q,t; (3)a,e,i,k,o,s.
S 4. O 1a,2b,3b,4b.
C B&Rb,2h,3(2/6)h,4d,6j.
PC; BLb; BLc
*AR 1936/7. Welsh glossary note is printed to
the right of the scale bar.*

1941 Outline **1000/11/41 LR**
PC *AR 1941/2.*

[1944 or 1945 Outline; not seen]
AR 1944/5.

92 GLOUCESTER & FOREST OF DEAN

Surveyed 1877-87; published 1892-3; revised
1894-6 and 1903-8; 3rd revision 1913.

1919
I 2/1919. M 1919.
L (1)a; (2)b,n,q,r,t; (3)a,k,o,s.
S 1. O 1a,2a,3a,4a.
C Buff,2a,3(1/6)a,4b²,5a²d,6e.
PC; BLa(13/10/19); Bod; CUL(28/9/19)
Supp. to Cat.Jun.1919.

1921 (l)6.21.
I 2/1919. M 1919.
L (1)a; (2)b,n,p,q,r,t; (3)a,k,o,u.
S 1. O 1a,2c[gap],3a,4a.
C Red,1b,3(3/6)c,5n,6d.
PC; BLb; BLc; RGS

1925 Outline 5 **600/25.**
I 2/1919. (1)24a; (4)25b
BLe

1928 3500/28. GLOUCESTER & FOREST OF DEAN.
I 2/1919; (1)24-8a; (4)28d; roads 5/26.
M Jan.1925.
L (1)a,b,c,i; (2)c,n,s,t; (3)c,q,s.
S 2. O 1a,2b,3b,4b.
C B&Ra,2a,3(2/6)d,4b²,5bd,6i.
PC; BLc
*Specification change: contours reinforced;
parks in green ruling.*

C cover: 271-81; I imprint: 259-62; L legend: 263-5; M magnetic variation; O other marginal data: 266-9;
S scale: 266; (k) left, between legend and map border; (l) left, below legend; location abbreviations: xii;
outline: 282; print codes: 84-7. *AR*: annual report; *Supp. to Cat.* see OS *Catalogues*: 394.

1933 3,000/33.
I 4/1919; (5)33c; (7)32a. **M** Jan.1925.
L (1)a,b,c,g; (2)e,n,s,u; (3)c,q,s.
S 4. **O** 1a,2b,3b,4b.
C B&Rb,2h,3(2/6)h,4d,5bd,6i.
PC; BLc

1936 3036.
I 6/1919. **M** Jan.1925.
L (1)g,i,j; (2)e,n,s,u; (3)c,i,q,s.
S 4. **O** 1a,2b,3b,4b.
C B&Rb,2h,3(2/6)h,4d,5bd,6j.
PC; BLb; BLc

1938 Outline 5 **538.**
Bod(16/3/40)
AR 1937/8.

1939 2539. **M39. R38.**
I 6/1919. **M** Jan.1925.
L (1)g,i,j; (2)e,j,n,s,t; (3)c,i,q,s.
S 4. **O** 1a,2b,3b,4b.
C BRed,1c,2f,3(2/6)i,5bd,6j.
PC

1941 Outline **1000/11/41 LR**
PC   *AR 1941/2.*

[1944 or 1945 Outline; not seen]
AR 1944/5.

93 STOW ON THE WOLD (STOW-on-the-WOLD *and* DISTRICT)
Surveyed 1872-85; published 1887-92; revised
1893 and 1902-3; 3rd revision 1914.

1919
I 2/1919. **M** 1919.
L (1)a; (2)b,n,q,t; (3)a,k,o,s.
S 1. **O** 1a,2a,3a,4a.
C Red,2a,3(2/6)d,4b²,5bd,6g.
PC; BLa(3/12/20); BLb; Bod;
CUL(30/11/20); RGS(16/2/20)
Supp. to Cat.Oct.1919.

1921 (l)9.21.
I 2/1919. **M** 1919.
L (1)a; (2)c,n,q,t; (3)a,o,s.
S 1. **O** 1a,2c[gap],3a,4a.
C Red,2a,3(3/6)a,5bd,6i.
BLc

1925 Outline 5
I (1)25a.
BLd(29/10/25); BLe; Bod
Supp. to Cat.1 Apr./30 Jun.1925.

1930 3000/30.
I 2/1919; (1)28a; (4)30b; roads (4)6-26.
M 1919.
L (1)a,b; (2)c,n,q,u; (3)a,o,s.
S 3. **O** 1a,2b,3b,4b.
C Red,2a,3(3/6)d,5bd,6i.
PC; BLb; KGM

1932 3000/30.3000/32.
I 2/1919; (1)32a; (4)32b; roads (4)5·32.
M 1919.
L (1)a,b; (2)c,n,q,u; (3)a,o,s.
S 4. **O** 1a,2b,3b,4b.
C B&Rb,2a,3(2/6)g,4d,5bd,6i.
PC; BLc; Bod; KGM; RGS

1935 1535.
I 5/1919. **M** 1919.
L (1)a,b; (2)e,n,q,u; (3)a,i,o,s.
S 4. **O** 1a,2b,3b,4b.
C B&Rb,2h,3(2/6)h,4d,5bd,6i.
PC

1936 1535.3036.
I 5/1919. **M** 1st.Jan.1936.
L (1)g,i,j; (2)e,n,q,u; (3)a,i,o,s.
S 4. **O** 1a,2b,3b,4b.
C B&Rb,2h,3(2/6)h,4d,5bd,6i.
PC; KGM
AR 1936/7.

1937 1535.3036.537.
I 5/1919. **M** 1st.Jan.1936.
L (1)g,i,j; (2)e,n,q,u; (3)a,i,o,s.
S 4. **O** 1a,2b,3b,4b.
C B&Rb,2h,3(2/6)h,4d,5bd,6j.
PC

1938 4038.M.36.R.36.
I 5/1919. **M** 1st.Jan.1936.
L (1)g,i,j; (2)e,n,s,t; (3)a,h,i,o,s.
S 4. **O** 1a,2b,3b,4b.
C B&Rb(wr),2h,3(1/9)c,4e,5bd,6j.
PC; BLb; BLc; Bod; KGM
AR 1937/8.

1941 Outline 8 **1,000/11/41 L.R.**
Southampton and date erased from imprint.
PC
AR 1941/2.

1942 Outline **1000/9/42 LR**
PC
AR 1942/3.

94 BICESTER

Surveyed 1872-85; published 1887-90; revised 1893 and 1902; 3rd revision 1914.

1919
I 2/1919. M 1919.
L (1)a; (2)b,n,q,r,t; (3)a,k,o,s.
S 1. O 1a,2a,3a,4a.
C Red,2a,3(2/6)b,5bd,6g.
PC; BLa(3/12/20); BLb; Bod;
CUL(30/11/20); RGS(12/12/19)
Supp. to Cat.Oct.1919.

1921 (l)10.21.
I 2/1919. M 1919.
L (1)a; (2)c,n,q,r,t; (3)a,o,s.
S 1. O 1a,2c[gap],3a,4a.
C Red,2a,3(3/6)a,5bd,6g.
BLc

  1925 Outline 5
  I (1)25a.
  BLd(29/10/25); BLe; Bod
  Supp. to Cat.1 Apr./30 Jun.1925.

1928 500/28.
I 2/1919; (1)26a; (4)28b; roads (5)8-26[sic].
M 1919.
L (1)a; (2)c,n,q,r,u; (3)a,o,s.
S 3. O 1a,2b,3b,4b.
C Red,2a,3(3/6)a,5bd,6h.
BLc

1930 500/28.2500/30.
I 2/1919; (1)30a; (4)30b; roads (1)6-26.
M 1919.
L (1)a,b,c,g; (2)c,n,s,u; (3)a,o,s.
S 4. O 1a,2b,3b,4b.
C B&Rb,2f,3(2/6)f,4c²,5bd,6i.
PC; BLb; BLc; KGM
Specification change: parish boundaries are shown.

1932 500/28.2500/30.3500/32.
I 2/1919; (1)32a; (4)32b; roads (1)6·31.
M 1919.
L (1)a,b,c,g; (2)c,n,s,u; (3)a,o,s.
S 4. O 1a,2b,3b,4b.
C B&Rb,2f,3(2/6)g,4d,5bd,6i.
PC; BLc; KGM

  [1936 or 1937 Outline; not seen]
  AR 1936/7.

1938 2038.M37.R37.
I 6/1919. M 1st.Jan.1937.
L (1)g,i,j; (2)e,n,s,u; (3)a,o,s.
S 4. O 1a,2b,3b,4b. Flat.
BLb; Bod
AR 1937/8.

  [1938 or 1939 not seen]
  AR 1938/9.

  1941 Outline 8 (l)1000/10/41.L.R.
  Imprint erased.
  BLf   *AR 1941/2.*

95 LUTON

Surveyed 1865-81; published 1887-9; revised 1893-4 and 1902-3; 3rd revision 1913-4.

[1919]
I 2[Close, F.R.S.; no date]. M 1919.
L (1)a; (2)b,n,q,u; (3)a,k,o,s.
S 1. O 1a,2a,3a,4a.
C Red,2a,3(2/6)a,4b²,5bd,6g.
PC; BLa(no date); Bod; CUL(27/9/21); RGS
Supp. to Cat.Jan.1920.

1921 (l)10·21.
I 2/1919. M 1919.
L (1)a; (2)c,n,q,u; (3)a,o,s.
S 1. O 1a,2c[gap],3a,4a.
C Red,2a,3(3/6)a,5bd,6g.
PC; BLb
All copies of this state so far seen lack any park fill.

  1923 Outline 4
  I 2/1923.
  BLd(19/10/23); BLe; Bod(13/12/23)
  Supp. to Cat.1 Jul./30 Sep.1923.

1926 500/26.
I 2/1923[sic]; (1)25a; (4)26b. M 1919.
L (1)a; (2)c,n,q,u; (3)a,o,s.
S 2. O 1a,2c,3b,4b.
C Red,2a,3(2/6)d,5bd,6g.
BLc

1927 500/26.500/27.
I 2/1923; (1)25a; (4)27b. M 1919.
L (1)a; (2)c,n,q,u; (3)a,o,s.
S 2. O 1a,2b,3b,4b.
C Red,2a,3(3/6)a,5bd,6i.
PC

C cover: 271-81; I imprint: 259-62; L legend: 263-5; M magnetic variation; O other marginal data: 266-9; S scale: 266; (k) left, between legend and map border; (l) left, below legend; location abbreviations: xii; outline: 282; print codes: 84-7. *AR*: annual report; *Supp. to Cat.* see OS *Catalogues*: 394.

328

1929 500/26.3000/29.
I 2/1923; (1)25-8d; (3)24a; (4)29b; roads (5)9.28.
M 1919.
L (1)a; (2)c,n,q,u; (3)a,o,s.
S 3. O 1a,2b,3b,4b.
C Red,2a,3(1/6)b,4a,5bd,6i.
PC; BLb
No park fill.

1931 250/31.
I 2/1923. M 1919.
L (1)a; (2)c,n,q,u; (3)a,o,s.
S 4. O 1a,2b,3b,4b. Flat.
MCL

1932a 500/26.3000/29.4500/32. LUTON.
I 2/1923; (1)25-8d; (3)24a; (4)32b; roads (4)6-31. M 1932.
L (1)a,b,c,g; (2)c,o,u; (3)a,o,s.
S 4. O 1a,2b,3b,4b.
C B&Rb,2f,3(2/6)f,4c²,5bd,6i.
PC; BLc; Bod; RGS(9/2/34)
Parks in black Third Edition stipple (i.e. not the rouletted stipple of the first state); parish boundaries shown; rivers in light blue with darker blue casing.

[**1932b** 500/32; not seen; inferred from 1934]

1934 500/26.3000/29.4500/32.500/32. 375/34
I 2/1923. (1)1925-8d; 3(24a); (4)32b; (5)34l; roads (4)6-31. M 1932.
L (1)a,b,c,g; (2)c,o,u; (3)a,o,s.
S 4. O 1a,2b,3b,4b.
C Red, 1b,3(4/-)a,5q,6i.
PC

1935a 1035.
I 5/1923. M 1932.
L (1)a,b,c,g; (2)e,o,u; (3)a,i,o,s.
S 4. O 1a,2b,3b,4b.
C B&Rb,2h,3(2/6)h,4d,5bd,6i.
PC

1935b 1035.3535.
I 5/1923. M 1932.
L (1)a,b,c,g; (2)e,o,u; (3)a,i,o,s.
S 4. O 1a,2b,3b,4b.
C B&Ra,2h,3(2/6)h,4d,5bd,6j.
PC; BLc

[**1936** or **1937** not seen]
AR 1936/7.

1942 Outline 8 **1000/6/42.L.R.** [in blue]
Southampton and date erased from imprint.
M Jan.1941.
PC
AR 1942/3.

[**1944** or **1945** Outline; not seen]
AR 1944/5.

96 HERTFORD & BISHOP'S STORTFORD
Surveyed 1865-81; published 1886-8; revised 1893-4 and 1902-3; 3rd revision 1914-5.

1919
I 1/1919. M 1919.
L (1)a; (2)b,n,q,u; (3)a,k,o,s.
S 1. O 1a,2a,3a,4a.
C Red,2a,3(2/6)a,4b²,5be,6g.
PC; BLa; Bod; CUL(27/9/21); RGS(27/7/20)
Supp. to Cat.Jan.1920. On several examples of this first state, the rouletted park fill is so faintly printed that it can only be seen with a magnifying glass. The extrusion of Hoddesdon below the southern neatline has caused the legend to be printed lower in the margin than normal. As a result, on some examples which have been printed on a larger than usual sheet of paper, the bottom fold has a small amount of the margin folded in.

1919 Outline 1
RGS OS Specimen no. 62

1921 6.21.
I 2/1919. M 1919.
L (1)a; (2)b,n,s,u; (3)a,k,o,s.
S 1. O 1a,2c[gap],3a,4a.
C Red,2a,3(3/6)a,5be,6g.
PC; BLb
Lacks park fill.

1923 2000/23.
I 2/1919; (1)23a; (4)23d. M 1919.
L (1)a; (2)c,n,s,u; (3)c,o,s.
S 2. O 1a,2c,3b,4b.
C Red,2a,3(2/6)d,4b²,5be,6i.
PC
Specification change: parks shown by green ruling.

1923 Outline 4
I 2/1923.
BLd(13/9/23); BLe; Bod
Supp. to Cat.1 Apr./30 Jun.1923.

1930 2000/23.3000/30.
I 2/1919; (1)28a; (4)30d; roads (6)7·28.
M 1919.
L (1)a,b,g; (2)c,n,s,u; (3)c,q,s.
S 4. O 1a,2b,3b,4b.
C B&Rb,2a,3(4/-)b,5be,6i.
PC; BLb
Specification change: contours reinforced.

1933 3500/33.
I 4/1919; (5)33c; (7)32a.
M 1919.
L (1)h,g; (2)e,n,s,u; (3)c,q,s.
S 4. O 1a,2b,3b,4b.
C B&Rb,2f,3(2/6)g,4d,5be,6i.
PC; BLc

1936 3036.
I 6/1919. M 1.ˢᵗ Jan.1936.
L (1)g,i,j; (2)e,n,s,u; (3)c,i,q,s.
S 4. O 1a,2b,3b,4b.
C B&Rb,2h,3(2/6)h,4d,6be,6i.
PC; BLb; Bod
AR 1936/7.

[1936 or 1937 Outline; not seen]
AR 1936/7.

[1938 or 1939 Outline; not seen]
AR 1938/9.

1941 Outline 8 **1000/10/41.L.R.**
BLf

AR 1941/2.

97 COLCHESTER
Surveyed 1861-85; published 1884-9; revised
1893 and 1904; 3rd revision 1914-19.

1921
I 2/1921. M 1921.
L (1)a; (2)c,n,p,t; (3)c,f,o,w.
S 1. O 1a,2c,3a,4a,5a.
C Red,2a,3(3/6)a,5bd,6g.
PC; BLa(23/3/22); BLb; BLc; Bod;
CUL(20/3/22); RGS(29/7/27)
Supp. to Cat.1 Apr./30 Jun.1921.

1921 Outline 2
BLd(20/5/22); BLe(GSGS 16/2/23); Bod
Supp. to Cat.1 Jul./30 Sep.1921.

1932 3500/32.
I 2/1921; (1)32a; (5)32d; roads (5)1/32.
M Jan.1926.
L (1)a,b,c,g; (2)c,n,p,t; (3)c,q,u.
S 4. O 1a,2b,3b,4b,5a.
C B&Rb,2g,3(2/6)g,4d,5bd,6i.
PC
Specification change: contours reinforced.

1936 2536.
I 6/1921.
M 1.ˢᵗ Jan.1936.
L (1)g,i,j; (2)e,n,p,t; (3)c,i,q,u.
S 4. O 1a,2b,3b,4b,5a.
C B&Rb,2e,3(2/6)h,4d,5bd,6j.
PC

1936 Outline 5 **436.**
PC
AR 1936/7.

1938 2538,M.38,R.37.
I 6/1921.
M 1.ˢᵗ Jan.1936.
L (1)g,i,j; (2)e,j,n,p,t; (3)c,i,q,u.
S 4. O 1a,2b,3b,4b,5a.
C B&Rb,2e,3(2/6)h,4d,5bd,6j.
PC; BLb; BLc; Bod
AR 1938/9.

[1941 or 1942 Outline; not seen]
AR 1941/2.]

98 CLACTON ON SEA & HARWICH
Surveyed 1861-85; published 1884-9; revised
1893 and 1904; 3rd revision 1914-19.

1921
I 2/1921. M 1921.
L (1)a; (2)c,n,p,t; (3)c,f,o,w.
S 2. O 1b,2c,3a,4a,5a.
C Red,2a,3(2/6)a,4b¹,5bd,6g.
PC; BLa(23/3/22); BLb; Bod;
CUL(20/3/22); RGS(29/7/27)
*Supp. to Cat.1 Apr./30 Jun.1921. An example
of this state exists with a retailer's cover
originally printed for the Third Edition Large
Sheet series.*

1921 Outline 2
BLd(20/5/22); BLe; Bod
Supp. to Cat.1 Jul./30 Sep.1921.

C cover: 271-81; I imprint: 259-62; L legend: 263-5; M magnetic variation; O other marginal data: 266-9;
S scale: 266; (k) left, between legend and map border; (l) left, below legend; location abbreviations: xii;
outline: 282; print codes: 84-7. *AR:* annual report; *Supp. to Cat.* see OS *Catalogues*: 394.

1929 3000/29.
I 2/1921; (1)28a; (4)29d; roads (5)8/28.
M Jan.1925.
L (1)a,b,c,g; (2)c,n,p,t; (3)c,o,w.
S 3. O 1b,2b,3b,4b,5c.
C B&Rb,2a,3(4/-)b,6bd,6i.
PC; BLc

1932 3000/29.3000/32.
I 2/1921; (1)32a; (4)32d; roads (5)2·32.
M Jan.1925.
L (1)a,b,c,g; (2)c,n,p,t; (3)c,o,w.
S 4. O 1b,2b,3b,4b,5c.
C B&Rb,2a,3(2/6)f,4c^2,5bd,6i.
PC

1932 Outline 6
PC

1934 Outline 5 **300/34.**
I 4/1921; (5)34c; (7)32a.
PC

1936 3036.
I 6/1921. M Jan.1936.
L (1)g,i,j; (2)e,n,p,t; (3)c,i,o,w.
S 4. O 1b,2b,3b,4b,5c.
C B&Rb,2h,3(2/6)h,4d,5bd,6i.
PC; BLb; BLc

1939 2039.M.38.R.37.
I 6/1921.
M Jan.1936.
L (1)g,i,j; (2)e,j,k,n,p,t; (3)c,i,o,w.
S 4. O 1b,2b,3b,4b,5c.
C B&Rb,2h,3(2/6)h,4d,5bd,6j.
PC

[1939 or 1940 Outline; not seen]
AR 1939/40.

1941 Outline 8 (l)**1000/10/41.L.R.**
Southampton and date erased from imprint.
                    PC
AR 1941/2.

99 PEMBROKE & TENBY (PEMBROKE)
Inset: Grassholm Island, Barrels, Hats, The Smalls
Surveyed 1860-88; published 1892-4; revised 1897 and 1909; 3rd revision 1919-20.

1922
I 2/1922.
M 1922.

L (1)a; (2)c,n,p,t; (3)c,o,u.
S 2. O 1b,2c,3b,5a.
C Red,2a,3(2/6)f,4c^2,5bd,6i.
PC; BLa(26/7/23); BLb; Bod;
CUL(24/7/23); RGS
Supp. to Cat.1 Jan./31 Mar.1923.

1923 Outline 2
I 2/1923.
BLd(26/7/23); BLe(GSGS 16/3/1923); Bod
Supp. to Cat. 1 Jan./31 Mar.1923.

1930 2750/30.
I 2/1922; (1)21a; (4)30d.
M 1922.
L (1)a,b; (2)c,n,p,t; (3)c,o,u.
S 4. O 1b,2b,3b,4b,5a.
C Red,1b,3(3/6)a,5o,6i.
PC; BLc; RGS(15/6/37)

1934 3,000/34.
I 4/1922; (1)33b; (2)31a; (5)34c.
M 1922.
L (1)a,b; (2)e,n,p,t; (3)c,i,o,u.
S 4. O 1b,2b,3b,4b,5a.
C B&Rb,2h,3(2/6)h,4d,5bd,6i.
PC; BLc; RGS

1937 3037.M36.R31.
I 6/1922.
M Jan.1937.
L (1)g,i,j; (2)e,n,p,t; (3)c,i,o,u.
S 4. O 1b,2b,3b,4b,5a.
C B&Rb,2h,3(2/6)h,4d,5bd,6j.
PC; BLc
AR 1937/8. Welsh glossary note is printed below the price statement.

1938 4038.M38.R37.
I 6/1922.
M Jan.1937.
L (1)g,i,j; (2)e,j,n,p,t; (3)c,i,o,u.
S 4. O 1b,2b,3b,4b,5a.
C B&Rb,2h,3(2/6)h,4d,5bd,6j.
PC; BLb; BLc; Bod; KGM
AR 1938/9.

1941 Outline 8 **1000/12/41.L.R.**
BLf
AR 1941/2.

100 LLANELLY

Surveyed 1875-88; published 1888-94; revised 1893-7 and 1904-9; 3rd revision 1919-20.

1923
I 2/1923. M 1922.
L (1)a; (2)c,n,p,t; (3)c,o,u.
S 2. O 1b,2c,3b,4b,5bc.
C Red,2f,3(3/6)a,5bd,6g.
PC; BLa(19/10/23); BLb; Bod;
CUL(18/10/23); RGS
Supp. to Cat.1 Jul./30 Sep 1923.

1923 Outline 4
BLd(1/2/24); BLe; Bod(8/2/24)
Supp. to Cat.1 Oct./31 Dec.1923.

1932 3500·32.
I 2/1923; (1)31a; (5)32d; roads (4)8·31.
M 1922.
L (1)a,b; (2)c,n,p,t; (3)c,o,u.
S 4. O 1b,2b,3b,4b,5bc.
C B&Rb,2g,3(2/6)g,4d,5bd,6i.
PC

1937 Outline 5 **3500·32** (k)**537.**
I (5)32d
PC   *AR 1937/8.*

1938 3038.M37.R37.
I 6/1923. M 1ˢᵗ Jan.1937.
L (1)g,i,j; (2)e,j,n,p,u; (3)c,i,o,u.
S 4. O 1b,2b,3b,4b,5bc.
C B&Rb,2h,3(2/6)h,4d,5bd,6j.
PC; BLb; BLc; Bod; RGS
AR 1937/8. Welsh glossary note is printed to the left of the imprint.

1941 Outline 8 **1000/12/41.L.R.**
Southampton and date erased from imprint.
BLf   *AR 1941/2.*

101 SWANSEA & ABERDARE

Surveyed 1867-88; published 1887-94; revised 1893-4 and 1904-8; 3rd revision 1919-20.

1923
I 2/1923. M 1923.
L (1)a; (2)c,n,p,t; (3)c,o,u.
S 2. O 1b,2c,3b,4b,5a.
C Red,2c,3(3/6)a,5bd,6g.

PC; BLa(13/9/23); BLb; Bod;
CUL(13/9/23); RGS(11/5/23)
Supp. to Cat.1 Apr./30 Jun.1923.

1923 Outline 2
BLd(26/7/23); BLe; Bod
Supp. to Cat.1 Jan./31 Mar.1923.

[**1927 500/27** not seen; inferred from 1931]

[**1930 500/27.500/30** not seen; inferred from 1931]

1931 500/27.500/30.3250/31.
I 2[no date]; (1)31a; (4)31d; roads (1)8.31.
M 1923.
L (1)a,b; (2)c,n,p,u; (3)c,o,u.
S 4. O 1b,2b,3b,4b,5a.
C B&Rb,2f,3(2/6)f,4c²,5bd,6i.
PC; BLb

1935 2035
I 5/1923. M 1923.
L (1)g,i; (2)e,n,p,t; (3)c,i,o,u.
S 4. O 1b,2b,3b,4b,5a.
C B&Rb,2h,3(2/6)h,4d,5bd,6i.
PC; BLb; RGS

[**1936** or **1937** Outline; not seen]
AR 1936/7.

1938 2538.M.38.R.37.
I 5/1923. M Jan.1938.
L (1)g,i,j; (2)e,j,n,p,t; (3)c,i,o,u.
S 4. O 1b,2b,3b,4b,5a.
C B&Rb,2h,3(2/6)h,4d,5bd,6j.
PC
AR 1938/9. Welsh glossary note is printed to the right of the scale statement.

1941 Outline 8 (l)**1000/12/41.L.R.**
BLf *AR 1941/2.*

102 NEWPORT (Newport (Mon.) and District)

Surveyed 1872-87; published 1891-3; revised 1894 and 1904; 3rd revision 1913.

1919
I 2/1919. M 1919.
L (1)a; (2)b,n,p,q,t; (3)a,k,o,s.
S 1. O 1b,2a,3a,4a.
C Red,2a,3(2/6)d,4b²,5bd,6i.
PC; BLa(13/10/19); BLb; Bod;
CUL(23/9/19); RGS(29/7/19)
Supp. to Cat.Jun.1919.

C cover: 271-81; I imprint: 259-62; L legend: 263-5; M magnetic variation; O other marginal data: 266-9; S scale: 266;   (k) left, between legend and map border;   (l) left, below legend;   location abbreviations: xii; outline: 282;   print codes: 84-7. AR: annual report;   *Supp. to Cat.* see OS *Catalogues*: 394.

1919 [i.e. **1920**] No print code
I 2/1919. **M** 1919.
L (1)a; (2)b,n,p,q,t; (3)a,k,o,s.
S 1. **O** 1a,2c[gap],3a,4a.
C Red,1b,3(3/6)a,5n,6g.
PC
This printing lacks the 1/- price note which may have been removed after the price increase in January 1920.

1924 1000/24.
I 2/1919; (1)23b; (3)22a; (4)24d.
M 1919.
L (1)a; (2)c,n,p,q,t; (3)a,o,s.
S 1. **O** 1b,2c,3a,4b. No cover.
PC

  1924 Outline 5
  I 2/1924; (1)23b.
  BLd(7/8/25); BLe; Bod
  Supp. to Cat.1 Oct./31 Dec.1924.

1931 1000/24.3000/31.
I 2/1919; (1)30b; (3)28a; (4)31d; roads (1)5/26.
M 1919.
L (1)a; (2)c,n,p,q,t; (3)a,o,s.
S 4. **O** 1b,2b,3b,4b.
C B&Rb,2a,3(2/6)f,4c²,5bd,6i.
PC

1934 3,000/34
I 4/1919; (1)33b; (2)32a; (5)34c.
M 1919.
L (1)a,b; (2)e,n,p,q,t; (3)a,e,i,o,s.
S 4. **O** 1b,2b,3b,4b.
C B&Rb,2f,3(4/-)g,5bd,6i.
KGM; BLc

1935 2035
I 6/1919. **M** Jan.1935.
L (1)g,i; (2)e,n,p,t; (3)a,h,i,o,s.
S 4. **O** 1b,2b,3b,4b.
C B&Rb,2h,3(2/6)h,4d,5bd,6i.
PC; BLc
Specification change: parish boundaries are shown.

1937 M36.R32.537.
I 6/1919. **M** Jan.1935.
L (1)g,i,j; (2)e,n,p,u; (3)a,e,h,i,o,s.
S 4. **O** 1b,2b,3b,4b.
C B&Rb,2h,3(2/6)h,4d,5bd,6i.
PC *AR 1937/8.*

[**1937** or **1938** Outline; not seen]
AR 1937/8.

1938 3038.M37.R36.
I 6/1919.
M Jan.1935.
L (1)g,i,j; (2)e,n,q,t; (3)a,e,h,i,o,s.
S 4. **O** 1b,2b,3b,4b. Flat.
BLb; Bod
AR 1938/9. Welsh glossary note is printed below the price note.

  1941 Outline **1000/12/41 LR**
  PC
  AR 1941/2.

  [**1944** or **1945** Outline; not seen]
  AR 1944/5.

103 STROUD & CHEPSTOW
Surveyed 1873-87; published 1891-3; revised 1894-6 and 1903-4; 3rd revision 1913.

1919
I 2/1919. **M** 1919.
L (1)a; (2)b,n,p,q,t; (3)a,k,o,s.
S 1. **O** 1a,2a,3a,4a.
C Buff,2a,3(2/6)b,5a²e,6g.
PC; BLa(13/10/19); Bod; CUL(28/9/19); RGS(29/7/19)
Supp. to Cat.Jun.1919.

1921 (l)**6-21.**
I 2/1919.
M 1919.
L (1)a; (2)b,n,p,q,t; (3)a,k,o,s.
S 1. **O** 1a,2c[gap],3a,4a.
C Red,2a,3(3/6)a,5be,6g.
PC; BLb; BLc

  1924 Outline 5
  I (1)24a; (2)22b.
  BLd(29/10/25); BLe; Bod
  Supp. to Cat.1 Apr./30 Jun.1925.
  Specification change: contours reinforced.

1928 500/28.
I 2/1919; (1)27a; (3)22b; (4)28d; roads (5)5·26.
M 1919.
L (1)a; (2)c,n,p,q,u; (3)a,q,s.
S 1. **O** 1a,2b,3a,4b.
C Red,1b,5p,6g.
BLc

1929 500/28.3000/29.
I 2/1919; (1)29a; (3)28b; (4)29d; roads
(5)5·26. M 1919.
L (1)a; (2)c,n,p,q,t; (3)a,q,s.
S 1. O 1a,2b,3a,4b.
C Red,2a,3(2/6)f,4c²,5be,5i.
PC; BLb; BLc

[**1930** 500/30 not seen; inferred from 1932]

1932 500/28.3000/29.500/30.200/32.
I 2/1919; (1)31a; (3)28b; (4)32d; roads
(5)5.32.
M 1919.
L (1)a,b; (2)c,n,p,q,t; (3)a,q.
S 1. O 1a,2b,3b,4b.
C B&Rb,2a,3(2/6)f,4c²,5be,6i.
PC; BLc

1933 3,000/33.
I 4/1919; (1)31c; (2)32a; (3)28b; (5)33[right
of c]. M 1.ˢᵗ Jan.ʸ 1933.
L (1)a,b,c,g; (2)e,o,q,t; (3)a,h,o,s.
S 4. O 1a,2b,3b,4b.
C B&Rb,2f,3(4/-)g,5be,6i.
PC; BLc
*Specification change: parish boundaries
shown; contours no longer reinforced; wider
rivers shown by blue casing with stippled
infill.*

[**1935** 135. not seen; inferred from 1936a]

1936a 135.1036.
I 4/1919; (1)31c; (2)32a; (3)28b.
M 1.ˢᵗ Jan.ʸ 1933.
L (1)a,b,c,g; (2)e,o,q,t; (3)a,h,o,s.
S 4. O 1a,2b,3b,4b.
C B&Rb,2h,3(2/6)h,4d,5be,6i.
PC

1936b 2536.
I 6/1919. M 1.ˢᵗ Jan.ʸ 1933.
L (1)g,i,j; (2)e,o,p,q,t; (3)a,h,i,o,s.
S 4. O 1a,2b,3b,4b.
C B&Rb,2h,3(2/6)h,4d,5be,6j.
PC; BLc; RGS
AR 1936/7.

1938 3038.M37.R37.
I 6/1919. M 1.ˢᵗ Jan.ʸ 1933.
L (1)g,i,j; (2)e,j,o,p,t; (3)a,h,i,o,s.
S 4. O 1a,2b,3b,4b.

C B&Rb,2h,3(2/6)h,4d,5be,6j.
PC; BLb; BLc; Bod

[**1938** or **1939** Outline; not seen]
AR 1938/9.

1942 Outline 7 **1,000/4/42 L.R.** [in blue]
PC *AR 1942/3.*

1943 Outline **800/2/43 LR**
PC

[**1943** or **1944** Outline; not seen]
AR 1943.4.

104 SWINDON & CIRENCESTER
Surveyed 1872-84; published 1887-91;
revised 1893 and 1902-3; 3rd rev. 1913-14.

1919
I 2/1919. M 1919.
L (1)a; (2)b,n,r,t; (3)a,k,o,s.
S 1. O 1a,2a,3a,4a.
C Buff,2a,3(2/6)b,5a¹d,6g.
PC; BLa(13/10/19); Bod; CUL(28/9/19);
RGS(29/7/29)
Supp. to Cat.Jun.1919.

1921 (l)**8·21.**
I 2/1919. M 1919.
L (1)a; (2)c,n,r,t; (3)a,o,s.
S 1. O 1a,2c[gap],3a,4a.
C Red,2a,3(3/6)a,5bd,6g.
PC; BLb; BLc

[**1924**] Outline 5
BLd(7/8/1925); BLe; Bod
Supp. to Cat.1 Oct./31 Dec.1924.

1929 3000/29.
I 2/1919; (1)24-8a; (4)29d; roads (5)6·26.
M 1919.
L (1)a; (2)c,n,q,t; (3)a,o,s.
S 3. O 1a,2b,3b,4b.
C Red,2a,3(2/6)d,4b²,5bd,6i.
PC; BLb; Bod

1933 3,000/33.
I 4/1919; (5)33b; (7)32a.
M 1919.
L (1)a,b,g; (2)e,n,r,t; (3)a,o,s.
S 4. O 1a,2b,3b,4b.
C B&Rb,2f,3(2/6)g,4d,5bd,6i.
PC; BLc

C cover: 271-81; I imprint: 259-62; L legend: 263-5; M magnetic variation; O other marginal data: 266-9;
S scale: 266; (k) left, between legend and map border; (l) left, below legend; location abbreviations: xii;
outline: 282; print codes: 84-7. AR: annual report; *Supp. to Cat.* see OS *Catalogues*: 394.

1936 (l)3036.
I 6/1919. M 1936.
L (1)g,i,j; (2)e,n,r,u; (3)a,i,o,s.
S 4. O 1a,2b,3b,4b.
C B&Rb,2h,3(2/6)h,4d,5bd,6i.
PC; BLb; BLc
AR 1936/7.

1941 Outline 8 **1000/11/41.L.R.**
Southampton and date erased from imprint.
PC   *AR 1941/2.*

105 OXFORD & HENLEY ON THAMES
Surveyed 1872-83; published 1887; revised 1893 and 1902; 3rd revision 1913.

1919
I 1/1919. M 1919.
L (1)a; (2)b,n,q,t; (3)a,k,o,s.
S 1. O 1a,2a,3a,4a.
C Red,1d,2a,2(2/6)b,5bd,6g.
PC; BLa(29/5/20); Bod; CUL(27/5/20); RGS(12/12/19)
Supp. to Cat.Sep.1919.

1921 (l)7·21.
I 2/1919. M 1919.
L (1)a; (2)b,n,q,u; (3)a,k,o,s.
S 1. O 1a,2c[gap],3a,4a.
C Red,2a,3(3/6)a,5bd,7g.
PC; BLb; BLc

[**1925** 500/25 not seen; inferred from 1926]

1924 Outline 5
I (1)24a.
BLd(11/9/25); BLe; Bod(27/10/25)
Supp. to Cat.1 Jan./31 Mar.1925.

1926 500/25.2500/26.
I 2/1919; (1)24-6a; (4)26d; roads (5)5-26.
M 1919.
L (1)a,g; (2)c,n,q,u; (3)a,q,s.
S 2. O 1a,2b,3b,4b.
C Red,2a,3(2/6)e,4b^2,5bd,6i.
PC; BLb; BLc
Specification change: contours reinforced.

1928 500/25.2500/26.3500/28.
I 2/1919; (1)24-6a; (4)28d; roads (5)5-26.
M 1919.
L (1)a,g; (2)c,n,q,u; (3)a,q,s.
S 2. O 1a,2b,3b,4b.
C Red,2a,3(2/6)d,4b^2,5bd,6i.
PC; BLc; RGS

1931 500/25.2500/26.3500/28.4500/31.
I 2/1919; (1)31a; (4)31d; roads (5)5-26.
M 1919.
L (1)a,g; (2)c,n,q,u; (3)a,q,s.
S 4. O 1a,2b,3b,4b.
C B&Rb,2a,3(1/6)d,4c^2,5bd,6i.
PC; BLc; RGS

1934 3,500/34.
I 4/1919; (1)34b; (2)31a; (5)34c.
M 1919.
L (1)a,b,c,g; (2)c,n,q,u; (3)a,q,s.
S 4. O 1a,2b,3b,4b.
C B&Rb,2h,3(2/6)h,4d,5bd,6i.
PC; BLc

1936 3036.M36.R31.
I 6/1919. M 1ˢᵗ Jan.1936.
L (1) a,b,g,j; (2)e,n,q,u; (3)a,i,q,s.
S 4. O 1a,2b,3b,4b.
C B&Rb,2h,3(2/6)h,4d,5bd,6i.
PC; BLb; BLc
AR 1936/7.

1937 Outline 5 **437.**
PC
AR 1937/8.

1941 Outline 8 **W.0.20,000/9/41.**
Imprint erased.
PC
AR 1941/2.

[1944 or 1945 Outline; not seen]
AR 1944/5.

106 WATFORD
Surveyed 1862-80; published 1877-87; revised 1893-4 and 1902; 3rd rev. 1913-4.

1920
I 2/1920. M 1920.
L (1)a; (2)b,n,q,u; (3)c,k,o,s.
S 1. O 1a,2c,3a,4a.
C Red,2a,3(3/6)a,5bd,6g.
PC; BLa(5/12/21); Bod; CUL(2/12/21)
Supp. to Cat. Jun.1920.

1921 (l)7-21.
I 2/1920. M 1920.
L (1)a; (2)c,n,p,q,u; (3)c,o,s.
S 1. O 1a,2c,3a,4a.
C Red,2a,3(2/6)c,4b^2,5bd,6g.
PC; BLc; RGS

1921 WATFORD. Outline 2
BLd(20/5/22); BLe; Bod
Supp. to Cat.1 Jul./30 Sep.1921.

1924 5500/24.
I 2/1920; (1)24a; (3)22b; (4)24d.
M Jan.1924.
L (1)a; (2)c,n,p,u; (3)c,o,s.
S 2. O 1a,2c,3b,4b.
C Red,2a,3(2/6)d,4b^2,5bd,6g.
PC; BLc
The position of some marginalia, such as series statement has altered; the imprint is in different lettering, the first revision date has been changed to 1895-4 [sic]; even the number of hatches in the sheet diagram square is different.

1927 5500/24.3000/27.
I 2/1920; (1)26a; (3)24-6b; (4)27d; roads (4)5/25.
M Jan.1924.
L (1)a; (2)c,n,p,u; (3)c,q,s.
S 2. O 1a,2b,3b,4b.
C Red,2a,3(2/6)d,4b^2,5bd,6h.
PC; RGS
Supp. to Cat.1 July/30 Sept.1927. 'With special Road Revision.' The revision date in the imprint has been corrected. Specification change: contours are reinforced.

1927 Outline **5500/24.500/27.**
PC

Supp. to Cat.1 Jan./31 Mar.1927. 'With special Road Revision.'

1928a 5500/24.3000/27.5000/28.
I 2/1920; (1)27-8a; (3)27b; (4)28d; roads (5)11/27.
M Jan.1924.
L (1)a; (2)c,n,p,u; (3)c,q,s.
S 2. O 1a,2b,3b,4b.
C Red,1b,[no price],5p,6i.
PC; BLc; RGS

1928b
*The details for this printing are the same as for 1928a, **except** that legend (3) is c,o,s, and there is a specification change: contours are no longer reinforced.*
C Red,2a,3(2/6)e,4b^2,5bd,6i.
PC

1930 5500/24.3000/27.5000/28.8,500/30.
I 2/1920; (1)29a; (3)27b; (4)30d; roads (5)11/27.
M Jan.1930.
L (1)a,b,c,g; (2)c,n,p,q,u; (3)c,o,s.
S 3. O 1a,2b,3b,4b.
C B&Rb,2f,3(1/6)d,4c^2,5bd,6i.
PC

1932
5500/24.3000/27.5000/28.8500/30.8000/32.
I 2/1920; (1)32a; (3)27b; (4)32d; roads (5)6/31.
M Jan.1930.
L (1)a,b,c,g; (2)c,n,p,q,u; (3)c,o,s.
S 4. O 1a,2b,3b,4b.
C B&Rb,2f,3(2/6)f,4d,5bd,6i.
PC; BLc; Bod; RGS

1934 1,000/34.
I 4/1920; (1)33b; (2)31a; (5)34c.
M Jan.1930.
L (1)a,b,c,g; (2)e,n,p,q,u; (3)c,o,s.
S 4. O 1a,2b,3b,4b.
C B&Rb,2f,3(2/6)g,4d,5bd,6i.
PC; RGS

1935 1,000/35.
I 4/1920; (1)33b; (2)31a; (5)35c.
M Jan.1920.
L (1)a,b,c,g; (2)e,n,p,q,u; (3)c,o,s.
S 4. O 1a,2b,3b,4b.
C Red, 1b, 3(4/-)a,5q,6i.
PC

1936 1,000/35,2,000/36.
I 4/1920; (1)33b; (2)31a; (5)36c.
M Jan.1930.
L (1)a,b,c,g; (2)e,n,p,q,u; (3)c,o,s.
S 4. O 1a,2b,3b,4b.
C B&Rb,2h,3(2/6)h,4d,5bd,6j.
PC

[1936 or 1937 Outline; not seen]
AR 1936/7.

[1944 or 1945 Outline; not seen]
AR 1944/5.

C cover: 271-81; **I** imprint: 259-62; **L** legend: 263-5; **M** magnetic variation; **O** other marginal data: 266-9; **S** scale: 266; (k) left, between legend and map border; (l) left, below legend; location abbreviations: xii; outline: 282; print codes: 84-7. *AR*: annual report; *Supp. to Cat.* see OS *Catalogues*: 394.

336

107 N.E.LONDON & EPPING FOREST
Surveyed 1862-80; published 1886-8; revised 1893 and 1902-3; 3rd revision 1914.

1920
I 2/1920. M 1920.
L (1)a; (2)b,n,p,q,u; (3)c,k,o,s.
S 1. O 1a,2c,3a,4a.
C Red,2a,3(2/6)b,4b¹,5bd,6g.
PC; BLa(5/12/21); Bod; CUL(2/12/21); RGS

Supp.to Cat.Jun.1920. The RGS example has 'Price 1/6 net.' stamped in purple below the copyright statement. [500/20; inferred from 1927.]

1921a (l)7.21 [perhaps 6000/21; print code inferred from 1931]
I 2/1920. M 1920.
L (1)a; (2)c,n,p,q,t; (3)c,o,s.
S 1. O 1a,2c,3a,4a.
C Red,2a,3(3/6)a,5bd,6g.
PC; BLb; BLc

1921 Outline 2
BLd(20/5/22); BLe; Bod
Supp. to Cat.1 Jul./30 Sep.1921.

[**1921b 6000/21** not seen; inferred from 1931]

[**1921c 2400/21** not seen; inferred from 1927]

[**1925 500/25** not seen; inferred from 1926]

1926 500/25.5000/26.
I 2/1920; (1)25a; (4)26d; roads (5)7/25.
M Jan.1924.
L (1)a,g; (2)c,n,p,q,t; (3)c,q,s.
S 2. O 1a,2c,3b,4b.
C Red,1b,[no price],5p,6g.
PC; BLc; RGS
Specification change: contours reinforced.

[1927 Outline; not seen]
Supp. to Cat. 1 Jan./31 Mar.1927. 'With special Road Revision.'

[**1929a 5000/29** inferred from 1929b]

1929b 500/25.5000/26.5000/29.500/29.
I 2/1920; (1)28a; (4)29d; roads (4)11/27.
M Jan.1924.
L (1)a,g; (2)c,n,p,q,t; (3)c,q,s.
S 2. O 1a,2b,3b,4b.
C Red,2a,3(2/6)f,4c²,5bd,6i.
PC; BLc; Bod; KGM; RGS

[**1930 500/30** not seen; inferred from 1931]

1931
6000/21.6000/21.500/25.5000/26.5000/29.500/30.4500/31.
I 2/1920; (1)30a; (4)31d; roads (4)11/27.
M Jan.1924.
L (1)a,b,g; (2)c,n,p,q,t; (3)c,q,s.
S 4. O 1a,2b,3b,4b.
C B&Rb,2a,3(3/6)d,5bd,6i.
PC; BLb; KGM

1932
6000/21.6000/21.500/25.5000/26.5000/29.500/30.4500/31.8000/32.
I 2/1920; (1)32a; (4)32d; roads (4)1/32.
M Jan.1924.
L (1)a,b,g; (2)c,n,p,q,t; (3)c,q,s.
S 4. O 1a,2b,3b,4b.
C B&Rb,2f,3(2/6)g,4d,5bd,6i.
PC; RGS

1933 Outline 5
6000/21.6000/21.500/25.5000/29.500/30.4500/31.800/32.700/33.
I (1)33a; (4)33d; roads (4)1/32.
BLd

1934 8,000/34.
I 4/1920; (1)34b; (2)32a; (5)34c.
M Jan.1924.
L (1)a,b,g; (2)e,n,p,q,t; (3)c,q,s.
S 4. O 1a,2b,3b,4b.
C B&Rb,2h,3(2/6)h,4d,5bd,6i.
KGM; BLb

[**1935 2035** not seen; inferred from 1936]

[1937 or 1938 Outline; not seen]
AR 1937/8.

[1944 or 1945 Outline; not seen]
AR 1944/5.

108 SOUTHEND & DISTRICT
Surveyed 1860-75; published 1882-6; revised 1893-4 and 1904; 3rd rev. 1914-9.

1921
I 2/1921. M 1921.
L (1)a; (2)c,n,p,t; (3)c,o,w.
S 1. O 1a,2c,3a,4a,5a.
C Red,2a,3(2/6)a,4b¹,5bd,6g.
PC; BLa(1/3/22); BLb; Bod; CUL(27/2/22); RGS(10/2/21)
Supp. to Cat.1 Jan./31 Mar.1921. The 'District' in the cover title is, unusually, in lower case italic.

1921 Outline 2
BLd(20/5/22); BLe; Bod
Supp. to Cat.1 Jul./30 Sep.1921.

1926 3500/26.
I 2/1921; (1)24-5a; (4)26d; roads (5)7.25.
M 1921.
L (1)a; (2)c,n,p,t; (3)c,o,w.
S 1. O 1a,2c,3a,4b,5a.
C B&Ra,2a,3(2/6)e,4b^2,5bd,6i.
PC; BLc; Bod; KGM

1930a 3500/30.
I 2/1921; (1)24-9a; (4)30d; roads (5)7·25.
M 1921.
L (1)a,b; (2)c,n,p,t; (3)c,o,w.
S 1. O 1a,2b,3a,4b,5a.
C B&Ra,2a,3(2/6)e,4b^2,5bd,6i.
PC; BLc; KGM

   1930 Outline **3500/30.200/30.** PC

1930b 3500/30.200/30.
I 2/1921; (1)24-9a; (4)30d; roads (5)7·25.
M 1921.
L (1)a,b; (2)c,n,p,t; (3)c,o,w.
S 1. O 1a,2b,3a,4b,5a.
C WP,6i.
PC

[**1930c 500/30** not seen; inferred from 1932]

1932 3500/30.200/30.500/30.4500/32.
I 2/1921; (1)32a; (4)32d; roads (5)1·32.
M 1921.
L (1)a,b; (2)c,n,p,t; (3)c,o,w.
S 4. O 1a,2b,3b,4b,5a.
C B&Rb,2f,3(2/6)f,4c^2,5bd,6i.
PC; BLc

109 PONTYPRIDD & BARRY
Surveyed 1868-81; published 1887-91;
revised 1893-4 and 1904; 3rd rev. 1913-20.

1922
I 2/1922. M 1922.
L (1)a; (2)c,n,p,t; (3)c,o,u.
S 2. O 1b,2c,3b,5a.
C Red,2f,3(3/6)a,5bd,6g.
PC; BLa(26/1/23); BLb; Bod;
CUL(18/1/23); RGS
*Supp. to Cat.1 Jul./30 Sep.1922. The
statement 'Note - The Taff Vale, Rhymney,*

*and Cardiff Railways should read Great
Western Railway.' is printed to the right of
the scale bar.*

1922 Outline 2
BLd(26/1/23); BLe; Bod
*Supp. to Cat.1 Jul./30 Sep.1922. The Taff
Vale railway note is printed bottom left.*

[**1927 500/27** not seen; inferred from 1931]

1931 500/27.3500/31.
I 2/1922; (1)30d; (3)26a; (4)31e.
M 1922.
L (1)a,b,g; (2)c,n,p,u; (3)c,o,u.
S 4. O 1b,2b,3b,4b,5a. Flat.
RGS
The Taff Vale railway note is omitted.

1933 3,500/33.
I 4/1922; (1)32c; (2)31a; (3)26b; (5)33
[printed to the right of (1)32c.]
M 1922.
L (1)a,b,g; (2)e,n,p,t; (3)c,o,w.
S 4. O 1b,2b,3b,4b,5a.
C B&Rb,2h,3(2/6)h,4d,5bd,6i.
PC; RGS

1937a 537.
I 4/1922; (1)32c; (2)31a; (3)26b.
M 1922.
L (1)a,b,g; (2)e,n,p,t; (3)c,o,w.
S 4. O 1b,2b,3b,4b,5a.
C B&Rb,2h,3(2/6)h,4d,5bd,6j.
PC

1937b 937.
I 4/1922; (1)32c; (2)31a; (3)26b.
M 1922.
L (1)a,b,g; (2)e,n,p,t; (3)c,o,u.
S 4. O 1b,2b,3b,4b,5a.
C B&Ra,2h,3(2/6)h,4d,5bd,6i.
PC; BLc
*This printing has been judged to be later
than 1937a because the black plate is much
darker, indicating a new plate, and the
legend (3)w has been altered to u,
conforming with the 1938 state.*

1938 M36.R31. 3038.
I 6/1922; (5)36(k); 38(l).   M 1937.
L (1)g,i,j; (2)e,n,q,t; (3)a,e,i,o,u.
S 4. O 1b,2b,3b,4b,5a.

C cover: 271-81; I imprint: 259-62; L legend: 263-5; M magnetic variation; O other marginal data: 266-9;
S scale: 266; (k) left, between legend and map border; (l) left, below legend; location abbreviations: xii;
outline: 282; print codes: 84-7. *AR*: annual report; *Supp. to Cat.* see OS *Catalogues*: 394.

C B&Rb(wr),2h,3(1/9)c,4e,5bd,6j.
PC; BLb; BLc
AR 1938/9. Specification change: sea in blue stipple. Welsh glossary note is printed to the left of the scale bar.

1940 3040.M39.R39.
I 6/1922. M 1937.
L (1)g,i,j; (2)e,j,n,q,t; (3)a,e,i,o,u.
S 4. O 1b,2b,3b,4b,5a.
C BRed,1c,2e,3(2/6)i,5bd,6j.
BLc; BLb; RGS

[1941 or 1942 Outline; not seen]
AR 1941/2.

[1943 or 1944 Outline; not seen]
AR 1943/4.
[1944 or 1945 Outline; not seen]
AR 1944/5.

110 CARDIFF & MOUTH OF THE SEVERN
Surveyed 1873-86; published 1887-92; revised 1894-97 and 1905; 3rd revision 1913.

1919
I 2/1919. M 1919.
L (1)a; (2)b,n,p,q,t; (3)a,k,o,w.
S 1. O 1b,2a,3a,4a,5a.
C Red,2a,3(3/6)a,5bdg,6g.
PC; BLa(13/10/19); BLb; Bod;
CUL(28/9/19); RGS(29/7/19)
Supp. to Cat.Jun.1919.

1924 1000/24.
I 2/1919; (1)23-4a; (3)22b; (4)24j.
M 1919.
L (1)a; (2)c,n,p,q,t; (3)a,o,w.
S 1. O 1b,2c,3a,4b,5a.
C Red,2a,3(1/6)b,4a,5bdg,6g.
PC; BLc; KGM; RGS

1924 Outline 4
I 2/1924; (1)23-4a; (2)22b.
BLd(15/12/24); BLe; Bod(16/1/25)
Supp. to Cat.1 Jul./30 Sep.1924.

1932 1000/24.2000/32.
I 2/1919; (1)32a; (3)22b; (4)32j; roads, partially (1)4/32. M 1919.
L (1)a,b,g; (2)e,n,p,q,t; (3)a,q,w.
S 4. O 1b,2b,3a,4b,5a.
C B&Rb,2f,3(2/6)g,4d,5bdg,6i.
PC; BLc; RGS
Specification change: contours reinforced.

1936 2036.
I 6/1919; (5)36(l). M 1.st Jan.1936.
L (1)g,i,j; (2)e,n,p,q,t; (3)a,e,i,q,w.
S 4. O 1b,2b,3b,4b,5a.
C B&Rb,2h,3(2/6)h,4d,5bdg,6i.
BLc; BLb; Bod

[1944 or 1945 Outline; not seen]
AR 1944/5.

111 BATH & BRISTOL (Bath, Bristol and District)
Surveyed 1879-85; published 1891-2; revised 1896-7 and 1903-5; 3rd revision 1913.

1919
I 2(FRS)/1919. M 1919.
L (1)a; (2)b,n,p,q,t; (3)a,k,o,s.
S 1. O 1a,2a,3a,4a.
C Buff,2a,3(1/6)a,4b^2,5a^{1}e,6g.
PC; BLa(13/10/19); Bod; CUL(28/9/19)
Supp. to Cat.Jun.1919.

[1920 500/20 not seen; inferred from 1927]

1921a (l)7-21.
I 2(CMG)/1919. M 1919.
L (1)a; (2)c,n,q,r,t; (3)a,o,s.
S 1. O 1a,2c[**no** gap],3a,4a.
C Red,2a,3(1/6)b,4a,5be,6g.
PC; BLb

1921b (l)11-21.
I 2/1919. M 1919.
L (1)a; (2)c,n,q,r,t; (3)a,o,s.
S 1. O 1a,2c,3a,4a.
C Red,2a,3(2/6)a,4b^2,5be,6g.
PC; BLc

[1921c 2400/21 not seen; inferred from 1927. Could apply to 1921a or 1921b.]

1924 Outline 5
I (1)24b; (3)22a.
BLd(11/9/25); BLe; Bod(27/10/25)
Supp. to Cat.1 Jan./31 Mar.1925.

1925 500/25.
I 2/1919; (1)24b; (3)22a; (4)25d.
M 1919.
L (1)a; (2)c,n,q,r,t; (3)a,q,s.
S 2. O 1a,2c,3b,4b. Flat.
RGS(29/7/27)
Specification change: contours reinforced.

1927 500/20.2400/21.3500/27.
I 2(FRS)/1919; (1)23-6d; (3)22a; (4)27b;
roads (5)5-26.
M Jan.1926.
L (1)a,b,c,g; (2)c,n,p,t; (3)a,o,s.
S 2. O 1a,2b,3b,4b.
C Red,2a,3(2/6)d,5be,6i.
KGM; BLc
*Supp. to Cat.1 Apr./30 June 1927. 'With
special Road Revision.' Specification
change: contours not reinforced.*

1929 500/20.2400/21.3500/27.3500/29.
I 2/1919; (1)23-9d; (3)27a; (4)29b/e; roads
(4)5-26.
M Jan.1926.
L (1)a,b,c,g; (2)c,n,p,t; (3)a,o,s.
S 3. O 1a,2b,3b,4b.
C Red,2a,3(2/6)d,4b²,5be,6i.
PC; BLb; BLc; KGM

*The 'R' in the initials 'F.R.S.' in the imprint
has the appearance of a 'B'.*

1932
500/20.2400/21.3500/27.3500/29.3500/32.
I 2/1919; (1)32d; (3)27a; (4)32b,e; roads
(5)4-32.
M Jan.1926.
L (1)a,b,c,g; (2)c,n,p,t; (3)a,o,s.
S 4. O 1a,2b,3b,4b.
C B&Rb,2f,3(2/6)g,4d,5be,6i.
PC; BLc; KGM

1935 2035
I 6/1919. M 1.ˢᵗ Jan.1935.
L (1)a,b,c,g; (2)e,n,p,t; (3)a,i,o,s.
S 4. O 1a,2b,3b,4b.
C B&Rb,2i,3(2/6)h,4d,5be,6i.
PC

1936 2035.3036. M.36.R.32.
I 6/1919. M 1.ˢᵗ Jan.1935.
L (1)a,b,c,g; (2)e,n,p,t; (3)a,i,o,s.
S 4. O 1a,2b,3b,4b.
C   B&Rb,2d,3(2/6)h,4d,5bd,[lacks   back
cover].
PC
AR 1936/7.

1941 Outline **1000/12/41 LR**
PC   *AR 1941/2.*

[1942 or 1943 Outline; not seen]
AR 1942/3.

**112 MARLBOROUGH (Marlborough and
Devizes)**
Surveyed 1871-84; published 1882-92;
revised 1893-6 and 1901-2; 3rd revision
1913.

1919
I 2/1919. M 1919.
L (1)a; (2)b,n,q,r,t; (3)a,k,o,s.
S 1. O 1a,2a,3a,4a.
C Buff,2a,3(1/6)a,4b²,5a²d,6g.
PC; BLa(13/10/19); Bod; CUL(28/9/19);
RGS(29/7/19)
Supp. to Cat.Jun.1919.

1921a 5-21.
I 2/1919; (5)21(l). M 1919.
L (1)a; (2)b,n,s,t; (3)a,k,o,s.
S 1. O 1a,2c[gap],3a,4a.
C Red,2a,3(3/6)a,5bd,6g.
PC; BLb; BLc

[**1921b** 2000/21; not seen; inferred from
1927; may refer to 1921a]

1924 Outline 5
I (1)24a.
BLd(11/9/25); BLe; Bod(27/10/25)
*Supp. to Cat.1 Jan./31 Mar.1925.
Specification change: contours reinforced.*

1927 2000/21.500/27.
I 2/1919; (1)26a; (4)27d; roads(4)4·26.
M Jan.1925.
L (1)a,b,c,g; (2)c,n,s,u; (3)a,o,s.
S 2. O 1a,2b,3b,4b.
C Red,1b,5p,6g.
PC

1929 2000/21.500/27.4500/29.
I 2/1919; (1)26-9a; (4)29d; roads (4)4.26.
M 1925.
L (1)a,b,c,g; (2)c,n,s,u; (3)a,o,s.
S 3. O 1a,2b,3b,4b.
C B&Rb,2b,3(4/-)b,5bd,6i.
PC; BLb; KGM

1931 2000/21.500/27.4500/29.3000/31.
Special Edition, with hills
I 2/1919; (1)31a; (4)31d; roads (2) 4/26.

C cover: 271-81; I imprint: 259-62; L legend: 263-5; M magnetic variation; O other marginal data: 266-9;
S scale: 266; (k) left, between legend and map border; (l) left, below legend; location abbreviations: xii;
340   outline: 282; print codes: 84-7. *AR*: annual report; *Supp. to Cat.* see OS *Catalogues*: 394.

M Jan.1930.
L (1)a,b,g; (2)c,n,s,u; (3)a,o,s.
S 4. O 1a,2b,3c,4b.
C Similar to Browne (1991) no.8, p.125, but all black on a buff card, with wavy black border and the title 'ORDNANCE SURVEY [separated by a coat of arms from] ENGLAND & WALES [wavy line] MARLBOROUGH [in lettering 2g] SHEET 112 | (SPECIAL EDITION, WITH HILLS). [wavy line] Scale One Inch to a Mile.'
PC; KGM

Another copy: Cover design as above, but with different typography: the ampersand resembles a rounded upper case 'E' with a flourish; the sheet title is in lettering 2f; the sheet number lacks the special edition note and reads: 'Sheet 112 (Popular Edition)'; the lettering of the scale statement is also slightly different. PC

*Specification change: now shows parish boundaries. This map was apparently specially printed to be used with **Landforms and Life** by C.C. Carter, and **The Marlborough Country** by Carter and H.C. Brentnall. Both had taught in the Geography Department at Marlborough College. This map was still being issued to the pupils until about 1945. See **Sheetlines**, no.9 (Apr.1984), pp.19-20; information supplied by Dr. C. Board.*

1932 2000/21.500/27.4500/29.4000/32.
I 2/1919; (1)32a; (4)32d; roads (2)7/32.
M Jan 1930.
L (1)a,b,c,g; (2)c,n,s,u; (3)a,o,s.
S 4. O 1a,2b,3b,4b.
C B&Rb,2f,3(2/6)g,5bd,6i.
PC; KGM

1935 3035
I 6/1919. M Jan.1930.
L (1)a,b,c,g,j; (2)e,n,s,u; (3)a,i,o,s.
S 4. O 1a,2b,3b,4b.
C B&Rb,2h,3(2/6)h,4d,5bd,6i.
PC; BLb; BLc; KGM; RGS

[1937 or 1938 Outline; not seen]
AR 1937/8.

1941 Outline **1000/12/41 LR**
PC   *AR 1941/2.*

[1944 or 1945 Outline; not seen]
AR 1944/5.

113 READING & NEWBURY
Surveyed 1870-83; published 1880-9; revised 1893-4 and 1901-2; 3rd revision 1913-14.

1919
I 2/1919. M 1919.
L (1)a; (2)b,n,q,r,t; (3)a,k,o,s.
S 1. O 1a,2a,3a,4a.
C Buff,2a,3(2/6)b,5a^{2}d,6g.
PC; BLa(3/12/20); BLb; Bod;
CUL(30/11/20)
Supp. to Cat.Oct.1919.

1921a 5-21.
I 2/1919; (5)21(l). M 1919.
L (1)a; (2)b,n,q,r,t; (3)a,k,o,s.
S 1. O 1a,2c[gap],3a,4a.
C Red,2a,3(3/6)a,5bd,6g.
PC; BLc

[**1921b 1000/21** not seen; inferred from 1927; may refer to 1921a]

1924 Outline 5   I (1)24a.
BLd(11/9/25); BLe; Bod(27/10/25)
Supp. to Cat.1 Jan./31 Mar.1925.

1926 3000/26.
I 2/1919; (1)26a; (4)26d; roads (1)4.26.
M 1919.
L (1)a; (2)c,n,s,t; (3)a,q,s.
S 1. O 1a,2c,3a,4b.
C Red,1b,5p,6g.
BLc; BLb; RGS

1927 1000/21.3000/27.
I 2/1919; (1)26a; (4)27d. M Jan.1926.
L (1)a,b,c,g; (2)c,n,s,u; (3)a,o,s.
S 2. O 1a,2b,3b,4b.
C Red,2a,3(2/6)d,4b^2,5bd,6g.
PC; BLc; RGS

Supp. to Cat.1 Apr./30 June 1927. 'With special Road Revision.'

1929 1000/21.3000/27.,4000/29.
I 2/1919; (1)28a; (4)29d; roads (11)4.26.
M Jan.1926.
L (1)a,b,c,g; (2)c,n,s,u; (3)a,o,s.
S 3. O 1a,2b,3b,4b.
C B&Rb,2a,3(2/6)f,4c^2,5bd,6i.
PC; KGM

1933 **1000/21.3000/27.,4000/29.1500/33.**
I 2/1919; (1)32a; (4)33d; roads (11)31.
M Jan.1926.
L (1)a,b,c,g; (2)e,n,s,u; (3)a,o,s.
S 4. O 1a,2b,3b,4b.
C B&Rb,2f,3(2/6)g,4d,5bd,6i.
BLc

1934 **3,200/34.**
I 4/1919; (1)33b; (2)31a; (5)34c.
M Jan.1926.
L (1)a,b,c,g; (2)e,n,s,u; (3)a,o,s.
S 4. O 1a,2b,3b,4b.
C B&Ra,2f,3(2/6)g,4d,5bd,6i.
PC; BLb; BLc; KGM

[**1936** or **1937** Outline; not seen]
AR 1936/7.

1941 Outline 7 **3,200/34**
1000/11/41.L.R.
I 4/Southampton and date erased.
PC
AR 1941/2.

114 WINDSOR
Surveyed 1861-74; published 1874-80;
revised 1887-93 and 1901-2; 3rd revision
1912-4.

1920
I 2/1920. M 1920.
L (1)a; (2)b,n,p,q,u; (3)c,k,o,s.
S 1. O 1a,2c,3a,4a.
C Red,2a,3(2/6)a,4b^1,5bd,6g.
PC; BLa(5/12/20); BLb; Bod;
CUL(2/12/21); RGS
*Supp. to Cat.Jun.1920. 'Price 1/6 net.' is
stamped in purple below the copyright
statement on the RGS example.*

1921 **7.21.**
I 2/1920; (5)21(l).
M 1920.
L (1)a; (2)c,n,p,q,u; (3)c,o,s.
S 1. O 1a,2c[**no gap**],3a,4a.
C Red,2a,3(2/6)a,4b^1,5bd,6g.
PC; BLc; RGS

1921 Outline 2 **WINDSOR.**
BLd(20/5/22); BLe; Bod
Supp. to Cat.1 Jul./30 Sep.1920.

1923 **5000/23. WINDSOR**
I 2/1920. (1)23a; (4)23d. M 1920.
L (1)a; (2)c,n,p,q,u; (3)c,o,s.
S 1. O 1a,2c,3a,4a.
C Red,2a,3(2/6)d,4b^2,5bd,6g.
PC; BLc; KGM; RGS

1927 **5000/27.**
I 2/1920; (1)25a; (4)27b; roads (5) 7.25.
M Jan.1925.
L (1)a,b,c; (2)c,n,q,t; (3)c,q,s.
S 2. O 1a,2b,3b,4b.
C Red,2a,3(2/6)d,4b^2,5bd,6i.
PC; BLc; KGM
*Supp. to Cat.1 July/30 Sept.1927. 'With
special Road Revision.' Specification
change: contours reinforced.*

1927 Outline **5000/27.500/27.**
PC

[**1929a** **6000/29** inferred from 1929b]

1929b **5000/27.6000/29.500/29.**
I 2/1920; (1)28a; (4)29b; roads (5) 11.27.
M Jan 1925.
L (1)a,b,c; (2)c,n,p,q,t; (3)c,q,s.
S 2. O 1a,2b,3b,4b.
C Red,2a,3(2/6)d,4b^2,5bd,6i.
PC; BLc; KGM
*General Roy's baseline is shown for the first
time. Tablets commemorating the
bicentenary of Roy's birth (4 May 1726)
were fixed, belatedly, on 22 February 1927,
to the cannon which marked the end of the
baseline on Hounslow Heath (**Geographical
Journal**, LXIX, 4:350-55, 1927). It may be
that the suggestion to show the line on the
one-inch map was made just too late for its
inclusion on the 1927 state of this sheet.*

[**1931a** **6500/31** not seen; inferred from
1931b]

1931b WINDSOR.
5000/27.6000/29.500/29.6500/31.2500/31.
I 2/1920; (1)30a; (4)31b,d; roads (4)11.27.
M Jan.1925.
L (1)a,b,c; (2)c,n,q,t; (3)c,q,s.
S 4. O 1a,2b,3b,4b.
C B&Rb,2f,3(2/6)f,4c^2,5bd,6i.
PC

C cover: 271-81; I imprint: 259-62; L legend: 263-5; M magnetic variation; O other marginal data: 266-9;
S scale: 266; (k) left, between legend and map border; (l) left, below legend; location abbreviations: xii;
342 outline: 282; print codes: 84-7. *AR:* annual report; *Supp. to Cat.* see OS *Catalogues*: 394.

1932 WINDSOR
5000/27.6000/29.500/29.6500/31.6500/32.
I 2/1920; (1)31a; (4)32b;roads revisd[sic]
(5)12/31.
M Jan.1925.
L (1)a,b,c,g; (2)c,o,p,t; (3)a,o,s.
S 4. O 1a,2b,3b,4b.
C B&Rb,2f,3(2/6)g,4d,5bd,6i.
PC; BLc; KGM
*Specification change: contours not
reinforced; rivers in same specification as
Scottish Popular.*

   1932 Outline
   5000/27.6000/29.500/29.6500/31.6500/32.
   SG

1933 **10,000/33.**
I 4/1920; (1)33b; (2)32-33a; (5)33c.
M Jan.1925.
L (1)a,b,c,g; (2)e,o,p,t; (3)a,q,s.
S 4. O 1a,2b,3b,4b.
C B&Rb,2h,3(2/6)g,4d,5bd,6i.
PC; BLb; BLc

   [1936 or 1937 Outline; not seen]
   AR 1936/7.

115 S.E.LONDON & SEVENOAKS
Surveyed 1861-71; published 1876-9;
revised 1887-93 and 1901-3; 3rd revision
1913-4.

1920
I 2/1920. M 1920.
L (1)a; (2)b,n,p,t; (3)c,k,o,s.
S 1. O 1a,2c,3a,4a.
C Red,2a,3(2/6)a,4b^1,5bd,6g.
PC; BLa(5/12/20); Bod; CUL(2/12/21)
Supp. to Cat.Jun.1920.

1921a **1.21.**
I 2/1920; (5)21(l). M 1920.
L (1)a; (2)b,n,p,q,u; (3)c,o,s.
S 1. O 1a,2c,3a,4a.
C Red,2a,3(2/6)a,4b^1,5bd,6g.
PC; BLc; KGM; RGS

1921b **9.21.**
I 2/1920; (5)21(l). M 1920.
L (1)a; (2)c,n,p,q,u; (3)c,o,s.
S 1. O 1a,2c,3a,4a.
C Red,2a,3(3/6)a,5bd,6g.
PC; BLb; BLc

1920 LONDON & SEVENOAKS.
Outline 2
BLd(20/5/1922); BLe; Bod
Supp. to Cat.1 Jul./30 Sep.1921.

1924 **5000/24.**
I 2/1920; (1)23a; (4)24d.
M 1920.
L (1)a; (2)c,n,p,t; (3)c,o,s.
S 2. O 1a,2c,3b,4b.
C Red,2a,2(3/6)c,4b^2,5bd,6g.
PC; KGM; RGS

1926 **5000/24.5000/26.**
I 2/1920; (1)25a; (4)26d; roads (5)5/25.
M 1920.
L (1)a,g; (2)c,n,p,u; (3)c,q,s.
S 2. O 1a,2c,3b,4b.
C Red,2a,3(2/6)d,4b^2,5bd,6h.
PC; BLc; KGM; RGS
Specification change: contours reinforced.

   1927 Outline **5000/24.500/27.**
   PC

   *Supp. to Cat.1 Oct./31 Dec.1927. 'With
   special Road revision.'*

1928 **5000/24.5000/26.5000/28.**
I 2(Jack)/1920; (1)27-8a; (4)28d; roads
(5)11/27.
M 1920.
L (1)a,g; (2)c,n,p,u; (3)c,o,s.
S 2. O 1a,2b,3b,4b.
C Red,2a,3(2/6)d,4b^2,5bd,6i.
PC; BLc; RGS
*Only the contours on the eastern and
southern sides of the sheet are reinforced.*

[1929 **5000/29** not seen; inferred from
1930]

1930 **5000/24.5000/26.5000/28.5000/29.
5000/30.**
I 2(Close, no date); (1)29a; (4)30d; roads
(5)11.27.
M Jan.1930.
L (1)a,b,c,g; (2)c,n,p,t; (3)c,o,s.
S 3. O 1a,2b,3b,4b.
C Red,2a,3(3/6)a,4c^2,5bd,6i.
PC; BLc; KGM
*PC example is inscribed with the date June
1930. Specification change: contours not
reinforced; parish boundaries are shown.*

1931
5000/24.5000/26.5000/28.5000/29.
5000/30.8500/31.
I 2/(Close, no date); (1)30a; (4)31d; roads
(5)11.27.   **M** Jan.1930.
L (1)a,b,c,g; (2)c,n,p,q,t; (3)c,o,s.
S 4. **O** 1a,2b,3b,4b.
C B&Rb,2a,3(2/6)f,4c²,5bd,6i.
PC; BLc; Bod; KGM

1933a   5000/24.5000/26.5000/28.5000/29.
5000/30.8500/31.10000/33.
I 2/1920; (1)32a; (4)33a; roads (6)12/31.
M Jan.1930.
L (1)a,b,c,g; (2)e,n,p,q,t; (3)c,o,s.
S 4. **O** 1a,2b,3b,4b.
C B&Rb,2f,3(2/6)g,4d,5bd,6i.
PC

1933b   10,000/33.
I 4/1920; (5)33b; (7)32a.   **M** Jan.1930.
L (1)a,b,c,g; (2)e,n,p,q,t; (3)c,o,s.
S 4. **O** 1a,2b,3b,4b.
C B&Rb,2f,3(2/6)g,4d,5bd,6i.
PC; BLc; KGM

1934   8,000/34.
I 4/1920; (1)33b; (2)31a; (5)34c.
M Jan.1930.
L (1)a,b,c,g; (2)e,n,p,q,t; (3)c,o,s.
S 4. **O** 1a,2b,3b,4b.
C B&Rb,2h,3(4/-)h,5bd,6i.
PC; BLc

> 1934   Outline 5
> Imprint details as for 1934a
> BLe

> [1936 or 1937 Outline; not seen]
> *AR 1936/7.*

> 1942 Outline   **1000/1/42 CR**
> PC

116 CHATHAM & MAIDSTONE
Surveyed   1860-72;   published   1876-9;
revised 1893 and 1903-4; 3rd rev. 1914-9.

1921
I 2/1921. **M** 1921.
L (1)a; (2)c,n,p,t; (3)c,o,w.
S 1. **O** 1b,2c,3a,4a,5a.
C Red,2a,3(1/6)b,4a,5bd,6g.

PC; BLa(1/3/22); BLb: Bod; CUL(27/2/22)
Supp. to Cat.1 Jan./31 Mar.1921.

> 1921 Outline 2
> BLd(20/5/22); BLe; Bod
> *Supp. to Cat.1 Jul./30 Sep.1921.*

1925a   5000/25.
I 2/1921; (1)24-5d; (3)22a; (4)25e; roads
(5)Aug.1925.
M 1921.
L (1)a,g; (2)c,n,p,t; (3)c,o,w.
S 1. **O** 1b,2c,3a,4b,5a.
C Red,2a,3(2/6)d,4b²,5bd,6h.
KGM; RGS(12/11/28)

[1925b   2000/25 not seen; inferred from
1929]

1929   2000/25.5000/29.
I 2/1921; (1)28d; (3)22a; (4)29e; roads
(4)10.26.
M 1921.
L (1)a,g; (2)c,n,p,t; (3)c,o,w.
S 3. **O** 1b,2b,3b,4b,5a.
C Red,2a,3(2/6)d,4b²,5bd,6i.
PC; BLc; KGM; RGS

1932   2000/25.5000/29.6500/32.
I 2/1921; (1)31d; (3)22a; (4)32e; roads
(4)11.31.
M 1921.
L (1)a,b,g; (2)c,n,p,t; (3)c,o,w.
S 4. **O** 1b,2b,3b,4b,5a.
C B&Rb,2f,3(2/6)f,4c²,5bd,6i.
PC; BLc; KGM

1935   2035.
I 6/1921. **M** 1921.
L (1)a,b,g; (2)e,n,p,t; (3)c,i,o,w.
S 4. **O** 1b,2b,3b,4b,5a.
C B&Rb,2f,3(2/6)g,4d,5bd,6i.
PC; KGM; RGS

1936   2035 3036. M 36. R 31.
I 6/1921.
M 1ˢᵗ Jan.1937.
L (1)a,b,g,j; (2)e,n,p,u; (3)c,i,o,w.
S 4. **O** 1b,2b,3b,4b,5a.
C B&Rb,2h,3(2/6)h,4d,5bd,6i.
PC
AR 1936/7.

C cover: 271-81; **I** imprint: 259-62; **L** legend: 263-5; **M** magnetic variation; **O** other marginal data: 266-9;
S scale: 266;   (k) left, between legend and map border;   (l) left, below legend;   location abbreviations: xii;
344   outline: 282; print codes: 84-7. *AR*: annual report; *Supp. to Cat.* see OS *Catalogues*: 394.

1938 **3038.M 37.R 31.**
I 6/1921. **M** 1ˢᵗ Jan.1937.
L (1)a,b,g,j; (2)e,j,n,p,t; (3)c,i,o,w.
S 4. **O** 1b,2b,3b,4b,5a.
C BaRed,1c,2f,3(2/6)i,5bd,6j.
PC; KGM
AR 1938/9.

1939 **1239.M37.R31.**
I 6/1921. **M** 1ˢᵗ Jan.1937.
L (1)a,b,g,j; (2)e,j,n,p,t; (3)c,i,o,w.
S 4. **O** 1b,2b,3b,4b,5a.
C BaRed,1c,2f,3(2/6)i,5bd,6j.
PC; BLc; BLb; Bod; RGS
AR 1939/40. Faint traces of a former print code, perhaps '2035' are visible under the '1239'.

 1939 Outline 5
 PC
 AR 1939/40. Lacks the title '(Outline)' in orange, top right.

 1941 Outline 8 (l)**1000/10/41.L.R.**
 I 6/Southampton and date erased.
 PC
 AR 1941/2.

117 EAST KENT
Surveyed 1858-72; published 1878-9; revised 1893 and 1903-4; 3rd revision 1914.

1920
I 2/1920. **M** 1920.
L (1)a; (2)c,n,p,t; (3)c,o,w.
S 1. **O** 1b,2c,3a,4a,5a.
C Red,2a,3(2/6)a,4b²,5bdh,6g.
PC; BLa(21/1/22); BLb; Bod; CUL(17/1/22)
Supp. to Cat.1 Oct./31 Dec.1920.

 1920 Outline 2
 BLd(20/5/22); BLe; Bod
 Supp. to Cat.1 Jul./30 Sept.1921.

1923 **3000/23.**
I 2/1920; (4)23a. **M** 1920.
L (1)a; (2)c,n,p,t; (3)c,o,w.
S 1. **O** 1b,2c,3a,4b,5a.
C Red,2a,3(2/6)c,4b²,5bdh,6g.
PC; BLc; KGM

1926 **3500/26.**
I 2/1920; (1)23-6a; (3)26d; (4)26e; roads (10)7/26. **M** 1920.
L (1)a,g; (2)c,n,p,t; (3)c,o,s.

S 1. **O** 1b,2c,3a,4b,5a.
C Red,2a,3(2/6)d,4b²,5bdh,6h.
PC; BLc; KGM; RGS

1929 **5500/29.**
I 2/1920; (1)28a; (3)26d; (4)29g; roads (8)9·26. **M** Jan.1929.
L (1)a,b,c,g; (2)c,n,p,t; (3)c,o,u.
S 3. **O** 1b,2b,3b,4b,5c.
C Red,2a,3(2/6)d,4b²,5bd,6i.
PC

1931 **5500/29.6300/31.**
I 2/1920; (1)31a; (3)26d; (4)31g; roads (10)11-31. **M** Jan.1929.
L (1)a,b,c,g; (2)c,n,p,t; (3)c,o,u.
S 4. **O** 1c,2b,3b,4b,5c.
C B&Rb(wr),2d,3(1/9)a,4e,5bdh,6i.
PC; BLc; KGM
Note that this state lacks the adjacent sheet diagram in the bottom margin.

1935 **2035.**
I 8/1921. **M** Jan.1929.
L (1)a,b,c,g; (2)e,n,p,t; (3)c,i,o,u.
S 4. **O** 1b,2b,3b,4b,5c.
C B&Rb,2e,3(2/6)h,4d,5bdh,6i.
PC; BLc

1936 **4036.**
I 8/1920. **M** Jan.1929.
L (1)a,b,c,g; (2)e,n,p,t; (3)c,i,o,u.
S 4. **O** 1b,2b,3b,4b,5c.
C B&Rb,2e,3(2/6)h,4d,5bdh,6i.
PC; BLc; KGM

1938 **4038. M.37.R.31.**
I 8/1920. **M** 1937.
L (1)a,b,c,g,j; (2)e,n,p,t; (3)c,i,o,u.
S 4. **O** 1b,2b,3b,4b,5c.
C B&Rb,2e,3(2/6)h,4d,5bdh,6j.
KGM; BLb
AR 1937/8.

1939 **1239. M.37.R.31.**
I 8/1920. **M** 1937.
L (1)a,b,c,g,j; (2)e,j,n,p,t; (3)c,i,o,u.
S 4. **O** 1b,2b,3b,4b,5c.
C BRed,1c,2g,3(1/9)d,4d,5bdh,6j.
BLc; BLb; KGM; RGS

 1942 Outline 7 (k)**M.37.R.31.**
 (l)**1,000/3/42.L.R.**
 BLf
 AR 1942/3.

118 BARNSTAPLE & EXMOOR (Inset: Lundy Island)
Surveyed 1883-8; published 1892-4; revised 1896-7 and 1906; 3rd revision 1913.

1919
I 1/1919. M 1919.
L (1)a; (2)a,n,p,q,t; (3)a,k,n,w.
S 1. O 1b,2a,3a,4a,5a.
C Buff(wr),2a,3(1/6)a,4b^2,5a^{2}d,6g.
PC; BLa(13/10/19); BLb; Bod;
CUL(28/9/19); RGS(29/7/19)
Supp. to Cat.Jun.1919. Contours are printed in orange, the same colour as secondary roads.

1923 2500/23.
I 1/1918[sic]. (4)23a. M 1910 [sic].
L (1)a; (2)c,n,p,q,t; (3)a,o,w.
S 1. O 1b,2c,3a,4b,5a.
C Red,2a,3(2/6)c,4b^2,5bd,6g.
PC; BLc; KGM
On many of the examples seen, the contours are printed in a distinct yellow, the same colour as secondary roads; other variants are pale orange, or a distinct orange. This either indicates distinct printings or a marked lack of colour control.

    1924 Outline 4
I 2/1924.
BLd(16/9/24); BLe; Bod(9/10/24)
Supp. to Cat.1 Apr./30 June 1924.

1927 2500/23.3500/27.
I 1/1918; (1)26d; (4)27a; roads (5)5/25.
M 1919.
L (1)a; (2)c,n,p,q,t; (3)a,o,w.
S 1. O 1b,2b,3a,4b,5a.
C Red,2a,3(2/6)d,4b^2,5bd,6g.
PC; BLc; KGM
Supp. to Cat.1 July/30 Sept.1927. 'With special Road Revision.' Contour colour is now reddish, similar to first class roads.

1929 2500/23.3500/27.4000/29.
I 1/1918; (1)26d; (4)29a; roads (5)5/25.
M 1919.
L (1)a; (2) c,n,p,q,t; (3)a,o,w.
S 1. O 1b,2b,3a,4b,5a.
C B&Rb,2a,3(4/-)b,5bd,6i.
PC; BLc; KGM

1932 2500/23.3500/27.4000/29.4500/32.
I 1/1918; (1)30d; (4)32a; roads (5)5/25.
M 1919.
L (1)a,b; (2)c,n,p,q,t; (3)a,o,w.
S 4. O 1b,2b,3b,4b,5a.
C B&Rb,2f,3(2/6)g,4d,5bd,6i.
PC

1934 2500/23.3500/27 4000/29.4500/32. 3500/34.
I 1/1918; (1)30d; (4)34a; roads (5)5/25.
M 1919.
L (1)a,b; (2)c,n,p,q,t; (3)a,o,w.
S 4. O 1b,2b,3b,4b,5a.
C B&Rb,2h,3(2/6)h,4d,5bd,6i.
PC; BLb; BLc; Bod; KGM; RGS

119 EXMOOR
Surveyed 1884-8; published 1893-4; revised 1896-7 and 1906; 3rd revision 1913.

1918 [1919]
I 1/1918. M 1918.
L (1)a; (2)a,n,q,t; (3)a,k,n,s.
S 1. O 1b,2a,3a,5a.
C Red,2a,3(2/6)a,4b^1,5bdk,6g,
PC; BLa(13/10/19); BLb; Bod;
CUL(28/9/19); RGS(29/7/19)
Supp. to Cat.Jun.1919. The sea is shown by blue bathymetric layering.

[**1922**   1500/22 not seen; inferred from 1931]

1923 1500/23.
I 1/1918; (4)23b. M 1918.
L (1)a; (2)c,n,q,t; (3)a,k,n,s.
S 1. O 1b,2c,3a,5a.
C Red,2a,3(2/6)c,4b^2,5bdk,6g.
PC

    1923 Outline 5
I (1)23b.
BLd(7/8/25); BLe; Bod
Supp. to Cat.1 Oct./31 Dec.1924.

1925 3500/25.
I 1/1918; (1)25b; (4)25a; roads (5)5.25.
M 1918.
L (1)a,g; (2)c,n,q,t; (3)a,o,s.
S 1. O 1b,2c,3a,4b,5a.
C Red,2a,3(2/6)d,4b^2,5bdk,6g.
PC; KGM; RGS

C cover: 271-81; I imprint: 259-62; L legend: 263-5; M magnetic variation; O other marginal data: 266-9;
S scale: 266; (k) left, between legend and map border; (l) left, below legend; location abbreviations: xii;
outline: 282; print codes: 84-7. *AR*: annual report; *Supp. to Cat.* see OS *Catalogues*: 394.

1928 3500/25.3500/28.
I 1/1918; (1)25-6b; (4)28a,d; roads
(5)4[sic].25.　M 1918.
L (1)a,g; (2)c,n,p,t; (3)a,o,s.
S 3. O 1b,2b,3b,4b,5a.
C Red,2f,3(2/6)d,4b²,5bdk,6i.
PC; BLc; KGM; RGS
Specification change: sea now shown by
solid tint. The second print code is printed
beneath the first code and the word 'reprint'
is represented by ditto marks.

1931 1500/22.3500/25.3500/28.6500/31.
I 2/1918; (1)30a; (4)31d; roads (5)4.25.
M 1918.
L (1)a,b,g; (2)c,n,p,t; (3)a,o,s.
S 4. O 1b,2b,3b,4b,5a.
C B&Rb,2h,3(2/6)h,4d,5bdk,6i.
PC; BLc; KGM; RGS

1936a
1500/22.3500/25.3500/28.6500/31.600/36.
I 2/1918; (1)30a; (4)36d; roads (5)4·25.
M 1918.
L (1)a,b,g; (2)c,n,p,t; (3)a,o,s.
S 4. O 1b,2b,3b,4b,5a.
C B&Rb,2h,3(2/6)h,4d,5bdk,6j.
PC; KGM

1936b
1500/22.3500/25.3500/28.6500/31.
600/36.500/36.
I 2/1918; (1)30a; (4)36d; roads (5)4.25.
M 1918.
L (1)a,b,g; (2)c,n,p,t; (3)a,o,u.
S 4. O 1b,2b,3b,4b,5a.
C B&Rb,2h,3(2/6)h,4d,5bdk,6i.
PC; BLb; BLc; KGM
AR 1936/7.

120 BRIDGWATER & QUANTOCK HILLS
Surveyed 1882-7; published 1892-4; revised
1896-7 and 1905; 3rd revision 1913.

1918 [1919]
I 1(CMG)1918. M 1918.
L (1)a; (2)a,n,q,t; (3)a,k,n,s.
S 1. O 1a,2a,3a,5a.
C Buff,2a,3(2/6)b,4b²,5a²dj,6g.
RGS; BLa(13/10/19); BLb; Bod;
CUL(28/9/19); RGS(29/7/19)
Supp. to Cat.Jun.1919. The sea is shown by
blue bathymetric layering.

1924 Outline 5
I 2/1918; (1)24a. M Jan.1924.
BLd(7/8/25); Bod
Supp. to Cat.1 Oct./31 Dec.1924.

1926 2500/26.
I 2/1918; (1)26a; (4)26d; roads (5)6.26.
M Jan.1924.
L (1)a,g; (2)c,n,q,u; (3)c,o,w.
S 2. O 1a,2c,3b,4b,5a.
C Red,2a,3(2/6)d,4a,5a²dj,6g.
PC; KGM; RGS
Specification change: parks in green ruling.

1929 3000/29.
I 2/1918; (1)29a; (5)29d; roads
(1)5[sic]·26.
M Jan.1924.
L (1)a,g; (2)c,n,q,t; (3)c,o,w.
S 2. O 1a,2b,3b,4b,5a.
C Red,2a,3(2/6)e,4b²,5a²dj,6i.
BLc; KGM

1931 3000/29.4500/31.
I 2/1918; (1)30a; (5)31d; roads (1)5-26.
M 1931.
L (1)a,b,c,g; (2)c,n,p,u; (3)a,h,o,w.
S 4. O 1a,2b,3b,4b,5a.
C B&Rb,2f,3(2/6)f,4c²,5a²dj,6i.
PC; RGS
Specification change: sea is shown by a
solid tint; parks have reverted to rouletted
stipple; parish boundaries are shown.

1935 2535.
I 5/1918.
M 1931.
L (1)a,b,c,g; (2)e,n,p,t; (3)a,h,i,o,w.
S 4. O 1a,2b,3b,4b,5a.
C B&Rb,2f,3(2/6)g,4d,5a²dj,6i.
PC; BLc; KGM; RGS

1936 2535.2036.M.36.R.32.
I 5/1918.
M 1931.
L (1)a,b,c,g,j; (2)e,n,p,t; (3)a,h,i,o,w.
S 4. O 1a,2b,3b,4b,5a.
C B&Rb,2h,3(2/6)h,4d,5adj,6i.
BLc; BLb; KGM; RGS
AR 1936/7.

1941 Outline **1000/11/41 LR**
PC　*AR 1941/2.*

121 WELLS & FROME (Wells, Frome and District)

Surveyed 1882-5; published 1892-3; revised 1897 and 1903-5; 3rd revision 1913.

1919
I 2/1919. M 1919.
L (1)a; (2)b,n,q,r,t; (3)a,k,o,s.
S 1. O 1a,2a,3a,4a.
C Buff,2a,3(1/6)a,4b^2,5a^{2}d,6g.
PC; BLa(13/10/19); Bod; CUL(28/9/19); RGS(27/7/19)
Supp. to Cat.Jun.1919.

1921a 5.21.
I 2/1919; (5)21(l). M 1919.
L (1)a; (2)b,n,s,t; (3)a,k,o,s.
S 1. O 1a,2c[gap],3a,4a.
C Red,2a,3(3/6)a,5n,6g.
PC
The print code of 1000/21, which is recorded on the 1931 printing, may apply to this state.

1921b 7.21.
I 2/1919; (5)21(l). M 1919.
L (1)a; (2)c,n,s,t; (3)a,o,s.
S 1. O 1a,2c[gap],3a,4a.
C Red,2a,3(2/6)c,4b^2,5bd,6g.
PC; BLb; BLc; KGM; RGS
The print code of 2500/21, which is recorded on the 1931 printing, may apply to this state.

1924 Outline 4
I 2/1924.
BLd(7/8/25); Bod
Supp. to Cat.1 Oct./31 Dec.1924.

1925 7.21.
I 2/1919; (1)25a; (5)21(l). M 1919.
L (1)a; (2)c,n,s,t; (3)a,o,s.
S 1. O 1a,2c,3a,4b. Flat.
BLb

[1928 500/28 not seen; inferred from 1931]

1931 1000/21.2500/21.500/28.2800/31. WELLS & FROME.
I 2/1919; (1)29a; (4)31b; roads (5)7.26.
M 1919.
L (1)a,b,c,g; (2)c,n,s,u; (3)a,o,s.
S 4. O 1a,2b,3b,4b.

C B&Rb,2a,3(2/6)f,4c^2,5bd,6i.
PC; BLc; KGM
Specification change: parish boundaries are shown; larger bodies of inland water are shown in blue ruling.

1934 2,000/34. (WELLS and FROME)
I 4/1919; (1)33b; (2)32a; (5)34c.
M 1919.
L (1)a,b,c,g; (2)e,n,s,u; (3)a,i,o,s.
S 4. O 1a,2b,3b,4b.
C B&Rb,2e,3(2/6)h,4d,5bd,6i.
PC

1937 2037.M36.R32.
I 6/1919. M Jan.1st 1936.
L (1)a,b,c,g,j; (2)e,n,s,u; (3)a,i,o,s.
S 4. O 1a,2b,3b,4b.
C B&Rb,2e,3(2/6)h,4d,5bd,6j.
PC; BLb; BLc; Bod; KGM
AR 1937/8.

1941 Outline 8 1000/11/41.L.R. BLf

[1942 or 1943 Outline; not seen]
AR 1942/3.

122 SALISBURY & BULFORD

Surveyed 1865-84; published 1877-92; revised 1893-7 and 1901-3; 3rd revision 1913.

1919
I 2/1919. M 1919.
L (1)a; (2)b,n,q,r,t; (3)a,k,o,s.
S 1. O 1a,2a,3a,4a.
C Buff,2a,3(2/6)b,4b^2,5a^{2}e,6g.
PC; BLa(13/10/19); Bod; CUL(28/9/19); RGS(29/7/19)
Supp. to Cat.Jun.1919.

1921a 6.21.
I 2/1919; (5)21(l). M 1919.
L (1)a; (2)b,n,s,t; (3)a,k,o,w.
S 1. O 1a,2c[gap],3a,4a.
C Red,2a,3(3/6)a,5be,6g.
PC; BLb; BLc

1921b 12.21
I 2/1919; (5)21(l). M 1919.
L (1)a; (2)b,n,s,t; (3)a,o,w.
S 1. O 1a,2c,3a,4a.
C Red,2a,3(1/6)a,4b^2,5a^{2}e,6g.

C cover: 271-81; I imprint: 259-62; L legend: 263-5; M magnetic variation; O other marginal data: 266-9; S scale: 266; (k) left, between legend and map border; (l) left, below legend; location abbreviations: xii; outline: 282; print codes: 84-7. *AR*: annual report; *Supp. to Cat.* see OS *Catalogues*: 394.

348

BLc
1924 Outline 5
I (1)24a.
BLd(11/9/25); Bod(27/10.25)
*Supp. to Cat.1 Jan./31 Mar.1925.
Specification change: contours reinforced.*

1927 3500/27.
I 2/1919; (1)25a; (4)27d; roads (4)10.25.
M 1919.
L (1)a,g; (2)c,n,s,t; (3)a,q,s.
S 2. O 1a,2b,3b,4b.
C Red,2a,3(2/6)d,4b²,5be,6i.
PC; BLc; Bod; KGM; RGS

Supp. to Cat.1 Apr./30 June 1927. 'With special Roads Revision.'

1931 3500/27 3500/31.
I 2/1919; (1)31a; (4)31d; roads (4)4.31.
M 1919.
L (1)a,b,g; (2)c,n,s,t; (3)a,q,s.
S 4. O 1a,2b,3b,4b.
C B&Rb,2a,3(2/6)f,4c²,5be,6i.
PC; BLc; KGM; RGS

1935 2035.
I 6/1919.
M 1919.
L (1)a,b,g; (2)e,n,s,t; (3)a,i,q,s.
S 4. O 1a,2b,3b,4b.
C B&Rb,2h,3(2/6)h,4d,5be,6i.
BLc

1937 2037.M.37.R.31.
I 6/1919. M 1919.
L (1)a,b,g,j; (2)e,n,s,t; (3)a,i,q,s.
S 4. O 1a,2b,3b,4b.
C B&Rb(wr),2h,3(1/9)c,5be,6j.
BLc

AR 1937/8.

1938 538.M37.R31.
I 9/1919. M 1.1.37.
L (1)a,b,c,g,j; (2)e,n,s,t; (3)c,h,i,q,s.
S 4. O 1b,2b,3b,4b.
C B&Rb,2h,3(2/6)h,4d,5be,6j.
PC

The back cover is inscribed in ink: 'SALISBURY -3.6.38'. Specification change: parish boundaries are shown; parks are in green ruling.

1941 Outline 8 **1000/12/41.L.R.**
BLf

AR 1941/2.

123 WINCHESTER (Winchester and District)
Surveyed 1865-78; published 1876-82; revised 1893 and 1901; 3rd rev. 1912-13.

1919
I 2/1919. M 1919.
L (1)a; (2)b,n,q,r,t; (3)a,k,o,s.
S 1. O 1a,2a,3a,4a.
C Buff,2a,3(2/6)b),5a²d,6g.
PC; BLa(13/10/19); Bod; CUL(28/9/19); RGS(29/7/19)
Supp. to Cat.Jun.1919.

1919 [1920]
I 2/1919. M 1919.
L (1)a; (2)b,n,q,r,t; (3)a,k,o,s.
S 1. O 1a,2c[gap],3a,4a.
C Buff,2a,3(2/6)b,5bd,6g.
KGM
The attribution of this state to a 1920 printing is made on the basis of the absence of a price note. It is possible that this printing never bore a month and year code, since the 4mm space below the legend on this example would be ample to have accommodated any notation. The colour of the contours is a reddish orange, rather than the more yellow tones of the first printing.

[**1921a 1000/21** not seen; inferred from 1929]

1921 12.21.
I 2/1919; (5)21(l). M 1919.
L (1)a; (2)c,n,q,r,t; (3)a,o,s.
S 1. O 1a,2c[**no gap**],3a,4a.
C Red,2a,3(2/6)a,4b²,5bd,6g.
PC; BLb; BLc; KGM
The print code of 1600/21 which is recorded on the 1929 printing may refer to this state.

1923 2000/23.
I 2/1919; (4)23a. M 1919.
L (1)a; (2)c,n,q,r,t; (3)a,o,s.
S 1. O 1a,2c,3a,4a.
C Red,2a,3(2/6)d,4b²,5bd,6i.
PC; BLc; KGM

1923 Outline 2 **WINCHESTER.**
I 2/1923.
BLd(26/7/23); Bod
Supp. to Cat.1 Jan./31 Mar.1923.

1929 **1000/21.1600/21.2000/23.3500/29.**
I 2/1919; (1)25-9d; (4)29a; roads (5)10/25.
M Jan.1927.
L (1)a,b,c,g; (2)c,n,r,u; (3)a,o,s.
S 3. O 1a,2b,3b,4b.
C Red,2a,3(2/6)f,4c^2,5bd,6i.
BLc

1932
1000/21.1600/21.2000/23.3500/29.3500/32.
I 2/1919; (1)31d; (4)32a; roads (5)1930.
M Jan.1932.
L (1)a,b,c,g; (2)c,n,r,u; (3)a,o,s.
S 4. O 1a,2b,3b,4b.
C B&Rb,2f,[price unclear],4e,5bd,6i.
KGM; BLb

1936
1000/21.1600/21.2000/23.3500/29.
3500/32.800/36.
I 2/1919; (1)31d; (4)36a; roads (5)1930.
M Jan.1927.
L (1)a,b,c,g; (2)c,n,r,u; (3)a,o,s.
S 4. O 1a,2b,3b,4b.
C B&Rb,2h,3(2/6)h,4d,5bd,6i.
PC; KGM
AR 1936/7.

   [1936 or 1937 Outline; not seen]
   AR 1936/7.

1938
1000/21.1600/21.2000/23.3500/29.
3500/32.500/38.
I 2/1919; (1)31d; (4)38a; roads (5)1930.
M Jan.1927.
L (1)a,b,c,g; (2)c,n,r,u; (3)a,o,s.
S 4. O 1a,2b,3b,4b.
PC *AR 1938/9.*

124 GUILDFORD & HORSHAM
Surveyed 1866-75; published 1874-82;
revised 1887-94 and 1901; 3rd rev. 1912-4.

1920
I 2/1920. M 1920.
L (1)a; (2)b,n,q,u; (3)c,k,o,s.
S 1. O 1a,2c,3a,4a.
C Red,2a,3(2/6)a,4b^1,5bd,6g.
PC; BLa; BLb; Bod; CUL(21/12/21); RGS
Supp. to Cat.1 Jul./30 Sep.1920.

1923 **5000/23.**
I 2/1920; (4)23a. M 1920.
L (1)a; (2)c,n,q,u; (3)c,k,o,s.
S 1. O 1a,2c,3a,4a.
C Red,2a,3(2/6)c,4b^2,5bd,6g.
PC; BLc; KGM; RGS

   1924 Outline 4
   I 2(Jack)/1920; (1)24a.
   BL(7/8/25); Bod
   Supp. to Cat.1 Oct./31 Dec.1924.

1926a **3000/26.**
I 2(Close)/1920; (1)25a; (4)26d; roads
(5)12.24. M 1920.
L (1)a; (2)c,n,q,u; (3)c,q,s.
S 2. O 1a,2c,3b,4b.
C Red,2a,3(2/6)a,4b^2,5bd,6g.
PC; BLc
Specification change: contours reinforced.

[**1926b** **1000/26** not seen; inferred from
1928]

1927 **5000/23.3000/26.3000/27.**
I 2/1920; (1)25a; (4)27d; roads (3)12.24.
M 1920.
L (1)a; (2)c,n,q,u; (3)c,q,s.
S 2. O 1a,2b,3b,4b.
C Red,2a,3(2/6)d,4b^2,5bd,6h.
PC; KGM
*Supp. to Cat.1 July/30 Sept.1927. 'With
special Road Revision.'*

1928 GUILDFORD & HORSHAM.
5000/23.,1000/26.,3000/28.
I 2/1920; (1)25a; (4)28d; roads (4)11·25.
M Jan.1927.
L (1)a,b,c,g; (2)c,n,p,u; (3)c,o,s.
S 3. O 1a,2b,3b,4b.
C Red,2a,3(2/6)d,4b^2,5bd,6i.
PC; BLc; KGM; RGS
*Specification change: contours not
reinforced.*

1929 **5000/23.,1000/26.,3000/27.,6000/29.**
I 2/1920; (1)25a; (4)29d; roads (4)11·25.
M Jan.1927.
L (1)a,b,c,g; (2)c,n,p,u; (3)c,o,s.
S 3. O 1a,2b,3b,4b.
C B&Ra,2a,3(2/6)f,4c^2,5bd,6i.
PC; KGM

C cover: 271-81; I imprint: 259-62; L legend: 263-5; M magnetic variation; O other marginal data: 266-9;
S scale: 266; (k) left, between legend and map border; (l) left, below legend; location abbreviations: xii;
outline: 282; print codes: 84-7. *AR:* annual report; *Supp. to Cat.* see OS **Catalogues**: 394.

1931
5000/23.,1000/26.,3000/27.,6000/29.
6500/31.
I 2/1920;(1)31a; (4)31d; roads (4)11.25.
M Jan.1927.
L (1)a,b,c,g; (2)c,n,s,u; (3)c,o,s.
S 4. O 1a,2b,3b,4b.
C B&Rb,2a,3(2/6)f,4c^2,5bd,6i.
PC; BLc; KGM; RGS

1932
5000/23.,1000/26.,3000/27.,6000/29.
6500/31.8000/32.
I 2/1920; (1)31a; (4)32d; roads (4)8.29.
M Jan.1927.
L (1)a,b,c,g; (2)e,n,p,u; (3)c,o,s.
S 4. O 1a,2b,3b,4b.
C B&Rb,2f,3(2/6)g,4d,5bd,6i.
PC; BLb; BLc; KGM; RGS

1935
5000/23.,1000/26.,3000/27.,6000/29.
6500/31.8000/32.1000/35.
I 2/1920; (1)31a; (4)35d; roads (4)8·29.
M Jan.1927.
L (1)a,b,c,g; (2)e,n,p,u; (3)c,o,s.
S 4. O 1a,2b,3b,4b.
C B&Rb,2h,3(2/6)h,4d,5bd,6i.
PC

1937
5000/23.,1000/26.,3000/27.,6000/29.
6500/31.8000/32. 1037.
I 2/1920; (1)23a; (4)32d; (5)37k; roads
(4)8.29. M Jan.1927.
L (1)a,b,c,g; (2)e,n,p,u; (3)c,o,s.
S 4. O 1a,2b,3b,4b.
C B&Rb,2h,3(2/6)h,4d,5bd,6j.
PC

AR 1937/8.

125 TUNBRIDGE WELLS
Surveyed 1865-75; published 1878-82;
revised 1887-93 and 1901-3; 3rd revision
1914-7.

1920
I 2/1920. M 1920.
L (1)a; (2)c,n,s,u; (3)c,o,s.
S 1. O 1b,2c,3a,4a.
C Red,2a,3(3/6)a,5bd,6g.
PC; BLa(21/1/22); BLb; Bod;
CUL(17/1/22); RGS
Supp. to Cat.1 Oct./31 Dec.1920.

1920 Outline 2
BLd(20/5/22); Bod
Supp. to Cat.1 Jul./30 Sep.1921.

1924 3500/24.
I 2/1920; (1)24d; (4)24a. M 1920.
L (1)a; (2)c,n,s,u; (3)c,o,s.
S 1. O 1b,2c,3a,4b.
C Red,2a,3(2/6)c,4b^2,5bd,6g.
PC; BLc; RGS

1927 5000/27.
I 2/1920; (1)24-5a; (4)27d. M 1920.
L (1)a; (2)c,n,s,u; (3)c,q,s.
S 1. O 1b,2b,3a,4b.
C Red,2a,3(2/6)d,4b^2,5bd,6h.
PC; BLc; KGM
Specification change: contours reinforced.

1929 5000/27.2000/29.
I 2/1920; (1)24-5a; (4)29d. M 1920.
L (1)a; (2)c,n,s,u; (3)c,q,s.
S 1. O 1b,2b,3a,4b.
C Red,2a,3(3/6)a,5bd,6i.
PC

1930 5000/27.2000/29.4000/30.
I 2/1920; (1)24-7a; (4)30d; roads (5)8/29.
M 1920.
L (1)a; (2)c,n,s,u; (3)c,q,s.
S 3. O 1b,2b,3b,4b.
C B&Rb,2a,3(2/6)f,4c^2,5bd,6i.
PC; BLb

1932 5000/27.2000/29.4000/32.
I 2/1920; (1)31a; (4)32d; roads (5)8/29.
M 1920.
L (1)a,b; (2)c,n,s,u; (3)c,q,s.
S 4. O 1b,2b,3b,4b.
C B&Rb,2a,3(2/6)f,4c^1,5bd,6i.
PC; BLc; RGS

1934 3,400/34.
I 4/1920; (1)34b; (2)29a; (5)34c.
M 1920.
L (1)a,b; (2)e,n,s,u; (3)c,i,q,s.
S 4. O 1b,2b,3b,4b.
C B&Rb,2e,3(2/6)h,4d,5bd,6i.
PC; BLc; Bod; RGS

1935a 3,400/34.1,500/35.
I 4/1920; (1)34b; (2)29a; (5)35c.
M 1920.
L (1)a,b; (2)e,n,s,u; (3)c,i,q,s.
S 4. O 1b,2b,3b,4b.

C B&Rb,2e,3(2/6)h,4d,5bd,6i.
PC

[1935b 300/35 inferred from 1936]

1936 3,400/34.1,500/35.300/35.2000/36.
I 4/1920; (1)34b; (2)29a; (5)36c,f.
M 1920.
L (1)a,b; (2)e,n,s,u; (3)c,i,q,s.
S 4. O 1b,2b,3b,4b.
C R&Bb,2e,3(2/6)h,4d,5bd,6i.
BLc; RGS
AR 1936/7.

1938 2038,M.38.R.37.
I 6/1920. M Jan.1938.
L (1)a,b,g,j; (2)e,j,n,s,u; (3)c,i,q,s.
S 4. O 1b,2b,3b,4b.
C B&Rb,2e,3(2/6)h,4d,5bd,6j.
BLc; BLb; Bod
AR 1938/9.

1942 Outline 8 **1,000/1/42 L.R.**
BLf   *AR 1941/2.*

126 WEALD OF KENT
Surveyed 1864-70; published 1878-9; revised 1893,1903-10; 3rd rev. 1914-9.

1921
I 2/1921. M 1921.
L (1)a; (2)c,n,p,u; (3)c,o,w.
S 1. O 1b,2c,3a,4a,5a.
C Red,2a,3(2/6)a,4b¹,5bd,6g.
PC; BLa(1/3/22); BLb; Bod; CUL(27/2/22); RGS(29/7/27)
Supp. to Cat.1 Jan./31 Mar.1921.

1921 Outline 2
BLd(20/5/22); Bod
Supp. to Cat.1 Jul./30 Sep.1921.

1927 3500/27.
I 2/1921; (1)27a; (4)27d; roads (4)8.25.
M 1921.
L (1)a,b,c,g; (2)c,n,p,u; (3)c,o,w.
S 3. O 1b,2b,3b,4b,5a.
C Red,2a,3(2/6)d,4b²,5bd,6i;
PC; BLb; BLc; RGS
Supp. to Cat.1 July/30 Sept.1927. 'With special Road Revision.'

1931 3500/27.4500/31.
I 2/1921; (1)29a; (3)27b; (4)31d; roads

(4)8.25.   M 1921.
L (1)a,b,c,g; (2)c,n,p,t; (3)c,o,s.
S 4. O 1b,2b,3b,4b,5a.
C B&Rb,2e,3(2/6)g,4d,5bd,6i.
KGM; BLc

1935 2535.
I 5/1921. M 1921.
L (1)a,b,c,g; (2)e,n,p,u; (3)c,i,o,w.
S 4. O 1b,2b,3b,4b,5a.
C B&Rb,2e,3(2/6)h,4d,5bd,6i.
PC; BLc; KGM

[1936 or **1937** not seen; but see next entry]
AR 1936/7.

1937 3037.M36.R31.
I 5/1921. M 1ˢᵗ Janʸ 1937.
L (1)a,b,c,g,j; (2)e,n,p,t; (3)c,i,o,w.
S 4. O 1b,2b,3b,4b,5b.
C B&Rb,2e,3(2/6)h,4d,5bd,6i.
PC; GM
AR 1937/8. The print code on this state is written over an imperfectly erased earlier print code; either the first code was an error, or it may have belonged to a previous state, perhaps 1936 or 1937. The digits 3 [or 8?] and 7 can just be identified.

1938 3038.M37.R31.
I 5/1921. M 1ˢᵗ Janʸ 1937.
L (1)a,b,c,g,j; (2)e,j,n,p,t; (3)c,i,o,w.
S 4. O 1b,2b,3b,4b,5a.
C BRed,1c,2g,3(1/9)d,5bd,6j.
PC; BLb; BLc
AR 1938/9.

1941 Outline 8 (l)**1,000/10/41.L.R.**
Imprint erased. BLf *AR 1941/2.*

127 RIVER TORRIDGE (River Torridge and District)
Surveyed 1882-8; published 1889-94; revised 1894-6 and 1907-8; 3rd rev. 1913.

1919
I 2/1919. M 1919.
L (1)a; (2)b,n,p,q,t; (3)a,k,o,w.
S 1. O 1b,2a,3a,4a,5a.
C Buff(wr),2a,3(2/6)a,4b¹,5a²d,6g.
PC; BLa(13/10/19); BLb; Bod;
CUL(28/9/19); RGS
Supp. to cat.Jun.1919.

C cover: 271-81; I imprint: 259-62; L legend: 263-5; M magnetic variation; O other marginal data: 266-9; S scale: 266; (k) left, between legend and map border; (l) left, below legend; location abbreviations: xii; outline: 282; print codes: 84-7. *AR*: annual report; *Supp. to Cat.* see OS *Catalogues*: 394.

1923 500/23.
I 2/1919; (4)23a. M 1919.
L (1)a; (2)c,n,p,q,t; (3)a,k,o,w.
S 1. O 1b,2c[gap],3a,4a,5a.
C Red,2a,3(3/6)a,5bd,6g.
PC; BLc

> 1924 Outline 5
> I (1)24d.
> BLd(1/4/26); Bod(13/4/26)
> *Supp. to Cat.1 Jul./30 Sep.1925.*

1927a 1000/27.
I 2/1919; (1)24-6d; (3)26a; (4)27e; roads
(5)10/26. M 1919.
L (1)a; (2)c,n,p,q,t; (3)a,o,u.
S 1. O 1b,2b,3a,4b,5a.
C Red,2a,3(3/6)a,5bd,6h.
PC; BLb; KGM; RGS

*Supp. to Cat. 1 July/30 Sept.1927. 'With
special Road Revision.'*

[1927b 2500/27 not seen; inferred from
1931]

1928 2500/28.
I 2/1919; (1)24-6d; (3)26a; (4)28e; roads
(5)10/26. M 1919.
L (1)a; (2)c,n,p,q,t; (3)a,o,u.
S 1. O 1b,2b,3a,4b,5a.
C Red,2a,3(2/6)d,4b^2,5bd,6h.
PC; BLc

*Supp. to Cat.1 Jan./31 Mar.1928. 'With
special Road Revision.'*

[1930 500/30 not seen; inferred from 1931]

1931 2500/27.500/30.2500/31.
I 2/1919; (1)24-6d; (3)26a; (4)31e; roads
(5)10/26. M 1919.
L (1)a,b; (2)c,n,p,q,t; (3)a,o,u.
S 4. O 1b,2b,3b,4b,5a.
C B&Ra,2a,3(3/6)a,5bd,6i.
KGM; BLc

1934 2,500/34.
I 4/1919; (1)31b; (2)31a; (5)34c.
M 1919.
L (1)a,b; (2)e,n,p,q,t; (3)a,o,w.
S 4. O 1b,2b,3b,4b,5a.
C B&Rb,2f,3(2/6)g,4d,5bd,6i.
PC; BLb; Bod; KGM

128 TIVERTON (Tiverton and District)
Surveyed 1876-89; published 1893-4;
revised 1896-7 and 1906-7; 3rd rev. 1913.

1918 [1919]
I 1/1918. M 1919.
L (1)a; (2)a,n,q,u; (3)a,k,o,s.
S 1. O 1a,2a,3a,4a,5a.
C Buff,2a,3(2/6)b,5a^{1}d,6g.
PC; BLa(13/10/19); BLb; Bod;
CUL(28/9/19); RGS(29/7/19)
Supp. to Cat.Jun.1919.

[1920] [?]0.
I 2/1918; (5)?0(l). M 1920.
L (1)a; (2)b,n,q,u; (3)a,k,o,s.
S 1. O 1a,2c,3a,4a.
C Red,2a,3(2/6)d,4b^2,5bd,6g.
RGS; KGM

> 1925 Outline 5
> I 2/1918; (1)25a.
> Bod
> *Supp. to Cat.1 Apr./30 June 1925.*

1934 500/34.
I 2/1918; (1)26a; (5)34b; roads (4)9.26.
M 1920.
L (1)a; (2)c,n,q,u; (3)a,o,s.
S 1. O 1a,2b,3b,4b.
C B&Rb,2f,3(2/6)g,4d,5bd,6i.
PC

1935 835.
I 6/1918; Roads (4)9.26. M 1920.
L (1)a; (2)c,n,q,u; (3)a,o,s.
S 1. O 1a,2c,3a,4b.
C B&Rb,2h,3(2/6)h,4d,5bd,6i.
BLc

129 CHARD & AXMINISTER
Surveyed 1884-8; published 1892-4; revised
1896-7 and 1904-8; 3rd revision 1913-14.

1919
I 2/1919. M 1919.
L (1)a; (2)b,n,q,r,t; (3)a,k,o,s.
S 1. O 1b,2a,3a,4a.
C Buff,2a,3(1/6)c,4b^2,5a^{1}e,6g.
PC; BLa(13/10/19); Bod; CUL(28/9/19);
RGS(29/7/19)
Supp. to Cat.Jun.1919.

1921 1-21
I 2/1919; (5)21(l). M 1919.
L (1)a; (2)b,n,q,r,t; (3)a,k,o,s.
S 1. O 1b,2c,3a,4a.
C Red,2a,3(3/6)a,5be,6g.
BLc; BLb

1924 Outline 5
I (1)24a.
BLd(1/4/26); Bod(13/4/26)
Supp. to Cat.1 Jul./30 Sep.1925.

1928 500/28
I 2/1919. (1)24-5a; (4)28d; roads (4)7/26.
M 1919.
L (1)a; (2)c,n,q,r,t; (3)a,o,s.
S 2. **O** 1a,2b,3b,4b. Flat.
BLb

1931 500/28.2300/31.
I 2/1919; (1)24-8a; (4)31d; roads (4)7/26.
M 1919.
L (1)a,b; (2)c,n,q,r,t; (3)a,o,s.
S 4. **O** 1b,2b,3b,4b.
C WPBuff,6i.
PC; BLb; BLc; KGM; RGS

1935 835.
I 6/1919. **M** 1919.
L (1)a,b; (2)e,n,r,u; (3)a,i,k,o,s.
S 4. **O** 1b,2b,3b,4b.
C B&Rb,2a,3(2/6)f,4d,5be,6i.
PC

1936 835.436.
I 6/1919; (5)36(l). **M** 1919.
L (1)a,b; (2)e,n,q,r,u; (3)a,i,k,o,s.
S 4. **O** 1b,2b,3b,4b.
C B&Rb,2f,3(2/6)g,4d,5be,6i.
PC

1937 835.436.1037.M36.R32.
I 6/1919; (5)37(l). **M** 1919.
L (1)a,b,j; (2)e,n,r,u; (3)a,i,k,o,s.
S 4. **O** 1b,2b,3b,4b.
C B&Ra,2h,3(2/6)h,4d,5be,6i.
PC; KGM
AR 1936/7.

130 YEOVIL & BLANDFORD
Surveyed 1862-88; published 1892-3; revised 1896-7 and 1903-5; 3rd rev. 1913-14.

1919
I 2/1919. **M** 1919.
L (1)a; (2)b,n,q,r,t; (3)a,k,o,s.
S 1. **O** 1b,2a,3a,4a.
C Buff,2a,3(2/6)b,4b^2,5a^{2}d,6g.
PC; BLa(13/10/19); Bod; CUL(28/9/19);
RGS(29/7/19)
Supp. to Cat.Jun.1919.

1921 9.21.
I 2/1919; (5)21(l). **M** 1919.
L (1)a; (2)c,n,q,r,t; (3)a,o,s.
S 1. **O** 1b,2c[gap],3a,4a.
C Red,2a,3(3/6)a,5bd,6g.
PC; BLb; KGM

1925 Outline 5
I (1)25a.
BLd(1/4/26); Bod(13/4/26)
Supp. to Cat.1 Jul./30 Sep.1925.

1928 500/28.
I 2/1919; (1)25·6a; (4)28b; roads (5)7.26.
M 1919.
L (1)a; (2)c,n,r,u; (3)a,o,s.
S 1. **O** 1b,2b,3a,4b.
C B&Ra,2a,3(2/6)d,4b^2,5bd,6i.
PC; KGM

1931 500/28.2800/31.
I 2/1919; (1)28a; (4)31b; roads (5)7.26.
M 1919.
L (1)a,b; (2)c,n,q,r,u; (3)a,o,s.
S 4. **O** 1b,2b,3b,4b.
C B&Rb,2f,3(2/6)g,4d,5bd,6i.
PC; KGM; RGS

1935a 1535.
I 6/1919.
M 1935.
L (1)a,b,c,g; (2)e,n,q,r,u; (3)a,h,i,o,s.
S 4. **O** 1b,2b,3b,4b.
C B&Rb,2h,3(2/6)g,4d,5bd,6i.
PC; BLb; KGM
*Specification change: parish boundaries are
shown; the parish boundary symbol in the
legend is drawn with every fourth dot
enlarged.*

1935b 1535.2535.
I 5/1919.
M 1935.
L (1)a,b,c,g; (2)e,n,q,r,u; (3)a,h,i,o,s.
S 4. **O** 1b,2b,3b,4b.
C B&Rb,2f,3(2/6)g,4d,5bd,6i.
PC; BLb

1941 Outline 8 **1000/11/41.L.R.**
BLf
AR 1941/2.

C cover: 271-81; **I** imprint: 259-62; **L** legend: 263-5; **M** magnetic variation; **O** other marginal data: 266-9;
S scale: 266; (k) left, between legend and map border; (l) left, below legend; location abbreviations: xii;
outline: 282; print codes: 84-7. *AR*: annual report; *Supp. to Cat.* see OS *Catalogues*: 394.

131 WIMBORNE & RINGWOOD

Surveyed 1861-86; published 1876-93; revised 1893-4 and 1901-3; 3rd revision 1913.

1919

I 2/1919. M 1919.
L (1)a; (2)b,n,r,t; (3)a,k,o,s.
S 1. O 1b,2a,3a,4a.
C Buff,2a,3(2/6)b,4b^2,5a^{2}e,6g.
PC; BLa(13/10/19); Bod; CUL(28/9/19); RGS(29/7/19)
Supp. to Cat.Jun.1919.

1921 10·21.

I 2/1919; (5)21(l). M 1919.
L (1)a; (2)c,n,p,q,t; (3)a,o,s.
S 1. O 1b,2c[gap],3a,4a.
C Red,2a,3(3/6)a,5be,6h.
PC; BLb

> 1925 Outline 5
> I (1)25a.
> BLd(29/10/25); Bod
> *Supp. to Cat.1 Apr./30 Jun.1925.*

1928 500/28.

I 2/1919; (1)25a; (4)28b; roads (5)10.25. M 1919.
L (1)a; (2)c,n,q,r,t; (3)a,o,s.
S 2. O 1b,2c,3b,4b.
C Red,2a,3(3/6)a,5be,6h.
PC; BLb

Supp. to Cat.1 Jan./31 Mar.1928. 'With Special Road Revision.'

[1929 2000/29 not seen; inferred from 1932]

1930 500/28.2000/30. WIMBORNE & RINGWOOD.

I 2/1919; (1)29a; (3)25d; (4)30b; roads (5)10.25. M 1919.
L (1)a,g; (2)c,n,t; (3)a,o,s.
S 3. O 1b,2b,3b,4b.
C Red,2a,3(1/6)b,4a,5be,6i.
BLc

1932 500/28.2000/29.6500/32.

I 2/1919; (1)32a; (3)25d; (4)32b; roads (5)2.32. M 1919.
L (1)a,b,g; (2)c,n,q,u; (3)a,o,s.
S 4. O 1b,2b,3b,4b.
C B&Rb,2a,3(2/6)f,4c^2,5be,6i.
PC; BLb; BLc; KGM; RGS

1937 637.

I 4/1920[sic]; (2)35a; (6)33b; roads (5)2·32.   M 1919
L (1)a,b,g; (2)c,n,q,u; (3)a,o,s.
S 4. O 1b,2b,3b,4b.
C B&Rb,2h,3(2/6)h,4c^2,5be,6i.
PC; BLb
AR 1937/8.

> [1937 or 1938 Outline; not seen]
> *AR 1937/8.*

> 1941 Outline 7 **500/28.2000/29.6500/32.(k)1000/11/41.L.R.**
> BLf
> *AR 1941/2.*

132 PORTSMOUTH & SOUTHAMPTON

Surveyed 1855-76; published 1876-77; revised 1893-4 and 1901; 3rd revision 1913.

1919

I 2/1919. M 1919.
L (1)a; (2)b,n,p,q,t; (3)a,k,o,w.
S 1. O 1b,2a,3a,4a,5a.
C Buff,2a,3(1/6)a,5adf,6g.
PC; BLa(13/10/19); Bod; CUL(28/9/19); RGS(29/7/19)
Supp. to Cat.Jun.1919.

1921 7.21.

I 2/1919; (5)21(l).
M 1919.
L (1)a; (2)c,n,p,q,t; (3)a,o,w.
S 1. O 1b,2c[gap],3a,4a,5a.
C Red,2a,3(3/6)a,4a,5bdf,6g.
KGM; BLb

1923 4000/23.

I 2/1919; (3)23a; (4)23d.
M 1919.
L (1)a; (2)c,n,p,q,t; (3)a,o,w.
S 2. O 1b,2c,3b,4b,5a.
C Red,2a,3(2/6)a,4b^2,5bdf,6g.
PC; KGM

> 1923 Outline 4
> I 2/1923; (3)23a.
> BLd(1/2/24); Bod(8/2/24)
> *Supp. to Cat.1 Oct./31 Dec.1923.*

1925 2000/25.

I 2/1919; (1)25a; (3)25d; (4)25e; roads (5)5.25.
M Jan.1925.
L (1)a,b,c,f,g; (2)c,n,p,q,t; (3)c,o,u.

S 2. O 1b,2c,3b,4b,5a.
C Red,2a,3(2/6)d,4a,5bdf,6g.
PC
The magnetic variation diagram has been moved from the sea area to the north-east corner. Specification change: parks are shown by green ruling.

1928 2000/25.3000/28.
I 2/1919; (1)25-8a; (3)25d; (4)28e; roads (5)5.25.
M Jan.1925.
L (1)a,b,c,g; (2)c,n,p,q,t; (3)c,o,u.
S 3. O 1b,2b,3b,4b,5a.
C Red,2a,3(2/6)d,4b²,5bdf,6i.
PC

1929 2000/25.3000/28.5000/29.
I 2/1919; (1)29a; (3)25d; (4)29e; roads (5)5.25.
M Jan.1925.
L (1)a,b,c,f,g; (2)c,n,p,q,t; (3)c,o,u.
S 3. O 1b,2b,3b,4b,5a.
C B&Rb,2a,3(2/6)f,4c²,5bdf,6i.
PC; BLb; BLc; KGM

1932 2000/25.3000/28.5000/29.5000/32.
I 2/1919; (1)32a; (3)25d; (4)32e; roads (5)4.32.
M Jan.1925.
L (1)a,b,c,f,g; (2)c,n,p,q,t; (3)c,o,u.
S 4. O 1b,2b,3b,4b,5a.
C B&Rb,2f,3(2/6)g,4d,6i.
PC; RGS

1935 4035.
I 6/1919. M Jan.1925.
L (1)a,b,c,g; (2)e,n,p,q,t; (3)c,i,o,u.
S 4. O 1b,2b,3b,4b,5a.
C B&Rb,2h,3(2/6)h,4d,5bdf,6i.
PC; BLc; KGM

  1935 Outline 6 **4035.**
  PC

1938 2538.M.37.R.32.
I 6/1919. M Jan.1925.
L (1)a,b,c,f,g,j; (2)e,j,n,p,q,t; (3)c,i,o,u.
S 4. O 1b,2b,3b,4b,5bc.
C B&Rb,2h,3(2/6)h,4d,5bdf,6j.
PC; KGM
AR 1938/9.

133 CHICHESTER & WORTHING
Surveyed 1860-76; published 1881; revised 1893-4 and 1901; 3rd revision 1914.

1920
I 2/1920.
M 1920.
L (1)a; (2)b,n,p,t; (3)c,k,o,s.
S 1. O 1a,2c,3a,4a,5a.
C Red,2a,3(2/6)c,4b²,5bdg,6g.
PC; BLa(23/12/21); BLb; Bod; CUL(21/12/21)
Supp. to Cat.1 Jul./30 Sep.1920.

  1920 Outline
  Heading printed in red: 'Transferred from Copper (engraved)'
  SG

1923 2500/23.
I 2/1920; (4)23a.
M 1920.
L (1)a; (2)c,n,p,t; (3)c,o,w.
S 1. O 1a,2c,3a,4b,5a.
C Red,2a,3(2/6)c,4b²,5bdg,6g.
BLc; KGM

  1923 Outline 2
  I 2/1923.
  BLd(26/7/23); Bod
  Supp. to Cat.1 Jan./31 Mar.1923.

1924 2500/23.3000/24.
I 2/1920; (1)24d; (4)24a; roads (13)8.24.
M 1920.
L (1)a; (2)c,n,p,t; (3)c,o,w.
S 1. O 1a,2c,3a,4b,5a.
C Red,2a,3(2/6)c,4b²,5bdg,6g.
PC; BLc; KGM; RGS

1926 2500/23.3000/24.3500/26.
I 2/1920; (1)24-6d; (4)26a; roads (13)3.26.
M 1920.
L (1)a; (2)c,n,p,t; (3)c,q,w.
S 1. O 1a,2c,3a,4b,5a.
C Red,2a,3(2/6)d,4b²,5bdg,6g.
PC
Specification change: contours reinforced.

1928 2500/23.3000/24.3500/26.3500/28.
I 2/1920; (1)24-6d; (4)28a; roads (1)3.26.
M 1920.
L (1)a; (2)c,n,p,t; (3)c,q,w.

C cover: 271-81; I imprint: 259-62; L legend: 263-5; M magnetic variation; O other marginal data: 266-9; S scale: 266; (k) left, between legend and map border; (l) left, below legend; location abbreviations: xii; outline: 282; print codes: 84-7. *AR*: annual report; *Supp. to Cat.* see OS *Catalogues*: 394.

356

S 1. O 1a,2b,3a,4b,5a.
C Red,2a,3(2/6)d,5bdg,6i.
PC; KGM

Supp. to Cat.1 Jan./31 Mar.1928. 'With Special Road Revision.'

1929
2500/23.3000/24.3500/26.3500/28.6000/29.
I 2/1920; (1)24-9d; (4)29a; roads (13)3.26.
M 1920.
L (1)a,g; (2)c,n,p,t; (3)c,q,w.
S 3. O 1a,2b,3b,4b,5a.
C Red,2a,3(2/6)d,4b²,5bdg,6i.
PC; BLc; KGM

[**1930** 500/30 not seen; inferred from 1931]

1931
2500/23.3000/24.3500/26.3500/28.6000/29.500/30.4500/31.
I 2/1920; (1)30d; (4)31a; roads (13)8.29.
M 1920.
L (1)a,b,g; (2)c,n,p,u; (3)c,q,w.
S 4. O 1a,2b,3b,4b,5a.
C B&Rb,2a,3(2/6)f,4c²,5bdg,6i.
PC; KGM

1933 5,000/33.
I 4/1920; (2)29a; (5)33c; (6)33b.
M 1920.
L (1)a,b,g; (2)e,n,p,t; (3)c,q,w.
S 4. O 1a,2b,3b,4b,5a.
C B&Rb,2f,3(2/6)g,4d,5bdg,6i.
PC; BLb; BLc; KGM

1935 5,000/33.3000/35.
I 4/1920; (2)35a; (5)35c; (6)33b.
M 1920.
L (1)a,b,g; (2)e,n,p,u; (3)c,i,q,w.
S 4. O 1a,2b,3b,4b,5a.
C B&Rb,2h,3(2/6)h,4d,5bdg,6i.
PC; KGM; RGS

1936 5,000/33.5,000/36.
I 4/1920; (2)35a; (5)36c/d; (6)33b.
M 1920.
L (1)a,b,g; (2)e,n,p,u; (3)c,i,q,w.
S 4. O 1a,2b,3b,4b,5a.
C B&Rb,2h,3(2/6)h,4d,5bdg,6i.
PC; KGM

1937 5,000/33, 1037.
I 4/1920; (2)35a; (5)37c/d; (6)33b.
M 1920.
L (1)a,b,g; (2)e,n,p,t; (3)c,q,w.

S 4. O 1a,2b,3b,4b,5a. Flat.
RGS(16/7/38)

1938 4038.M.37.R.33.
I 6/1920. M 1937.
L (1)a,b,g,j; (2)e,j,n,p,q,t; (3)c,i,q,w.
S 4. O 1a,2b,3b,4b,5a.
C B&Rb,2h,3(2/6)h,4d,5bdg,6j.
PC; BLc; KGM

134 **BRIGHTON & EASTBOURNE**
Surveyed 1860-76; published 1880-1; revised 1893-4 and 1901-3; 3rd revision 1914-6.

1920
I 2/1920. M 1920.
L (1)a; (2)b,n,p,t; (3)c,o,w.
S 1. O 1b,2c,3a,4a,5a.
C Red,2a,3(2/6)a,4b¹,5bdg,6g.
PC; BLa(21/1/22); Bod; CUL(17/1/22)
Supp. to Cat.1 Oct./31 Dec.1920.

   1920 Outline 2
   BLd(20/5/22); Bod
   Supp. to Cat.1 Jul./30 Sep.1921.

1923 4000/23.
I 2/1920; (1)23d; (4)23a. M 1920.
L (1)a; (2)c,n,p,t; (3)c,o,w.
S 1. O 1b,2c,3a,4b,5a.
C Red,2a,3(2/6)d,4b²,5bd,6g.
PC; BLb; BLc; KGM

'New Anzac on Sea' has been re-named 'Peacehaven'.

[**1926** 3500/26 not seen; inferred from 1928 outline]

1927 4000/23.3500/27.
I 2/1920; (1)23d; (4)27a; roads (4)12/24.
M 1920.
L (1)a; (2)c,n,p,t; (3)c,q,u.
S 2. O 1b,2b,3b,4b,5a.
C Red,2a,3(3/6)a,5bd,6g.
PC; BLc; Bod; KGM; RGS
Supp. to Cat.1 Apr./30 June 1927. 'With special Road Revision.' Specification change: contours are reinforced.

[**1928a** 500/28 not seen as a standard coloured sheet; inferred from 1928b; may refer to 1928 outline]

   1928 Outline **4000/23.3500/26.500/28.**
   PC

1928b 4000/23.3500/27.500/28.5000/28.
I 2/1920; (1)23-8d; (4)28a; roads (4)12.24.
M Jan.1928.
L (1)a,b,c,g; (2)c,n,p,t; (3)c,o,u.
S 3. O 1b,2b,3b,4b,5a.
C Red,2a,3(2/6)f,4c^2,5b,6bd,8i.
PC; BLc; KGM
*Specification change: contours are not
reinforced. The figures '5000/28' in the
print code are faintly printed on all copies
so far seen.*

1930
**4000/23.3500/27.,500/28.,5000/28.,
5500/30.**
I 2/1920; (1)30d; (4)30a; roads (4)8.29.
M Jan.1928.
L (1)a,b,c,g; (2)c,n,p,u; (3)c,o,u.
S 4. O 1b,2b,3b,4b,5a.
C B&Rb,2f,3(2/6)f,4c^2,5bd,6i.
PC; BLb; BLc; KGM; RGS

1933 5,500/33.
I 4/1920; (2)29a; (5)33c; (6)33b.
M Jan.1928.
L (1)a,b,c,g; (2)e,n,p; (3)c,o,u.
S 4. O 1b,2b,3b,4b,5a.
C B&Rb,2f,3(2/6)g,4d,5bd,6i.
PC; BLc; KGM; RGS

1936a 5,500/33.2000/36.
I 4/1920; (2)29a; (5)36c/d; (6)33b.
M Jan.1928.
L (1)a,b,c,g; (2)e,n,p,u; (3)c,o,u.
S 4. O 1b,2b,3b,4b,5a.
C B&Rb,2h,3(2/6)h,4d,5bd,6i.
PC; BLc
*The figures '2000/36' are faintly printed on
some examples.*

1936b 5,500/33.2000/36. 4/36.
I 4/20; (2)29a; (5)36d; (6)33b.
M Jan.1928.
L (1)a,b,c,g; (2)e,n,p,u; (3)c,o,u.
S 4. O 1b,2b,3b,4b,5a.
C R&Bb,2h,3(2/6)h,4d,5bd,6i.
PC

1936c 3036.M36.R33.
I 6/1920. M Jan.1928.
L (1)a,b,c,g,j; (2)e,n,p,t; (3)c,i,o,u.
S 4. O 1b,2b,3b,4b,5a.

C B&Rb,2h,3(2/6)h,4d,5bd,6j.
PC; BLc; KGM
AR 1936/7.

[1936 or 1937 Outline; not seen]
AR 1936/7.

1938 3038.M38.R33.
I 6/1920. M Jan.1928.
L (1)a,b,c,g,j; (2)e,j,n,p,t; (3)c,i,o,u.
S 4. O 1b,2b,3b,4b,5a.
C B&Rb,2h,3(2/6)h,4d,5bd,6j.
PC; KGM; RGS
AR 1938/9.

1939 1239.
I 6/1920. M Jan.1928.
L (1)a,b,c,g,j; (2)e,j,n,p,t; (3)c,i,o,u.
S 4. O 1b,2b,3b,4b,5a.
C BRed,1c,2f[&],3(2/6)i,5bd,6j.
PC; KGM
AR 1939/40.

1941 Outline 8 (l)**1000/10/41.L.R.**
Imprint erased.
BLf
AR 1941/2.

135 HASTINGS (RYE)
Surveyed 1868-73; published 1878-80;
revised 1893 and 1903-10; 3rd revision
1914-9.

1921
I 2/1921. M 1921.
L (1)a; (2)c,n,p,t; (3)c,o,w.
S 1. O 1b,2c,3a,4a,5a.
C Red,2a,3(2/6)a,4b^1,5bd,6g.
PC; BLa(1/3/22); BLb; Bod; CUL(27/2/22)
Supp. to Cat.1 Jan./31 Mar.1921.

1921 Outline 2
BLd(20/5/22); Bod
Supp. to Cat.1 Jul./30 Sep.1921.

1926 3.500/26.
I 2/1921; (1)24-5a; (4)26d; roads (4)8/25.
M Jan.1925.
L (1)a,b,c,g; (2)c,n,p,t; (3)c,o,w.
S 2. O 1b,2c,3b,4b,5c.
C Red,2c,3(3/6)a,5bd,6i.
PC; BLb; BLc; KGM; RGS

C cover: 271-81; I imprint: 259-62; L legend: 263-5; M magnetic variation; O other marginal data: 266-9;
S scale: 266; (k) left, between legend and map border; (l) left, below legend; location abbreviations: xii;
outline: 282; print codes: 84-7. *AR*: annual report; *Supp. to Cat.* see OS *Catalogues*: 394.

1928 3500/26.5000/28.
I 2/1921; (1)24-8a; (3)27b; (4)28d; roads (4)8/25. M Jan 1925.
L (1)a,b,c,g; (2)c,n,p,u; (3)c,o,w.
S 2. O 1b,2b,3b,4b,5c.
C Red,2a,3(1/9)b,4a,5bd,6i.
PC; BLc; KGM; RGS

1933 3,500/33.
I 4/1921; (5)33b; (7)33a. M Jan.1925.
L (1)a,b,c,g; (2)e,n,p,u; (3)c,o,w.
S 4. O 1b,2b,3b,4b,5c.
C B&Rb,2f,3(2/6)g,4d,5bd,6i.
PC; BLc; KGM

1935 30.35.
I 6/1921. M Jan 1925.
L (1)g,i; (2)e,n,p,t; (3)c,h,i,o,w.
S 4. O 1b,2b,3b,4b,5c.
C B&Rb,2e,3(2/6)h,4d,5bd,6i.
PC; BLb; Bod; KGM

1937 3037.M.36.R.31.
I 6/1921. M Jan.1925.
L (1)a,b,c,g,j; (2)e,n,p,t; (3)c,h,i,q,s.
S 4. O 1b,2b,3b,4b,5c.
C B&Rb,2e,3(2/6)h,4d,5bd,6i.
PC; BLc; Bod; KGM
AR 1936/7, reprinted. Specification change: contours reinforced.

1941 M39.R38.3041.L.R.
I 6/1921. M Jan.1925.
L (1)a,b,c,g,j; (2)e,j,n,p,t; (3)c,h,i,q,w.
S 4. O 1b,2b,3b,4b,5c.
C B&Rb,2e,3(2/6)h,4d,5bd,6j.
PC; RGS
Specification change: contours are not reinforced. A partly deleted number to the left of the print code is illegible.

    1941 Outline 8 **1,000/10/41.L.R.**
    BLf
    AR 1941/2.

136 BOSCASTLE & PADSTOW
Surveyed 1879-83; published 1888-9; revised 1894 and 1907-9; 3rd revision 1913.

1919
I 2/1919. M 1919.
L (1)a; (2)a,n,p,q,t; (3)a,k,o,w.
S 1. O 1b,2a,3a,4a,5a.
C Red,2a,3(2/6)c,4b²,5beg,6g.
PC; BLa(13/10/19); Bod; CUL(28/9/19)
Supp. to Cat.Jun.1919.

1921 9.21.
I 2/1919; (5)21(l). M 1919.
L (1)a; (2)c,n,p,q,t; (3)a,o,w.
S 1. O 1b,2c[gap],3a,4a,5a.
C Red,2a,3(1/6)b,4a,5beg,6g.
PC; BLb; KGM

    1925 Outline 5
    I (1)25a.
    BLd(1/4/26); Bod(13/4/26)
    Supp. to Cat.1 Jul./30 Sep.1925.

1928 3000/28.
I 2/1919; (1)25a; (4)28d; roads (13)9.26.
M 1919.
L (1)a; (2)c,n,p,q,t; (3)a,o,s.
S 3. O 1b,2b,3a,4b,5a.
C Red,2a,3(2/6)d,4b²,5beg,6i.
PC; BLc; Bod; KGM

1931 3000/28.3800/31.
I 2/1919; (1)27a; (4)31d; roads (1)9.26.
M 1919.
L (1)a,b; (2)c,n,p,q,t; (3)a,o,s.
S 4. O 1b,2b,3b,4b,5a.
C B&Rb,2f,3(2/6)f,4c²,5beg,6i.
PC; BLc; KGM

1934 3,500/34.
I 4/1919; (1)27b; (2)26a; (5)34c.
M 1919.
L (1)a,b; (2)e,n,p,q,u; (3)a,o,w.
S 4. O 1b,2b,3b,4b,5a.
C B&Rb,2h,3(2/6)g,4d,5beg,6i.
PC; BLc; KGM

137 DARTMOOR, TAVISTOCK & LAUNCESTON (Tavistock and Dartmoor)
Surveyed 1881-88; published 1889-93; revised 1894-96 and 1907-08; 3rd revision 1912-13.

1919
I 2(CMG)/1919. M 1919.
L (1)a; (2)b,n,q,t; (3)a,k,o,s.
S 1. O 1b,2a,3a,4a.
C Buff,2a,3(3/6)b,5a²d,6g.
PC; BLa(13/10/19); BLb; Bod; CUL(28/9/19); RGS
Supp. to Cat.Jun.1919.

1921 1.21.
I 2/1919; (5)21(l).
M 1919.

L (1)a; (2)b,n,q,t; (3)a,k,o,s.
S 1. O 1b,2c[gap],3a,4a.
C Red,2a,3(3/6)a,5bd,6g.
KGM

1925 Outline 5
I (1)25a.
BLd(1/4/26); Bod(13/4/26)
Supp. to Cat.1 Jul./30 Sep.1925.

1928 3500/28.
I 2/1919; (1)27-8a; (4)28d; roads (4)9/26.
M 1919.
L (1)a; (2)c,n,q,t; (3)a,o,s.
S 3. O 1b,2b,3b,4b.
C Red,2a,3(2/6)d,4b²,5bd,6i.
PC; BLb; BLc; KGM; RGS(12/11/28)
*An example of this state exists with the title
'Dartmoor, Tavistock and Launceston'
printed on the cover.* PC

1932 3500/28.1200/32.
I 2(FRS)/1919; (1)30a; (4)32d; roads (4)9/26.
M 1919.
L (1)a,b; (2)c,n,q,t; (3)a,o,s.
S 4. O 1b,2b,3b,4b.
C B&Rb,2f,3(2/6)g,4c²,5bd,6i.
PC; BLb; KGM

1933 3500/28.1200/32.3000/33.
I 2/1919; (1)30a; (4)33d; roads (4)9/26.
M 1919.
L (1)a,b; (2)c,n,q,t; (3)a,o,s.
S 4. O 1b,2b,3b,4b.
C B&Rb,2f,3(2/6)g,4d,5bd,6i.
PC; KGM

138 DARTMOOR & EXETER
Surveyed 1876-88; published 1891-94; revised 1896 and 1907-08; 3rd rev. 1912-13.

1919
I 2/1919.
M 1919.
L (1)a; (2)b,n,p,q,t; (3)a,k,o,w.
S 1. O 1b,2a,3a,4a,5a.
C Buff,2a,3(1/6)a,4b²,5a²df,6g.
PC; BLa(13/10/19); BLb; Bod;
CUL(28/9/19)
Supp. to Cat.Jun.1919.

1919 [1920]
As for 1919, but without a price, and with
a gap where the price was formerly printed.
OSRML

1924 Outline 5
I (1)24a; roads (5)10.24.
BLd(11/9/25); Bod(27/10/25)
Supp. to Cat.1 Jan./31 Mar.1925.

1925 3000/25.
I 2/1919; (1)24a; (4)25b; roads (5)10.24.
M 1919.
L (1)a; (2)c,n,p,q,u; (3)a,q,w.
S 1. O 1b,2c,3a,4ab.
C Red,2a,3(1/6)b,4a,5bdf,6g.
PC; BLb; RGS(2/8/27)
Specification change: contours reinforced.

1927 5000/27.
I 2/1919; (1)26a; (4)27d; roads (5)10.24.
M 1919.
L (1)a; (2)c,n,p,q,u; (3)a,q,s.
S 1. O 1b,2b,3a,4ab.
C Red,2a,3(2/6)d,4b²,5bdf,6i.
PC; BLc; RGS
*Supp. to Cat. 1 Apr./30 June 1927. 'With
special Road Revision.'*

1931 5000/27.3300/31.
I 2/1919; (1)30a; (4)31d; roads (5)10.24.
M 1919.
L (1)a,b; (2)c,n,p,q,u; (3)a,q,w.
S 4. O 1b,2b,3b,4b.
C B&Rb,2a,3(2/6)f,4c²,5bdf,6i.
PC; BLc; KGM

1932 5000/27.3300/31.1000/32.
I 2/1919; (1)31a; (4)32d; roads (4)1931.
M 1919.
L (1)a,b; (2)c,n,p,q; (3)a,q,w.
S 4. O 1b,2b,3b,4b.
C B&Rb(wr),2f,3(1/9)a,4e,5bdf,6i.
PC

1933 2,500/33.
I 4/1919; (1)32b; (2)31a; (5)33c.
M 1919.
L (1)a,b; (2)e,n,p,q,u; (3)a,q,w.
S 4. O 1b,2b,3b,4b,5a.
C B&Rb,2f,3(2/6)g,4d,5bdf,6i.
PC

C cover: 271-81; I imprint: 259-62; L legend: 263-5; M magnetic variation; O other marginal data: 266-9;
S scale: 266; (k) left, between legend and map border; (l) left, below legend; location abbreviations: xii;
360   outline: 282; print codes: 84-7. *AR*: annual report; *Supp. to Cat.* see OS *Catalogues*: 394.

1936 **2,500/33.1,000/36.**
I 4/1919; (1)32b; (2)31a; (5)36c.
M 1919.
L (1)a,b; (2)e,n,p,q,t; (3)a,q,w.
S 4. O 1b,2b,3b,4b.
C B&Rb,2h,3(2/6)h,4d,5bdf,6i.
KGM; BLb

139 SIDMOUTH & BRIDPORT
Surveyed 1884-8; published 1892-4; revised
1896-7 and 1904-8; 3rd revision 1913-14.
1919
I 2/1919. M 1919.
L (1)a; (2)b,n,p,q,t; (3)a,k,o,w.
S 1. O 1b,2a,3a,4a,5a.
C Buff,2a,3(2/6)b,5a^{2}dk,6g.
PC; BLa(13/10/19); BLb; Bod;
CUL(28/9/19); RGS
Supp. to Cat.Jun.1919. An example of this
state is known in a red cover with the
printed title: Lyme Regis and Sidmouth. PC

1922 **6.22.** (Seaton and District)
I 2/1919; (5)22(l).   M 1919.
L (1)a; (2)d,n,p,q,t; (3)a,k,o,w.
S 1. O 1b,2c[gap],3a,4a,5a.
C Red,2a,3(1/6)b,4a,5bdk,6g.
PC; BLc

1924 **2000/24.** (SEATON AND DISTRICT)
I 2/1919; (1)23-4a; (4)24b; roads
(5)10·24. M 1919.
L (1)a; (2)c,n,p,q,t; (3)a,o,w.
S 1. O 1b,2d,3a,4b,5a.
C Red,2f,3(2/6)d,4b^2,5bdk,6i.
PC; BLc; KGM; RGS

  1924 Outline 5
  I (1)23-4a; roads (5)10·24.
  BLd(11/9/25); Bod(27/10/25)
  Supp. to Cat.1 Jan./31 Mar.1925.

1928 **2000/24.3500/28.** (LYME REGIS
and SIDMOUTH)
I 2/1919; (1)23-5a; (4)28b; roads (5)10.24.
M 1919.
L (1)a; (2)c,n,p,q,t; (3)a,q,w.
S 3. O 1b,2b,3b,4b,5a.
C Red,2a,3(2/6)d,4b^2,5bdk,6i.
PC; KGM; RGS
Specification change: contours reinforced.

1932 **2000/24.3500/28.4000/32.**
I 2/1919; (1)31a; (4)32b; roads (5)12·31.
M 1919.
L (1)a,b; (2)c,n,p,q,u; (3)a,q,w.
S 4. O 1b,2b,3b,4b,5a.
C B&Rb,2f,3(2/6)f,4c^2,5bdk,6i.
PC; BLc; KGM; RGS

1933 **5,000/33.**
I 4/1919; (1)33b; (2)31a; (5)33c. M 1919.
L (1)a,b; (2)e,n,p,q,t; (3)a,q,w.
S 4. O 1b,2b,3b,4b,5a.
C B&Rb,2h,3(2/6)g,4d,5bdk,6i.
PC; BLc; Bod; KGM
Examples of this state are known with the
following sticker titles on the covers:
Axminster; Lyme Regis; Seaton and district.
PC

1937 **R.31.M.36.2537.**
I 6/1919. M 1st Jan.1937.
L (1)a,b,g,j; (2)e,n,p,q,t; (3)a,h,i,q,w.
S 4. O 1b,2b,3b,4b,5a.
C B&Rb,2h,3(2/6)h,4d,5bdk,6i.
PC; BLb; Bod; KGM; RGS
AR 1936/7.

  1941 Outline **1000/10/41 LR**
  PC   *AR 1941/2.*

  [**1942** or **1943** Outline; not seen]
  AR 1942/3.

140 WEYMOUTH & DORCHESTER
Surveyed 1862-88; published 1892-3;
revised 1896-7 and 1903-5; 3rd revision
1913-14.
1919
I 2(CMG)/1919. M 1919.
L (1)a; (2)b,n,p,q,t; (3)a,k,o,w.
S 1. O 1b,2a,3a,4a,5a.
C Buff,2a,3(2/6)b,4b^2,5a^{1}i,6g.
PC; BLa(13/10/19); BLb; Bod;
CUL(28/9/19)
Supp. to Cat.Jun.1919.

1922 **11-22.**
I 2/1919; (5)22(l).
M 1919.
L (1)a; (2)c,n,p,q,t; (3)a,k,o,w.
S 1. O 1b,2c[gap],3a,4a,5a.
C Red,2a,3(3/6)a,5bi,6g.
BLc

1924 1000/24.
I 2/1919; (1)24a; (4)24b; roads (9)9·24.
M 1919.
L (1)a; (2)c,n,p,q,t; (3)a,o,w.
S 1. O 1b,2c[gap],3a,4b,5a.
C Red,2a,3(3/6)a,5bi,6h.
PC; BLb

> 1924 Outline 5 **1000/24.**
> BLd(7/8/25); Bod
> *Supp. to Cat.1 Oct./31 Dec.1924.*

1930 1000/24.,3000/30.
I 2(FRS)/1919; (1)29a; (4)30d; roads
(14)9·24.
M Jan.1930.
L (1)a,b,c,g; (2)c,n,p,t; (3)a,h,o,u.
S 3. O 1b,2b,3b,4b,5a.
C B&Ra,2a,3(2/6)d,4b²,5bi,6i.
PC; BLc; KGM
*Specification change: parish boundaries
shown. The publication date for the large-
scale plans has been changed from 1892-3
to 1892-5.*

1933 2,000/33.
I 4/1919; (5)33b; (7)31a.
M Jan.1930.
L (1)a,b,c,d,g; (2)e,n,p,t; (3)a,h,o,u.
S 4. O 1b,2b,3b,4b,5a.
C B&Rb,2f,3(2/6)g,4d,5bi,6i.
PC; BLc; KGM

1934 2034.
I 5/1919.
M Jan.1930.
L (1)a,b,c,d,g; (2)e,n,p,t; (3)a,h,i,o,u.
S 4. O 1b,2b,3b,4b,5a.
C B&Rb,2f,3(2/6)g,4d,5bi,6i.
PC; KGM; RGS

1936 2036.
I 9/1919.
M Jan.1930.
L (1)g,i,j; (2)e,n,p,t; (3)a,h,i,o,u.
S 4. O 1b,2b,3b,4b,5a.
C Red,1b,3(4/-)a,5q,6i.
PC; BLb; RGS
AR 1936/7.

141 BOURNEMOUTH & SWANAGE
Surveyed 1862-88; published 1892-3;
revised 1893-96 and 1903; 3rd rev. 1913.

1919a
I 2/1919.   M 1919.
L (1)a; (2)b,n,p,q,t; (3)a,k,o,w.
S 1. O 1b,2a,3a,4a,5a.
C Buff,2a,3(1/6)a,4b²,5a²dm,6g.
PC; BLa(13/10/19); BLb; Bod;
CUL(28/9/19); RGS(29/7/19)
Supp. to Cat.Jun.1919.

1919b [1920]
I 2/1919. M 1919.
L (1)a; (2)b,n,p,q,t; (3)a,k,o,w.
S 1. O 1b,2c[gap],3a,4a,5a.
C Red,2a,3(3/6)a,5bdm,6g.
PC; OSRML
*This state has no print code, but lacks the
price note.*

1923 4000/23.
I 2/1919; (3)22a; (4)23d.
M 1919.
L (1)a; (2)c,n,p,q,t; (3)a,o,w.
S 2. O 1b,2c [no gap],3b,4b,5a.
C Red,2a,3(2/6)a,4b²,5bdm,6g.
PC; BLc

> 1924 Outline 4
> I 2/1924; (1)24b; (3)22a.
> BLd(7/8/25); Bod
> *Supp. to Cat.1 Oct./31 Dec.1924.*

1926 4000/23.3500/26.
I 2/1919; (1)26b; (3)22a; (4)26d; roads
(13)10/25.
M 1919.
L (1)a,g; (2)c,n,p,q,t; (3)a,o,w.
S 2. O 1b,2c,3b,4b,5a.
C Red,2a,3(2/6)d,4b²,5bdm,6i.
PC; BLb; BLc

1928 4000/23.3500/26.5000/28.
I 2/1919; (1)26b; (3)22a; (4)28d; roads
(13)10/25.
M 1919.
L (1)a,g; (2)c,n,p,q,t; (3)a,o,w.
S 2. O 1b,2b,3b,4b,5a.
C B&Ra,2a,3(2/6)d,4b²,5bdm,6i.
PC; BLc; KGM; RGS

C cover: 271-81; I imprint: 259-62; L legend: 263-5; M magnetic variation; O other marginal data: 266-9;
S scale: 266; (k) left, between legend and map border; (l) left, below legend; location abbreviations: xii;
outline: 282; print codes: 84-7. *AR*: annual report; *Supp. to Cat.* see OS *Catalogues*: 394.

1931 4000/23.3500/26.5000/28.5500/31.
I 2/1919; (1)26b; (3)22a; (4)31d; roads (13)10/25.
M 1919.
L (1)a,g; (2)c,n,p,r,t; (3)a,o,w.
S 4. **O** 1b,2b,3b,4b,5a.
C B&Rb,2a,3(2/6)f,4c^2,5bdm,6i.
PC; KGM; RGS
The price statement is printed in blue.

1933 5,000/33.
I 4/1919; (2)32a; (5)33c; (6)33b.
M 1919.
L (1)a,b,c,g; (2)e,n,p,q,t; (3)a,e,h,o,s.
S 4. **O** 1b,2b,3b,4b,5a.
C B&Rb,2f,3(2/6)g,4d,5bdm,6i.
PC; BLc; KGM; RGS

1935 2535.
I 5/1919. **M** 1919.
L (1)a,b,c,g; (2)e,n,p,q,t; (3)a,h,i,o,s.
S 4. **O** 1b,2b,3b,4b,5a.
C B&Rb,2h,3(2/6)h,4d,5bdm,6i.
PC; BLc; KGM; RGS
An illegible four-digit number has been erased left of the print code.

  1935b Outline 6 **2535.**
  PC

1936 2535.3036.
I 5/1919. **M** 1919.
L (1)a,b,c,g; (2)e,n,p,q,t; (3)a,h,i,o,s.
S 4. **O** 1b,2b,3b,4b,5a.
C B&Rb(wr),2h,3(1/9)c,4e,5bdm,6i.
PC; BLc; KGM; RGS
AR 1936/7.

1937 3037 M37.R32.
I 5/1919. **M** 1919.
L (1)a,b,c,g,j; (2)e,n,p,q,u; (3)a,h,i,o,w.
S 4. **O** 1b,2b,3b,4b,5a.
C B&Rb,2h,3(2/6)h,4d,5bdm,6j.
PC
AR 1937/8.

142 ISLE OF WIGHT
Surveyed 1856-69; published 1873-6; revised 1893-4 and 1901; 3rd revision 1913.

1919
I 2/1919. **M** 1919.
L (1)a; (2)b,n,p,q,t; (3)a,k,o,w.
S 1. **O** 1b,2a,3a,4a,5a.
C Buff,2a,3(1/6)a,4b^2,5a^{2}dg,6g.

KGM; BLa(13/10/19); Bod; CUL(28/9/19); RGS(29/7/19)
Supp. to Cat.Jun.1919.

1920 12.20.
I 2/1919; (5)20(l). **M** 1919.
L (1)a; (2)b,n,p,q,t; (3)a,k,o,s.
S 1. **O** 1b,2c[gap],3a,4a,5a.
C Red,2a,3(1/6)b,4a,5bdg,6g.
PC; BLb

1923 4000/23.
I 2/1919; (1)23a; (4)23d. **M** 1921.
L (1)a; (2)c,n,p,q,t; (3)a,o,w.
S 2. **O** 1b,2c[no gap],3b,4b,5a.
C Red,2a,3(2/6)c,4b^2,5bdg,6g.
PC; BLc; KGM; RGS

  1923 Outline 4
  I 2/1923; (1)23a.
  BLd(1/2/24); Bod
  Supp. to Cat.1 Oct./31 Dec.1923.

1926a 4000/26.
I 2/1919; (1)25a; (4)26d; roads (5)10/25.
M Jan.1925.
L (1)a,b,c,g; (2)c,n,p,q,t; (3)a,o,u.
S 2. **O** 1b,2c,3b,4b,5a.
C Red,2a,3(1/6)b,4a,5bdg,6h.
PC; BLb; KGM; RGS

[1926b 3000/26 not seen; inferred from 1928]

1928 3000/26.4500/28.
I 2/1919; (1)28a; (4)28d; roads (5)10/25.
M Jan.1925.
L (1)a,b,c,g; (2)c,n,p,q,t; (3)a,o,u.
S 2. **O** 1b,2b,3b,4b,5a.
C Red,2a,3(2/6)d,4b^2,5bdg,6i.
PC; BLc

  1928 Outline 6 [but lacks squaring]
  PC

1930 3000/26.4500/28.6500/30.
I 2/1919; (1)30a; (4)30d; roads (5)10/25.
M Jan.1925.
L (1)a,b,c,g; (2)c,n,p,q,t; (3)a,o,u.
S 4. **O** 1b,2b,3b,4b,5a.
C B&Rb,2a,3(2/6)f,4c^1,5bdg,6i.
PC; KGM

  1931 Outline **M** Sept.1931. PC
  Printed in grey; no outline edition title.

1932 **3000/26.4500/28.6500/30.6000/32.**
I 2/1919; (1)32a; (4)32d; roads (5)7/32.
M Sep! 1931.
L (1)a,b,c,g; (2)e,n,p,q,t; (3)a,o,w.
S 4. O 1b,2b,3b,4b,5a.
C B&Rb(wr),2e,3(1/9)a,4e,5bdg,6i.
PC; BLc; KGM; RGS

  1933 Outline **500/33** PC

1935 **3035.**
I 6/1919. M Sep! 1931.
L (1)a,b,c,g; (2)e,n,p,q,t; (3)a,i,o,w.
S 4. O 1b,2b,3b,4b,5a.
C B&Rb,2e,3(2/6)h,4d,5bdg,6i.
PC; BLb; BLc; GM; RGS

  1942 Outline 8 (k)**W.O.6,000/40.**(l) [in
blue:]**1,000/3/42 L.R.**
BLf
AR 1941/2.

  [**1942** or **1943** Outline; not seen]
AR 1942/3.

143 TRURO
Surveyed 1866-81; published 1877-90;
revised 1894 and 1905-6; 3rd revision 1913.

1918 [1919]
I 1/1918. M 1918.
L (1)a; (2)a,n,p,q,t; (3)a,k,o,w.
S 1. O 1b,2a,3a,4a,5a.
C Buff,2a,3(2/6)b,5a²df,6g.
PC; BLa(13/10/19); Bod; CUL(28/9/19)
Supp. to Cat.Jun.1919.

1919 **11-19.**
I 1/1918; (5)19(l). M 1918.
L (1)a; (2)a,n,p,q,t; (3)a,k,o,w.
S 1. O 1b,2a,3a,4a,5a.
C Red,2a,3(2/6)c,4b²,5bdf,6g.
PC; BLb; BLc; KGM; RGS
*The print code of 3500/19 which appears on
the 1927 state may apply to this printing.*

  1924 **TRURO AND ST.AUSTELL**
  Outline 5 I (1)24a.
  BLd(7/8/25); Bod
  Supp. to Cat.1 Oct./31 Dec.1924.

[**1924b** **1000/24** not seen; inferred from
1927]

1925 **1000/25. (Truro)**
I 1/1918; (1)24a; (4)25b; roads (1)11.24.
M 1918.
L (1)a; (2)c,n,p,q,u; (3)a,q,w.
S 1. O 1b,2c,3a,4b,5a.
C Red,2a,3(2/6)a,4b²,5bdf,6g.
KGM
Specification change: contours reinforced.

1927 **3500/19.1000/24.3500/27. TRURO
& ST.AUSTELL**
I 2/1918 [lacks 'Director General']; (1)26a;
(4)27d; roads (5)10/26. M Jan.1927.
L (1)a,b,c,g; (2)c,n,p,t; (3)a,o,u.
S 2. O 1b,2b,3b,4b,5a.
C Red,2a,3(2/6)d,4b²,5bdf,6h.
PC; BLb; BLc; KGM
*Supp. to Cat.1 Oct./31 Dec.1927. 'With
special Road Revision.' Specification
change: contours not reinforced.*

1930a
3500/19.1000/24.3500/27.4000/30.
I 2/1918; (1)29a; (4)30d; roads (5)
10/24.[sic]. M Jan.1927.
L (1)a,b,c,g; (2)c,n,p,t; (3)a,o,u.
S 2. O 1b,2b,3b,4b,5a.
C Red,3(3/6)a,5bdf,6i.
PC; BLc

1930b (Newquay)
3500/19.1000/24.3500/27.4000/30.
All details as for 1930a except for I roads
(5)10/24.-26.
PC; KGM; RGS

1931 (Truro and St.Austell)
**3500/19.1000/24.3500/27.
4000/29.5500/31.**
I 2/1918; (1)30a; (4)31d; roads (5)10/26.
M Jan.1927.
L (1)a,b,c,g; (2)c,n,p,t; (3)a,o,u.
S 4. O 1b,2b,3b,4b,5a.
C B&Rb,2f,3(4/-)g,5bdf,6i.
PC; KGM
*The road revision date of 9/24 has been
crossed out in print in red and the date of
10/26 has been substituted in red. The
St.Austell bypass is shown by a red road
without black casing. Covers with title
stickers: Newquay (PC); Perranporth
(KGM).*

C cover: 271-81; I imprint: 259-62; L legend: 263-5; M magnetic variation; O other marginal data: 266-9;
S scale: 266; (k) left, between legend and map border; (l) left, below legend; location abbreviations: xii;
outline: 282; print codes: 84-7. *AR*: annual report; *Supp. to Cat.* see OS *Catalogues*: 394.

144 PLYMOUTH (Plymouth and District)

Surveyed 1855-88; published 1893; revised 1894-7 and 1908-9; 3rd revision 1912-13.

1919

I 2(CMG)/1919. M 1919.
L (1)a; (2)b,n,p,q,t; (3)a,k,o,w.
S 1. O 1b,2a,3a,4a,5a.
C Buff,2a,3(2/6)b,5a^{2}dl,6g.
PC; BLa(13/10/19); Bod; CUL(28/9/19)
Supp. to Cat.Jun.1919.

1920 Outline   SG
Heading printed in red: 'Transferred from copper (engraved)'

1922 6.22.

I 2/1919. (5)22(l).   M 1919.
L (1)a; (2)d,n,p,q,t; (3)a,k,o,w.
S 1. O 1b,2c[gap],3a,4a,5a.
C Red,2a,3(3/6)a,5a^{2}dl,6g.
BLc; BLb

1925 Outline 5   I (1)25a.
BLd(1/4/26); Bod(13/4/26)
Supp. to Cat.1 Jul./30 Sep.1925.

1927a 3500/27.

I 2/1919; (1)25a; (4)27d; roads (5)9·26.
M 1919.
L (1)a; (2)c,n,p,q,t; (3)a,o,w.
S 1. O 1b,2b,3a,4b,5a.
C Red,2a,3(3/6)a,5a^{2}dl,6g.
PC; BLc; RGS

Supp. to Cat.1 Apr./30 June 1927. 'With special Road Revision.'

1927b 5000/27.

I 2/1919; (1)25a; (4)27d; roads (5)9·26.
M 1919.
L (1)a; (2)c,n,p,q,t; (3)a,o,w.
S 1. O 1b,2b,3a,4a,5a.
C Red,2a,3(1/9)a,4b^2,5a^{2}dl,6g.
PC; BLc

1927c 5000/27.

I 2(FRS)/1919; (4)27b.
C Red,1b,[no price],5p,6g.
PC

All details are the same as for 1927b except that the print code is in position b; and Close's honours have changed from CMG to FRS. This state also lacks the letters and numbers of the alpha-numerical squaring in the border.

1927d 5000/27.

C Red,2a,3(1/6)b,4a,5a^{2}dl,6i.
PC; BLb

This state is the same as (1927)c except that the numbers and letters have been restored to the border.

1931 5000/27.2000/31.

I 2/1919; (1)31a; (4)31d; roads (5)9·26.
M 1919.
L (1)a,b; (2)c,n,p,q,t; (3)a,o,w.
S 4. O 1b,2b,3b,4b,5a.
C B&Rb,2a,3(2/6)f,4d,5adl,6i.
KGM; BLc

1933 3,500/33.

I 4/1919; (1)33b; (2)29a; (5)33c.
M 1919.
L (1)a,b; (2)e,n,p,q,t; (3)a,o,w.
S 4. O 1b,2b,3b,4b,5a.
C B&Rb,2h,3(2/6)h,4d,5adl,6j.
PC; BLb; Bod

[1941 or 1942 Outline; not seen]
AR 1942/2.

145 TORQUAY & DARTMOUTH

Surveyed 1858-89; published 1892; revised 1896-7 and 1908-9; 3rd revision 1912-13.

1919

I 2/1919.
M 1919.
L (1)a; (2)b,n,p,q,t; (3)a,k,o,w.
S 1. O 1b,2a,3a,4a,5a.
C Buff,2a,2(2/6)b,5a^{1}el,6g.
PC; BLa(13/10/19); Bod; CUL(28/9/19)
Supp. to Cat.Jun.1919.

1921 10·21.

I 2/1919; (5)21(l). M 1919.
L (1)a; (2)c,n,p,q,u; (3)a,o,w.
S 1. O 1c,2c[gap],3a,4a,5a.
C Red,2a,3(1/6)b,4a,5bel,6g.
PC; BLb; BLc

1925 2000/25.

I 2/1919; (1)24a; (4)25d; roads (8)4.25.
M 1919.
L (1)a; (2)c,n,p,q,u; (3)a,q,w.
S 1. O 1b,2c,3a,4ab,5a.
C Red,2a,3(2/6)c,4b^2,5bel,6g.
PC; BLc; KGM; RGS
Specification change: contours reinforced.

<u>1925</u> Outline 5 **2000/25.**
BLd(29/10/25); Bod
*Supp. to Cat.1 Apr./30 Jun.1925. The
print code may refer to the black plate of
the coloured edition.*

1926 2000/25.4000/26.
I 2/1919; (1)24-5a; (4)26d; roads (8)4.25.
M 1919.
L (1)a; (2)c,n,p,q,u; (3)a,q,w.
S 1. O 1b,2c,3a,4ab,5a.
C Red,2a,3(2/6)d,4b²,5bel,6h.
PC; BLb; BLc; KGM; RGS

1929 2000/25.4000/26.4000/29.
I 2/1919; (1)24-8a; (4)29d; roads (8)4.25.
M 1919.
L (1)a; (2)c,n,p,q,t; (3)a,q,w.
S 3. O 1b,2b,3b,4b,5a.
C Red,2a,3(2/6)c,4b²,5bel,6i.
PC; BLc; KGM

1931 2000/25.4000/26.4000/29.5000/31.
I 2/1919; (1)31a; (4)31d; roads (8)4.25.
M 1919.
L (1)a,b; (2)c,n,p,q,t; (3)a,q,w.
S 4. O 1b,2b,3b,4b,5a.
C B&Rb,2a,3(2/6)f,4c²,5bel,6i.
PC; BLc; KGM

1934
2000/25.4000/26.4000/29.5000/31.3500/34.
I 2/1919; (1)31a; (4)34d; roads (8)4.25.
M 1919.
L (1)a,b; (2)c,n,p,q,t; (3)a,q,w.
S 4. O 1b,2b,3b,4b,5a.
C B&Rb(wr),2f,3(1/9)a,4e,5bel,6i.
PC; BLc; KGM

146 LAND'S END & LIZARD
Surveyed 1875-8; published 1887-90;
revised 1893-4 and 1905; 3rd revision 1913.

1919
I 2(CMG)/1919. M 1919.
L (1)a; (2)b,n,p,q,t; (3)a,k,o,w.
S 1. O 1b,2a,3a,4a,5a.
C Buff,2a,3(1/6)a,4b²,5a²e,6g.
PC; BLa(13/10/19); Bod; CUL(28/9/19)
Supp. to Cat.Jun.1919.

1921 'Reprinted in 1921'.
I 2(FRS)/1919; (4)21a. M 1921.
L (1)a; (2)c,n,p,t; (3)c,o,w.

S 2. O 1b,2c,3a,4a,5a.
C Red,2a,3(3/6)a,5be,6g.
PC; BLb; BLc; KGM
*Specification change: parks shown by green
ruling.*

1925 2000/25.
I 2/1919; (1)24d; (4)25j; roads (5)11.24.
M 1921.
L (1)a; (2)c,n,p,t; (3)c,q,s.
S 2. O 1b,2c,3a,4b,5a.
C Red,2a,3(2/6)c,4b²,5be,6g.
PC; BLc; KGM
Specification change: contours reinforced.

<u>1925</u> Outline 5 **2000/25.**
BLd(29/10/25); Bod
*Supp.to Cat.1 Apr./30 Jun.1925. The
print code may refer to the black plate of
the coloured edition.*

**1926 2000/25.3000/26. LAND'S END &
LIZARD.**
I 2/1919. (1)24-6d; (4)26j; roads (5)11.24.
M 1921.
L (1)a; (2)c,n,p,t; (3)c,q,s.
S 2. O 1b,2c,3a,4b,5a.
C Red,2a,3(3/6)a,5be,6h.
PC; BLc; KGM; RGS

**1928 2000/25.3000/26.5000/28. LAND'S
END & LIZARD**
I 2/1919; (1)28d; (4)28j; roads (5)11.24.
M 1921.
L (1)a; (2)c,n,p,t; (3)c,q,s.
S 2. O 1b,2b,3a,4b,5a.
C Red,2a,3(2/6)d,4b²,5be,6i.
KGM; BLc

1931 2000/25.3000/26.5000/28.5500/31.
I 2/1919; (1)30d; (4)31j; roads (3)11.24.
M 1921.
L (1)a,b; (2)c,n,p,t; (3)c,o,s.
S 4. O 1b,2b,3a,4b,5a.
C B&Rb(wr),2f,3(1/9)a,4e,5be,6i.
PC; BLc; Bod; KGM; RGS

1933 3,000/33. LAND'S END & LIZARD.
I 4/1919; (1)33b; (2)32a; (5)33c. M 1921.
L (1)a,b,c,g; (2)e,n,p,t; (3)c,o,w.
S 4. O 1b,2b,3b,4b,5a.
C B&Rb,2f,3(2/6)g,4d,5be,6i.
PC; KGM

C cover: 271-81; I imprint: 259-62; L legend: 263-5; M magnetic variation; O other marginal data: 266-9;
S scale: 266; (k) left, between legend and map border; (l) left, below legend; location abbreviations: xii;
outline: 282; print codes: 84-7. *AR*: annual report; *Supp. to Cat.* see OS *Catalogues*: 394.

CHECK-LIST 1

LIST OF SHEET NAMES

1	RIVER TWEED	38	DONCASTER
2	HOLY ISLAND	39	SCUNTHORPE & MARKET RASEN
3	THE CHEVIOT HILLS	40	GRIMSBY & LOUTH
4	ALNWICK & ROTHBURY	41	ANGLESEY
5	SOLWAY FIRTH & RIVER ESK	42	LLANDUDNO & DENBIGH
6	HEXHAM	43	CHESTER
7	NEWCASTLE UPON TYNE	44	NORTHWICH & MACCLESFIELD
8	WORKINGTON & COCKERMOUTH	45	BUXTON & MATLOCK
9	CARLISLE	46	THE DUKERIES
10	ALSTON & WEARDALE	47	LINCOLN
11	DURHAM & SUNDERLAND	48	HORNCASTLE & SKEGNESS
12	KESWICK & AMBLESIDE	49	PORTMADOC & CRICCIETH
13	KIRKBY STEPHEN & APPLEBY	50	BALA
14	DARLINGTON	51	WREXHAM & OSWESTRY
15	MIDDLESBROUGH & HARTLEPOOL	52	STOKE ON TRENT
16	WHITBY & SALTBURN	53	DERBY
17	ISLE OF MAN	54	NOTTINGHAM
18	WASDALE	55	GRANTHAM
19	WINDERMERE & ULVERSTON	56	BOSTON
20	KIRKBY LONSDALE & HAWES	57	FAKENHAM
21	RIPON & NORTHALLERTON	58	CROMER
22	PICKERING & THIRSK	59	DOLGELLY & LAKE VYRNWY
23	SCARBOROUGH	60	SHREWSBURY
24	LANCASTER & BARROW	61	WOLVERHAMPTON
25	RIBBLESDALE	62	BURTON & WALSALL
26	HARROGATE	63	LEICESTER
27	YORK	64	PETERBOROUGH
28	GREAT DRIFFIELD & BRIDLINGTON	65	WISBECH & KING'S LYNN
29	PRESTON, SOUTHPORT & BLACKPOOL	66	SWAFFHAM & EAST DEREHAM
30	BLACKBURN	67	NORWICH & GREAT YARMOUTH
31	LEEDS & BRADFORD	68	BARMOUTH & ABERYSTWYTH
32	GOOLE & PONTEFRACT	69	LLANIDLOES
33	HULL	70	BISHOP'S CASTLE
34	MOUTH OF THE HUMBER	71	KIDDERMINSTER
35	LIVERPOOL & BIRKENHEAD	72	BIRMINGHAM
36	BOLTON & MANCHESTER	73	RUGBY
37	BARNSLEY & SHEFFIELD	74	KETTERING & HUNTINGDON
		75	ELY

76 THETFORD
77 LOWESTOFT & WAVENEY VALLEY
78 LAMPETER
79 LLANDRINDOD WELLS
80 KINGTON
81 WORCESTER
82 STRATFORD ON AVON
83 NORTHAMPTON
84 BEDFORD
85 CAMBRIDGE
86 BURY ST.EDMUNDS & SUDBURY
87 IPSWICH
88 ST.DAVID'S & CARDIGAN
89 CARMARTHEN
90 BRECON & LLANDOVERY
91 ABERGAVENNY
92 GLOUCESTER & FOREST OF DEAN
93 STOW ON THE WOLD
94 BICESTER
95 LUTON
96 HERTFORD & BISHOP'S STORTFORD
97 COLCHESTER
98 CLACTON ON SEA & HARWICH
99 PEMBROKE & TENBY
100 LLANELLY
101 SWANSEA & ABERDARE
102 NEWPORT
103 STROUD & CHEPSTOW
104 SWINDON & CIRENCESTER
105 OXFORD & HENLEY ON THAMES
106 WATFORD
107 N.E.LONDON & EPPING FOREST
108 SOUTHEND & DISTRICT
109 PONTYPRIDD & BARRY
110 CARDIFF & MOUTH OF THE SEVERN
111 BATH & BRISTOL
112 MARLBOROUGH
113 READING & NEWBURY
114 WINDSOR
115 S.E.LONDON & SEVENOAKS
116 CHATHAM & MAIDSTONE
117 EAST KENT
118 BARNSTAPLE & EXMOOR
119 EXMOOR
120 BRIDGWATER & QUANTOCK HILLS

121 WELLS & FROME
122 SALISBURY & BULFORD
123 WINCHESTER
124 GUILDFORD & HORSHAM
125 TUNBRIDGE WELLS
126 WEALD OF KENT
127 RIVER TORRIDGE
128 TIVERTON
129 CHARD & AXMINISTER
130 YEOVIL & BLANDFORD
131 WIMBORNE & RINGWOOD
132 PORTSMOUTH & SOUTHAMPTON
133 CHICHESTER & WORTHING
134 BRIGHTON & EASTBOURNE
135 HASTINGS
136 BOSCASTLE & PADSTOW
137 DARTMOOR, TAVISTOCK &
    LAUNCESTON
138 DARTMOOR & EXETER
139 SIDMOUTH & BRIDPORT
140 WEYMOUTH & DORCHESTER
141 BOURNEMOUTH & SWANAGE
142 ISLE OF WIGHT
143 TRURO
144 PLYMOUTH
145 TORQUAY & DARTMOUTH
146 LAND'S END & LIZARD

Abbreviated print codes: coloured sheets

The following information is intended as a check-list for librarians and collectors. It comprises the shortest form of reference necessary to identify the different printings of each sheet. In the majority of cases all that is required is the year of printing for the first issues, or the latest part of the print code for subsequent printings. In a few cases it has been necessary to supplement this with a short description of the salient features which mark the difference between one state and another: these are fully explained in the catalogue. Dates and codes in square brackets indicate that these states have not been seen by the author and their existence has been inferred from other sources. An 'a' indicates that the inferred state has been included within a later print code. A 'b' indicates that the sheet is described as having been reprinted in an annual report. No punctuation is used.

1 1926
15/37

2 1925
3000/32
1537

3 1926
2150/34
3038

4 1925
2500/34
2038

5 1925
3000/32

6 1925
3500/32
2538

7 1925
500/29
[1000/30]a
3500/32
2035
3036

8 1925
3000/32

9 1925
1035
1536

10 1925
2200/34
2038

11 1925
3000/32
537
2038
[1938/9]b

12 1925
2500/29
2200/34
3036
3038

13 1925
3300/30
1537
2039

14 1925
3300/30
1535
2038

15 1925
3750/31
2538

16 1925
3000/29
3000/32
3035

537
3038

17 1921
6000/24
5000/27
5500/31
4000/34
4038

18 1925
1035
538
2039

19 1925
2500/28
2250/34
3036

20 1925
4000/29
3000/33
1535
2536
838
2538
1040

21 1925
3000/29
1535
25/36

22 1925
3800/30
3000/34
737
3039
[1939/40]b

23 1925
3000/32
2035
3036

24 1924
3030/30
1535

25 1924
3500/28
3500/32
3500/34
3037
[3040]a
3500/40

26 1925
3000/27
[3000/29]a
[500/30]a
4500/31
2035
3036
3039
[1939/40]b

27 1924
3000/29
2035
638
2539

28 1924
2500/30
3000/31
3039

29 1924
3500/28
2250/30
638
3039

30 1924
6000/29
5000/33
3038

31 1925
[500/29]a
3000/29
3500/32
2035
3036

32 1924
2000/34
2038

33 1924
3000/31
1536

34 1924
2039

35 1923
3500/27
2535
2537

36 1924
500/28
2000/29
2500/31
3000/34
4037

37 1924
500/29
4000/31
2536
3039

38 1923
3000/29
2035
539
[2040]a
2000/40

39 1923
1535
1537

40 1923
1035
2038

41 1922
3500/27
[500/29]a
[6500/31]a
3750/31
3000/34
3036
538
3039

42 1922
3500/28
[2500/30]a
2300/31
3000/33
3036
3538

43 1924
6000/27
3200/34
3036
[3039]a
3400/40

44 1923
500/27
3000/30
3000/34
3036
3039

45 1923
1000/27
1928 *see (1936)*
3000/30
3200/34
*(1936) Same as
3036, but lacks
print code.*

3036
3040

46 1923
3000/30
[500/30]a
4000/32
3036
[1938/9]b
3040

47 1923
2250/30
2500/34
2538

48 1923
2200/34
2039

49 1922
3000/27
3500/30
3700/33
4000/36
4038

50 1921
2700/34
3037
[2539]a
2500/40

51 1921
3000/32
2035
2037
3039

52 1921
3200/33
3039

53 1921
3500/32
2535
638
3039

54 1921
3000/31
3000/33
3036
3038

55 1922
3800/30
2038

56 1922
2200/34
1539

57 1921
1535
2038

58 1922
3500/29
1536
2038

59 1921
2036
2040

60 1921
1535
2036
2039

61 1921
2700/33
2036
538
2539

62 1921
2700/33
2036
2539

63 1921
3000/30
2500/33
3036
3038

64 1922
2500/30
1035
2037
2040

65 1922
3500/32

66 1921

67 1921
1000/24
[1000/24-5]a
[500/29]a
3750/31
2535
2539

68 1922
3000/29
3000/32
2035
4036
4039

69 1922
2700/34
2039

70 1920
3000/32
2000/35
538 *Print code
indented from left
edge of legend.*
538 *Print code in
line with left edge
of legend.*
2538

71 1921
3000/29
3200/34
3036
538
2539

72 1921
3500/27
3500/31
4500/34
4036
5038

73 1920
[3300/31]a
800/31
2036
2039

74 1920
2500/30
2036
2038

75 1920
1537
2039

76 1920
1537
2040

77 1921
2500/33
2037
1537
2538

78 1923
1535
2038

79 1923
2500/33
2538

80 1920 *White
circular stations*
1920 *Red circular
stations*
3000/32
20/38

81 1920
5000/28
3036
3038

82 1919
1000/23
3500/30
3000/33
2535
4037
4040

83 1919
500/25
3000/30
1535
435
3036

84 1919
750/24
2500/30
1535
2036
2038

85 1920
3000/29
3500/32
3036
3039

86 1921
2735
2538

87 1921
2700/33
2036
25/37
[1937/8]b

88 1923
1535
2037
3039

89 1923
2036
2540

90 1923
3500/31
2038
2040

91 1919 *White
circular stations*
1919 *Red circular
stations*
7·21
1000/24
2000/34
2537

92 1919
6.21
3500/28
3000/33
3036
2539

93 1919
9.21
3000/30
3000/32
1535
3036
537
4038

94 1919
10.21
500/28
2500/30
3500/32
2038
[1938/9]b

95 (no date, 1919)
10·21
500/26

500/27
3000/29
250/31
4500/32
[500/32]a
375/34
1035
3535
[1936/7]b

96 1919
6.21
2000/23
3000/30
3500/33
3036

97 1921
3500/32
2536
2538

98 1921
3000/29
3000/32
3036
2039

99 1922
2750/30
3000/34
3037
4038

100 1923
3500·32
3038

101 1923
[500/27]a
[500/30]a
3250/31
2035
2538

102 1919
1919 (1920) *No
print code; lacks
price*
1000/24
3000/31
3000/34
2035
537
3038

103 1919
6-21
500/28
3000/29
[500/30]a
200/32
3000/33
[135]a
1036
2536
3038

104 1919
8·21
3000/29
3000/33
3036

105 1919
7·21
[500/25]a
2500/26
3500/28
4500/31
3500/34
3036

106 1920
7-21
5500/24
3000/27
5000/28
5000/28 *As
above* **except:**
*contours not
reinforced.*
8500/30
8000/32
1000/34
1000/35
2000/36

107 1920
7.21
[6000/21]a
[6000/21]a
[2400/21]a
[500/25]a
5000/26
[5000/29]a
500/29
[500/30]a
4500/31
8000/32

8000/34
[2035]a

108 1921
3500/26
3500/30
200/30
[500/30]a
4500/32

109 1922
[500/27]a
3500/31
3500/33
537
937
3038
3040

110 1919
1000/24
2000/32
2036

111 1919
[500/20]a
7-21
11-21
[2400/21]a
500/25
3500/27
3500/29
3500/32
2035
3036

112 1919
5-21
[2000/21]a
500/27
4500/29
3000/31 (With
hills)
4000/32
3035

113 1919
5-21
[1000/21]a
3000/26
3000/27
4000/29
1500/33
3200/34

114 1920
7.21
5000/23
5000/27
[6000/29]a
500/29
[6500/31]a
2500/31
6500/32
10000/33

115 1920
1.21
9.21
5000/24
5000/26
5000/28
[5000/29]a
5000/30
8500/31
10000/33
10000/33
8000/34

116 1921
5000/25
[2000/25]a
5000/29
6500/32
2035
3036
3038
1239

117 1920
3000/23
3500/26
5500/29
6300/31
2035
4036
4038
1239

118 1919
2500/23
3500/27
4000/29
4500/32
3500/34

119 1918
[1500/22]a
1500/23

3500/25
3500/28
6500/31
600/36
500/36

120 1918
2500/26
3000/29
4500/31
2535
2036

121 1919
5.21
[1000/21]a
7.21
[2500/21]a
7.21 *minor
corrections 1925*
[500/28]a
2800/31
2000/34
2037

122 1919
6.21
12.21
3500/27
3500/31
2035
2037
538

123 1919
1919 (1920) *No
print code; lacks
price.*
[1000/21]a
12.21
[1600/21]a
2000/23
3500/29
3500/32
800/36
500/38

124 1920
5000/23
3000/26
[1000/26]a
3000/27
3000/28
6000/29

6500/31
8000/32
1000/35
1037

125 1920
3500/24
5000/27
2000/29
4000/30
4000/32
3400/34
1500/35
[300/35]a
2000/36
2038

126 1921
3500/27
4500/31
2535
[1936/7]b
3037
3038

127 1919
500/23
1000/27
[2500/27]a
2500/28
[500/30]a
2500/31
2500/34

128 1918
1918 [2?]0
500/34
835

129 1919
1-21
500/28
2300/31
835
436
1037

130 1919
9.21
500/28
2800/31
1535
2535

131 1919
10·21
500/28
[2000/29]a
2000/30
6500/32
637

132 1919
7.21
4000/23
2000/25
3000/28
5000/29
5000/32
4035
2538

133 1920
2500/23
3000/24
3500/26
3500/28
6000/29
[500/30]a
4500/31
5000/33
3000/35
5000/36
1037
4038

134 1920
4000/23
[3500/26]a
3500/27
[500/28]a
5000/28
5500/30
5500/33
2000/36
4/36
3036
3038
1239

135 1921
3500/26
5000/28
3500/33
3035
3037
3041LR

136 1919
9.21
3000/28
3800/31
3500/34

137 1919
1.21
3500/28
1200/32
3000/33

138 1919
1919 *No print
code; lacks price*
3000/25
5000/27
3300/31
1000/32
2500/33
1000/36

139 1919
6.22
2000/24
3500/28
4000/32
5000/33
2537

140 1919
11-22
1000/24
3000/30
2000/33
2034
2036

141 1919
1919 *No print
code; lacks price*
4000/23
3500/26
5000/28
5500/31
5000/33
2535
3036
3037

142 1919
12.20
4000/23
4000/26
[3000/26]a
4500/28

6500/30
6000/32
3035

143 1918
11-19
[3500/19]a
[1000/24]a
1000/25
3500/27
4000/30 *Rds
10/24*
4000/30 *Rds
10/24-26*
5500/31

144 1919
6.22
3500/27
5000/27
5000/27 *As above
except: print
code in position
b; Close is FRS;
also lacks the
letters and
numbers of the
alpha-numerical
squaring in the
border.*
5000/27 *As above
except that the
numbers and
letters have been
restored to the
border.*
2000/31
3500/33

145 1919
10·21
2000/25
4000/26
4000/29
5000/31
3500/34

146 1919
'Reprinted   in
1921'
2000/25
3000/26
5000/28
5500/31
3000/33

CHECK-LIST 3

Abbreviated print codes: outline sheets

The following check-list is by no means complete because the search for outline states has been less rigorous than that made for the coloured sheets. It therefore merely reflects what has been seen so far, or is inferred to exist. This list is the shortest form of reference necessary to identify the different printings of each sheet. This comprises the year of printing for the first issues, or the latest part of the print code for subsequent printings. Dates in square brackets indicate that these states have not been seen by the author and their existence has been inferred from other sources. An 'a' indicates that the inferred state has been included within a later print code. A 'b' indicates that the sheet is described as having been reprinted in an annual report, and 'c' denotes information contained in the *Supplement to Catalogue* (see p.394). No punctuation is used.

1 1926 1000/10/41LR	**12** 1925 336 1000/11/41LR	**21** 1925 1000/12/41LR 2040 846Cr	**30** 1924 1000/11/41LR 1000/10/42LR
2 1925 1000/11/41LR	**13** 1925 1000/11/41LR	**22** 1925 1000/1/42LR	**31** 1925 500/29 538 [1942/3]b 600/8/43Wa [1944/5]b 446
3 1926 1000/8/42LR	**14** 1925 1000/11/41LR	**23** 1925 1000/1/42LR	
4 1925 1000/11/41LR	**15** 1925 [1930]c 1000/11/41LR	**24** 1924 [1930]c 1000/8/42LR	**32** 1924 [1936/7]b 1000/11/41LR 846/Cr
5 1925 1000/8/42LR	**16** 1925 1000/11/41LR	**25** 1924 1000/11/41LR	
6 1925 1000/11/41LR	**17** 1921 1000/11/41LR [1942/3]b	**26** 1925 1000/1/42LR 1000/10/42LR	**33** 1924 1000/12/41 LR
7 1925 1000/11/41LR 846/Cr	**18** 1925 1000/11/41LR	**27** 1924 1000/12/41LR [1942/3]b	**34** 1924 WO8 24 [1930]c 1000/12/41LR [1942/3]b
8 1925 1000/11/41LR	**19** 1925 1000/12/41 LR [1944/5]b	**28** 1924 1000/11/41LR	
9 1925 1000/1/42LR	**20** 1925 1000/11/41LR 1000/12/42LR	**29** 1924 [1930]c 500/31 1000/11/41LR	**35** 1923 1000/12/41LR [1942/43]b 446
10 1925 1000/11/41LR			
11 1925 1000/11/41LR [1944/5]b			

36 1924
500/30
1000/11/41LR
[1944/5]b
446

37 1924
500/27
1000/8/42LR
[1944/5]b

38 1923
539
1000/11/41LR

39 1923
[1939/40]b
1000/4/42LR

40 1923
1000/1/42LR

41 1922
1000/11/41LR
1000/9/42

42 1922
[1937/8]b
1000/11/41LR
[1944/5]b

43 1924
[1941/2]b

44 1923
500/30
1000/11/41LR
[1943/4]b
846Cr

45 1923
1000/8/42LR
[1944/5]b

46 1923
500/30
[1938/9]b
[1941/2]b
446

47 1923
1000/1/42LR

48 1923
1000/11/41LR

49 1922
1000/6/42LR

50 1921
1000/11/41LR

51 1921
1000/11/41LR
800/2/43LR
[1943/4]b

52 1921
1000/11/41LR

53 1921
[1936/7]b
1000/11/41LR
846Cr

54 1921
3000/31
1000/11/41LR
1000/9/42LR
[1944/5]b
446

55 1922
[1936/7]b
1000/10/41LR

56 1922
1000/3/42LR

57 1921
1000/1/42LR

58 1922
1000/4/42LR

59 1921
1000/11/41LR

60 1921
2039
1000/11/41LR

61 1921
1000/12/41LR
[1942/3]b
[1944/5]b

62 1921
[1937/8]b
1000/11/41LR
[1944/5]b

63 1921
[1941/2]b
1000/12/42LR
[1943/4]b

64 1922
1000/11/41LR

65 1922
1000/11/41LR

66 1921
1000/3/42LR
[1942/3]b

67 1921
1000/8/42LR

68 1922
1000/11/41LR

69 1922
1000/6/42LR

70 1924
1000/4/42LR
600/7/43Ch
[1944/5]b

71 1921
[1939/40]b
[1941/2]b
[1942/3]b

72 1921
500/28
1000/11/41 LR
[1942/3]b
[1943/4]b
846/Cr

73 1924
1000/10/41LR
1000/2/43LR

74 1923
1000/10/41LR

75 1923
1000/10/41LR

76 1920
1000/11/41LR

77 1921
[1937/8]b
1000/11/41LR

78 1923
1000/3/42LR
[1942/3]b

79 1923
[1937/8]b
1000/11/41LR

80 1924
1000/11/41LR

81 1924
[1942/3]b

82 1923
[1939/40]b
1000/11/41LR
800/2/43LR

83 1924
500/31
1000/10/41LR

84 1923
436
1000/10/41LR

85 1923
1000/10/41LR
1000/10/42LR

86 1921
1000/10/41LR

87 1921
1000/11/41LR

88 1923
1000/11/41LR

89 1923
1000/11/41LR
[1942/3]b

90 1923
1000/11/41LR

91 1923
1000/11/41LR
[1944/5]b

92 600/25
538
1000/11/41LR
[1944/5]b

93 1925
1000/11/41LR
1000/9/42LR

94 1925
[1936/7]b
1000/10/41LR

95 1923
1000/6/42LR
[1944/5]b

96 1919
1923
[1936/7]b
[1938/9]b
1000/10/41LR

97 1921
436
[1941/2]b

98 1921
1932
300/34
[1939/40]b
1000/10/41LR

99 1923
1000/12/41LR

100 1923
537
1000/12/41LR

101 1923
[1936/7]b
1000/12/41LR

102 1924
[1937/8]b
1000/12/41LR
[1944/5]b

103 1924
[1938/9]b
1000/4/42LR
800/2/43LR
[1943/4]b

104 1924
1000/11/41LR

105 1924
437
W0 20000/9/41
[1944/5]b

106 1921
500/27
[1936/7]b
[1944/5]b

107 1921
[1927]c
700/33
[1937/8]b
[1944/5]b

108 1921
200/30

109 1922
[1941/2]b
[1943/4]b
[1944/5]b

110 1924
[1944/5]b

111 1924
1000/12/41LR
[1942/3]b

112 1924
[1937/8]b
1000/12/41LR
[1944/5]b

113 1924
[1936/7]b
1000/11/41LR

114 1921
500/27
6500/32
[1936/7]b

115 1921
500/27
8000/34
[1936/7]b
1000/1/42LR

116 1921
1939
1000/10/41LR

117 1920
1000/3/42LR

118 1924

119 1923

120 1924
1000/11/41LR

121 1924
1000/11/41LR
[1942/3]b

122 1924
1000/12/41LR

123 1923
[1936/7]b

124 1924

125 1920
1000/1/42LR

126 1921
1000/10/41LR

127 1924

128 1925

129 1924

130 1925
1000/11/41LR

131 1925
[1937/8]b
1000/11/41LR

132 1923
4035

133 1920
1923

134 1920
500/28
[1936/7]b
1000/10/41LR

135 1921
1000/10/41LR

136 1925

137 1925

138 1924

139 1924
1000/10/41LR
[1942/3]

140 1000/24

141 1924
2535

142 1923
1928
1931
500/33
1000/3/42LR
[1942/3]b

143 1924

144 1920
1925
[1941/2]b

145 2000/25

146 2000/25

CHECK-LIST 4

Calendar of first publication of coloured sheets

The months of publication are taken from the Ordnance Survey *Supplement to Catalogue of England & Wales. Publications issued.* The date of printing/publication appearing on the map is given in brackets after the sheet number, where it differs from the date in the publications lists.

1919 (June)	91, 92, 102, 103, 104, 110, 111, 112, 118(1918), 119 (1918), 120 (1918), 121, 122, 123, 127, 128 (1918), 129, 130, 131, 132, 136, 137, 138, 139, 140, 141, 142, 143 (1918), 144, 145, 146.
1919 (September)	105
1919 (October)	82, 84, 93, 94, 113
1919 (December)	83
1920 (January)	95 (no date), 96 (1919)
1920 (February)	85
1920 (June)	106, 107, 114, 115
1920 (July/September)	70, 73, 75, 80, 124, 133
1920 (October/December)	74, 76, 81, 117, 125, 134
1921 (January/March)	17, 108, 116, 126, 135
1921 (April/June)	71, 72, 86, 87, 97, 98
1921 (July/September)	52, 53, 60, 61, 62, 63
1921 (October/December)	51, 54, 57, 59
1922 (January/March)	50, 64, 66 (1921), 67, 77 (1921)
1922 (April/June)	58
1922 (July/September)	55, 56, 65, 109
1922 (October/December)	42, 68, 69
1923 (January/March)	41 (1922), 99 (1922)
1923 (April/June)	49 (1922), 88, 89, 101
1923 (July/September)	39, 45, 46, 47, 48, 78, 79, 90, 100
1923 (October/December)	35, 38, 40, 44
1924 (January/March)	29, 43

1924 (April/June)	36, 37
1924 (July/September)	24, 25, 27, 28, 32, 33, 34
1924 (October/December)	30
1925 (January/March)	23, 26, 31
1925 (April/June)	14, 20, 22
1925 (July/September)	5, 9, 13, 16, 21
1925 (October/December)	4, 12, 15, 18, 19
1926 (January/March)	2, 3, 6 (1925), 7 (1925), 8 (1925), 10 (1925), 11 (1925)
1926 (July/September)	1

CHECK-LIST 5

Calendar of reprints of coloured sheets

Inferred states, which are noted in square brackets in the catalogue, are not included in this list.

1919   91, 143

1920   80, 102, 123, 128, 138, 141, 142

1921   91, 92, 93, 94, 95, 96, 103, 104, 105, 106, 107, 111 (x2), 112, 113, 114, 115 (x2), 121 (x2), 122 (x2), 123, 129, 130, 131, 132, 136, 137, 145, 146

1922   139, 140, 144

1923   82, 96, 114, 117, 118, 119, 123, 124, 127, 132, 133, 134, 141, 142

1924   17, 67, 84, 91, 102, 106, 110, 115, 125, 133, 139, 140

1925   83, 111, 116, 119, 121, 132, 138, 143, 145, 146

1926   95, 105, 107, 108, 113, 115, 117, 120, 124, 133, 135, 141, 142, 145, 146

1927   17, 26, 35, 41, 43, 44, 45, 49, 72, 95, 106, 111, 112, 113, 114, 118, 122, 124, 125, 126, 127, 134, 138, 143, 144 (x4)

1928   19, 25, 29, 36, 42, 81, 92, 94, 103, 105, 106 (x2), 115, 119, 124, 127, 129, 130, 131, 132, 133, 134, 135, 136, 137, 139, 141, 142, 146

1929   7, 12, 16, 20, 21, 27, 30, 31, 36, 37, 38, 58, 68, 71, 85, 95, 98, 103, 104, 107, 111, 112, 113, 114, 116, 117, 118, 120, 123, 124, 125, 132, 133, 145

1930   13, 14, 22, 24, 28, 29, 44, 45, 46, 47, 49, 55, 63, 64, 74, 82, 83, 84, 93, 94, 96, 99, 106, 108 (x2), 115, 125, 131, 134, 140, 142, 143 (x2)

1931   15, 17, 26, 28, 33, 36, 37, 41, 42, 54, 67, 72, 73, 90, 95, 101, 102, 105, 107, 109, 112, 114, 115, 117, 119, 120, 121, 122, 124, 126, 127, 129, 130, 133, 136, 138, 141, 143, 144, 145, 146

1932   2, 5, 6, 7, 8, 11, 16, 23, 25, 31, 46, 51, 53, 65, 68, 70, 80, 85, 93, 94, 95, 97, 98, 100, 103, 106, 107, 108, 110, 111, 112, 114, 116, 118, 123, 124, 125, 131, 132, 137, 138, 139, 142

1933   20, 30, 42, 49, 52, 54, 61, 62, 63, 77, 79, 82, 87, 92, 96, 103, 104, 109, 113, 114, 115 (x2), 133, 134, 135, 137, 138, 139, 140, 141, 144, 146

1934   3, 4, 10, 12, 17, 19, 22, 25, 32, 36, 41, 43, 44, 45, 47, 48, 50, 56, 69, 71, 72, 91, 95, 99, 102, 105, 106, 107, 113, 115, 118, 121, 125, 127, 128, 136, 140, 145

1935   7, 9, 14, 16, 18, 20, 21, 23, 24, 26, 27, 31, 35, 38, 39, 40, 51, 53, 57, 60, 64, 67, 68, 70, 78, 82, 83 (x2), 84, 86, 88, 93, 95 (x2), 101, 102, 106, 111, 112, 116, 117, 120, 122, 124, 125, 126, 128, 129, 130 (x2), 132, 133, 135, 141, 142

1936   7, 9, 12, 19, 20, 21, 23, 26, 31, 33, 37, 41, 42, 43, 44, 45 (x2), 46, 49, 54, 58, 59, 60, 61, 62, 63, 68, 71, 72, 73, 74, 81, 83, 84, 85, 87, 89, 92, 93, 96, 97, 98, 103 (x2), 104, 105, 106, 110, 111, 116, 117, 119 (x2), 120, 123, 125, 129, 133, 134 (x3), 138, 140, 141

1937   1, 2, 11, 13, 16, 22, 25, 35, 36, 39, 50, 51, 64, 75, 76, 77 (x2), 82, 87, 88, 91, 93, 99, 102, 109 (x2), 121, 122, 124, 126, 129, 131, 133, 135, 139, 141

1938   3, 4, 6, 10, 11, 12, 14, 15, 16, 17, 18, 20 (x2), 27, 29, 30, 32, 40, 41, 42, 47, 49, 53, 54, 55, 57, 58, 61, 63, 70 (x3), 71, 72, 74, 77, 78, 79, 80, 81, 84, 86, 90, 93, 94, 97, 99, 100, 101, 102, 103, 109, 116, 117, 122, 123, 125, 126, 132, 133, 134

1939   13, 18, 22, 26, 27, 28, 29, 34, 37, 38, 41, 44, 48, 51, 52, 53, 56, 60, 61, 62, 67, 68, 69, 71, 73, 75, 85, 88, 92, 98, 116, 117, 134

1940   20, 25, 38, 43, 45, 46, 50, 59, 64, 76, 82, 89, 90, 109

1941   135

CHECK-LIST 6

Sheets issued in buff covers

This list is not exhaustive. The following sheets (first printings) are known to have been issued in buff covers:

91	104	113	121	128	132	139	143
92	110	118	122	129	136	140	144
102	111	119	123	130	137	141	145
103	112	120	127	131	138	142	146

CHECK-LIST 7

Sheets printed on Place's waterproof paper

According to contemporary printed Ordance Survey sources (see pp.187-8) the following sheets were printed on Place's waterproof paper; they may not all have been issued in the special buff 'waterproof' style covers (see fig.46g, p.271):

2	17	40	53	72	101	118	136
3	19	41	54	73	102	119	137
5	22	42	55	82	103	120	138
6	23	43	56	83	105	121	140
7	24	44	61	87	106	122	141
8	26	45	62	90	107	124	142
9	28	46	63	91	108	125	143
10	29	47	64	93	109	126	144
11	32	48	65	94	113	127	145
12	33	49	67	96	114	129	146
13	35	50	69	97	115	130	
14	36	51	70	99	116	133	
15	37	52	71	100	117	134	

CHECK-LIST 8

Sheets issued in Bender covers

This list is not exhaustive. The following sheets, together with their print codes (not including punctuation), are known in Bender covers. An asterisk denotes the presence of the sheet title on the spine:

3	(3038*)	41	(3039)	63	(3038*)	89	(2540)
6	(2538)	43	(3400/40)	64	(2040)	90	(2042)
7	(3036)	45	(3040)	68	(4039)	92	(2539)
12	(3038)	46	(3040)	69	(2039)	93	(4038)
13	(2039)	47	(2538)	70	(2538)	98	(2039)
14	(2038*)	48	(2039)	71	(2539)	99	(4038)
16	(3038)	49	(4038)	72	(5038)	101	(2538)
21	(25/36)	50	(2500/40)	75	(2039)	109	(3040)
22	(3039*)	51	(3039)	76	(2040)	116	(1239*)
25	(3500/40)	53	(3039)	78	(2038)	117	(1239*)
26	(3039)	54	(3038)	79	(2538)	126	(3038)
27	(2539)	56	(1539)	80	(20/38)	133	(4038*)
28	(3039)	59	(2040)	81	(3038)	134	(1239)
30	(3038)	60	(2039)	82	(4040)	135	(3041LR)
31	(3036)	61	(2539*)	83	(3036)		
37	(3039)	62	(2539)	85	(3039)		

SOURCES

ARCHIVES

Charles Close Society Archive (CCS)

The Charles Close Society Archive of Ordnance Survey Material is housed in Cambridge University Library Map Library. The Society archives are in the charge of the Hon. Secretary.

Revision & Specials Job Files:

R.3352 1" Tourist Sheet Middle Thames (1939-1945)
R.3376 1" District Sheet Leicester (1940-1941)
R.3382 1" District Sheet Manchester (1939-1940)

Indexes

National Library of Scotland (NLS)

Bartholomew Archive, Acc.10222. B9-26, outgoing correspondence 1896 to 1914.

Bartholomew Printing Archive. These volumes, held in the Map Library, contain specimen copies of printed maps and advertising material, annotated in manuscript with the date of printing and the number of copies printed and occasionally with the colours of the inks, and their proportions used. Items are arranged in chronological order.

Ordnance Survey Library (OSL)

Director General's Conference Minutes. Duplicated typescripts of the Technical Post War Planning Conferences, the first of which was held on 14/6/1943, and of the Director General's Conferences. No reference number:

1st Technical Post War Planning Conference 14/6/1943
2nd Technical Post War Planning Conference 15/7/1943
3rd Technical Post War Planning Conference 17/8/1943
Conference on One-Inch Drawing 20/1/1944
Director General's Conference no.3 13/7/1944
Director General's Conference no.4 10/8/1944
Director General's Conference no.6 12/10/1944
Director General's Conference no.7 30/11/1944
Director General's Conference no.14 15/3/1945
Director General's Conference no.19 26/4/1945

Cassini coords of one-inch. Quarter Inch. Half Inch. 1" Section. Small Sheet Series grid cuts (Scotland) ... revision dates Pop. Edn. (Box TL23 A19 C1 S3 B2 held in Departmental Records).

[Ordnance Survey Committee (OSC). Minutes, memoranda, and other papers relating to the Davidson Committee.] (G5186).

Southampton Circulars, Book 1, 11/2/1880-3/9/1912. (G3962)
Southampton Circulars, Book 2, 1904-1922. (G3964)
Southampton Circulars, Book 3, 1892-1902 (some to 1946. G3963)
Southampton circulars and decisions from 25th March 1913. To 17th Sept.1919. (G7094)
Southampton circulars and decisions from 16 Sept.1919 to 1925. (G7095)
Southampton circulars and decisions from 7th June 1925 to 31 December 1931. (G7096)
Southampton circulars [mainly on administrative matters, 1920-1936]. (G2795)

Public Record Office

OS 1/2/5   1893-1932 Organisation of Ordnance Survey.
OS 1/4/3   1913   Publications and Debates Report: Director General's evidence.
OS 1/6/2   1883-1911 Crown copyright in Ordnance Survey maps.
OS 1/6/3   1886-1907 Copyright of OS maps.
OS 1/6/4   1911-1918 Revision of copyright regulations.
OS 1/6/5   1914   Departmental Committee on the sale of small scale maps.
OS 1/7/4   1923-1925 Reorganisation of clerical staff.
OS 1/8/4   1825-1926 Magnetic declination.
OS 1/8/5   1913-1924 Magnetic survey of the British Isles.
OS 1/8/6   1925-1927 Magnetic resurvey of Great Britain.
OS 1/9/2   1899-1902 One-inch maps of Ireland: omission of Parish boundaries.
OS 1/9/5   1923-1928 Abolition of engraving.
OS 1/18/1 1915-1926 Miscellaneous historical informaton.
OS 1/20   1927-1932 Committee of Enquiry into Government printing establishments.
OS 1/22   1932   Analysed statements of O.S. costs by processes, operations, etc.
OS 1/24A 1924-1933 Technical and industrial grades.
OS 1/24B 1933-1936 Technical and industrial grades.
OS 1/24C 1927-1936 Unestablished grades; standardisation of rates of pay.
OS 1/25   1936-1949 Industrial grades.
OS 1/34   1932-1935 Revision of Ordnance Survey maps.
OS 1/35   1932-1934 Acceleration of revision.
OS 1/37   1932-1935 Mine surveys and Ordnance Survey.
OS 1/38   1933-1935 Organisation of Field Divisions.
OS 1/39   1937-1939 Organisation of the Publication and Drawing Divisions.
OS 1/48   1928-1933 One-inch map of England & Wales on Gauss conformal projection.
OS 1/49   1931-1935 1″ Gazetteer.
OS 1/52   1932-1940 1-inch Popular Edition map.
OS 1/54   1932-1940 Quarter-inch map series.
OS 1/63-7 1927-1938 Magnetic Survey.
OS 1/68   1927-1931 Ordnance Survey Datum: enquiries.
OS 1/69   1927-1937 Levels: Isle of Wight.
OS 1/70   1923-1937 Supply of OS maps to Dr.G.B.Grundy, Oxford.
OS 1/84B 1935-1955 National grid: proposed single meridian for Great Britain.
OS 1/85A 1935-1955 National grid: memo on resurveyed maps and plans.
OS 1/85B 1935-1936 Director General's memorandum on scales and sheet sizes.
OS 1/90   1933-1935 1/M map of the Roman Empire.
OS 1/96   1935-1938 Director General's conferences.
OS 1/97   1939-1940 Annual report, 1939-1940.
OS 1/111 1933-1951 National Grid.
OS 1/113 1935   Davidson Committee: general correspondence.
OS 1/125 1929-1933 Jersey: maps and revisions.
OS 1/126 1931-1935 Select committee on estimates.
OS 1/128 1933-1955 Edward Stanford: agency for Ordnance Survey maps.
OS 1/134 1927-1948 Re-levelling of Greater London.
OS 1/139 1941   Annual report, 1940-1941.
OS 1/140 1942   Annual report, 1941-1942.
OS 1/141 1943   Annual report, 1942-1943.
OS 1/146 1932-1933 Administrative costs.
OS 1/173 1944   Annual report, 1943-1944.

OS 1/175 1918-1919 Record copies of maps.
OS 1/181 1931-1935 Half-inch District maps - general file; experimental map of Skye.
OS 1/206 1927-1960 Imprints on OS maps.
OS 1/208 1921-1947 Maps of the Isle of Man.
OS 1/213 1933-1955 Guernsey: drawing of 1933 three-inch map.
OS 1/219 1939-1944 War Office maps of GB: conversion to new grid and sheet lines.
OS 1/233 1931   History of copyright of OS publications.
OS 1/250 1928-1939 Security deletions.
OS 1/256 1936-1938 Prices of Ordnance Survey maps.
OS 1/283 1927-1949 Committee of enquiry into Government printing establishments.
OS 1/289 1928-1952 Map travellers.
OS 1/312 1928-1950 One inch map conventional signs.
OS 1/334 1932-1956 Style of lettering.
OS 1/369 1935-1952 Drawing and reproduction of small-scale maps.
OS 1/374 1937-1957 One inch map Sixth Edition.
OS 1/375 1938-1947 One inch tourist and district maps.
OS 1/460 1937-1958 Map folding.
OS 1/536 1927-1943 Awards to staff for suggested improvements.
OS 1/541 1933-1962 Electricity transmission lines on OS maps.
OS 1/751 1907-1909 Reproduction of maps without permission by Bacon and Bartholomew.
OS 1/755 1925-1930 Miscellaneous Crown Copyright considerations.
OS 3/260 1816-1820 Letter Book.

Royal Engineers Corps Library (Institution of Royal Engineers)

The history of the formation and work of M.I.4. War Office/Geographical Section of the General Staff. Class no.355.486 (RE/GSGS/M.I.4.). Accession no.8785.

Royal Geographical Society (with IBG)

Archives

Close Correspondence 1886-1951
Jack Correspondence 1921-1930
MacLeod Correspondence 1922-1938

Winterbotham Correspondence 1920-1933
1/M Map Correspondence 1911-1920
OS, papers relating to, 1930-1940

Map Room

Ordnance Survey Specimens

GENERAL BIBLIOGRAPHY

Account of the methods and processes adopted for the production of the maps of the Ordnance Survey of the United Kingdom (1875). London: HMSO.
-- *Account of the methods and processes ...* (1902). Revised in 1901 under the direction of Colonel Duncan A. Johnston, R.E., Director-General. London: HMSO.
Adams, B., (1989a) '198 years and 153 meridians, 152 defunct' *Sheetlines* 25:3-7; (1989b) [part 2] *Sheetlines* 26: 15-20; (1990) [concluded] *Sheetlines* 27:3-9.
Adams, B., (1994a) ' "Parallel to the Meridian of Butterton Hill" - do I laugh or cry?' *Sheetlines* 38:15-19.
Adams, B., (1994b) 'From eighteen minutes west to Longitude zero - episodes from the lives of a cartographer and a meridian' *Sheetlines* 40:7-16.
Aldcroft, D.H., (1973) *The inter-war economy: Britain, 1919-1939.* London: Batsford.

Andrews, J.H., (1975) *A paper landscape : the Ordnance Survey in nineteenth-century Ireland*. Oxford: Clarendon Press.

Andrews, J.H., (1997) *Shapes of Ireland : maps and their makers 1564-1839*. Dublin: Geography Publications.

Annual Report, see Ordnance Survey, Annual Reports.

Anon., (1916) *Map reading and panorama sketching*. By an Instructor. London: Sifton Praed.

Anon., (1985) 'Grid-lines and the 1912 Kilworth map' *Sheetlines* 14:17.

Askew, J.E., (1960) 'Half & Quarter Inch Series' in *Précis of technical lectures given on Small and Medium Scales Division*. [O.S. 1960] Part 2:15-18.

Aylward, J., (1971) 'The retail distribution of Ordnance Survey maps and plans in the latter half of the nineteenth century - a map seller's view' *The Cartographic Journal* 8, 1:55-8.

Baker, A.R., (1960) 'One Inch Seventh Series' in *Précis of technical lectures given on Small and Medium Scales Division*. [O.S. 1960] Part 2:13-14.

Baker, T.D., (1892) *Report of Committee on a military map of the United Kingdom*. London: War Office. A237. (Together with minutes of evidence and appendices. President (i.e., Chairman) T.D. Baker, Q.M.G)

Barker, T.C. and Savage, C.I., (1974) *An economic history of transport in Britain*. Third (revised) Edition. London: Hutchinson University Library.

Bignall, W., (1993) 'Conventional signs and the Ordnance Survey: the case of mills and the New Series' *Sheetlines* 35:10-13.

Bigwood, M.J., (1960) 'The photographic processes employed in Small Scales studio' in *Précis on technical lectures given on reproduction processes*. [O.S.1960.] Part 2:1-12.

Board, C., (1981) 'The Third Edition of the Quarter-inch map: a working note' *Sheetlines* 1:2-4.

Board, C., (1991) 'Things maps won't show us: reflections on the impact of security issues on map design' in *Mapping the nations*. London: ICA. (Proceedings of the ICA 15th Conference. Edited by K. Rybaczuk and M. Blakemore. Vol.1:136-141)

Board, C., (1993) 'Neglected aspects of map design' *The Cartographic Journal* 30, 2:119-122.

Booth, J.R.S., (1980) *Public boundaries and Ordnance Survey 1840-1980*. [Southampton]: Ordnance Survey.

Bramhall, C.W., (1960) 'Printing' in *Précis on technical lectures given on reproduction processes*. [O.S. 1960] pp.13-19.

Bramhall, C.W., (1972) 'The pin register system' *Ordnance Survey Bulletin* 20:1-5.

Browne, J.P., (1991) *Map cover art*. Southampton: Ordnance Survey.

Brunker, H.M.E., (1905) *Notes on maps and map-reading for the guidance of majors preparing for the 'tactical fitness' examination; and for Officers in instructing their N.C. officers and men*. Second Edition. London: William Clowes.

Butcher, N.E., (1983) 'The advent of colour-printed geological maps in Britain' *Proceedings of the Royal Institution of Great Britain* 55:149-161.

Bygott, J., (1938) *An introduction to mapwork and practical geography*. Second Edition. London: University Tutorial Press.

C., S., (1934) 'The new Ordnance Survey magnetic maps of Great Britain' *The Geographical Journal* LXXXIII, 6:527-8.

Carter, C.C., (1915) 'Cartographic needs of physical geography' *The Geographical Journal* XLV, 1:46-68.

Catalogues see Ordnance Survey, Catalogues

Chapman, J.C., (1971) 'The new map marketing arrangment for OS maps' *The Ordnance Survey Bulletin* 18:4-6.

Chapman, J.C., (1974) 'The launch of the 1:50,000 map series' *The Ordnance Survey Bulletin* 25:5-8.

Chasseaud, P., (1984) 'The development of artillery squares and artillery training maps of the U.K. 1914-1918' *Sheetlines* 10:2-8.

Cheetham, G., (1929) 'Notes on the reproduction of maps and plans' in *Empire Conference of Survey Officers. 1928. Report of Proceedings*. London: HMSO. (pp.49-65)

Cheetham, G., (1945) 'The post-war programme of the Ordnance Survey of Great Britain' *Empire Survey Review* VIII, 57:93-102.

Circulars see Ordnance Survey, Circulars

Clark, C.F., (1960) 'Hill-shading', in *Précis of technical lectures given on Small and Medium Scales Division*. [O.S., 1960.] Part 2:19-21.

Clark, P.K., and Jones, Y., (1974) 'British military map-making in the Peninsular War'. (Paper presented to the Seventh International Conference on Cartography, Madrid)

Clark, P.K. and Mumford, I., (1982) 'Note on the "1941 style" of coded imprint adopted by the Ordnance Survey and War Office' *Sheetlines* 5:9-12.

Clark, P.K., (1983) 'Maps for the army' *Sheetlines* 7:2-6. (Notes of a talk given by Peter Clark and written up by R. Oliver).

Clarke, A.R., (1852:58) *Ordnance Trigonometrical Survey of Great Britain and Ireland Account of the observations and calculations, of the Principal Triangulation; and of the figure, dimensions and mean specific gravity, of the earth as derived therefrom*. (1858) Published by order of the Master-General and Board of Ordnance. Drawn up by Captain Alexander Ross Clarke, R.E. F.R.A.S. under the direction of Lt. Colonel H. James, R.E. F.R.S. M.R.I.A. &c. Superintendent of the Ordnance Survey. London: Eyre and Spottiswoode. [Another volume, plates:] *Ordnance Trigonometrical Survey. Principal Triangulation. Plates*. (1852). London: Eyre and Spottiswoode.

Clinker, C.R., (1978) *Clinker's register of closed passenger stations and goods depots in England, Scotland and Wales 1830-1977*. New Edition. Bristol: Avon-Anglia Publications & Services.

Close, C.F., (1898) *Text book of military topography*. Part I [and] Part II. London: HMSO.

Close, C.F., (1905) 'The ideal topographical map' *The Geographical Journal* XXV, 6:633-647.

Close, C.F., (1913) *Text book of topographical and geographical surveying*. London: HMSO. (Revised by Captain E.W. Cox, R.E.)

Close, C.F., (1914) 'Relief in cartography' *The Geographical Journal* XLIII, 3:347.

Close, C.F., (1915) 'Correspondence: a reply to C.C. Carter' *The Geographical Journal* XLV, 5:443-4.

Close, C.F., (1922) *The second geodetic levelling of England and Wales 1912-1921*. London: HMSO.

Close, C.F., (1928) 'Some aspects of the work of the Ordnance Survey' *The Journal of the Manchester Geographical Society* 44:49-63.

Close, C.F., (1929) Obituary of Col. Hellard *The Geographical Journal* LXXIII, 4:399-400.

Close, C.F., (1931) 'The new one-inch Ordnance map' *The Geographical Journal* LXXVIII, 5:496.

Close, C.F., (1932) *The map of England or about England with an Ordnance map*. London: Peter Davies.

Close, C.F., (1933) 'Land Utilization maps of Great Britain' *The Geographical Journal* LXXXI, 6:541-3.

Close, C.F., (1934) A review of *Maps and survey* by A.R. Hinks *The Geographical Journal* LXXXIII, 1:64-6.

Close, C.F., (1947) *Geographical by-ways*. London: Edward Arnold.

Conolly, W.P., (1976) *British railways pre-grouping atlas and gazetteer*. Fifth Edition. London: Ian Allan.

Coote Hedley, W., (1938) Obituary of, *Empire Survey Review* 4, 28:381-3.

Correspondence respecting the scale for the Ordnance Survey, and upon contouring and hill delineation. (1854) London: HMSO. (BPP (1854) [1831] XLI).

Cox, C.H., (1924) *Exercises on Ordnance maps*. London: G. Bell and Sons.

Cox, C.H. & Maggs, A.J., (1939) *Exercises on Ordnance maps*. London: G. Bell and Sons.

Craster, J.E.E., (1925) 'Photo-mechanical processes of map production' *The Geographical Journal* LXXV, 4:301-314.

Crook, H.T., (1890) 'On the present state of the Ordnance Survey and the paramount necessity for a thorough revision' *The Journal of the Manchester Geographical Society* VI:228-238.

Cruickshank, J. and Archer, D., (1987) 'O.S. covers - a glossary of terms' *Sheetlines* 18:2-9.

Dale, G.H.C., (1921) *Map reading*. London: MacMillan. (With an introduction by E.M. Jack)

Davidson, J. (1936) *Interim report of the Departmental Committee on the Ordnance Survey*. London: HMSO.

-- (1938) *Final report of the Departmental Committee on the Ordnance Survey*. London, HMSO.

Dean, R., (1983) 'The Peak District and its approaches' *Sheetlines* 6:14.

Dean, R., (1984) 'The "1941" style of coded imprint' *Sheetlines* 9:18-19.

Dear, J.R., and Reid, P.E., (1975) 'The Ordnance Survey 1:50 000 map' *The Cartographic Journal* 12, 2:120-2.

'Discussion on the Final Report of the Departmental Committee on the Ordnance Survey' *The Geographical Journal* XCIII, 4:314-332.

Doodson, A.T., (1924) 'The tides and the work of the Tidal Institute, Liverpool' *The Geographical Journal* LXIII, 2:134-147.

Dorington, (1893a) *Report of the Departmental Committee appointed by the Board of Agriculture to inquire into the present condition of the Ordnance Survey*. London: HMSO. (With copy of the Minute appointing the Committee. Chairman, Sir John Edward Dorington. London: HMSO. BPP 1893-4, C.6895, LXXII)

-- (1893b) *Report from the Select Committee of Public Accounts*. London: HMSO. (Together with the Proceedings of the Committee. minutes of evidence, appendices and index)

-- (1893c) *Report of the Departmental Committee appointed by the Board of Agriculture to inquire into the present condition of the Ordnance Survey*. London: HMSO. (With minutes of evidence, appendices and index)

-- (1893d) Ordnance Survey. Copy of Minute of the Board of Agriculture dated the [blank] November 1893 upon the Report of the Departmental Committee appointed by the Board of Agriculture in April 1892 to inquire into the present condition of the Ordnance Survey. London: HMSO. (PRO OS 1/2/5.)

-- (1894) *Copy of Minute of the Board of Agriculture dated the 22 December 1893 upon the Report of the Departmental Committee appointed by the Board of Agriculture in April 1892 to inquire into the present condition of the Ordnance Survey*. London, HMSO. (C.7257.)

Dowson, A.H., [1961] *The one-inch maps of Great Britain*. (Copy of a typescript which it was proposed to issue as an OS Professional Paper. PC)

Drewitt, B.D., (1973) 'The changing profile of the map user in Great Britain' *The Cartographic Journal* 10, 1:42-48.

Drewitt, B.D., (1975) *The map market in Great Britain.* Southampton: Ordnance Survey. (Ordnance Survey Professional Papers New Series No.28)

Edwards, A.E., (1981) *The design of suburbia: a critical study in environmental history.* London: Pembridge Press.

Fairbairn, D.J., (1993) 'On the nature of cartographic text' *The Cartographic Journal* 30, 2:104-111.

Farquharson, Sir J., (1900) 'Twelve years' work of the Ordnance Survey 1887-1899' *The Geographical Journal* XV, 6:565-598.

Ford, B. (Ed.), (1992) *Early twentieth-century Britain.* Cambridge: Cambridge University Press. (The Cambridge Cultural History of Britain vol.8)

Fortescue, F.S., (1967) *A comparison of modern colour proofing methods.* Southampton: Ordnance Survey. (Ordnance Survey Technical Paper 18)

Freeman, T.W., (1985) 'Charles Frederick Arden-Close' *Geographers Biobibliographical Studies* 9:1-13.

Frith, G.R., (1906) *The Topographical Section of the General Staff: with an account of the geographical services of the Austrian, French, German, and Russian, armies.* Chatham: School of Military Engineering.

Galletley, W.H., (1932) 'The advancement of surveying practice' *The Colliery Guardian and Journal of the Coal and Iron Trades* CXLIV, 3721:771-2.

Gerken, R.F., [1960] '1:25,000 series' in *Précis of technical lectures given on Small and Medium Scales Division.* [O.S. 1960] Part 2:9-12.

Gilbert, B.B., (1973) *British social policy 1914-1939.* London: Batsford.

Goodman, J., (1920) 'Lithographic map printing at the Ordnance Survey Office, Southampton' *The Modern Lithographer,* pp.73-74.

Griffith, D.L., (1964) 'The Cairngorms' *Ordnance Survey Technical Bulletin* 9:1-2.

Griffith, D.L., (1965) 'Keeping small scale maps up to date' *Ordnance Survey Technical Bulletin* 11:5-7.

Hansard, see *Parliamentary Debates.*

Harley, J.B., (1964) *The historian's guide to Ordnance Survey maps.* London: The National Council of Social Service for The Standing Conference for Local History. (Reprinted from 'The Amateur Historian' with additional material)

Harley, J.B., (1975) *Ordnance Survey maps   A descriptive manual.* Southampton, Ordnance Survey.

Harley, J.B., (1979) *The Ordnance Survey and land-use mapping: parish books of reference and the county series 1:2500 maps, 1855-1918* [London]: Institute of British Geographers, Historical Geography Research Group. Historical Geography Research Series 2.

Harris, L.J., (1959) 'Hillshading for relief depiction in topographical maps with some recent applications' *Commonwealth Survey Officers' Conference.* Paper no.20(a). (This paper was reprinted in the *Scottish Geographical Magazine* (1960) 76, 1:14-20)

Harvey, P.D.A. and Thorpe, H., (1959) *The printed maps of Warwickshire 1576-1900.* Warwick: Records and Museum Committee of the Warwickshire County Council in collaboration with the University of Birmingham.

Hayes Fisher. (1896a) *Report of the Departmental Committee appointed by the Board of Agriculture to consider the arrangements to be made for the sale of Ordnance Survey maps.* London: HMSO. (With copy of the minute appointing the Committee. Chairman, William Hayes Fisher.) BPP 1896, C.8147, LXVIII. (The Committee sat in 1895, but the proceedings were published in 1896)

-- (1896b) *Minutes of evidence taken before the Departmental Committee appointed by the Board of Agriculture to consider the arrangements to be made for the sale of Ordnance Survey maps*; With appendices and index. London, HMSO. BPP 1896, C.8148, LXVIII.

-- (1897) *Copies of three contracts entered into by the Board of Agriculture, with the Agents appointed for the sale of Ordnance Survey maps in London, Edinburgh, and Dublin ...* London: HMSO. C.8488. (This seems to have been intended as an addendum to the Hayes Fisher Report. It includes a copy of the conditions upon which agents are appointed in provincial towns; list of the agents appointed in England and Wales, Scotland, and Ireland; and a list of Post Offices at which Ordnance Survey maps may be ordered.)

Heawood, E., (1932) 'Early map indexing' *The Geographical Journal* LXXX, 3:247-249.

Hellyer, R., (1992a) 'The physical maps of the Ordnance Survey' *Sheetlines* 32:18-32.

Hellyer, R., (1992b) *The 'ten-mile' maps of the Ordnance Surveys.* London: The Charles Close Society for the Study of Ordnance Survey Maps.

Hellyer, R., (1999) *Ordnance Survey small-scale maps indexes 1801-1998.* Kerry: David Archer.

[Hinks, A.R.], (1913) 'The forthcoming new edition of the one-inch Ordnance Survey map' *The Geographical Journal* XLII, 4:371-2.

Hinks, A.R., (1922) 'The Ordnance Survey: retirement of Sir Charles Close' *The Geographical Journal* LX, 3:229-230.

Hinks, A.R., (1923) *Maps and survey.* Second Edition. Cambridge: Cambidge University Press.

Hinks, A.R., (1924) 'The choice of a grid for British maps: the grid in civil use' *The Geographical Journal* LXIII, 6:499-508 (including discussion).

Hinks, A.R., (1925) 'The science and art of map-making' *The Scottish Geographical Magazine* 4:321-336.

[Hinks, A.R.], (1931) 'The One-Inch to the mile Ordnance Survey map of England' *The Geographical Journal* LXXVIII, 4:353-356.

[Hinks, A.R.], (1932) 'The new One-Inch map' *The Geographical Journal* LXXX, 4:358-9.

[Hinks, A.R.], (1933) 'The national grid on the map of London' *The Geographical Journal* LXXXII, 4:357-8. (A review of the Ordnance Survey 3-inch map of London.)

Hodgkiss, A.G., (1969-70) 'The Ordnance Survey one-inch to one mile map - an outline history with special reference to the early editions' *SUC Bulletin* 4, 1:19-34.

Hodson, D., (1974) *The printed maps of Hertfordshire 1577-1900.* London: Dawson.

Hodson, Y., (1989) *Ordnance Surveyors' Drawings 1789-c.1840 : the original manuscript maps of the first Ordnance Survey of England and Wales from the British Library Map Library.* Reading: Research Publications. (With an introduction, summary listing and indexes by Tony Campbell.)

Hodson, Y., (1991a) 'A little light relief: a personal view of collecting OS maps' *The Map Collector* 54:10-15.

Hodson, Y. (Ed.), (1991b) *An inch to the mile : the Ordnance Survey One-Inch map 1805-1974.* London: The Charles Close Society for the Study of Ordnance Survey Maps. (Catalogue of an exhibition to commemorate the bicentenary of the Ordnance Survey.)

Hodson, Y., (1991c) 'The evaluation of older maps' *Rights of Way Law Review* Section 9, 3:29-32.

Hodson, Y., (1991d) 'Board of Ordnance Surveys 1863-1820' in *Proceedings of the Symposium to celebrate the Ordnance Survey Bicentenary.* Chichester: Survey and Mapping Alliance.

Hodson, Y., (1994) 'More on the map of East Anglia' *Sheetlines* 38:11.

Hodson, Y., (1995) *The Ordnance Survey Popular Edition one-inch map of England and Wales 1919-1942: a cartographic anatomy.* PhD thesis, University of London.

Hodson, Y., (1999) 'Roads on OS 1:2500 plans 1884-1912' *Rights of Way Law Review* Section

9,3: 107-118.

Horner, A.A., (1974) 'Some examples of the representation of height data on Irish maps before 1750, including an early use of the spot-height method' *Irish Geography* VII:68-70.

Hotine, M., (1929) 'Surveying from air photographs' in *Empire Conference of Survey Officers. 1928. Report of Proceedings*. London: HMSO.

Hotine, M., (1936) 'A grid system for Ordnance Survey maps' *The Royal Engineers Journal* L:597-605.

House, J.W. and Fullerton, B., (1960) *Tees-side at mid-century: an industrial and economic survey*. London: Macmillan.

Ilkeston. (1911a) *Departmental Committee on the remuneration of the Ordnance Survey staff*. London: HMSO. (Cd.5825. Report of the Departmental Committee appointed by the Board of Agriculture and Fisheries to inquire into the pay and classification of the Ordnance Survey staff.)

-- (1911b) *Departmental Committee on the remuneration of the Ordnance Survey Staff*. London: HMSO. (Cd.5826. Minutes of evidence taken before the Departmental Committee of Enquiry into the pay and classification of the Ordnance Survey staff. With appendices, index and analysis of evidence. Chairman, Lord Ilkeston, formerly Sir Walter Foster)

-- (1912) *Ordnance Survey. Copies of Minutes of the Board of Agriculture & Fisheries Dated the 23rd November, 1911 and the 7th March, 1912 upon the Report of the Departmental Committee appointed in June, 1910 (Cd.5825) To Inquire into the Pay and Classification of the Ordnance Survey Staff. Revised scales of pay, 1912*. London: HMSO. (Cd.6156)

Jack, E.M., (1924) 'The choice of a grid for British maps: the National Grid' *The Geographical Journal* LXIII, 6:496-9.

Jack, E.M., (1925) 'The work of the Ordnance Survey'. See *Papers read ...* (1926).

Jack, E.M., (1926) 'The work of the Ordnance Survey' *The Scottish Geographical Magazine* XLII:220-227.

James, N.N., (1993) *A list of Ordnance Survey catalogues, publication reports & other publications*. Oxford: Bodleian Library, University of Oxford. (Maplist Nº 2)

Johnston, W.J., (1920) 'The new one-inch and quarter-inch maps of the Ordnance Survey' *The Geographical Journal* LV, 3:192-200.

Jones, Y., (1974) 'Aspects of relief portrayal on 19th century British military maps' *The Cartographic Journal* 11, 1:19-33.

Keates, J.S., (1962) 'The perception of colour in cartography' in *Proceedings of the Cartographic Symposium held in the Department of Geography, University of Edinburgh 21-24 September 1962*.

Keates, J.S., (1989) *Cartographic design and production*. Second Edition. New York: Longman Scientific & Technical with John Wiley & Sons.

King, J., (1995) 'Subtle change in symbol meaning' *Sheetlines* 42:27-8.

Kitiro, T., (1932) 'The orthographical method of representing hill features on a topographical map' *The Geographical Journal* LXXIX, 3:213-219.

Langstaff, A.E. and Sainsbury, E.G., (1974) 'A glimpse into the Thirties' *The Ordnance Survey Bulletin* 25:14-18.

Law, C.M., (1981) *British regional development since World War I*. London & New York: Methuen.

Leach, G.A., (1892) *Report of the Departmental Committee appointed to inquire into the position of the Civil Assistants employed on the Ordnance Survey*. London: HMSO. (Cd.6692. Chairman, Lieut.-Col. G.A. Leach)

Llewellyn Brown, R., (1951) 'The revision problems of the Ordnance Survey' *Journal of the Institution of Chartered Surveyors* XXX, X:70-80.

Lockey, B., (1942) *The interpretation of Ordnance Survey maps and geographical pictures*. Second Edition. London: George Philip.

Loveless, W.C., [1960] 'The six-inch series' *Précis of technical lectures given on Small and Medium Scales Division*. [O.S. 1960] Part 2:1-8.

Lyons, H.G., (1914) 'Relief in cartography' *Geographical Journal* XLIII, 3:233-248 and XLIII, 4:395-407.

MacLeod, M.N., (1923) 'Military survey' *Royal Engineers Journal* XXXVII, 4:619-626.

MacLeod, M.N., (1925a) 'The International Map'. See *Papers read ...* (1926)

MacLeod, M.N., (1925b) 'The International Map' *The Geographical Journal* LXVI, 5:445-9.

MacLeod, M.N., (1929) 'Some problems of revision' in *Empire Conference of Survey Officers. 1928. Report of Proceedings*. London: HMSO. pp.123-133.

MacLeod, M.N., (1939) 'The Ordnance Survey and its work' *The Royal Engineers Journal* LIII, 2:183-192.

MacLeod, M.N., [1946] *Autobiographical notes*. [Post 1946]. Typescript. (OSL G5127)

Maling, D.H., (1989) *Measurements from maps: principles and methods of cartometry*. Oxford: Pergamon Press.

Manual of map reading air photo reading and field sketching. (1955) Part I. Map reading. London, HMSO.

Margary, H., (1975-1992) *The Old Series Ordnance Survey maps of England and Wales scale: 1 inch to 1 mile. A reproduction of the 110 sheets of the Survey in early state in 10 volumes*. Lympne Castle: Harry Margary. (Introductory essays and cartobibliographies by J.B. Harley and Y. O'Donoghue/Hodson, vols I-III; J.B. Harley, and B.A.D. Manterfield, vols.IV-V; J.B. Harley and R.R. Oliver, vols. VI-VIII)

Marles, A.C. and Goodhall, A., (1972) 'Colour printing in the Ordnance Survey : an extract from an old file with commentary' *The Ordnance Survey Bulletin* 21:20-22.

Marriott, S.F., (1946) *Map reading for the countrygoer*. London: Ramblers' Association.

Martin, D.R., (1931) 'The Ordnance Survey map-mounting machine' *Empire Survey Review* I, 1:15-21.

Mathieson, J., (1932) 'The new one-inch to a mile Ordnance Survey map. (Popular Edition)' *Scottish Geographical Magazine* XLVIII, 2:98-103.

Messenger, K.G, (1988) *The Ordnance Survey one-inch map of England and Wales Third Edition (Large Sheet Series): a descriptive and cartobibliographical monograph*. London: The Charles Close Society for the Study of Ordnance Survey Maps.

Messenger, K.G. and Oliver, R.R., (1992) 'A miscellany on covers' *Sheetlines* 32:53-58.

Mosley, J. and Hodson, Y., (1982) 'Egyptian lettering on OS and other maps' *Sheetlines* 5:12.

Morrow, F., (1913) *Contours and maps explained and illustrated*. London: Meiklejohn.

Mowat, C.L., (1968) *Britain between the wars 1918-1940*. London: Methuen.

Mumford, I., [1951] 'New light on old methods of relief representation on topographic maps' (unpublished paper)

Mumford, I., (1972) 'Lithography, photography and photozincography in English map production before 1870' *The Cartographic Journal* 9, 1:30-6.

Mumford, I. and Clark, P.K., (1986) 'Marketing of maps before 1918' *Sheetlines* 15:1-8.

Mumford, I., (1991) 'Monochrome to polychrome at the Ordnance Survey in the 19th century' in *Proceedings of the Symposium to celebrate the Ordnance Survey Bicentenary*. Chichester: Survey and Mapping Alliance.

Murray, J. and Pullar, L., (1905) 'Bathymetrical surveys of the freshwater lochs of Scotland' *The Geographical Journal* XXVI, 1:42-68.

Murray, and Pullar, L., (1910) *Bathymetrical survey of the Scottish freshwater lochs. Conducted ... during the years 1897-1909. Report on the scientific results.* Edinburgh: Challenger Office.

Newbigin, M.I., (1920) *Ordnance Survey maps : their meaning and use with descriptions of typical 1-inch sheets.* Second Edition. Edinburgh: W. & A.K. Johnston.

Nicholson, T.R., (1983a) *Wheels on the road : maps of Britain for the cyclist and motorist 1870-1940.* Norwich: Geo Books.

Nicholson, T.R., (1983b) 'Fifty-seven varieties? First notes towards a listing of OS leaflets, 1919-1939' *Sheetlines* 7:9-12.

Nicholson, T.R., (1984) 'Lies, damned lies, and imprints - some tourist and district map anomalies' *Sheetlines* 11:9-11.

Nicholson, T.R., (1985) 'Ordnance Survey maps on Place's waterproof paper: some notes' *Sheetlines* 14:10-13.

Nicholson, T.R., (1991a) 'The first Ordnance Survey district maps of England, Wales and Scotland 1847-1898' *The Cartographic Journal* 28, 2:181-187.

Nicholson, T.R., (1991b) 'Ordnance Survey ephemera to 1939' *The Map Collector* 54:2-7.

Nicholson, T.R., (1994a) 'Theme and variations: the retitled small-scale map' *Sheetlines* 40:29-32.

Nicholson, T.R., (1994b) 'The Ordnance Survey one inch/mile black outline, coloured roads district map 1899-193?' *The Cartographic Journal* 31, 2:123-31.

Notes on the making of maps and plans. (1937) London: HMSO.

Nowell-Smith, S., (Ed.) (1964) *Edwardian England 1901-1914.* London: Oxford University Press.

O'Brien, C.I.M., (1992) 'A man for his time? Sir Charles Arden-Close 1865-1952' *Sheetlines* 34:1-7.

O'Donoghue, K.P., (1972) 'Work of the OS sales representative' *The Ordnance Survey Bulletin* 21:9-12.

Ogilvie, A.G., (1915) 'Cartographic needs of physical geography' *The Geographical Journal* XLV, 1:46-68.

Ogilvie, A.G., (1939) 'The future work of the Ordnance Survey: a review' *Scottish Geographical Magazine* LV, 2:107-111.

Oliver, R., (1982a) 'Fourth Edition one-inch map of England and Wales sheet 34' *Sheetlines* 2:8.

Oliver, R., (1982b) 'What's what with the New Series' *Sheetlines* 5:3-8.

Oliver, R., (1985a) 'New light on the New Series' *Sheetlines* 12:7-11.

Oliver, R., (1985b) *The Ordnance Survey in Great Britain 1835-1870.* PhD thesis, Sussex.

Oliver, R., (1988) 'Edition codes on Ordnance Survey maps' *Sheetlines* 22:4-7.

Oliver, R., (1989a) *A guide to the Ordnance Survey one-inch Fifth Edition.* London, The Charles Close Society for the Study of Ordnance Survey Maps. Second Edition.

Oliver, R., (1989b) *A guide to the Ordnance Survey one-inch New Popular Edition and Scottish Popular Edition with National Grid.* Second edition. London: The Charles Close Society for the Study of Ordnance Survey Maps.

Oliver, R., (1990) 'Steeples and spires: the use of church symbols on Ordnance Survey maps' *Sheetlines* 28:24-31.

Oliver, R., (1991) *An introduction to the Ordnance Survey One-Inch Seventh Series map with a list of edition numbers.* Southampton: Ordnance Survey.

[Oliver, R.,] (1992a) 'The "King Alfred map" found' *Sheetlines* 32:6.

Oliver, R., (1992b) 'The "unpopular" one-inch Fourth Edition: an insight into early twentieth century Ordnance Survey small-scale revision policy' *Sheetlines* 32:38-46.

Oliver, R., (1993) *Ordnance Survey maps: a concise guide for historians.* London: The Charles Close Society for the study of Ordnance Survey Maps.

Oliver, R., (1996) 'The rivals' *Sheetlines* 47:3-36.

Olivier (1914a) *Departmental Committee on the sale of small-scale Ordnance Survey maps.* (Confidential. For Departmental use only. Minutes of Evidence. Chairman, Sir Sydney Olivier. Only one copy known, on PRO OS 1/6.)

-- (1914b) *Report of the Departmental Committee on the sale of small-scale Ordnance Survey maps; with appendices.* (26/8/1914).

Ordnance Survey publications and printed texts

The items listed under this heading can be found in the Ordnance Survey Library, the copyright libraries, and the Royal Geographical Society, as well as in private collections. All items were published or produced by Ordnance Survey in Southampton, or Chessington (1943-69) unless otherwise stated.

Abridged list of the Ordnance Survey small scale maps of England and Wales. For motoring, cycling, walking and general purposes. (Jan.1925). (OS Leaflet No.6. Issued annually until at least 1939.)

Abridged list Ordnance Survey small-scale maps of Scotland for motoring, cycling, walking and general purposes. [1935] (OS Leaflet No.7. Issues also known in 1936 and 1939.)

A brief description of the National Grid and reference system. (Nov.1945). Ordnance Survey Booklet No.1/45.

Administrative regulations and instructions (1908) London: HMSO (For Departmental use only.) See under *Rules and regulations ...* for later issues.

Annual reports

Report of the progress of the Ordnance Survey [Annual Reports] Titles vary. A full listing of the reports consulted, from 1872 to 1944, is given in Hodson (1995). The typescripts of unpublished wartime reports are in the Public record Office (see listing under PRO on pp.384-5).

Catalogues

The 'Supplement' to the Catalogue which contains 'Publications issued' since the previous catalogue, were published at weekly, monthly, and then quarterly intervals. These are invaluable for giving a more precise date of publication, and are quoted with dates in the main text and Appendices. A skeleton listing of those in the Bodleian Library is given in James (1993). They are too numerous to list individually here, but are referred to by short title and date in the footnotes. All were published in London by HMSO.

Catalogue of the maps and plans and other publications of the Ordnance Survey of England and Wales, to 1st March 1863. (1863)

Catalogue of the maps and plans and other publications of the Ordnance Survey of England and Wales, and the Isle of Man, to 16th March 1870. (1870). (Later editions published in 1885, 1887, 1896, 1898, 1899, 1900, 1901.)

Catalogue of the one-inch and smaller scale maps, and other publications of the Ordnance Survey of the United Kingdom. To 1st January, 1902. (1902). (Another edition was published in 1903.)

Catalogue of the 6-inch and 25-inch county maps and town plans of England and Wales and the Isle of Man, and of the one-inch and smaller scale maps, and other publications of the Ordnance Survey of the United Kingdom. To 1st January, 1904. (1904). (Later editions were published in 1905, and annually from 1907 to 1915, 1917, 1918, and 1920.)

Ordnance Survey publications ...

Catalogue of maps and other publications of the Ordnance Survey. (1924) (The index to the Popular Edition on p.75 shows sheets 34 and 42 in the wrong position. A reduced facsimile of this catalogue, together with an introduction by R. Oliver, was published in 1991 by David Archer.

Circulars

These entries are arranged in alpha-numerical order for ease of reference, but it should be noted that this does not necessarily follow the chronological order of issue; the exact significance of the difference between C/C and C.C. (Chief Clerk's Circulars) has not been discovered, although it is evident that they do represent different sequences. Those items which are evidently circulars, but which have no numbers, are placed in date order at the end. Many circulars and notices have no formal title, and in these cases the formula: [Begin:] followed by all or most of the first sentence is used. Where necessary, the content of the circulars is summarised in square brackets. Most of these documents survive in single numbers only. Those listed below are kept in the books of circulars in the Ordnance Survey Library (for full references to these see above under the heading 'Ordnance Survey Library') at Southampton unless otherwise noted.

C/C 31/10. 25/10/1919. [Begin:] Sir, I am to inform you that owing to the number and positions of aerodromes in the United Kingdom not having been definitely decided upon, it is not considered advisable to show them on Ordnance Survey maps ... (Copy of a letter from the Air Ministry dated 25/10/1919.) Annotated to the EO by Close: 'the meaning of this may be taken to be that the word aerodrome is not to be printed.')

C/C 425/10. 19/1/1910. [Begin:] No spelling of names should be taken from the Admiralty charts ... (Charts to be used for lightships and sea contours. Duplicated MS)

C/C 460/11. 20/1/1911. [Begin:] It has been decided in future to omit the dotted line on the one-inch map round areas of rough pasture ...

C/C 659/96. 12/2/1896. *Engraving contour figures on 1" sheets of Great Britain.*

C/C 842/95. 27/2/1895. [Begin:] E.O. Please instruct O.E. that on the Tablet of Characteristics on the margin of the 1-inch sheets ... (Instruction to remove the symbols for lighthouse, lightship and beacon from the marginal tablet of characteristics for the inland one-inch sheets)

C/C 1259/8. 9/3/1908. [To EO thro' OID. Begin:] The following small points should I think receive attention on the Revision of the one inch of Ireland ... (Characteristic sheets for the one-inch maps of Great Britain and Ireland. pp.4)

C/C 2726/16. 7/6/1916. [Begin:] Extract from the 'Times' dated June 3rd 1916 ... (giving details of Closes's Order of the Bath, the initials 'C.B.' to be added to imprints)

C/C 6835/19. 17/5/1919. [Begin:] E.O. For engraved maps &c, "Colonel Sir Charles Close, K.B.E., C.B., F.R.S.

C/C 7052/13. 7/11/1913. [Begin:] E.O. An inspection of black proofs of sheets 144 & 145, England 1", shows that the method of filling up the interrupted railway symbol is not satisfactory ...

C/C 7677/13. 5/12/1913. *Railway lines on 1" map.*

C.C.14. 17/10/1895. *Alterations to published names.* pp.2.

C.C.146. 16/9/1901. *Classification of roads on the 1/2500 and 6-inch scales.* pp.2.

C.C.324. 8/4/1909. [Begin:] The work of the one-inch revision is now very expensive ... (revised allowances for work in the field. pp.4)

C.C.433. 28/8/1912. [Begin:] From 2nd September 1912 inclusive, the Engraving Department will cease to be a separate Department ...

C.C.520. 23/2/1915. *Money awards for suggestions regarding improvements in methods or material tending to economy or efficiency.*

Ordnance Survey publications ...

C.C.775. 28/11/1921. *Aerodromes.*

C.C.819. 5/5/1923. *Abolition of engraving, and rules as to the disposal of engravers.*

C.C.844. 15/3/1924. *Information shown or omitted from sales editions of Ordnance Survey maps with regard to Naval and Military defence works, explosives factories, naval dockyards, wireless telegraph stations, Aerodromes, &c.*

C.C.863. 5/12/1924. [Tests, imposition of bar and deferred increments for draftsmen and litho-draftsmen]

C.C.882. 13/6/1925. [Begin:] In accordance with War Office letter no.81/2431 (M.I.4.) dated 9th June, 1925, all buildings in connection with explosives factories which have a noticably characteristic form are to be omitted from the public sales editions of Ordnance Survey maps of all scales. Circulars C.C.844 (15/3/1924) and C.C.846 (24/4/1924) should be read in conjunction with these later War Office instructions.

C.C.885. 5/8/1925. *Instructions for Test of Draftsmen as required by para.1 of Circular (C.C.863).*

C.C.913. 17/5/1926. *Railway names under the 1921 Grouping.*

C.C.926. 16/2/1927. *Defence security information to be omitted or deleted from 'Official Use Only' and sales editions of maps on all scales.*

C.C.944. 12/1/1928. *Defence security information to be admitted or deleted from "Official Use Only" and sales editions of O.S. maps on all scales.* For Official Use Only. pp.4. (PRO OS 1/250)

C.C.953. 14/5/1928. *New rates of pay for technical grades.* (Sanctioning the introduction of the new occupation of Map Mounting Machine Minder to grade IV on the Technical Grades pay scale.)

C.C.958. 8/10/1928. *Progress of Levellers.*

C.C.966. 25/5/1929. (Amendments to *Instructions to levellers and contourers (1926)*)

C.C.1051. 6/4/1934. *Photographers' qualifications for grading.* pp.2.

C.C.1065. 1/11/1934. *Establishment.* (Transfer of the Engraver from the Small Scale Revision Department to the Zinc and Litho Department)

C.C.1081. 6/8/1935. *1/25,000 series - Great Britain.* (Security information)

C.C.1082. 23/8/1935. (Experimental work to be recorded not only on the appropriate file, but a summary to made also on form 157)

C.C.1087. 3/10/1935. *Secret documents.*

C.C.1088. 18/10/1935. *Instructions for test of draughtsmen for (a) qualifying for entry to Group II. (b) passing the Bar in Scale III.* (Cancels C.C.978. The writing part of the test was to be based on the 'Ordnance Survey Alphabets' and the Perth drawing)

C.C.1122. 16/12/1936. (Consolidated rates of allowances, including those for Map Travellers, from 1/10/1936. PRO OS 1/289)

Copy C.6201. 14877/12. A.1931/1912. 27/9/1912. [Begin:] To note. The words 'Crown Copyright Reserved' should be substituted for 'All rights of reproduction reserved' on Ordnance Survey maps for the future ... (Copy of a letter from H.M. StationeryOffice instructing that the imprint on OS sheets should be 'Crown Copyright Reserved'. With covering minute from the E.O. dated 30/9/1912)

CR 8294. 16/6/1932. (Request for information about revision of the large scale plans)

O.S.307. *Instructions to surveyors.* [1908] (A reprint of an 1882 document. pp.13. PC Xerox of an original in Boundaries Section, OS, 1974)

O.S.318. [1913]. *Application for Ordnance Survey maps for educational purposes.* (PRO OS 1/4/3)

Ordnance Survey publications ...

O.S.404. *Character of writing for Ordnance Survey plans.* (This number and title appeared on a blue cover of the booklet *Ordnance Survey maps of the United Kingdom. A description of their scales, characteristics, and character of writing. q.v.* under 'Ordnance Survey')

O.S.463. 11/10/1897. *Instructions for insertion of railways, &c., for 1-inch map.* With reference to D.G's circulars of 7th November, 1879, and 20th July, 1886.

[Number indistinct:] 1?9060/1919. 29/11/1921. [Begin:] E.O. On 1″ and ½″ draw aerodromes to scale and write 'Aerodrome' ...

[No number] Circular. 25/6/1884. *Roads, carriage drives &c.* (Cancels circular dated 18/4/1884; not seen)

[No number] 27/11/1894. *Instructions for keeping the History Sheet of English 1″ Revision Sheets.* (Together with a blank sample: 'History Sheet. 1″ revision, England sheet No. ...')

[No number] 18/6/1908. *Revision of one-inch map. W.D. information.*

[No number] 1909. *Instructions for the revision of the 1″ map 1909.* (Duplicated typescript. pp.6. No specific date, nor signature)

[No number] 1913. *Tender for the supply of lithographic and other papers, required for use at the Survey Offices, Southampton and Dublin.* [1913]. (pp.5 PRO OS 1/4/3)

Descriptions: 1890-1917

Ordnance Survey maps of the United Kingdom. A description of their scales, characteristics, and character of writing ... [1890] [London: HMSO]

-- *Ordnance Survey maps ... A description* ... [1891] OS 404. [London: HMSO.] (Revised to November, 1891; includes *Character of writing for Ordnance Survey plans.* Later editions were published in 1899 and 1913.)

Ordnance Survey maps of the United Kingdom. A description of their characteristics and character of writing; also diagrams and explanatory notes to facilitate reference whilst using them. [1914] (For Office use only. OS 404. No imprint. The 'Character of writing for Ordnance Survey plans' on p.9 is dated June 1914.)

Ordnance Survey maps of the United Kingdom. A description of their scales, characteristics, &c. (1917) London: HMSO.

Descriptions: medium scales

A description of Ordnance Survey medium scale maps. (1947). (Later editions were printed in 1948, 1949, 1951, and 1955.)

Descriptions: small scales

A description of the small scale Ordnance Survey maps with specimens and indexes. [1919]. *Supplement to catalogue* 1-31/12/1919. (Later editions were published in 1920 (Second Edition); 1921 (Third Edition); 1923 (Fourth Edition); 1925 (Fifth Edition); 1927 (Sixth Edition); 1931 (Seventh Edition); 1935 (8th Edition); 1937 (9th Edition). The booklet was published in a new format in 1947, and further editions of this were printed in 1949, 1951, and 1957.)

England & Wales, 3rd Revision 1-Inch maps. General instructions for guidance of Departments. 6/3/1913. (In PRO OS 1/4/3)

Glossary of the most common Welsh words used on the Ordnance Survey maps. [1930s]

High and low water marks as shown on Ordnance Survey plans. [1940]. (OS Leaflet No.20/40)

Important notice relating to Ordnance Survey maps on Place's waterproof paper. (OS Leaflet No.48/36)

Instructions: arranged in chronological order

(1896) *Instructions for the revision of the one-inch map in the field.* (16/3/1896). (OSL G93963)

(1901) *Instructions to one-inch field revisers.*

Ordnance Survey publications ...

(1909) *Instructions for the revision of the 1-inch map.* (i.e. the 'first', abortive Third Revision)

(1912) *Instructions to field examiners and revisers.* (Jul.1912)

(1914) *Instructions for the revision of the small scale maps (Provisional). Section dealing with drawing and examination (1" scale).* (Jan.1914). (i.e. the 'second' Third Revision.)

(1924) *Instructions to field revisers and draftsmen for the revision and preparation of the small scale maps for reproduction by heliozincography.*

(1926) *Instructions for levellers and contourers.*

(1932) *Instructions to field revisers 1/2500 scale.*

(1936) *Instructions for the revision and drawing of the one-inch (Fifth Edition) map.* (1936)

(1961) *Instructions for small scales revision (The Green Book 1961).* (Sept.1961). (Much of this has been transcribed in *Sheetlines* (1998) 52)

(1962-4) *Drawing instructions one inch Seventh Series.* [1962-4]

Methods and processes used by the Ordnance Survey for map reproduction by photo-lithography. Notes on map reproduction. (1927)

Notes on the printing of maps for the Ordnance Survey. (1943)

1:50 000 Second Series specification. [1975]. (Duplicated typescript; issued before April 1975.)

Ordnance Survey alphabets. pp. 24. (*Supplement to catalogue of England & Wales* 1/1 to 31/3/1934. It was intended to publish this as an OS Professional Paper, but this does not seem to have been approved by HMSO. See PRO OS 1/111)

Ordnance Survey. A short outline of the duties of the various departments at Headquarters. (1934)

Ordnance Survey. Notice. [Begin:] 'In future it will not always be possible to supply demands for Copper-plate impressions of the 1-inch ...' (1/4/1918). (Single-sided leaflet.)

[*Ordnance Survey of Great Britain.*] (1/8/1895). pp.29 (No title-page; the supplied title is taken from the heading of the text on p.1 which is preceded by two unnumbered pages. The first is headed 'Departments', and gives the names of the Superintendents together with their physical location which is keyed to a map, which forms the cover of this example, of the OSO at London Road; the OS Establishment as at 1/8/1895 is also given. The second unnumbered page is headed 'Preface'. Photocopy (PC); location of original unknown. A brief account of the work and processes of map reproduction at OS)

Price list of Ordnance Survey small scale maps revised 1st January, 1934. O.S. Leaflet No.18/33. (PRO OS 1/213)

-- *Price list ... revised 1st January, 1935.* O.S. Leaflet No.18/34. (PRO OS 1/90)

-- *Price list ... revised 1st January, 1938.* O.S. Leaflet No.18/37. (With ms. annotations revised to 1939. PRO OS 1/256)

-- *Price list ... revised to 1st January, 1939.* O.S. Leaflet No.18/38. (PRO OS 1/256)

Publication Division one-inch issues 1961-71. (Xerox, in a yellow cover; 7 pages of figures for the issues of the standard and tourist sheets for the calendar years 1961-1971. PC)

Regulations governing the reproduction of Ordnance Survey maps. O.S.23D. (BL B.S.56/2)

Report on the levelling network of London & Kent. (1932) (Printed for Departmental use)

Report on the levelling network of Wales. (1932) (BL B.S.56/5)

Report on the transference of levels to the Isle of Wight, 1927. (1928)

[*Research Bulletin* no.3; ca May 1938]. pp.vi,90. (Duplicated typescript; lacks title-page and pp.i-ii.Arranged in eighteen sections covering the following topics: Drawing & reproduction using non-distorting mediums; reproduction of 1/2500 KM plans; lithographic printing plates; strip films; transparent transfer papers; the use of film in place of glass negatives; the photonymograph; map folding and sheet sizes; waterproofing maps; new methods of map

Ordnance Survey publications ...

reproduction; economics of printing machines; dry plate photography; testing machine plates for fit; extracts from PATRA literature; miscellaneous; reviews of literature. The idea for these Bulletins, whose principal purpose appears to have been to summarise recent technical experiments and developments, may have grown out of the Director Generals' Conferences at which these problems were discussed. PC)

Routes through towns ... with indexes and descriptions of the Ordnance Survey small scale maps. [1935]

Rules and regulations (in abridged form) of the Ordnance Survey. [1936]. See **Ordnance Survey** *Administrative regulations and instructions* for earlier issues.

-- *Rules and regulations ...* [1938]

Small-scale maps of the Ordnance Survey. [ca 1929] (Two-sided leaflet; index to Popular Edition on reverse. PRO OS 1/144)

Specification for the production of the one-inch Seventh Series. Issued July 1952 and amended to November 1957. (pp.13; with full colour, and outline copies of sheet 180 folded in; together with 'Specification to One Inch Seventh Series Appendix No 3 Index to sheets', on which the sheet lines are overprinted in red on the grey base of 'Great Britain 1:1,250,000' (1946). On each page is printed the number '(92287)'. PC)

Specimens of type. Letterpress Department. (1937)

Specimens of type held in the Letterpress Printing Section of the Ordnance Survey. (1947)

Specimens of type used in the production of Ordnance Survey plans. [1934]

Technical Bulletin No.2 (Dec.1960). (Note on road revision)

Technical Bulletin No.4 (Jan.1962). (Note on map mounting and folding)

The Newlyn Datum and Ordnance Survey levels. (1929) (Single-sided leaflet)

The Ordnance Survey. An outline of its origin, and of the organisation & administration of its military side. (24/2/1932). (PRO OS 1/110)

'Ordnance Survey Departmental Committee: memorandum of evidence from the Royal Geographical Society' (1936) *The Geographical Journal* LXXXVII, 6:540-3.

'Ordnance Survey maps: discussion, with special reference to the grid system' (1936) *The Geographical Journal* LXXXVII, 4:308-327.

Owen, T. and Pilbeam, E., (1992) *Ordnance Survey map makers to Britain since 1791.* Southampton and London: Ordnance Survey and HMSO.

-- Reprinted with amendments, [1995].

Palmer, H.S., (1873) *The Ordnance Survey of the kingdom; its objects, mode of execution, history and present condition.* London: Edward Stanford.

Papers read at the British Association meeting of 1925 on the work of the Ordnance Survey including an account of the work of the International Bureau of the 1/M Map which is located at the Ordnance Survey Office, Southampton. (1926) London: HMSO. (Ordnance Survey Professional Papers, New Series, no.10)

Parliamentary Debates: *The Parliamentary Debates* (Official Report) [Hansard, House of Commons Debates]. Fifth Series (abbreviated in footnotes to: H.C.Deb.5s+vol.no.+date). A full listing of the entries consulted, dating from 1917 to 1938 is given in Hodson (1995).

Pilkington White, T., (1886) *The Ordnance Survey of the United Kingdom.* Edinburgh and London: William Blackwood and Sons.

Price, J.G., (1975) 'A review of design and production factors for the Ordnance Survey 1:50000 map series' *The Cartographic Journal* 12, 1:22-9.

Publications issued ..., see Ordnance Survey, *Catalogues*

Ravenhill, W., (1991) 'The South West in the eighteenth-century re-mapping of England', in *Maps and history in south-west England* K. Barker and R.J.P. Kain (Eds). Exeter: University of Exeter Press. (Exeter Studies in History No.31)

Report from the Select Committee on Publications and Debates' Reports; together with the Proceedings of the Committee, minutes of evidence and an appendix. (1913) London: HMSO.

Results of the magnetic observations made by the Ordnance Survey in the Channel Islands and in southern England in 1926. (1927) London: HMSO.

Results of the magnetic observations made by the Ordnance Survey in England in 1927 and preliminary results (declination only) of those made in England and Wales in 1928 (1930) London: HMSO.

Results of the magnetic observations made by the Ordnance Survey in England & Wales in 1928 and preliminary results (declination only) of those made in Scotland in 1929 (1930) London: HMSO.

Reynolds, J.H., (1932) 'The new One-Inch Ordnance map' *The Geographical Journal* LXXIX, 1:79-80.

Roberts, D.E., (1946) *An analysis of the One-Inch to the Mile Ordnance Survey map of Great Britain with special reference to the methods of production and the persistence ... of conventional signs.* M.Sc. thesis, University of Wales. (This thesis is based on very little documentary research; no revision or drawing instructions have been used; the bibliography is short and few maps were studied.)

Robertson, J., (1931) 'A few thoughts on map construction' *Empire Survey Review* I, 2:76-78.

Sankey, H.R., (1995) *The maps of the Ordnance Survey: a mid Victorian view.* London: Charles Close Society. (With an introduction by Ian Mumford. Originally published in 1888 in *Engineering*, a weekly illustrated journal)

Sauvain, S.J., (1997) *Highway law.* Second Edition. London: Sweet & Maxwell.

Select Committee of Public Accounts (1929-1930). V. Class VI. Surveys of Great Britain.

Select Committee of Public Accounts (1930-1931). V. Class VI. Surveys of Great Britain.

Select Committee of Public Accounts (1931-1932). IV. Class VI. Surveys of Great Britain.

Seymour, W.A. (Ed.), (1980) *A history of the Ordnance Survey.* Folkestone: Dawson.

Stamp, L. D., (1931) 'The Land Utilization Survey of Britain' *The Geographical Journal* LXXVIII, 1:40-53.

Stanford, E., (1890) *A résumé of the publications of the Ordnance Survey for England & Wales.* London: Edward Stanford. (With an introductory description of the Survey by Major Francis P. Washington, R.E., and a supplement on methods of map mounting. No.17.)

Stanford, E., (1891) *The Ordnance Survey from a business point of view.* London: Edward Stanford. (Published for private circulation)

Stanford, E., (1898) *A résumé of the publications of the Ordnance & Geological Surveys of England & Wales.* London: Edward Stanford. (With indexes to the 1-inch maps of the British Isles, and a supplement on methods of map mounting)
-- (1912) *A résumé ...*

Steers, J.A., (1962) *An introduction to the study of map projections.* Thirteenth Edition. London: University of London Press.

Stevenson, J., (1984) *British Society.* London: Penguin Books. (Penguin Social History of Britain)

Supplement to catalogue see Ordnance Survey, Catalogues.

Tanaka, K., (1932) 'The orthographical relief method of representing hill features on a topographical map' *The Geographical Journal* LXXIX, 3:213-219.

Taylor, A.J.P., (1973) *English history 1914-1945*. Harmondsworth: Pelican Books.

Thompson, A.G., (1927) *Map reading for ramblers: how to use the 1-inch Ordnance map*. London: Edward Stanford.

Thorpe, A., (1992) *Britain in the 1930s: the deceptive decade*. Oxford: Blackwell.

Verner, W., (1893) *Map reading and the elements of field sketching*. London, R.H. Porter and Simpkin, Marshall, Hamilton, Kent.

Wallis, H.M., and Robinson, A.H., (1987) *Cartographical innovations. An international handbook of mapping terms to 1900*. [Tring], Map Collector Publications.

War Office, (1912) *Manual of map reading and field sketching*. London: HMSO

War Office, [1914] *Manual of map reading and field sketching*. London: HMSO.

War Office, (1921) *Manual of map reading and field sketching*. London: HMSO.

War Office, (1929) *Manual of map reading, photo reading, and field sketching*. London: HMSO.

War Office, (1939) *Manual of map reading, photo reading, and field sketching*. London: HMSO.

War Office, *Notes on map reading*. London: HMSO.

War Office, (1943) *Hints on map reading instruction*.

Washington, F.P., (1890) *Lecture on the methods & processes of the Ordnance Survey*. (Delivered at the Royal Engineers Institute, Chatham, 18th March 1890. Printed for private circulation)

Waterhouse, J., (1870) *Report on the cartographic applications of photography as used in the topographical departments of the principal states in central Europe, with notes on European and Indian surveys*. Calcutta: Office of Superintendent of Government Printing.

Willis, J.C.T., (1932) *An outline of the history and revision of 25-inch Ordnance Survey plans*. London: HMSO.

Willis, J.C.T., (1935) Obituary of Capt.J.G. Withycombe, *Empire Survey Review* III, 15:63.

Wilson, C.W., (1890) [Letter in reply to an article by Crook], *Journal of The Manchester Geographical Society* VI:236-7.

Winterbotham, H.StJ.L., (1913) *An investigation into the accuracy of the Principal Triangulation of the United Kingdom*. ... London, HMSO. (With an Introduction by Colonel C.F. Close. Ordnance Survey. Professional Papers, New Series, no.2)

Winterbotham, H.StJ.L., (1924) 'The choice of a grid for British maps: the National Grid' *The Geographical Journal* LXIII, 6:491-496.

Winterbotham, H.StJ.L., (1925) 'Survey grids and map references' *The Royal Engineers Journal* XXXIX:81-86.

Winterbotham, H.StJ.L., (1932a) 'The small-scale maps of the Ordnance Survey' *The Geographical Journal* LXXIX, 1:17-31.

Winterbotham, H.StJ.L., (1932b) 'Sheet-lines' *The Geographical Journal* LXXX, 6:512-518.

Winterbotham, H.StJ.L., (1932c) 'Note on Professor Kitiro's method of orthographical relief' *The Geographical Journal* LXXX, 6:519-520.

Winterbotham, H.StJ.L., (1933a) 'Some Norwegian maps' *The Geographical Journal* LXXXI, 1:65-6.

Winterbotham, H.StJ.L., (1933b) 'The use of the new grid on Ordnance Survey maps' *The Geographical Journal* LXXXII, 1:42-54.

Winterbotham, H.StJ.L., (1934a) *The national plans (The Ten-foot, Five-foot, Twenty-five-inch and Six-inch scales)*. London: HMSO. (Ordnance Survey Professional Papers. New Series, no.16)

Winterbotham, H.StJ.L., (1934b) *Sidelights. Being notes on Ordnance Survey matters; some dictated in the cold reason of the office; some scribbled in the greater license of an after dinner chair; some written as memoranda at different times and at greater length.* ('Handover' notes from Winterbotham to MacLeod. Typescript. OSL G05172)

Winterbotham, H.StJ.L., (1936a) 'Map-grids' *Empire Survey Review* III, 20:322-325.

Winterbotham, H.StJ.L., (1936b) *A key to maps.* London and Glasgow: Blackie & Son.

Winterbotham, H.StJ.L., (1938) '150 years and 150 meridians' *Empire Survey Review* IV, 28:322-6.

Withycombe, J.G., (1925) 'Recent productions of the Ordnance Survey' *The Geographical Journal* LXVI, 6:533-9.

Withycombe, J.G., (1929a) 'Lettering on maps' in *Empire Conference of Survey Officers. 1928. Report of Proceedings.* London: HMSO. pp.158-165.

Withycombe, J.G., (1929b) 'Lettering on maps' *The Geographical Journal* LXXIII, 5:429-446.

Wolff, A.J., (1919) *The mathematical basis of the Ordnance maps of the United Kingdom.* Southampton: Ordnance Survey.

Wood, M., (1939:1945) *Map-reading for schools.* London: George Harrap (First published 1939; reprinted 1942, 1943, 1944, 1945)

Youth Hostels Association, *Handbook of hostels.* (1931-) Welwyn Garden City, YHA. Vol.I, *et seq.*

INDEX

Figures in **bold** refer to illustrations; numbers in parentheses, preceded by the letter f refer to footnotes

Notes

Notes

Notes

Notes

Notes